Uno
Dos
Tres.

British Airways now offers scheduled services
to the three Andalucian gateways of
Jerez de la Frontera, Malaga and Gibraltar.
Ask your travel agent for further details or
call us direct on 0345 222111.

BRITISH AIRWAYS

Andalucía
Handbook

Rowland Mead

Footprint Handbooks

*Oh lovely Spain! It is a goodly sight to see. What
heaven hath done for this delicious land!*

Byron *Childe Harold*

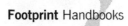

Footprint Handbooks

6 Riverside Court, Lower Bristol Road
Bath BA2 3DZ England
T 01225 469141 F 01225 469461
E mail handbooks@footprint.cix.co.uk
www.footprint-handbooks.co.uk

ISBN 0 900751 94 0 ISSN 1363-7517
CIP DATA: A catalogue record for this book is
available from the British Library

In North America, published by

PASSPORT BOOKS
a division of *NTC Publishing Group*

4255 West Touhy Avenue, Lincolnwood
(Chicago), Illinois 60646-1975, USA
T 847 679 5500 F 847 679 24941
E mail NTCPUB2@AOL.COM

ISBN 0-8442-4868-1
Library of Congress Catalog Card
Number: on file
Passport Books and colophon are registered
trademarks of NTC Publishing group

Every effort has been made to ensure that
the facts in this Handbook are accurate.
However travellers should still obtain
advice from consulates, airlines etc about
current travel and visa requirements and
conditions before travelling. The authors
and publishers cannot accept responsibility
for any loss, injury or inconvenience,
however caused.

Cover design by Newell and Sorrell; cover
photography by The Travel Library/A Amsel,
Emma Lee, and Travel Ink/Ronald Badkin

Production: Design by Mytton Williams;
Typesetting by Jo Morgan, Ann Griffiths and
Melanie Mason-Fayon; Maps by Sebastian
Ballard and Kevin Feeney; Charts by Ann
Griffiths; Original line drawings by Rowland
Mead; Proofread by Rod Gray.

Printed and bound in Great Britain by
Clays Ltd., Bungay, Suffolk

Contents

Author

Rowland Mead

A teacher by profession, Rowland first went to Spain in the late 60's with a minisail on the roof of his car and binoculars round his neck. He has been hooked ever since with the culture, language, wildlife and food. He has a house in Andalucía and lives there for 3 to 4 months a year. Andalucía satisfies all his main interests - church architecture, wildlife, geology, the sociology of the beach and good food and wine - all at a leisurely pace. Only rugby is not catered for, but even Marbella now has a rugby team!

Acknowledgements

The author wishes to acknowledge the initial help given by Anne and Keith McLachlan, in whose North African Handbook the original Andalucía text first appeared. Thanks are also due to Andrew Prideaux of Footprint Handbooks for his patience and discreet guidance.

The Spanish National Tourist Office in London and the Lookout magazine have provided useful reference material, while the regional *oficinas de Turismo* in Andalucía were always cooperative, despite often overwhelming pressure of work. Finally, my thanks to countless friends and acquaintances in Andalucía who contributed, often unwittingly, to this Handbook.

Introduction and hints

DURING THE late 1980's, the Spanish National Tourist Office adopted as its slogan the phrase **'Everything Under The Sun'**, suggesting that Spain was not just sand and sex, but had a variety of attractions to suit all tastes. Whilst this campaign was referring to the whole of Spain, nowhere was it more appropriately aimed than towards its most southerly region of Andalucía. Consider it's attractions:

A superb all year round **climate**, with the mildest winters in mainland Europe and high sunshine records in every month.

A varied **scenery**, with coastal cliffs, dunes and tidal estuaries, while, especially W of Gibraltar, there are some of the most unspoilt sandy beaches to be found anywhere. Inland, there are the highest mountains in mainland Spain, dense forests, rolling farmland and even, in Almería, semi- desert.

A wealth of **history** stretching from Prehistoric times to the present and giving opportunities to visit Chalcolithic sites, Roman amphitheatres, Moorish baths and Gothic cathedrals.

One of the best **wildlife** locations in Europe, with birds, flowers and butterflies in abundance, plus some of Europe's rarest mammals. Amongst the many nature reserves and natural parks, the incomparable Coto Doñana stands out as Europe's premier wetland site.

Wide opportunities for **sport**, from water sports along the coast to rock climbing, skiing, golf and tennis in inland areas.

A healthy regional **cuisine**, which relies on simple, fresh food, washed down with some outstanding, but cheap, wines.

The 'Everything Under the Sun' campaign was, of course, designed to attract the discriminating tourist to Spain at the expense of the lager lout, to promote rural tourism to counteract depopulation and to stress the diversity of the landscape – all aspects with which the Handbook deals.

Getting to Andalucía is no problem. There are international airports at Málaga, Sevilla, Jerez and Almería. The AVE high speed train from Madrid to Sevilla is faster than travelling by air and sufficiently reliable for the authorities to refund the fare in full if it is more than 5 mins late. **When to go** is a more tricky decision and will depend on the visitors interests. All seasons have their attractions.

Andalucía - main routes

Winter is probably the best time for visiting the major sites, such as the Alhambra at Granada or the cathedral at Sevilla, which will be mercifully free of fellow tourists. Despite the risk of rain, the coast can be surprisingly warm at this season. Spring is the time for wildlife enthusiasts, with flowers at their best and resident birds in full song. Autumn also has its attractions, although the landscape can look parched and the first rains surprisingly heavy. Summer on the coast is strictly for hedonists, with the resorts throbbing and the heat searing. This is not a recommended time for exploring inland – stay on the coast where at least there will be a sea breeze.

Travelling around Andalucía presents few difficulties. Although hitchhiking is not recommended, all the main cities and towns are linked by cheap and reliable bus services. Hire car rates are some of the cheapest in Europe, while the road system has improved dramatically in recent years with all the major provincial capitals linked by *autovia*. Even the remotest corner of Andalucía can be reached within 3-4 hrs driving from Málaga airport, so that 'fly/drive holidays' have become increasingly popular.

The Footprint Handbook on Andalucía has its origins in the Trade and Travel North African Handbook, in which the original text was included because of the Moorish connection. It differs from many Footprint Handbooks in that its subject is not a Third World country, but an area of mainland Europe which is also one of the continent's most popular tourist destinations. The **Andalucían Handbook**, therefore, should appeal to a wide variety of readers, from the individual traveller on a budget to the tourists with money in their pockets who are looking for comfortable accommodation and good food. The accommodation section **'Something different'** is listed with the latter in mind. Research has shown that the majority of package tourists, when choosing their destination, look for opportunities for exploring inland, often by hired car.

The Handbook will prove useful to them and also to the many visitors who come to Andalucía on specialist holidays such as sailboarding, skiing, golf, painting, botany and birdwatching.

The Handbook also aims to help the traveller in a hurry who does not wish to look at yet another poverty stricken church which will probably be closed anyway. If time is at a premium, the visitor needs to know what to miss out and what to avoid. Andalucía may have 'Everything under the Sun', but the trick is informed selection.

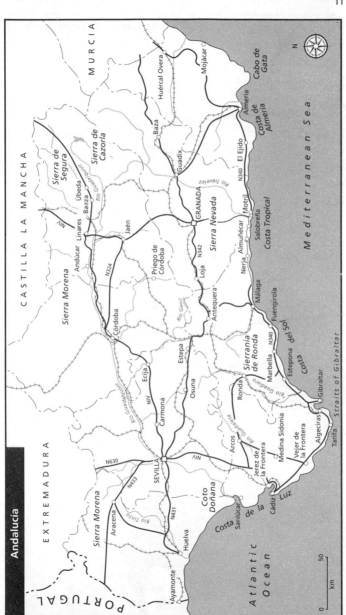

Andalucía

Horizons

THE NAME Andalucía is properly applied to the area of Iberia occupied by the Muslims in the period from 711 AD for approximately five centuries. Because Arab rule encompassed all of Iberia immediately after the conquest, indeed, pushing deep into France before being reversed at the battle of Poitiers in 732, the term Andalucía can in a historical sense loosely be applied to almost any area of Spain. The longest and most concentrated rule of the Moors was in the south. This lasted until the fateful battle of Navas de Tolosa in 1212, after which the residual territories under Muslim rule broke up to leave only the Kingdom of Granada as an effective independent state until 1492. Present day Andalucía takes in this area of the south which was longest and most thoroughly under Arab control.

OFFICIAL NAME

Comunidad Autónoma de Andalucía (Autonomous Community of Andalucía). One of 17 communidads.

REGIONAL FLAG

Rectangular with three equal horizontal fields of green, white and green.

OFFICIAL LANGUAGE

Castilian Spanish.

POPULATION INDICATORS

Population: 6.86 million; *Urban population*: 80%; *Religion*: Roman Catholic 97%; *Birth rate*: 10.7 per 1,000; *Death rate*: 8.2 per 1,000; *Life expectancy*: 74 (men)/80 (women).

LAND

Andalucía is some 87,000 sq km in area, occupying 17% of Spain and being the largest of the Autonomous Communities. It is larger than countries such as Austria or Ireland. Andalucía comprises 8 administrative provinces – Almería, Cádiz, Córdoba, Granada, Huelva, Jaén, Málaga and Sevilla, each with a capital city of the same name. Its northern boundary is formed by a range of mountains, known as the Sierra Morena in the W and their eastward extension of the Sierra Madrona and the Sierra Aguila. The one major pass through these mountains to the interior of Spain is the

Despeñaperros Pass, followed by both road and railway. To the W, Andalucía borders with the Portuguese Algarve and the Atlantic Ocean. The southern boundary provided by the Mediterranean Sea is interrupted only by the small peninsula of Gibraltar, which remains in British hands.

GEOGRAPHICAL REGIONS

Andalucía falls neatly into four zones:

The Northern Mountains

Dominated by the Sierra Morena, this region rises to rugged hills topping in places 1,000m. This region is the one most rarely visited by tourists and has suffered considerable depopulation during the present century.

The Guadalquivir Valley

Derived from the Arabic *Wad Al-Kebir*, the valley and its delta form flatlands, rich in alluvial soils and with abundant water for irrigation. The river itself is the fifth longest in Spain, rising in the mountains of Jaén province and flowing for 657 km through Córdoba and Sevilla to enter the Atlantic via the marshlands of the Coto Doñana in Huelva province. In Roman times, when the river was known as *Betis*, it was navigable as far as Córdoba, but now ships can only reach as far inland as Sevilla. The valley was extensively farmed in Roman times, while the Moors introduced complicated irrigation systems. It remains today the hub of Andalucía's agricultural production. The delta itself has only comparatively recently been reclaimed from marshes to permanent agriculture and water taken for farming has seriously lowered levels in the Coto Doñana, one of Europe's foremost wetland nature reserves.

The Southern Sierras

These may divided into the **Sistema Subbetico**, which rises to its highest point of 3,398m in the Cazorla Natural Park in the NE of Andalucía, and the **Sistema Penibetico** in the S, which in the Sierra Nevada range provides Spain's highest mainland mountain in Mulhacén at 3,482m, where Europe's most southerly skiing resort may be found. The lower slopes in the N of the sierras are dotted with olive groves, particularly in Jaén and Códoba provinces, while the spectacular higher slopes have a high concentration of natural parks and nature reserves.

The Mediterranean Coastal Plain

Although narrow and discontinuous, the coastal plain has the highest density of population in Andalucía, due to the growth of the tourist industry. From Málaga westwards to Gibraltar, the coast is known as the *Costa del Sol* and has developed into a linear conurbation, swollen by tourists throughout the year and providing employment for Andalucíans, thereby depopulating the interior. West of Gibraltar to the Portuguese border, the *Costa de la Luz* is less developed, but the fierce *levante* wind provides a Mecca for sail boarders. In Almería province, the coastal plain is wider and is extensively used for the production of fruit and vegetables grown under plastic and transported all over northern Europe. The Granada stretch of the coast, known as the *Costa Tropical*, is mountainous and its distance from a major international airport has meant that it is largely underdeveloped from a tourist point of view.

RIVERS AND WATER SUPPLY

The Guadalquivir has a large number of tributaries, from the mountains both to the N and the S, and is the dominant river system of Andalucía, draining the entire region, with the exception of the generally short S flowing rivers which descend rapidly to the Mediterranean. Flying over the region, the visitor is always impressed by the large number of reservoirs which have been constructed and with normal winter rainfall, precipitation is usually sufficient to cope with the de-

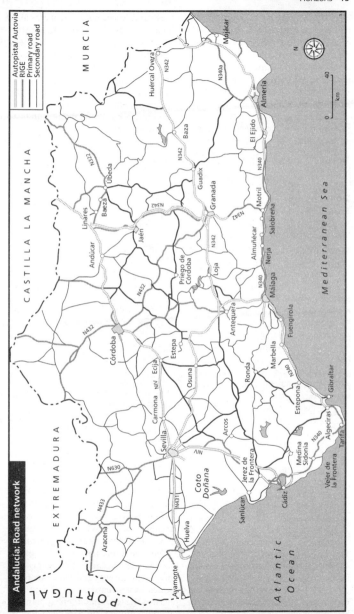

Andalucía: Road network

mands of the dry Andalucían summer. During the period 1990-1995, however, the winter rains failed. In addition, EXPO '92 at Sevilla, caused severe strains on water supplies, so that water rationing has been common during recent summers. Mindful of the effect that this situation could have on the tourist industry, many towns on the Costa del Sol are considering the construction of desalinization plants. This is not a recent problem – the remains of both Roman and Moorish water channels and aqueducts can be seen in many parts of Andalucía even today.

CLIMATE

In an area which extends 400 km from W to E and an average of 225 km from N to S and with altitudes varying from sea level to 3,482m in the Sierra Nevada, it is hardly surprising that there are subtle variations in climate. Andalucía has, in general, what is known as a Mediterranean climate, which involves hot, dry summers and mild wet winters, with high sunshine totals. The wind pattern is generally westerly in winter and easterly in summer. The coastal areas, particularly the Costa del Sol, have the most agreeable climate on mainland Europe, which explains the high number of northern Europeans who settle here. West of Gibraltar, the *levante* wind from the E can blow fiercely for days on end. In summer, the strong, hot *sirocco* blows up from North Africa, bringing airborne sand, high temperatures and low humidity, usually for shorter periods.

While the summer temperatures on the coast are moderated by sea breezes, inland the heat can be searing. Ejica, in Seville province, is known as the *sartenilla de Andalucía* ('frying pan of Andalucía'), and temperatures of over 40°C in summer are not uncommon. In the E, the province of Almería is noted for aridity. The city of Almería itself may have a mere 1 or 2 days rain a year and the interior warrants the description of semi-desert.

Inland, the height of the sierras leads to an increase in precipitation during the winter months. The 'white village' of Grazalema, in the Serrania de Ronda, is reputed to be the wettest place in Spain, while the snowfall on the Sierra Nevada supports a thriving winter sports industry.

Average maximum temperatures for the provincial capitals are shown below:

	Feb	Aug
	(°C)	(°C)
Almería	12	27
Cádiz	12	25
Granada	8	26
Huelva	12	25
Jaén	10	28
Málaga	13	25
Sevilla	11	28

LAND USE

Land use is highly polarized in Andalucía. The Mediterranean coastal rim is densely used for either farming, settlement or tourism, but rising altitudes a few km inland bring extensive farming and only modest use of the land for tourism. The lowlands of the Guadalquivir Valley and the plateau to the W, on the other hand, are intensively farmed for cereals and fruit, often with the aid of irrigation.

Land tenure

The Spanish S is a region of large farms and estates, especially away from the Mediterranean coast. The system derives from the Reconquest when land was redistributed in huge plots or *'latifundia'*. The landlords of these estates (often absent) created appalling conditions for the farm workers, who were often hired on a daily basis – a situation which has only marginally improved today. Elsewhere there are middle-ranking private farms or *fincas*. On the poorer land, farms are often no more than small holdings used for self sufficiency and some small scale commercial cropping.

For the traveller, there is plenty of opportunity to buy fresh produce in season at the roadside from privately-run stands and kiosks for very reasonable prices. Oranges, lemons, potatoes and a variety of vegetables, including asparagus, are sold in this way.

Stringent rules against trespass on farmland, particularly for hunting, are in evidence and areas marked either with the sign *coto privado de caza* (hunting by licence), or with a small rectangle carrying a black and white triangle, are to be treated as private land. Similarly, there are large areas of land in Andalucía still under military administration, indicated by the warning *zona militar*. These areas are best avoided, particularly by bird watchers armed with binoculars and telescopes, which are bound to arouse military suspicion.

Potential

The region's potential has scarcely been touched, except for coastal tourism where that is, arguably, over-developed. The historical sites, particularly the Moorish cores of Granada, Códoba and Sevilla, concentrate attention, but elsewhere a full range of castles, monuments and other remains are lightly visited and under-valued by the local authorities. The treatment of some archaeological sites is occasionally despairing for the visitor. There is, nevertheless, enormous scope for the traveller to both escape the tourist throngs and see some excellent sites throughout the region. The Andalucían government is actively promoting 'rural tourism' in the interior and encouraging minority interests such as horse riding, botany and bird watching. The idea is to attract the more discerning type of tourist and at the same time to halt the rural depopulation which has blighted the inland areas for some time. Hopefully, 'rural tourism' will not result in the same ill thought out mass tourist developments of the *costa*. Certainly, at the moment, large parts of Andalucía remain virgin territory, and the discriminating tourist will find much to enjoy.

WILDLIFE

The wide diversity of wildlife found in Andalucía is truly amazing. There are a number of reasons for this.

1. Andalucía is located at the geographical crossroads where Europe meets Africa and where the Atlantic Ocean connects to the Mediterranean Sea. Its wildlife reflects all of these influences.

2. The wide range of habitat within Andalucía, varying from semi desert in the E to wetlands in the W, from broad river valleys to high mountain ranges. The coastline, too, provides contrasts, with dunes, cliffs and salt marshes. The almost landlocked Mediterranean is virtually tideless, but W of Gibraltar the tidal estuaries and beaches provide yet another environment. The original Mediterranean forests were destroyed in prehistoric times and these have been replaced by cork oaks, pines and *maquis*. Farmland, in contrast with northern Europe, also provides a rich habitat, as methods of production are often still primitive.

3. Large areas of Andalucía remain wild and undeveloped.

4. The government of Andalucía has enthusiastically promoted the cause of nature conservation. There are over 80 protected areas covering nearly 15,000 sq km, which amounts to 17% of Andalucía.

Because of the geographical isolation of the Iberian peninsula and in particular Andalucía, cut off to the N by high ranges, the area is rich in **endemic species** – found nowhere else in the world.

PLANTS

There are more than 5,000 species of flowering plant to be found in Andalucía, a total which includes over 150 which are endemic, mainly found in the Sierra Nevada and the Cazorla range. A favoured spot for botanists is the 'painted fields'

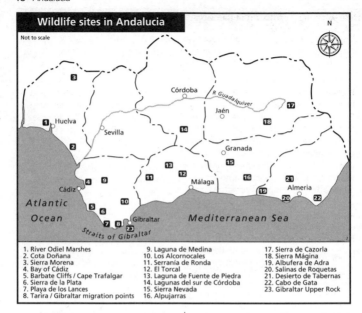

Wildlife sites in Andalucia

Not to scale

N

1. River Odiel Marshes
2. Cota Doñana
3. Sierra Morena
4. Bay of Cádiz
5. Barbate Cliffs / Cape Trafalgar
6. Sierra de la Plata
7. Playa de los Lances
8. Tarira / Gibraltar migration points
9. Laguna de Medina
10. Los Alcornocales
11. Serranía de Ronda
12. El Torcal
13. Laguna de Fuente de Piedra
14. Lagunas del sur de Córdoba
15. Sierra Nevada
16. Alpujarras
17. Sierra de Cazorla
18. Sierra Mágina
19. Albufera de Adra
20. Salinas de Roquetas
21. Desierto de Tabernas
22. Cabo de Gata
23. Gibraltar Upper Rock

area between Vejer and Tarifa, where meadows which have never known pesticides are a riot of colour in Spring, with mallows, convolvulus, lupins, irises and squills in abundance. There are, however, flowers to be seen at all seasons, with roadside verges covered with Bermuda Buttercups and Narcissi as early as Jan. Even in the aridity of Aug, coastal dunes can produce surprising numbers of Sea Daffodils. Those visitors looking for Alpine plants should head for the Sierra Nevada, where by early to mid summer the snow is melting from the upper slopes. In the *maquis* areas, cistus, rock roses and aromatic herbs are abundant. A wide range of orchids can be found in all the habitats, but particularly on the limestone soils.

Recommended reading

Flowers of the Mediterranean, Polunin and Huxley, Pub Chatto and Windus; *Mediterranean Wild Flowers*, Roger Phillips, Pub Elm Tree Books; *Wild Flowers of Spain*, Clive Innes, Pub Cockatrice; *Wildflowers of Southern Spain*, Betty Molesworth Allen, Pub Mirador Books.

MAMMALS

There is a wide variety of mammals in Andalucía, although it must be said that many of the species are either very scarce or nocturnal and therefore highly unlikely to be seen. Of the three North African species, the Mongoose and the Genet are quite common, while the Barbary Macaques have been introduced to Gibraltar. Of the more endangered species, the Wolf hangs on in small numbers in the Sierra Morena, while the Pardel Lynx (of which Andalucía has 60% of the surviving world population) can occasionally be spotted in the Coto Doñana. The Otter, on the other hand, whilst rarely seen is still common. Of the herbivores, both Red and Fallow Deer appear in a number of locations, as does the Wild Boar. The Spanish Ibex seems to be increasing its numbers and can be readily

Making sense of rhe wildlife acronyms

Visitors to Andalucía are often confused by the various organizations and classifications involved in wildlife conservation and the inevitable acronyms which occur. The following clarifications may help.

Firstly the **organizations** involved:

ICONA   This is the National Institute for Nature Conservation, which is a branch of the *Ministerio de Agricultura Pesca y Alimentacion* (the Ministry of Agriculture, Fish and Food), based of course in Madrid. Many environmentalists in Spain consider that the title is a misnomer, as the organization is dominated by engineers, rather nature conservationists. Fortunately, it only controls National Parks and in Andalucía there is only one.

AMA   The *Agencia de Medio Ambiente*. This is the environmental agency of the *Junta de Andalucía*, the autonomous regional government and it has done a marvellous job in giving protected status of some type or another to all the key wildlife sites of the area. Its educational efforts in making the inhabitants of Andalucía more environmentally aware are under recognized. It can be contacted at Avda Eritaña 1, 41071 Sevilla, T (954) 627202.

SEO   *Sociedad Española de Ornitologia*. The Spanish birdwatching equivalent of Britain's RSPB or the US AOU. Based in Madrid, it has branches in Andalucía and has recently opened a splendid new hide/interpretation centre over looking the marshes at El Rocio. It can be contacted at the Facultad de Biología, University of Madrid, 28040, Madrid, Spain, T (91) 5493554.

Next the **reserves**:

RESERVA NATURAL (Natural Reserve)   Equivalent to the British SSSI (Sites of Special Scientific Interest), these are small scale affairs such as lagoons or small patches of woodland. Activities which threaten the survival of the ecosystem are banned.

PARAJE NATURAL (Natural Locality)   Similar to the above, but generally protecting a wider area of scenic or ecological interest.

PARQUE NATURAL (Natural Park)   Covers a large area of, say, mountains or coastline and prevents unsuitable development, while allowing traditional activities, such as charcoal burning or cork cutting, to continue. Recreational and educational facilities are provided, with interpretation centres, hides and wardens. Examples include the Odiel Marshlands in Huelva province, El Torcal limestone complex in Málaga province, the Sierra Nevada in Granada province and the Cabo de Gata coastal headland in Almería province.

PARQUE NACIONAL (National Park)   The top of the conservation ladder, with only nine National parks in the whole of Spain, and one in Andalucía – the incomparable Coto Doñana. These are areas of international importance with restricted access and strong control of human activities.

seen in the Sierra Nevada, Cazorla, and the Serrania de Ronda, while Mouflon have been introduced locally as a game species.

Common Hedgehogs are joined along the Costa del Sol by the Algerian variety. Rabbits and Hares are common, despite widespread hunting. The Garden Dormouse is often found in trees close to houses, where it is often persecuted in mistake for a 'tree rat'. There are numerous varieties of Bats. Most are of the small pipeitrelle type, which will often fly during the day. Indeed they have frequently been seen hunted by Kestrels. The larger Noctules are also common.

The cetaceans are represented by both Common and Bottle Nosed Dolphins which can always be seen in the Straits of Gibraltar, where there are also regular sightings of Pilot Whales and occasionally Killer Whales. Dolphin watching trips depart from the marina at Gibraltar.

Recommended reading

The Mammals of Britain and Europe, Corbett and Overton, Pub Collins.

BUTTERFLIES

With over 130 species of butterfly, including more than 30 types of Blue alone, Andalucía is a lepidopterists nirvana. Many of the butterflies seen in northern Europe have in fact bred in Andalucía, such as the Clouded Yellow, while others migrate to the area from North Africa, like the Painted Lady. There are also a small number of endemics, including the Nevada Blue and the Nevada Grayling. Amongst the more spectacular and common butterflies are two varieties of Swallowtail, Spanish Festoon, Cleopatra, the ubiquitous Speckled Wood and the Moroccan Orange Tip. Most striking of all is the huge Two Tailed Pasha, which one could be forgiven for mistaking for a small bird when it is in flight. On occasions, large numbers of American vagrants turn up, including the Monarch. There are also a number of day flying moths, of which the Great Peacock Moth and the Hummingbird Moth are most likely to be noticed.

Recommended reading

The Butterflies of Britain and Europe, Higgins and Hargreaves, Pub Collins.

REPTILES AND AMPHIBIANS

There are some 17 species of amphibian represented, including a variety of frogs, toads and newts. Of these, the noisy Marsh Frog and the delightful little green Tree Frog are notable, while the Salamander can often be seen.

Reptiles are widespread, particularly the lizards, which vary from the iguana-like Ocellated Lizard, which can grow up to a metre in length down to the common Wall Lizards and Geckoes. The latter can often be observed at night hunting insects close to electric lights on the side of houses. Also common are the Spiny Footed Lizards found in dunes and other dry habitats, the young being very noticeable with their bright red tails. At waterside margins, two varieties of terrapin can be seen, the European Pond Terrapin and the Striped Neck Terrapin. Both terrapins and the land based Spur Thighed Tortoise seem to survive predation for the pet trade. Finally, in the southern coastal fringes of Andalucía, the highly protected Chameleon may still be seen with luck in a few places.

Of the eight species of snake, only one, the Latastes Viper, is venomous, while the largest is the Montpellier Snake, which can grow to 2m. Most common are the familiar Grass Snake and the Southern Smooth Snake.

Amongst the insects the most fascinating is the Praying Mantis, which may be brown or green. Noisy cicadas, crickets and grasshoppers are heard everywhere during the summer months. Dung beetles make fascinating watching. The plethora of ants and flies are less welcome.

BIRDS

While Andalucía is attractive for many forms of wildlife, it is the wide selection of birds which is a magnet for naturalists from far afield. There are over 400 birds on the systematic list and nearly half of these breed. It is the only place in Europe where you will find, for example, White-headed Duck, Marbled Duck, Black Shouldered Kite, Spanish Imperial Eagle, Purple Gallinule, Black-bellied Sand Grouse, Red-necked Nightjar,

Identifying Raptors

The following raptors may be seen in Andalucia and many can be spotted crossing the Straits of Gibraltar in spring and autumn. The first name shown is Spanish, followed by the Latin name and the English name. The figure on the right shows the wingspan. All birds seen from below.

BUITRE NEGRO
Aegypius monachus
BLACK VULTURE

295 cm

BUITRE LEONADO
Gyps fulvus
GRIFFON VULTURE

280 cm

QUEBRANTAHUESOS
Gypaetus barbatus
LAMMERGEIER
(Bearded Vulture)

277 cm
(very rare)

AGUILA REAL
Aquila chrysaetus
GOLDEN EAGLE

227 cm

AGUILA IMPERIAL
Aquila adalberti
SPANISH IMPERIAL EAGLE   200 cm

ALIMOCHE
Neophron percnopterus
EGYPTIAN EAGLE   180 cm

AGUILA PERDICERA
Hieraetus fasciatus   180 cm
BONELLI'S EAGLE

AGUILA CALZADA
Hieraetus pennatus   121 cm
BOOTED EAGLE

AGUILA PESCADORA
Pandion haliaetus   170 cm
OSPREY

RATONERO
Buteo buteo   128 cm
BUZZARD

AGUILA CULEBRERA
Circaetus gallicus   190 cm
SHORT TOED EAGLE

HALCON ABEJERO
Pernis apivorus   135 cm
HONEY BUZZARD

MILANO NEGRO
Milvus migrans   155 cm
BLACK KITE

MILANO REAL
Milvus milvus   175 cm
RED KITE

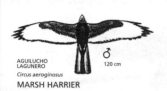

AGUILUCHO
LAGUNERO
Circus aeroginosus
MARSH HARRIER

120 cm

AGUILUCHO PALIDO
Circus cyaneus
HEN HARRIER

110 cm

AGUILUCHO CENIZO
Circus pygarqus
MONTAGU'S HARRIER

105 cm

AZOR
Accipiter gentilis
GOSHAWK

135 cm

GAVILAN
Accipiter nisus
SPARROWHAWK

55 cm

HALCON PEREGRINO
Falco peregrinus
PEREGRINE

110 cm

HALCON DE ELEONOR
Falco eleonorae
ELEONORA'S FALCON

100 cm

ALCOTAN
Falco subbuteo
HOBBY

90 cm

CERNICALO VULGAR
Falco tinnunculus
KESTREL

75 cm

CERNICALO PRIMILLA
Falco naumanni
LESSER KESTREL

60 cm

ESMERJON
Falco columbarius
MERLIN

55 cm

109c

The effect of wind on migration routes over the Straits of Gibraltar

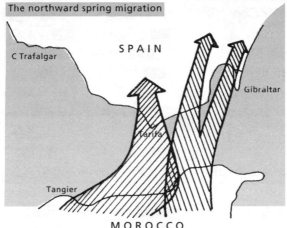

The northward spring migration

SPAIN

C Trafalgar

Gibraltar

Tarifa

Tangier

MOROCCO

◩ routes followed during westerly winds
◩ routes followed during easterly winds

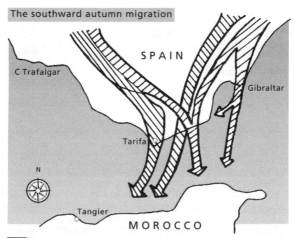

The southward autumn migration

SPAIN

C Trafalgar

Gibraltar

Tarifa

N

Tangier

MOROCCO

◩ routes followed during easterly winds
◩ routes followed during westerly winds

Source: Garcia & Patterson *Where to watch birds in Southern Spain*, Helm

Passage periods of Raptors at Gibraltar

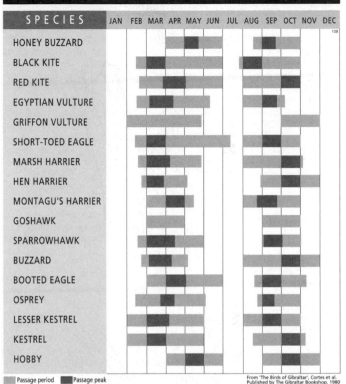

SPECIES	JAN	FEB	MAR	APR	MAY	JUN	JUL	AUG	SEP	OCT	NOV	DEC
HONEY BUZZARD												
BLACK KITE												
RED KITE												
EGYPTIAN VULTURE												
GRIFFON VULTURE												
SHORT-TOED EAGLE												
MARSH HARRIER												
HEN HARRIER												
MONTAGU'S HARRIER												
GOSHAWK												
SPARROWHAWK												
BUZZARD												
BOOTED EAGLE												
OSPREY												
LESSER KESTREL												
KESTREL												
HOBBY												

▨ Passage period ▪ Passage peak

From 'The Birds of Gibraltar', Cortes et al.
Published by The Gibraltar Bookshop. 1980

Dupont's Lark, Black Wheatear, Azure-winged Magpie, Spotless Starling and Trumpeter Finch. This is enough to wet the appetite of all keen bird watchers, let alone the most fanatical 'twitchers'. It also ensures that the tourist industry is swollen, particular in Spring, by visits organized by specialist bird watching organizations – a fact which the Andalucían government has recently begun to appreciate and is reflected in the increasing number of reserves and protected areas.

The reasons for the wide range of birds are twofold. Firstly, the strategic location of Andalucía at the meeting point of bird migration routes, and secondly the wide variety of available habitats. The assemblage of birds varies according to the season. There are **Resident** birds which are present all the year round, which includes many typical Mediterranean species, such as the Crested Lark, Crag Martin, Blue Rock Thrush, Fan-tailed Warbler, Short-toed Treecreeper and Serin. **Winter Visitors** include a range of wildfowl and gulls, plus passerines such as Meadow Pipits, White Wagtails, Blackcaps and Chiffchaffs. **Summer Visitors** include such spectacular species as Little Bitterns, Purple Herons, Black Storks,

White Storks, Short-toed Eagles, Booted Eagles, Collared Pratincoles, Bee Eaters, Rollers and Golden Orioles. Other birds simply pass through Andalucía on their way N and S – these are called **Passage Migrants** and include a whole range of warblers, terns, waders and raptors.

All the varying habitats have their attractions, even the man-made environment. Hordes of Pallid Swifts can be seen screaming around unfinished apartment blocks, while golf courses, with their well-watered greens, are particularly appealing to Hoopoes, many of which now remain in coastal Andalucía throughout the year. In the W of the region, especially in Cádiz province, church towers and railway pylons are favourite nesting spots for White Storks. Nearly all the cathedrals of Andalucía have their colonies of Lesser Kestrels. Even the well tended gardens of villas along the Costa del Sol provide suitable territory for Blackbirds and, in the winter, Robins and Chiffchaffs.

It is the wetlands, however, which attract most birds and bird watchers. The incomparable Coto Doñana at the mouth of the Guadalquivir is arguably Europe's best wetland reserve. Apart from over 300,000 wintering wildfowl, its breeding species include Cattle and Little Egrets, Grey, Night and Purple Herons, Spoonbills and White Storks. Raptors include Black and Red Kite, Short-toed Eagle and Marsh Harrier, while there are some 15 pairs of the rare Spanish Imperial Eagle within the park boundary. Among other coastal wetlands are the Odiel Marshes to the W of Huelva city and the Cabo de Gata-Nijar in Almería province. There are also a number of inland wetlands, such as the group of freshwater lakes S of Córdoba and the Laguna de Medina E of Cádiz. The salt lake of Fuente de Piedra in Málaga province can have as many as 40,000 breeding Flamingoes when conditions are right.

The mountain areas have their own bird communities, which will include raptors such as Golden Eagle, Griffon Vulture and Bonellis Eagle. Blue Rock Thrush and Black Wheatear are typical of rocky slopes, while at the highest levels Raven, Chough, Alpine Accenter and Rock Bunting are the specialities.

There are still many roads in Andalucía with telephone wires and these make excellent vantage points and song posts for Corn Bunting, Stonechat, Roller, Bee Eater and shrikes, while the adjacent farmland with its extensive methods of production can contain Great and Little Bustard, Red-legged Partridge and Montagus Harrier. The forests, olive groves and *maquis* are also rich in bird life.

Observing the migration The soaring birds, such as raptors and storks, which migrate to Africa for their winter quarters, face the problem of crossing the Mediterranean Sea. They are obliged to head for the narrowest point, which is the Straits of Gibraltar. Here they gain height in thermals over the land and then attempt to glide the 16 km over the water (where thermals are usually lacking) to the other side. Observing this movement when conditions are right and numbers are high can be an unforgettable sight. For more details and advice, see the section on Tarifa in the regional descriptions.

Andalucía (and indeed Spain in general) used to have a particularly bad reputation for cruelty to animals, indiscriminate shooting and the liming and trapping of birds. This has begun to change in recent years. There is now a network of Natural Parks and Nature Reserves, an increasing number equipped with hides, wardens, nature trails and information and interpretation centres. Young people, in particular, have a much more educated approach to conservation. You are just as likely to share a hide with a foreign bird watcher as you are with a Spanish schoolchild armed with binoculars and identification book – surely an encouraging sign.

For a list of recommended wildlife sites, see the map below. For full descriptions and details of access, see the regional sections.

Recommended reading

Where to Watch Birds in Southern Spain, Garcia and Patterson, Pub Helm; *A Birdwatchers Guide to Southern Spain and Gibraltar*, Clive Finlayson, Pub Prion.

The two best field guides are: *Field Guide to the Birds of Britain and Europe*, Peterson, Mountford and Hollom, Pub Collins and *Guide to the Birds of Britain and Europe*, Heinsel, Fitter and Parslow, Pub Collins.

HISTORY

Located at the junction of land and sea routes, Andalucía has always been open to invasion and colonization. The influence of this settlement often spread to the rest of the Iberian peninsula, as in the case of the Moors. In the 15th century the role was reversed as Andalucía sent sailors and explorers on their conquests of the Americas.

THE PREHISTORIC SCENE

The caves of Andalucía have revealed considerable evidence of prehistoric man. A female skull found in a cave in Gibraltar has been dated as Neanderthal. (It's significance was not realized at the time, otherwise we might have been talking about 'Gibraltar Woman' rather than 'Neanderthal Man'). In Palaeolithic times, homo sapiens reached the area. The caves of Nerja and the cave at Pileta, near Ronda, both have fine cave paintings which give an indication of the way of life of those times. In the Neolithic period, the cave paintings at Velez Blanco have been dated at around 4000 BC. The remains of the Chalcolithic settlement at Los Millares show that a thousand years later metal was being used for weapons and utensils. The dolmens at Antequera also probably date from this period.

The Iberians

The Iberians established their kingdom of **Tartessus** during the first millennium BC, possibly located around the mouth of the Guadalquivir. It is known that they were literate and had skills in music and art. The most valuable artefact from this time is the **Dama de Basa**, a statue found at Basa in Granada province and believed to date from the 4th century BC.

Phoenicians and Carthaginians

The Phoenicians came to Andalucía in a trading capacity, establishing settlements at places such as Málaga and Almuñecar, dealing in metals, fish, salt and dyes. They were superseded by the

Carthaginians, who set up their capital at Cartagena, in Murcia, but eventually occupied the whole of Andalucía.

Romans and Visigoths

The second Punic War ended the domination of Carthage and the Romans soon occupied the whole of the Iberian peninsula. Their most southerly province was called **Hispania Baetica**, which was approximately the area of modern Andalucía, with its capital at Córdoba, and this soon became one of the wealthiest parts of the Roman empire. The Romans developed the mines at Río Tinto in Huelva province and grew a variety of agricultural produce, particularly along the Guadalquivir valley. Their settlement at Baelo Claudia in Cádiz province exported *garum* – a type of fish sauce – throughout the empire. Baetica provided three Roman emperors during this period, Theodosius, Hadrian and Trajan, plus philosophers such as Seneca. Before the decline set in, the Romans had built temples, amphitheatres, aqueducts and a network of fine roads linking the major cities.

As the Roman domination weakened, there were invasions from the N by firstly the **Vandals** (incorporated in the name Andalucía) and later by the **Visigoths**. Although they first brought Christianity to the area, their hold was never strong and by the 8th century the way was open for the Moorish invasion.

The Moors

The first move in the Moorish Conquest took place in 711 when **Tarik**, the governor of Tangier, crossed the straits from North Africa with a force of 7,000 Berbers and defeated the Visigoth ruler King Roderic by the Río Guadalete near Tarifa. Within the decade the invaders conquered most of the peninsula which became part of a vast Muslim empire known as **al-Andalus**.

When the Ommayyad Dynasty in North Africa was overthrown by the Abbasids, the sole surviving Ommayyad prince, **Abd Al-Rahman**, escaped to al-Andalus and set up an independent Caliphate with its capital at Córdoba, which became one of the largest, wealthiest and most cultured cities in the western world. A power struggle within the régime led to civil war after 1008 and the last of the Ommayyad caliphs was expelled in 1031.

Al-Andalus split up into a number of petty principalities or *taifas*. The rulers of several of the *taifas* were patrons of high culture and art and thereby played a crucial role in the transmission of Greek thought, via Arabic, to Europe at the start of the Renaissance.

The *taifas*, however, were caught between the expanding Christian powers to the N and the Islamic revivalism of the **Almoravid** rulers of Morocco, who particularly objected to the taifa rulers' payment of tribute to the Christians. In 1086 Almoravid troops crossed the Straits to help the *taifas* defeat Castilla. The newcomers then overthrew the taifa rulers and re-established unity in al-Andalus. The defeat of the Almoravids in 1145 by the **Almohads**, led to fresh invasions both from the Christian kingdoms and from Africa. The high point of Almohad power in al-Andalus was reached around 1200 with a series of attacks on Castilla and Aragón, but in 1212 the severe defeat by Christian forces at Las Navas de Tolosa was the beginning of the end of Moorish domination in Spain.

How should one evaluate the Moorish period of occupation? The main thing to remember is that it was not so much a military conquest as a benevolent occupation, typified by a tolerant attitude towards other religions. Jews and Christians were allowed to retain their religions and were known as 'Mozarabs', while their places of worship were rarely destroyed. From the social point of view, the Moors made a tremendous impact. They made their mark not only in scholarship, but in trade and urban life. Their agriculture was aided by complex irrigation projects, which sophisticated the existing Roman models. It is their architecture, however, which has left the strongest influence, as shown in the impressive monuments in Córdoba, Granada and Sevilla.

The Christian Reconquest

The reconquest of Moorish lands by the Christians was a gradual process and advances intermittent. The frontier be- tween the opposing forces was always changing and this accounts for the place name 'de la frontera' which is common in SW Andalucía. After the crucial bat- tle of Las Novas de Tolasa in 1212, the Christian forces led by Fernando ('el Santo') quickly captured Córdoba in 1236 and then Sevilla in 1248. Only Granada survived as a Nasrid King- dom for, remarkably, another 250

The Spanish Inquisition

The Spanish Inquisition was established in 1480 by King Fernando V and Queen Isabella I, *Los Reyes Católicos*, with the authority of the Pope. It was introduced initially to meet the supposed threat posed by the *conversos*, Jews who through coercion or social pressure had converted to Christianity. many were suspected of continued secret observance of Judaism. Later attention turned to the *Moriscos* (converted Muslims) and in the 1520's to persons suspected of Protestantism. Its authority did not extend to non-Christians. Within a few years of the founding of the Inquisition, the Papacy relinquished virtually all supervision of it to the sovereigns. This the Spanish inquisition became more an instrument of the state than of the church, furthering the absolute monarchy and abridging the power of the nobles

The Spanish Inquisition continued actively in the time of Philip II, who further oppressed the Protestants, particularly in Holland and the Moriscos. The latter rebelled in 1568 and after suppressing the revolt, Philip expelled the entire group, to the great detriment of the country.

The inquisition, with powers to investigate and try suspects, worked through tribunals in the principal towns and was controlled by an Inquisitor General appointed by the Monarch. The harshest tribunal was in Sevilla, seen as a hotbed of *conversos*, where 20,000 cases were tried between 1481 and 1524.

Each region was visited annually by an Inquisitor who published an Edict of Faith, a type of questionnaire for all adult Christians, covering their beliefs and requiring them to report known heretics. Those accused of serious crimes were imprisoned to wait investigation and trial, which could take years. The accusers were never named, but the prisoner could produce a list of his enemies whose evidence was supposedly ignored. The most notorious inquisitor was Tomas de Torquemada, who was said to have executed thousands of supposed heretics.

Although there were controls on interrogation methods, three forms of torture were allowed – the rack, the hoist and water torture. Those who confessed were given lighter sentences. Various fates awaited those who were found guilty – absolution, flogging, fines, galley service, confiscation of property or being burned at the stake. As a consolation, those who confessed after being sentenced to death were strangled before being burnt.

About 5,000 people were executed up to 1530, thereafter the Inquisition's ferocity declined and between 1560 and 1700 only 500 death sentences were passed from 50,000 cases. The Inquisition was not suppressed in Spain, however, until 1834.

years, protected by a chain of castles and paying heavy tribute to Castilla. The decline of **Marinid** power in Morocco after 1415 left Granada without allies. The marriage of Isabella I of Castilla and Fernando V of Aragón united the two Christian kingdoms and paved the way for the final assault on Granada, led by Gonzalo Fernández de Córdoba – 'El Gran Capitan', who had developed the Christian army into a large and effective force. The advance culminated in a 9 month siege in 1491. In Jan 1492, Boabdil surrendered the keys of the city and fled to the Alpujarras.

Although Muslims were promised the right to practise their religion the expulsion of the Jews in 1492 indicated religious intolerance in Spain. Forcible mass baptism of Muslims began in 1499, provoking a quickly suppressed rebellion. Muslims in Granada had the choice of conversion or emigration on unfavourable terms (children and property to be left behind). In 1502 the same policy was extended to Castilla and in 1525 to Aragón. Many 'converted' Muslims, known as Moriscos, practised their faith in secret. In 1609 Philip III expelled all Moriscos. The 300,000 people who left included many of the country's finest craftsmen and artisans (those Moors who had worked on Christian buildings had produced an architectural style known as Mudejar). Thus the 780 year long Muslim presence in Iberia came to an end, commemorated now only in the Spanish language, in Spanish place names and in the few remaining examples of its architectural greatness.

The fall of Granada in 1492 coincided with the first of the voyages of Christopher Columbus to the New World. Over the next 3 decades there was a systematic exploration and exploitation of the Americas, followed later by colonisation. Power in Andalucía now moved to Sevilla, where the riches of the New World were brought ashore. Little of this wealth, however, found its way to the ordinary people of Andalucía.

16th to 20th centuries

The 16th and 17th centuries found Spain, and Andalucía in particular, in the doldrums. The Inquisition had led eventually to the expulsion of the Jews and the Moriscos, which created a void in the labour force and in commerce and trade. Financially in huge debt, despite the New World riches, Spain lost its possessions in France and the Netherlands.

When Felipe V, a Bourbon, succeeded to the Spanish throne in 1700, a rival claimant, Archduke Charles of Austria, was supported by British forces, leading to the War of Spanish Succession. The war ended in 1713 with the Treaty of Utrecht, whereby Spain lost its territory in Belgium, Luxembourg, Italy and Sardinia. Gibraltar, which had been taken by the British during the war, was to remain in their hands. The Bourbon connection meant that Spain was drawn into the Napoleonic Wars and the Spanish fleet was defeated by Nelson at the battle of Trafalgar, near Cádiz in 1805. Within 3 years Napoleon had installed his brother Joseph on the Spanish throne and the French army set out on a systematic destruction and theft of much of the country's artistic heritage, which Andalucía was unable to escape. This led to the War of Independence, when the Spanish initially defeated the French at the Battle of Bailen in Jaén province. Later, helped by Wellington's army, the French were finally driven out of Spain. Meanwhile, in 1812, the first democratically elected parliament was set up in Cádiz and although this was not to last long, the written constitution was to form the basis of future democracy in Spain.

The remainder of the 19th century saw the political turmoil continue, the further loss of overseas territories and, in Andalucía, the phylloxera plague which severely hit the wine and sherry industry.

Looking at Andalucían cathedrals

For the visitor from Britain or France, a first glance at an Andalucían cathedral gives an impression of disorientation. In Britain the design of a cathedral concentrated on length order to give the observer a vista. In France, it was height which provided the vista. Well known patterns of window tracery, columns and arches place the building into clear architectural styles, such as Norman, Early English, Decorated and Perpendicular. The windows make the interiors well lit with natural light, showing stained glass off to good effect, while the Dissolution of the Monasteries meant that much of the internal ornamentation and statuary were removed leaving an essential simplicity.

Andalucían cathedrals, on the other hand, are nearly always square in shape and as a result do not attain great height. Pillars and arches abound and some buildings may have as many as five parallel naves. This shape is explained by the fact that they were usually built on the site of a mosque, occupying its rectangular ground plan. Furthermore, the High Altar and the choir, or *coro*, are centrally placed and even walled in, forming the *capilla mayor*, so that the general impression is of one building contained within another. This does not give any sort of vista, so that the size of the building is rarely appreciated. Sevilla cathedral, for example, is the largest cathedral in the world (according to the Guiness Book of Records), but the visitor does not get that impression when standing in the interior.

Another strong immediate feeling is one of gloom, due to the lack of natural light. Windows tend to be few and small. In coastal cathedrals, such as Almería, this was because they had a defensive function, as the inhabitants fled to the cathedral when raiding Berbers approached the city. This also explains the paucity of good quality stained glass. The lack of windows also makes the identification of architectural styles more tricky. Most cathedrals have some **Mudéjar** elements, which were passed on by the Moorish craftsmen who stayed to work for the Christians. The latter introduced the **Gothic** style, which in Spain was sub divided into **Fernandine** and **Isabelline** after the Catholic Monarchs. During Renaissance times the **Plateresque** style, which covered surfaces in richly decorated stonework, was predominant in Andalucía. It gained its name from its resemblance to the work of silversmiths. A much plainer type of Renaissance work was known as **Herreran**, after the architect who designed the Escorial in Madrid. Finally, there was the **Baroque**, flourishing in the 17th and 18th centuries and perhaps the dominating style in the Andalucían cathedrals. **Churrigueresque**, named after José Churriguera its main exponent, was a particularly flamboyant form of Baroque.

Visitors to Andalucían cathedrals are bound to be impressed by the ornamentation of the interiors. They are full of statuary, silverwork, and decorated iron grills or *rejas*, plus rich art work and imposing tombs (which is indeed a feature of the smallest church). The central feature is always the *retablo*, the altarpiece behind the High Altar, which is invariably rich in carving and dripping with gold leaf. Look too, for the effigies, such as the Virgen, which are carried on the *pasos* on the Easter processions.

Each Andalucían provincial capital city has a cathedral and while Sevilla is undoubted the most stunning, they are all worth an inspection. Unfortunately, Málaga cathedral, the nearest to the Costa del Sol where the majority of visitors will be based, is the least impressive.

The early 20th century

Protest from the landless peasants in the early years of the century led to calls for more regional autonomy and reform of the agricultural system. Spain remained neutral during the First World War and the post war recession led to disillusionment with the parliamentary government. General Primo de Rivera sensed the feeling of the time and organized a successful military coup in 1923. He later organized the Ibero-American Exhibition of 1929 at Sevilla. This was something of a fiasco as it coincided with the Wall Street crash and led to the collapse of the peseta and Rivera's departure.

The success of the anti-monarchist parties in the 1931 elections forced Alfonso XIII off the throne and the Second Republic was born. Republican and moderate Socialist leaders were released from jail to form a government. Two features of the new constitution were particularly controversial: home rule for the Basque and Catalonia which was opposed by Spanish nationalists and the army; separation of the Church and the State which antagonized many Catholics. A mild land reform and other social policies stirred up right wing hostility. Disputes between Socialists and Republicans led to their defeat in the 1933 election and the coming to power of the right who reversed earlier reforms. Left wing groups rose in revolt in 1934 and were brutally put down by General Franco and the Spanish Foreign Legion. The Feb 1936 elections were held in an atmosphere of extreme tension. The victory of the left wing parties united in the popular Front was followed by the formation of a minority Republican government and growing violence as Socialists and Anarchists seized land while right wing leaders plotted with army officers to seize power.

The Civil War

The military rising on 18 July 1936 failed in the main cities but succeeded in the Catholic North. In Andalucía and Catalonia workers seized land and factories. General Franco borrowed planes from Hitler to transport his best Spanish troops, then stationed in Morocco, into Andalucía to crush the revolt before marching them N towards Madrid. With the accidental death of General Sanjurjo, Franco became leader of the rebel (Nationalist) forces.

The Civil War was prolonged and bloody. The Nationalists enjoyed the assistance and weaponry of Nazi Germany and Fascist Italy. Despite the support of the volunteer International Brigade, the Republicans could not compete against the professional army, and their resistance collapsed in Mar 1939. The war had turned factions within villages and towns against each other and reprisals were violent. It was also the first 'modern' war, when aircraft showed their ability to wipe out whole populations, as the example of Guernica showed. Franco's revenge was harsh and many were sent to labour camps or executed.

Post War Spain

Spain was too weak and exhausted to be anything but neutral during WW2 and post war recovery was slow. Conditions for workers on the land in Andalucía was appalling and many emigrated to Madrid, Northern Spain and to Latin America. American aid in the mid fifties initiated a recovery, but it came with a price – the establishment of American nuclear bases, such as that at Rota in Cádiz province. The aid did, in fact, kick start the economy, and with the growth of tourism, such as that along Andalucía's Costa del Sol, prosperity began to increase.

When Franco finally died in Nov 1975, he had already nominated Juan Carlos, grandson of Alfonso XIII as his successor. He duly became King and successfully steered Spain towards parliamentary democracy. The centrist UDC party won the elections in 1977 and drafted a new constitution. The King showed his authority in Feb 1981 when there was an attempted army coup led by Col Tejero, whose men stormed the Cortes. When it was clear that the King would not support the plotters, the coup disintegrated, but the crisis had briefly been serious.

The PSOE (Partido Socialista Obrero Español), led by Felipe González, took over in 1982. Since then, under González's leadership, Spain has joined the EU and NATO and has enjoyed rapid economic growth accompanied by improvement in the infrastructure and large scale foreign investment. Tight control of government spending has brought down inflation at the cost of increased unemployment and the hostility of the PSOE's former allies in the unions. Unemployment in Andalucía is currently at 28%, compared with 18% for Spain as a whole, and many of the workless are agricultural labourers. Whilst the landowners have benefited from EU grants and been able to modernize their farms, the day labourers have had fewer job opportunities due to the increased mechanization. Spending on the highly successful EXPO at Sevilla in 1992 resulted in a modernization of the infrastructure of Andalucía, particularly the road system and the major airports.

In the General Election in 1996, following a number of scandals, the PSOE government of Felipe González was defeated, but the conservative Partido Popular, led by Jose María Aznar, could only form a government with the help of various regional parties. The new Prime Minister has promised to take a firm line on Gibraltar, but it seems doubtful whether Andalucía will benefit from the new government in the same way that it did from its predecessor.

MODERN ANDALUCIA

GOVERNMENT

The Kingdom of Spain, according to the 1978 Constitution, is 'parliamentary monarchy' in which 'sovereignty resides in the people'. Parliament contains two Chambers, the Congress of Deputies with 350 members elected by proportional representation and the Senate with 208 elected members (four from each province) and 49 appointed members. The main political parties are the socialist PSOE, the conservative Popular Party and the left wing United Left.

Although the Constitution emphasizes the 'indissoluble unity of the Spanish nation', it also guarantees the right of autonomy of the nationalities and regions. Andalucía is one of the 17 autonomous communities with its own assembly elected for a 4 year term and its own government (Junta de Andalucía) with powers over local functions including town planning, housing and tourism. It has benefited financially from the policies of the PSOE. Felipe González and several other leading figures in the national government are from Andalucía, which is one of the PSOE strongholds, the party controlling the Junta de Andalucía and the larger towns.

Gibraltar is a democratically self governing colony of the UK though its territory is claimed by Spain, for which the dispute over the Rock is long-running and bitterly contested. Border controls continue to exist between Spain and Gibraltar.

ECONOMY

Agriculture

Despite the advent of mass tourism and a degree of industrialization in the region, farming is still the economic backbone of Andalucía. The variety and mildness of the climate combined with generally reliable rainfall and generous

Economic indicators - Spain	
Gross domestic product, GDP (billion Ptas)	64,669
GDP per head (US$)	12,331
Public consumption (% of GDP)	16.9
Government revenue (%of GDP)	39.5
Government deficit (% of GDP)	6.6
Exports of goods and services (Billion US$)	107.6
Imports of goods and services (Billion US$)	107.2
Source: OECD, Paris Economic Surveys Spain 1996	

surface water flows provide a considerable, albeit increasingly overstretched, irrigation potential. Irrigated lands provide a series of world famous products – Seville's oranges, lemons, the grapes for wine and sherry from Jerez, the olive crop which is the largest in the world – in addition to a wide range of vegetables, cotton and fruits. Away from the lowlands, farming is hard and until recent years the mainly self-sufficient cultivators and herders of the sierras were very poor, eking a living from poor soils. The higher, marginal environments have now been abandoned as families move to employment in the towns and tourist complexes. Livestock is important, Andalucía producing cattle in great numbers for meat and milk as well as specimens for bull fighting. Most farms keep sheep and despite conservation laws, flocks of goats still graze (often over-graze) the hillsides. There are approximately 800,000 cattle, 4 million sheep and 2.25 million pigs in Andalucía.

The most flourishing sector of farming is that of the private estates, generally in large holdings. Average farm sizes of commercial enterprises on the lowlands are in the region of 1,000 ha and on the uplands more than 5,000 ha with a large range of sizes in both areas. In the Mediterranean coastlands the farms are small and intensively cultivated on the **Huerta** model, inherited from a Moorish tradition, in which horticultural techniques are used to produce high quality and high value crops for the local markets and for export. The citrus,

vine and olive districts use similar techniques but for virtual monocultures over fairly wide areas. New plantings of orange and lemon groves are to be seen, developing the specialisms introduced by the Moors centuries ago. Olive cultivation is tending to decline slightly as a result of competition from cheaper producers in North Africa. Spain has the world's third largest grape harvest. Although Andalucía is well-known for table grapes, it has few remarkable wines and vintages, except for those of Jerez where the bulk are converted into sherry, much for export. A fall in the popularity of sherry in the UK has adversely affected the prosperity of the Jerez farming region, despite the fact that *fino* is a hugely popular Andalucían drink. The main national crops in which Andalucía has an approximate 20% share are barley 9.4 million tonnes, grapes 6.5 million tonnes and olives 2.2 million tonnes.

The most remarkable agricultural development in recent years has been the growth of *plasticultura* – fruit and vegetables grown in plastic greenhouses – mainly in the province of Almería. Grown with the aid of drip feed irrigation, the produce is transported by refrigerated lorries to destinations throughout northern Europe.

Energy/petroleum

Spain is able to produce little of her energy requirements. It has some poor quality coal available in Asturias providing some 36 million tonnes a year, but is otherwise import-dependent. Imports of crude oil run at 50 million tonnes a year against a domestic output of 7 million tonnes. Andalucía itself has no coal but an active subsidized oil refining industry is located at Algeciras, exporting oil products as well as supplying the domestic market. A major experiment in the use of wind-generated electricity can be seen on the heights immediately inland from the Straits of Gibraltar. Many propeller type generators have been installed to catch the strong wind funnelling in from the Atlantic. A small amount of hydro electric power is produced in the mountains N of Málaga.

Economic plans

Regional development plans exist as master plans for each of the sub districts within Andalucía. They are mainly indicative land use plans for urban areas provided to act as guide lines for the control of building permissions. There is great variation in the scope and level of the provisions of the local plans. In very recent years, local authorities have become more conscious of the need to improve and protect the environment to prevent the complete destruction of the coast through the over building of hotels and tourist sites. The controls are belated and much of the coast is already severely blighted by ill considered property development, much of it incomplete, and by the crowding of properties onto the beaches. National laws *(leys de la costa)* protecting beaches are gradually taking hold and might save some residual areas from encroachment.

Industry

Industry is an important element of the economy in Andalucía. The major centre is Sevilla, where there is a highly diversified industrial manufacturing base including food processing, brewing, textiles, light engineering and energy related plants. Elsewhere in the urban centres of the Guadalquivir – Cádiz, Chiclana, San Fernando and to a lesser extent, Córdoba – there are food process-

ing and packing plants and other smaller industries which service the thriving agricultural sector. In Málaga there are breweries and consumer goods industries together with plants making items for the tourist sector. The tourist industry is large and Andalucía earned approximately one tenth of Spain's total income in this sector. Gibraltar is gradually developing an economy based on international financial services.

Economic trends

Andalucía experienced a boom in land prices, wages, and employment in the 15 years to 1991. This trend was generated by confidence in the newly democratic structures of the state and its accession to the EU. Large flows of foreign finance came to Spain and much of it was invested in projects and properties on the Mediterranean coast, especially in Andalucía. There was a slump in the tourist trade and building industry between 1991 and 1994, but by 1995, recovery was underway.

The Andalucían people

Considering the vast number of settlers and invaders who have come to the region during historical times, it is not surprising that in appearance it is hard to describe a 'typical' Andalucían. Although predominantly dark haired and olive skinned, fair haired people are not uncommon, particularly in Cádiz province. An *Andaluz* is usually somewhat shorter than his northern European counterpart, but his life expectancy is similar and in the cities in particular his lifestyle differs little.

The family is still the strongest influence on everyday life, with the mother the dominant figure, but the catholic church is less authoritative than in the past. The home is a private place and strangers are rarely invited in. Even friends are met on the street or in a bar or restaurant. Noise is an everyday fact of life (if a travel company claims that a resort is 'quiet', it lies – there is no such place in Andalucía!). Despite the archetypal picture of the Andalucían, laziness is not in his makeup, simply a cavalier attitude towards time, with the idea that *mañana* might be a better time to complete a job. It is often said that the Andalucían loves a bandit (there is even a Museum of Banditry in Ronda). Certainly anyone who outsmarts bureaucracy and authority is highly regarded. Children are often over-indulged and their noise tolerated, while the elderly and the handicapped are well cared for.

Above all the Andalucíans love their leisure. Extended weekends and holidays are enjoyed with intensity. So called

Domestic architecture

Although the majority of Andalucíans live in high or low rise apartments in the suburbs of towns or cities, a significant minority still live in the older parts of urban areas or in country towns and villages, where a distinct style of architecture still remains and indeed has been adapted for some of the better modern *urbanisacións* in the tourist areas.

The style owes much to the Moors, but is also influenced by the climate, which leads to subtle differences within Andalucía. Villages have narrow, winding alleyways more suited to the donkey than the car, which often lead to small squares or *plazuelas*, sometimes with a fountain or communal washing areas. Houses are small and whitewashed to reflect the sun, with only small openings on the outside. Within the house, there is often an inner courtyard or *patio*, around which family life centres. Many patios will have a small fountain playing, while the walls are hung with pot plants, particularly geraniums. There is full use made of decorated ceramic tiles or *azulejos*. Roofs are either flat or gently sloping and pantiled. The flat roof of one house may be the terrace of another, where fruit and washing can be dried. Windows are usually covered with iron grilles or *rejas*, allowing security, but at the same time letting air circulate. Ground floor rooms with high ceilings are often used as bedrooms in the summer, while sunny top floor rooms are warmer in the winter – the continuance of an old Moorish tradition.

The influence of climate is everywhere obvious. In the drier areas, such as Almería, flat roofs predominate. In the SE of Granada province, the inhabitants have found that there are still advantages in living in caves, with their constant temperatures throughout the year. In wetter, mountainous regions, tiled roofs are the norm, while stonework tends to replace whitewashed plaster and chimneys put in an appearance. One of the most distinctive forms of domestic architecture is to be found in the Alpujarras on the southern slopes of the Siera Nevada. Here, despite the high rainfall and snow, roofs are flat. They are composed of thin stone slabs covered with shards of slate. The circular chimneys with their mushroom-like cappings reflect the need for fires for much of the year.

In the more prosperous rural areas, particularly in the W of Andalucía, large agricultural estates known as *latifundios* are found, dating back to Roman times and carried on by the Moors. At the centre of the estate is a large farmstead, known as a *cortijo* in the corn growing areas and a *hacienda* in the olive and wine growing regions. They are often quite palatial, with a central courtyard surrounded by living quarters. There were, additionally, living quarters for seasonal workers, stables, stores, oil mills and wine cellars. The main entry to the *cortijo* was often impressive, with a large studded doorway topped with a bell tower. The specially planted palm trees add a note of distinction as well as shade.

religious events such as *fiestas* and *romerias* are times for eating, drinking, fireworks and dancing. The highlight of all the festivities comes at *Semana Santa* (Holy Week), with its eerie processions. Each small town will have its *feria* or fair, which although originally agricultural, has now lost this purpose. The *Feria de Abril* in Sevilla is the best known of these jamborees, lasting for a full week during the second half of April.

Andalucían society has changed rapidly over the past 20 years, particularly in the urban areas. For the wealthy land-owners and aristocracy little has altered, but for many ordinary people the opportunity for upward social mobility is there and the new found affluence is clear to see. What has not changed is the friendliness and essential decency of the Andalucían, which the visitor will find endearing.

Málaga Province

MALAGA IS the smallest of the eight provinces of Andalucía, but for much of the year it is the most heavily populated, with its influx of summer tourists and a permanent clutch of resident expats.

Inland are a number of historic towns, such as Ronda, deeply cut by the gorge of El Tajo, and Antequera with its prehistoric dolmens. Caves at Nerja and Ronda and abundant evidence of Roman and Moorish occupation, plus the attractive scenery, mean that the hinterland is rich in interest for the tourist who becomes bored with the pleasures of the coast.

HORIZONS

It is the province of Andalucía with the greatest variety of scenery. Inland, there are mountain ranges, such as the Serranía de Ronda and the limestone block of El Torcal, with its weirdly eroded shapes. Rivers flowing south to the Mediterranean have cut deep gorges, such as that of El Chorro, while many have been dammed to form reservoirs like the Guadalhorce complex. Agriculturally, the most fertile area is the Antequera basin, where amongst the small lagoons one finds the salt lake of Fuente de Piedra, home to several thousand breeding flamingos.

The long coastline, which is made up of generally gritty beaches and low cliffs, is typified by resort developments, such as the Costa del Sol stretching from Málaga to the border with Cádiz province. The largest port and city is Málaga. East of the city is the remote area of La Axarquia, bandit country until recent times

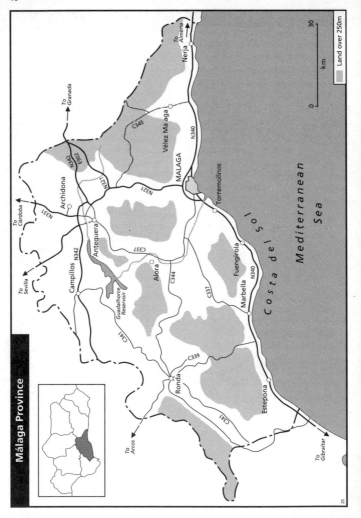

Málaga Province

MALAGA

(*Pop* 555,000; *Alt* sea level; *STD code* 95)
Málaga is located at the mouth of the Guadalmedina River (usually dry) at the head of a broad bay, with its suburbs stretching away to the foot of the surrounding mountains. Climatically, it is located in one of the most favoured parts of Spain, with the mountains to the N cutting out cold winter winds, so that average Jan temperatures are around 15°C, while in the summer, sea breezes usually make the heat bearable. Rainfall figures for Málaga itself are low, but plentiful rain in the sierras inland, along with a plethora of reservoirs, ensure that water supply is not usually a problem.

Málaga has a long history dating back to the Phoenicians, who founded a settlement called *Malaka*, a word derived from *malac*, meaning to salt fish. Málaga became a busy trading port during Roman times, exporting minerals and agricultural produce from the interior. From the 8th century Málaga was occupied by the Moors, when it was the main port for the province of Granada. It was the Moors, under Yusef I, who built the Gibralfaro fortress in the 14th century. The city fell to the Catholics in 1487 after a long and violent siege. The Moorish population was subject to considerable persecution, which led to a revolt in 1568. This was brutally put down and the remaining Moors expelled.

Deprived of its most able citizens, the fortunes of Málaga declined. It was not, in fact, until the 19th century when an agricultural based revival began. During the Civil War, Málaga supported the Republicans and saw a considerable amount of vicious fighting. Italian planes bombed the city, destroying part of its ancient centre. Over the last 35 years mass tourism has transformed the area, but has had little effect on the city itself. Only a very small proportion of tourists visit Málaga – the airport is to the W of the city, close to Torremolinos and the other resorts of the Costa del Sol, while the new ring road to the N of Málaga carries traffic to the E without entering the city. This is in many ways a pity, because there is much to interest the visitor.

Today Málaga is a busy regional centre. Industry is increasingly important, with a number of industrial estates on the outskirts. Unemployment figures, however, are high, with over 20% out of work (but bear in mind that official statistics are notoriously unreliable and there is a thriving 'grey economy'). The port does not handle its former volume of shipping, but it is a regular port of call for cruise liners.

ACCESS Air Málaga's busy airport (6.23 million passengers in 1995) is located at San Julián, some 7 km W of the city centre. A new international terminal was completed in Nov 1991 and the former international terminal is now the national terminal. **Transport to town**: the cheapest and most convenient link to the city is by the Fuengirola-Málaga electric railway which runs half-hourly between 0714 and 0014 from the airport, 190 ptas, takes 15 mins. There are two Málaga stations – stay on until the *Guadalmedina* stop, which is the end of the line and most convenient. The previous stop is the main *RENFE* station

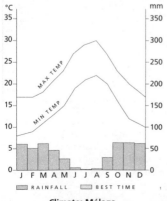

Climate: Málaga

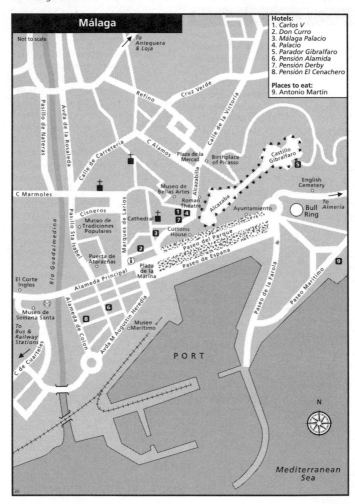

Málaga

Not to scale

To Antequera & Loja

Hotels:
1. *Carlos V*
2. *Don Curro*
3. *Málaga Palacio*
4. *Palacio*
5. *Parador Gibralfaro*
6. *Pensión Alamida*
7. *Pensión Derby*
8. *Pensión El Cenachero*

Places to eat:
9. *Antonio Martín*

Refino
Cruz Verde
Calle de Carretería
C Álamos
Plaza de la Mercad
Birthplace of Picasso
Castillo Gibralfaro
Calle de la Victoria
Alcazabilla
English Cemetery
C Marmoles
Museo de Bellas Artes
Avda de la Rosaleda
Pasillo de Nateras
Cisneros
Pasillo Sta Isabel
Marques de Larios
Cathedral
Museo de Tradiciones Populares
Roman Theatre
Alcazaba
Ayuntamiento
Bull Ring
To Almería
Río Guadalmedina
Puerta de Atarazñas
Customs House
Paseo del Parque
Alameda Principal
Plaza de la Marina
Paseo de España
El Corte Inglés
Museo de Semana Santa
To Bus & Railway Stations
Alameda de Colón
Avda M Augustin Heredia
Museo Marítimo
Paseo de la Farola
Paseo Marítimo
C de Cuarteles

PORT

Mediterranean Sea

N

and further from the city centre. There is also a bus service from the airport running to the cathedral area every 20 mins between 0640 and 2230. The taxi fare to the centre is currently about 1500 ptas.

Train Train travellers arrive at the station on C/Cuarteles.

Bus A new bus station has recently opened conveniently close to the RENFE (5 mins N) on Paseo de los Tilos.

It is a 20-min walk to the city centre. Local buses also cover the route. Both the bus and train stations have small tourist offices. The main tourist office is at Pasaje de Chinitas 4.

WARNING As in any large city, watch out for pickpockets and be sure to leave no valuables accessible in cars, even when driving through the city.

PLACES OF INTEREST

Fortunately most of the places of interest in Málaga are contained within a small area N of the main E-W thoroughfare and can be covered easily on foot. This thoroughfare starts in the E at the Plaza de Toros and passes first through the Paseo del Parque, a tree lined promenade, past the Plaza de la Marina, along the Alameda Principal, a 19th century boulevard, over the dried up bed of the Río Guadalmedina, ending in the area around *El Corte Inglés*, the post office and the Fuengirola line railway station.

Málaga's oldest monuments date back to **Moorish** times.

The Alcazaba This former fortress and palace was started by the Moors in the 700s, but most of the structure dates from the mid-11th century. The site was originally occupied by both the Phoenicians and the Romans, and in fact there is a considerable amount of Roman masonry in the walls. The Alcazaba suffered badly during the Catholic Reconquista, but was carefully restored in the 1930s. Today, it consists of a series of terraced, fortified walls and fine gateways, laid out with gardens and running water in typical Moorish style.

The main palace building now houses the **Archaeological Museum**. Exhibits cover the prehistoric, Phoenician, Roman and Moorish periods, consisting of pottery, statues, coins and mosaics, presented in a rather haphazard fashion. From the terraces of the museum there are fine views over the port and the city. Open 1000-1300 and 1700-2000, Sun 1000-1400. Entrance a mere 20 ptas.

The Castillo Gibralfar 'Lighthouse Hill' is a ruined Moorish castle built by Yusef I of Granada in the early 14th century. It is linked to the Alcazaba below by parallel walls. A path leads up to it from the side of the Alcazaba, but this is a stiff walk and in the summer heat it might be prudent to approach it by the road which leads from the city up towards the *parador*, some 500m

from the car park. Take the No 25 bus from the Paseo del Parque. Open 1000-1300. Free entry.

There are two other Moorish curiosities in Málaga. In the underground car park at the W end of the Parque de Paseo are the remains of the **Moorish City Walls** (plus part of the 18th century harbour wall). Formerly protected by a brick wall, they are now being restored and the plan is for them to be displayed behind glass sheets. The Moorish walls are believed to date from the 14th century Nasrid period. Further W at the entrance to the city market is the **Puerta de Atarazañas**. This was originally the gateway into the Moorish dockyard and it displays the crest of the Nasrid dynasty.

Roman Theatre The Teatro Romano was unearthed in the 1950s when it was planned to extend the 19th century **Casa de Cultura**. It consists mainly of banks of seating, but more will be exposed when the Casa de Cultura is eventually demolished. The Teatro Romano is close to the entrance to the Alcazaba and is easily viewed, with free access.

The Cathedral Málaga's cathedral, as with many others in Andalucía, was built on the site of a mosque and dates from the 16th century, with numerous modifications at later dates. One of its two towers was never completed, giving it a lopsided appearance, leading to the nickname of *la Manquita*, variously translated as 'the cripple' or 'the one-armed lady'. An ugly, gloomy building, its interior could benefit from some imaginative lighting. Its one saving grace is the choir, where behind the stalls are some 40 superb carvings of saints produced by Pedro de Mana in 1662 (de Mana's house, incidentally, is located in a back street about 500m from the cathedral). Open 1000-1300 and 1600-1730. 'Tourists' will be charged an entrance fee of 100 ptas. There are a number of interesting **churches** in the central area of Málaga, outstanding of which are the

Iglesia del Sagrario, adjacent to the cathedral with an outstanding Plateresque retablo, and **Nuestra Señora de la Victoria**, in C\Victoria, which has further work by de Mana. The main problem, as with many Andalucían churches, is gaining entry. The times of services are often the best bet.

The English Cemetery This curiosity is located E of the Paseo del Parque and just past the bull ring. It dates from the days when 'infidels' ie non Catholics, were buried on the beach, where after storms their remains were often washed up. In the mid-1800s a British consul persuaded the authorities to allow him to start an English cemetery. Look for the small Church of St.George. From here a path leads into the walled cemetery. The inscriptions on the gravestones make absorbing reading.

Paseo del Parque Between the Alcazaba and the port is a delightful tree-lined avenue, giving welcome shade during the heat of summer days. Built on land reclaimed from the sea, the Parque has a fine collection of rare, well labelled plants, along with sculptures and fountains (look

The Alcazaba, Málaga

for the Genoa Fountain, now on a traffic island). There are some distinguished buildings on the N side of the Parque, including the flamboyant **Ayuntamiento** or town hall, **La Aduana**, the old customs house, and **El Correo**, the old post office.

Casa Natal de Picasso Often erroneously described as a museum, Picasso's birthplace is now the headquarters of the Picasso Foundation. It is located in the Plaza de la Mercad, a once impressive square which is now a little seedy. The building is open during office hours and the staff do not seem too bothered if you go in to look around. There is the occasional Picasso print to be seen on the walls.

MUSEUMS

Museo De Belle Artes Conveniently close to the cathedral, the Fine Arts Museum is located in C\San Agustín, housed in a restored 16th century palace. It mainly displays work by Spanish artists such as Belgrano, Murillo and Cano. There are some interesting seascapes by Ocon y Rivas and some more modern pieces by Villa and Oliva. In an upstairs room are some ink and wash sketches by **Picasso**, who lived in Málaga until he was 14. Look particularly for his drawing of his father which he produced at the age of nine. There are also a few uninspiring works by Muñoz Degrain, who was Picasso's first tutor. Open 1000-1330 and 1700-2000, Sat, Sun and festivals 1000-1300. Entrance fee 250 ptas pensioners and students under 21 from EU countries free.

Museo De Artes Y Tradiciones Populares, C\Pasillo Santa Isabel 10. Any visitor interested in social history should make a particular effort to see this museum which is located by the dried up bed of the river Guadalmedina, a 2-min walk from the Alameda. Look for the inn sign labelled Mesón de Victoria, as this museum is housed in an old 17th century hostelry. The museum consists of a somewhat haphazard collection of items of everyday life going back several centuries, including fishing boats, an olive press, guns, farming implements and a whole range of household relics. There is much to appeal to visitors of all ages. Open 1000-1300 and 1700-2000. Closed Sat afternoon and Sun. Entrance free.

Museo De Semana Santa, Plaza de San Pedro (opposite *El Corte Inglés*). Holy Week museum with exhibits of processional regalia. Open Mon-Fri 1030-1230 and 1900-2100.

Museo Diocesano de Arte Sacro, Palacio del Obisco (near cathedral). Museum of religious art located in the recently restored Episcopal Palace. Only open when an exhibition is being held.

Acuario Museo Aula del Mar (Museo Maritimo), Avda Manuel Augustin de la Heredia (near the port). Marine museum with aquaria and underwater caves containing turtles, octopuses and coral. Runs marine ecology courses and boat excursions in Málaga Bay, T 2229287. Open Tues-Fri 1700-1900, Sat and Sun 1100-1300 and 1715-1900. Entrance 400 ptas, children 300 ptas.

OUT OF TOWN

Their are two 'botanical gardens' within easy reach of both Málaga and the Costa del Sol. They are entirely different from each other in concept and aims, but are both well worth a visit, particularly as a change from the heat of the city or the beach.

La Concepción Botanical Gardens The gardens have an interesting history, being created over 150 years ago by Amalia Heredia and her husband, the American George Loring, a mining tycoon, who later became the Marquis of Casa-Loring. They collected plants from many parts of the world and also accumulated an important archaeological collection. The estate, covering some 120 acres, eventually passed into the hands of the Echevarrieta family who sold it to the Málaga city hall in 1990.

Any excuse for a party!

One of the most bizarre of all the extraordinary fiestas in Andalucía takes place in the hills N of Málaga during the last week in Dec. Known as the *Fiesta de Verdiales*, it is one of the noisiest, booziest and most wild dates in the *malagueñas* calendar. Groups of folk singers and dancers from the surrounding villages home in on La Venta del Tunel, just off the Málaga – Antequera autovia, joined by thousands of merrymakers. The groups are called *pandas* and must have at least eight members, including musicians, dancers and flag wavers. They are led by an *alcade* (mayor) and wear white shirts, black leggings with a red sash and extraordinary headgear decorated with flowers, beads, mirrors and bells. From these hats fall lengths of multi coloured ribbons. Their instruments include guitars, fiddles, tambourines and anything else which will make a loud noise – for that is the object of the exercise. The songs themselves are made up by the pandas and certainly wouldn't make the top 20, generally extolling the virtues of their particular *pueblo*. The greatest cacophony occurs when two groups of *pandas* encounter each other, (known as a *choque*) when a frenzy of noise and energy erupts in an effort to drown the rivals.

Although each *panda* performs on a stage, in fact they rarely stop playing throughout the festival, lubricated by vast quantities of the sweet Málaga wine. The followers of the Verdiales join in the fun, consuming litres of wine and sausages.

The history of the Verdiales is long and complex. Experts believe that they are older than flamenco itself, possibly originating during the time of the Moors, with the songs of the olive pickers. The fiesta was held until 1931 at the shrine of the Virgen de los Dolores, when a mass was held and alms collected. When the shrine was demolished, the groups kept up the tradition by playing at rural inns or *ventas*. The permanent site of the fiesta de Verdiales at Venta del Tunel was fixed in 1961, since when the event has gone from strength to strength. The Málaga city authorities now support the jamboree to the tune of over one million ptas in prize money, but one suspects that who wins is less important than having a good party!

The local authorities then spent 4 years classifying the plants, restoring the fountains and clearing paths. The gardens were finally open to the public in Jun 1994. Visits take the form of guided tours, with multi-lingual guides, lasting around 1½ hrs. The tone is set at the entrance, which is through a 3m thick bourgainvilea hedge and then follows what resembles a tamed jungle with some 30 species of palms, dragon trees, a huge pergola of Wisteria, whole banks of Swiss cheese plants, some in flower, Camellia, Jacarandas, a Norfolk Island pine claimed to be the largest in Andalucía, a vast variety of rhododendrons and much more. Curiously, this part of the gardens is known as the 'English garden'; nearby is a typical Spanish *paseo* known equally curiously as the 'French garden'. The latter leads to a mirador giving stunning views over Málaga (the cathedral and castle can be clearly seen) and the enormous stone dam of La Concepción reservoir. The tour returns via a small archaeological museum in the form of a reproduction of a Greek temple, containing artefacts filched from a variety of sites, as was the custom of the time. Particularly impressive are the articles from the 1st century Roman site at nearby Cártema, including statuary, mosaics, milestones and a sarcophagus with interior pillow. The museum itself may not always be open, but there are sufficient artefacts lying around outside to provide interest. The house or *palacio* will open some time in the future as an interpretation centre. Access to La Concepción is easy as it lies alongside the Málaga-Antequera *autovia*, just off the Málaga by-pass, and is well signposted. Local buses stop nearby. Entrance 400 ptas; children up to 14, 200 ptas. Open daily, 0900-1900, 1000-1730 in winter, T 2252148. Thankfully, there is no bookshop or bar, but there is a somewhat sleepy venta 200m to the N.

El Retiro Parque Ornitológico Botánico The estate, which was once a 17th century monastery, consists of three parts – a bird park, a formal garden and a small collection of buildings. The **Bird Park** comprises a series of large aviaries set in pinewoods containing a variety of species. There are few raptors (apart from a rather forlorn looking South American Condor and a family of Eagle Owls) and, regrettably, hardly any local species. There are a number of threatened species and a comprehensive collection of the world's toucans and hornbills, while a small lake has a group of Greater Flamingoes and wildfowl. The aviaries themselves are large and well vegetated, with one huge walk-through cage containing some stunning Scarlet Ibises. The birds are in excellent condition and many breed. The **Formal Gardens** are also impressive, with walks, lawns and well-labelled trees and plants and a number of water features, including fountains, ponds and a 'canal'. Particularly attractive is the Courtiers' Garden, a slope of cascades, fountains and statues ending in a view over Málaga and the airport. The **Hamlet**, dating from the 17th century, contains the old monastery buildings and manor house or *palacio*, which is being restored and will eventually contain artisans' workshops with demonstrations of local crafts. Other plans include a simulated Mexican desert and Amazon rain forest. There are a number of picnic sites, a restaurant and a small gift shop. El Retiro is located on the C344 Málaga-

Coín road, some 3 km from the N340 *autovia*, and is well signposted. Open daily, 1000-1900. Entrance 950 ptas, children 600 ptas. Note that El Retiro can be very crowded at weekends and it is a popular venue for Spanish school parties in the spring.

LOCAL FESTIVALS

Málaga is noted for its *fiestas*, starting with the *Carneval* in late Feb. Then comes the Easter *Semana Santa* when local brother hoods mount processions each day and a prisoner is released from Málaga jail. The ceremonies rival those of Sevilla and are arguably the best in Spain. *San Juan*, 23 Jun, sees huge bonfires on which satirical images are burnt. On 16 Jul, the *Virgen del Carmen* is taken in procession to the sea by local fishermen. In Aug, Málaga has its annual *Feria*, with bullfights, flamenco, processions and fireworks. In Dec, *Verdiales*, folk song competitions, take place in the mountains N of Málaga.

LOCAL INFORMATION

Price guide

Hotels:

AL	over US$90	D	US$20-40
A	US$75-90	E	US$10-20
B	US$60-75	F	under US$10
C	US$40-60		

Places to eat:

♦♦♦	expensive	♦♦	average
♦	cheap		

● **Accommodation**

Despite its size and importance, Málaga has a surprisingly poor range and choice of accommodation. Nearby Torremolinos, however, can rectify this, providing that the visitor can tolerate the distractions.

AL *Guadalmar*, Ctra de Cádiz, Km 238, T 2231703, F 2240385, 185 rm, all facilities, close to the beach; **AL** *Málaga Palacio*, Calle Cortina del Muelle 1, T/F 2215185, 225 rm, imposing, traditional, centrally placed, rooftop pool, a/c, TV; **AL** *Parador del Golf*, Apdo 324, T 2381255, F 2382141, 60 rm, a/c, pool, golf course, 10 km to the W of the city.

A *Don Curro*, C/Sancha de Lara 7, T 2227200, F 2215946, 105 rm, central location close to cathedral, usual city noises are accentuated by the hotel's bingo hall; **A** *Las Vegas*, Paseo de Sancha 22, T 2217712, F 2224889, 107 rm, large traditional establishment, located nr bull ring, convenient for city's attractions, tropical gardens; pool; **A** *Los Naranjos*, C/Paseo Sancha 35, T 2224317, F 2225975, 41 rm, parking, a/c, restaurant, some way from the city centre; **A** *Parador de Gibralfaro*, Paseo García del Olmo, T 2221902, F 2221904, a small regional style hotel on the hill next to the Moorish castle, marvellous views, TV, parking, restaurant, only 12 rm, booking essential.

B *Bahia de Málaga*, C/Somera 8, T 2224305, F 2229268, 44 rm, parking, restaurant, close to the port.

C *Carlos V*, C/Cister 10, T 2215120, 51 rm, parking, in the shadow of the cathedral; **C** *Don Paco*, C/Salitres 53, T/F 2319008, 25 rm, parking, a/c.

Pensiones: there are over 60 pensiones to choose from in Málaga, but as is often the case in a seaport, they need to be chosen with care, as some can be rather squalid, particularly in the central area. Insist on seeing the room first. The following, however, can be rec: **D** *Derby*, C/San Juan de Dios1 No 4, T 2221301, 16 rm, clean, some good views over the harbour; **D** *El Cenachero*, C/Barroso 5, T 2224088, 14 rm, friendly, clean and good value.

E *Chinitas*, Pasaje Chinitas 2, T 2214683, F 2286642, 5 rm, a/c, small and clean; **E** *Córdoba*, C/Bolsa 9-11, T 2214469, 11 rm, cheap, family run, nr the cathedral.

Youth hostels: *Plaza de Pio XII 6*, T 2308500, 100 beds, suitable for wheelchairs, meals provided, reservations rec, nr Carranque multi-sports facilities. The hostel can be difficult to find. Take the No 18 bus to the last stop and ask from there.

Camping: the nearest is *Balneario del Carmen*, Avda Pintor Sorolla on the coast road E of Málaga, T 2290021, bar, restaurant, beach, tennis. There are other sites at Torre del Mar and Torremolinos.

● **Places to eat**

Despite the nearby tourist area and the obvious attractions of Málaga to visitors, the restaurants in the city are designed to cater primarily for *malagueñas* (other Spaniards actually refer to them as *boquerones* because of their liking for this fish). The emphasis, therefore, is on regional cooking, especially seafood. Do not expect to see many menus with an English translation.

Fish restaurants: many of the best fish restaurants are to the E of the city in the old fishing villages of Pedregalejo and El Palo, now part of the Málaga suburbs. The best known are: ◆◆◆*El Cabra*, C/Copo 21, and ◆◆◆*Casa Pedro*, C/Quitapeñas 4, an enormous building which actually has an English translation of the menu. Nearby on the Playa del Dedo is the remarkable ◆*Tintero*, where the dishes are auctioned as they leave the kitchen.

Back in Málaga, the best known fish restaurant is ◆◆◆*Antonio Martín*, Paseo Maritimo, long established, popular and expensive. It closed in 1994 after financial difficulties, but new owners hope to reopen it in late 1996. Another favourite is ◆◆*Marisquería Las Dos RR*, C/Carpio 4, in the Huelin district, which specializes in *pescaito frito*, mixed small fishfood fried in batter. ◆*Los Culitos*, C/Circo 1, inexpensive and usually crowded. ◆*Los 21*, C/Martínez Maldonado, small, cheap, but excellent food.

Other restaurants: ◆◆◆*La Taberna del Pintor*, C/Maestranza 6, arguably the best meat restaurant in Málaga; ◆◆*Al-Yamal*, C/Blasco de Garay 3, medium priced Moroccan food; ◆◆*El Corte Inglés*, department store's top floor buffet libre and grill is a popular snap for shoppers; ◆◆*El Mesón Gallego*, C/Casas de Campos 23, Galician specialities.

At the cheaper end of the market, try: ◆*Restaurante Arcos*, Alameda 31, good variety of *platos combinados*; ◆*La Cancela*, C/Denis Belgrano 3, good family cooking. A number of Chinese restaurants and pizzerias have recently begun to appear in Málaga and the former, particularly, might appeal to visitors on a budget. Try ◆*Chino Hong Kong*, Paseo las Farolas 25; ◆*La Tarantella*, C/Granada 61, for fast food.

● **Bars**

Tapas bars: these are to be found everywhere. On of the best areas is along the pedestrianized Calle Marín García. Look in particular for *La Tosca*, No 12, noted for its jamón serrano, and the atmospheric *La Manchega* at No 4. Along the Alameda try *Antigua Casa Guardia*, where according to the photograph on the wall, a youthful Picasso drank. Also rec on the Alameda is *Bar Don Jamon* at No 11.

● **Banks & money changers**
All the main Spanish banks and savings banks have branches in Málaga, mainly concentrated at the W end of the Alameda Principal. There are few branches of foreign banks as yet. *Telebancos* (cash machines) are found at most banks. There are a few change shops in the central area, but the commission can be high.

● **Embassies & consulates**
Canada, Plaza de Malagueta 3 – 1°, T 2223346; **France**, Duquesa de Parcent 8, T 2226590; **Germany**, Paseo de Limonar 28, T 2227866; **Italy**, C/Palestina 3, T 2306150; **Netherlands**, Alameda de Colon, Pasaje Linaje 3P, 2 – 4°D; T 2379954; **UK**, Duquesa de Parcent 8, T 2217571.

NB The nearest US consulate is in Fuengirola.

● **Entertainment**
Art galleries: there are a number of excellent art galleries in the city. The best is undoubtedly the *Colegio de Arquitectos*, Avda de las Palmeras – the building itself is worth the visit – which has regular exhibitions by artists, photographers and architects. The *Sala Miramar* in the old Hotel Miramar on the Paseo Maritimo has major exhibitions, while *Aula 7*, C/ Médez Nuñez, concentrates on photographic shows.

Cinemas: there are numerous cinemas in the city, which show the latest films invariably dubbed in Spanish. For more out of the ordinary films there is the *University Film Club* at Patio San Agustín (next to the Museo de Belle Artes) most Tues and Thur evenings.

Nightclubs: Malagueñas love the *juerga*, so nightlife is not hard to find particularly in the summer. Student life centres around Plaza Mitjana, while there is a host of disco bars in the Malagueta area, S of the bullring, where *Ragtime*, Paseo de Reding 12, is a favourite jazz venue. *H20*, C/Fernando Camino, is another throbbing club in this area. The bohemian crowd focus on *Café Teatro*, C/Afligidos 8, while *La Casa del Conde*, C/Sta Lucía 9, is the haunt of Málaga's yuppies. The nightlife in summer tends to spill out towards El Palo and its beachside discos.

Theatres: the *Teatro Cervantes*, C/Ramos Martín 2, was restored in 1987 and all opera, theatre and dance buffs should check the programme as international performers frequently appear. It is also the home of the Málaga Symphony Orchestra and the Málaga Danza Teatro. More modest is the *Teatro*

Estable de Málaga whose productions feature at the Casa de Cultura in C/Alcazabilla.

● **Post & telecommunications**
Area code: 95 (2). **NB** As with much of the province of Málaga, a 2 prefix has been added to most telephone numbers, in which case the code is 95.

Post Office: the main *Correos* can be found in the Avda de Andalucía, almost opp *El Corte Inglés*, T 2359008.

Telephones: numerous *locutorios* throughout the central area of the city. Open Mon-Sat 0900-2100, Sun 1000-1300. Credit cards accepted.

● **Shopping**
The main shopping area is W of the cathedral and N of the Alameda Principal and in the streets around the Plaza de la Constitución. Further W in the Avda de Andalucía is *El Corte Inglés*, the comprehensive department store. It has a popular restaurant, convenient parking and is opp the terminus of the Fuengirola railway line. In the central area of the city is the rather more down market department store of *Félix Sáenz*, which dates back to 1886. Fashion shops are centred around C/Larios, where you will find most of the well known international franchises. For jewellery try *Tierra*, C/Especerías 10, while visitors interested in perfumes and scents could do no better than the tiny *Perfumería y Mercería Lagarterana* in C/Careterí 93. There is an interesting group of street stalls between *El Corte Inglés* and the river, with bargain jewellery and souvenirs offering good value. A street market is held every Sun in the Paseo de los Martiricos, 1000-1500. A new shopping complex, the *Larios Centro*, opened in Mar 1996. Located between *El Corte Inglés* and the new bus station, it has over 100 shops, a hypermarket, a multi-cinema and luxury apartments.

● **Sports**
Aeronautics: at *Aeroclub de Málaga*, Ctra de Cádiz, T 2230595.

Equestrian centre: Apartado 94, Alaurin de la Torre, T 2412818.

Football: Málaga's team are currently in the Spanish second division. Estadio de Futbol La Roselada, P Martirincos, T 2243926.

Golf: a vast number of golf courses to choose from along the Costa del Sol to the W of the city. Nearest is *Club de Golf 'El Cabdado'*, T 2294666.

Marina: has berths for over 200 pleasure craft.

Tennis: *Club de Tenis*, C/Pinares de San Antón, T 2291092.

● **Tour companies & travel agents**

There are over 30 travel agents' offices in Málaga, so the following are a small selection: *Benamar*, Avda Aurora 2, T 2349800; *Larios Travel*, Aeropuerto, T 2352463; *Melia*, Alameda Principal 1, T 2211071; *Wagon-Lits Cook*, C/Strachen 20, T 2212664.

● **Tourist offices**

The main **Regional Government Tourist Office** is at Pasaje Chinitas 4, T 2213445. Open Mon-Fri 0900-1400, Sat 0900-1300. There is also an office in the main hall at the international airport. The **Municipal Tourist Office** is located at the main bus station, Paseo de los Tilos, T 2350061. For the hire of tourist guides, ring T 2386042.

● **Useful addresses**

Car repairs: *Citroën*: Ctra Cádiz 239, T 2315400; *Renault*: Ctra Cádiz 178, T 2315000; *Volkswagon*: Ctra Cádiz, T 2313630; *Ford*; Ctra Cádiz, Km 239, T 2233489; *Volvo*: Avda Juan XXIII, T 2316108; *Peugeot*, C/Bodegueros 19, T 2346862; *Seat*, Poligono Santa Bárbara, T 2241880.

● **Transport**

Local Car hire: this is most conveniently arranged at the airport, where all the main international firms have their offices. Local Spanish firms are equally reliable and may offer better deals. The larger firms have offices below the arrival lounge and you can collect a car from the airport car park. Smaller firms have their offices on the airport approach road to which they will transport customers by minibus (allow 30 mins for this process when departing). The following firms have offices in the city: **Avis**, C/Cortina del Muelle, T 2216627; **Hertz**, Alameda de Colón 17, T 2225597; **Málaga**, Paseo Maritimo, T 2210010; **Miramar**, Avda Pries, T 2226933. **Scooter and motorcycle hire**: Victoria Racing, C/Victoria 6, T 2220483. **Taxi**: there are taxi ranks at the bus and train stations and in the Alameda Principal; *Radio Taxi*, Plaza de Toros Vieja, T 2327950/2328062.

Air Málaga has a busy airport from which Iberia and its subsidiaries run internal flights to **Madrid, Valencia, Almería, Sevilla, Melilla, Tanger** and **Palma de Mallorca**. British Airways offer regular scheduled services to **Málaga** (information and reservations on UK T 0345 222111 or Málaga T 902 0111333). There are charter and scheduled flights to many North European cities. Information: **T 2136166. NB** If taking the train to the airport, remember that there are stops labelled 'cargo', 'nacional' and 'internacional'. Buses to the airport leave the Alameda at half-hourly intervals between 0630 and 2300.

Train The RENFE station is on C/Cuarteles, but there is an office in the city in C/Strachen, T 2312500. There is a twice daily *Talgo 200* to **Madrid** which now takes only 4 hrs as it joins the high speed AVE track at Córdoba. They leave Málaga at 0635 and 1605. The 4 other daily trains to Madrid might take 2-4 hrs longer. The same trains stop at **Córdoba**, while there is also a direct link with **Sevilla**. Other Andalucían destinations involve a change at **Bobadilla** junction. The Fuengirola-Málaga electric line has an additional station almost opp *El Corte Inglés* department store, while another branch runs N to **Alora**. The electric railway has newly introduced air conditioned rolling stock, playing classical music over the public address system. Strains of Vivaldi are particularly welcome travelling through the rather seedy suburbs of Málaga. Tickets may be purchased at the termini or on board the train. Non-payers and others who misbehave are likely to be ejected by the travelling security guards.

Road Bus: the main bus station is on Paseo Tilos, T 2350061. A number of bus companies use the station, with Portillo covering the area to the W of Málaga and Alsina Graells running services to the E. Local connections are generally at 30 mins intervals and links with other cities every 2 hrs. Printed timetables are, as usual, difficult to obtain and travellers may have to rely on the information on the wall. **Coches de Caballo**: for a stately tour around central Málaga, horse drawn carriages may be picked up at the Paseo del Parque.

Trams A San Francísco style tourist tram opened in Aug 1996. The tour takes 90 minutes and visits all the main sites. Multi-lingial guides provide a commentary. The tours start near El Corte Ingles and costts 1,000 ptas for adults and 500 ptas for children.

Sea Ferry: there are regular daily sailings (except Sun) to Melilla, the Spanish enclave in North Africa. The crossing takes around 10 hrs. For information, Transmediterranea, C/Juan Díaz 4, T 2224391/93.

EAST FROM MALAGA

The coastline E of Málaga (strictly speaking the eastern Costa del Sol) is in the main an uninspiring stretch of ribbon development with small, unattractive resorts largely shunned by international tourists, but crowded with *malagueñas* at weekends. In the initial Málaga suburbs there is a *paseo maritimo* (named inevitably after Pablo Picasso) fronted by imported sand. Then comes the old fishing villages of Pedregalejo and El Palo, with

little to commend them except their fish restaurants. The first resort of any size is **Rincón de la Victoria**. Despite two modest hotels and a newly built *paseo maritimo*, there is little to delay the discriminating tourist. 2 km before Rincón, however, is a road leading inland to the **Cueva del Tesoro** (Treasure Cave – a name allegedly derived from some Moorish kings' gold which was secreted here). There are the usual fairly standard karst features such as stalactites, stalagmites, columns and tufa screens, but the

The Carretera Nacional N340

👣 Visitors to the Costa del Sol should be warned about the dangerous nature of the N340 which runs along the full length of the Mediterranean coast of Andalucía. In the 1980's it was dubbed 'the most dangerous road in Europe', a reputation which was fully justified. Literally hundreds of lives were lost each year in accidents, particularly in the stretch between Fuengirola and San Pedro.

The reasons for this situation were obvious, except apparently to the Spanish authorities. The N340 was not only a 4-lane highway without a central reservation, but it also acted as a local road linking *urbanisacións* with each other. It also cut off *urbanisacións* from the beach. This led to horrific situations such as cars stationary in the fast lane waiting to turn left and, because of the lack of footbridges, pedestrians running across 4-lanes of traffic. Add to this the Spanish drivers love of speed and his general naiveté on the road, then you have a recipe for disaster.

Fortunately, the early 1990's saw a massive introduction of funds to improve the infrastructure in Andalucía, spurred on by EXPO '92 at Sevilla and the availability of money from the EU Regional Fund. The N340 is now a 2 or 3-lane *autovia* from Málaga to Estepona, with a central reservation, flyovers, tunnels and pedestrian footbridges.

But, it is still a very dangerous road, for the following reasons:

● There is no hard shoulder, so there is nowhere to go to avoid an accident or sudden hold up.

● There are few slip roads, so cars cannot join the *autovia* at speed. Cars join the road from STOP signs into traffic travelling at up to 120 kph. Similarly, vehicles must slow down considerably before leaving the *autovia*.

● The sheer volume of traffic, especially during the height of the season.

● Many tourists collect hire cars from the airport at Málaga and drive straight on to the *autovia* in a strange car with left hand drive heading for unknown destinations.

● After the summer drought, the heavy autumn rains fall on an oily surface which soon resembles a skating rink.

● Visitors should also beware of Moroccan guestworkers returning from France and Germany to the ferries at Algeciras. Their ancient cars are usually overloaded with family and possessions and the drivers have rarely stopped for sleep.

Drivers are strongly advised to take the utmost care at all times and certainly not drink and drive.

main interest is in the Palaeolithic wall paintings and other remains. Unfortunately, the wall paintings are not always on view, but with a mere 200 ptas entrance fee, these caves are refreshingly uncommercialized, compared with those at Nerja further E. Open Mon-Fri 1000-1400 and 1500-1900, Sat and Sun 1100-1900. There are also some ruins of **Roman baths** at nearby Benagalbón. After a half hearted attempt at some restoration by the regional government, the site has now been totally abandoned.

Back on the coast, the Málaga ring road ends just to the E of Rincón. Many of the place names in this area have the prefix 'torre', referring to the *atalayas* (watchtowers) which are found at intervals along the shore. The square towers are probably Moorish in origin, while the round towers were more likely to be built by the Christians.

Torre del Mar, the next coastal resort has made recent efforts to improve its image, but it is a soulless spot with a pebbly beach, backed by a huge promenade and high rise apartment blocks. Some good seafood restaurants, however, can be found. For those looking for accommodation, there are two small hotels, four reasonable pensiones and a rather basic camp site. From Torre del Mar, a road leads inland to **Vélez Málaga**, the regional capital of *la Axarquía*. It gets its name from *Ballix-Malace*, meaning rock fortress, and today there are remains of the Moorish castillo on a steep crag above the town. Fernando's army eventually ejected the Moors in 1487, leaving the way open for the assault on Granada 5 years later. Today it functions as the main market town for the fertile Vélez valley. Take a look at the church of Santa María la Mayor, dating from the 16th century and the first building to be erected by the victorious Christian forces. It was built on the site of the mosque and the minaret can still be distinguished. Inside, the triple nave,

typical of the period, and the Mudéjar ceiling, are noteworthy. There are two or three other churches of interest along with the Palacio del Marques de Beniel, a 16th century mansion which was once the town hall. Drivers looking for an inland route to return to Málaga have plenty of possibilities. Those with time on their hands and a bent for curiosity, could head N to Zaffaraya and then head for **Alfarnate**. The attraction here is the Antigua Venta de Alfarnate, claimed to be the oldest inn in Andalucía. Once the haunt of assorted highwaymen and robbers, including the notorious El Tempranillo, it now houses a small 'outlaws museum' including a prison cell. More to the point, the venta serves excellent country food, although avoid the weekends when it is crowded with the inhabitants of Málaga and Granada. Return to Málaga via Colmenar, joining the motorway at Casabermeja.

Back on the coast the ribbon development continues towards **Torrox Costa**, a featureless resort favoured by Germans and Scandinavians. The village of **Torrox** itself is some 4 km inland and has some Roman remains, while recent archaeological evidence suggests that the area immediately to the W was an important Phoenician stronghold and several graveyards have been found dating from the 4th and 5th centuries. Approaching Nerja, the coastal plain begins to widen out and there are some of the first signs of the *plasticultura* which disfigures the coast further E in Almería.

NERJA

ACCESS Road Located on the N340 coast road. The nearest airport and railway station are in Málaga. Buses stop on the main road N of the town, the Avda de Pescia, or the bus station on C/San Miguel.

Some 50 km from Málaga, Nerja is situated on a low cliff littered with sandy coves. Sheltered by the mountains, Nerja has a mild winter climate, making

Hotels:
1. Balcón de Europa
2. Portofino
3. Parador
4. Pensión Don Peque
5. Pensión Fontainebleu
6. Pensión Miguel

Places to eat:
7. El Chispa
8. Jiminez
9. La Familia
10. Patanegra
11. Pepe Rico

it attractive to northern Europeans. Despite tourist development, Nerja has been spared the excesses of the western Costa del Sol, most of the buildings being low rise and the *urbanizacions* tastefully designed.

Nerja started life as the Moorish settlement of *Narixa*, suggesting reliable spring waters. Unfortunately, an earthquake in 1884 destroyed much of the town and no Moorish constructions survived. For centuries the inhabitants eked out a living by making silk, growing sugar cane and fishing. None of these activities thrive today and the sugar refining buildings are part of the industrial archaeology. The main attraction within the town is the **Balcón de Europa**, a tree lined promenade jutting out into the sea giving fine views along the coast and to the mountains inland. Beware, however, of the inflated prices charged in the bars and restaurants around the Balcón. On the E side of the Balcón is the small, former fishermens'

beach of Calahonda. There are a few token fishing boats left, but it has now been largely taken over by tourists. Further E, and out of sight behind a headland is the popular beach of Burriana. Other beaches, near to the main tourist hotels, stretch away to the W of the town. To the W of the Balcón is a small square at the end of which is the whitewashed **Church of El Salvador**, dwarfed by its Norfolk Island Pine. It has elements of Mudéjar and Baroque work plus an interesting mural representing the Annunciation on a Nerja beach. On the main N340, in the N of the town, is the **Hermitage of the Virgen of las Angustias**, a 17th century chapel with Granada style paintings on the cupola. Inland from the Balcón is a maze of small streets, with some quality shops.

EXCURSIONS FROM NERJA

Cuevas de Nerja These caves were discovered in 1959 by a group of local schoolboys on a bat hunting expedition and are now a national monument. In addition to the usual features of limestone caves, such as stalactites and stalagmites, there is evidence that the caves were occupied by Cro-Magnon man as indicated by pottery, ornaments, implements of stone bone and flint, and tools of copper and bronze. The boys found a group of skeletons and it is believed that small communities were in occupation from 2000 BC until a major earth tremor blocked the cave entrance and sealed in the occupants and their artefacts. The most important finds were the wall paintings, probably Upper Palaeolithic in age and largely of animals – believed to be part of a magical rite to ensure success in hunting and guarantee the fertility of domestic animals. Regrettably, the paintings are not on public view. The lighting of the caves and the piped music may appear to some visitors to be somewhat overdone, but this is a highly popular excursion as the number of tourist coaches in the car park proves. There is a small archaeological museum near the entrance and a restaurant on site, but this can get crowded – far better to walk the 200m to the delightful Hotel al Andalus, with excellent views from its terrace restaurant. The caves are open all year daily 1030-1800; entrance fee adults 400 ptas, children 200 ptas. During the summer season, the main chamber of the caves is used as an auditorium for a festival of music, often with internationally known performers. Contact the tourist office in Nerja for the programme.

The small village of **Maro** is located on the cliff top 4 km E of Nerja, close to the caves. The white washed houses stand above an attractive cove. Originally the Roman settlement of *Detunda*, Maro has three items of particular interest, all dating from the 18th century: the small, but charming village church of Nuestra Señora de la Maravillas de Maro; the ruined sugar factory; and best of all, the magnificent 4-tiered aqueduct which carried water across a valley to the factory. Regular buses run from Nerja to both the caves and to Maro.

La Axarquia (also spelt Ajarquia) is defined as the area inland from the coast E of Málaga city. Parts of the region are remote and settlement, by and large, consists of small villages. Once notorious bandit country and a hotbed of guerrilla activity during the Civil War (and after), it has only been in comparatively recent times that La Axarquia has been safe for travel. Some of the more southern villages are within easy reach of Nerja. **Frigiliana**, a mere 6 km N, steeped in Muslim atmosphere, was the site of one of the last battles between the Christians and the Moors in 1569 and ceramic plaques record the events on the walls of the houses in the older part of the town. It is a pretty village, with narrow streets and whitewashed houses festooned with hanging plants and geraniums. The only accommodation here is at *Las Chinas*, Plaza Capitán Conés, T 2533073, 9 rm, good restaurant. Further W, some 20 km from the coast, is the village of **Competa**. Around the village the slopes are clothed with vineyards and drying racks for the Moscatel grapes making the strong, sweet wines for which the area is well known. A riotous wine festival is held in the main square in mid-Aug. Competa has attracted large numbers of northern European ex pats in recent years, particularly from UK and Denmark, and many have set up craft industries. There is a pleasant main square, dominated by the bell tower of the Church of la Asunción, with two or three bars serving economical meals.

In an effort to sponsor 'rural tourism', five routes have been devised for visiting La Axarquia by car, each colour coded and way marked. The **Ruta del Sol y del Aguacate** (the Sun and Avocado Route) starts at Rincón de la Victoria and visits the agricultural villages of the Vélez valley, including Macharaviaya, Benamacarra and Iznate. The **Ruta del Sol y del**

Vino (the Sun and Wine Route) starts in Nerja and includes the main wine producing villages such as Competa and Frigiliana. The **Ruta Mudéjar** concentrates on architecture, looking at villages such as Archez, Salares and Sedilla. The **Ruta de la Pasa** (the Route of the Raisin) looks at the more mountainous villages in the NW of the area. Finally, the **Ruta del Aceite y los Montes** (the Route of the Oil and the Mountains) examines the olive growing villages such as Periana and Alaucín in the N of the area. Unfortunately, owing to the terrain, most of the routes are not 'round tours' and involve retracing one's steps in places, but they are, nevertheless, highly recommended. A detailed brochure describing the routes can be obtained from the tourist office in Nerja. Be prepared, in the more remote parts of La Axarquia, for some erratic signposting. The Nerja tourist office will also put you in touch with Elma Thompson, an English woman resident in the town who organizes guided local walks during the cooler months.

Local festivals

16-17 Jan: *San Anton* – procession and fireworks in Maro.

Feb: *Carnival* – for 3 days in Feb with parades and singing of *chirigotas* (popular songs).

3 May: *Cruces de Mayo* – flower crosses made locally with singing and dancing.

14-15 May: *San Isidro* – romería.

23-24 Jun: *San Juan* – beach barbecues, with local cake speciality 'tortas de San Juan'.

Jul: *Festival de la Cueva* – flamenco, classical music and ballet in the Nerja caves.

16 Jul: *Fiesta de la Virgen del Carmen* – the fishermens fiesta, where the statue of the Virgin is carried down to the sea at Calahonda beach.

7-9 Sep: *Feria Maravillas de Maro* – local Saints Day festival with fair in Maro.

9-13 Oct: *Feria de Nerja* – local Saints Day week long festival.

Semana Santa – Holy Week processions.

Local information
● **Accommodation**

There is a good choice of accommodation to suit all pockets. It is best to book in advance during the height of the summer and during *Semana Santa*.

AL *Monica*, Playa de Torrecilla, T 2521100, F 2521162, 234 rm, modern beach hotel with everything on tap for the package tourist; **AL** *Parador de Nerja*, C/Almuñécar 8, T 2520050, F 2521997, 73 rm, pool, tennis, a/c, TV, relatively modern parador set on cliff top with attractive gardens, lift to the beach, all that one would expect from a parador.

A *Balcón de Europa*, Paseo Balcón de Europa 1, T 2520800, F 2524490, 102 rm, TV, sauna, garage, private beach, convenient for shops but can be noisy from merrymakers and breaking waves; **A** *Perla Marina*, C/Merida 7, T 2523350, F 2524083, 106 rm, beach, pool, TV, parking, beach hotel to the W of the town.

B *Nerja Club*, Ctra Almería, Km 293, T 2520100, F 2522608, 47 rm, a/c, pool, tennis, on the coast road E of town; **B** *Playa de Maro*, Apdo Correos 7, T 2529598, F 2529622, 22 rm, pool, small quiet hotel close to the beach in Maro.

C *Portofino*, Puerta del Mar 2, T 2520150, 12 rm, central location, closed Oct-Mar.

Pensiones: **D** *Don Peque*, C/Diputacion 13, T 2521318, 10 rm, small comfortable, central position; **D** *Fonteinbleu*, C/Alejandro Bueno 5, T 2520939 F 2521475, 22 rm, NE side of town, British run, good range of facilities; **D** *Mena*, Calle Alemania 15, T 2520541, 10 rm; **D** *Miguel*, C/Almirante Ferrándiz 31, T 2521523, 8 rm, good ambience in the older part of town, close to the Balcón.

Those looking for an out of town location could try **C** *Al-Andaluz*, Ctra de la Cueva s/n, T 2529648, F 2529557, 18 rm, small, quiet hotel close to the caves and Maro village, good restaurant.

Camping: *Almayate-Costa*, Ctra Málaga-Almería, Km 267, nr Maro, top category, bar, restaurant, beach, booking necessary in high season.

● **Places to eat**

There is a wide selection of restaurants to suit all pockets and tastes in Nerja, although those around the Balcón tend to have inflated prices and be directed at the tourists.

Seafood restaurants: ◆◆*Hermanos Pulguilla*,

C/San Pablo 6, T2521892; **Marisquería la Familia**, C/Diputación 17, T 2520046; **Marisquería Jiminez**, Plaza Marina.

Other restaurants: ***Casa Luque**, Plaza Cavana 2, T 2521004, Spanish and international cuisine, good value for money; **Pepe Rico**, C/Cristo 26, T 2520247, good international cuisine; **Rey Alfonso**, T 2520195, varied menu. **Meson Patanegra**, Plaza la Marina, T 2520222, good Spanish cooking at moderate prices; **La Noria**, Ctra de Frigiliana, Km 1.5, Spanish style mesón in an old farm building, good fish and game dishes at moderate prices. * Those on a tight budget could try the lunch time offerings of fish and shellfish in the *chiringuitos* on Burriana beach or *Pizzeria Jiménez*, Avda de Pescia 17, T 2521998.

● **Bars**
Tapas bars: try *El Chispa*, C/San Pedro 12 and *Las 4 Esquinas*, C/Pintada.

● **Entertainment**
Disco and karaoke bars cluster around Plaza Tutti Frutti. For *flamenco* shows, try **Bar El Colono**, C/Granada 6.

● **Hospitals & medical services**
Chemists: *Lucía Molina*, C/Diputacíon 18; *Luis Sáenz*, C/Pintada 48; *Victor Navas*, C/Pintada 33.

First aid: T 2520935.

Hospitals: *Clinic*, C/Bronce 8, T 2520358, open 24 hrs.

● **Post & telecommunications**
Area code: 95(2).

Post Office: *Correos* is located nr the junction of Puerta del Mar and C/Carabeo.

Telephones: cabins are available around the town, incl on the Balcón de Europa.

● **Shopping**
Street market: held every Tues.

● **Tour companies & travel agents**
Benamar, C/G Franco 35, T 2521745; *Jaime Tours*, C/Pintada 79, T 2522790; *Latitud 7*, Plaza Cantarero s/n, T 2522512; *Verano Azul*, C/ Castilla Pérez 60, T 2523700.

● **Tourist offices**
The *turismo* is located at the landward end of the Balcón de Europa with very cooperative staff who will provide a useful town plan. Check their noticeboard for vacancies and events. Open 1000-1400 Mon-Fri, 1000-1300 Sat, T 2521531.

● **Transport**
Local Car hire: Autos Andalucía, C/Pintada 51, T 2521534; Autos Costasol, C/Jaen, Edf La Marina, T 2522796; Autos Nerja, C/Cruz 22, T 2520694; Autos Unidos-Hertz, C/Diputación 7, T 2524250; Lual, C/Castilla Pérez s/n, T 2523066. **Taxis**: taxi rank at Plaza Ermita on the old N340.

Road Bus: daily bus departures from Calle San Miguel 3, are as follows: 12 to **Málaga** and the coastal towns to the W; 8 to **Motril** and **Almuñécar**; 2 connect directly to **Granada**, which can also be reached by changing at **Motril**. There are daily long distance coaches to **Córdoba**, **Cádiz** and **Sevilla**, plus local buses to the inland villages of the Axarquía such as **Frigiliana**, **Torrox** and to the hospital at **Velez**.

NORTH FROM MALAGA

The autovia N from Málaga is a well engineered road, making full use of tunnels and bypassing villages such as **Casabermeja** and **Colmenar**. Northeast of **Antequera** it joins the N342 linking **Sevilla** and **Granada**. (As yet there is no autovia link with **Córdoba**.)

A more interesting route is the MA 402 NW from Málaga. This passes initially through **Pizarra** – fortunately bypassed – don't be detained here, move on to **Alora**, which is a white hill village capped with a ruined Moorish alcazaba (now the cemetery). It is well worth taking a stroll through the narrow streets – aim for the main square, where you will find the impressive church of La Incarnación, dating from the early 18th century and claimed to be the largest in Málaga province after the cathedral.

Just N of Alora fork right and after 12 km you will arrive at **Garganta del Chorro** (El Chorro Gorge), a deep ravine cut into the limestone by the river Guadalhorce, a route used by the railway which cuts in and out of tunnels along the side of the gorge. Also following the

side of the gorge is a narrow path, *El Camino del Rey*, which was built in the early 1920s and used by King Alfonso XIII when he opened the nearby hydro electric works. The path today is **extremely dangerous** and is marked with a 'No Entry' sign. This does not, however, seem to stop people making the attempt. The HEP scheme itself is of interest. The river is dammed S of the gorge and water is pumped to a storage reservoir at the top of the nearby hill. When electricity demand is high the water returns back down through the turbines to increase the supply.

The road continues N from El Chorro into the **Bobastro** valley. Look for the sign 'Iglesia Mozárabe' which leads up the mountain side to the hilltop site where there are the remains of a Mozarab hill fort, once the home of over 3000 people. It was the headquarters of Omar Ibn Hafsun, a bandit from Ronda who was a *muwallad* (of mixed Arab-Christian parentage) who at one time controlled much of Andalucía. In 899 he converted to Christianity and constructed the church where he was interred on his death in 917. The church is the only recognizable

Rock climbing in El Chorro Gorge

Spain is not generally thought of as a 'Mecca' for rock climbing, but it is, nevertheless, a popular sport and Málaga province offers some superb climbs. Indeed, some of Spain's foremost rock climbers come from Málaga. The place where most *aficionados* head for is the **El Chorro Gorge**, where there are 300m cliffs cut by the Rio Guadalhorce which can be glimpsed from the train as it spasmodically emerges from the tunnels which line the gorge.

Unlike climbing routes in Britain which are generally unassisted, climbs in Andalucía are Sport Climbs, that is they are 'equipped' already with bolts and rings, thereby removing much of the danger involved in case of equipment failure. If the climber becomes detached from the rock face, he or she will not fall completely to the ground. Although this does not entirely eliminate accidents, serious casualties are rare and the enthusiast has more time to enjoy the climb.

For those interested in this multi national sport, the main meeting place in El Chorro is *Isabel's Bar*. There are other challenging equipped climbs at Benhavís, Casares, El Torcal, Mijas, Puerto del Viento at Ronda and at Benaojan. For further details, contact: Sociedad Excursionista de Málaga, C/República Argentina 9, 29016, Málaga, T 2650258.

structure left and the nave, aisles, a transept and some side chapels can be clearly identified. Back in the valley, the rocky walls contain a number of formerly inhabited caves.

Further N are the **Guadalhorce Reservoirs**, a collection of four man made lakes, which supply the drinking water for Málaga and have earned the title Andalucía's 'Lake District'. In much of the early 1990s when the winter rains failed, the reservoirs have been well under capacity (as low as 8% in 1995, when 30% is needed to supply Málaga for the summer), but when they are full they make a valuable leisure resource. With their blue water, pine clad sides and perfect swimming they are an obvious tourist attraction. Camping sites, picnic areas and restaurants are gradually appearing, but the area sees few visitors, except on summer weekends, when the reservoirs are best avoided. Although the reservoirs themselves are rather sterile from a wildlife point of view, the pinewoods have Crested Tits and Crossbills, while the surrounding hills have a good range of raptors, including Golden and Bonelli's Eagles, Griffon Vultures and the occasional Osprey on migration. Flowers and butterflies are also outstanding, particularly in the early summer.

For a different return route, take the MA 444 to SW end of the reservoirs at **Ardales**, a village which clothes the side of a rocky hill capped by the remains of a Roman fort and a Moorish alcázar. The central square has a number of bars where *tapas* are available. Ardales is the nearest place to the Guadalhorce Reservoirs for accommodation, but this is limited to **E** *El Cruce*, Ctra Alora-Campanillos, T 2459012, 7 rm. At Ardales take the road SE, arriving after 5 km at **Carratraca**, well known for its sulphur spa, which has attracted bathers since Roman times. The baths were at their most famous during the 19th century, when they attracted nobility from all over Europe. When not frolicking in the

sulphurous water, the socialites could visit one of three casinos. The elegant *Hostal El Principe* is also a throwback from these times. After being closed for many years, the baths have recently reopened for the summer months and the water which issues forth at a constant 16°C is claimed to work wonders for skin and respiratory complaints. From Carratraca, the road rejoins Alora for the return journey to Málaga.

ANTEQUERA

(*Pop* 41,000; *Alt* 512m; *STD code* 95(2))

ACCESS Air The nearest airport is at Málaga 45 km away.

Train The train station, in Avda Estación, is 3 km from the town centre. Walk past the Campsa petrol station via C/Cruz Blanca and C/Lucena to the central Plaza San Sebastián. Taxis and buses await the trains.

Road From the bus station on Paseo García del Olmo it is downhill to the town via the nearby bull ring, turning left onto the Alameda de Andalucía. Antequera can be reached easily by road from the cities of Granada, Málaga and Sevilla using the excellent *autovia* system.

Antequera today is a modest sized market town serving the fertile plain (*vega*) to the N which grows cereals, vegetables and sunflowers. To the S is the Sierra de Chimenea, rising to over 1,300m. Antequera's strategic position as a focus of routes has resulted in a long and important history. The clutch of dolmens to the E of the town show that the area was occupied in prehistoric times, while recent excavations to the W demonstrate that *Antikaria* was an important Roman city. The Moorish past is evident in the hilltop *alcazaba*, which dominates the town. In 1410, Antequera was the first city in Andalucía to fall to the Christian armies and was later an important base for the attacks on other Moorish strongholds. During the next 2 centuries Antequera built up its wealth and many of its churches and other monuments date from this time.

Antequera

To Railway Station & Córdoba

To Parador

To Málaga and the Dólmenes

Bull Ring
7
Paseo Real
To Sevilla

Alta

Calle Juan Casco

Avda. Estacion

Vega

Herreruelos

Calle Sta Clara

Calle Martin de Luque

San Pedro

Obispo

C de Archidona

Alameda de Andalucia
8

Calle Merecillas

Cruzblanca

C Cantareros

C Diego Ponce

C Fresca

Iglesia de los Remedios
6

3

Infante D Fernando

4

Calle Lucena

Herrera

Iglesia de la Encarnación

C Calzada

N

Plaza San Sebastián

C Encarnación

Iglesia del Carmen

2
1

C Nájera

1. Iglesia de la Incarnación
2. Palacio de Nájera

C Carreteros

5

Zapateros

C del Rio

C Colegio

Hotels:
3. *Nuevo Infante*
4. *Pensión Colón*
5. *Pensión Manzanito*
6. *Pensión Reyes*

C Nueva

Arco de los Gigantes

Iglesia de Santa María

Places to eat:
7. La Espuela
8. Noelí

C Herradores

Not to scale

Castillo de Santa María

Places of interest

The castle hill, close to the centre of the town, makes an excellent starting point as the view over Antequera is outstanding and all the main features can be identified. The area can be reached on foot or by car (there is a small parking place beneath the walls). The **Castillo de Santa María** is a Moorish alcazaba built in the 14th century over the remains of a Roman fort. The most impressive features are the two towers, the 13th century Torre de Homenaje (Tower of Homage) and the earlier Torre Blanco (White Tower). Both are undergoing restoration and should not be entered without the guide (if you can find him). The castle was captured from the Moors by a royal prince, the future King Fernando I of Aragón, in a Christian victory of such significance that he was henceforth known as *El de*

Antequera. The courtyard of the alcazaba now consists of well kept gardens with welcome shade, while the walls provide panoramic views over the surrounding countryside. Look E towards the oddly shaped hill known as the **Peña de los Enamorados** (lovers rock). Legend has it that two lovers, a Christian girl and a Moslem boy, threw themselves off the top when their liaison was forbidden. Next to the castillo is the **Arco de los Gigantes**, a type of triumphal arch built in 1585 for Philip II, but believed to incorporate stone from older monuments, possibly Roman. Behind the arch is the church of **Santa María la Mayor**, with an ornate Plateresque facade and recently restored Mudéjar ceilings. Today it functions as an art restoration centre, where students can learn stone masonry and the treatment of iron and woodwork. A display in the nave shows the development plans for Antequera and future restoration details for the towns monuments. Stripped of all its religious paraphernalia, the church has a wonderful simplicity which gives the visitor a chance to appreciate its basic architecture.

The Dólmenes Antequera was originally a prehistoric site prior to successive occupation by the Romans, Moors and Christians and its Megalithic dólmens, a National Monument on the NE outskirts of the town off the road to Granada, are some of the best preserved burial chambers in Europe. The **Cueva de Menga**, the oldest, dates back to 2500 BC with huge, roughly cut stone slabs, believed to weigh 180 tons, from a location 8 km away, forming the roof. The gallery leads to an oval burial chamber. Much is made of the fact that Menga's gallery lines up with the Lovers Rock, behind which the sun rises at the summer solstice. The visitor is left to decide whether this is coincidental or not. The nearby **Cueva de Viera** is smaller and slightly less ancient, but has better cut stones, while the domed ceiling of **Cueva de Romeral**, c 1800 BC, 3 km N, is regarded as one of the earliest examples of Spanish architecture. Menga and Viera can be reached on foot from the town by following the signs for Granada and looking out for the petrol station on the left. The local bus also runs this way. Open Tues-Fri 1000-1400 and 1500-1700, Sat and Sun 1000-1400. You may or may not be charged an entrance fee. Don't despair if the caves are closed as you will almost certainly be approached by some local *pensionistas* who will miraculously produce a key and even give a somewhat suspect guided tour for which they will expect a tip. Romeral is a few kilometres further along the main road along a rough track off left in the grounds of a sugar refinery (look for the chimney). The cave itself is on the far side of the railway line (leave you car before crossing the line). Open Tues 1600-1800, Wed-Sat 0930-1430 and 1615-1830, Sun 1000-1400. Entrance is free, but the guardian will expect a tip.

Singlia Barba The recently excavated Roman ruins of Singlia Barba are at Finca Castillon, 6 km W of Antequera on the old road to Sevilla. The team of archaeologists from Málaga university have revealed a cemetery, theatre, houses and many Roman artefacts. The land is privately owned, but the town hall in Antequera may be able to arrange a visit.

Antequera has 26 churches and convents and many are well worth a visit. Just below the castillo to the E is the **Iglesia Nuestra Señora del Carmen**, built in the 17th century. It is now being restored – look for the Mudéjar woodwork ceiling, chiaroscuro panel and the main altar's *retablo*, over 10m in height. The 16th century **Iglesia de la Incarnación** also has a Mudéjar ceiling, while the **Iglesia de Los Remedios**, a National Monument, is dedicated to Antequera's patron saint. Many of the convents provide *dulces*.

Museums

Ancient mansions are much in evidence in Antequera, including the Renaissance style **Palacio de Nájera** on Plaza Coso Viejo, which now houses the **Museo Municipal**. There are, oddly, hourly guided tours, but it has to be said that many of the displays are uninspiring. The visit is worthwhile, however, for two remarkable exhibits. A bronze Roman statue – a life size figure of a boy, *El Efebo* – was ploughed up in a field in the 1950s and is believed to date from the 1st century. An American museum is said to have offered a million dollars for it, but the offer was turned down! The other exhibit is a wood carving of St Francis of Assisi, variously attributed to either Alonso Cano or Pedro de Mena. Open Tues-Fri 1000-1300, Sat 1000-1300, Sun 1100-1300. Entrance 100 ptas. The **Plaza de Toros** also has a small museum. Open 1830-2100. Entrance free.

Local festivals

The *Carneval* is celebrated in Feb with satirical songs and fancy dress parades through the streets; during *Semana Santa*, Holy Week, there are the usual processions. The *Feria de Primavera* (Spring Fair), which includes a flamenco contest, is seen as a practice for the *Real Feria de Agosto* (Royal August Fair) during the third week of Aug and marked by bullfights and flamenco; during the *Fiesta de Nuestra Señora de los Remedios*, 8 Sep, Antequera's patron saint is paraded through the streets on her silver platform.

Local information

● Accommodation

A *Parador de Antequera*, C/García del Olmo s/n, T 2840051, F 2841312, 55 rm, pool, parking, restaurant, garden, TV, avoid during Spring and Summer fairs if you want any sleep.

B *La Sierra*, Ctra Málaga-Madrid, Km 583, T 2845410, F 2845265, 30 rm, restaurant, parking, TV, laundry, out of town.

C *Las Pedrizas*, Ctra Madrid-Málaga, Km 527, T 2742081, 20 rm, parking, out of town; **C** *Lozano*, Polígono Industrial A6-A7, T 2844712, 17 rm, TV, good restaurant, out of town dolmen site; **C** *Nuevo Infante*, C/Infante Don Fernando 5, 2°, T 2700293, 12 rm, excellent new apartment style accommodation, garage, quiet, central, bar.

Pensiones: **D** *Colon*, C/Infante Don Fernando 29, T 2844516, F 2841164, 35 rm, renovated, central; **D** *Manzanito*, Plaza de San Sebastián 5, T 2841023, 33 rm, showers, in main square.

E *Bella Vista*, C/Cuesta de Archidona 27, T 2841997, 15 rm; **E** *La Yedra*, Ctra Sevilla-Málaga, T 2842287, 15 rm, a/c, restaurant; **E** *Madrona*, C/Calzada 31, T 2840014, 10 rm, clean, central, good restaurant with local specialities; **E** *Numero Uno*, C/Trinidad de Rojas 40, T 2843334, 9 rm; **E** *Pepe*, C/Najera 1, T 2844354, 6 rm; **E** *Reyes*, C/Tercia 4, T 2841028, 14 rm, central.

Youth hostels: none in the Antequera area. Nearest is in Málaga.

Camping: the site at El Torcal does not figure in the official list for Andalucía, but is regarded as legitimate by the Antequera authorities, who are happy to advertise it. Located at Río de la Villa, on the slopes of El Torcal.

● Places to eat

♦♦♦*Parador de Antequera*, Paseo García de Olmo, T 2840261, good, but pricey, regional food.

♦♦*La Espuela*, Ctra de Córdoba s/n, T 2702633, newish restaurant inside the bull ring, atmospheric, local dishes with a good *menu*; *Madrona*, C/Cazada 31, T 2840014, good pensión restaurant serving local dishes; *Méson-Bar Noelía*, Alameda de Andalucía 12, T 2845407, functional but good.

♦*Manzanito*, Plaza San Sebastián 5, T 2841023, another good pensión restaurant. There are also a number of cafeterías/heladerías in the commercial centre serving pastries, ice cream, etc, incl *Manolo*, C/Calzada 24; *Berrocal*, C/Tercia 8; and *Lozano Chico*, C/Diego Ponce 29.

● Bars

For *tapas bars* try those around Plaza Abartos.

● Banks & money changers

The main banks are located in C/Infante Don Fernando, though many do not open on Sat in the summer. A few have *telebanco* machines.

● Entertainment

Not much goes on in Antequera, except at *feria* times. The 19th century bull ring is used mainly during the *Feria de Primavera* and *Feria Real* (see local festivals). A flamenco contest also takes place during the former, while more of the art can be seen during the *Noche Flamenco de Santa María* in Aug. There is a small theatre, *Teatro Torcal*, C/Cantareros 8, T 2841196. Three cinemas operate, one at the theatre just mentioned plus *Ideal Cinema*, Infante Don Fernando 73, T 2842130 and *Delicias*, C/San Pedro. The pick of the rather uninspiring discotheques are *Rockefella*, C/La Silla 25; *Top Kapi*, C/San Pedro 24 and *Triangulo*, Camino de Santa Catalina s/n.

● Hospitals & medical services

Casa de Socorro, Calle Picadero, T 2844411; *Centro de Salud*, Parque María Cristina s/n, T 2842929; *Cruz Roja*, Paseo Cristina s/n, T 2842283; *Hospital General Basico*, C/Infante Don Fernando 135, T 2844411.

● Post & telecommunications

Area code: 95.

Post Office: *Correos*, C/Nájera s/n, nr Museo Municipal, T 2822083, Mon-Fri 0800-1500, Sat 0900-1300. Telegrams by telephone, T 2222000.

Telephones: all numbers have the prefix 2. There are no *locutorios*, but there are plenty of public telephones on C/Infante Don Fernando and Alameda de Andalucía.

● **Shopping**

The main shopping area is along C/Infante Don Fernando, the Alameda de Andalucía and C/Canteros.

Flea market: held in Avda de la Estación on Sun mornings.

● **Sports**

Gliding: contact Town Hall, T 2844211.

Football: Estadio de Futbol, close to the bull ring.

Swimming: there are 2 pools – *Piscinas Albarizas*, Ctra de Sevilla s/n, and *Piscina Municipal*, C/Antonio Mohedano, s/n, T 2844153.

● **Tour companies & travel agents**

Viajes Ibermar, C/Infante Don Fernando 49; *Viajes Toral*, Plaza Pintor Cristobel Toral 2, T 2840112.

● **Tourist offices**

The **Regional Government Tourist Office** is inside the Palacio de Nájera, Plaza Coso Viejo, T 2842180. Open Tues-Fri 1000-1330, Sat 1000-1300, Sun 1100-1300. The **Municipal Tourist Office** is in Edificio San Luis, C/Infante Don Fernando, T 2700405, open daily 1000-1400 and 1700-2000.

● **Useful addresses**

Car repairs: as usual in Spain, these cluster in an out of town situation, in this case along the Ctra de Córdoba. *Seat/Audi/Volkswagen*, Ctra de Córdoba s/n, T 2843661; *Opel/GM*, Ctra de Córdoba s/n, T 2842940; *Renault*, Pol Industrial, T 2841559; *Austin/Rover*, Taller Soto, C/Porterías 48, T 2841567; *Citroën*, Automobiles Martos, C/Camino Villaba s/n, T 2843463; *Ford*, Ctra Sevilla-Granada, Km 159, T 2844051; *Peugeot*, Ctra de Córdoba 7, T 2841685.

● **Transport**

Local Car hire: Autos Malu, c/o Viajes Toral, Plaza Pintor Cristóbel Toral, T 2840112; Rentacar Antequera, C/San Agustín 4, T 2702892. **Taxi**: T 2841076/2841008.

Air National and international flights from Málaga.

Train The major train junction is at Bobadilla Estación, several kilometres W of Antequera. Only 3 trains/day visit **Antequera**, 2 go direct to **Sevilla**. For **Cádiz** change at **Dos Hermanos**, for other locations change at **Bobadilla**. RENFE office, C/Divina Pastora 8, reservations on T 2844068.

Road Bus: bus station on Paseo García del Olmo, T 2481957. Local tickets from Ranca SA (to **Teba** and **Archidona**) and Casado SA upstairs, incl 5/day to **Bobadilla** train junction. Intercity routes downstairs, Alsina Graells, T 2841365. Frequent service to **Málaga**, **Sevilla** and **Granada**. No buses to **Ronda**.

EXCURSIONS FROM ANTEQUERA

Teba on the C341 is a walled Moorish town on a hilltop above the Río Almargen and is accessible by bus from Antequera. Lord James of Douglas died here in 1330 in a battle when the Christians defeated the Moors. He may have been encumbered by a casket hanging around his neck which contained the heart of Robert the Bruce. He was taking the heart to the Holy Land, so what he was doing in Teba is anyone's guess. The heart was recovered and returned to Melrose Abbey where it was buried, but in 1989 a monument in Scottish granite was erected in the centre of Teba to mark the connection. The Moorish castle, built on Roman foundations, is largely in ruins, but worth a visit if only for the view.

3 km W of the town is **Garganta de Teba** (Teba Gorge) cut by the Río la Venta. This is a splendid area for wildlife enthusiasts. Bonelli's Eagles, Egyptian Vultures and Eagle Owls have traditionally bred in the gorge, but they may have been deterred by rock climbers in recent years. Other birds around in summer include Chough, Black Wheatear, Blue Rock Thrush and Crag Martin. It is also an excellent spot for butterflies. Access into the gorge depends very much on the amount of water running – it can be quite a scramble in winter.

El Torcal This upland limestone block is 16 km S of Antequera, and has been designated a National Park, covering 1,171 ha. The grey limestone has been weathered into fantastic shapes giving an eerie atmosphere. The thin alkaline soil supports stunted trees and bushes such as elder, maple and hawthorn. There is a huge variety of wild flowers, including over 30 species of orchids, dwarf irises, peonies, rock roses and many more. Spring and early summer are the best times to visit, but there are flowers to see at all times of the year. Bird watchers might see Booted and Short Toed Eagles, Blue Rock Thrushes and Black Wheatears, while there is an abundance of reptiles, including the rare Green-eyed lizard. Keen naturalists should, however, avoid the weekends, when large numbers of Spaniards will ensure that any self respecting fauna remains well hidden. Apr and May are the peak periods for visits by the dreaded Spanish school parties on their dubious 'educational visits'.

To reach El Torcal by car, take the C3310 from Antequera towards Villanueva de la Concepción, turning off after about 12 km towards the interpretation centre at the foot of the mountain which reaches 1,369m at its highest point. Buses towards Villanueva de la Concepción are infrequent and drop you at the turn off with several kilometres still to walk. The best options are hitchhiking or a taxi. From the interpretation centre there are two circular routes marked with arrows. With the aid of substantial footwear, the yellow circuit can be walked in under 1 hr, while the red path can take up to 5 hrs. The paths are generally well marked with arrows painted on the rocks, but in thick mist keeping to the trail can be tricky. Visitors should consult the weather forecast, as El Torcal can not only be covered in thick cloud, but frost and snow are not uncommon in winter. The interpretation centre has excellent displays and audio visual presentations. Keen geologists from the UK will find that the grey limestone of El Torcal is not of Carboniferous age, but was formed in Jurassic times and has the fossil assemblage of that era, which can

be very confusing. Near to the centre is a terrace giving exceptional views down towards Málaga and the coast. Visitors from the Costa del Sol should consider returning along the scenic minor roads via Villanueva, from where there is a choice of two routes to Málaga.

Archidona 15 km E of Antequera lies the once strategic town of Archidona. Occupied by the Iberians, the Romans and the Moors and defended by a hilltop *castillo*, it was captured by Christian forces in 1462. Later it was the chief town of the Counts of Ureña and the Dukes of Osuna. Today it is a backwater, bypassed by both the main road and the *autovia* to Granada. Its pride and joy, however, is the *Plaza Ochavada*, a late 18th century octagonal square, accompanied by buildings using ornamental brickwork and stone. One of the main aims in building the Plaza was to provide work for the many unemployed at that time. Surprisingly, apart from the Convent of las Minimas, which is not open to the public, there are few monuments of interest in the town. The surrounding hills contain a significant reminder of the area's Moorish past in the shape of a church high in the Sierra de Archidona. The **Santuario de la Virgen de Gracia** is signposted up a steep, narrow tarmac road from the town. It was originally a 9th century mosque, Moorish settlements having been established in the area under Emir Abd Al-Rahman in 756 AD. Following the reconquest of Archidona in 1462 the mosque was converted into a Christian church, although there may have been a church on the site prior to the arrival of the Moors, since the three arches inside the door are Visigothic. The mosque's *mihrab* was converted by the Christians into an altar to the Virgen de Gracia, the local patron saint whose fiesta is celebrated on 14 Aug. Restoration work began in 1988. Open Nov-Jan 0900-1400 and 1500-1900, Feb-Apr 0800-1400 and

1600-2000, May-Oct 0700-1400 and 1700-2200. Entrance free. There is very limited parking at the summit.

Nearby are the scant remains of an Arab fortress, the scene of much fighting amongst various factions of the occupying Moors and later between the Moors and the Christians during the Reconquista.

Laguna de la Fuente de Piedra, located close to the town of the same name, lies just off the N334 to the W of Antequera. The lagoon, which is eliptical in shape covering around 1,300 ha, is notable as one of only two regular breeding sites for the Greater Flamingo in SW Europe. In winter, this saline lagoon extends up to 14,000 ha. In summer, however, the heat and the wind induce high levels of evaporation. Until the 1950s it was used as a *salinera* producing salt commercially and in 1963 the first recorded breeding took place. By 1982, the importance of the lagoon was officially recognized and it was listed under the Ramsar convention as a wetland of international significance. By 1984 it was a fully protected reserve and controlled by AMA, the department of environment of the Andalucían government. The lagoon now has an information and display centre (open 1000-1500 and 1600-1900) with information panels, audio visual and computer displays regarding the way of life of the flamingoes and the other wildlife of the reserve. Next to the centre is a mirador located under a shady tree giving perfect viewing. The breeding success of the flamingoes depends entirely on the amount of winter rainfall. In 1990, for example, after a wet winter, the flamingoes produced 10,400 chicks. In 1993-95, on the other hand, the lake had dried out by Easter and the flamingoes dispersed to other areas. The consistent precipitation of the winter of 1995/6 produced perfect conditions and by Apr there were some 25,000 flamingoes on the lake. The demands by local farmers for irrigation water has not

helped the overall situation. The chicks are counted by photographs taken from the air and then they are rounded up before they can fly and are ringed. This process has shown that the flamingoes are amazing wanderers and birds ringed at Fuente de Piedra have been recorded on the Camargue, in Tunisia and even in Senegal. The lagoon also has 200 breeding pairs of Gull Billed Terns, plus Black Winged Stilts, Avocets, Kentish Plovers and the rare White Headed Duck. During the winter months there are a host of waders, wildfowl and even cranes. Within the lake's zone of influence are halophytic plant communities which can cope with the saline conditions. On the sandier stretches, Tamarisk is abundant. The best time to visit Fuente de Piedra is between Jan and Jun. Try to arrive before 1100 as the heat haze and sun shining from the S make watching difficult later in the day. Bird watchers travelling from Málaga airport to the Coto Doñana will find Fuente de Piedra a profitable port of call.

ACCESS Drive through the town of Fuente de Piedra, cross the railway and take a track to the left of a rubbish dump to a small hill, on the top of which is the conservation centre. Parking is not a problem.

● **Accommodation** There are some accommodation possibilities in Fuente de Piedra itself for those wishing to stop over: **B** *Tropical*, Ctra Sevilla-Málaga, Km 136.5, T 2735218, 13 rm, pool, rather overpriced; **D** *La laguna*, Autovia Sevilla-Málaga, Km 135, T 2735292, restaurant, a/c. There is a **campsite** in the village close to the reserve – *La Laguna de Fuentepiedra*, Camino de la Rabíta, s/n, T 2735294, open throughout the year, but with few facilities.

WEST OF MALAGA

THE COSTA DEL SOL

This is the name given to the stretch of coast from Málaga westwards to Gibraltar, which consists of a narrow coastal strip of ribbon development. Beginning in the late 60s, it has grown into a collection of resorts, *urbanisaciós* and leisure complexes which on first sight can be quite a shock to the uninitiated. It is difficult to explain the success of the *costa*. It is certainly not the quality of the beaches, which are generally gritty or rocky; nor is it the access provided by the coast road, which is one of the most dangerous in Europe; it cannot be the cultural background, which with one possible exception is almost non-existent. A British journalist who wrote a quasi sociological account of his experiences on the Costa del Sol possibly has the answer. He concluded that, at 35, he was "too young for Fuengirola, too old for Torremolinos and too poor for Marbella". In other words there is something for everyone. Certainly the climate, particularly in winter, is the best on mainland Europe, as thousands of northern Europeans who spend the colder months here will agree. Inland, the scenery can be spectacular. Historic cities such as Ronda and Antequera are within 45 mins of the coast. Drive for 2 to 3 hrs and you can be in Sevilla, Granada or Córdoba. Even on the coast itself there are compensations for the persistent and enquiring visitor.

Many of the worst architectural features in the form of tower blocks were put up in the 60s and 70s; since then the main trend has been to build low rise *urbanisaciós*, which in the 80s and 90s have been dominated by the 'time share' business. Many of these developments have been stylish and well designed, but often the original landscape of dunes, heath and pine woods has been destroyed. Nevertheless it is estimated that around 350,000 foreigners live on the Costa del Sol, either legally or illegally, vast numbers owning their own property. Tourist numbers have fluctuated and the early '90's were lean years with European recession, high Spanish inflation and the attraction of other package venues such as Florida and the Caribbean. 1995, however, showed that recovery was well under way, with over 3 million visitors passing through Málaga airport and high hotel occupancy rates.

TORREMOLINOS

The first of the resorts as one travels W from Málaga, Torremolinos was also the first to be developed. Known as 'Torrie' to the early English package tourists, it is loud, brash and dedicated to providing enjoyment. Many visitors might be appalled by its vulgarity, but out of season it is far less offensive and the local authorities are working hard to raise its image. It is difficult to appreciate that 40 years ago there were hardly any buildings here apart from the water mills which gave Torremolinos its name (and which only stopped working in 1924), and a few fishermen cottages behind la Carihuela beach. The centre of what old town existed is Calle San Miguel, now a busy pedestrianized alley full of boutiques, restaurants, and even a Moorish tower. Torremolinos has four beaches, separated by a rock headland. To the E are the Playa de Bajondillo and the Playa de Playamar, while to the W are Playa de Carihuela and Playa de Montemar. All four are identically heaving with browning bodies during the height of the season. The most interesting area in Torremolinos is undoubtedly la Carihuela, the old fishermens quarter. There are a few token fishing boats still hauled up on the beach, but the majority now operate out of Benalmádena marina to the W. There are still some excellent fish restaurants, however, including *La Lonja* and *Los Pescadores*, both right on the beach. Try also *La Langusta* and *La Can-*

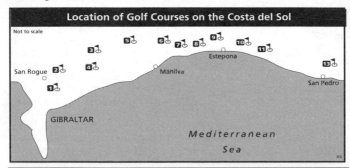

Location of Golf Courses on the Costa del Sol

Not to scale

San Roque

Estepona

Manilva

San Pedro

GIBRALTAR

Mediterranean Sea

Golfers paradise

There are nearly 60 golf courses in Andalucía, which represents over a third of all the courses in Spain. More than 30 of the courses are along the Costa del Sol and include such championship courses as Las Brisas, Sotogrande, Los Naranjos, San Roque and Valderrama. The great expansion came in the 1980's and during this golden era both resident and visiting golfers had the financial means not to be deterred by prohibitive green fees. By the end of the decade the recession was beginning to bite and the cost of living in Spain began to match that of the other countries of northern Europe. Golfers began to look at other destinations such as Portugal and Florida and the fairways and bars of Andalucía began to empty – a reflection of the overall malaise in the Spanish tourist industry.

Fortunately the authorities came to their senses and the diversification in tourism took in golf, which was perceived as a largely winter activity from Oct to Apr. In most cases green fees are much reduced, the surrounding infrastructure has improved and the approach of the service sector is much more accommodating. The result has been that the golfers have come flooding back.

There is a golf course for everybody on the Costa del Sol, from the pro to the hacker, from the affluent to the cash strapped. Admittedly the courses in the W of the region have high green fees – at 20,000 ptas, a round at Valdarrama does not come cheap – but for courses designed by such as Ballesteros, Jacklin, Thomas and Trent Jones, there is no lack of takers. East of Marbella, the green fees become more reasonable and there are bargains to be had at courses such as El Chaparral and Mijas. Here the problem is more likely to get a slot to actually play because of the heavy demand particularly during the peak period around Easter. Golfers experiencing such problems could contact **Vacation Golf**, T 2837272, who, as well as arranging reservations and competition entries, can provide corporate arrangements and lessons. There is also a great variety of courses to play from the semi-links course at Alcaidesa overlooking Gibraltar to the mountain side course at Alhaurín. One can even play floodlit golf at night at Dama de Noche near Marbella.

The Valdarrama course at Sotogrande has been chosen as the venue for the 1997 Ryder Cup between the European and American teams, the first time in the 70 year history of the tournament that the home match has not been played in Britain. The course has a capacity for 26,000 spectators, while the infrastructure of the area can provide 48 hotels with 17,000 beds. The only problem is the coast road, and there is frenzied activity to bring it up to *autovia* standard to cope with the expected traffic.

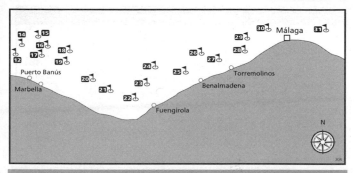

Golf on the Costa del Sol – Where to play

COURSE	TELEPHONE	LOCATION
ALCAIDESA (1)	(956) 791040	East of Gibraltar
SAN ROQUE (2)	(956) 613030	East of San Roque
VALDERRAMA (3)	(956) 795750	Sotogrande
SOTOGRANDE (4)	(956) 795050	Sotogrande
LA DUQUESA (5)	289 0726	West of Estepona
ESTEPONIA GOLF (6)	281 0982	Estepona
FRANHOUSE GOLF (7)		West of Estepona
COTO LA SERENA (8)	280 4700	Estepona
MONTEMAYOR (9)	281 0805	Estepona
EL PARAISO (10)	288 3846	East of Estepona
ATALAYA (11)	288 2812	East of Estepona
ATALAYA ROSNER (11)	288 2812	East of Estepona
GUADALMINA NORTH (12)		San Pedro
GUADALMINA SOUTH (13)	288 3375	San Pedro
LOS ARQUEROS (14)	278 6437	Between Marbella and San Pedro
LA QUINTA (15)	278 2277	
LOS NARANJOS (16)	281 5206	Marbella
LAS BRISAS (17)	281 0875	Marbella
ALOHA (18)	281 2388	Marbella
DAMA DE NOCHE (19)	281 8150	Marbella
RIO REAL (20)	277 9509	Marbella
THE GOLF CLUB		
MARBELLA (21)	283 5786	Marbella
SANTA MARIA (22)	283 0386	Between Marbella and Fuengirola
MIRAFLORES (23)	283 7353	Between Marbella and Fuengirola
LA CALA SOUTH (24)	258 9100	La Cala
LA CALA NORTH (24)	258 9100	La Cala
EL CHAPARRAL (25)	249 3800	La Cala
MIJAS (OLIVOS) (26)	247 6843	Mijas
MIJAS (LAGOS) (26)	247 6843	Mijas
TORREQUEBRADA (27)	244 2742	Torremolinos
PARADOR (28)	238 1255	Torremolinos
LAURO (29)	241 2767	West of Málaga
GUADALHORCE (30)	224 3682	West of Málaga
ANORETA (31)	240 5000	East of Málaga

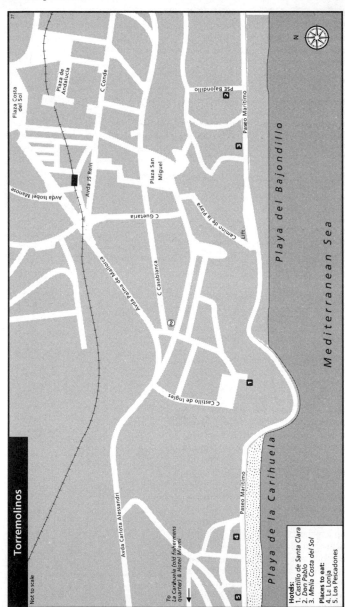

Torremolinos

Not to scale

Plaza de Andalucía

Plaza Costa del Sol

C. Conde

Avda Isabel Manoso

Avda 15 Rein

PSE Bajondillo

Paseo Marítimo

Plaza San Miguel

C Guetaria

Camino de la playa

Lift

C Casablanca

Avda Palma de Mallorca

Avda Carlota Alessandri

C Castillo de Ingles

Paseo Marítimo

To Carihuela (old fishermens quarter) & Hotel Miami

Playa del Bajondillo

Mediterranean Sea

Playa de la Carihuela

N

Hotels:
1. Castillo de Santa Clara
2. Don Pablo
3. Melia Costa del Sol

Places to eat:
4. La Lonja
5. Los Pescadones

tana on the Paseo Maritimo. While in La Carihuela, look in at the simple little fishermens church of the Virgen del Carmen, in C/Carmen, one block back from the Paseo.

● **Accommodation** This should not be a problem, except at the height of the season. Most of the large package tour hotels are located behind the eastern beaches and incl: **A** *Melia Costa del Sol*, P Maritimo Playa de Bajondillo, T 2386677, 540 rm, all the facilities expected of a familiar hotel chain; *Don Pablo*, Paseo Maritimo s/n, T 2383888, F 2383783, 419 rm, pool, a/c, wheelchair access; **B** *Don Pedro*, Avda de Lido s/n, T 2386844, F 2386935, 272 rm, pool, leisure facilities, restaurants, wheelchair access. A further clutch of hotels are found behind the Montemar beach incl: **A** *Al-Andaluz*, Avda de Montemar s/n, T 2381200, F 2381906, 164 rm, pool, a/c, tennis; **B** *La Barracuda*, Avda España 1, 3 and 5, T 2385400, F 2389121, 234 rm, a/c, pool, restaurant, tennis. At the cheaper end of the range, try: **E** *Miami*, C/Aladino 14, T 2385255, 26 rm, quiet, small hotel in suburban road, nice gardens, pool. There are also 2 pensiones in la Carihuela which can be rec: *Prudencio*, C/Carmen 43, T 2381452, 35 rm, on the beach, many rooms with sea views; *Pedro*, C/Bulto 1, T 2380536, 12 rm, simple but clean, right on the Paseo.
  Something different: **B** *Finca La Mota*, Ctra de Mijas, Alhaurín el Grande, T 2490901, 12 rm in a 300-year-old converted farmhouse.

Just to the E of Torremolinos and quite close to Málaga airport is a quite unexpected nature reserve. This is at the mouth of the **Río Guadalhorce**. This area consists of the narrow estuary and a series of ponds and scrub. Although protected by AMA the site suffers from industrial pollution, sewerage and human disturbance from hunters and the occasional nudist. Despite these problems this minute little wetland site turns up a remarkable number of birds, particularly during passage periods. There is a wide range of winter wildfowl, waders, heron and egrets. No fewer than seven varieties of terns have been recorded. Access is via the old N340 just E of the river at Finca la Isla.

Benalmádena Torremolinos merges imperceptibly into Benalmádena, its less frenetic neighbour to the W. There are some well kept beaches which are less gritty than those at Torremolinos while most of the developments are low rise with tasteful villas straggling up the hillside. Less attractive on the paseo is a red mock Moorish building known as Bil-Bil Castle, an eyesore used as a conference and exhibition centre. Benalmádena's most noticeable feature is its *Puerto Deportivo* (Marina), which is still undergoing construction. It provides 978 berths for boats of up to 30m in length and includes apartments, chandlers, shops and restaurants. Try to find *Le Resaca*, a bodega serving excellent fish food and *tapas*. Within the marina is *Sea Life*, a submarine park with plastic tunnels taking you into the aquariums for eyeball to eyeball contact with sharks and other sea creatures. Open 1000-1800 daily, adults 900 ptas, children 600 ptas, over 65s 700 ptas. 3 km inland is *Benalmádena pueblo*, a village which has a few narrow streets and a square. It has made some effort to be regarded as a 'typical Andalucían village' and thereby attract tourists. Certainly the views are good. Other attractions include a small archaeological museum and a folly type castle, the *Castillo de Aguilas*, where birds of prey are flown daily at 1300 and 2000. There are some 150 raptors on display, including eagles, owls, falcons and vultures. Admission 850 ptas, children 550 ptas.

FUENGIROLA

ACCESS **Air** Fuengirola, in the province of Málaga, is now only 25-min drive away from Málaga airport since the new motorway was opened.
Train The train station is in Avda Santos Rein, opposite the indoor market.
Road The bus station is 100m from the train station on the corner of Avda Ramón y Cajal and C/Alfonso XIII. Much of the life of the town revolves around the Plaza

Anyone for time share?

Walk along to Fuengirola's massive Tuesday outdoor market or take a stroll around Benalmádena's marina and one thing is absolutely certain – you will be pestered by time share touts. They are usually young people, often students, and their task is to persuade tourists to come along to a time share sales office. They are looking for couples, preferably those who are not short of a bob or two, and their methods of persuasion are varied and ingenious. There may be enticements (free lunch, free gin/whisky/champagne), a personal appeal regarding their own poverty (they are paid according to the numbers they bring in), the statement 'I'm not trying to sell you time share' (they lie) or just sheer persistence. The latest ruse is the scratchcard and if a tourist finds that they have won something, and they invariably have, then it takes a strong will not to go along to collect it.

Those who weaken will be taken by car or taxi to the sales office, often on the time share complex itself, and handed over to a sales person, for a presentation which may take up to an hour and might include a video film. The sales person spends some time chatting and putting people at ease but at the same time they are analysing the background of the visitor and judging their credit worthiness. After viewing one of the show apartments, which will be lavishly furnished and equipped, the hard sell begins. The time share usually involves some variation of buying an apartment for life for a certain period each year. The amount which you pay will depend on the time of year and these periods are identified by, say, colours. A blue zone in the height of the summer, for instance, might cost twice as much as a yellow zone in February. Reductions are always available if the visitor agrees to pay on the spot. If the visitor is still reluctant, a senior salesperson is called in and will probably make a further reduction. Time to consider the proposal is not encouraged. Those who decide not to buy are then shown the door, where the smiling secretary who received you now hands over the champagne (which turns out to be sparkling wine) with bad grace.

de la Constitución, where the main church is located.

At first glance this resort might be a carbon copy of its neighbours to the E, but in fact it has much to recommend it, especially the fishermens' quarter of Santa Fé which has somehow managed to retain its original whitewashed cottages. Fuengirola is located at the mouth of the Fuengirola River, which forms a broad valley extending inland. It has a climate similar to that of Málaga, but being further W, it is more open to Atlantic influences and has slightly cooler summers.

Fuengirola is linked by a 7 km promenade with Los Boliches and Carajel to the E. The name Los Boliches was derived from the Bolicheros, who were sailors and traders from Genoa and who are

believed to have settled here in the early 1300s. It is from Los Boliches that the Virgen del Carmen fishermens fiesta takes place every Jul.

Places of interest

Unlike Torremolinos, Fuengirola has a long history. Roman remains are currently being excavated at Torreblanca, while at Los Boliches on the Paseo Maritimo a Roman arch has been erected from remains recovered from the sea bed by divers. It was the Romans, too, who probably built the first structure at the **Castillo de Sohail** located on a hill by the river at the W end of the town. In the 8th century it was extensively rebuilt by Caliph Abd Al-Rahman III after which much of the history of the town was linked with the castle. Its protection at-

So is there any advantage at all in buying time share? The answer is that for some people, yes, for others, no. Certainly many thousands have bought timeshare in its various guises and are very happy with it. The time share business has cleaned up its act considerably since the early days when there were some very dubious operators. Clearly, many visitors would prefer to buy their own property, where they can keep there own possessions, use when they like and even get some renting revenue from it. Time share does not have these advantages. You cannot leave your possessions there and cannot even guarantee getting the same property each year. Annual service charges may also be high. The benefits are that you get a luxurious property which is well maintained with a variety of services and leisure facilities, without having the worries of property maintenance which a home owner might have. Time share appeals particularly to golfers, who may have excellent concessions regarding green fees and booking at busy times of the year.

Another point to remember is that you can swap your week for a similar booking anywhere else in the time share world. Many people never ever use the property which they have bought, such as the hundreds of South Africans who have bought time share on the Costa del Sol, but always swap it for locations in the southern hemisphere such as the Seychelles or Kenya.

One economic aspect of time share, is the effect that it has had on the package tour industry. Tour reps often give dire warnings about time share touts and how to avoid them. The reason is not hard to see, for one time share purchaser is one less package tour holidaymaker and the luxury of a time share apartment may compare very favourably with a battered hotel room.

If you decide that time share might be a viable option, prepare your self thoroughly beforehand. Do some reading, see more than one resort, compare prices and facilities, ask about inheritance and tax avoidance when you die and check if the organization will buy back the property if you decide to sell.

tracted farmers and fishermen and led to the beginnings of the present town, which until the last century was under the administration of Mijas. The castle was destroyed in 1485 in the Christian reconquest of the area, the Moors surrendering on the day of San Cayetano, the patron saint of Fuengirola today. In 1730 the castle was rebuilt to defend the coast against the British who had taken Gibraltar in 1704. During the Peninsular War in 1810, a British expedition of 800 men under General Blayney landed at the Castle and advanced on Mijas, but later they retreated to the Castle, where, humiliatingly they were obliged to surrender to 150 Polish mercenaries. It is interesting to note that at this time the population of Fuengirola was a mere 60 people. The town became independent

of Mijas in 1841, but the big expansion was not to come until the tourist boom of the 1960s and 70s.

The Castillo de Sohail is currently undergoing renovation. There are plans to turn it into a cultural centre and outdoor auditorium and the first outdoor concerts took place in the summer of 1996. Meanwhile the exterior can be viewed by taking the track from the coast road along to the river mouth and then proceeding along the beach to the W of the castle.

Other places of interest

Travellers with younger visitors to entertain might find the following venues helpful:

Parquesam Zoo, C/Camilo José Cela, small and certainly not the best example of a zoo, but it is the only one on the coast. Reptile house, children's playground, mini train and boats, open daily 1100, closure according to season. Adults 550 ptas, pensioners 300 ptas, children 225 ptas.

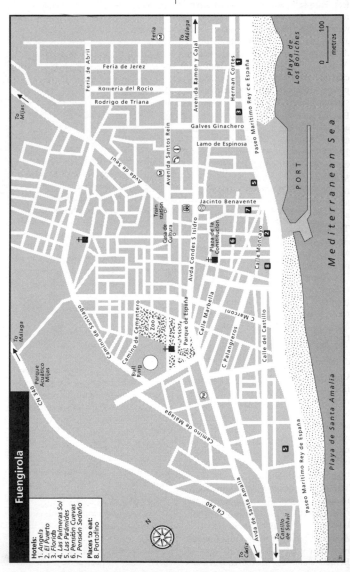

Fuengirola

Hotels:
1. Angela
2. El Puerto
3. Florida
4. Las Palmeras Sol
5. Las Pirámides
6. Pensión Cuevas
7. Pensión Sedeño

Places to eat:
8. Portofino

Aquaparks can be found on Torremolinos and Fuengirola bypasses with similar opening hours, attractions and entrance fees. **Parque Aquático Mijas** at Fuengirola, for example, has a variety of pools, watershoots including a 'kamikaze', slides and rapids, restaurant, free parking. Open daily at 1000, closure according to season. Adults 1,550 ptas, children 1220 ptas (no charge for second child), pensioners 900 ptas. Connections from Fuengirola bus station, T 2460404.

Piccolo Park, Paseo Maritimo. Play park with slides, climbing mazes, remote controlled cars and laser games. Open daily 1900-0100 (times which certainly reflect the hours Spanish children keep).

Minitrain Children will enjoy the tourist train which chugs around Fuengirola. It leaves the port at 30 min intervals and cost adults 300 ptas and children 200 ptas.

Tivoli World Large amusement park at Arroyo de la Miel, near Banalmádena with gardens, computerized fountains, rides, restaurants, *flamenco* shows and a large outdoor theatre featuring internationally known stars. The entrance price includes all the entertainment. The nearest railway station is at Arroyo de la Miel, T 2441896, open 1800-0200. Entrance 600 ptas, children under 5 free. A 'supertivolino' ticket, aimed at children, includes all the rides for 1,000 ptas.

Coin Film City Constructed for the ill-fated Eldorado TV series, the complex was used for the production of Spanish TV films and had a cinema school for around 60 students. The whole site has now closed (although it may still be advertised in some of the older tourist material) so don't waste any time trying to find it.

The **Museo Abierto de Pintura** is in reality a series of colourful outdoor murals painted on the walls of various buildings in the town centre.

A popular **boat trip** runs from Fuengirola harbour to the marina at Benalmádena. The *Joven María II* runs

approx hourly in each direction. Adults one way 800 ptas (return 1,300 ptas), children under 10 one way 400 ptas (return 600 ptas).

NB: that substantial reductions can be made on entrance fees to places such as Tivoli World and the Aquaparks, by booking through travel agents such as Maxy's on the Paseo Maritimo.

Local festivals

There are the usual Semana Santa processions during Holy Week. On 16 Jul, the *Fiesta de la Virgen del Carmen* is one of the best of its type along the coast. The statue of the virgin is carried from the church in Los Boliches in a 2-hr procession to the beach and into the sea. An amazing spectacle, with half the inhabitants on the beach and the other half in the sea, either swimming or in boats. There is a small *Romería* in late Sep with decorated carts and horse riders heading for the hills. This precedes the *Feria del Rosario*, which is celebrated during the first 2 weeks of October on the permanent showground site between Los Boliches and Fuengirola, where there are *casetas* for the various societies and brotherhoods. All this is accompanied by fireworks, bullfights and *flamenco*.

Local information
● Accommodation

A *Angela*, Paseo Rey de España, T 2475200, F 2462087, 261 rm, close to beach, pool, parking, wheelchair access, restaurant, used by tour parties; **A** *El Puerto*, Paseo Maritimo 32, T 2470100, F 2470166, 300 rm, a/c, rooftop pool, used by tour parties, opp harbour; **A** *Las Palmeras Sol*, Paseo Maritimo, T 2472700, F 2472908, 398 rm, parking, Pool, a/c, restaurant, shops in the hotel complex, used by package tours, can be noisy at night; **A** *Las Pirámides*, C/Miguel Márquez 43, T 2470600, F 2583297, 320 rm, at the quieter end of the Paseo, restaurant, parking, pool, tennis, convenient for the beach, often live entertainment in the evening.

B *Florida*, Paseo Maritimo s/n, T 2476100, F 2581529, 116 rm, pool, a/c restaurant, nr beach, another popular package venue, but good value; **B** *Fuengirola Park*, Ctra Cádiz, Km 213, T/F 2470000, 391 rm, restaurant, pool, popular with tour parties.

C *Mas Playa*, Urb Torreblanca del Sol, T 2475300, pool, restaurant, tennis, wheelchair access; **C** *Stella Maris*, P Príncipe de España s/n, T 2475450, 196 rm, a/c, restaurant, pool, wheelchair access.

All the above hotels have much reduced winter rates.

Pensiones: **D** *Agur*, C/Tostón 4, T 2476662 F 2488708, 33 rm, parking, conveniently situated for town and beach; **D** *Cuevas*, C/Capitán 7, T 2460606 13 rm, small, well kept and handily placed; **D** *El Amigo*, Avda los Boliches 71, T 2470333, 20 rm, on the main street; **D** *Santa Fé*, Avda de los Boliches 66, T 2474181, 27 rm, probably the best of the *pensiones*; **D** *Sedeño*, C/Don Jacinto 1, T 2474788, 30 rm, pleasant garden.

E *El Cid*, Avda Conde San Isidro s/n, 46 rm, 100m W of the bus station, breakfast available; *Las Islas*, Urb Torreblanca del Sol, T 2475598, 12 rm, pool, gardens, good value; **E** *Costabella*, Avda los Boliches 114, T 2474631, 18 rm, on the main street.

Something different: **A** *El Castillo de Monda*, 29110 Monda, Málaga, T 2457142, F 2457336, 23 rm in sympathetically converted ruins of a Moorish castle, pool, restaurant; **B** *Santa Fé*, Ctra de Monda, Km 3, Coín, T 2452916, F 2595524, 5 rm in a converted olive mill, gourmet restaurant.

Youth hostels: the nearest are in Málaga and Marbella.

Camping: there are numerous sites close to the sea to the W of Fuengirola. *La Roselada*, Ctra Nacional 340, Km 211, Camino la Salina, Loma Baja, T 2460191, bar, pool, tennis, beach; *Fuengirola*, Ctra Nacional 340, Km 207, T 2474108, bar, restaurant, games area, beach; *Calazul*, Ctra Nacional 340, Km 200, Mijas Costa, T 2493219, bar, restaurant, beach, watersports.

● **Places to eat**

There is a vast and cosmopolitan range of choice in Fuengirola, varying from simple Spanish fish food through to Indian, Chinese and exotic Indonesian. Street musicians often entertain diners to add to the ambience, although they are usually vigorous in their attempts at remuneration.

◆◆◆*La Langosta*, C/Lopa de Vega, T 2475049,

shellfish specialities; *Portofino*, Paseo Maritimo, T 2470643, Italian and international menu, quite expensive, booking rec; *Valparaiso*, Ctra Fuengirola-Mijas, Km 4, T 2485996, international menu, dancing, terrace, closed Sun.

◆◆*City Grill*, C/Juan Sebastian Elcano, T 2474369, steak specialities; *El Sultan*, Parque Doña Sofia, C/Heroes de Balar, well established Moroccan restaurant, house spec incl lamb and couscous; *Bali Mas*, C/Martínez Catena, T 24/1994, authentic Indonesian rijstafel; *Bélgica Antiqua*, Avda Condes San Isidro 67, T 2471596, Danish and Belgian cuisine and fish dishes; *Rajdoot*, C/Lamo de Espinosa, T 2462910, tandoori specialities.

◆ For those who enjoy simple Spanish food, especially fish, the pedestrianized Calle Moncayo can be rec. There are numerous restaurants here, such as *La Gondola*, *Las Chanquetes*, *Sal y Pimiento* and *Romy*, where an excellent *menu del dia* with wine can be had for under 1,000 ptas. There are also small fish bars for *raciones* around the sport harbour. Cheaper still are the *buffet libre* restaurants, where for a set price diners can eat as much as they like. The following are located along the Paseo Maritimo: *Buffet Pyr* at *Hotel Palmeras*; *Buffet Saturno* and *Buffet Versalles*. The price is invariably the same at each establishment and is currently 700 ptas. In the summer, locals and long term residents head for the *ventas* on the Mijas Golf Rd, incl *Venta Perea* and *Venta La Marena*. At the Mijas-Alhaurin crossroads, the *Venta los Morenos* is as good as any. All offer good basic Spanish country cooking at reasonable prices, but they can be crowded at weekends and at the height of the golfing season.

● **Bars**

The main *tapas* bars in Fuengirola are located in the area to the W of the train station and in C/San Rafael, which leads off the main square. Try La Campana El Parillo and Casa Flores.

● **Banks & money changers**

All the main Spanish banks and *cajas de ahorros* have branches in Fuengirola, mainly close to the Plaza de la Constitución. Some English and other foreign banks are also represented. Cash dispensers are commonly found.

● **Embassies & consulates**

Most of the nearest consulates are located in Málaga, except **USA**, Centro Commercial las Rampas, T 2474891 and **Ireland**, Avda los Boliches, T 2475108.

● **Entertainment**

Adults might be interested in *Casino Torreque-bradna*, Ctra de Cádiz, Km 226, Benalmádena-Costa, T 2442545, games room, Fortuna nightclub with cabaret, piano bar and restaurant, open Fri and Sat from 2230. *Salon Varietes*, a small, but highly popular theatre with entertainment in English. Performances from Mid Sep to mid Jun. Located in C/Varietes.

Nightclubs: just to the W of the main bus station is a cluster of nightclubs, incl a number providing 'adult' entertainment. Discotheques are mainly found either along the Paseo Maritimo, try *Disco Maxy*, or at the W end of town close to Hotel Pirámides, such as *La Marcha* and *Jaguar*.

● **Hospitals & medical services**
Ambulance: T 2472929.
First aid clinic: T 2472929.
Hospital: T 2307700.
Cruz Roja: T 2250450.

● **Post & telecommunications**
Area code: 95.

Post Office: new building on the site of the old indoor market in C/España, T 2474384.

Telephones: *locutorios* containing several booths and accepting credit cards are located on the Paseo Maritimo and next to the Tourist Office in Avda Santos Rein.

● **Shopping**

There is a daily indoor market located in a modern building at the junction of Avda Suel and Avda Santos Rein. The huge outdoor weekly market is held on Tues at the permanent fairground site on Avda Santos Rein. The large *hipermercado Euromarket* is situated on the Fuengirola bypass and also has a regular Sun car boot sale. The main fashion shops are located around the Plaza de la Constitución. The so-called 'leather market', close to the Hotel Palmeras Sol, sells a variety of goods in addition to leather work and bargaining can take place.

● **Tour companies & travel agents**
Rusadir, C/Marbella 37, T 2474885; *Perla Travel*, Paseo Maritimo, T 2463076; *Centro*, Las Rampas, T 2470208; *Benamar*, Paseo Maritimo, Edf El Yate, T 2473762. *Maxy*, Paseo Maritimo, T 2470610.

● **Tourist offices**

The **Municipal Tourist Office** is at the old railway station, Avda Santos Rein, T 2467457, very cooperative staff. The office also acts as a centre for foreign residents' organizations and clubs.

● **Transport**
Local Car hire: probably best arranged at the airport, but local firms incl: **Helle Hollis**, T 2479800 and **Marinsa**, T 2382180. **Taxis**: the main taxi rank is opp the bus station in C/Alfonso XIII; also **Radio taxis**: T 2471000.

Train The electric railway runs half-hourly to Málaga via the airport. The RENFE station is in Avda Santos Rein, T 2360202.

Road Bus: the bus station is on the corner of Avda Ramón y Cajal and C/Alfonso XIII, T 2475066. Portillo buses run half-hourly along the coast road and to **Mijas** while there are a number of long distance coaches – 4 daily to **Granada, Ronda, Coín** and **La Linea**; 11 daily to **Algeciras**, with 3 proceeding to **Cádiz**; 1 daily to **Jerez** and **Almería** and 5 daily to **Madrid**. The buses are cheap and reliable and therefore crowded, so booking is advisable well in advance, especially in the summer.

EXCURSION FROM FUENGIROLA

Mijas A visit to Mijas, a small village of 5,000 people, is on the itinerary of most tourists who come to the Costa del Sol. It is described in the brochures as a 'typical Spanish hill village'. This is only partly true. The village is geared to catering for the tourist, with donkey rides, garish souvenirs and English run restaurants. Despite all this, Mijas has a certain charm and is well worth a visit. It has a long history, certainly going back to Roman times, while the Moors built the defensive walls which partially remain today. The village is located 425m above sea level at the foot of pine covered mountains. The *vista panoramica* in well kept gardens above the cliffs gives superb views along the coast. Visitors will note on arrival the imposing new town hall, largely built with taxes from foreign residents, who, in the Mijas administrative district which stretches to the sea at Mijas-Costa, outnumber Spaniards by two to one. The newly constructed Plaza Virgen de la Peña is the venue for concerts and fiestas. Head for the Plaza de la Constitución, which leads to the cliffs and old walls. The church here is the **Iglesia de la Concepción Immaculada**, built in the 17th century on the site of a Moorish mosque (the town fell to the Christian armies in 1487 and most of the Moorish population were expelled). Most of the church was built in Mozarabe style. While it was being re-roofed and renovated in 1992, some ancient wall paintings were discovered on the main pillars. Inscriptions in Old Spanish date them as early 17th century. To the N of the church is the tiny **bull ring**. Built in 1900, it is one of the very few non-round bull rings in Spain. Because it is so small, traditional bull fights with mounted picadors cannot take place here, so it is restricted to the fighting of novice bulls on foot. Entrance to the bull ring is via the uninspiring **Museo Taurino** with an extortionate entrance fee of 600 ptas. The other museum in the village is the **Carromato de Max**, a portacabin on stilts which claims to display the 'smallest curiosities in the world'. Give it a miss and save yourself 300 ptas. Near to the bull ring is an outdoor **auditorium**, where concerts are held and plays performed. Adjacent is the **Universidad Popular**, an adult education college.

● **Accommodation** Mijas has some high class hotels incl: **AL** *Byblos Andaluz*, Mijas Golf, T 2473050, F 2476783, 144 rm, one of the top hotels in Spain, with outstanding sports and leisure facilities; **A** *Club Puerta del Sol*, Ctra de Fuengirola, Km 4, T 2486400, F 2486441, 330 rm, large new hotel in Andalucían style, fitness centre; **A** *Mijas*, Urbanización Tamisa, T 2485800, F 2485825, 101 rm, a well appointed establishment in a quieter part of the village; **D** *El Mirío Blanco*, Plaza de la Constitución 13, small, cosy, on the main square; a good value pensión is **E** *Romana*, C/Coín 47.

● **Places to eat** ◆◆◆ *Le Nialhac*, Hotel Byblos, T 2460250; ◆◆*El Olivar*, Avda de la Peña, good ambience and value; ◆◆*El Padrastro*, Paseo de Compas, T 2485000, International food in a picturesque tower. For a meal under 1000 ptas try ◆*La Malagueña*, Plaza de la Paz, T 2485128.

FUENGIROLA WEST TO MARBELLA

The N340 initially hugs the coast as it passes through the administrative area of Mijas Costa with a series of dreary *urbanizacións* until the former fishing village of **La Cala** is reached. There is a broad shingle beach and a few reasonable restaurants, but little else to stop for. Further W is the vast spread of **Calahonda**, a mini town of villas, low rise apartments and leisure facilities, with its own commercial centre containing shops, bars, banks and supermarkets, but it is without a decent beach. The *autovia* now enters the Marbella district, a fact confirmed by the blue and white paint on the central reservation and footbridges. On the seaward side of the road is **Cabopino**, a pleasant high rise development around a small marina with a number of waterside restaurants. There is a good sandy beach, while the nearby dunes are an official naturist area.

From here into Marbella the developments and hotels step up a social grade, until **Marbella** itself is reached, signalled by an imposing 'triumphal arch' across the road.

MARBELLA

(*Pop* 80,000; *Alt* Sea level; *STD Code* 95)

ACCESS **Air** Nearest airports are at Gibraltar and Málaga.

Train The nearest train stations are at Fuengirola to the E and Algeciras to the W.

Road Marbella can only be reached by road from the N340, one of the most dangerous in Europe. The Marbella bypass opened in Jul 1993 and has significantly reduced traffic in the town and shortened the journey time along the coast. The bus station is located at the junction of Avda Ricardo Soriano and C/Calvario. **NB** Work has started on a new bus station which is due to open in late 1996. It will be located in C/Trapiche and will be complemented by a small 20 rm hotel and a number of shops.

Marbella has a long history, having been

populated at various times by Phoenicians, Visigoths and Romans, as well as being the most important Moorish town between Málaga and Gibraltar. Historians suggest that Moorish Marbella was a fortified town, with an oval shaped, 2m thick encircling wall containing 16 towers and three gates – to Ronda, Málaga and the sea. The town was taken by the Christians in 1485 and they set about remodelling the layout of the fortress, but much of the Moorish street plan remains today. In the early years of this century, Marbella was little more than a large village struggling to earn a living from agriculture and iron mining.

The iron industry is believed to have employed over 1,000 men in the mid-19th century, with main centre of operations along the banks of the Río Verde. An iron pier was built near the present fish dock to export the finished product and a few stanchions remain today. The industry finally closed in 1931, not through shortage of iron ore, but because of the depletion of local trees which provided the charcoal for the smelting process.

The changes began in the mid 1950s when a Spanish nobleman named Ricardo Soriano introduced his friends to the area. His nephew, Prince Alfonso von Hohenlohe, built the Marbella Club, attracting a wealthy international set to the area.

Marbella's inhabitants include Arab kings, arms dealers, stars of the media, famous sportsmen and notorious criminals. A visitor to Marbella might be surprised at its reputation as life seems entirely normal on the surface, but the social life of the celebrities goes on behind closed doors in luxury yachts, palatial villas and private clubs. Marbella was in danger of becoming rather seedy in the late 1980s, particularly when the property market collapsed, but the new, larger than life mayor, Jesus Gil, has given the town a facelift and it continues to thrive. Amongst his many grandiose schemes is a plan to build a 'millionaires' island off the shore at Puerto Banus.

Places of interest

Casco Antiguo (Old Town) Marbella's Old Town is a compact area located to the N of Avda Ramon y Cajal. In its centre is the **Plaza de Naranjos** (Orange Square), opened up in the 16th century by the Christian town planners by demolishing the maze of alleyways which comprised the Moorish *medina* (and incidentally finding Roman remains on the site). On the N side of the square is the 16th century **ayuntamiento** (town hall). In the SW corner of the square is a delightful stone fountain, the **Fuente de la Plaza**, which dates from 1604. Nearby is the **Ermita de Nuestro Señor Santiago**, Marbella's first Christian church, a small and simple building thought to date from the late 15th century. Look also for the **Casa Consistorial**, built in 1572. It has a fine wrought iron balcony and Mudéjar entrance, while on its exterior stonework is a coat of arms and inscriptions commemorating the bringing of water to the town. Finally in the square is the **Casa del Corregidor**, with a 16th century stone facade, now a cafe.

Armed with a map from the tourist office in the *ayuntamiento*, you can now explore the rest of the old town. Head for the NE corner, particularly around C/Trinidad, where there are good stretches of the old Moorish walls and at the western end of this street stands one of the towers of the original **castillo**, built by the Moors in the 9th century. The old walls continue into C/Carmen and C/Salinas. Also at the E end of the old town are two 'hospitals'. **Hospital Real de San Juan de Dios**, in C/Misericordia, was founded by *los Reyes Catolicos* at the time of the reconquest to minister to foreign patients. It has a chapel with a panelled Mudéjar ceiling and a tiny cloister. The **Hospital Bazán**, with its attractive exterior of pink stone and

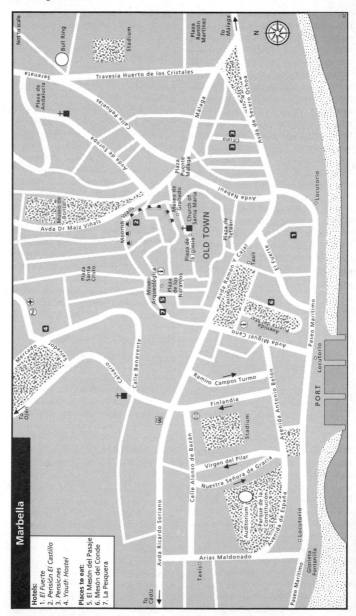

Marbella

Hotels:
1. El Fuerte
2. Pensión El Castillo
3. Pensicnes
4. Youth Hostel

Places to eat:
5. El Mesón del Pasaje
6. Mesón del Conde
7. La Pesquera

brickwork, dates from Renaissance times. Inside, there is a chapel, large rooms with intricate ceilings and a gallery. Originally a palace, the building was bequeathed by its owner Don Alonso de Bazán to be a local hospital; today, it is an art gallery. Do not miss the fine **Church of Santa María de la Encarnación**. Started in 1618, it has an impressive stone Baroque doorway, three sizeable naves and an interesting upper choir loft. Try to ignore the ghastly modern organ and concentrate on the high altar, where you will find the image of San Bernabé, the patron saint of Marbella. The main enjoyment of the old town, however, is in simply wandering around its maze of narrow alleyways, small squares and whitewashed houses festooned with flowers. Half a day will probably suffice.

Museums

Museo Arqueológico, Plaza de Naranjos 1, open Mon-Fri afternoons only. Contains Visigothic, early Christian and Roman artefacts.

Museo del Grabado Español Contemperáneo, Hospital Bazán. Exhibition of contemporary Spanish prints in the sympathetically restored Palácio de Bazán with strong Mudéjar influence. Open Mon 0930-1400, Tues-Fri 0930-1400 and 1730-2030, Sat closed, Sun 1100-1400. Entrance 300 ptas, children under 14, 100 ptas.

Museo de Bonsai, Parque Arroyo de la Repressa, T 2862926. This museum is an absolute gem and has become a major tourist attraction. Housed in a modern building surrounded by landscaped gardens and lakes, the miniature trees are imaginatively displayed on a wooden raft-like structure over water containing turtles and fish. Very Japanese! There is no problem with parking, and indeed this is a good place to leave a car when visiting Marbella's old town. Open 1000-1330 and 1600-1900. Adults 400 ptas, children 200 ptas, pensioners 300 ptas.

Parks

Marbella prides itself on the number of parks and open spaces around the town. **La Alameda**, close to the main street, has now been extended into the **Avenida del Mar**, linking the town centre with the *paseo marítimo*. Further W is the **Parque de la Constitución**, consisting of attractive gardens and a large outdoor auditorium. **Parque Arroyo de la Repressa** occupies a dry valley in the E of the town and comprises of a series of terraced gardens and lakes set off by a modern suspension bridge and providing a pleasant walk if you are obliged to visit the police station at the top of the hill.

Local festivals

Usual *Semana Santa* processions. The *Feria y Fiesta de San Bernabé* celebrates Marbella's patron saint with concerts and firework displays.

Local information
● **Accommodation**

AL *Don Carlos*, Ctra de Cádiz, Km 192, T 2831140, F 2833429, 238 rm, 10 km E of Marbella, the ultimate beach hotel, with sub tropical gardens leading down to a beach club, TV, pool, restaurant, Womens World Tennis Centre located in grounds; **AL** *El Fuerte*, Avda El Fuerte, T 2861500, F 2824411, 263 rm, luxury hotel close to the beach; **AL** *Meliá Don Pepe*, Finca las Merinas, T 2770300, F 2770300, 202 rm, faces the sea with a sports and leisure complex which incl 18 hole golf course, indoor and outdoor pools, TV, parking, garage, restaurant, squash and tennis courts.

A *Club Pinomar*, Ctra de Cádiz, Km 189, T 2831345, F 2833948, 46 rm, 5 km E of Marbella, small beach hotel with watersports facilities; **A** *Las Chapas*, Ctra de Cádiz, Km 192, T 2311375, F 2831377, 117 rm, on N340 2 km from beach, pool, restaurant, a/c.

B *Artola*, Ctra de Cádiz, Km 194, T 2831390, F 2830450, 31 rm, 12 km E of Marbella, small traditional Andalucían hotel with modern extension and 9-hole golf course, pool, restaurant, parking; **B** *Guadalpin*, Ctra de Cádiz, Km 179, T 2771100, F 2773334, 103 rm, situated on the coast road between Marbella and Puerto Banus, good value.

Something different: **B** *Refugio de Juanar*,

Sierra Blanca, Ojén, T 2881000, F 2881001, 20 rm, formerly a hunting lodge and parador, now a management run cooperative, peaceful mountain location with ibex and eagles and good walking possibilities, functional but comfortable, cosy fires in winter, tennis, pool, no dogs allowed.

Pensiones: the cheaper accommodation is mainly located around the fringes of the old town, particularly in C/Luna. Try **D** *La Estrella*, C/San Cristóbal 36, T 2779472; **E** *El Castillo*, Pza de San Bernabé 2, T 2771739, 26 rm, simple and clean, marvellous location in small square in old town; **E** *Isabel de Pacheco*, C/Luna 24, T 2771978, 4 rm; **E** *Juan*, C/Luna 18, T 2779475, 4 rm; **E** *La Luna*, C/Luna 7, T 2825778, 10 rm.

San Pedro de Alcantara: visitors requiring easy access to Marbella without wishing to pay inflated prices might consider the town of San Pedro de Alcantara just 10 km W for accommodation. **A** *El Cortijo Blanco*, Ctra de Cádiz, Km 172, T 2780900, F 2780916, 311 rm, Andalucían style with pleasant gardens, pool, wheelchair access; **D** *El Cid*, C/Extramadura 11, T 2780639, 28 rm, simple, but good value.

Youth hostels: C/Trapiche 2, T 2771491, 113 beds, suitable for wheelchair users, meals provided, kitchen, pool, central location.

Camping: there are 3 excellent camp sites in the vicinity of Marbella, all on the main coast road, but close to the beach. All are open all year round and winter use by recreational vehicles is high. Booking is advisable during the height of the season and on fiesta weekends. *La Bouganvilla*, Ctra Nacional 340, Km 188, T 2831973, top category, bar, restaurant, laundry, beach, pool, watersports, golf, riding tennis; *Marbella 191*, Ctra Nacional 340, Km 184, bar, laundry, beach, watersports; *Marbella Playa*, Ctra Nacional 340, Km 190, located 12 km E of town despite its name, close to one of the best beaches in the area, bar, restaurant, pool, supermarket.

● **Places to eat**

It is no surprise to find that there is a huge variety of eating places in Marbella and the surrounding area. Despite the affluent reputation of the town it is possible to find food which will not cost the earth.

♦♦♦ At the top of the range is *Gran Marisquería Santiago*, Paseo Maritimo, T 2770078, good seafood and other dishes, favoured by locals; *La Hacienda*, Urb Las Chapas, T 2821267, inaugurated by the late Paul Schiff, the famous Swiss chef, unique menu, very expensive; *La Meridiana*, Camino de la Cruz, Las Lomas, T 2776190, modern restaurant with inventive international cooking, one of Marbella's top eating spots, very expensive; *Meson del Conde*, Avda del Mar 18, T 2771057, Swiss restaurant specializing in meat and cheese fondues; *El Castillo*, Urb Pinomar, Ctra de Cádiz, Km 189, T 2832746, Castilian style restaurant with 8 types of paella, suckling pig and much more.

♦♦*Albahaca*, C/Lobotas 31, T 2863520, a rare Andalucían vegetarian restaurant in a 400-year-old town house, lunchtime *menu* at 975 ptas; *El Mesón del Pasaje*, C/Paseje, T 2771261, traditional restaurant in the old town; *Rama*, Urb Marbesa, T 2832438, family restaurant which has risen from beach bar origins to number cabinet ministers among its clientele (is this a recommendation?); *El Palenque*, Ctra de Cádiz, Km 176, T 2823112, Argentinian style steaks; *La Pesquera*, Plaza de la Victoria, T 2778054, reasonably priced fish menus under a thatched roof in a quiet square in the W part of the old town; *Pizzeria Portofino*, Paseo Maritimo, T 2775043, pizzas, couscous and great sea views.

♦ For those seeking reasonable prices and American fast food at *mañana* pace the Avda Ricardo Soriano can provide; *Burger King*, *McDonald's* and *Kentucky Fried Chicken*. Locals looking for cheap food out of doors head for the collection of 3 *ventas* located on the mountain road 3 km S of Ojén on the C337, which specialize in game dishes, especially rabbit and partridge.

● **Bars**

The following *tapas bars* are rec: *Bar Figuerado*, C/Haza del Méson (opp Municipal market); *El Mediterranito*, C/Tetuan; *Los Tres Pepes*, C/Peral, good ambience; *Trebol*, C/Ancha, always busy; *Bodegón El Chorrón*, C/Chorrón, good seafood.

● **Banks & money changers**

Branches of all the main Spanish banks and savings banks, plus some foreign banks may be found in Marbella, mainly along Avda Ricardo Sorriano. Cash dispensers abound.

● **Hospitals & medical services**

Chemists: these are open on Sat morning and weekdays 0900-1400 and 1700 2030. The name of the duty night chemist is shown on the window of each shop.

Hospitals: *Marbella Clinic*, T 2774282, is located on the Avda de Severo. A new hospital, *Hospital Comarcal*, has recently opened 5 km E of Marbella on the N340, opp Los Monteros Hotel. A recent grant of £1 million to the hospital by King Faud ensures that he will get good medical treatment should he be taken ill while resident in Marbella. *Marbella Medical Services*, T 2823135, have British trained doctors and do not charge travel insurance holders.

● **Post & telecommunications**
Area code: 95.

Post Office: *Correos* is located in C/Alvaro de Bázan, T 2772898.

Telephones: *locutorios* are placed at intervals along the sea front, Avda de Duque de Ahumada. Payment can be made by credit card.

● **Shopping**
Good quality shops abound in Marbella, particularly along Avda Ricardo Sorriano and in the alleyways of the old town. Many of these specialize in expensive, good quality jewellery and fashion goods. There are also numerous art galleries and craft shops. A new branch of *El Corte Inglés* at the *Centro Commercial Costa Marbella* at Puerto Banus opened in Mar 1996 and incl a hypermarket. Despite the 2,600 parking spaces, this development has added to the chronic traffic congestion in the area. There is an indoor market in C/Benevente selling fresh fruit and vegetables, open daily. There is also a large outdoor market held on Mon nr the football stadium, which is well worth a visit. The nearby San Pedro market is held on Thur. A flea and antique market is held at Puerto Banus next to the bullring on Sat mornings.

● **Sports**
Football: Marbella's team is in one of the lower divisions of the Spanish league. Stadium located in the NE of the town 1 km from the autovia.

Golf: Marbella is surrounded by golf courses, incl *La Dama de la Noche*, the first floodlit course in Europe, T 2812352. Others include *Río Real*, T 2779509; *Aloha*, T 2812388; *Los Naranjas*, T 2815206; *Las Brisas*, T 2810875; *Guadalmina*, T 2883375 (at San Pedro); *La Quinta*, T 2783462 (road to Benhavís).

Riding: at Club Hípico Elvira, T 2835272, Club Hípico Los Monteros, T 2770675, Centro de Equitación, Lakeview, T 2786934.

Tennis: Manola Santana, Hotel Puente Romano, T 2770100; Club Deportivo Sierra Blanca, T 2863829; Los Granados, Puerto Banus, T 2818832. In addition, the majority of hotels in the Marbella area have tennis courts with equipment to hire.

● **Tour companies & travel agents**
Marbesol, Avda Ricardo Sorriano 10, T 2773139; *Tourafrica*, Avda Ricardo Sorriano, Edif Molino, T 2771596; *Viajes Melía*, Avda Ricardo Sorriano, T 2773548.

● **Tourist offices**
The main office is located at the *ayuntamiento* in the Plaza de Naranjos, T 2771442. An additional office is open in the summer under the 'triumphal arch' at the E entrance to Marbella. Another summer only office may be found Avda Principal, Puerto Banus, T 2817474.

● **Useful addresses**
Garages/workshops: showrooms and workshops of all the major European car firms are clustered along the N340 on the E fringe of the town. Ford, T 2776450; Renault, T 2771616; Seat, T 2778800; VAG 2828409.

Should your car be parked illegally and towed away, contact **Municipal Car Tow**, T 2773692.

● **Transport**
Local Car hire: both international and local firms have their headquarters at Málaga airport. **Taxi**: ranks are located at C/Arias Maldonado (close to the outdoor auditorium); at the Alameda and next to the bus station, both in Avda Ricardo Sorriano. **Radio Taxi**: T 2770053. For the San Pedro area, T 2783838.

Air The nearest airport is at Málaga, 56 km E. There is an *Iberia* office on Paseo Maritimo, Complejo Marbella 2000, T 2770284, reservations T 2773082.

Road Bus: bus station, C/Ricardo Sorriano, T 2772193 (note that new bus station opens late 1996 in C/Trapiche). Local buses operate half-hourly along the coast road to the E and W. 5 buses a day link Ojén, Monda and Coín inland to the N. Coaches run to **Algeciras** 8 times a day, **Ronda and La Linea** 4 times a day. **Cádiz, Sevilla** and **Jerez** are also served and there are 5 coaches daily to **Madrid**.

EXCURSIONS FROM MARBELLA

There are a number of villages located in the hills inland from Marbella. **Istán**, described by the developers as 'the village on the lake', is, in fact, some distance from a recently built reservoir, and has little to commend it. The village of **Benhavís**, on the other hand, has an attractive setting just N of a picturesque gorge. It is the home of a number of artists and sculptors and has a number of excellent restaurants, of which the following can be particularly rec: ♦♦*La Sarten*, T 2855577, good Spanish cooking accompanied by twice monthly jazz and *flamenco. Las Griegas*, T 2855465, authentic Greek cooking; *Cuarto Hondo*, T 2855136, international cuisine, incl suckling pig. ♦*Venta Román*, T 2886421, typical country style Spanish restaurant popular on Sun lunchtimes.

Just 8 km N of Marbella is the expanding village of **Ojén**, which was Moorish until 1570 and still retains much of the flavour of that time. There is an annual *Fiesta de Flamenco* during the first week in Aug. The road above and below Ojén is winding and dangerous, but in late 1995 a new well engineered road was opened which bypasses the town. Continue through Ojén and over the pass and after 4 km turn left through the pine forests to the **Refugio de Juanar** (see accommodation, page 79). From this former parador a track leads through woodlands of sweet chestnut and almonds and on past olive groves to a *mirador* at 1,000m, from where there are stupendous views over Marbella, the coast and often Morocco. Allow 1½ hrs for this walk. There are many other walking trails, mostly leading from the Refugio. The adventurous could even walk back down through the woods to Ojén. The whole area is a naturalists delight, with a wide range of flowers, including orchids, butterflies and birds. Small family groups of Ibex are not uncommon, but should these prove elusive there is a compensatory bronze statue of one set on a rock above the mirador. During the spring and autumn passages birds of prey can be seen en route to and from the Straits, while Booted and Bonellis Eagles breed in the vicinity. Other breeding birds include Crossbills, Dartford Warblers, Blue Rock Thrushes, Firecrests and Crested Tits. Avoid Sun, when hordes of Spaniards picnic in the area. A return route to Marbella could be made via **Monda**, **Coín**, a bustling market town of some 22,000 people, **Mijas** and **Fuengirola**.

Puerto Banus A marina development some 6 km W of Marbella and the haunt of the famous and the notorious. Floating gin palaces alongside gold Rolls Royces and tourists hoping to glimpse the famous are just some of the sights. As someone once remarked, here the ultimate in posing is to actually put to sea! The harbour is backed by expensive apartments, boutiques, restaurants and nightclubs.

The area between Marbella and Puerto Banus is known as the 'golden mile', lined with expensive properties including that of King Faud of Saudi Arabia with an adjacent mosque – a return of the arabs to the area bringing the history full circle.

Casino Nueva Andalucía at *Hotel Andalucía Plaza*, Nueva Andalucía, T 2810919. Games room with American and French Roulette, Black Jack, Punto y Banca and fruit machines, restaurant.

Centro de Observación Marina Following the success of the Marine Observation Centre at Banalmádena, the same company *Sea Life España* have opened a new centre at Puerto Banus. The chief aim is to study marine species, but the centre is open to the public. Visitors can see 22 tanks holding 50 different species, including sharks, conger eels and sun fish. Open 1000-midnight, admission 700 ptas.

Cortylandia Visitors with children visiting *El Corte Ingles/Hipercor* shopping complex at Puerto Banus could park them at Cortylandia, a 19th century style amusement park. Amongst the dozen rides are a 2-tiered merry-go-round and a train running 3m off the ground. Admission is free for shoppers at *Hipercor*, otherwise 500 ptas.

WEST OF MARBELLA

About 10 km W of Marbella is **San Pedro de Alcantara**, which recently voted to become part of Marbella – its reward was a 'triumphal arch' to mark the western limits of the administrative area. San Pedro is largely undeveloped, being a kilometre or so back from the beach. This area of wasteland, however, is rapidly becoming urbanized and with a planned marina, San Pedro is confident of its future affluence. The town itself is unremarkable and even its church is 19th century.

Roman remains There are three important archaeological sites in the area W of Marbella dating from Roman times. All are easily accessible.

The **Basílica de Vega de Mar** To find the site leave the N340 at the roundabout at San Pedro Alcántara and take the beach road. Turn along the last road on the right before the beach. After 500m look for a grove of mature Eucalyptus trees on the left. Alternatively go to the end of the beach promenade and walk along the beach for 150m before turning inland to the Eucalyptus trees. The centre of the site consists of a Roman basilica dating from the 7th century. The plan is still clear to see, with three naves which would have separated major clergy, men and women, and the bases of some substantial pillars. The basilica is aligned E/W and at each end are semi-circular apses, showing the link with the North African churches of the time. At the N end of the westerly apse is a remarkable baptismal font, some 2m deep and often filled with rain water to give a realistic idea of the total immersion practised at that time. Surrounding the basilica is a necropolis where 187 tombs of various types have been unearthed. They date from late Roman to the start of the 8th century and all are aligned E/W. The earliest tombs were triangular in cross section and probably made of wood. They were later square shaped and lined with round stones.

Later still there were family tombs of brick. The more affluent had their tombs lined with marble. There are some small tombs, apparently of children who died in infancy.

The second site is 400m along the beach to the W of the basilica next to the urbanisación of Guadalmedina. Look for the round watch tower, which is adjacent. These are the **Roman Baths** or the **Ternas de las Bovedas** (or vaults), which date back to the 3rd century and were possibly part of the town of *Silniana*, which was destroyed by an earthquake in 365 AD. It is a building of two octagonal floors, constructed with stone bonded with a mortar of limestone and beach sand – a combination which has proved extremely durable. The building was constructed around an octagonal patio nearly 10m in diameter. Parallel to the walls are the remains of a 1.2m deep octagonal pool. The upper floor consists of a circular gallery with access to several small rooms. Discovered in the subsoil are the remains of a hypercaust and a praeforium (where the water was heated). Assuming that they are in fact baths, then they are clearly some of the most important discoveries of early Roman times, but archaeologists are divided in their opinions and some experts consider them to be storage tanks for water carried in nearby aqueducts (these were noted in a manuscript by a historian in 1663 who described them as 'over a league in length', but which have now been lost). Having survived since the 3rd century, Las Bovedas are now, ironically, in danger of falling down and it is planned to spend some 4 million pesetas in securing the structure.

The third site is the **Roman villa** at **Río Verde**, which is located to the S of the coast road between Marbella and Puerto Banus. Owing to the problems of turning left from the *autovia*, it must be approached from the W, so if arriving from Marbella go to the Puerto Banus underpass and return. After crossing the

Río Verde bridge, take the first road to the right and follow the signs. The remains are tucked in amongst modern day villas. This was a large Roman villa located near the mouth of the Río Verde and believed to be built at the end of the 1st century or at the beginning of the 2nd century. The remains show the peristilo (round patio with columns) surrounded by three corridors and five rooms. The main interest is in the mosaics, which are mainly in black and white. The room which faces N (and which can easily be seen from the road) contains a splendid mosaic of Medusa's head, with four snakes among the strands of her hair and two more coiled around her neck. She is surrounded by geometrical patterns enclosing ducks and herons. The other rooms have mosaics showing culinary items and nautical themes. The mosaics suggest that the owner of the villa was of the dominant social class at the time and probably involved in commerce and trade.

All three sites are enclosed by railings, from which good views can be had, but for detailed viewing it is well worth getting keys, which can be supplied by both the Marbella and San Pedro tourist offices. The Marbella office organizes occasional guided tours of all three sites.

San Pedro is the first location in Spain for **Cable Ski**, whereby water skiers are towed by cable for distances of up to 20 km. Situated on the landward side of the coast road, cable-ski provides full equipment and charges vary from 1,000 ptas for four rounds to 10,000 ptas for 100 rounds. Instruction is also available. There is an artificial beach with *chiringuitos* and children's play areas. **Ronda** is an easy excursion from here. Then follows a ribbon development of coastal urbanizations until Estepona is reached.

ESTEPONA

The most Spanish of the Costa resorts, Estepona has an attractive sea front with a promenade backing a shingle beach, with a few low rise apartment blocks. The town itself has some interesting corners, including two attractive squares, the Plaza Arce and the Plaza las Flores. The main restaurants and *tapas* bars are along C/Terraza. As far as accommodation is concerned, there should be no problem except at the height of the summer. There are two luxury hotels, both on the main road, but close to the beach: **AL** *Atalaya Park*, Ctra de Cádiz, Km 168.5, T 2884801, F 2885735, 246 rm, pool, golf, tennis a/c; **AL** *El Paraiso*, Ctra de Cádiz, Km 167, T 2883000, F 2882019, 195 rm, a/c, pools, tennis, golf. More modest is **C** *Santa Marta*, Ctra de Cádiz, Km 167, T 2888177, F 2888180, 37 rm, pool, restaurant. There are around 10 **pensiones** of which the following nr Plaza las Flores can be rec: **E** *La Malagueña*, C/Castillo s/n, T 2800011, 14 rm; **E** *San Miguel*, C/Terraza 16, T 2802616.

Estepona is also the location of the first 'ecological hotel' on the Costa del Sol. This is the **C** *Diana Park*, Km 168, on N340, which opened in Spring 1996 and stresses its anti-allergy paint, use of natural fibres in furnishings, no fitted carpets, environmentally friendly soap and detergents and the treatment of its swimming pool water with ozone instead of chlorine.

On the W edge of Estepona is the new port. Less pretentious than its neighbours to the E and W, it is very much the working harbour, with a large fishing fleet as well as the usual luxury craft. There are also a number of restaurants to suit all pockets.

The new bypass around Estepona has removed traffic congestion from the town. 3 km W of Estepona is **Costa Natura**, a long established naturist complex with accommodation and a wide variety of facilities. Casual visitors are discouraged and membership cards from naturist clubs in your own country must be produced. For information T 2801500.

Baring all on the Costa

Even during the Franco dictatorship, topless sunbathing was beginning to appear on the Costa del Sol, even though enthusiasts risked being advised to 'cover up' by the patrolling *Guardia Civil*. Today, the practice is commonplace and full nudism is permissible in certain areas.

Nudism (or naturism) probably began in Scandinavia in the early years of this century, but the first purpose built nudist resort did not appear on the Costa del Sol until 1979 at Costa Natura, just to the west of Estepona. Here, there are apartments, a supermarket, water sports and many other facilities. Local authorities have recently begun to realise that nudist beaches can be part of the wide range of facilities a resort might offer and they have officially designated certain sites as being set aside for naturism. Indeed some sites may have signs banning the wearing of costumes (a good ploy to deter the 'Peeping Tom'). Other beaches, whilst not officially designated, are widely accepted as locations for nudism.

Such locations, of course, often attract the poseur and voyeur, but the atmosphere is generally healthy, particularly at weekends, when Spanish families appear in droves. Visitors to Andalucía wishing to sample the delights of nudism (and don't forget to apply high factor cream to the parts which the sun does not normally reach!) could try the following sites: **Benalnatura**, beneath the cliffs to the W of Benalmádena; the dunes to the W of **Puerto Cabopino**; the beach at **Almarat** in the Velez Málaga district; in Cádiz province, the southern part of the beach at **Bolonia** and at **Caños de Meca** near Cape Trafalgar.

There are also a number of sites in Almería province, where the Andalucían Nudist Association has its headquarters. For further information, contact C/Principe Felipe 11, Apartado de Correos 301, Almería.

Prado World is a children's amusement park and water park rolled into one, with pools, rides, bouncing castles on a 21 acre site just off the main coastal highway. Open in summer 1000-2100; open until 0100 at weekends, T 2791174.

3 km W of Estepona, a winding road leads inland for 18 km to **Casares**, which claims to be the 'most photographed village in Spain'. Its whitewashed houses clothe the side of a hill which is capped by the ruins of a 13th century Moorish fortress on Roman foundations built in the time of Ibn al Jatib. The fort was a centre of resistence against the French during the Peninsular War. Next to the fort is the Church of the Incarnación. It was built in 1505 and has a brick Mudejar tower (the remainder of the church is constructed of brick and stone, partly covered in plaster). The interior has three naves and a small chapel, but as it was partially destroyed during the Civil War, it is nowadays boarded up. The castle and church share their hilltop position with the local cemetery, which is meticulously kept (the view from the hill top shows a new one being built on the outskirts). On the cliff below is a breeding colony of Lesser Kestrels, while there are spectacular views down to the coast towards Gibraltar and North Africa. Casares is said to have derived its name from Julius Caesar, who may have been cured of his liver complaints by the sulphur springs at nearby Manilva. The 17th century Church of San Sebastián, which can be visited on the way to the fortress, is a simple white washed 17th century building containing the image of the Virgen del Rosario del Campo. In the adjacent square is a statue of Blas Infante who was a native of Casares

and leader of Andalucías nationalist movement. He was executed by Franco's supporters. There are possibilities for eating in the square, with *Bar Restaurant Claveles* having walls festooned with farming implements and specializing in game dishes such as rabbit, partridge and quail. Across the road is *Bar los Amigos*, busy with locals and providing a good range of *tapas*. There is another decent restaurant and craft shop at the entrance to the village. From their terrace there are fine panoramic views of Casares. The alternative route back to the coast at Manilva passes through attractive vineyards and limestone scenery, although the road surface is poor. There are two buses a day from Estepona to Casares, but should you decide to stay overnight, the only viable possibility is the pensión **E** *Plaza*, in the main square, T 2894088, 9 rm. From Casares, it is an exciting 20-min drive to **Gaucín** (see page 94), the road initially dipping down into the valley of the Río Genal before climbing up a series of hairpin bends to the village. There are few accommodation possibilities in Gaucín, apart from one small *pensión*, but the surrounding area has some interesting ideas. **Something different**: there are two English owned farmhouses offering bed and breakfast in peaceful surroundings: **C** *Cortijo El Puerto del Negro*, Apto 25, 29480 Gaucín, T/F 2151239, 4 rm plus 2 cottages in wilderness surroundings; and **C** *Finca la Almuña*, Apto 20, 29480 Gaucín, T/F 2151200, 6 rm, good home cooking, good riding and walking possibilities.

At the end of the Estepona by-pass, the N340 reverts to single carriageway causing huge tailbacks during the summer months. The infrastructure will hopefully improve before the 1997 Ryder Cup on the Valderrama course at Sotogrande.

West of the growing village of Manilva is the new marina of Puerto Duquesa, an attractive development and a carbon copy of those further W. The usual apartments, restaurants, boutiques and chandlers line the harbourside.

RONDA

(*Pop* 34,000; *Alt* 750m; *STD code* 95)

ACCESS Air The nearest airport is at Málaga, some 122 km E.

Train The train station is located in the N edge of the town in Avda de Andalucía. Rail links SW to Algeciras and E to Antequera and Málaga.

Road Ronda is at the centre of a network of roads, the one S to San Pedro de Alcántara is particularly well engineered and ensures that Ronda can be reached from the Costa del Sol in under an hour. Other roads lead SW to Algeciras, W to Arcos de la Frontera, NE to Antequera and SE to Coín and Málaga. The bus station is in Plaza Concepción García Redondo, just 5 mins walk from the centre.

Ronda is a charming, historic town some 55 km N of the coast and should be a priority for an traveller in S Andalucía. It is located on a plain in the Serranía de Ronda mountains, the town being cut in half by a spectacular gorge – **El Tajo** – some 120m deep. It has a more extreme climate than the coast with colder winters (snow is not uncommon on the surrounding mountains) and very hot summers when mid afternoon temperatures can average 33°C.

History

Ronda has a long and fascinating history. The Iberians named it Arunda; the Romans changed it to Munda. It enjoyed its most prosperous times, particularly under Abu Nur, during the Moorish occupation which lasted for more than 8 centuries. The Moors fortified it so well that it took a Christian army of 13,000 cavalry and 25,000 infantrymen 7 days to capture it in 1485. What remained of the Moorish Alcazaba was almost totally destroyed by the French during the Penin-

Ronda

sular War in 1809. Ronda also saw plenty of action in the Civil War, when representatives of both sides were thrown into the Tajo. In the early years of this century Ronda was a popular retreat for British officers based in Gibraltar. Now the British come in coaches from the Costa, but this does not seem to spoil the essential charm of the town.

Places of interest

The Tajo, formed by the river Guadalevin, splits Ronda into two unequal sections. To the E is the old town, known as the *cuidad*, and its suburb of San Francisco, which lies outside the old walls. To the W is the much more recent *mercadillo*.

The Tajo is spanned by three bridges. The lowest and oldest is the **Puente Arabe**, a

Moorish structure which has been much restored. Next is the **Puente Viajo**, dating from the 17th century and still taking vehicular traffic. Thirdly, there is the so called **Puente Nuevo** or new bridge, which began with tragedy when on completion the architect, Martín Aldehuela, was lowered over the parapet to inspect his work. A gust of wind blew away his hat and in making a grab for it he fell to his death. Beneath the Puente Nuevo was the former prison, which in recent times acted as a *tapas* bar. This has now, regrettably, closed. Despite its foul smelling raw sewerage, the photogenic gorge makes for excellent bird watching, with Rock Doves, Choughs and Crag Martins whirling through the gorge. At the N end of the gorge are the **Baños Arabes** (Moorish Baths). Reached from the Puente Viejo, the roof cupolas are soon seen. Made of brick with typical Moorish arches, there are the typical hot and cold rooms, which were fed by a nearby stream. The baths have had some minor renovations in recent years and the site may with luck be found open, but the *Turismo's* confident opening times are something of a joke. The author has only found the baths open once in 16 years of visiting Ronda. The most recent excuse (Jan 1995) was that a stream had flooded the baths, leaving a thick layer of mud and rubbish, and it would be a year before they reopened.

There are other Moorish remains in the *cuidad*. Along the main road, the C/Armiñán, is the **Minarete de San Sebastián**, a 14th century Nasrid style tower from a mosque. At the end of the same road are two gates in the town walls. The oldest is the Arab **Puerta del Almocábar** with a horseshoe arch and two matching towers. Next to it the road runs under the **Puerta de Carlos V**, dating from the 16th century. Alongside the ramparts is the **Iglesia del Espíritu Santo** (Church of the Holy Spirit), built in 1505. Open 1000-1930, entrance 75

ptas. The focal point of the *cuidad* is the **Plaza Duqueza de Parcent**, which is dominated by the **Iglesia de Santa María Mayor**. Originally a 13th century mosque, it was rebuilt by the Christians but retains much of the Moorish architecture. It has a late Gothic nave and heavily carved wooden Baroque choir stalls and an impressive retablo. There is also a *tesoro* – a museum of church treasures, including a large amount of silver ware and ancient bibles. In the entrance porch are some Moorish arches covered with Arab calligraphy and nearby part of a *mihrab* has been exposed. On the frontal exterior of the church is a balcony facing the square which provided a position for dignitaries to watch bull fights before the main ring was built. Open winter 1000-1800, summer 1000-2000, entrance 150 ptas, pensioners 75 ptas. At the far end of the Plaza is the site of the **Alcázar**, destroyed by the French in 1809. Completing the square are the *ayuntamiento* (in a building which was formerly the 18th century barracks), the police station, law courts and two small convents.

Moving further W in the *cuidad* in the Plaza del Gigante is the **Casa del Gigante**, a 14th century Moorish palace, which unfortunately is not open to the public. In the extreme S, on the top of the cliff is the **Casa de Mondragón**, undoubtedly the most important civil monument in Ronda. It was believed to be the residence of Abomelic, son of the Sultan of Morocco in the early 14th century. Later Ronda became part of the kingdom of Granada and the last Moorish governor of Granada also resided in the palace. When Ronda fell to the Christians, Fernando and Isobel adapted the palace for their use. The outer façade of the building dates from the 18th century, but much of the interior is Moorish or Mudéjar, with filligree work and horseshoe arches and mosaics. There are a number of delightful patios with fountains and stunning views over the Tajo. Much of the Casa de Mondragón is taken up with the **Museum of Ronda and the Serrania**. The history section looks at the world of caves, Roman and Moslem funeral remains, and the historical evolution of the town of Ronda. The ethnography section has displays on the production of cork oak, cheese and pig products. The third section deals with the environment and in particular the local natural park of Grazalema. The audio visual displays are well presented and include a 'walk in' cave and a metallurgy room. The palace also acts as the local cultural centre with adult education classes and lectures. Open 1000-1900, Sat and Sun 1000-1500, entrance 200 ptas, pensioners 100 ptas.

All Andalucía loves a bandit

Banditry or *bandolerismo* has always, until quite recently, been an acceptable occupation in Andalucía. With its rugged countryside, dense forest, caves and mountains, Andalucía has been profitable territory for the brigand and smuggler. Many of the *bandoleros* were Robin Hood-like characters, who stole from the rich but made sure that the less fortunate in society were well looked after. Many were forced into banditry because of the appalling social conditions in the rural areas. As such, their activities functioned as a safety valve against social dissent, a point noted by Gerald Brenan, "In the eyes of the country people he was a hero, the friend of the poor and a champion against their oppressors". The more privileged in society were not, however, so appreciative and their protests led in 1844 to the formation of the Civil Guard, whose main role was to protect the affluent against the brigands.

Undoubtedly the most notorious bandit was José María Hinojosa Cobacho – *El Tempranillo* – who was born near Lucena in Córdoba province in 1800. At the age of 22 he claimed that "The king may reign in Spain, but in the sierra I do". He was referring to the Sierra Morena, which runs along the entire length of northern Andalucía and through which all transport to Madrid had to pass as it delivered the riches from the New World. Profitable territory for a bandit, especially as *El Tempranillo* demanded an ounce of gold for each wagon or carriage which crossed his land. Said to be blond (he may have been a descendant of one of the German settlers who came to the area in the mid-18th century), *El Tempranillo* was noted for his gallantry towards women (kissing their hands as he removed the rings) and for his sense of humour. It is said that on one occasion he arrived at a venta and asked to share some soup. He was told by the diners that there were no spoons left, so he fashioned a spoon from a piece of bread and consumed the soup and his bread. He then produced a gun and revealed his identity, requesting that the terrified diners eat their spoons, as he had done, until their teeth cracked. *El Tempranillo* was eventually treacherously murdered by a former comrade.

The last of the notorious *bandoreros* was José Mingolla Gallardi, known to all and sundry as 'Pasos Largos' (Big Feet). Hailing from the village of El Burgo, he took to the hills after committing several murders. He quickly became a legendary figure and although once captured and gaoled, he soon returned to his bandit's way of life. He was eventually killed in 1934, after a shoot out with the *Guardia Civil*.

This long history of banditry does much to explain the Andalucían's tolerant attitude towards law breaking. A man who can get away with a swindle or a scam is often respected, while one who can put one over bureaucracy or authority is something of a hero.

Back in C/Armiñán, is the newly opened **Museum of Banditry**. Ronda is an apt place for such a museum to be located as the mountains around the town abounded with 'Robin Hood' type characters in the 18th, 19th and even the early 20th centuries. There are five rooms in the museum displaying documents, weapons, maps, and a mock up of a tavern of the times. Some of the great figures of banditry are illustrated, including José María Hinojosa Cobacho, alias 'El Tempranillo', José Mingolla Gallardi, alias 'Pasos Largos' (Big Feet), and 'Shotgun Getares'. The forces of law and order are also not forgotten. Open 1000-1800, 175 ptas.

The *mercadillo* part of the town has less in the way of monuments, but is not without interest. It is dominated by the **Plaza de Toros** (Bull ring), built in 1785 and claimed to be the oldest in Spain. It holds 5,000 people and was used as the setting for the film 'Carmen'. Under the bull ring is a small **Museo de Toros** and whatever ones feelings about bull fighting this is a fascinating place, full of 'torobilia' such as photographs, posters, toreadors' clothing and bulls' heads, all with suitable background music. Open summer 1000-1400 and 1600-1900, winter 1000-1400. En-

trance 200 ptas. Tickets can be obtained from the souvenir shop to the right of the bull ring entrance.

Suggested walking route

A convenient start is at the main bridge, the **Puente Nuevo** (2). Move NW into the recently cleaned up **Plaza de España**. Note on the left the new **Parador** which opened in 1994, occupying the shell of the old town hall. At the far end of the Plaza is the **Tourist Office** where a town plan can be obtained (100 ptas). Take the alleyway to the left of the office which brings you to the **Bull ring**, beside which is a pay and display car park. You are now in the **Paseo de Blas Infante**, which forms a sort of linear mirador with superb vertiginous views over the cliff and down to the river Guadalevín. Apart from the view, this is a marvellous bird watching spot as Peregrine Falcons breed on the cliffs and during the summer Alpine Swifts and Crag Martins can also expect to be seen. Proceed NW past the new concert hall and into the **Alemeda**. This is a shady park with fountains and a small aviary. At *Corpus Cristi*, the central pathway is covered with flowers laid out in patterns.

Returning via the Plaza de Toros, go to the Plaza de España and turn left down C/Villanueva. Take the first right

The modern bullfight

The original bullfights were fought from a horse using a long spear. The modern form of bullfighting on foot began in Ronda, when Francisco Romero jumped into the ring to save a dismounted rider who was being gored by distracting the bull with his hat. But it was his grandson, **Pedro Romero** (1754-1839), who laid down the ritual of modern bullfighting using a sword and red cape. With his formal style, Romero killed nearly 6,000 bulls without once being gored. Today there is a monument to Romero in the Alameda. The nearby bullring was opened in 1785 and it is unusual in that the seating is fully covered. There has been a long string of famous *toreros* from Ronda, the latest being Antonio Ordóñez, who owns a nearby estate.

The artist Goya painted a number of pictures at the Ronda bullring. Every Sep there is a Pedro Romero festival, when *corridas goyescas* take place with the bullfighters wearing the costumes of Goya's time.

The Ronda style of bullfighting is regarded by *aficionados* as rather severe and ascetic, compared with the more exhibitionist approach of, say, Sevilla.

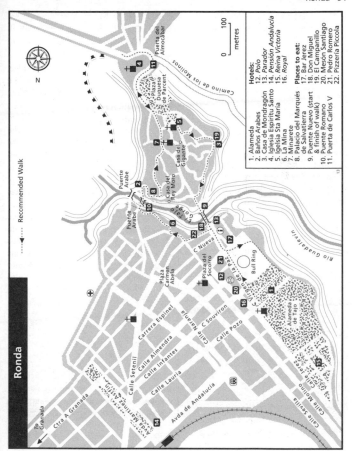

Hotels:
1. Alameda
2. Baños Arabes
3. Casa de Mondragón
4. Pensión Andalucía
5. Reina Victoria
16. Royal

12. Polo
13. Parador
14. Pensión Andalucía
15. Reina Victoria
16. Royal

Places to eat:
17. Bar Jerez
18. Don Miguel
19. El Campanillo
20. Mesón Santiago
21. Pedro Romero
22. Pizzeria Piccola

1. Alameda
2. Baños Arabes
3. Casa de Mondragón
4. Iglesia Espíritu Santo
5. Iglesia Sta María
6. La Mina
7. Minarete
8. Palácio del Marqués de Salvatierra
9. Puente Nuevo (start & finish of walk)
10. Puente Romano
11. Puerta de Carlos V

into C/Los Remedios. After 200m any alleyway to the right will bring you into a series of beautifully terraced gardens, known as **La Mina** (4), affording stupendous views of El Tajo. Emerging from the gardens, cross the gorge by the **Puente Viejo** (5), originally a Roman bridge, but re-built in 1616. Note to the left the Church of Nuestre Padre Jesús, outside of which is the water trough known as El Fuente de los Ocho Caños – the Fountain of the Eight Springs. From here the distinctive roof of the

Baños Arabes (6) can be seen.

Now pass through the arch, the **Puerta de Filipe V**, which dates from 1742, and turn right up the steep hill of C/Santa Domingo. **WARNING** The street cobbles are highly polished by countless feet and are extremely slippery. On the left is the **Palácio del Marqués de Salvatierra** (8), an ornate privately owned Renaissance building with handsome balconies of typical Ronda wrought iron work. Note the curious frieze of Adam and Eve above the entrance. The palace is open 1100-

1400 and 1600-1800, visits taking place every 30 mins; just wait at the door for the guide. Entrance 200 ptas. To the right is the **Casa del Rey Moro** (8), the House of the Moorish King, an 18th century mansion, built on Moorish foundations. At the rear of the house is a footpath cut into the rocky side of the gorge, said to have been used by Christian slaves to bring water to their Moorish masters. Hopefully the water was less polluted in those days than it is today. The Casa del Rey Moro is not open to the public.

At the top of the hill, near a cluster of antique shops, is C/Armiñán, the main street through the old town. Turn left and follow this road to the old city walls marking the edge of the town, passing on the way the free standing Moorish **Minarete de San Sebastián** (9). Note the two gates in the city walls and the **Iglesia del Espíritu Santo** (10). Continue back into town, turning left up C/Escalona into the old quarter via Plaza Duquesa de Parcent, dominated by the church of **Santa María la Mayor** (11). Proceed now via the **Casa del Gigante**, in the Plaza of the same name to the **Palacio de Mondragón** (12). Walk now into the Plaza del Campillo with excellent views of the gorge. For the energetic there is a path down into the valley. Return to the Puente Nuevo via C/Tenorio. The full walk could be completed in 2 hrs, but shade and restaurant will be needed in the heat of summer.

TOURIST GUIDES There is a lively tourist guide business. For an informative tour of Ronda's historic sites, phone José Paez Carroscosa, T 2873468. **NB** Unofficial guides may fasten on to tourists while they are sightseeing, impart a few words of wisdom and then demand money. Don't get involved.

Local festivals

These include *Fiesta de la Virgen de la Paz*, patron saint of Ronda, 24 Jan, the processions during *Semana Santa*, and *Corpus Cristi*, when flowers cover the ground in the Alameda. The *Feria de Mayo*, the May Fair celebrates the Reconquest, while on the second Sun in Jun there is a *romería* for Our Lady of the Cabeza. In early Sep there is the Pedro Romero Festival with *corridas goyescas* (bull fights in Goyaesque attire). There is also an International Folk Festival in Sep and a *flamenco* festival on the last Sat in Aug as part of the *Feria de Ronda*.

Local information
● Accommodation

AL *Parador de Ronda*, Plaza de España, T 5590069, F 2878080, 71 rm, 8 suites, restaurant, opened Jul 1994, built within the original façade of the old town hall with spectacular views over the gorge.

A *Reina Victoria*, C/Jerez 25, T 2871240, F 2871075, 89 rm, beautifully located Edwardian hotel built by the English, 1 room is a small museum dedicated to the German poet Rainer María Rilke, good views, pool, garage.

B *Don Miguel*, C/Villanueva 8, T 2877722, F 2878377, 19 rm, small hotel adjacent to the gorge, comfortable, clean, excellent restaurant, garage; *Polo*, C/Mariano Soubiron 8, F 2872449, 33 rm, traditional town centre hotel, restaurant, a/c.

C *El Tajo*, C/Dr Cajal 7, T 2876236, F 2875099, 67 rm, garage, in the centre of the *mercadillo*; *Royal*, C/Virgen de la Paz 42, T 2871141, F 2878132, 29 rm, on main rd opp Alameda, can be noisy, a/c, restaurant.

Pensiones: most of the pensiones are located in the heart of the *Mercadillo* area of the town. **E** *Aguilar*, C/Naranja 28, T 2871994, 17 rm; **E** *Andalucía*, Avda Martínez 19, T 2875450, 11 rm, opp railway station, clean, with bath, highly rec; *Biarritz*, C/Cristo 7, 21 rm, pets accepted; *Casa Huespedes la Española*, off Plaza España, rooms with bath, clean, good views over the Tajo; *El Atico*, C/Cañada Real 12, T 2875903, 7 rm; *Morales*, C/Sevilla 51, T 2871538, 13 rm; *Rondasol*, C/Cristo 11, T 2877497, 15 rm, some with bath; *San Francisco* C/Prim 8, T 2873299, 16 rm; *Virgen del Rocío*, C/Nueva 18, T 2877425, 6 rm.

Travellers wishing to stay in a nearby village could consider **E** *Moneda*, C/Luis Armiñán, Gaucín, T 2151156. Gaucín, which lies 37 km SW of Ronda on the C341, was a favourite stop for British officers en route from Gibraltar to Ronda.

Something different: **AL** *La Posada Real*, C/Real 42, T 2877176, F 2878370, 10 rm, small hotel in the E side of the town nr to the gorge. Formerly a palace, convent and town hall. Full of antiques, but all mod cons incl pool, sauna and roof top mirador. Restaurant serving local dishes; **B** *Molino del Santo*, Barriada del Estación, 29370, Benaoján, T 2167151, F 2167327, 12 rm in renovated water mill in village to the W of Ronda close to Cueva de la Pileta. Good base for walking.

Camping: there are no official camp sites in the vicinity of Ronda, the nearest being on the Costa del Sol and in the Parque Natural Sierra de Grazelema to the W.

● **Places to eat**

The better restaurants in Ronda serve the traditional food of the area, incl *cocidos* and game dishes.

♦♦♦*Don Miguel*, Plaza de España, T 2871090, probably the best food in Ronda, certainly the best view, with its terraces overlooking the bridge and gorge; *Pedro Romero*, C/Virgen de la Paz, opp bull ring, regional decor and food.

♦♦*Bar Restaurant Jerez*, Paseo de Blas Infante 2, T 2872098, by the bull ring, happily caters for both tourists and locals with av costs; *El Campanillo*, Plaza del Campanillo s/n, good food, cliff top location with mirador in old town; *Hermanos Andrades*, C/Los Remedios 1, good value; *Mesón Santiago*, C/Marina 3, T 2871367, traditional Ronda restaurant with local dishes; *Pizzería Piccola Capri*, C/Villanueva 18, T 2873943, one of the few restaurants in Ronda serving international food, nice atmosphere and views over the Tajo; *Polo*, C/Mariano Souvirón 8, hotel restaurant; *Tenorio*, C/Tenorio 1, T 2874936, local dishes.

♦*Cervecería El Patio*, C/Carrera Espinel 100, T 2871015, patio dining area; *Flores*, C/Virgen de la Paz 9, popular with tourist, cheap *menu del día*; *La Ibense*, C/Espinel 42, good for ice creams and snacks. Restaurant at railway station is good. Try also the café at the bus station for a small snack and a large slice of Spanish life.

● **Bars**

For the best *tapas* bars try the Plaza del Socorro, particularly *Marisquería Paco*. Elsewhere, the following are rec: *Bodega la Esquina*, C/Remedios 24, and *Bodega la Giralda*, C/Nueva 19.

● **Banks & money changers**

The main bank in the town is the Caja de Ahorros de Ronda in C/Virgen de la Paz opp the bull ring. Some other banks have appeared in recent years, but they are still rather thin on

the ground, while the commission they charge on TCs varies enormously. There are also a few establishments offering change facilities in the bull ring area.

● **Hospitals & medical services**

Emergencies: *Clínica Espinillo*, T 2875882; *Cruz Rojo*, C/Jerez 56, T 2871464.

Hospitals: *Hospital General Basico de la Serrania*, Ctra del Burgo 1, T 2871540.

● **Post & telecommunications**
Area code: 95.

Post Office: *Correos*, Virgen de la Paz 20, T 2872557, open Mon-Fri 0800-1500, Sat 0900-1300.

Telephones: *locotorios* on C/de la Bola and C/El Niño.

● **Shopping**

Ronda's function as a regional centre means that it does not go out of its way to cater for tourists (apart from a few souvenir shops around the bull ring). The main pedestrianized shopping street is the C/de la Bola (confusingly shown on some maps as C/Carrera Espinel) which runs E from the bull ring for approx 1 km. Regional specialities incl saddlery, wrought iron work and antiques. There is a street market held on Sun at the Barrio de San Francisco nr the S walls of the old town. Shops on the C/Nueva sell equipment for camping. Local craft shops incl *Artesania Arte Ronda*, Pza del Teniente Arce s/n; and *Ceramica Rondeña Ramon*, Pza de España s/n.

● **Sport**

The municipal sports stadium is on the industrial estate to the N of the town, T 2870506. For tennis, T 2871438. For hot air balloon flights contact Aviación del Sol, T 2877249.

● **Tourist offices**

Located at Plaza de España 1, usually very helpful, unless harassed by hordes of tourists, T 2871272.

● **Useful addresses**

Garages/repairs: filling stations are thin on the ground. One is located on the S edge of the town, another on the N bypass. Note that there are no petrol stations between Ronda and the coast. There are several garages and repair workshops on the El Fuerte industrial estate.

● **Transport**

Local Bicycle hire: *Biciserrania*, opp bus station. **Car hire**: local firms only, **Francisco Sánchez**, C/Los Remedios 26, T 2871343; **Velesco**, C/Lorenzo Borrego 11, T 2871272.

Taxis: the main taxi rank is in the Plaza Carmen Abela. **Radio taxi**: T 2872316.

Train Station in Avda Andalucía, T 2871662. Ronda is on the line from **Bobadilla** to **Algeciras**; 5 trains a day run in each direction, incl 2 *expressos*. You should change at **Bobadilla** for **Málaga**. Madrid-Algeciras express, 1 in each direction daily. The line W runs through a number of towns and villages, incl **Gaucín**, **Castellar de la Frontera** and **San Roque**, but the timetable should be checked carefully to see where each train stops.

Road Bus: most routes are operated by the Portillo company. There are 4 buses a day directly to **Málaga**, one to **La Linea** and 3 to **Cádiz** (one of which proceeds to **Jerez**). The most direct and frequent buses link with **Marbella** and these can be boarded in the Plaza de España. Both the Comes and Lara companies serve the *pueblos blancos* to the W and N of Ronda.

EXCURSIONS FROM RONDA

Ronda La Vieja These are the ruins of the 1st century Roman town of Acinipo. To reach the site take the C339 Arcos road out of Ronda towards Algodonales. Turn right after 9 km along a minor road signposted to Ronda la Vieja. 6 km later you will arrive at a farmhouse, where the farmer will give you a plan of the site. Entrance is free. Acinipo was once a Neolithic and later a Phoenician settlement, but had its peak period as a Roman town in the 1st century AD, when it was a prosperous agricultural centre. Much of the site is rubble strewn and only the Roman theatre survives in any recognizable form. There are superb views of the surrounding countryside, particularly towards Olvera to the NNW. Open 1000-1800 Tues-Fri, 1200-1830 Sat, Sun and festivals.

Cueva de la Pileta This prehistoric cave is located some 20 km SW of Ronda and is reached either by taking the C339 and turning off left after 6 km S through Montajaque and Benoaján, or by taking the C341 towards Jimena and turning right just after passing through Atajate. (If you take the Montajaque route, look out for the huge dam built in the 1920s, but lacking a reservoir because the water insists on seeping underground.) For those without private transport, the nearest train and bus stops are in Benoaján. The caves were discovered in 1905 by Jose Boullon, while searching for guano to use as a fertilizer. Later exploration found skeletons of Paleolithic Man plus shards of pottery and other artefacts dating from 25,000 BC, but the most significant finds were the wall paintings of fish, a goat, a deer and a pregnant mare, which had been executed in charcoal and red and yellow ochres. There are also some abstract signs and symbols, which it is suggested might be connected with magic ritual, but most visitors will come to the conclusion that they are some form of tallying system. There are also some fine limestone formations, such as stalactites and stalagmites, but as these are not lit they are difficult to appreciate. There are also thousands of bats hanging from the roof of the cave. Your guide will be one of the Boullon family, who live in the farmhouse in the valley. If there is nobody around when you arrive, don't worry, you will be seen from the farmhouse and a guide will soon appear. If a party is inside the cave there will be a notice on the grill at the entrance. One in every two or three visitors will be given an oil lamp to carry. Extra torches are useful. The lack of commercialization of the cave adds to its charm. Open daily 1000-1300 and 1600-1700 (entry times of last group). Visits last approximately 1 hr. Take warm clothing.

Visitors to Ronda from the Costa del Sol with their own transport could consider returning to the coast along the slower, but more interesting C341, which passes through **Atajate**, **Algatocin** and **Gaucín**. The latter, in particular, is well worth a stop. The Moorish castle, the Castillo de Aguila, so called for its eagle's views to Gibraltar and North Africa, has been partially restored, and it was here that Guzmán el Bueno of Tarifa fame died in 1309 while attempting to capture the fortress. Motorists will find the alarming one-way system around the narrow streets a considerable challenge. In truth, Gaucín, set on its ridge, looks considerably better from a distance than by closer inspection. For those wishing to stay the night, there are two possibilities, the old *Fonda Nacional*, C/San Juan de Dios 8, T 2151156, a favourite with British officers in the old days travelling from Gibraltar to Ronda and *Pensión Moncada*, C/Luis Armillán s/n, T 2151156. After passing through Gaucín, take the road S to **Casares**, from where there is a choice of two routes to the coast.

Los Pueblos Blancos – the white towns

Oh, white walls of Spain!" wrote Federico García Lorca in one of his deeply felt poems, presenting this colour as one of the most personal characteristics of the popular architecture of Spain. Andalucía typifies this architecture and the classic *pueblo blanco* territory is best seen in the triangle of land between Málaga, Sevilla and Algeciras. Let us zoom in to the area immediately W of Ronda for the archetypal *pueblos blancos* – in this case villages rather than towns. The area is mountainous, green, forested and remote. Until recently it was bandit territory. Today the *pueblos* retain much of their early Moorish flavour. Try to visit the following:

Setenil de las Bodegas A curious village with cave-like streets with houses built into the overhanging rock, which was once carved out by the river Guadalporcun. Formerly a wine producing area (the caves were used as wine cellars) the industry was decimated by the phylloxera disease. The Moorish castle, which was conquered by the armies of Ferdinand and Isabel in 1485, is largely in ruins. The Church of the Encarnación is 15th century Gothic.

Olvera Located, as its name suggests, in an olive growing area. The church, despite being built over a mosque, is 19th century. The Moorish castle, dating from the 12th century, is of more interest and the keep and defensive walls are in good condition.

Zahara de la Sierra Reached by the Puerto de las Palomas (the Pass of the Doves) which is the highest pass in Andalucía, Zahara is a delightful fortified hill village. Beneath the inevitable ruined Moorish castle (taken by the Catholic Monarchs in 1483) is an unexpected 18th century Baroque church, with an impressive *retablo*. Just outside the village is the largest surviving stand of *pinsapo*, the rare Spanish Fir.

Ubrique This white village spreads along the valley of the river of the same name. Noted for producing guerrilla fighters, Ubrique was one of the last strongholds of the Republicans in the Civil War. Today, its traditional leather industry is thriving.

Grazelema The gem of all *pueblos blancos*, Grazelema is notorious as the wettest location in Spain. The rain ensures lush vegetation throughout the year. It is the main centre for the Sierra de Grazalema Natural Park, which supports a wide range of birds, flowers and mammals (including the Otter). To visit the Park it is necessary to obtain a permit from the park offices in Grazalema, Calle Piedras 11, where maps of walking routes can be obtained. The traditional industry in Grazelema is the making of blankets and *ponchos* (they are even exported to Argentina) and woodwork. The British sociologist Pitt-Rivers wrote a classic study of the town, *People of the Sierra*.

Pleasure craft harbours

Andalucía has a long seafaring tradition. Some of the world's oldest civilisations came across the seas to its shores, while it was largely Andalucían sailors who crewed the ships of Columbus and others who discovered and mapped the New World. Of the eight provinces of Andalucía, six have a coastline, either on the Atlantic Ocean or the Mediterranean Sea. There are major seaports such as Cádiz or Málaga, which have had to adapt with the changing times and convert to the container trade or cater for cruise liners. There are also countless smaller fishing ports, such as Barbate or Fuengirola, which are suffering from the problem of over fishing and the consequent depletion of stocks.

In more recent history a major change has been the adaptation to the demands of the thriving tourist industry and this has led to the growth of puertos deportivos or pleasure craft harbours. There are now over 30 of these ports, with more under construction. They range from the small harbours, such as that at Garrucha in Almería province, which caters for little more than a tiny fishing fleet, to the large, glitzy and rather vulgar Puerto Banús, which can cope with nearly a thousand boats, many of them floating gin palaces with their own on-board helicopters. Some have become tourist attractions in their own right – coaches full of pensioners flock to Benalmádena port during the winter months.

The successful pleasure craft harbours generate their own spin-offs. Apart from chandler's shops and the provision of fuel and repairs, many have popular restaurants, bars, boutiques and discos, while the attraction of water has led to the development of up-market apartment blocks. Benalmádena has a thriving sea water aquarium. Many have regular flea markets and other popular attractions, while in many cases, as at Estepona, the local fishing fleets have moved into the puertos deportivos and no longer have to haul up on the beach. Along with the tourists come others who feed off them, such as the jugglers, street musicians and pickpockets. The time share touts, too, have found pleasure craft harbours to be fertile ground. But the emphasis is on pleasure and they have rapidly become an integral part of the Andalucían tourist scene.

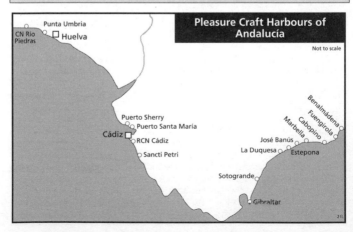

Pleasure Craft Harbours of Andalucía

Pleasure craft harbours of Andalucía

	Berths	Harbour/entrance width/depth	Anchorage	Services
GARRUCHA	221	170m/14m	sandy	WEFITRC
SAN JOSE	243	35m/6m	sandy	WE ITRC
CLUB DE MAR ALMERIA	185	300m/10m	stone & mud	WEFITRCMS
AGUADULCE	764	60m/6m	stone & sand	WEFITRCMS
ROQUETAS DE MAR	183	90m/4m	mud	WEFIT CMS
ALMERIMAR	1100	140m/2m	sand	WEFITRCMS
ADRA	120	65m/7m	mud	WE IT CMS
MOTRIL	168	92m/11m	muddy	WE ITRCMS
PUNTA DE LA MONA	227	45m/4m	rocky	WEFITRCMS
CALETA DE VELEZ	200	80m/5m	sand	CMS
EL CANDADO	215	30m/3m	sand & mud	WE TR M
R.C. MEDITERRANEO	20	70m/5m	mud & stone	WE TRC
BENALMADENA	961	180m/8m	sand	WEFITRCMS
FUENGIROLA	226	70m/4m	mud & sand	WE ITRCMS
CABO PINO	169	60m/4m	sand	WEF CMS
MARBELLA	377	20m/4m	sand	WEF CMS
JOSE BANUS	915	80m/7m	sand	WEFITRCMS
ESTEPONA	443	80m/5m	rocky	WE ITRCMS
LA DUQUESA	328	70m/7m	sandy	WEFIT CMS
SOTOGRANDE	545	80m/5m	sandy	WEFITRCMS
RCN ALGECIRAS	70	40m/9m	sandy	WE ITR
CLUB NAUTICO BARBATE	105	150m/5m	mud & sand	WE R MS
CN SANCTI PETRI	250	100m/2m	mud	WEFI R
RCN DE CADIZ	200	80m/8m	mud	WEFITRC S
SANTA MARIA	200	100m/5m	mud	WE ITRCMS
SHERRY	753	100m/4m	sandy	WEFITRCMS
RCN HUELVA	400	river/12m	muddy	ITRCMS
PUNTA UMBRIA	175	river/1m	muddy	ITRC
RIO PIEDRAS	0	50m/3m	sandy	ITRCMS
CN SEVILLA	52	river/2m	mud & sand	WE ITRCMS

Key: **W**ater, **E**lectricity, **F**uel, **I**ce, **T**elephone, **R**amp, **C**rane, **M**echanic, **S**hop.

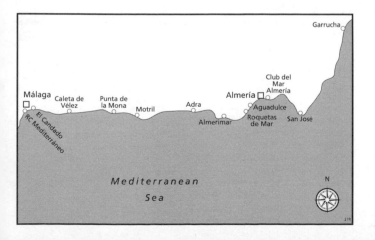

Almería Province

THIS IS THE most easterly of the provinces of Andalucía. It is the driest and least populated province, with only 400,000 people living in its 8,000 square kilometres. Despite the airport at Almería, neither residential nor hotel tourism has made much progress here, especially when compared with the Costa del Sol. One has the distinct feeling that much of the area has more in common with North Africa than with mainland Europe. There are few towns of any size in the interior. After Almería, the second largest town is El Ejido (which has grown as a marketing centre for the *plasticultura* industry) and remarkably this is still not shown on many maps of the province.

HORIZONS

The mountains belong to the Sistema Penibetico, within which are the Sierra de Gádor to the Northwest of Almería city and the Sierra de Alhamilla to the Northeast. The Sierra Nevada extends into the west of the province and provides its highest mountain, Chullo, at 2,609m. In the extreme northeast of the province are the mountains of the Parque Natural de Sierra María rising to over 2,400m. Many of the rivers are dry, their valleys having been eroded away during wetter historic periods.

Almería's **climate** is the driest and sunniest in Andalucía. Humidity is low and the hours of sunshine high. Cloud and rain are restricted to a mere 17 days a year. The highest recorded temperature is 38°C. The reliable climate led to the growth of a film making industry in the 1970s, but this has declined in recent years.

The scenery is varied with barren semi desert, mountains and an ever changing coastline with impressive cliffs, remote coves and occasional dunes. Much of the coastal lowland is marred by vast areas of *plasticultura*.

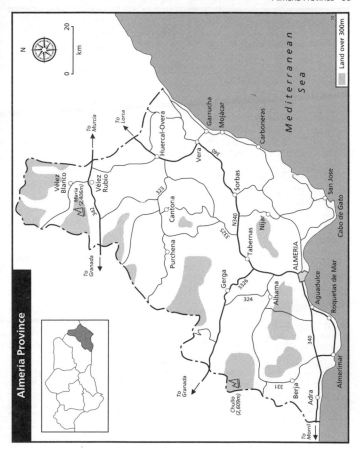

Almería Province

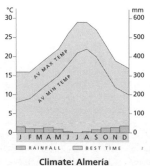

It was the Moors who introduced their *huertas*-fertile horticultural plots to the region. After centuries of decline, the industry has revived with the benefit of plastic sheeting and market gardening produce now supplies both Spain and much of northern Europe too.

RAINFALL   BEST TIME

Climate: Almería

ALMERIA CITY

(Pop 155,000; *Alt* Sea level; *STD code* 951)
The city is a regional and market centre
and a busy port with ferry links to Melilla
in North Africa, Genoa and Palma, and a
sizeable fishing industry. The old part of
the town lies between the Moorish castle
and the port, while the modern town centre
focuses on the tree lined Paseo de Almería.
Recent development of suburbs is mainly
to the N, while tourist development is
spreading along the coast to the east.

The city dates from 10th century
Moorish times, when the newly built
port at the mouth of the river Andarax
was known as Al-Mariyat (the mirror of
the sea). Later, after the collapse of the
caliphate at Córdoba, it became capital
of a separate *taifa*. By the 14th century
it had a population of over 300,000, with
prosperity based on ship building and
silk weaving. This period of affluence
ended with the Christian Reconquest in
1490 and the expulsion of the Moors.
Decline set in, not helped by the earthquake of 1522, which destroyed much of
the town and the castle. By the 17th
century the population had fallen to under 600. Recovery had to wait until the
20th century with the coming of the
railway line and the export of minerals
such as iron and lead. Almería did not
escape unscathed during the Civil War
as it was bombarded for a time by German warships. It was not until the last 2
decades that prosperity returned,
spurred on by horticulture and tourism.

PLACES OF INTEREST

The Alcazaba This is the largest Moorish castle in Andalucía and its hill site
dominates the city of Almería. Although
it can be easily seen from most parts of
the city, it can be quite complicated to
find the entrance. The historic parts of
the city are clearly signposted, but the
streets in the old part are narrow and
confusing, so obtain a town plan from the
tourist office first. Approach via the cathedral and C/Almanzor. If you are lost
you will find the local inhabitants very
helpful. There is limited parking at the
entrance of the Alcazaba and also in the
nearby Plaza Vieja.

The Alcazaba has had a chequered
history reflecting that of the town itself.
Work on the building started in 955
under Abd ar-Rahman 111 of Córdoba,
who gave the city the classification of
'medina'. Its most glorious period was
during the 11th century during the
reigns of Jayran, Zuhayr and Almotocin,
but it has also experienced periods of
total neglect. Although in the beginning
the Alcazaba served as the headquarters
of the governors and the Muslim kings
and in later times as the residence of the
Christian rulers, it was always first and
foremost a military base. This use, combined with the effects of the earthquake

The Alcazaba at Almería

in 1522, plus subsequent renovations, has substantially altered the original appearance.

It consists of three defensive compounds, all containing construction from different periods of history. The **first compound**, the largest of the three, is approached through an exterior gate, then up a zig-zag ramp (a defensive ploy not uncommon in Moorish fortifications) before arriving at the **Justice Gate** (1), overlooked by the **Tower of Mirrors** (2) which was added in the 15th century. The mirrors were apparently used to contact ships approaching the harbour. This compound originally served as a military camp and could also house several thousand people in times of siege. A constant supply of fresh water was pumped up through wells by **windmills** (3). Today the first compound is a garden with attractive areas of flowing water. To the E is the **Salient Bastion** (4) which was used as a lookout point. The ramparts eventually arrive at the **Wall of the Watch** (5) which served as a bell tower. From here the massive **Moorish Wall** (6) stretches away to the NE spanning a deep valley and up to the mirador of San Cristóbel on the hill of the same name, reminding visitors inevitably of the Great Wall of China.

The **second compound** served as a residence for the Muslim Kings and Governors and also housed their guards and servants. One can only wonder at its former magnificence, for there are only scant remains today. You can identify the remnants of **watermills** (7), a **mosque** (8) (converted into a Mudéjar style shrine by the Catholic Kings), some **Muslim houses** (9) and **military baths** (10) in the Roman style. Archaeological work is continuing in this compound, concentrating on the **Palace of Almotacin** (11) and the **Odalisk window** (12) in the N wall. There is a poignant tale concerning the latter. Apparently a prisoner fell in love with a Moorish slave girl who tried to help him escape, but the

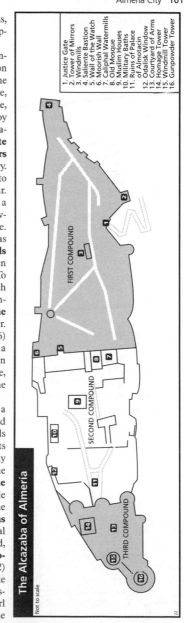

1. Justice Gate
2. Tower of Mirrors
3. Windmills
4. Salient Bastion
5. Wall of the Watch
6. Moorish Wall
7. Caliphal Watermills
8. Old Mosque
9. Muslim Houses
10. Military Baths
11. Ruins of Palace of Almotacin
12. Odalisk Window
13. Courtyard of Arms
14. Homage Tower
15. Windmill Tower
16. Gunpowder Tower

FIRST COMPOUND

SECOND COMPOUND

THIRD COMPOUND

The Alcazaba of Almería

Not to scale

plot was discovered and he jumped to his death from the window, the girl inevitably dying from a broken heart some days later.

The **third compound** is entirely post Muslim. After the reconquest of Almería, the Catholic Kings, seeing the earthquake wreckage, ordered the construction of a castle with thicker walls in the westernmost and highest part of the Alcazaba. Entrance was by a bridge over a moat protected by three semi-circular towers. The interior **Courtyard of Arms** (13) is dominated by the **Torre del Homenaje** (Tower of Homage) (14). The two other buildings are the **Windmill Tower** (15) and the **Torre de Pólvora** (16). There are excellent views from these towers over the port and the gypsy area below the castle known as **La Chanca**. The Alcazaba is open daily, summer 1000-1400 and 1630-2000; winter 0930-1400 and 1630-1900. Entrance fee 250 ptas, but free for EU citizens with proof of identity.

The Cathedral is a large uninspiring building begun in 1524 on the site of an old mosque, but most of the work was carried out in the 17th century. Designed by Diego de Siloé, it was built for defence against attacks by Berber pirates as well as for worship. It consequently has massive stone walls and small high windows, while its corner towers had positions for cannons. The only exterior feature of note is the stylish Renaissance doorway. Inside, amongst the severity, look for the altar designed by Ventura Rodríguez and paintings by Alonso Cano. Note, too, the 16th century choirstalls carved in walnut by Juan de Orea. Open 0900-1200 and 1730-2000, but it is recommended that tourists visit from 1030 to 1200 and 1730 to 1830 and should on no account disturb services. Entrance is free.

Of the other churches worth mentioning in Almería, the best is the **Iglesia de San Juan**, just to the W of the cathedral, which was built in the 17th century on the site of a mosque. There is a *mihrab* on the S wall, but unfortunately you will only gain entry at service times.

Cerro de San Cristóbal This hill is the best vantage point in town. Next to the *mirador* is an enormous figure of Christ and an outdoor altar. This area can be reached from the town centre via the Puerta de Purchena and C/Antonio Vico, but visitors will be unimpressed by the vandalism and graffiti at the site.

Centro de Rescate de la Fauna Sahariana (Sahara Wildlife Rescue Centre) This is located in the valley behind the Alcazaba and was established in 1971 with help from the World Wildlife Fund to save Saharan species in danger of extinction. The surrounding scenery ensures that the desert species feel at home and the venture has been extremely successful. The centre is not generally open to the public, but it is possible to obtain a permit from the organization's headquarters close to the tourist office.

Los Alijibes Town plans of Almería show these old Moorish water cisterns at C/ de los Alijibes 20. Visitors wishing to see the cisterns will find that the location is actually a *flamenco* bar, which is usually closed until mid-evening. Curiously, some performances actually take place partially within the cisterns – certainly a unique venue.

Museo Arqueológico The Museo de Almería in C/Jávier Sanz, which contained largely archaeological displays, has now been replaced by the Archaeological Museum at Ctra Ronda 13, T 225058. At the time of writing the new building is still not open. The archaeologists seem to spend most of their time at the Chalcolithic site (see page 106) at Los Millares, from where artefacts will no doubt eventually be displayed. Check with the tourist office for up-to-date details.

Hospital Real, C/Hospital. Built in the mid 18th century, this building is still a

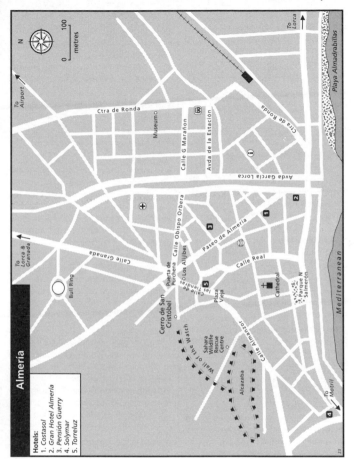

Hotels:
1. Costasol
2. Gran Hotel Almería
3. Pensión Guerry
4. Solymar
5. Torreluz

working hospital. If you can get inside, look for the delightful tiled patio.

La Plaza Vieja (the Old Square, more correctly known as the Plaza de la Constitución) With only one access road, it is easy to miss this delightful pedestrianized square, with its late 19th century *Ajuntamiento*. One block away to the N is the 17th century Church of Las Claras.

Calle de las Tiendras Just S of the Puerta de Purchena, this is the oldest street in Almería and during the 1800s it was full of fashionable shops, but now it is looking a little run down.

LOCAL FESTIVALS

The *Winter Festivals* take place in late December and early Jan and culminate in the *Romería de la Virgen del Mar* when Our Lady of the Sea is taken in procession to Torre García beach. During Holy Week there are processions on Wed, Thur and Good Friday. The main *Feria* is in the last week in Aug, when there are sports events, bullfights and dancing. There is a Festival of Puppet Theatre in Feb. In Aug there is an Iberian and Mediterranean Folklore event, while Nov sees the International Jazz Festival in the Cevantes Theatre.

LOCAL INFORMATION

Price guide

Hotels:

AL	over US$90	D	US$20-40
A	US$75-90	E	US$10-20
B	US$60-75	F	under US$10
C	US$40-60		

Places to eat:

♦♦♦	expensive	♦♦ average
♦	cheap	

● **Accommodation**

There is a variety of hotels available, incl traditional hotels in Almería itself without package tourists, but likely to be noisy, or alternatively in the surrounding resorts with wider facilities.

AL *Gran Sol Almería*, Avda Reina Regente 8, T 238011, F 270691, 117 rm, traditional, comfortable, Andalucían city centre hotel, a/c, TV, garage, disco, pool; *Torreluz*, Plaza Flores, T and F 234799; this is in fact a series of 4 hotels, offering various prices and facilities in the range **AL** to **C**.

A *Solymar*, Ctra Málaga 110, T 234622, F 277010, 15 rm, small modern hotel in good location overlooking the port and the Moorish castle, good but expensive restaurant, guests will be relieved that the nearby gypsy portacabin rehousing site has now gone.

B *Costasol*, Paseo de Almería 58, T/F 234011, 55 rm, good value, convenient for bus and train stations; **B** *Indalico*, C/Dolores R Sopeña 4, T 231111, F 231028, 52 rm, central location, can be noisy, a/c, garage.

C *Embajador*, C/Calzada de Castro 4, T 255511, F 259364, 67 rm, on the train station side of the city centre, a/c; **C** *La Perla*, Plaza del Carmen 7, T 238877, F 275816, 44 rm, just off the Puerta de Purchena, a/c.

Pensiones: there are 9 pensiones to choose from plus a number of *fondas*; most are in the central area in streets leading off the Puerta de Purchena. **D** *Americano*, Avda de la Estación 4, T 258011, garage, close to train station;

D *Bristol*, Plaza San Sebastián 8, T 231595, 27 rm, right in the centre of things, good value rooms; **D** *Estación*, C/Calzada de Castro 37, T 267239, modest pensión close to both the bus and train stations; **D** *Nixar*, C/Antonio Vico 24, T 237255, F 237255, 40 rm, probably the best of the pensiones, rooms with a/c and some with bath.

E *Andalucía*, C/Granada 9, T 237733, 76 rm, large and faded but clean and good value; **E** *Maribel*, Avda Federico García Lorca 153, T 235173, 16 rm, adequate cheap rooms on the Rambla de Belén.

Youth hostels: *Isla Fuerte Ventura*, 04007 Almería, T 269788, 173 beds, meals available, suitable for wheelchair users.

Camping: *La Garrofa*, Ctra Motril-Almería, Km 8, T 235770, 2nd category site, open all year round. There are other sites nearby at San José and Roquetas de Mar, both 2nd category.

● **Places to eat**

There are plenty of eating places in Almería, but except in the major hotel restaurants, there are few concessions to international food. The best restaurants are either on, or just off, the Paseo de Almería. Local specialities to look for incl *gachas* (a hot clam stew), *trigo* (a stew with grains of wheat, pork, beans and herbs), *choto al ajo y en ajillo* (kid with garlic or garlic sauce) and spiced sardines. Almería is not noted for classical wines but small cellars can be found in the villages of Alboloduy, Berja, Fondón, Luajar and Ohanes.

♦♦♦*Anfora*, C/Acosta Lainez 3, T 231374, specializes in local produce; *Club de Mar*, C/Muelle 1, T 235048, wharfside setting, semi international cuisine; *Rincon de Juan Pedro*, Plaza del Carmen 5, T 235184, expensive local specialities.

♦♦*Meson la Reja*, C/Arapiles 7, T 235702, moderately priced local dishes; *Los Gauchos*, C/Granada 25, T 273594, specialist steak restaurant.

♦ Those on a more limited budget might try *Buffet Libre Almería*, C/Jerez 10, T 260137, eat as much as you like for a set price; *Hong Kong*, C/Hermanos Machado 2, T 264338, the cheaper of the 2 Chinese restaurants in the city. There is also a number of bar-restaurants offering cheap *menús* in the Parque de Nicolás Salmerón opp the port.

● **Bars**

There are good bars for *tapas* in and around

the Puerta de Purchena at the N end of the Paseo de Almería. Try *Bodega las Botas*, C/Fructuoso Perez 3, good atmosphere with sherry barrels and legs of serrano ham hanging from the ceiling – you may even get a free *tapa*. Also *Bar El Alcázar*, Paseo de Almería 4, good sea food *tapas*. *Bar Restaurant Imperial*, Puerta de Purchena, spoilt only by the traffic noise. In the cathedral area there are numerous bodegas catering mainly for lunchtime trade, of which *Bodegas Montenegro* is highly rec.

● **Banks & money changers**
There are branches of all the main Spanish banks, mostly at the N end of the Paseo de Almería. Opening hours Mon-Fri 0900-1400, Sat 0900-1300.

● **Embassies & consulates**
Finland, Avda Cabo de Gata, T 243238; **France**, Avda de Cabo de Gata 81, T 252284; **Germany**, Centro Comercial Satélites Park, Ctra de Málaga s/n, Aguadulce, T 340555; **Netherlands**, C/Reyes Católicos 26, T 268504; **Sweden**, C/Dr Aráez Pacheco 2, T 250033; **UK**, contact Málaga, T 952 217571.

● **Entertainment**
Cinemas: Almería boasts 4 cinemas, of which the *Imperial*, Avda de Pablo Iglesias s/n, is probably the best.

Discos: *Lord Nelson*, C/Canónigo Molina Alonso 1, T 254026; *Grants Club*, C/Reina Regente s/n, T 241099. During the height of the season, the local authority erects disco marquees along part of the Paseo Maritimo, which at least keeps the noise in one place.

Flamenco: the only spot worth mentioning is *Peña El Taranto*, C/Los Alijibes 20.

Theatres: *Cevantes*, C/Poeta Vilaespesa s/n, T 237093; *Auditorio Municipal 'Maestro Padilla'*, Avda del Mediterraneo s/n, T 276922.

● **Hospitals & medical services**
Emergencies: T 257198.

Hospitals: *Cruz Roja*, T 222222; *Hospital Provincial de Almería*, Plaza Dr Gómez Campana 1, T 241455.

● **Post & telecommunications**
Area code: 951.

Post Office: *Correos*, Plaza J Casinello 1, Paseo de Almería, T 237207.

Telephones: *Locutorio* in C/Navarro Rodríguez 9. Open Mon-Sat.

● **Shopping**
The commercial centre is in the Paseo de Almería, the Puerta de Purchena, the C/de las Tiendas and the surrounding area. Handicraft items typical of the region incl ceramics and pottery, *jarapas* (blankets made from rough cloth and rag strips), bedspreads, esparto grass items, basketwork and small carved marble goods. There are street markets on Tues in Avda Mediterraneo; on Fri at the Plaza de Toros; and on Sat at the Plaza del Zapillo.

● **Sport**
The Cabo de Gata area is popular for scuba diving and underwater fishing; the nearest golf courses are at Almerimar, T 480234, Roquetas de Mar, T 333055 and Turre, T 479164; for watersports contact the *Centro de Actividades Náuticas*, Avda de Cabo de Gata. The Municipal Sports Centre is in the Avda de Mediterraneo, T 229820.

● **Tourist offices**
The **Regional Government Tourist Office** is in C/Hermanos Merchado in the Edificio Multiple (Multiple Ministries Building), T 230858. The staff are multilingual and extremely helpful. This should be the first stop for all first time visitors to Almería.

● **Tour companies & travel agents**
Koral, Paseo Almería 47, T 251133; *Indamar*, Paseo de Almería 73, T 237883; *Paris*, Paseo San Luis 2, T 265022; *Viajes Alysol*, Paseo de Almería 34, T 237622; *Viajes Sur*, Paseo de Almería 4, T 244677.

● **Useful addresses**
Garages/car repairs: Ford: Automecánica Almeriense, Ctra N340, Km 117, T 237033; **Peugeot**: Talleres Sur, C/Padre Santaella 4, T 238101; **Renault**: Ctra N340, Km 446, T 259312; **Rover**: Codasa, C/Doctoral 16, T 224266; **Volvo**: Ctra de Granada, T 238963.

● **Transport**
Local Car hire: Avis, C/Canónigo Molina Alonso s/n, T 252578; **Europcar**, C/Rueda López 23, T 234966; **Hertz**, Avda de Cabo de Gata 1, T 243229; **Rucar**, Aeropuerto, T 297815. **Horse drawn carriages**: provide sightseeing tours of the city and may be picked up nr the port. **Taxis**: Radio Taxi, T 226161; **Tele Taxi**, T 251111; Taxis Nocturnos, T 235757

Air Information, T 221954. In addition to international charter flights, there are internal connections with **Madrid**, **Melilla** and **Barcelona**. *Iberia* have an office in town at Paseo de Almería 44, T 230933. Buses to airport every 30 mins between 0700 and 2130 during the week and every 45 mins Sat and Sun.

Train It is difficult to mistake the RENFE station on Ctra de Ronda, T 251122, with its neo Moorish style frontage and ultra modern extension. There are 4 *talgos* a day to **Madrid** and other connections with **Barcelona**, **Granada** and **Valencia**. An overnight train goes to **Córdoba** and **Sevilla**. RENFE also have an office in the town centre, C/Alcade Muñoz, T 231207.

Road Bus: the bus station is in the Plaza de Barcelona, T 210029, and is a modern building with a cafetería and a comfortable waiting room. There are daily connections to **Madrid**, **Barcelona**, **Algeciras**, **Málaga**, **Granada** and **Sevilla**. Locally, there are 5 buses a day to **Berja**, 7 to **Adra** and 2 daily to **Cabo de Gata**, **Nijar**, **Mojácar** and **Tabernas**. There are hourly buses to the resorts of **Aguadulce** and **Roquetas de Mar**. Timetables are more easily obtained from the tourist office than the bus station, although they are displayed on the wall there.

Sea Ferry: car ferries run to **Melilla**, the Spanish enclave in N Africa, on Tues, Thur and Sat leaving at 1400, the voyage taking just over 6 hrs. **Aucona-Transmediterránea**, Parque Nicolás Salmerón 28, T 236356.

NORTH OF ALMERIA

Take the N340 N out of Almería and after 12 km fork left along the N324. Just after the village of **Gador**, fork left again along the C332 towards **Alhama de Almería**. This is a small spa town which dates back to Moorish times and you can still take the waters here today, which explains the unexpectedly grand *Hotel San Nicolas*, which is located at the site of the original baths. Another reason to stay here, however, is the proximity of the Chalcolithic archaeological site of **Los Millares**, just 4 km away. It was discovered in 1891 when the Almería-Linares railway line was being constructed. The early excavations were carried out by two mining engineers, Louis and Henri Siret, who were employees of the railway company. They found a Chalcolithic (or Copper Age) fortified settlement dating from circa 2700 BC. The excavations spread over 5 ha and show a series of defensive walls enclosing circular huts, a foundry, a simple aqueduct bringing water from Alhama and a silo. Most remarkable of all, however, is the Necropolis, where over 100 tombs have been discovered. Artefacts recovered include pottery, jewellery, basketware and a variety of utensils. The inhabitants, who may have numbered 2,000, were hunters and farmers. The evidence suggests that the climate and vegetation were much kinder than the barren semi desert which surrounds the site today. The farm stock included sheep, goats and pigs, while it is clear that cereals and vegetables were grown. The surrounding forest sheltered wild boar and deer. It also seems that the Río Andarax, the dry bed of which runs round part of the site, was navigable in those days and was used for bringing the copper ore from the Sierra de Gador to the SW. The site is open 0930-1330 and 1700-1930, Sun 0930-1430, closed Mon, entrance 200 ptas.

Back on the N340, the road runs N

through the **Parque Natural del Desierto de Tabernas**, a fascinating area of semi desert, the bare treeless mountain slopes showing the rock structure, dried up river beds and flat topped plateaux. This is probably the only area of true semi desert on mainland Europe and not surprisingly it has some desert birds more common in North Africa, such as Trumpeter Finch and Duponts Lark, of which there are believed to be around 150 pairs.

Mini Hollywood 12 km along the N340 and just past a road junction, almost immediately on the right hand side of the road is Mini Hollywood. This is a relic of the golden age of 'spaghetti western' films, such as *A Fistful of Dollars* and *Indiana Jones*, which were made in this area in the 1960s and 1970s. The film makers were attracted by the arid scenery, reminiscent of the American midwest, plus the clear air and almost unbroken sunshine, all of which were ideal for shooting. The film makers have now moved on but the sets remain, with bars, a bank, stables and Red Indian encampments. 'Cowboys' enact shoot outs and stunts. Open 0900-2100 in summer, 0900-1800 in winter. Entrance for adults a pricy 1,000 ptas, children 600 ptas. There is a smaller, rival, Mini Hollywood lookalike about a kilometre away, but this has few facilities and is best avoided.

At the road junction near Mini Hollywood a road leads northwards to the village of **Gérgal**, which has a ruined castle and is the main gateway to the **Sierra de los Filabres**. A winding road from Gérgal leads up to Calar Altar, which at 2,168m is the highest point in the sierra. Just beneath the summit is the Observatorío Astronómico, which clearly benefits from the cloudless skies of the region. From the Observatory, a network of tracks, passable with 4WD vehicles, fans out over the Sierra linking with the villages to the N on the C323

Heurcal-Baza road, such as Purchena, Tijola and Olula. The E part of the Sierra de los Filibres can be seen by passing through Tabernas and after 11 km taking the 3325 road N towards Uleila. Then follows a spectacular mountain drive over the Puerto de la Virgen pass before descending into Albanchez and joining the C323 near Cantoría.

Tabernas lies 2 km beyond Mini Hollywood and is dominated by a conical hill capped by a small Moorish castle. While the town itself has little of interest, the castle, where Ferdinand and Isobel stayed during the siege of Almería, looks more promising. There is no tourist office and, although the *ayuntimiento* are helpful, there is no information about the castle. It is best approached by heading for the municipal sports stadium and taking the wide, but rough, track to the summit. There has been some half hearted restoration work on the castle, from where there are superb views, but one is left with the feeling that the town could make more of this asset.

● **Accommodation** There are no hotels in Tabernas, but 3 *pensiónes* are located on the N340, which by-passes the town. **D** *Hermanos García* is probably the best of the 3, but possibly over-priced.

18 km E of Tabernas is the small town of **Sorbas**, located on a deep gorge, over which houses hang alarmingly. Sorbas is a pottery making centre and, at the lower part of the town, there are a number of shops in front of small workshops where the goods are sold at wholesale prices.

A return route to Almería could be made by missing out Sorbas and instead encircling the Sierra Alhamilla, turning off the N340 to **Lucainena de la Torres** and following a dramatic scenic road before dropping down into **Nijar**. This is an attractive little town with some scant remains of a Moorish castle, but most visitors come here for its craftwork. It produces some distinctive hand-made pottery, a craft carried on from Moorish times. Nijar is also a centre for the production of *jarapas*, the rugs and blankets made from wool and rags. There are a surprising number of accommodation possibilities in the town, with 2 small hotels and 5 *pensiones*. Good value is **C** *Venta de Pobre*, T/F 385192, 21 rm, a/c, wheelchair access. Return to Almería by joining the N332, 6 km to the S.

EAST OF ALMERIA

The N332 E from Almería is now virtually of *autovia* standard all the way to the border with Murcia. Almería airport is located some 5 km out of town. Shortly after this, fork right to **El Cabo de Gata**, a small undeveloped resort with a long beach of coarse sand. There is little in the way of accommodation here. The village takes its name from the vast area of succulents growing around it. You are now in the **Parque Natural de Cabo de Gata-Nijar** which covers 29,000 ha. There are two distinct types of landscape. Firstly there are the coastal dunes with saline lagoons behind them. The first line of dunes are mobile, but further inland the dunes are fixed by vegetation. Secondly, there are the hills of volcanic origin, known as the Sierra de Cabo de Gata and still exhibiting some laval columns. There are some interesting flora within the park, including the thorny Jujube tree, the dwarf fan palm or palmetta, which is Europe's only native palm and Sand Wort which occurs in the dunes. Reptiles are represented by the Italian Wall Lizard (the only place in Spain where this is found), the Tawny Lizard, Viper and Grass Snake. Hares and foxes are common. The Mediterranean Monk Seal last bred here in 1974, but has recently been re-introduced. It is the birds, however, which are the main attraction of this reserve. The most rewarding location is the area known as **Las Salinas**, a series of salt pans which are still commercially operated just S of Cabo de Gata village. Fortunately AMA has an arrangement with owners and large parts of the 350 ha of water are undisturbed and they form a wetland of major importance. Greater Flamingoes have attempted unsuccessfully to breed here, but there can be as many as 2,000 non breeders around in the summer. Breeding birds include Black Winged Stilts, Avocet and Little Terns, while passage species include Osprey, storks, Purple

Herons and egrets. There is a good range of wildfowl in the winter, while the rarer gulls include Slender-bulled and Audouins. For access, look for the life guards' tower on the side of the coast road; immediately opposite this is an entrance with a sign saying 'Entrada Prohibida'. Ignore this and drive into the car park, which is alongside the hide which overlooks the *salinas*.

South of the hills of salt, the road continues to the headland of Cabo de Gata with its lighthouse. The mirador is a good spot for observing migratory birds, while the clear waters off the point are a favourite spot for scuba divers. The Cape actually protrudes further S than the northern tip of Tunisia. Beneath the headland is a rocky reef, El Arrecife de la Sirenas – Mermaids' reef – named not after mermaids, but the Monk Seals which were once found here in large numbers. The road from here on is narrow and tricky with numerous hairpin bends. To reach the small resort of **San José** it is probably prudent to return inland from Cabo de Gata. For those without private transport, San José can be reached by bus from Almería. It is fairly unspoilt still, but the newly built marina will probably alter that. There are some accommodation possibilities here, including *San José*, Bda. San José, T 380116, curiously decorated but with fine sea views; and *Bahia Vista*, Correo s/n, T 380019, an economical alternative. The Hotel San José has a good dining room, while there are 2 good fish restaurants, *El Ganandero* at nearby Retamar and *Bar Fonda Mediterraneo* on the beach at San Miguel.

The coastline now runs to the NE, with a series of cliffs, inaccessible coves and cliff top tracks which might prove challenging to owners of 4WD vehicles. Most visitors will prefer to head back inland and return to the coast at **Carboneras**. Initial impressions will probably be coloured by the enormously ugly cement works at the S end of the town.

There is a broad beach with a large number of fishing boats, backed by a collection of bars and *pensiones*. A new marina is under construction and behind it is a small resort area. Amongst the *pensiones*, **D** *Felipe*, T 454015, has the best facilities, while **E** *La Marina*, T 454070, is the cheapest. There is one unusual hotel: **B** *El Dorado*, Playa de Carboneras, T 454050, F 130102, 17 rm, different parts of the hotel are decorated as film sets, such as Dr Zhivago and the Three Musketeers; pool, restaurant.

From Carboneras the road towards Mojácar is one of the most spectacular coastal drives in Andalucía, winding along the cliff top with hairpin beds and tantalizing views of isolated coves, some with access along rough tracks.

MOJACAR

There are two parts to Mojácar – Old Mojácar and Mojácar Playa. The former is the more interesting as it is a hill village with a distinctly Moorish flavour, with its cube-like, sugar lump, whitewashed houses, Arab gateways and the original Moorish street pattern. Until quite recently, the women half-covered their faces with *cobijas* (triangular shawls) and drew *indalos* on their doors to keep away bad luck. *Indalos* are stick like figures holding an arc above their heads, thought to have originated in Neolithic times in the caves at Vélez Blanco.

A settlement at Mojácar goes back to Iberian times and during the Roman occupation it was one of the most important towns of *Baetica*, when it was believed to be known as *Murgis*, a name the Moors later changed to *Muxacra*. The Moors defended Mojácar stoutly against the armies of the Catholic Kings, who eventually allowed them to keep their customs provided they swore allegiance to the Christian crown. Mojácar prospered in the early years of the 20th century and in the 1920s it had a population of 9,000, but after the Civil War and the years of emigration, the numbers shrank as low as 400. Its recovery began in the 1960s when it was discovered by an intellectual set of artists and writers. In 1969 it was declared 'Spain's Prettiest Village', which resulted in the intellectuals mostly moving away to fresh untouched paradises. In their place came an English travel company who were largely responsible for developing Mojácar Playa. The travel firm soon went into liquidation, but by then the boom was well underway. Today, Mojácar has a population of 5,000 people, half of whom are foreign residents, mainly British, with a significant number of artists and potters. A long established English language magazine is produced monthly.

Old Mojácar *pueblo*, despite the picture postcard views, is a little disappointing. The Moorish atmosphere of the alleyways and squares is attractive and there is a *mirador* on the N side giving fine views over the countryside inland towards Turre. The Church of Santa María dates from the 15th century, but has been vastly restored. Bars, restaurants and souvenir shops abound. And that is about it!

Local festivals

The highlight of the year is the *Fiesta Moros y Cristianos*, a mock battle between the Moors and Christians, lasting 3 days and accompanied by fireworks, music and giant paellas. One of the best on the coast.

Disney Land – or not?

Read any number of travel guides and speak to the inhabitants of Mojácar and they will tell you that this is the birthplace of the film maker Walt Disney. For a small, unimportant, although admittedly attractive village, this is a serious claim to fame. But unfortunately it is almost certainly a myth.

The citizens of Mojácar, however, will give you chapter and verse. They will tell you that Disney was known as Waldo and was born out of wedlock. His father was the village doctor and his mother was a laundry women. Because of the embarrassment, the mother, Waldo and his brother were exiled to Valencia. There the brother was employed on an American ship, the skipper of which was known as (yes, you've got it) Captain Disney. He fell in love with Waldo's mother, married her, adopted the two boys and carted the lot off the California. What happened after that is well-known.

The American version is somewhat different and goes like this – Walt Disney was born on 5 December 1901 in Chicago, where his mother was a schoolteacher and his father a carpenter. He went briefly to Art Schools in both Chicago and Kansas City, before gaining his first employment delivering newspapers in Kansas City. He died in 1966. What is certain, however, is that some of Walt Disney's associates visited Mojácar a few years ago to see if they could obtain some documentary evidence of baptisms from the church archives. No luck – everything had been destroyed in the Civil War. There is no record of Walt Disney himself ever having visited Mojácar, but if he had, he might have concluded that there are worse places to claim as a birth place.

Local information
● Accommodation
There are some excellent hotels in Mojácar Playa, but the lower end of the accommodation scale tends to be overpriced.

A *Continental*, Playa de Palmeral, T 478225, F 475136, 23 rm, only hotel on the beach side of the road, a/c, wheelchair access; **A** *Parador Reyes Católicos*, Playa s/n, T 478250, F 478183, 98 rm, modern building on sea front, in landscaped grounds, pool, tennis, garage.

B *El Moresco*, Avda Horizón s/n, T 478025, F 478176, 147 rm, another package hotel, on the edge of the *pueblo* with superb views, 2 pools; open summer only; **B** *Indalo*, Ctra de Carboneras s/n, T 478001, F 478176, 308 rm, largest hotel in Mojácar, heavily used by package tours, pool, range of sports activities incl tennis and wind surfing, wheelchair access.

C *Río Abajo Playa*, Playa de Mojácar, T 478928, 18 rm, small beach front hotel with pool.

Pensiones: the pensiones at Mojácar Playa tend to charge hotel prices. The better ones incl **D** *Flamenco*, Playa Mojácar (Puntal del Cantal), T 478227, F 475195, 25 rm; **D** *Hostal Puntazo*, Paseo Mediterráneo s/n, T 478265, 36 rm (incl a modern extension); **D** *Provenzal*, Playa de Descargador, T 478308, 26 rm, a/c.

In the *pueblo*, there is **D** *Mamabels*, C/Embajadores 1, T 475126, which also has a decent restaurant; one could try cheaper possibilities such as **E** *La Esquinica*, C/Cano s/n, T 475009; **E** *Casa Justa*, C/Morote 5, T 478372.

Camping: *El Cantal de Mojácar*, Ctra Nacional 340, Desvío Vera-El Cantal, T 478204, 2nd category, restaurant.

● Places to eat
The vast range of eating places reflects Mojácar's international character.

◆◆◆*Bistro Breton*, Playa Mojácar, T 478008, French cuisine, closed Thur; *La Lubina*, Pueblo Indalo, T 458376, terrace, fish dishes; *Palacio*, Plaza del Cano, in old town, nouvelle cuisine and traditional; *Tito's*, Playa de Ventanicas, T 478711, beachside fish restaurant.

◆◆*Saturno*, Avda Mediterráneo, T 478202, good *tapas*; *El Bigote*, in the pueblo, international and Spanish food; *Estrella de Mar*, Rambla de Cantal, excellent seafood restaurant, with *tapas*.

◆ For cheap *tapas*, try those round the main square in the *pueblo*, such as *Bar Indalo*. There are also a number of ice cream parlours (*heladerías*), such as the genuine Italian *Alberto's*, nr the *Hotel Indalo*, where fresh ice cream is made daily along with excellent capucino.

● Tourist offices
In Plaza Nueva at the entrance to Old Mojácar, T 475162, very helpful, bus timetables posted on the window when closed on Sat afternoon and Sun. Town plans available.

● Tour companies & travel agents
Aysol, Urb El Cruce, T 478175; *Indalo*, Ctra Carboneras, T 478700; *Solar*, Urb Gaviota, T 478700.

● Transport
Local Car hire: Autos Mojácar, C/Glorieta 3, T 478125; Indalo, Playa de Mojácar, T 478376; Solvicar, C/Plaza Nueva, T 478246.

NORTH FROM MOJACAR
5 km inland from Mojácar, the agricultural village of **Turre** is a delightful change after the coast. There is an attractive church with a Mudéjar tower and a Wed street market. Nearby is a Bronze Age site, although the archaeologists from Almería seemed to have removed most things of interest. 6 km away is the tasteful development of Cortijo Cabrera, which as well as the David Bryant Lawn Bowling Centre, has golf, horse riding and tennis. Visitors looking for more unusual accommodation could try *Finca Listonero*, Cortijo Grande, T 345147.

Back on the coast, Mojácar merges into **La Garrucha**, a small fishing port with pretensions of grandeur. The marina stubbornly refuses to take off, but villas are appearing thick and fast in the hills behind the port. The fair sized fishing fleet ensures that the fish restaurants around the port at least serve fresh food, but it does not come cheap. There is a beach of coarse sand and more than acceptable litter.

The coast road now swings inland to the agricultural village of **Vera**, with 5,000 inhabitants and an interesting collection of monuments, including the parish church of La Encarnación, dating from the 16th century; the Real Hospital de San Agustín built in 1521 for Carlos V; the early 17th century convent in C/Juan Anglada; and the Casa Consistorial which was completed in the early 18th century. The latter also houses a small Historical Museum of mild interest, open 1000-1400 and 1700-2200. Closed Mon. Vera also has a stretch of beach E of la Garrucha, with three typical beach hotels, one of which is a naturist complex – **C** *Vera-Hotel*, Ctra Vera-Garrucha, Km 2, T 390382, F 390361, 20 rm, restaurant, 2 pools, a/c, sports.

East of Vera, close to the estuary of the Río Almanzora, is the village of **Palomares**, which achieved notoriety in 1966, when after a mid-air collision an American B-52 lost its cargo of H-bombs. Three fell in fields outside the village and were quickly recovered. The fourth fell in the sea and it took a sizeable US fleet several weeks to reclaim it. None, fortunately, exploded.

20 km N of Vera is the unremarkable agricultural town of **Huercal-Overa**. The C321 leads N into the NE corner of Almería province to the area known as Los Vélez, flanked by the Sierra María. On the N342 is the town of **Vélez Rubio**, which is a rather ordinary spot apart from it's magnificent Church of the Encarnación, claimed to be the largest parish church in the province. It dates from the mid-18th century and its construction was funded by local noblemen, whose crests appear on the superbly carved façade. If you can gain entry, look for the impressive *retablo*. **Vélez Blanco** has rather more interest. It is located below a hill capped by a Renaissance castle which envelops the original Moorish structure, mostly dating from the early 16th century. It is, however, a mere shell, the interior having been gutted and transported stone by stone to the USA by an American millionaire. It now rests inside the New York Metropolitan Museum. Other buildings of note include the Convent of San Luís, dating from the 16th century, the Church of Santiago and some fine mansions in C/Palacios, while the narrow streets of the old Moorish quarter are worth wandering around. Between Vélez Rubio and Vélez Blanco is the **Cueva de los Letreros**, approached by a rough track and some concrete steps. The cave is in fact a rock overhang, shielded by an iron grille, from where you can just about see some drawings of animals and the famous *indalo* sign – not really a high priority visit.

Just W of Vélez Blanco is the **Parque Natural de Sierra de María**, consisting of some 19,000 ha of dolomitic limestone covered with Mediterranean scrub at lower levels and pines and oaks higher up. Excellent for wild flowers, particularly orchids in the spring and early summer, the area has a wide range of butterflies including rarities such as the Spanish Argus and the Nevada Grayling. Red Squirrels are not uncommon in the pines. The sierra is noted for its raptors, with Golden Eagle, Goshawk, Buzzard and Peregrine resident, joined in the summer by Short Toed and Booted Eagles. There is also a wide range of other birds, with Nightingales in the denser scrub and Little Bustards and Stone Curlew in the semi steppe areas. For the best access, take the local road from Vélez Blanco to María. Just past this village is a small road S to the Ermita de la Virgen de la Cabeza. From here there are tracks leading up into the higher parts of the sierra.

WEST OF ALMERIA

The N340 initially hugs the coast using a series of recently constructed tunnels until, after 8 km, **Aguadulce** is reached. This is a long-established and sedate holiday resort, originally the domain of weekenders from Almería, but with recent expansion it is appealing to a more international clientele. There is a large pleasure craft harbour, a tree lined promenade backing a beach of rather gritty sand and a range of mainly low rise apartment blocks and hotels. It has the usual entertainment of a holiday resort, but nothing of historical or other interest, although fortunately Almería is within easy reach, with local buses running at frequent intervals.

From Aguadulce, leave the N340 and follow the coast road to **Roquetas de Mar**. This was originally a small agricultural and fishing village. The port still operates, but the fishing boats now have to compete with pleasure craft. There are a number of fish restaurants adjacent to the port, but these are surprisingly expensive, considering their location. The main development has been 3 km to the S, where a huge new resort has been built, known as Playa Serena, with a collection of high rise hotels, aparthotels and apartments, tailor made for the package tour industry. In amongst the hotels are concentrations of shops, bars and restaurants. On the S side of the resort are some tasteful villas. There is plenty of opportunity for tennis and watersports, including sailing and sail boarding. There is an 18-hole golf course at Golf Playa Serena, where equipment can be hired, T 322055. For a visitor looking for sun, sport and a safe environment for children (there is no coast road between hotel and beach) the Playa Serena part of Roquetas is ideal, but you would not know that you were in Spain.

● **Accommodation** Those wishing to satisfy the above requirements could do no better than: **AL** *Bahia Serena*, Avda de las Gaviotas, Urb Playa Serena, T 334950, F 336247, 221 rm, a clone of the above; **AL** *Golf Trinidad*, Avda Principal, Urb Playa Serena, T 333011, F 333118, 390 rm, good sports facilities, a/c, pool; **AL** *Playacapricho*, Urb Playa Serena H-10, T 333100, F 333806, 331 rm, garage, a/c, pools, tennis, everything for the demanding package tourist; **A** *Las Salinas*, Ctra Faro Sabinal, T 333327, F 333331, 111 rm, pool, wheelchair access; **A** *Playalinda*, Urb Playa Serena, T 334500, F 334111, 124 rm, 2 pools, tennis, wheelchair access; **B** *Sabinal*, Urb Roquetas de Mar, Avda Gaviotas, T 333600, F 333533, 416 rm, the largest and cheapest of the package giants. **Pensiones**: for cheaper accommodation it is necessary to go the older part of town: **D** *El Faro*, Puerto de Roquetas, T 321015, harbourside pensión with garage; **D** *Los Angeles*, C/Estación 2, T 320125; **E** *Juan Pedro*, Plaza de la Constitución, T 320482, 30 rm, well used hostel in the main square. **Camping**: *Roquetas*, Ctra Los Parrales s/n, T 343809, 2nd category, open all year, good sports facilities.

The route continues W running between the *invernaderos* (Plastic greenhouses) of the *plasticultura* industry and the coastal dunes, lagoons and salt marsh, until down to the left is the new, purpose built resort of **Almerimar**. This consists of a number of hotels, apartment blocks and other facilities built around a marina for over 1,000 craft, with a nearby Gary Player designed golf course. Started by British developers, it suffered from the economic downturn of the early 90s, but has had its fortunes revived by the Japanese. The whole complex seems under siege from the acres of plastic surrounding it.

● **Accommodation** There are 3 large hotels in the Almerimar complex: **A** *Beach Hotel Almerimar*, Urb Almerimar, T 497150, F 497019, 278 rm, a/c, wheelchair access, good sports facilities; **A** *Florida Park Aguamarina*, Urb Almerimar, T 484611, F 484923, 543 rm, right on the marina; **A** *Golf Hotel Almerimar*, Urb Almerimar, T 497050, F 497019, 149 rm, a/c, all facilities for golf and other sports.

The whole idea of Almerimar is that

Plasticultura – life and death in the greenhouse

👣 Some 15,000 ha of the Almería coast are covered in plastic greenhouses, creating a curious illusion so that it is often difficult to see where the land ends and the sea begins. In Moorish times the coastal area was extremely fertile, but after the ReConquest the infrastructure of the agriculture began to crumble away, so that by the early years of this century the area was barren and desolate. Things began to change in the 1950's when the 'sand-plot technique' of cultivation was introduced. This involves firstly levelling the land and then surfacing it with a layer of compacted clay, followed by well rotted manure and finally a layer of well washed beach sand. The clay prevents water percolating downwards, while the sand prevents evapotranspiration. The manure is replaced every 3 or 4 years. In 1962 the first sand plot was covered with a greenhouse, but the plastic 'explosion' did not occur until the mid-70's. The typical greenhouse is 25m long and 3.5m high in the centre and supported by eucalyptus poles and wire. The crops are watered by drip (or trickle) irrigation, which cuts down on evaporation. The plants are dependent on soluble fertilisers and pesticides are added to the water. Crops are mainly grown between Oct and Jun (the summer temperatures being too high). The main crops are peppers, cucumbers, courgettes, tomatoes, water melons and flowers, which are transported to the countries of northern Europe by refrigerated lorry. In recent years lettuces have been flown to the USA and Canada. The produce is marketed by cooperatives known as *alhondigas* (derived from the Arabic word for corn exchange).

Despite its economic success, *plasticultura* is not without its problems. The biggest difficulty is with **water supply**. Most supplies come from wells, but the aquifers are becoming exhausted and the remaining water more saline. There are plans to divert water from the High Alpujarras, but this has led to protests by environmentalists and the farmers in the mountains. Desalinisation plants may be a solution. Secondly, **pesticide residues** have built up and some northern European countries have refused to accept some consignments due to high chemical levels. The third problem concerns **transportation**. There is no rail link westwards, while the road system in Almería is poor. Refrigerated lorries and tourist traffic are not happy bedmates. Finally, the rapid growth of *plasticultura* has led to serious **social problems**, including alcoholism, drug abuse, bankruptcies and particularly suicide. Many of the *plasticultura* farmers are illiterate peasants from the hill villages of the Alpujarras, who have lost their close knit support systems when moving to the coast and have been unable to cope with the sudden wealth and tensions of a highly competitive industry. As far as the tourist is concerned, the *plasticultura* leads to a similarly depressing feeling and most visitors are glad to flee the area as quickly as possible.

there is everything on site and the visitor has no need to leave the complex. Not that this is likely, as Almerimar often looks like an island, with no obvious break between the plastic and the sea. Unfortunately there is worse to come as the road now swings inland to **El Ejido**, the centre of the *plasticultura* industry. A surprising number of maps and brochures still do not show El Ejido, but it has grown into a linear conurbation along the N340 of nearly 45,000 people, making it the second largest town in the province. Largely unplanned, El Ejido is not a pretty place and its convoys of refrigerated lorries, carrying cargoes of fruit and vegetables, make life difficult for the touring motorist.

18 km W of El Ejido is the equally depressing **Adra**, whose main claim to fame is that it was the place where Boabdil, the last Moorish King, stayed before leaving Spain for good. Fortunately Adra is soon to be by-passed. Some 20 km inland along the C331 is the small agricultural town of **Berja**, the slopes around covered with orchards and vineyards. Steeped in history, there is a ruined Moorish alcazaba and some remnants of Moorish baths, while a little to the N is the hermitage of La Virgen de Gádor. Berja's neighbour to the E, **Dalías**, is sited on the Roman town of *Murgis*.

Birdwatching

At first sight the area W of Roquetas, dominated by market gardening and tourism, would seem unpromising for wildlife, but in fact this is a prime location for birdwatching with some rich wetland sites. There are four *salinas* or old salt production sites, most of which have nearby dunes, reeds and scrub. The first is *Salinas de San Rafael*, which is to the E of Roquetas and is partly overgrown and rubbish strewn, but there are a few salt pans left near the sea. West of Roquetas and S of the village of San Agustín is the largest complex of *Salinas Viejas* and *Salinas de Cerillos*, divided by a raised bank. The most westerly site is the *Salinas de Guardias Viejas*, just to the W of Almerimar. Watching is rewarding throughout the year, but least so between Jun and Aug, when the heat can be blistering, especially with the lack of shade. A wide range of gulls and wildfowl visit the salinas during the winter, but it is the passage periods of spring and autumn when the real rarities appear, including six varieties of tern, Collared Pratincole and Cream Coloured Courser. Breeding water birds include White headed Duck, Marsh Harrier, Black Winged Stilt and Avocet, while the surrounding reeds and scrub hold Water Rail, Great Reed Warbler, Lesser Short Toed Lark and Woodchat Shrike. This list is just a fraction of the species which could turn up.

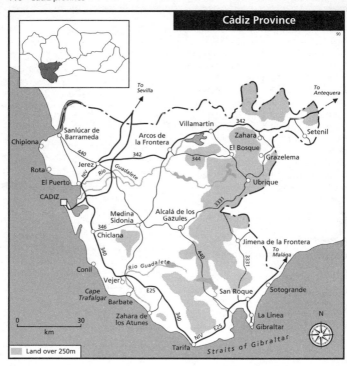

Cádiz Province

CADIZ IS the most westerly and southerly of the provinces of Andalucía. It is bordered in the North by Sevilla province and in the East by Málaga. The Atlantic coastline, known as the *Costa de la Luz*, which is tidal and generally backed by dunes or low cliffs. Its beaches are the best and least used in Andalucía. In the South, the strong *Levante* wind gives some of the best wind surfing conditions in the world, while the narrow Straits of Gibraltar provide a routeway for thousands of migrating storks, eagles and other raptors during Spring and Autumn.

Inland, the western half of the province is typified by open rolling agricultural land, while the eastern portion is more hilly, merging into the Serrania de Ronda on the Málaga border.

CADIZ CITY

(Pop 157,000; *Alt* 4m)

ACCESS Air The nearest national and international airport is at Jerez.

Train Trains run daily from Jerez and Sevilla to the station close to the entrance to the old part of the town.

Road The approach to Cádiz by road is somewhat dreary, the causeway being flanked by endless marsh and salt pans of interest only to bird watchers. The road then passes through modern suburbs of mainly low rise apartments, until the city walls mark the entrance to the old town located at the end of an isthmus. Street parking is inevitably difficult, but fortunately there are three large underground car parks (see map), which, because of the Spaniards' in-built resistance to paying for parking, usually have plenty of free places.

Bus: buses of various firms arrive next to the port or in the adjacent Plaza de España.

Sea Ferry: ferries also arrive opposite the Plaza de España, which is convenient for the centre of the town. The *vapor* from Sanlúcar is a pleasant way of arriving in Cádiz for a day visit.

Cádiz is a seaport located at the end of an E/W aligned isthmus protruding into the Atlantic. The capital, but not the largest town in the province, Cádiz has a long and fascinating history, claiming to be the oldest continuously occupied urban settlement in Western Europe. In Phoenician times it was known as *Gadir*, the port exporting minerals from the interior. It's strategic position also attracted the Romans, who called it *Gades* (the inhabitants of Cádiz are still known as *Gaditanos*) and Julius Caesar was given his first public office here. The Moors, whilst occupying the area, were not great seafarers, and there followed a period of decline until the 16th century when Spain became an important maritime power. With the colonization of the Americas Cádiz was ideally placed to benefit and when the river to Sevilla began to silt up, it became a great seaport once again. This strategic importance inevitably attracted the attentions of rival seafaring nations such as England, France and Holland, who regularly came to sack, pillage and "singe the King of Spain's beard". Much of the wealth from the Americas ended up in Cádiz and much of the older part of the city, including the cathedral, dates from the 18th century. In the early part of the 19th century, during the Peninsular War, some of the radical citizens of Cádiz set up the first Spanish Parliament or Cortes. It was short-lived, but was the blue print for the Spanish democracy of today, which ironically took more than 150 years to evolve.

Cádiz survived and today it is well worth a visit. Do not expect, however, another Córdoba or Granada. Cádiz has a unique atmosphere. Its people are more cosmopolitan than those in the rest of Andalucía and have more varied features and colouring. They are tolerant of minorities, particularly gays, as anyone who has witnessed the *Carnaval* will verify. In contrast to other Andalucían cities, the visitor will not feel threatened in Cádiz, even at night. What's more, even the motorists in Cádiz seem more courteous than elsewhere in Andalucía!

PLACES OF INTEREST

Fortunately, all the worthwhile features of Cádiz are contained within a very small area of the old part of the city and can easily be covered in half a day, although if time is to be spent in museums, then longer should be allocated. The streets are on a grid pattern and therefore navigation is easy, although finding the name of a street can often be frustrating. Many visitors will be content to wander at will around the narrow streets, but the following itinerary will cover all the recommended places (see page 120).

The start of the older part of the town is marked by the old **City Walls** (1) to the E, dating back to 1757. Traffic swirls round the nearby Plaza de la Constitución before passing through the Puerta de Tierra, the old land gate to the city. Proceed along the Avda del Puerto, from where the busy container dock can be seen, to the **Plaza de España** (2). Here in the middle of the square stands the **Monument to the Cortes** (3), built for the centenary of the short-lived liberal constitution of 1812. It is an impressive white stone monument, crowded with dignitaries and inscriptions and topped with a book representing the constitution – this itself is now capped with a large occupied storks nest.

From the corner of the plaza, take C/Antonio López into the attractive, tree-lined **Plaza Mina** (4), on the corner of which is the helpful **Tourist Office** (5) which can provide an excellent town plan (100 ptas) to assist the tour. Across the square is the **Museo de Bellas Artes y Arqueológico** (6). Housed in a restored mansion, with excellent lighting, this must be one of the best museums in Andalucía. The ground floor has a magnificent collection of archaeological remains from the Cádiz region. There are some significant Phoenician artefacts from the necropolis at *Gadir*, but it is the five Roman rooms which are absolutely outstanding. There is a comprehensive collection of sarcophagi from the Roman necropolis at *Gades*, showing the gradual evolution of shapes, while in room 5 there is a wide range of amphoras. Household and domestic items are well represented, including some fine mosaics and coins. There are busts, sculptures and models of the Roman theatre in Cádiz and the Roman city of *Baelo Claudia*. The Fine Arts collection is on the first floor, where the most important paintings are the 18 by Zurbaran, including a series of panels from the Carthusian monastery at Cartuja, near Jerez. (Note that the faces of the saints were painted from monks he had met.) Murillo fans will want to see 'Los Desposorios de Santa Catalina' which was his last work and completed by a pupil. Much of the more modern paintings are by local artists and of mixed quality, although those by Godoy and Prieto are notable. The second floor contains an unusual 'ethnographic' section, including the 'Tia Norica' marionettes, from Cádiz's long established and popular satirical marionette theatre. Note that this floor is often closed. Visitors from EU countries are allowed free entry (otherwise 200 ptas) and may be given a detailed guide in their own language. Visitors may be put off, however, by the over-zealous attendants who 'tail' people around as though they were potential terrorists. Open 0930-1400, Tues to Sun, closed Mon and public holidays, T 212281.

From the Plaza Mina proceed W to the equally attractive **Plaza de San Antonio** (7). The square has been stripped of its trees and cobbled over to form an underground car park. From here it is a short walk along C/Veedor W to the **Parque Genovés** (8) and the shore of Cádiz Bay. The shady park with its palms and cypresses has an open air theatre where there are performances during the summer evenings. At the end of the park and before reaching the Hotel Atlantico, turn E along C/Benito Pérez Galdós, noting on the left the venerable Dragon Tree. We are now in the university quarter and ahead, in a small square, is the Mudejar style, brick built **Falla Theatre** (9), named after the composer Manuel de Falla, who was a native of the city.

We are now in C/Sacramento and at the junction with C/San Jose is the **Oratorio San Felipe Neri** (10) where the 1812 Declaration of Independence was made by a group of refugees from Napoleon's occupation of the rest of Spain. The Baroque, oval-shaped building has a fascinating façade covered with plaques sent from other countries. There is a double row of balconies, above which a series of windows flood light into the light blue dome. A Murillo *Immaculada* dominates the high altar's *retablo*, while a series of seven chapels surround the oval nave. The Oratory is open every day, but at the inconvenient hours of services – 0830-1000 and 1930-2200. It may be possible to latch on to a group visit, however. These generally take place between 1000 and 1200.

Almost next door (officially in C/Santa Inés), is the **Museo Histórico Municipal** (11), which was set up in 1912 to mark the centenary of the 1812 Constitution. It consists of a rambling series of rooms containing a collection of uninspiring portraits of civic dignitaries, bishops and wealthy *gaditanos*, plus a few uninspiring archaeological artefacts. The highlight is on the first floor, where there is an immense scale model of Cádiz carved of wood and ivory depicting the city as it was in 1779. Behind the model is an impressive mural showing the signing of the 1812 Constitution. There are also some documents from 1812 in a showcase in an upper room. Entrance is free. Closed Mon. Open Tues-Fri 0900-1300 and 1600-1900 (Jun to Sep 1700-1900). Sat and Sun 0900-1300, T 221788.

Continue along C/Sacramento which now becomes C/Solano and shortly on the left is the **Torre Tavira**

(12). The tower, built in Baroque style, was part of the Palace of the Marquis of Recaño, whose first watchman, Antonio Tavira, gave it its name. In 1778, the Tavira Tower was appointed the official watchtower for the town. Above the reception area there are two exhibition

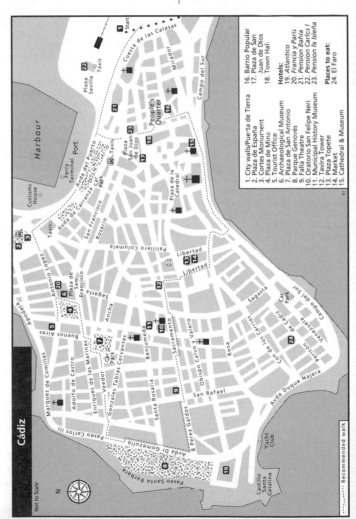

Cádiz

1. City walls/Puerta de Tierra
2. Plaza de España
3. Cortes Monument
4. Plaza de Mina
5. Tourist Office
6. Archaeological Museum
7. Plaza de San Antonio
8. Parque Genovés
9. Falla Theatre
10. Oratorio San Felipe Neri
11. Municipal History Museum
12. Tavira Tower
13. Plaza Topete
14. Market
15. Cathedral & Museum
16. Barrio Popular
17. Plaza de San Juan de Dios
18. Town Hall

Hotels:
19. Atlántico
20. Francia y París
21. Pensión Bahía
22. Pensión Carlos I
23. Pensión la Isleña

Places to eat:
24. El Faro

------ Recommended walk

Not to Scale

The cathedral at Cádiz

halls, which are of moderate interest. Above these is a *camera obscura* room, where a moving image of the roof top view of the city is projected. (The principle of *camera obscura* is quite simple and has been used since the days of Leonardo de Vinci. What is required is a completely darkened room, a screen, a hole through which light enters, a mirror and a magnifying glass.) The result in this case is spectacular and well worth a visit. The Torre Tavira is open daily, 1000-2030 from Jun to Aug and 1000-1800 from Sep-May. Entrance 400 ptas, T 212910.

From here fork right into the **Plaza Topete** (13), which is the site of a Phoenician temple where first born babies were said to be sacrificed. The square is now almost completely occupied by the covered **Market** (14) where appetizing displays of fruit, vegetable, meat and fish can be seen. There is also an outdoor flower market. The *Correos* is also located here and there are a number of cheap bars in the plaza offering lunchtime *tapas*.

From the Plaza Topete take C/Libertad to the shore and to one of the best photo opportunities in Cádiz – the view of the gold-domed **Cathedral** (15), flanked by a row of colour washed houses. Known officially as the Cathedral Nueva because it replaced the earlier Catedral of Santa Cruz, which was largely destroyed by fire in 1596, it was built in Gothic style and begun in 1722. It was not until 1853, however, that it was finally completed with the two towers at the western end. The older parts of the cathedral are built of a brown coarse sandstone, which does not lend itself to fine masonry work, so the later construction was of a light grey limestone, giving the building a curiously attractive patchwork appearance. Windows are almost non-existent, while the 'gold' dome is in fact composed of yellow glazed tiles. The interior is rather severe, but well lit and mercifully lacking in the over ornate gilding of many Spanish cathedrals. Have a look at the choirstalls, which date from 1702 and were originally in the Cartuja in Sevilla. The composer, Manuel de Falla, is buried in the crypt. Artwork includes some sculptures by Montañes and Lucia Roldan. The cathedral is only open between 1200 and 1300 Mon to Sat, entrance 100 ptas. At other times the main doors of the building are closed except when a service is being held, so it will be necessary to gain entrance via the Cathedral

Museum, the door of which is located on the corner nearest the sea. Look in the Treasury for the famous and quite hideous 'million jewel monstrance', a 3m high piece of ceremonial silver, believed to be a present from a grateful colony. The museum is open Tues-Sat 1000-1200, adults 400 ptas, children 200 ptas. In front of the cathedral is the Plaza de la Catedral, where there are numerous bars and restaurants.

The route continues from the cathedral striking inland along C/San Juan de Dios and into the **Barrio del Pópulo** (16) (Peoples' Quarter), a labyrinth of narrow streets, with some houses dating from the 13th century, having survived the attentions of Drake and others. Nearby is the **Plaza de San Juan de Dios** (17), the social centre and meeting place for *gaditanos* and visitors alike and flanked by the **Ayuntamiento** (18) (Town Hall), an impressive building in Elizabethan Neoclassical style. Immediately W of the square are the main pedestrianized shopping streets and to the E the town walls where the tour begins.

The beach on the S side of the old town of Cádiz is the **Playa de la Caleta**, which is tightly sandwiched between the ruined defensive castles of Santa Catalina and San Sebastian. It is not always particularly clean. Most *gaditanos* prefer to use the longer **Playa de la Victoria**, which extends the full length of the new part of the city. It has plenty of sports facilities and beach bars and is backed by hotels, apartments and restaurants. It can get very crowded in the summer.

LOCAL FESTIVALS

The usual religious celebrations take place at Semana Santa and Corpus Cristi. 7 Oct is the day of the city's Patron Saint, La Virgen del Rosario. At the beginning of Aug is La Velada de los Angeles, a popular fair which has been revived in recent years. On the eve of All Saints Day, 1 Nov, the central Market receives some

elaborate decoration. Cádiz is best known, however, for its **Carnaval**, which lasts for 10 days in Feb. Dating from the 19th century, even Franco was unable to suppress it. The Carnaval is a riot of eating, drinking, dancing, singing and masquerades with a certain South American flavour. A distinctive feature are the 'bands' – groups of people who parade around the city in fancy dress making music with any instruments they can lay their hands on, singing satirical songs particularly about politicians. The gay element in the city (and it is quite large) play an important part in proceedings, and prizes are awarded for the most original and outrageous presentations. It is hopeless to attempt to get accommodation in Cádiz during Carnaval unless booked well ahead.

LOCAL INFORMATION

Price guide

Hotels:			
AL	over US$90	**D**	US$20-40
A	US$75-90	**E**	US$10-20
B	US$60-75	**F**	under US$10
C	US$40-60		

Places to eat:			
♦♦♦	expensive	♦♦	average
♦	cheap		

● **Accommodation**

The top hotel in Cádiz is **AL** *Atlantico*, Avda Duque de Nájera 9, T 226905, F 214582, 153 rm, pool, garage, wheelchair access, a/c, state run hotel located at the point of the isthmus, good views over the Atlantic and Cádiz Bay.

A *Husa Puertatierra*, Avda Andalucía 34, T 272111, 98 rm, garage, a/c, wheelchair access, modern chain hotel in new part of city; **A** *La Caleta*, Avda Amilcar Barca s/n, T 279411, F 259322, 143 rm, garage, a/c, restaurant, wheelchair access, in the newer part of the city; **A** *Playa Victoría*, Pza Ingeniero Lacierva s/n, large modern hotel close to the main beach, a/c, garage, pool.

B *Francia y Paris*, Pza San Francisco 2, T 222348, F 222431, 57 rm, small hotel in charming square in old part of city; **B** *Regio I and Regio II*, Avda Andalucía 79, T 253008, both with 40 rm in newer part of town.

The *pensiones* are numerous and vary tremendously in quality. As is often the case in seaports, some are very scruffy, particularly some of those in the alleyways leading off Plaza San Juan de Dios. Insist on seeing a room first. The following are at least clean: **D** *Bahia*, C/Plocia 5, T 259061, 21 rm, just off the main plaza, good value; **D** *Carlos I*, Pza de Sevilla s/n, T 286600, 30 rm, a/c, good facilities; **D** *Centro Sol*, C/Padre Elejalde 7, T 279747, 19 rm, will provide breakfast.

E *La Isleña*, Pza Juan de Dios 12, T 287064, 10 rm, simple but clean; **E** *Manolita*, C/Benjumeda 2, T 211577, 6 rm, small family run.

For the cheapest accommodation, look for the *camas* signs in windows. There are plenty of these around and it might be possible to haggle over a price.

Youth hostels: none in Cádiz. The nearest are in Jerez and Algeciras.

Camping: there are no camp sites around Cádiz itself, but plenty nr Puerto de Santa María, Puerto Real and Rota. *Las Dunas de San Anton*, Las Dunas de la Puntilla, T 870112, 1st category, beachside, pool, excellent facilities; *Guadalete*, Ctra N IV, Km 655, Puerta de Santa María, T 561749, 3rd category, pool; *El Pinar*, Ctra N IV, Km 666, Puerto Real, T 830897, 2nd category, open Apr-Oct only; *Punta Candor*, Ctra Rota-Chipiona, Km 13, T 813303, 1st category, good facilities.

● **Places to eat**
Not surprisingly, fish comes top of the menu in Cádiz. Two of the most outstanding (and expensive) fish restaurants in Andalucía are: ◆◆◆*El Faro*, C/San Felix 15, T 253613, some excellent house specialities, but also a moderately priced *menu del dia*; ◆◆◆*Achuri*, C/Plocia 15, T 253613.

For cheaper sea food, try the *freidurias*, of which ◆◆*Las Flores*, Plaza las Flores, is one of the best. Many visitors will be quite happy with *tapas* and in Cádiz, fish and shellfish are the dominant ingredients. Those fancying a 'tapas crawl' could head for C/Zorilla which runs from Plaza de Mina to the N shore and is made up almost entirely of small tapas bars. Particularly rec is ◆*Gaditana*, which has an amazing range on offer. There are plenty of other tapas bars in the Plaza de San Juan de Dios and the surrounding alleyways.

Visitors looking for a change from Spanish food, could try ◆*Chino Marco Polo*, Paseo Maritimo, nr the main beach in the new part of town, with a *menu* at 900 ptas. This area is also excellent in summer for *heladerias*.

● **Banks & money changers**
The main Spanish banks and regional savings banks have their branches close to the Plaza de San Juan de Dios/Calle Nueva area. Some savings banks may be reluctant to cash TCs or Euro cheques.

● **Embassies & consulates**
Denmark, Alameda Apodaca 21, T 221364; **France**, Ctra Madrid-Cádiz, Km 634, T 302354; **Holland**, Plaza Tres Carabelas 5, T 224500; **Italy**, C/Ancha 8, T 211715; **Norway**, Alameda Apodaca 21, T 221364.

● **Entertainment**
Outside of *Carnaval*, Cádiz can appear rather staid, but things liven up in the summer along the Playa Victoria. For **Discos**, try the following: *Las Pergolas*, Paseo Marítimo 11, T 280949 or *Holiday*, Nereidas, Paseo Marítimo, T 273775. Cádiz has 3 excellent theatres: *Teatro Andalucía*, C/Londres 2, T 223029; *Teatro Jose Peman* (open air theatre in Parque Genovés, summer only), T 223534; and *Gran Teatro Falla*, Plaza de Falla s/n, T 220828. There are no fewer than 7 cinemas in Cádiz, 2 of which are multi screen.

● **Hospital & medical services**
Residencia Sanitaria (for urgent cases), Avda Ana de Viya 21, T 279011; *Red Cross*, C/Santa María de la Solidad 10, T 254270; *Hospital de Traumaticos/Clinica de San Rafael*, C/Diego Arias 2, T 226408.

● **Post & telecommunications**
Post Office: the main *Correos* is in Plaza Topete.

● **Shopping**
The chief shopping streets are Calles San Francisco, Nueva, Columela and San José. The more gaudy tourist items seen in other Andalucían cities are happily rarely in sight. There are a number of shops selling local handicraft incl: **Ceramica Popular 'La Cartuja'**, C/Nicaragua 2; **Ceramica Compañia**, C/Compañia s/n; and **Estereria Acuaviva**, C/Rosario 21.

● **Sports**
Tennis: *Real Tenis Club*, Avda Doctor Gómez Ulla, T 221945.

Watersports: not surprisingly, watersports figure prominently at Cádiz: *Club Nautico Deportivo Alcazar*, Plaza de San Lorenzo 2,

T 260914; *Club Maritimo Gaditano La Caleta*, C/Duque de Nájera, s/n, T 213680; *Club Nautico Deportivo*, Bda Puntales s/n, T 260914; and *Real Club Nautico de Cádiz*, Pza de San Felipe s/n, T 212991.

● **Tourist offices**
Regional Government Tourist Office, C/Calderón de la Barca 1 (corner of Plaza de Mina), T 211313, very helpful multilingual staff; **Municipal Tourist Office**, C/Marqués de Valdenigo 4, T 253254. There is also a further temporary municipal office in the summer months at Victoría beach.

● **Useful addresses**
Garages/repairs: all the firms listed below are clustered together in the Zona Franca industrial area on the SE edge of the city. **Citröen**, C/Algeciras s/n, T 281438; **Fiat**, C/Cdad. de San Roque s/n, T 251309; **Ford**, C/Algeciras s/n, T 271054; **GM**, Tainy SA, Ronda de Puente s/n, T 276298; **Renault**, Ronda del Puente s/n, T 280300; **Rover**, C/Gibraltar s/n, T 264308; **Seat/VAG**, Automóviles Bahia, C/Algeciras s/n, T 250207.

Parking: there are 3 large underground parking places in the old part of the city.

● **Transport**
Local Car hire: Atesa, Pza. de San Juan de Dios 16, T 258207; **Autos Pua**, Avda. de Portugal 77, T 252344; **Autos Santa María**, C/Cuesta de las Caleas 41, T 278250; Avis, Avda Cayetano del Toro 16, T 258250; **Europcar**, C/Velazquez s/n, T 262811; **Hertz**, C/Condesa Villafuente Bermeja, T 271895; **Imperial Alquiler de Coches**, C/Cuesta de las Calesas 45, T 264477. **Coches de Caballo**: carriage stand in Plaza de San Juan de Dios. A pleasant and leisurely way to see the city. **Taxis**: there are taxi ranks in the Plaza de San Juan de Dios and nr the Plaza de España. Radio Taxi, T 221006; Tele Taxi, T 286969.

Train There are 3 daily trains to Granada; 18 trains daily to Jerez; and 8 daily to Sevilla. Information, T 254301.

Road Bus: 2 bus companies serve Cádiz. Los Amarillos covers the area N to Rota and Sanlúcar, with their buses leaving from Avda Ramón de Carranza 31, close to the port, T 285852. The Comes company serves the area S and E of Cádiz to Medina Sidonia, Tarifa and Algeciras; their station is located in the Plaza de la Hispanidad, T 211763.

Sea Ferry: a ferry service runs from the port to Puerto de Santa María, taking 45 mins and leaving at 0900, 1100, 1300 and 1530 with extra trips on Sun and public holidays. Seagoing ferries leave Cádiz weekly for Almería, Genoa and the Canary Islands. Contact the Transmediterrania office in Avda Ramón de Carranza 26, T 284311.

NORTH FROM CADIZ

The area N of Cádiz as far as the estuary of the Río Guadalquivir consists of rolling farmland given over largely to the production of grapes. Along the attractive coastline are a series of fishing ports and holiday resorts, the latter being very popular with *sevillaños*, many of whom have built villas along the shore.

Immediately across the Bay of Cádiz is **El Puerto de Santa María**, which is very much a multi-purpose town. One of the three towns making up the 'sherry triangle', it is also a fishing and commercial port as well as being a minor resort. A pleasant way to arrive at the town is to take the *vapor* from Cádiz. Adriano 111 is an elderly wooden tub with an equally ancient crew and pitches and rolls alarmingly if there is an Atlantic swell in the bay. The *vapor* leaves Cádiz at 1000, 1200, 1400 and 1830; it departs from El Puerto at 0900, 1100, 1300 and

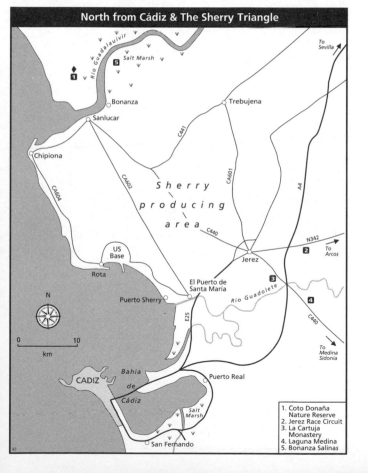

North from Cádiz & The Sherry Triangle

1. Coto Doñana Nature Reserve
2. Jerez Race Circuit
3. La Cartuja Monastery
4. Laguna Medina
5. Bonanza Salinas

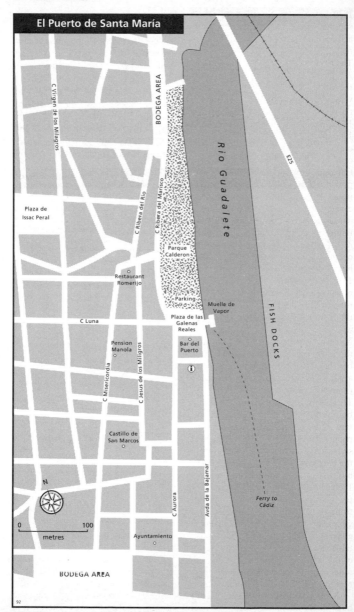

El Puerto de Santa María

BODEGA AREA

C Virgen de los Milagros

Plaza de Issac Peral

C Ribera del Rio

C Ribera del Marisco

Rio Guadalete

E25

Parque Calderon

Restaurant Romerijo

Parking

Muelle de Vapor

FISH DOCKS

C Luna

Plaza de las Galenas Reales

Pension Manola

Bar del Puerto

C Misericordia

C Jesus de los Milagros

ⓘ

Castillo de San Marcos

N

C Aurora

Avda de la Bajamar

Ferry to Cádiz

0   100

metres

Ayuntamiento

BODEGA AREA

92

1530. On Sun and festivals there are supplementary services leaving Cádiz at 1630 and El Puerto at 1730. There are no sailings on Mon, except at festivals. The 10 km voyage takes 40 mins and cost 225 ptas each way. The *vapor* docks at the Muelle de Vapor, where there is convenient parking for those wishing to do the reverse journey. The tourist office is 100m away in C/Guadalete, open 1000-1400 and 1730-1930, T 857545. Worth noting by the muelle, is the ornate 18th century stone fountain, El Fuente de las Galeras, with its four spouts, built to provide water for the sailing ships leaving for the New World. Nearby in C/Federico Rubio is the Castillo San Marcos, dating from the 13th century and containing a Mudejar church with the Moorish *mihrab* still intact. The building operates today as a conference centre, but is officially open on Sat only, 1100-1330, but a generous tip to the guardian might persuade him to open up at other times. Other buildings of note include the Baroque Church of San Francisco, with a fine S door and the monastery of Nuestra Señora de la Victoria built in the 12th century. There are also a number of impressive *palacios* dispersed around the town, built largely with the profits of the trade with the Americas. The bullring in El Puerto, which was built in 1880, is one of the most important in Andalucía and can hold 15,000 people. The *corrida* is celebrated in great style during the May *feria*, when some of the best known matadors perform. The bullring can be visited Mon-Fri 1000-1300. El Puerto de Santa María is famous for its *marisquerías* which line the river front in C/Ribero del Marisco. Select your seafood which is then weighed and given to you in a paper bag. Take it to a table and order your drink. The largest of the *marisquerías* is *Romerijo*, but another place worth trying is *Bar del Puerto* opposite the Muelle del Vapor.

A familiar sight in El Puerto are the huge sherry warehouses lining the river front. It is possible to visit some of the *bodegas* by private arrangement, but telephone first: **Terry**, C/Gilos s/n, T 483000; **Osborne**, C/Fernan Cabellero 3, T 855211. The Osborne family also breed many of the fearsome fighting bulls which can be seen in the fields in the area (as well as providing the large black bulls which are the advertising hoardings for Osborne *coñac* and a common feature of the Andalucían countryside).

● **Accommodation** Top of the range in every respect is the exclusive **AL** *Puerto Sherry Yacht Club*, Avda de la Libertad s/n, T 812000, F 853300, 58 rm, every possible facility and prices to match. Also rec in the El Puerto area is: **AL** *Meliá Caballo Blanco*, Avda de Madrid 1, T 562541, F 562712, 94 rm, with all the usual features one associates with the Meliá chain. For more affordable prices in El Puerto try **E** *Manolo*, C/Jesús de los Milagros 18, T 857525; or the basic **E** *Tiburón*, C/Sudamérica s/n, T 875334.

Just outside El Puerto is a new British built luxury development known inevitably as **Puerto Sherry**. There are the usual apartments, chandlers and restaurants around the harbour, plus an enormous 'multi storey car park' for small boats and dinghies, which is a landmark for miles around. Puerto Sherry was a casualty of the recession in the early 90's, but work has now resumed and the latest phase is an attractive residential development, known as **Pueblo Sherry**. Nearby is the Aquasherry Parque Acuatico with a range of slides, shoots and other water attractions. On the N IV at Km 647, it can be reached by bus from El Puerto. Open Jun to Sep, 1100-1800. For latest prices and concessions, T 870511.

The CA603 now leads along the coast, looping inland to avoid the US naval base at **Rota**, one of three in Spain. If the graffiti in the area is to be believed, relations between the Americans and the locals is not always smooth, but at least the base provides employment and sustains local businesses. The town of

Rota itself is a pleasant little holiday resort with a good sandy beach, an elegant *paseo marítimo* and a small sport harbour. The Castillo de Luna dates from the 13th century, but has been much restored. The Torre de la Merced is all that remains of the Convent of the same name which was built in 1600 and largely destroyed by a hurricane in 1722. The only other historical feature is the parish church of Nuestra Señora de la O, dating from the 16th century and displaying a mixture of Gothic, Plateresque and Baroque styles.

The coast road runs N to Punta del Perro where the town of **Chipiona** is located. A quiet family resort with some Roman remains and pretensions to be a spa, it is popular with Spaniards and during the height of the season its many *pensiones* are usually fully booked.

The road, with its accompanying railway line, now runs along the estuary of the Río Gaudalquivir to the town of **Sanlúcar de Barrameda**, the third part of the 'sherry triangle'. Sanlúcar has Roman origins and the Moors built a defensive fort here, while later under the Christians it became an important port. Columbus left here on his second Atlantic crossing and it was Magellan's last port of call before his attempt to circumnavigate the world. The town is divided into the older Barrio Alto, occupying the higher ground and containing most of the monuments, and the newer Barrio Bajo towards the river, the two being linked by a tree lined avenue, the Calzada de Ejercito, on which the tourist office is located. The centre of the old town is the charming Plaza del Cabildo and just to the N of here are the main monuments. There are numerous churches worth a visit, particularly Nuestra Señora de la O in the small Plaza de la Paz, with a 16th century Mudejar doorway. It also has a curious tower, with a 3-tier belfry, which if you can gain admittance gives marvellous views over the town. Adjacent is the *palacio* of the Duques de Medina Sidonia. The present incumbent is the Duchess of Medina Sidonia, a larger than life character known as the 'Red Duchess' for her political views. A direct descendant of Guzman 'el Bueno' of Tarifa, she has made herself a thorn in the side of authority in her defence of the less fortunate of the area. Today, the *palacio* functions as a small, exclusive guest house. Just to the W is the Moorish Castillo de Santiago, which in its ruined state has little to reward the climb, except the views across the estuary.

Sanlúcar is famous for its very dry *manzanilla* sherry, its flavour caused by the salt laden winds blowing off the ocean, giving a *flor* (the yeasty skin within the barrels) throughout the year. The largest of the sherry producers is the Barbadillo family, who make four varieties – a Fina (*manzanillas* are feminine), an Olorosa, a Pasada and Solear Muy Vieja, plus an excellent table wine from Palomino grapes. The *bodega* is located at C/Egualiz 11, in the old town, and is open Mon-Fri 0730-1500; T 365103 in advance for a tour.

Sanlúcar is also noted for its horse racing, Carreras de Caballos de Sanlúcar, which has taken place for over 150 years during Aug. The thoroughbred horses race along a 1,800m stretch of sand at the mouth of the Río Guadalquivir.

Up river from Sanlúcar is the small fishing village of Bonanza, which is the actual spot where both Magellan and Columbus left on their voyages. Today, a busy auction takes place each afternoon when the fishing fleet returns. North of Bonanza is an area of commercial salt production, the Salinas de Bonanza, which is an excellent area for bird watching, particularly for migrant and wintering wildfowl and waders. The salinas are private, but the owners are sympathetic to responsible bird watchers. A day permit is essential, however, and should be obtained at the company's office at the entrance.

Across the river from Sanlúcar is the nature reserve of **Coto Doñana** (dealt with in detail in the section on Huelva).

Foot passengers can cross the river by motor boat from the fishing quarter of Bajo de Guia, but to get there by car, however, requires a 150 km, 3 hrs round trip via Sevilla, which is the lowest

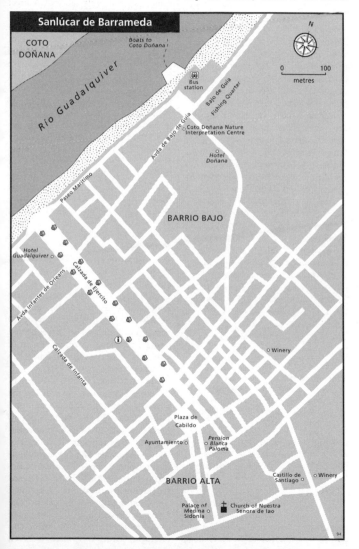

Sanlúcar de Barrameda

COTO
DOÑANA

Boats to
Coto Doñana

Río Guadalquivir

N

0   100
metres

Bus
station

Bajo de Guia
Fishing Quarter

Avda de Bajo de Guia

Coto Doñana Nature
Interpretation Centre

Hotel
Doñana

Paseo Marítimo

BARRIO BAJO

Hotel
Guadalquiver

Calzada de Ejercito

Avda Infantes de Orleans

Calzada de Infanta

Plaza de
Cabildo

Ayuntamiento

Pension
Blanca
Paloma

Winery

BARRIO ALTA

Castillo de
Santiago

Winery

Palace of
Medina
Sidonia

Church of Nuestra
Senora de lao

bridging point of the river. It is now possible to visit the Coto Doñana from Sanlúcar. The riverboat *Real Fernando* (named after Spain's first steamship) leaves twice daily in summer and once a day in winter. Times vary according to the season – from 21 Sep until 30 Apr at 1000; from 1 May until 30 Jun at 0900 and 1600; from 1 Jul until 20 Sep at 0830 and 1630. Check with the Centro de Interpretación located opposite the departure jetty for any changes. Cost 2,100 ptas, children 1,050 ptas. No sailings on Mon. Real Fernando is a substantial boat, with a snack bar and other facilities. The excellent guides are multilingual and there is a video on the Coto shown on board. The first stop is at La Plancha, a restored settlement of thatched huts originally occupied by charcoal burners. The second stop is at the *marismas*, where salt was once produced. The heat can be searing here in the summer as there is a total lack of shade. Wild boar and deer are more or less guaranteed, plus a wide range of birds including terns, Little Owl, egrets, Black Kite and a variety of waders along the rivers edge. Binoculars are useful. Tickets can be obtained from the Centro, T 363813. Board the boat 15 mins before departure.

The return journey to Cádiz can be made inland following the CA440 to Jerez and then using the E25.

● **Accommodation** There is a good choice in Sanlúcar, apart from at the budget end of the scale. Everything is likely to be taken in Jul and Aug. **A** *Doñana*, Avda Cabo Noval s/n (at Bajo de Guía), T 365000, F 367141, 96 rm, garage, a/c, pool, wheelchair access; **A** *Tartaneros*, C/Tartaneros 8, T 362044, F 360045, 22 rm, garage, wheelchair access, a/c; **B** *Guadalquivir*, C/Calzada de Ejército 10, T 360742, F 360745, 80 rm, disco; *Posada de Palacio*, C/Caballeros 11, T 364840, F 365060, 11 rm, restaurant; **C** *Los Helechos*, C/Madre de Dios 9, T 361349, F 369650, 56 rm, garage, a/c, restaurant; **D** *Las Marismas*, Pza La Salle 2, T 366008, 9 rm, small pensión close to the bus station; **E** *Blanca Paloma*,

Plaza San Roque 9, T 363644, 8 rm, small economical pensión in the older part of town.

● **Places to eat** ✦✦✦*Casa Bigote*, Bajo de Guía s/n, T 362696, one of several excellent fish restaurants along the same road, one back from the river.

JEREZ DE LA FRONTERA

(*Pop* 187,000: *Alt* 55m)

ACCESS Air There is an airport 10 km N of the town for internal flights and a few international flights. There is no bus link with the town, taxi is approx 1,300 ptas. **Train & road** The bus station on C/Medina Cartuja and the train station in Plaza de la Estación at the end of C/Medina Cartuja are close together within walking distance of the central C/Larga and Plaza del Arenal. There are normally taxis at the train station. **NB** The one-way system in Jerez is extremely confusing, while street parking is difficult. Car crime is rife, but fortunately there is fairly secure underground parking in the Alameda Cristina, in C/Madre de Dios and in Plaza Monti. Visitors should also take sensible precautions against petty street crime.

Jerez de la Frontera lies 83 km S of Sevilla and 30 km NE of Cádiz, in the agricultural plains S of the Río Guadalquivir. The city was known as *Ceret* in Roman times, but renamed *Scherish* by the Moors. This later changed to *Xeres* and finally Jerez. The 'de la Frontera' element of the city's name, as with many other towns in the area, dates from around 1380 when it marked a Moorish frontier and also reflects the fact that Jerez changed hands numerous times during the course of the Reconquista. Despite being outnumbered by almost 10 to 1, the Moors under Tarik first captured Jerez in 711 following a battle against its Visigoth residents on the plains to the E of the town. Jerez was reconquered in 1251 by Fernando III, but subsequently lost in 1264 by his son Alfonso X. The commander of the Christian forces, García Gómez Carillo, so impressed the Moorish victors that they spared his life. This was clearly a mistake, because after a major siege lasting 5 months, Alfonso and Carillo were able to recapture the town permanently.

The white, chalky soil in the area, known as *albariza*, has proved ideal for cultivating the Palamino grapes which produce the sherry for which Jerez has been famed for centuries, although, curiously, it is many kilometres out of town before one finds vineyards. Many of the powerful sherry families were originally English, some having been involved in sherry production since the time of England's Henry VII. Today the town presents deep contrasts, with sterile high rise suburbs and a fascinating ancient centre, with a close knit gypsy *barrio* and the upper class villas of the sherry barons.

Places of interest

Fortunately all the places of interest and most of the sherry *bodegas* are within easy walking distance of the *plaza mayor*, the Plaza del Arenal. It is said that this name originated when two knights accused each other of treason and fought for 2 days and nights in the sandy arena, before King Alfonso stopped the fight personally and pardoned both knights.

Just to the S of the Plaza del Arenal is the **Alcazar**, which dates back to the 11th century when it was built by the Almohads. It was once the residence of the Caliphs of Sevilla. It has been heavily restored and consists mainly of walls and the 12th century octagonal tower. The interior contains a mosque which was transformed into the **Iglesia de Santa María la Real** by Alfonso X when he recaptured the town. Open 1030-1400 and 1700-1900.

Cathedral of San Salvador Located on the Plaza de la Encarnación, the cathedral, although sited on a mosque, dates only from the 18th century and is in Baroque style. Amongst its treasures are a 14th century figure of Christ, 'Cristo de la Viga' and Zurbarán's painting 'La Virgen Niña' (Our Lady as a Child). Open daily 1730-2000. In the same area, a further

reminder of Jerez's past role as a defensive outpost can be seen in the fragments of the original city walls from the Almohad-Almoravid period which still remain, including the **Puerta del Arroyo** at the junction of C/Calzada del Arroyo and Puerta del Rota.

Banos Arabes Situated on the same hill as the Alcazar, these *hamman* date back to the period when Jerez was part of the Caliphate of Córdoba. Open Mon-Sat 1100-1330 and 1700-2000, Sun 1100-1330. Entrance free.

Iglesia-Convento de Santa Domingo Originating from the time of the Reconquest, the convent is an odd mixture of architectural styles. It was badly damaged by fire during the Civil War, but has been carefully restored. Note the 17th century *retablo*. Open 0730-1000 and 1730-2130.

Museums

Museo de Arte Flamenco, Palacio de Penmartín, Plaza San Juan 1. Located in an 18th century building, this museum has a collection of musical instruments and the history of the art of flamenco, which *jerezanos* claim began in their town. Audio visual presentations every hour on the hour. Open Mon-Fri 0930-1330 and 1800-2100, Sat 1000-1300. Entrance free.

Museo de Reloj (Clock Museum), La Atalaya Palace, C/Lealas. A fascinating collection (once owned by disgraced tycoon Ruiz-Mateos) of more than 300 clocks from the 16th to the 19th centuries. Be sure not to be around when they are all striking on the hour. Open Mon-Sat 1000-1330. Entrance 300 ptas.

Museo del Vino, Casa del Vino, Avda Domecq. Traces the history of sherry making. Open Sun-Fri 1000-1300.

Other places of interest

Parque Zoológico, C/Taxdirt on the NW suburbs of Jerez. Has botanical gardens and a park in addition to the zoo. One of the few decent zoos in Andalucía, making a big effort to preserve and breed endangered species. Open Tues-Sun all year,

Sherry – amber nectar Spanish style

Sherry is produced largely within a triangle formed by the towns of Jerez de la Frontera, El Puerto de Santa María and Sanlúcar de Barrameda, covering some 20,000 hectares of agricultural land. Any fortified wine grown outside this area cannot officially be termed 'sherry'. The best growing areas have a white chalky soil called *albariza*. Its porosity soaks up the winter rains and gradually releases the moisture to the vine roots during the long, hot summer. Two thirds of the grapes are of the *palomino* variety, while the remaining one third are of the *Pedro Ximénez* variety which are used to give sweetness, particularly in cream sherries.

The grapes are harvested in early Sep and taken to special houses for pressing. The resulting pulp goes into vats, where the juice is separated by gravity. It is only now that the amber liquid arrives at the *bodegas* where it spends several weeks in fermentation. By Jan it is clear and a thin crust of *flor* begins to grow on its surface. The *flor del vino* or flower of the wine, is a type of yeast which is unique to the area. It grows most strongly in Spring forming a crinkly white skin on the surface of the wine. *Flor* is only allowed to continue to grow on the *fino*, a light dry sherry. In the case of the heavier, darker *olorosos* the *flor* is killed by increasing the volume of alcohol in the wine to 17 to 18%. The design of the *bodegas* helps to develop the cool humid environment needed to encourage the *flor*. They have thick walls and high roofs, while windows are shaded with esparto grass. The floors are made of hard packed soil, which is sprayed with water during the heat of the summer.

Sherry does not have a vintage. The essence of its production is the blending using the *solera* system. This consists of hundreds of barrels (or butts) made of American oak and arranged in rows called scales. Three times a year 10% of each barrel in the bottom row is drawn off. This is replenished by 10% of the row above, known as the *criadera* or nursery casks; this is topped up by 10% from

---

summer 1000-2000, winter 1000-1800. Entrance 500 ptas.

Real Escuela de Arte Equestre (Royal Andalucían School of Equestrian Art), Avda Duque de Abrantes s/n, T 311111. Located in the Palace of the Cadenas, a 19th century mansion built by Garnier, the architect of the Paris Opera. The training sessions can be watched, plus a tour of the stables, on 4 days a week, 1100-1300; entrance 425 ptas. On Thur an 'equestrian ballet' is performed by the Dancing Horses of Andalucía at 1200, entrance 1750 ptas. Many tour companies combine the horse show with a *bodega* visit. Jerez's equestrian tradition is further demonstrated at the **Feria del Caballo** (Horse Fair), see Local festivals below.

Bodegas Most visitors to Jerez will want to visit one of the famous sherry cellars, most of which welcome visitors and offer guided tours and free tasting. There is usually a demonstration by a vintner who dips his *venencia* (a silver cup on the end of a long pole) into a barrel and pours the sherry into the four glasses in his left hand without, of course, spilling a drop. It is best to phone beforehand as the largest bodegas may be fully booked with organized tours. The largest bodegas are **González Byass**, C/Manuel María González, T 340000, whose tour used to feature a famous drunken mouse, but he is long gone, believed to have been consumed by a snake – no doubt he was inebriated at the time. Visits at 1000, 1045, 1130, 1215, 1300 and 1345 by prior reservation; Cost – 300 ptas; **Pedro Domecq**, C/San Ildefonso 3, T 331900, visits at 1000, 1100 and 1200 by prior reservation. Visits are free. The smaller bodegas include **Sandeman**, C/Pizzaro 10,

the row above and so on. The top row is then filled up from the current vintage. The *solera* system ensures that the wine keeps the characteristics of the older stock and maintains its quality and taste. The success of the *solera* system relies on the skills of the *bodega* manager and his foreman the *capataz*. Samples of wine are taken from the butts by means of a *venencia*, which is a small silver cup attached to a flexible stick. The amber liquid cascades down into tall glasses called *cavatinos* and by taste, sight and smell the *capataz* decides on the future of the wine and its route through the barrels . The main sherry types are:

Fino – a very dry, delicate sherry, drunk cold and very popular in Andalucía as an accompaniment to sea food and *tapas*. It has a light straw like colour.

Oloroso – darker, sweeter, with a higher alcohol content and matures without *flor*.

Amontillado – in between a fino and an oloroso, it carries *flor* throughout its maturing, but is darker and sweeter with a rather 'nutty' aroma.

Manzanilla – comes from the coastal *bodegas* of Sanlucár where the higher humidity, lower temperatures and salt laden air produce *flor* throughout the year, giving a very distinctive flavour. Usually drunk with seafood.

Cream sherries – smooth and sweetened by the addition of *muscatel* or *Pedro Ximénez* grapes. Very popular in northern European countries such as UK and Holland.

Some well known sherries are a blend of different sherry types. Williams and Humberts Dry Sack, for example, is a blend of oloroso, amontillado and *Pedro Ximénez*. Surprisingly, apart from in Andalucía, sherry is not a popular drink in Spain, but this has not affected production as most of the sherry is exported. Some 70% goes to Britain, continuing the connection which has lasted since the 14th century. The members of the sherry 'dynasties' often appear more 'English than the English', with their polo horses, tweeds and British public school education, leading to the derisive description of them as 'señoritos' or little gentlemen – the nearest you will get to snobbery is this land of the amber nectar.

T 301100, visits 1030 and 1330, highly recommended; **Williams and Humbert**, C/ Nuno de Canas 1, T 331300, visits at 1200 and 1300. Cost-300 ptas; **Wisdom and Walker**, C/ Pizarro 7, T 184306, visits at 1230 and 1345, except Thur at 1100 and 1400. Cost – 250 ptas; **Harveys**, C/Arcos 53, T 151030, visits at 1200. Cost – 300 ptas. The bodega buildings themselves are of considerable interest as each has a unique character. The domed structure at González Byass, for example, was designed by Gustav Eiffel, architect of the Eiffel Tower, while that at Domecq is a mass of rounded arches based on the Mezquita at Córdoba. Note that the bodegas may be closed in late Aug/early Sep when the grape harvest or *vendimia* takes place, but this in itself is a marvellous festival, so the visitor should not feel deprived.

Local festivals

Traditional Easter processions take place during *Semana Santa*. The impressive *Feria del Caballo* (Horse Fair) is held in May, marked by races, shows and competitions featuring the locally bred Cartuja horses and 17th century traditions. In the week prior to 24 Aug the *Fiesta de la Vendimia* takes place celebrating and blessing the grape harvest. The *Circuito de Jerez* race track hosts the Spanish Grand Prix in Sep. Also in Sep during the first fortnight is the *Fiesta de la Bulería*, a festival of song and dance. The month ends with the feast day of the patron Saint of Jerez, La Virgen de la Merced.

Local information
● **Accommodation**
There are a number of luxury hotels in Jerez, all of which can be confidently rec, and plenty of cheap *pensiones* nr to the town centre.

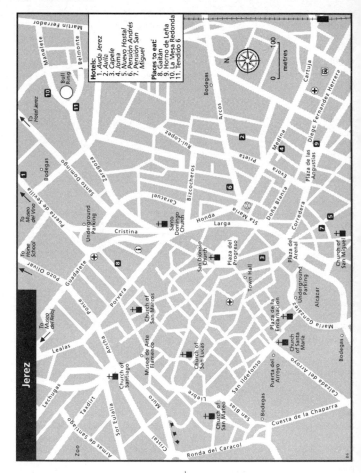

Hotels:
1. Avda Jerez
2. Avila
3. Capele
4. Joma
5. Nuevo Hostal
6. Pensión Andrés
7. Pensión San Miguel

Places to eat:
8. Gaitán
9. Horno de Leña
10. La Mesa Redonda
11. Tendido 6

There is little choice, however, in the intermediate range. **NB** High season rates in Jerez tend to be charged during the *feria* rather than in high summer.

AL *Cueva Park*, Ctra de Arcos, Km 10, T 189120, F 189121, 44 rm, garage, pool, a/c, wheelchair access, out of town location with every facility; **AL** *Don Tico*, Ctra NIV, Km 628.5, T 185906, F 181604, 70 rm, a/c, pool, tennis, out of town location; **AL** *Guadalete*, C/Duque de Abrantes 50, T 182288, F 182293, 137 rm, garage, pool, a/c; **AL** *Jerez*, Avda Alcade Alvaro Domecq 35,

T 300600, F 305001, 120 rm, quiet location on N side of town, pool, sports facilities; **AL** *Montecastillo*, Ctra Jerez-Arcos, Km 9.6, T 151200, F 151209, 120 rm, pool, a/c, wheelchair access, quiet location; **AL** *Royal Sherry Park*, T 303011, F 311300, 173 rm, recently built, pool, gardens, a/c, wheelchair access, quiet location.

A *Avenida Jerez*, Avda Alcade Alvaro Domecq 11, T 347411, F 337296, 95 rm, a/c, garage, walking distance of the centre; **A** *Doña Blanca*, C/Bodega 11, T 348761, F 348586, 30 rm, garage, a/c.

B *Capele*, C/Corredera 58, T 346400, F 346242, 30 rm, garage, a/c, central position; **B** *Joma*, C/Higueras 22, T 349689, 29 rm, close to the town centre.

C *Aloha*, Ctra Jerez-Madrid, Km 637, T 302500, a/c, pool, quiet out of town location; **C** *Avila*, C/Avila 3, T 334808, F 336807, 32 rm, a/c.

D *Torres*, C/Arcos 29, T/F 323400, a/c, wheelchair access.

Most of the *pensiones* are located in the area immediately to the E of the town centre, conveniently close to both the bus and train stations.

D *Nuevo Hostal*, Caballeros 23, T 331600, 27 rm, in an elderly building of some charm, in the shadow of the Iglesia de San Miguel.

E *Las Palomas*, C/Higueras 17, T 343773, 41 rm, clean, quiet location; **E** *San Andrés*, C/Morenos 12, T 340983, 26 rm, basic, central location; **E** *Santa Rosa*, C/Gaspar Fernández 8, T 347082, F 323400, 42 rm, garage, central position.

Youth hostels: Avda Carrero Blanco 30, 11408 Cádiz, T 342890, S edge of town, 128 beds, shared rooms, meals available, suitable for wheelchair users, sports facilities. IYHF card required.

Camping: there are no camp sites in the Jerez vicinity. The nearest sites are approx 25 km W on the Atlantic coast between **Rota** and **El Puerto de Santa María**. El Pinar de Chipiona, Ctra Chipiona-Rota, Km 3, Chipiona, T 372321, restaurant, bar, beach; **Punta Candor**, Ctra Chipiona-Rota, Km 13, Rota, T 813303, 1st category, restaurant, beach, bar, fishing; **Guadalete**, Ctra Madrid-Cádiz N IV, Km 658, 1st category, restaurant, bar beach, pool, launderette; **Playa las Dunas de San Antón**, Paseo Marítimo, Playa de la Puntilla, El Puerto de Santa María, T 8701112, 1st category, restaurant, bar, launderette, beach, tennis, fishing.

● **Places to eat**

The best restaurants of international standard are undoubtedly in the *comedores* of the luxury hotels, such as: ♦♦♦*El Cartujo*, Hotel Jerez, Avda Alvaro Domecq, T 300600; ♦♦♦*Las Cadenas*, Hotel Sherry Park, Avda Alvaro Domecq, T 303011; ♦♦♦*Montecastillo*, Ctra Arcos, Km 8, T 189210.

For a more local flavour at reasonable prices: ♦♦*Gaitán*, C/Gaitán 3, T 345859, modern and traditional cuisine, good seafood, closed Sun; ♦♦*El Bosque*, Avda Alvaro Dornecq, T 303333, traditional Andalucían specialities; ♦♦*La Mesa Redonda*, C/Manuel de la Quintana 3, T 340069, more local cuisine; ♦♦*Tendido 6*, C/Circo 3, T 344835, located nr the bullring, fish specialities.

As in nearby El Puerto, it is the local habit to buy fresh fish and shellfish from *freiduria* and *marisquerias* and take them to a bar to eat with a drink. One of the most popular *freidurias* is **El Boqueron de Plata**, Plaza Santiago.

● **Bars**

There is a multitude of *tapas* bars to choose from, with the local *fino* the usual accompaniment. Try **Bar Juanito**, C/Pescadería Vieja 4 (just off the Plaza del Arenal), and **Bar La Valencia**, C/Larga 3, right in the main shopping area.

● **Banks & money changers**

Branches of the main Spanish banks and savings banks are found around the Plaza Romero Martínez and in C/Larga. There are numerous Telebanco cash dispensers.

● **Embassies & consulates**

Denmark, C/Manuel González 12, T 340000; France, Ctra Madrid-Jerez, Km 634.6, T 302354; Germany, C/Pizzaro Bodegas Sandeman, T 301100; Italy, C/Manuel González 12, T 340000; Portugal, C/Manuel Gonzalez 12, T 340000.

NB There are no British or American consulates in the area. The nearest are in Sevilla.

● **Hospitals & medical services**

First Aid from **Casa de Socorro**, C/Diego Fernández Herrera 5, T 341349; *Cruz Roja*, C/Alcubillas s/n, T 341549. For urgent treatment *Sanitorio de Santa Rosalla*, C/Cañada de Miraflores, T 181650; also *Hospital de Santa Cruz*, Avda de la Cruz Roja s/n, T 307454.

● **Entertainment**

Cinemas: there are 3 cinemas in Jerez: *Delicias*, Paseo de la Delicias s/n, T 349642; *Jerezano*, Plaza de San Andrés s/n, T 341845; *Luz Lealas*, C/Lealas s/n, T 183347.

Discos: much of the night life of Jerez goes on in the area around and to the N of the bullring. Some of the more popular discos incl: *Cupola*, Plaza Aladros s/n; *Mool*, Avda de México s/n; and *Scorpio*, Ctra de Arcos.

Flamenco: can be seen at the *Bar Rociero*

Camino del Rocío, C/Velázquez; *Tablao Flamenco los Jereles*, Plaza Cocheras. For the real thing, however, go to the gypsy quarter of Santiago to the *peñas* (flamenco clubs). Try *Peña la Buena Gente*, C/Lucas 9; or *Peña Antonio Chacon*, C/Salas 2. No point in arriving before 2230. *Flamenco* festivals are often held in the town during the summer. Ask the tourist office for details.

Theatre: the one theatre in Jerez is the *Teatro Villamarta*, C/Romero Martínez s/n. The tourist office will have details of performances.

● **Post & telecommunications**
Area code: 956.

Post Office: *Correos*, C/Veracruz, off C/Santa María. Open Mon-Fri 0800-2100, Sat 0900-1400, T 349295. Telegrams by telephone T 341692.

Telephones: there are numerous call boxes throughout the city.

● **Shopping**
The main shopping streets are between Plaza del Arenal and Plaza Romero Martínez, particularly C/Larga and C/Veracruz. Shops selling local craftwork incl *La Esparteria*, C/Ramón de Cala 17, for wickerwork; *Cerámica Amaya*, Avda Carrero Blanco 16, for pottery; and *Ferros*, C/La Torre 4, for lanterns. There is a street market in the Plaza de la Asunción on Sun.

Sherry: the *fino* and brandy for which the town is renowned can be bought direct from the *bodegas* or from supermarkets.

● **Sport**
There is an Olympic standard all purpose stadium in Jerez – *Complejo Deportivo Chapin*, located on the E outskirts of the town, T 342131. There are 2 swimming pools – *Piscinas Jerez*, Ctra Arcos, T 340207; and *Piscina Cubierta*, C/Poseidón s/n, T 312245.

● **Tour companies & travel agents**
Ecuador, C/Consistorio 8, T 331150; *Marsans*, C/Larga 53, T 341010; *Sherrytours*, Plaza de la Yerba 4, T 343912.

● **Tourist offices**
C/Alemeda Cristina 7, T 331150. Helpful staff, with a good supply of town plans, will give information on sherry visits and flamenco possibilities.

● **Useful addresses**
Garages/car repairs: most of the large car firms cluster along the Ctra Madrid-Cádiz on the N outskirts of the town. *Citroën*, J Paez SA, Ctra Madrid-Cádiz s/n, T 344401; *Ford*, Ctra Madrid-Cádiz, Km 634, T 305200; *GM*, Ctra N IV, Km 635, T 304766; *Peugeot*, Autosherry, Ronda Muleres 12, T 344663; *Renault*, Ctra Madrid-Cádiz, Km 634, T 306900; *Seat/VAG*, Ctra Madrid-Cádiz, Km 635, T 306300.

● **Transport**
Local Bike hire: from Casa de la Juventud, C/Rosario 14, T 344314, 250 ptas a day with 1,500 ptas deposit. **Bus**: there are 12 local bus lines, mostly departing Plaza del Arenal, Plaza Esteve or Plaza Angustias. Lines 8 and 9 are circular. **Car hire**: ATASA, Hotel Royal Sherry Park, Avda Alcade Alvaro Domecq 11, T 311313; **ATESA**, Avda Alvaro Domecq 41, T 305831; **Avis**, C/Sevilla 25, T 344311 and Aeropuerto, T 325284; **Europcar**, C/Honda 18, T 334856; **Hertz**, C/Sevilla 10, T 335520; **Imperial**, T 324520; **Ital**, Plaza San Isabel s/n, T 348202; **Romecar**, C/Armas 10, T 338054. **Coches de Caballo** (horse drawn carriages): can be picked up in Alameda Cristina, nr to the tourist office. **Taxi**: tele taxi, T 344860.

Air National flight tickets and information from **Iberia**, Plaza del Arenal 2, T 339908. Daily flights to **Madrid**, less frequent to other cities and the Canary Islands. Airport information, T 334300.

Train Jerez is on the Sevilla-Cádiz line. There are numerous trains to both cities. Destinations in other parts of Andalucía will involve rather tortuous connections and changes, so the bus is usually quicker. Madrid can be reached via Sevilla and the high speed link.

Road Bus: long distance buses connect with Algeciras, Arcos, Chipiona, Conil, Granada, Jerez, Málaga, El Puerta de Santa María, Sanlúcar, Sevilla and Tarifa.

EXCURSIONS FROM JEREZ

Laguna de Medina This small fresh water lake is on most birding itineraries in SW Andalucía. It is located by the C440 Jerez-Los Barrios road, about 11 km from Jerez. Look for the large cement works opposite the lake. It is well signposted and there is a small car park. In the generally monotonous rolling landscape around Jerez, the path along the S side of the reserve provides a pleasant walk, even for those who are not bird watchers. In winter, there can be large concentrations of wildfowl including rarities such as Marbled Duck and Crested Coot. Breeding birds include Black-necked Grebe and Purple Gallinule, while raptors such as Marsh Harrier, Red Kite and Montagus Harrier are often around. The margins of the lake are particularly attractive to waders in the passage periods. This is also an excellent spot for dragonflies, butterflies and wild flowers. After a winter of low rainfall, the Laguna de Medina may dry up completely by Aug, as happened in 1993. Visitors are requested to keep to the path and avoid the N shore, which is privately owned.

La Cartuja Lying 4 km along the C440 to Medina Sidonia is the Carthusian monastery of La Cartuja. It has a long history, being founded in 1477. During the Peninsular War it was used as a barracks by French soldiers, who caused considerable destruction to the building and in 1835 it was closed down. It was given back to the Carthusians in 1949 and now supports a small closed order which continues its archaic traditions by refusing to allow women to participate in its late afternoon visits. The grounds are entered through an impressive gateway which leads to the church, which has a marvellous Baroque façade dating from the 1660s and is rich in carved stonework in a golden sandstone with a colony of Lesser Kestrels breeding among the niches and gargoyles. The interior of the monastery can be viewed with a guided tour on Tues, Thur and Sat, 1700-1830.

Medina Sidonia About 35 km SE of Jerez along the C440 is the ancient hill town of Medina Sidonia. Here a dukedom was created in the 15th century to the family of Guzmán el Bueno of Tarifa fame, who led the capture of Medina Sidonia from the Moors. It was one of the early Dukes who led the Spanish Armada in its ill-fated attack on England. The town is dominated by the 15th century Church of Santa María, built on the site of an old castle, parts of which still survive. The church is usually open for visitors, who will find the interior dominated by the massive Plateresque *retablo*. The church tower can be climbed and the exertion is rewarded by the impressive views N over the cliff edge and across the plains towards Arcos. Other places of interest include the three surviving Moorish gates, the churches of San Agustín and Santiago, the 18th century *ayuntamiento* and the ducal palace. There is little in the way of accommodation – Medina Sidonia is not really used to tourists – but visitors who reach the top of the hill will find that the small square outside the church has a good restaurant *Meson Bar Machín*, T 410850, with a dining room full of farming antiques, a terrace providing a wonderful view over the rooftops of the town and an economical *menu*.

Arcos de la Frontera Arcos, the most westerly of the *pueblos blancos*, has an unrivalled position sitting on a long ridge above a steep limestone cliff dropping down to the Río Guadalete. There is a sprawl of white houses, comparing dramatically with the brown sandstone of the castle and the churches. Remote from the Mediterranean coast, Arcos does not attract visitors to the same extent as, say, Ronda, but is all the more pleasant as a result. The town goes back to Roman times, when it was known as *Arco Briga*, but it was during Moorish times that it began to assume importance. It was once part of the Córdoba Caliphate and then later a *taifa* until in 1103 it came under the influence of Sevilla. It held out against the Christian forces until 1264 – an indication of its wonderful strategic location.

There is no rail link to Arcos, but *Comes* buses run regularly to Cádiz, Jerez and Ronda. The bus station is in the newer part of the town, in C/Corregidores. Visitors arriving by car should follow the advice on the signs and leave their car in the parking spaces in the square on the western edge of the town and walk from here. (There is a Tourist Office kiosk in the middle of the square which supplies a town plan.) The *barrio antiguo* or old part of the town is a maze of narrow streets which retain their Moorish pattern and is more suitable for donkeys than cars. The centre of the old quarter is the Plaza de España, with a *mirador* looking out over the cliff to the rolling countryside to the S. On the W side of the square is the 11th century Castillo established by the Ben Jazrum dynasty and now privately owned. Also in the square is the Church of Santa María de la Asunción. It was built on the site of a mosque in gothic-Mudejar style. The original bell tower fell during the 1755 Lisbon earthquake and the replacement was never completed, giving a certain asymmetry to the overall effect. The Plateresque S side is impressive. The interior is rather dismal, although the choir stalls attributed to Roldan should be viewed. The church is open 1000-1300 and 1600-1900, entrance 150 ptas. Moving E one passes the Convento de la Encarnación with just the church surviving, and on the right the Convent of the Mercedarias Nuns (dulces available). Ahead is the Church of San Pedro, built in the 15th century over a Moorish fort in Gothic style with pointed arches. It is worth looking around inside where the *retablo* is believed to have been designed by La Roldana, the daughter of Pedro Roldano. For a few pesetas it is worth climbing the tower for the spectacular view over the town and away to the Bornos reservoir to the NE. A further walk to the E end of the old town brings one to the Church of San Agustín, a former convent dating from 1539, and the Puertas Matrera, with an 11th century wall and tower.

The main, and rather sleepy, tourist office is on the C/Cuesta de Belén and you may be able to persuade them to produce details of the festivals in Arcos. The Holy Week processions are impressive and the floats have to be specially customized to negotiate the narrow streets. Also in Apr is the Bull Running day, when fighting bulls rampage through the streets, the local teenagers running before them, dodging into doorways and jumping up on street signs and balconies to evade the horns.

● **Accommodation** Most of the accommodation in the old part of the town is at the upper end of the range. Those looking for budget options will need to go to the newer area to the W. **AL** *Cortijo Faín*, Ctra de Algar, Km 3, T and F 701167, 6 rm, a small luxury alternative on the SE outskirts of the town, converted 17th century *cortijo*; **AL** *Parador Casa de Corregidor*, Plaza de España s/n, T 700500, F 701116, 24 rm, a/c, parking difficult in the square outside, great views; **B** *Los Olivos*, C/San Miguel 2, T 700811, F 702018, 19 rm, a/c, small hotel at quiet end of the town with good views over the cliff, can be reached by car without problems; **C** *El Convento*, C/Moldanado 2, T 702333, 8 rm, atmospheric accommodation in the old 17th century convent at the back of the *parador*. For something completely different: **C** *Meson de la Molinera*, Ctra Arcos-El Bosque, Km 6, T 700511, F 702967, 20 rm, pool, located at a development on the banks of the Bornos reservoir, watersports and a replica Mississippi paddle steamer. At the cheaper end of the range are: **D** *Andalucía*, Poligno Ind El Retiro, T 702718, 5 rm, restaurant, on the edge of an industrial estate on the Jerez road; **D** *Málaga*, C/Luis Cernuda 1, T 702010, 14 rm, a/c, clean, traditional, rooms with TV.

● **Places to eat** There is a surprising variety with a little detective work: ♦♦♦*El Convento*, C/Marqués de Torresoto 7, restaurant of the hotel of the same name, expensive local game dishes a speciality; ♦♦*Mesón Las Callejas*, C/Callejas 19, hostel restaurant with an economical *menu*. Those bored with Spanish food could try the following: ♦♦*Los Faraones*, C/Debajo del Corral, T 700612, genuine Turkish restaurant with regular belly dancers to aid the digestion, *menu del día* at 1300 ptas; ♦*La Gran Muralla*, C/Josefa Moreno Segura 2, T 704120, Chinese restaurant offering a *menu* at 800 ptas, plus set meals for groups of people at a variety of prices.

SOUTH FROM CADIZ

This part of Cádiz province along the Atlantic coast is known as the **Costa de la Luz** and remains mercifully under-developed, containing fine beaches, flower strewn meadows, salt flats, rolling farmland, mountains and a number of small, but fascinating villages.

The shore of the **Bay of Cádiz** is an officially designated National Park, covering some 10,000 hectares. The Bay itself is outstanding for its wintering wildfowl and seabirds. The shoreline has patches of dunes merging into salt marsh, much of which is used for the production of salt, so that entry is often forbidden. Although the N IV and the N340 cross the salt pans and bird watching is possible from a car on the hard shoulder, this is not encouraged and those who stop will often be subjected to a barrage of horns from passing motorists. The banks between the *salinas* are also of interest for botanists with a wide range of halophytic plants.

Leaving behind the salt marshes, the first town of note is **Chiclana de la Frontera**, a growing settlement of some 50,000 inhabitants, which is increasingly becoming a dormitory of Cádiz. Once known for its manufacture of traditional dolls, it now has a broader manufacturing base, with a ring of industrial estates to the S and E. The main development is to the SW of the town, where a road cuts through the pine woods to the Barrosa beach area. Offshore stands the island of Sancti-Petri, with the remains of a Temple of Hercules, a 13th century castle and a more modern lighthouse. Novo Sancti-Petri is a new tourist complex, with a 27-hole Ballesteros designed golf course (which was a contender for the 1997 Ryder Cup venue), a range of other sports facilities, apartments and three luxury hotels.

Back on the coast road, the N340, known here as the *Ruta de la Dos Mares*, runs S past the luxury development of **Roche**, where a road runs through pine woods and villas to the beach which is backed by low cliffs. The next settlement is **Conil de la Frontera**, surrounded by a prosperous market gardening area: it was once a minor fishing village but is now developing as a holiday resort, although as yet still unspoiled. It has two things in its favour – the old part of the town, which has plenty of character, and the broad sandy beach stretching for miles in each direction. The mouth of the small river Salado has been cleaned up from its formerly disgusting state with the construction of a new sewage works a kilometre or so upstream. To the NW of Conil are low cliffs and a scattering of small hotels, while to the S the dunes extend all the way through the hamlet of El Palmer to Cape Trafalgar.

Further along the coast road is the hill village of **Vejer de la Frontera** (*Pop* 13,000) located on a cliff above a gorge eroded by the Río Barbate. Dating back to Roman times, Vejer retains the atmosphere of its Moorish past, with its narrow streets, whitewashed patios and a ruined alcazar. Many guide books mention the fact that the women in Vejer still wear the *cobija*, a dark cloak which veils the face, a habit claimed to originate in North Africa. In fact, this habit died out some time ago. The only monument worth looking at is the 13th century Church of El Salvador. Built on the site of a mosque, it has a strange mixture of architectural styles, with gothic dominating. If you can gain admittance, look for the reredos, containing statues and tilework. The joy of Vejer is to wander around the maze of alleyways and narrow streets and drivers are advised to leave their cars in the newer part of the town. Visitors arriving by bus will probably find themselves dropped on the main road in the gorge. To get to the old part of Vejer on the top of the cliff will involve either a taxi, a long walk up the winding road or tackling a rough track. Each Easter Sunday, Vejer holds its annual *encierro* or running of the bulls. There are runs at midday and 1600. The good news is that this is a *toro embalao*, where the points of the bulls horns are wrapped in a protective sheath.

A minor road leads S from Vejer to the **Cabo de Trafalgar**, off which the Battle of Trafalgar took place in 1805. It was probably the most decisive sea battle of the Napoleonic war as nine French and nine Spanish ships were either captured or sunk without the loss of a single British ship. The British commander, Admiral Nelson, was unfortunately killed, his body being pickled in rum and taken to Gibraltar before being returned to London and the pomp of a burial in St Paul's Cathedral. Cape Trafalgar today displays no such drama. The actual cape is a small island marked by a lighthouse and linked to the mainland by a road along a sandy spit (geographers will recognize this feature as a 'tombolo'). Immediately to the E is the rather scruffy village of **Los Caños de Meca**. Its beach is magnificent but the overall effect is spoilt by unattractive apartment blocks. There are a couple of good camp sites and three *pensiones*, while some of the bars can get lively during the height of summer.

From here a road winds up into the pine woods and heads E to Barbate. Beneath the woods are some precipitous sandstone cliffs, the site of a large colony of over 2,500 pairs of nesting Cattle Egrets, along with smaller numbers of Little Egrets, Peregrines and Ravens. The road eventually drops down into **Barbate de Franco**, which must be one of the least attractive towns in Andalucía. Situated to the W of the estuary of the none too clean Barbate River, it is a fishing port with an important canning industry. The fish dock spreads for 2 km between the town and the cliffs, while the town itself has few attractions. The fishing and canning industries provide work for many of the inhabitants of Conil, Zahara and Barbate, with tuna the most important catch. The methods of catching the tuna have changed little for centuries. Shoals pass along the coast between Apr and Jun on their way to spawn in the Mediterranean, returning in Jul and Aug. The tuna, which can weigh up to 800 kg, are herded into nets where they are hooked and hauled into the boats. Much of the tuna goes to Japanese and Korean factory ships waiting off shore, but the catch has dwindled in recent years, no doubt due to over fishing. Southeast of Barbate is an area of rubbish dumps and salt pans, before an extensive area is reached which is occupied by the military. The magnificent beach is unfortunately out-of-bounds and drivers should not stop on the road.

After 5 km, **Zahara de los Atunes** is reached. The place name is literally translated as 'Flower of the Tuna Fish' and the village has, along with Barbate and Tarifa, an important tuna fishing industry. Its chief attraction is its broad sandy beach, which for much of the year is totally deserted. For an 'away from it all' weekend or for birding breaks, there are four small hotels and a *pensión*. East of Zahara is a small upland area known as the Sierra de la Plata, whose main claim to fame is that it was the first European breeding site of the White-rumped Swift, which uses the old nests of Red Rumped Swallows. The sierra also has breeding colonies of Griffon and Egyptian Vultures.

Further military land means returning to the N340 before coming back to the coast at **Bolonia**, the road leading through the famous 'painted fields', noted for their wild flowers attracting botanists from throughout Europe. In Jan the Paper White Narcissus are in full display and the colours and varieties increase during the spring. By late Apr

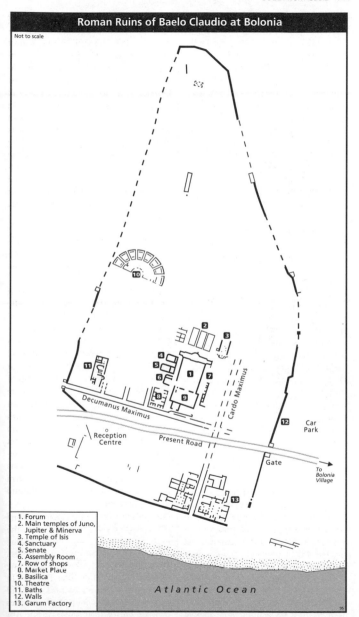

Roman Ruins of Baelo Claudio at Bolonia

Not to scale

Decumanus Maximus

Cardo Maximus

Reception Centre

Present Road

Car Park

Gate

To Bolonia Village

Atlantic Ocean

1. Forum
2. Main temples of Juno, Jupiter & Minerva
3. Temple of Isis
4. Sanctuary
5. Senate
6. Assembly Room
7. Row of shops
8. Market Place
9. Basilica
10. Theatre
11. Baths
12. Walls
13. Garum Factory

the verges and fields, which have never experienced weedkiller or plough, are a riot of colour, with squills, clovers, lupins, irises, vetch and many more. Reaching Bolonia itself, the major attraction (apart from the magnificent beach) is the remains of the old Roman town of **Baelo Claudia**. Thought to have been founded in 171 BC, the town was at the height of its importance during the 1st century AD. Under Emperor Claudius it was given the rank of 'municipum' thriving on the salting of fish and production of fish sauces, as well as being an administrative centre for the surrounding area. Its decline came with the restaurant of the Roman empire, hastened in all probability by earthquakes. The excavations began in 1917 and have continued intermittently since then. The remains have been partially excavated from the sand, revealing a main street; temples to Jupiter, Juno and Minerva; and a rectangular forum, on one side of which is a basilica and lines of shops or *tabernae*. The town evidently extends much further up the hill, where a theatre has been discovered, although this cannot be seen at the moment. The baths are in the E of the city and were probably private. Three aqueducts brought water to the city, where it was stored in tanks. The necropolis was situated, as was the custom, outside the city walls. For most visitors, however, the most interesting feature will probably be the fish factory which is located right on the beach. Large stone vats have been discovered, which apparently contained *garum*, a type of soupy fish paste composed of the otherwise unwanted bones, heads and entrails, which were stored in the vats with salt until mature. Garum was highly regarded and exported in amphorae throughout the Roman Empire. Guided tours of Baelo Claudia are available Tues-Sat at 1000, 1100, 1200, 1300, 1700, and 1800. Sun and festivals morning tours only. Closed Mon. A notice informs that entrance for Spaniards is free on production of their DNI, while 'foreigners' are obliged to pay 250 ptas. There is a small reception area nearby. If there is no sign of life, ask for Isodoro at the nearest bar. The village of Bolonia itself is rather a scruffy sprawl, redeemed only by some good fish restaurants. The 4 km long beach is superb (although wind can be a problem). There is a naturist area to the S and, apart from during Jul and Aug, your only companions are likely to be the local cattle, who seem to be able to wander around at will.

Approaching Tarifa, the coast road nears the beach. This is the **Playa de los Lances**, the best of the many fine sandy beaches along the Costa de la Luz. Behind the dunes, several small rivers form a shallow lagoon, backed by rough pasture with a wide variety of spring flowers. This is now a nature reserve and, as it is on a main migration route, it is usually productive, while the rivers here are said to contain otters. The beach is highly popular with wind surfers, but the same wind which makes this sport so thrilling here also means that anyone just wanting to loaf around on the beach will have to put up with an element of sand blasting.

An alternative inland route to the coast road runs through **Facinas**, past the Almodovar reservoir and over the Puerto de Ojén pass and down to **Los Barrios**, an attractive dormitory town for Algeciras. Delightful as this route is, it is currently in a very bad state, with some of the best potholes in Andalucía. The laying of pipes has also damaged the surface and one can only recommend 4WD vehicles attempting this route at present. The road passes through the SW part of **Los Alcornocales National Park**. Alcornocales means 'cork oaks' and these trees clothe the lower slopes, along with white poplars, myrtles, ash and alder along with a variety of ferns, contrasting with the bare rock of the upper slopes. A wide variety of mammals inhabit the park, including Mongoose, Otter, Polecat and Wildcat. Among the birds, there is a good selection of birds of prey, such as Griffon Vulture, Short Toed Eagle, Booted Eagle and Goshawk.

● **Accommodation** In the area S of Cádiz, the luxury accommodation is limited to the 3 golf hotels at Nuevo Sancti Petri: **AL** *Costa Golf*, Urb Novo Sancti Petri, T 494535, F 494626, 195 rm, a/c, sports facilities, wheelchair access, pool; **AL** *Playa la Barrosa*, Urb Novo Sancti Petri, T 494824, F 494860, 264 rm, garage, sports facilities, pool, wheelchair access, a/c; **AL** *Royal Andalus Golf*, Urb Novo Sancti Petri, T 494109, F 494490, 263 rm, garage, a/c, sports facilities, pool, wheelchair access.

At **Conil** the following are rec: **A** *Fla-*

Cork in the bottle

The native evergreen Cork Oak *Quercus suber*, which flourishes in the humid and gentle hillslopes of SW Iberia is highly prized for its commercial value. It is instantly recognized by its orange brown smooth trunk where the bark has been stripped away from the ground up to the main branches. Growing to a height of 10-15m, the Cork Oak can live for up to 800 years, although harvesting its bark can reduce its life span by up to 200 years. It takes 20 years for the first bark to be ready to cut and thereafter it takes another 7 years for the bark to regenerate, although it will not be until the third harvest, when the tree is approaching 50-years-old, that the top quality cork is produced.

Many of the old cork estates have been split up and used for housing development, but a number of the cork trees have survived, so that many a villa owner has been surprised to receive a visit from the 'cork man', who will negotiate a price for the product. He will be followed later by the *peladores*, who working in pairs can cut around 600 kilos of bark a day. The cylinders of bark are cut off with axes and the tree immediately starts to bleed resin. This protects the tree until the new bark begins to grow the following spring. The flattened slabs of bark called *planchas* are taken away by lorry to processing plants, such as those in the Jimena valley and near San Roque, where they are left in the sun to season before being boiled to reduce the tannin content and soften the material. The sheets are then taken away to factories for the final processing.

Cork is, of course, best known as a stopper in wine bottles, a practice widely introduced in the 17th century, thereby revolutionizing the storage of wines. Previously the wine had been stored in barrels and was only poured into bottles for consumption, where it could not be kept long before deteriorating. The advent of corks meant that the wine could now mature in the bottle. It is essential that the stopper is kept in contact with the wine, which is the reason why the bottles are usually stored on their sides. The corks are often printed with the bodegas name or crest, usually branded under heat. Despite much research, no synthetic substitute has yet been produced which is better than the natural cork stopper.

The Cork Oak tree itself is a valuable part of the landscape, being attractive to birds and insects. The acorn or *alconoque* is the main food of the black Iberian pig, which gives the desirable ham known as *Jamon iberico*. The bark, of course, has many other uses as well as a bottle stopper. Its lightness, buoyancy and resistance to burning means that it makes an excellent material for insulation, while it has also been used for floor tiles, wall covering, gasket seals and formerly for cricket balls. Furthermore, there is evidence that the ancient Egyptians, seeking comfort to the end, used this most versatile of materials for lining coffins.

menco, C/Fuente de Gallo s/n, T 440711, F 440542, 120 rm, a/c, pool, wheelchair access, clifftop location, closed Nov-Mar; **C** *Garum*, Ctra N340, Km 24, T 443131, 19 rm, recently opened on the main coast road; **C** *Tres Jotas*, C/San Sebastián 27, T/F 440450, 39 rm, garage, comfortable small hotel on the road into town.

Unique accommodation at **Vejer** is at the restored monastery of **A** *Convento de San Francisco*, Plazeula s/n, T 451001, F 451004, 25 atmospheric rm, the hotel was previously occupied by Franciscan monks, good restaurant in the former refectory. At the other end of the range is **E** *La Posada*, C/Los Remedios 21, T 450258, 6 rm above a restaurant, garage.

Few visitors will want to stay at Barbate, but nearby **Zahara** offers some good possibilities: **B** *Gran Sol*, C/Sánchez Rodríguez s/n, T 439301, F 439197, 22 rm, garage, a/c, beach location, spotless, excellent restaurant; **C** *Doña Lola*, C/Thompson 1, T 439009, 11 rm, garage, a/c, by bridge over the tidal estuary.

Pensiones are hard to come by and are always full in the height of the summer.

For simple solitude in **Bolonia**, try **D** *Rios*, T 684320, a small pensión on a remote part of the beach with some modern rooms overlooking the sea; good fish restaurant.

● **Something different**: **AL** *Monte de la Torre*, Apto 66, Los Barrios, T 660000, 4 rm plus 2 apartments in an English owned, English style estate in one of Europe's largest cork oak forests, breakfast, but no other meals, good base for walking and bird watching.

● **Camping**: there is an abundance of camp sites in the area, incl 6 at Conil, 2 at Chiclana, 3 at Vejer and 3 at Barbate. Most are located on the coast or nr to the N340. The following are 1st category sites: *Caños de Meca*, Ctra Vejer-Caños, Km 10, T 750425, close to beach and Cape Trafalgar; *Camping Pinar Tula*, T 445500, good range of facilities, incl pool, on N340 nr Conil; *La Rana Verde*, Pago de la Rana s/n, Chiclana, T 494348; *Camping Vejer*, Ctra N340, Km 39, Vejer, T 450098, good range of facilities incl pool.

THE CAMPO DE GIBRALTAR

The southern part of Cádiz province (and the most southerly tip of mainland Spain) is known as the Campo de Gibraltar and stretches from Tarifa in the W to the border with Málaga province in the E, including the sea port of Algeciras. If the graffiti on the walls is anything to go by, the locals would prefer some autonomy from Cádiz.

TARIFA

(*Pop* 14,500; *Alt* Sea level)

ACCESS Air The nearest airport is in Gibraltar, which is accessible by international flights only. For internal Spanish flights, Jerez airport (120 km) can be reached by the daily Comes bus to Jerez or in 2 hrs by car. Málaga airport is 164 km E along the coast road.
Train The nearest station is in Algeciras at the end of the line from Madrid.
Road There are frequent buses from Algeciras to Tarifa. Car drivers should turn off the N340, part of the *Ruta de la Dos Mares*, which bypasses the town.

Tarifa, 21 km W of Algeciras and only 14 km N of Morocco, is the southernmost town on the Iberian peninsula. Its exposed position between the Atlantic Ocean and the Mediterranean Sea at the entrance to the Straits of Gibraltar has recently brought it new prosperity as a windsurfers' paradise, causing its population to double during the summer months. Tarifa has both Carthaginian and Roman origins (when it was known as *Julia Traducta*). Although its name is said to mean 'wind' in Arabic, it is generally accepted that Tarifa was named after Tarif Ibn Malik who in 710 led the first Moorish exploratory raid across the straits with 500 Berbers, returning the next year with a force of 12,000 men. The town was recaptured from the Moors in 1292 by Sancho IV, but their attempt to regain it 2 years later is more memorable. During the siege, the Moors threatened to murder the young son of the

Christian commander, Alonso de Guzmán, unless Tarifa surrendered. Guzmán's response was to throw down his own dagger preferring 'honour without a son to a son without honour'. Nobody apparently asked the opinion of the son who was duly murdered, while Guzmán acquired the title of *El Bueno* (the Good) and the lands which later formed the dukedom of Medina Sidonia under his descendants. Guzmán did not live much longer, however, for he was killed in the Battle of Sierra Gaucín in 1309. 50 years later Tarifa was again threatened by the Moors, led by Yusuf I of Granada. This time King Alfonso XI defeated them in the decisive Batalla del Salado in 1340. The fact that much of

Tarifa – the wind surfers mecca

Wind surfing or Sail boarding or fun boarding – whatever you like to call it – is probably the world's fastest growing sport. Surfing, as such, probably goes back 2 centuries or more to the Polynesian Islands, and by the 1960's it had become part of the 'hippie' way of life in California. It was not until the early-70's that the idea of fitting a sail to the board was put into motion with the first windsurfing board being constructed in Holland. In the early days sailboarding could only take place on calm waters and changing direction was a fraught manoeuvre, but gradually there have been considerable technological advances to cope with rough water and strong winds.

Aficionados of the sport have increasingly searched for areas with strong and reliable winds, and eventually Tarifa was discovered, transforming it from a sleepy frontier town to the Mecca of European windsurfers within a matter of 15 years. Today it ranks alongside Fuerte Ventura in the Canary Islands and Hoopika in Hawaii as the top three locations in the world. The winds, the eastern *Levante* and the western *Poniente*, can be so persistent as to drive local people to suicide, but these same conditions make wind surfing an all year round sport at Tarifa.

With the growth of the sport has come the trappings, such as shops selling windsurfing equipment and the associated fashion clothes, camp sites, hotels and other accommodation, and a string of wind surf schools providing coaching for surfers of all ability. All this has worked wonders for the economy of Tarifa and the surrounding area. The Playa de los Lances, immediately N of Tarifa is the main location for the windsurfing, but there is excellent sport to be had further N at Bolonia, Zahora, Barbate, Caños de Meca, Conil, Chiclana and even off the Playa de Victoría at Cádiz, but the wind strength tends to lessen the further N one goes.

Visitors to Tarifa who decide to have a go at wind surfing should certainly get some instruction first. The local windsurfing schools always stress these 10 commandments:

- Familiarize yourself with local conditions before taking to the water.
- Check your equipment thoroughly before going out.
- Never go sailboarding alone.
- Be very careful of offshore winds.
- Never sail too far from the coast.
- Always tie the board to the sail.
- Never let go of the board.
- Always wear a wet suit.
- Never go out late in the afternoon – latest is 2 hrs before sunset.
- Do not put others at risk, such as swimmers and other surfers.

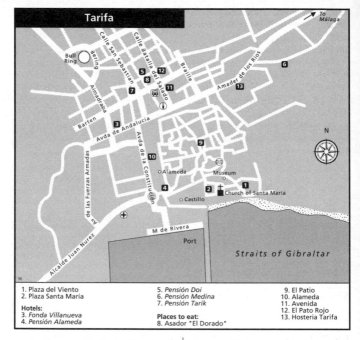

Tarifa

To Málaga

Calle San Sebastian

Calle batalla del Salado

Braille

Amader de los Ríos

Bull Ring

Almadraba

Barten

Avda de Andalucia

Avda de la Constitución

Av de las Fuerzas Armadas

Alcalde Juan Nurez

Alameda

Museum

Castillo

Church of Santa Maria

M de Rivera

Port

Straits of Gibraltar

N

1. Plaza del Viento
2. Plaza Santa María

Hotels:
3. *Fonda Villanueva*
4. *Pensión Alameda*

5. *Pensión Doi*
6. *Pensión Medina*
7. *Pensión Tarik*

Places to eat:
8. Asador "El Dorado"

9. El Patio
10. Alameda
11. Avenida
12. El Pato Rojo
13. Hosteria Tarifa

the land around Tarifa has historically been in the hands of the military and the fact that the exfoliating *levante* wind is blowing for much of the time, it explains why the magnificent beaches to the N of the town have remained undeveloped. On the hills to the NE of Tarifa, wind farms take advantage of the wind to generate enough electricity for Tarifa and a surplus to export to Morocco. From two or three experimental wind mills in 1981, there are now thousands covering the hillsides as far as the eye can see. Environmentalists are divided – they are certainly a clean and renewable form of energy – but it can be argued that they are a form of visual pollution, which certainly provide a hazard for the migrating storks, vultures and eagles. No research on the effect on the birds was carried out before the expansion.

Places of interest

The Castillo de Guzmán el Bueno was built between 950 and 960 when the Caliph of Córdoba, Abd Al-Rahman III, decided that the area needed defending against any invasion from North Africa. A small town grew up around the castle, in the quarter now known as the Barrio de Jesús. The tower known as the **Torre de Guzmán** is more modern. The whole site is still controlled by the Spanish army and although the castle is closed to the public, it is possible to climb up to the ramparts. The **Church of Santa María** stands in a delightful square of the same name adjacent to the castle. Also in the square is the *ayuntamiento* and a small museum (entrance free). East of the square is a charming promenade with a *mirador* looking out towards North Africa. Close to the town walls is the **Church of San Mateo**, a 15th century Gothic church built on the site of a mosque. Unusual for a church in this position, it has some interesting stained glass windows, while the rib vaulting in the nave is also of importance.

The *Al-Medina Bar* in C/Almedina off Plaza Santa María is also worth a visit for a quick drink since it has an entrance arch which was originally a point of access to the castle.

Local festivals

6 Jan: procession for the *Día de los Reyes*; **Feb**: *Carneval* marked by dancing, costumes, masquerades, etc; Traditional processions mark *Semana Santa*; **15 May**: *Romería del Conejo*, pilgrimage in honour of San Isidro; **24 Jun**: the fiesta of *San Juan* is celebrated with bonfires in nearby **Facinas**; **Jul**: first fortnight of Jul, *Feria de Tahivilla*; **16 Jul**: *Fiesta del Carmen*, the statue of the *Virgen del Carmen* is taken out to sea in a fishing boat to bless the waters; **Aug**: first fortnight in Aug, *National Folk Muisic Festival*; **Sept**: in early Sept a fair, fiesta and pilgrimage in honour of *Nuestra Señora de la Luz*, patron saint of Tarifa.

Local information
● **Accommodation**

NB Hotels in the area tend to be relatively expensive due to Tarifa's windsurfing resort status. Beach hotels are often closed in the winter, but those which remain open have much reduced rates.

A *Balcón de España*, Ctra Nacional 340, Km 76, T/F 684326, 40 rm, garden, pool, riding, tennis, parking; **A** *Dos Mares*, T 684035, F 681078, 17 rm, pool, tennis, bike hire, restaurant, wind surfing school, parking; **A** *Hurricane*, Ctra Nacional 340, Km 77, T 684919, 28 rm, garden, pool, squash, horse riding, wind surfing, health club, beach, parking.

C *La Cordoniz*, Ctra N340, Km 79, T 684744, F 684101, 35 rm, wheelchair access, parking; **C** *La* **Ensenada**, Ctra N340, Km 76, T/F 680637, 22 rm, garage, pool; **C** *Mesón de Sancho*, Ctra N340, Km 94, T 684900, F 648721, 17 rm, garage, pool, tennis.

Pensiones: it is very difficult to find cheap accommodation in Tarifa, owners of even the most basic *pensión* ask and get inflated prices due to the massive influx of tourists during the season. The following *pensiones* all have rooms with bath: **C** *Tarik*, C/San Sebastián 36, T 685240; **D** *Alameda*, Paseo Alameda 4, T 681181, 11 rm, central position; **D** *Correo*, opp Post Office, popular, clean; **D** *Dori*, C/Batalla Salado 55, T 685317, 8 rm, can be noisy; **D** *La Calzada*, C/Justino Pertíñez 7, T 684366, in old town; **D** *Medina*, C/Algeciras 26, T 684904, 13 rm; **E** *Fonda Villanueva*, Avda Andalucía, nr tourist kiosk, some rooms with bath, clean, pleasant, secure and modern.

Youth hostels: the nearest is in Algeciras in the Parque Natural 'Los Canutos', T 679060, 10 km from Tarifa, 108 beds, meals, parking, sailing.

Camping: plenty of choice of camp sites all located close to the beach to the N of Tarifa. All those mentioned below are 2nd category: *Paloma*, Ctra N340, Km 70, T 684203, beach, restaurant, bar, riding; *Río Jara*, Ctra N340, Km 80, T 680570, beach, bar, riding; *Tarifa*, Ctra N340, Km 79, T 684778, restaurant, bar, launderette, beach; *Torre de la Peña I*, Ctra N340, Km 78, T 684903, restaurant, bar, launderette, beach; *Torre de la Peña II*, Ctra N340, Km 75, T 684174, restaurant, bar, beach.

● **Places to eat**

◆◆◆*Alameda*, Paseo de la Alameda, nicely positioned, good sea food and *platos combinados*; ◆◆◆*Méson de Sancho*, Ctra N340, Km 94, for those with transport this is worth the drive a few kilometres E to this excellent roadside restaurant; ◆◆◆*El Rincón de Manolo*, Ctra N340, Km 76, T 643410, probably the most expensive restaurant in Tarifa, with outstanding fish and shell fish.

◆◆*Avenida*, C/Batalla del Salado, reasonable *platos combinados*; *Hosteria Tarifa*, C/Amador de los Rios, T 684076, steak house.

◆ The cheaper food is found along and around the C/Batalla del Salado, the old main road W out of Tarifa. *Asador de Pollos*, 'El Dorado', C/Batalla del Salado 37, chicken and chips to take away; *Bar Freiduría Parame*, C/Huerta del Rey, T 681435, fresh fish; *El Pato Rojo*, C/Batalla del Salado 47, cheap *menú*; *Freiduría Sevilla*, C/Sancho IV el Bravo.

● **Banks & money changers**

There are 2 banks on C/Sancho IV el Bravo, 2 on C/Nuestra Señora de la Luz, 1 on Avda de Andalucía and 1 on C/Batalla del Salado.

● **Entertainment**

Bullfights: the Plaza de Toros is in C/Bering, check locally for the next bullfight.

● **Hospitals & medical services**
Hospitals: *Cruz Roja*, C/Juan Nuñez 5, T 684896; *Servio de Urgencia* (emergencies), C/Calzadilla Téllez s/n, T 680779.

● **Post & telecommunications**
Area code: 956.

Post Office: *Correos*, C/Colonel Moscardó 9. Open Mon-Fri 0900-1400, Sat 0900-1200.

Telephones: there are numerous private *locutorios*, incl *Estudio 21*, C/Batalla del Salado 35; *Baelo International*, C/Sancho IV El Bravo 19.

● **Shopping**
Handicrafts: the *Bazar Hispano Arabe* in Avda de Andalucía sells leather goods, mainly imported from Morocco and other North African countries.

● **Sports**
Horse riding: enquire at *Hotel Dos Mares* (T 684035) or *Hotel Balcón de España* (T 684326).

Windsurfing: 21 recognized 'spots' requiring various degrees of expertise. Several shops in the town are devoted to windsurfing gear.

● **Tour companies & travel agents**
Marrucotour, C/Batalla del Salado 57, T 680256, plus another office on the N340; *Tourafrica*, Estsción Marítima, T 684751.

● **Tourist offices**
Cabin on Avda de Andalucía. Open only in the summer, hours variable.

● **Useful addresses**
Garages/repair workshops: *Ford*, Frandomar Auto, C/Braille 5, T 681443; *Renault*, Auto-Silva, Ctra N340, Km 84.

● **Transport**
Local Bike hire: enquire at *Hotel Dos Mares* (T 684035). **Car hire**: Citroën-Dal Auto, Avda Andalucía 18, T 643726; **El Estrecho**, C/Batalla del Salado 20, T 684147; **Maruecotour**, C/Batalla del Salado 57, T 684241. **Taxis**: Avda de Andalucía, T 684241.

Train The nearest station is at Algeciras.

Road Bus: the buses are operated by the Comes company. There are 12 buses a day to Algeciras; 8 to Cádiz; 3 to both Sevilla and Málaga; and 1 daily to Almería, Huelva, Jerez, Barbate and Facinas. The bus station is at C/Batalla del Salado 19, open 0900-1100 and 1600-1900 for booking and advance tickets. Other long distance buses can be caught in Algeciras, T 684038.

Sea Ferry: to Morocco departs Tarifa 1000 daily except Sun, return departs Tangier 1530. Takes approx 1 hr, T 684751.

EAST FROM TARIFA

The N340 rises quickly out of Tarifa eastwards, reaching 340m at the Puerto de Cabrito, surrounded by the ubiquitous wind farms. Just past this point is a *mirador*, with a small kiosk, giving fine views of North Africa. On clear days, individual buildings and minarets can easily be picked out on the Moroccan side of the straits.

The road continues eastwards dropping quickly down to the city of **Algeciras**. A busy container port of over 100,000 people and with an important petro chemical industry, Algeciras can hardly be called an attractive place and few people would think of a reason for lingering, unless they were waiting for a ferry. Pollution frequently hangs over the town and its high rise suburbs are dreary in the extreme. Algeciras is notable chiefly for its position at the end of the train line from Madrid and its proximity to Morocco. It has views across Algeciras Bay towards Gibraltar and the equally depressing town of La Linea. The recent opening of the long awaited Algeciras bypass has helped to relieve the town's traditional traffic congestion. As a major embarkation point for Tangier and Ceuta with frequent daily ferries to both, Algeciras becomes congested during the summer months as migrant Algerians and Moroccans return home from France, Belgium, Germany and the Netherlands. Tickets for North Africa can be purchased from kiosks all round the Campo de Gibraltar and also at the port on embarkation, from Transmediterráne, Recinto de Puerto, T 663850.

Algeciras gained its name from the Moorish *el Gezira el-Khadra* (Green Island). The Moors landed here when they first invaded Iberian soil in 711 under their commanders Musa and Tarik. The 'Pillars of Hercules' at either side of the Straits of Gibraltar are named after the

Moorish leaders – Jebel Tarik (Gibraltar) on the European coast after the general who led the invasion and Jubel Musa on the African coast after Musa Ibn Nusayr, his lieutenant.

A major Christian victory was achieved by Alfonso XI in 1344. Participation in this assault was referred to by a character in Chaucer's *Canterbury Tales* as an indication of knightly valour. A few decades later, in 1379, Algeciras was destroyed during a Moorish raid and had to be reconstructed by Carlos III. Consequently, the Moorish placenames are the only remaining traces of the centuries they spent in the town.

Today, with persistence, a few attractive corners of the town can be found, mostly in the area around Plaza Alta, with two interesting churches, Nuestra Señora de la Palma, dating from the 18th century, and Nuestra Señora de Europa with a neat Baroque façade.

Algeciras is an important communication centre. **Trains** connect with Madrid (3 daily), Córdoba, Granada, Málaga and Sevilla (although some of the journeys are slow and tortuous), while **buses** connect with Cádiz, Jerez, La Linea (for Gibraltar), Madrid (1

A second Moorish invasion

Visitors to the Costa del Sol in August will soon become used to seeing (and avoiding) car loads of Moroccan families returning to their own country for a holiday. These are 'guestworkers' travelling from Germany or France where they live and work quite legally. Their cars, which often travel in convoys, are usually overloaded with family and possessions. By the time they reach the ferry ports of Algeciras and Tarifa, the drivers are exhausted after what is often a more or less non stop journey. 4 weeks later they will make the return drive N, minus the cookers, fridges and bicycles they have left with their relatives.

These are the lucky ones who are returning N to a job, accommodation and schools for their children, but there is another type of immigrant from Morocco, whose journey may end in death. These are the illegal immigrants. Known as *espaldas mojadas* or wetbacks, they come to Spain in the hope of securing employment and a brighter future, but are ruthlessly exploited by the boat mafia.

The trade began in the late '80s. The wetbacks pay anything up to £600 to risk their lives in small open boats known as *pateras*, powered only by a 50 horsepower outboard. Designed for no more than six people and normally used for inshore fishing, some have been intercepted with as many as 40 passengers on board, earning their owners up to £20,000 a trip. The Straits of Gibraltar, whilst only 13 miles wide, are dangerous waters, with swirling currents and strong winds. When the *levante* is blowing at full strength even 5,000 ton ferry boats may be confined to harbour. Inevitably, many *pateras* sink. Sometimes the wetbacks are put over the side well off the beach and non-swimmers may not make it to the shore. As the *pateras* have no radios or life saving equipment, they can sink without trace. The Spanish authorities believe that over 1,000 illegal immigrants may have perished in this way over the last 10 years.

But for every wetback drowned, thousands of the Moroccans do make it and quickly disappear into the interior. Many are picked up by the police and held in special camps where they are looked after by the Red Cross. As they have no papers and refuse to say where they have come from, it is difficult for the authorities to expel them. Those who do evade the police face an uncertain future, lacking documents and confined to low paid work.

Watching the migration

Many birds migrate according to the season in order to take advantage of the optimum conditions for breeding. Whereas small songbirds migrate on a broad front, soaring birds tend to concentrate their routes. This is because their method of travelling is to soar and glide, rather than to fly strongly in a direct line. Soaring birds must therefore constantly seek thermals in order to gain height. This gives them problems when it comes to crossing large stretches of water, so they must seek routes where the water is at its narrowest point. Soaring birds in Europe (and we include here Storks, Eagles, Vultures and other birds of prey) will either use the Bosphorus in the east or the Straits of Gibraltar in the west. This means that the majority of the soaring, migratory birds of the western side of Europe will pass over the Tarifa/Gibraltar area twice a year, travelling northwards in the Spring and southwards in the Autumn.

When to watch the migration

Migration across the Straits of Gibraltar takes place, in fact, almost the whole year round, but the most significant northward movements are between mid-Mar and the end of May, while the most important southbound movements are between late Aug to mid-Oct. Some species have concentrated periods of travel – the Honey Buzzard, for example, will be seen coming N during the first 3 weeks of May. Other species have a less exact timetable, with the White Stork moving north as early as Nov and as late as May. There are more birds involved in the Autumn, southbound migration which follows breeding, but on the other hand during the Spring, northbound migration the birds will seen at lower levels having just drifted across the straits. Generally speaking, the most rewarding months will be Apr and Sep.

Where to watch the migration

The most popular place is the *Mirador del Estrecho* on the N340 5 km E of Tarifa, a public viewing point with a small, overpriced kiosk. If this becomes too crowded with tourists there are a number of lay-bys in the vicinity. An alternative, especially for the northward Spring migration is *Punta Secreta*, a low headland due S of Algeciras, reached via the coast road from Algeciras to Getares Bay and moving on round the lighthouse. When westerly winds are blowing, Gibraltar can be rewarding. The Upper Rock Nature Reserve is an excellent spot for observing the migration, but there is a hefty entrance fee which includes admittance to the Apes Den and St Michaels Caves. There is, however, an observatory at Jews Gate, just past the entrance to the Reserve, manned by the Gibraltar Ornithological and Natural History Society who welcome visitors and can give information on the latest sightings. In selecting a viewpoint, remember that the wind direction is crucial as soaring birds will drift laterally with the wind. With westerly winds then, Gibraltar is likely to be the best bet, while with winds from the east the area around Tarifa is likely to be more profitable.

Other points to remember

● Binoculars are essential, and likely to be less cumbersome than a telescope.
● Birds of prey are most easily identified by their underwing pattern. A good field guide is therefore desirable. Any of the popular ones will do, but enthusiasts might want to obtain *Flight Identification of European Raptors*, RF Porter, *et al*, 1981, Poyser, London.
● Storks and larger raptors will not be active until around 1000, local time, when thermals are starting to form.

- Strong winds and persistent rain will stop movement.
- In very hot weather, the thermals will ensure that raptors will soar to high levels.

What species to expect

The following are the most common and regular migrants: Black Stork, White Stork, Honey Buzzard, Black Kite, Red Kite, Egyptian Vulture, Griffon Vulture, Short-toed Eagle, Marsh Harrier, Hen Harrier, Montagu's Harrier, Sparrowhawk, Buzzard, Booted Eagle, Osprey, Lesser Kestrel, Merlin , Hobby.

Rarer migrants include: Black Vulture, Goshawk, Spanish Imperial Eagle, Golden Eagle and Bonelli's Eagle.

For full details of the migration of raptors and storks in Andalucía, the following is recommended: *Where to Watch Birds in Southern Spain*, Ernest Garcia and Andrew Patterson, Christopher Helm, London

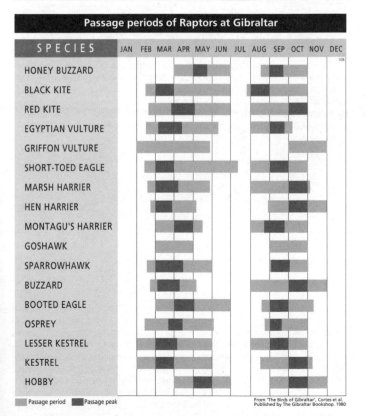

Passage periods of Raptors at Gibraltar

SPECIES	JAN	FEB	MAR	APR	MAY	JUN	JUL	AUG	SEP	OCT	NOV	DEC
HONEY BUZZARD												
BLACK KITE												
RED KITE												
EGYPTIAN VULTURE												
GRIFFON VULTURE												
SHORT-TOED EAGLE												
MARSH HARRIER												
HEN HARRIER												
MONTAGU'S HARRIER												
GOSHAWK												
SPARROWHAWK												
BUZZARD												
BOOTED EAGLE												
OSPREY												
LESSER KESTREL												
KESTREL												
HOBBY												

Passage period   Passage peak

From 'The Birds of Gibraltar', Cortes et al.
Published by The Gibraltar Bookshop. 1980

daily), Málaga, Sevilla and Tarifa. **Ferry boats** run to Tangier (6 daily) and Ceuta (9 daily), with seasonal hydrofoils to both of these ports. Note that the hydrofoils may not run in rough weather, which is a not infrequent occurrence.

• **Accommodation** There are a number of hotels in Algeciras for anyone unfortunate enough to need overnight accommodation. The best is **AL** *Reina Cristina*, Paseo de la Conferencia, T 602622, F 603323, 162 rm, a/c, pool, faded Victorian elegance. More reasonable in price are **A** *Alborán*, C/Alamo, Colonia San Miguel, T 632870, F 632320, 79 rm, a/c, wheelchair access; **A** *Al-Mar*, Avda de la Marina 2, T 654661, F 654501, 192 rm, garage, a/c, wheelchair access. As befits a sea port, there is

plenty of cheap accommodation to choose from, with over 30 *pensiones*. Many of these are pretty tatty – check the room before you part with any money. **E** *González*, C/José Santacana, T 652843, 19 rm, is at least brand new.

Continuing round the Bay of Algeciras, the hill village of **San Roque** appears to the left. It was founded in 1704 by people fleeing from Gibraltar, which had just been taken over by the British. They assumed that they would one day return to the Rock, but this, of course, was not the case. There is a pleasant main square, an 18th century church, an antiquated bullring and very little else. Even the view from the *mirador* is marred by the hideous petro-chemical works.

Will there ever be a land link to North Africa?

For many years there have been ferry links from Spain's most southerly ports of Tarifa and Algeciras to Tangier and to Spain's enclave of Ceuta, in North Africa. For those who suffer from motion sickness, the ferry crossing can often be rough, while the faster hydrofoil can frequently be cancelled because of the wind. So why not a land link in the form of a bridge or tunnel? After all, the Straits of Gibraltar are only 15 km wide at their narrowest point, while a tunnel has been constructed under the English Channel which is more than twice this distance.

Civil engineers have been applying themselves to this problem for years and now reject the idea of a bridge. Due to the depth of the water, it would be too expensive to construct, while the strong winds in the Straits would make it hazardous for vehicles making the crossing. So a tunnel it would have to be. But how would it be funded?

When the new Spanish Prime Minister, Jose María Aznar, came to power in mid 1996, one of the first things he did was to sign an agreement with the Moroccan Premier Abdellatif Filali giving the green light to the scheme. Although both countries would make a financial contribution, the bulk of the money would hopefully come from the EU structural funds. As the EU has shown a willingness to give aid to those countries, such as Morocco, who provide 'guestworkers' to the northern European countries, the possibility of funding is hopeful. Unlike the Eurotunnel, it is not felt that the tunnel would be sufficiently profitable to attract private investment.

Because of the depth of water at the narrowest point in the Straits, the tunnel would run well to the W, from near Tarifa to Tangier. In initial stage would involve the construction of a service tunnel 37.7 km long and dipping down to a dept of 450m. The main tunnel, in the second phase of the project, would have a diameter of 7.5m and contain a single track railway, which would use Eurotunnel type trains to carry vehicles. The completed project would aim to carry 12 million passengers, 2 million cars and 7 million tons of goods annually. Work *could* start in 1997 and if so it would provide welcome employment opportunities in both Andalucía and Morocco, where the numbers of those out of work are legendary. With an estimated completion date of 2009, however, no one is looking at this mega project in the short term.

From San Roque a road leads to **La Linea**, the main gateway to Gibraltar. If San Roque is dreary, La Linea is even worse. Its prosperity during this century has depended on the state of the border with Gibraltar. La Linea traditionally provided most of the workers in the naval dockyard and when Franco closed the border, many of the inhabitants were deprived of a livelihood. Today there is a poverty-stricken look about the place, particularly in the litter strewn fishing suburb to the E. There is, however, an attractive main square, the Plaza de la Constitución, with some good *tapas* bars in the side streets. The bus station is just off the main square and there is a regular bus service along the Costa del Sol to Málaga.

Things improve as the coast road runs E from San Roque over hills towards **Sotogrande**. This development is like a piece of Surrey stockbroker belt dropped down in southern Spain, with its manicured lawns, cricket pitches, polo fields and golf courses. On the coast is Puerto Sotogrande, probably the most upmarket of all the sport harbours along the *costa*. The Valderama golf course at Sotogrande is to host the Ryder Cup competition between Europe and the USA in 1997 and frantic efforts are being made to improve the infrastructure of this part of the coast.

The C3331 runs inland from San Roque following a parallel route to the railway line to Ronda. This is one of the best places in Andalucía for watching Storks, which nest enthusiastically on the railway pylons. After 10 km, a road branches off NW to **Castellar de la Frontera**, perched on a hilltop overlooking the Guadarranque reservoir. The original inhabitants were moved out in 1971 to Nuevo Castellar in the valley, their place taken by German and Dutch hippies looking for an alternative lifestyle. Old Castellar has a 13th century Moorish castle and considerable architectural interest, but the place has a rather sinister atmosphere and few visitors stay long. Plans to turn Castellar into a tourist complex with a *parador* (it has the potential) seem to have foundered.

A further 25 km away is **Jimena de la Frontera**, another hill town with a Moorish castle. This is in a good condition and has an impressive triple-arched entrance gateway. Jimena is notable for its surprisingly large colony of expat Brits, many of whom have their own businesses. From Jimena, the C341 climbs up through Gaucín, Algatocín and Benadalid to Ronda – one of the great scenic routes in Andalucía.

● **Accommodation**   Something different: **C Hostel El Anon**, C/Consuelo 34-40, 11330 Jimena de la Frontera, T 640113, F 641110, 12 rm, converted from 4 village houses and full of charming nooks and crannies, price for double room incl breakfast, restaurant, pool.

Córdoba Province

THE PROVINCE of Córdoba is the most northerly of the eight provinces of Andalucía and is completely landlocked. Spreading through the centre of the province is the broad Valley of the Rio Guadalquivir. At its heart lies Córdoba with its magnificent Mezquita. Olive trees stretch endlessly over the surrounding countryside. In the north is the little visited Sierra Morenna whilst in the south are the limestone ranges of the Sistema Subbético rising to over 1,000m in places.

HORIZONS

Three natural regions running east-west across the area. In the north is the **Sierra Morena**, which forms the border with Extremadura and Castilla, rising in places to over 900m. In the extreme northwest of the Sierra is the region known as Los Pedroches, which is a continuation of the steppe scenery from further north. The Sierra Morena has two natural parks: in the northeast is the Parque Natural de Sierra Cardeña Montoro, while in the west is the Parque Natural de la Sierra de Hornachuelos. Numerous reservoirs have been constructed on the lower slopes of the Sierra Morena. As in the neighbouring provinces, the Sierra Morena attracts few tourists, which is as good a reason as any for looking around.

The Río Guadalquivir, which rises to the E in Jaén province, flows to the W and over time has built up fertile plains, providing an important routeway for roads and railways.

In the S of the province is the **Sistema Subbético**, consisting of limestone ranges and narrow valleys covered with cork oaks. There are four ranges within the Subbetico rising to over 1,000m, the whole forming a Parque Natural. In the W of this region is an unexpected group of wetland sites or *zonas húmedas* covering some 10 sq km.

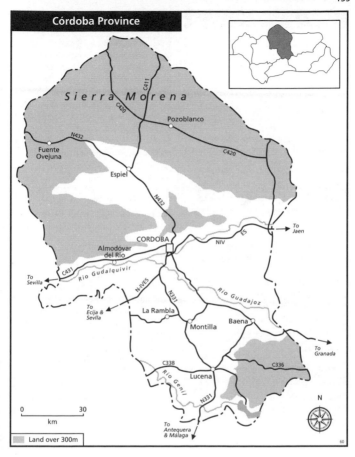

Córdoba Province

Sierra Morena

Pozoblanco

C411
C420
N432
C420

Fuente
Ovejuna

Espiel

N432

CORDOBA

ES
To
Jaen

NIV

Almodóvar
del Río

C431

Rio Gudalquivir

To
Sevilla

N-IVE5

N331

Río Guadajoz

To
Ecija &
Sevila

La Rambla

Montilla

Baena

To
Granada

C336

C338

Lucena

Río Genil

N331

0   30
km

To
Antequera
& Málaga

N

Land over 300m

60

CORDOBA

(*Pop* 300,000; *Alt* 124m)

ACCESS Air Nearest airport is in Sevilla.

Train The train station is on Avda de América on the N edge of town, a 20 mins walk from the old town via the commercial centre. Taxis are available and a local bus links with the centre.

Road The Ureña bus depot on Avda de Cervantes and the Alsina Graells on Avda de Medina Azahara are in the same area as the train station.

Córdoba is located on the fertile plains of the **Vega del Guadalquivir** 175 km N of the Mediterranean and some 140 km NE of Sevilla. The old part of Córdoba is situated on the N bank of Guadalquivir, which was once navigable as far as this point. Although known principally today for one building, the Mezquita or Moorish mosque, the city has a host of other attractions.

The history of Córdoba probably goes back to Neolithic times and there was certainly a Bronze Age settlement here based on the minerals of the Sierra Morena, but it was during Roman times that it sprang to prominence. Founded in 152 BC, it was known as *Corduba* and soon became a regional capital. Later it was the administrative centre for the wealthy province of *Baetica*. It was later overrun by both the Vandals and the Visigoths and had to wait for the Moors to take over for its golden age to come. In late 711, Córdoba was captured by Moorish troops led by Mugueiz El Rumí. By 756 Córdoba had become the capital of Moorish Spain and for several centuries it was the main centre of Muslim culture and learning, producing poets and philosophers such as Averoëss and Miamonides. In 758, Abd Al-Rahman I of the Ommayyad Dynasty arrived from Damascus and established an independent Emirate. Much of the Iberian peninsula was ruled from the city which was the capital of the western Caliphate from 929 to 1031 following independence from Baghdad. By now the city probably had as many as 500,000 inhabitants and an estimated 3,000 mosques. Córdoba grew in importance and influence under Abd Al-Rahman's successors, especially Abd Al-Rahman III and Hakkam II, until internal disputes and a revolt by the Berbers began to weaken the Ommayyads, leading to the abdication of Hisham II in 1031. The Caliphate of Córdoba then split up into a number of minor *tiafas* (kingdoms), while the city itself came into the hands of first the Almoravides in 1094 and subsequently the Almohades in 1149. Córdoba was captured by the Christians led by Fernando III in 1236 and with the Reconquest the decline soon set in. Little of the wealth from the New World found its way to Córdoba, and by the time the French occupied the city during the Peninsular War, the population had dropped dramatically.

During the Civil War, Córdoba was captured by the Nationalists, who perpetrated some appalling atrocities. The *Córdobeses* proved, however, to have long memories and in the first post Franco elections returned a communist local authority, a situation which remained until quite recently.

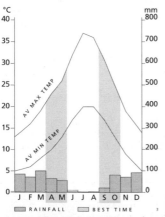

Climate: Córdoba

Puente Romano, Córdoba

PLACES OF INTEREST

The Mezquita (or mosque) is Córdoba's most famous example of Arab architecture. Although not quite as remarkable as Granada's Alhambra, it is in its own way an equally significant remnant of Spain's Moorish heritage and is a must for any visitor to Andalucía.

There are in fact four distinct stages in the construction of the Mezquita, representing distinct styles and periods corresponding to the Moorish rulers of the time. The building began in 785 in the time of Abd Al-Rahman I on the site of a Visigoth church and a Roman temple, with the intention of building Islam's most grandiose mosque. The architect, whilst demolishing the original church, had a ready source of building materials. To save time the west-facing wall was retained, but this meant that the *mihrab* does not exactly face Mecca. (An alternative explanation is that the *mihrab* was designed to face Damascus, from where many of the inhabitants had fled.) There were a vast number of pillars available

for use, both from the Visigoth church and also the earlier Roman temple, plus many more brought to the site from other places. There were of a variety of types (marble, jasper and porphyry), colours and lengths. The longer pillars were buried in the floor to match the height of the shorter ones, while a second row of pillars and arches were constructed to support the roof, a design which inevitably reminds the visitor of a Roman aqueduct. A distinctive feature of the arches is the striped red and white pattern produced by using red brick and white stone.

Abd Al-Rahman II extended the mosque during the period 833 to 848 with nine more arches added to the S. The third enlargement came in the time of Al Hakkim II, who demolished the S wall to add another 14 rows of columns, transforming the building into a huge rectangle. He also used Byzantine craftsmen to construct a new *mihrab*. The prayer niche, whilst indicating the direction of Mecca, also has the function of amplifying the voice of the prayer

Mezquita at Córdoba

Not to scale

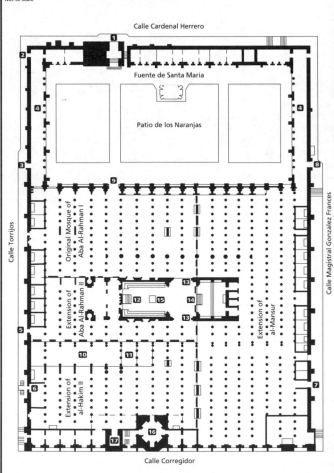

Calle Cardenal Herrero

Fuente de Santa Maria

Patio de los Naranjas

Calle Torrijos

Calle Magistral Gonzalez Frances

Original Mosque of
Aba Al-Rahman I

Extension of
Aba Al-Rahman II

Extension of
al-Mansur

Extension of
al-Hakim II

Calle Corregidor

1. Belfrey Tower (old minaret & Pardon Gate)
2. Postern Gate de la Leche
3. Deans' Gate
4. Cloisters
5. St Michael's Gate
6. Posten Gate del Palacio
7. Posten Gate of the Sagrarium
8. St Catherine's Gate (main entrance)
9. Gate of the Palms
10. Site of Visigoth Cathedral
11. Capilla Real (Royal Chapel)
12. Choir
13. Transepts
14. High Altar
15. Capilla Mayor (main chapel)
16. Mihrab
17. Tesoro (Treasury)

Understanding the mosque

👣 Before visiting the Mezquita in Córdoba, it is helpful to appreciate mosques in general and in particular those of the Moors in Andalucía. Large cities such as Córdoba would have had scores of mosques, but the Grand Mosque or *alijama* would have been located in the centre of the urban area, surrounded by its commercial area known as the *medina*. Nearby would be the *madraza* or college, while a maze of surrounding alleyways would contain numerous small shops.

The mosque itself would consist of three distinct elements – the minaret, the courtyard and the prayer hall. The minaret, from where the muezzin calls the faithful to prayer, is a square, narrow tower decreasing in size as it rises. Usually made of brick or stone, it is decorated with small arches, tiles and brickwork. It is capped with three golden spheres or *yamur*. The courtyard or *shan*, which was often shaded with trees and had fountains playing, was the place for the ritual washing or ablutions. There was frequently a covered gallery running around the outside. The prayer hall or *liwan* is little more than an empty space held up by arches and pillars forming parallel naves, with prayer mats on the floor. The *mihrab* is in the centre of the wall which faces Mecca. In small mosques, the *mihrab*, which amplifies the voice of the prayer leader, might be a simple hollow niche, but in the Grand Mosque the area might be ornately decorated. The exterior of the Mosque (and Córdoba is an excellent example) usually has high stone walls with minimal decoration and no windows, as the mosque might need to be defended. There would be a small number of doors, invariably with horseshoe arches.

It should also be remembered that the mosque acted as a central point for many of the activities of the city such as teaching, carrying out the law and the administration for the community.

leader. Today, the *mihrab* is railed off, but try to see the ceiling, which is carved into a shell from a single piece of marble and also the *maksura* or anti chamber, where the Caliph and his party would pray. This is distinguished by some richly coloured mosaics.

The fourth and final expansion of the Mezquita was during the time of Al-Mansur, the minister of the child-ruler Hisham II. This final enlargement added seven rows to the E side, which it can be claimed destroys the symmetry of the mosque, since the *mihrab* no longer occupies a central position. The building today comprises a huge rectangle measuring 129m by 179m.

To the N of the mosque is the **Patio de los Naranjos**, a courtyard of orange trees and fountains where the ritual ablutions took place before prayer. None of the original fountains remain today but their more modern successors give the flavour of Moorish times. Set into the N wall of the patio is the **Bell Tower** or belfry, built at the same time as the cathedral. The climb to the top is rewarded with fine views over the city.

After Córdoba was captured by Fernando III in the Christian Re-conquest, the mosque was gradually converted into a church, initially by adding a **Capilla de Villaviciosa** built by Mudéjar craftsmen in 1371. The most drastic alterations took place in 1523 under Charles V (also renowned for his interference with the Alhambra in Granada) who sanctioned the building, despite local objections, of a **Capilla Real** (Royal Chapel) and the **Cathedral Coro** in Renaissance style. On inspecting the finished work he did have the decency to comment that "You have built what you or others might have built anywhere, but you have destroyed something that was unique in the world". The cathedral is not without its worth, however, and of particular interest are the choir stalls, ornately carved in mahogany by Pedro Duque Cornejo in the 18th

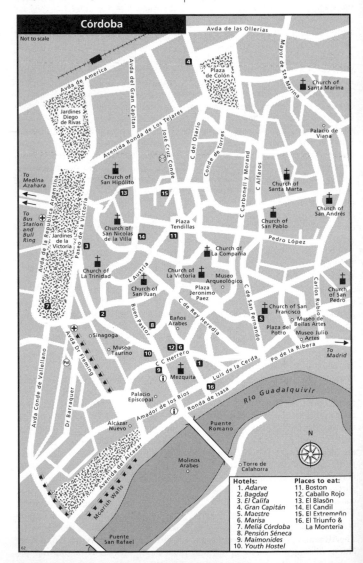

Córdoba

Not to scale

To Medina Azahara

To Bus Station and Bull Ring

Avda de las Ollerías

Avda de America

Avda del Gran Capitan

Mayor de Sta Marina

Church of Santa Marina

Plaza de Colón **4**

Jardines Diego de Rivas

Avenida Ronda de los Tejares

José Cruz Conde

C del Osario

Conde de Torres

C Carbonell y Morand

C Alfaros

Palacio de Viana

Church of San Hipólito **13**

15

Plaza Tendillas

Church of Santa Marta

Church of San Nicolás de la Villa **14**

11

Church of San Pablo

Church of San Andrés

Pedro López

Church of La Compañía

Paseo de la Victoria

Jardines de la Victoria

Avda de la República Argentina

Church of La Trinidad

Church of La Victoria

Museo Arqueológico

Carlos Rubios

Church of San Pedro

L Austria

Church of San Juan

Plaza Jeronimo Paez

C de San Fernando

Church of San Francisco **5**

Museo de Bellas Artes

7

Buen Pastor

C de Rey Heredia

Plaza del Potro

Museo Julio Artes

Baños Árabes

2

8

To Madrid

Avda Dr Fleming

+ Sinagoga

Museo Taurino

10

12 6

9

C C Herrero

1

Pol

Mezquita

Luis de la Cerda

Po de la Ribera

Río Guadalquivir

Palacio Episcopal

Amador de los Ríos

Ronda de Isasa

16

Avda Conde de Vallellano

Dr Barraquer

Alcázar Nuevo

Puente Romano

N

Avenida del Alcázar

Mcanth Walls

Molinos Árabes

Torre de Calahorra

Puente San Rafael

Hotels:
1. *Adarve*
2. *Bagdad*
3. *El Califa*
4. *Gran Capitán*
5. *Maestre*
6. *Marisa*
7. *Meliá Córdoba*
8. *Pensión Séneca*
9. *Maimonides*
10. *Youth Hostel*

Places to eat:
11. Boston
12. Caballo Rojo
13. El Blasón
14. El Candil
15. El Extremeñn
16. El Triunfo & La Monteria

century. There also some items of interest in the Christian side chapels. In the Capilla de la Concepción are some fine carvings by Pedro de la Mena, while in the Capilla de Cardinal Salazar is an impressive statue of Santa Teresa, sculpted by José de Mora. In the Tesoro (treasury), is a monstrance by Enrique de Arfe, which was first seen in the Corpus Cristi procession of 1518. It is more than $2\frac{1}{2}$m high, weighs 200 kilos and is a mass of jewels, crosses and relics. Nevertheless, having viewed the cathedral sitting awkwardly within the Moorish mosque, one is reminded of a famous Royal observation in a similar context that it is "like a carbuncle on the face of a well-loved friend".

The Mezquita can be crowded with visitors, but this need not be a disadvantage. Some of the tour guides are a fund of knowledge and it is quite easy to tag on to a group and get the benefit of an expert commentary. Open Apr-Sep 1030-1330 and 1600-1900; Oct-Mar 1030-1330 and 1530-1730. Entrance, via the Puerta del Perdón, 700 ptas, children 350 ptas.

The Palacio Episcopal, on the W side of the Mezquita, was originally constructed by the Visigoths, then became an alcázar which the resident Caliphs had linked to the mosque by means of a bridge. The Omayyad court abandoned this alcázar when they moved to Medina Azahara. However, the oldest surviving part of the building today is 15th century in age, but it is due to the existence of the early Moorish fortress that the nearby Christian building is known as the 'Alcázar Nuevo'. The Palacio is today partly used as a museum (mainly religious art, sculptures and tapestries) and partly as a venue for exhibitions and congresses. Open 0930-1330 and 1530-1730, Sat 0930-1330. Entrance 150 ptas or free with a Mezquita ticket.

The **Alcázar de los Reyes Cristianos** (or Nuevo Alcázar) was begun in the 13th century for Alfonso X and was later enlarged and used as a palace by the Catholic Kings. Ferdinand and Isobel received Columbus in this building, before he departed on his first voyage to the New World, while it was also the prison of Boabdil el Chico, the last of the kings of Moorish Granada. Along the riverside opposite the palace were a series of water wheels and flour mills. The wheels also brought water to the alcázars, but they are said to have infuriated Isobel as they prevented her from sleeping. One reconstructed wheel remains today. The Alcázar became a centre for the Inquisition from 1490 until 1821. Even as late as the middle of the 20th century, the building was functioning as a prison, so it is perhaps not surprising that there is little to see from its Golden Age. There is now a small municipal museum here, in which the locally discovered Roman mosaics are the most important exhibit. Most visitors will probably find more enjoyment wandering around the gardens to the S of the building, with its pools, fountains and rose beds, which are illuminated during the summer evenings. Open Tues-Sat, May-Sep 0930-1330 and 1700-2000; Oct-Apr 0930-1330 and 1600-1900, Sun 0930-1330. Entrance 200 ptas, Tues free.

The **Judería** Between the Mezquita and the city walls to the W lies the Judería, Córdoba's old Jewish quarter, a virtual labyrinth of narrow lanes and alleyways. It can be entered through the Puerta de Almodóvar, the ancient gateway of the Jews. From here turn right into C/Judias which leads to the **Synagogue**, one of only three in Spain and the only one in Andalucía. Built in 1315, this tiny building has some fine Mudéjar plaster work around attractive balconies. The fact that both the Judería and the Synagogue survived after the expulsion of the Jewish community by Ferdinand and Isobel in 1492, says much for the traditional religious and racial tolerance of the *Córdobeses*.

Open Tues-Sat 1000-1400 and 1330-1730, Sun 1000-1330, Entrance 50 ptas. South of the Synagogue, in a small *plazuela*, is a statue of Maimonides, the Jewish philosopher, who was born in Córdoba in 1135.

Also in the Judería is the **Museo Taurino y Arte Cordobés** in the Plaza de Maimonides, devoted largely to *tauromaquía* (the art of bullfighting), with special attention given to Manolete, the famous local matador killed by the bull Islero in 1947. (There is a statue to Manolete in Plaza Lagunilla.) Open Tues-Sat, May-Sep 0930-1330 and 1700-2000; Oct-Apr 0930-1330 and 1600-1900, Sun 0930-1330. Entrance 200 ptas, free Tues. EU students free.

Puente Romano (Roman Bridge) crosses the Río Guadalquivir from the Triumphal arch and Bridge Gate to the Torre de Calahorra on the other side. It has 16 arches and was built after Caesar's victory over Pompey. First restored by the Moors in the 8th century, it has been renovated many times since.

Torre de Calahorra Located on the S side of the Roman Bridge, this defensive tower is now an Interpretation Centre, giving an audio visual history of Córdoba in addition to displaying some armour which once belonged to *El Gran Capitán* – Gonzalo Fernández de Córdoba, and items connected with the local 16th century poet Luis de Góngora. Open May-Sep 1000-1400 and 1730-2030; Apr-Oct 1030-1800. Entrance 350 ptas plus 500 ptas for full audio visual programme. This, incidentally, uses some 18 projectors and other electronic wizardry, showing amongst other things 'The song of the waters of the land of Andalucia', and a 'Magic model of of the Alhambra of Granada', which may help you to make up your mind on whether to part with 500 ptas.

Baños Arabes In a private house at the rear of a shop in C/Velázquez Bosco in the Judería, there is a 10th century *hamman* or sauna. The owner claims these are the oldest baths in Andalucía. Adjacent to a small open patio surrounded by arches, they certainly have plenty of atmosphere. There was once a passage between the baths and the nearby Mezquita. The opening hours are dependent on the presence of the friendly and informative owner, who will deliver a 2-min lecture in rapid fire Spanish and leave you to it. Entrance 100 ptas.

Callejón de las Flores Worth seeking out is this small narrow street just a stone's throw from the NE of the Mezquita. Its whitewashed walls are festooned with pots and flowers. At the small plaza at the end of the alley, look back to see the belfry of the Mezquita perfectly framed. This street sets the scene for the rest of Córdoba, which maintains the patios passed on from the Romans and the Moors – from the humblest cottage to the grand *palacios*. Often framed by wrought iron doorways and complimented by decorative tiles and gentle fountains, the patio is an essential feature of the city, culminating in the annual Festival of the Patios during the first fortnight in May.

OTHER PLACES OF INTEREST

Although most day visitors will be constricted by time to the area around the Mezquita, those staying longer will find much to enjoy in other parts of the city, particularly to the E of the main monumental area.

Museo Arqueológico Provincial Located in the Plaza de Jerónimo Páez, the Córdoba Archaeological Museum is undoubtedly the best of its kind in southern Spain. Housed in a Renaissance mansion with an Italian style porch, the museum is entered via a delightful patio with a fountain and surrounding arches containing Roman capitals and assorted mosaics. There is much to appreciate in the Neolithic, Roman and Moorish periods, but certain items stand out such as the Christian sarcophagus, its side beautifully carved in marble and the bronze stag from the Moorish ruins of nearby Medina Azahara. The mosaics throughout are excellent and some were, in fact, discovered on the site, the mansion having been built over a Roman villa. Open Tues-Sat, May-Sep 1000-1400 and 1800-2000; Oct-Apr 1000-1400 and 1700-1900, Sun 1000-1330. Entrance 250 ptas, free to EU citizens with proof of identity. **NB** The Plaza Páez outside the museum is the meeting place of some of the more dubious youths of Córdoba and this is probably the only place in the city that the visitor is likely to feel even remotely threatened.

Plaza del Potro This is a delightful square about a kilometre E of the Mezquita, and well worth the walk. The square is named after the fountain, dating from 1577, which is decorated with a *potro* (or colt). At the S end of the Plaza is a monument to San Rafael, behind which is the Guadalquivir and the countryside stretching away in the distance. The square was once a livestock market and in the 16th and 17th centuries it was a popular meeting place for the wheeler dealers of the city. The square was certainly known to Cervantes, who mentioned it in *Don Quixote*. An interesting and balanced set of buildings, mostly in honey coloured sandstone, surround the square. To the W is the **Posada del Potro**, a carefully restored inn (Cervantes probably stayed here) with a courtyard surrounded by former stables and a wooden balcony containing the inn's rooms. The building is now the Casa de la Cultura and visitors are welcome to wander around. Opposite, on the E side of the square, is the **Museo de Bellas Artes** in a building which was once the Hospital de la Caridad – the Catholic Kings Hospital of Charity. Entry is through an attractive sculpture filled garden. The galleries contain works by all the usual names such as Valdés Leal, Zurburán,

Alonso Cano and Murillo, although not their better works. There are also, refreshingly, some works by modern painters, such as Benedito, Chicharro and Solana, T 473345. Open Tues-Sat, May-Sep 1000-1400 and 1800-2000; Oct-Apr 0930-1330 and 1600-1900. Sun 0930-1330. Entrance free. On the other side of the same building's courtyard, as you enter on the right, is the **Museo Julio Romero de Torres**. This museum is devoted to the work of the local Córdoban artist Julio Romero de Torres. Largely unheard of outside the city, this exponent of modernism and symbolism claims to provide 'a personal glowing serenade to the women of Córdoba'. Most of his work consists of semi-erotic nudes and smouldering gypsy women. He does, however, have a big following in the city, although probably mainly the male section of the population. Local feminists possibly think otherwise. Open Tues-Sat, May-Sep 0930-1330 and 1700-2000; Oct-Apr 0930-1330 and 1600-1900; Sun 0930-1330. Entrance free.

Plaza de la Corredera Just E of the Archaeological Museum and N of the Plaza del Potro is the remarkable Plaza de la Corredera, which is an extraordinary colonnaded square. It was enclosed in the 17th century and formed a multipurpose arena, which has been used for bullfights and even burnings during the Inquisition. Today, it has a rather faded air about it and is the location for an open and a covered market.

Palacio de Viana Located in Plaza Don Gome, this is an opulent mansion dating originally from the 14th century, which until quite recently was the home of the Marquess of Viana. The guided tour takes in the various rooms of the house, including art galleries, bedrooms, and a particularly fascinating kitchen. Visitors will probably enjoy mostly the 14 flower filled patios. Open Mon-Tues and Thur-Sat, Jan-May and Oct-Dec 1000-1300, Jun-Sep 0900-1400, Sun 1000-

1400; Entrance: adults 200 ptas, children 100 ptas.

The Churches of Córdoba After the Re-conquest Fernando III built 14 parish churches in Córdoba, mainly between the end of the 13th century and the beginning of the 14th century and incorporating a mixture of architectural styles including Roman, Gothic and Mudéjar. They were usually built with three naves, often with many-sided apses and built in the local cream-coloured sandstone. Several had additions in the Baroque style in the 17th and 18th centuries. For visitors keen on churches, then, Córdoba is fertile ground. With limited time, the following are the most rewarding. **Iglesia de San Nicholás de Villa**, in Plaza San Nicholás on the edge of the main shopping area, has an octagonal tower and battlements and, unusually, four square apses. **Iglesia Santa Marina**, in the plaza of the same name in the N part of the city, is a stout building with three porches with pointed arches above which is a delicate rose window. Outside the church is a monument to Manolete, the bullfighter who was born in the Santa Marina barrio. **Iglesia San Lorenzo**, located again in a square of the same name, has a distinctive tiled porch with three pointed arches. Above this is an ornate rose window surrounded by six rows of mouldings. The bell tower has a curious belfry set at an angle to the main structure. Finally, there is the **Iglesia de San Andrés** located in the old silk making district. Built mainly in the 18th century, it retains only its vaults from the times of the Re-conquest.

LOCAL FESTIVALS

Carneval takes place in Feb; during *Semana Santa* there are some 28 traditional Easter processions; 5-12 May, the *Fiesta de la Patios* is marked by concerts and *flamenco* in addition to the competition for the best decorated patio; 25-28 May, *Feria de Nuestra Señora de la Salud* for which the city's women dress in traditional garb; Córdoba's patron saint is celebrated during the *Fiesta de Nuestra Señora de la Fuensanta* in Sep; 24 Oct, fiesta of *San Rafael Arcángel*.

LOCAL INFORMATION

Price guide

Hotels:

AL	over US$90	D	US$20-40
A	US$75-90	E	US$10-20
B	US$60-75	F	under US$10
C	US$40-60		

Places to eat:

♦♦♦	expensive	♦♦ average
	♦ cheap	

● **Accommodation**

Visitors arriving by car will probably look for a hotel as nr as possible to the Mezquita and with the benefit of a garage, as street parking is very difficult. Accommodation is generally cheaper away from the historic quarter (off map).

AL *Adarve*, C/Magistral González Francés 15, T 481102, F 474677, 103 rm, modern, garage, a/c, cafeteria – no restaurant, immediately opp E side of the Mezquita; **AL** *Amistad Córdoba*, Plaza Miamonides 3, T 420335, F 420365, 69 rm, a/c, new hotel based on old mansions in the old wall of the Judería; **AL** *Husa Gran Capitán*, Avda de América 5, T 470250, F 474643, 96 rm, garage, a/c, in N part of town some way from the historic centre; **AL** *Meliá Córdoba*, Jardines de la Victoria, T 298066, F 298147, 147 rm, garage, a/c, wheelchair access, restaurant (but best to eat out), pool, good location overlooking fountains and gardens.

A *Los Gallos Sol*, Avda de Medina Azahara 7, T 235500, F 231636, 115 rm, pool, modern facilities, originally constructed by the bullfighter El Cordobés; *Maimonides*, C/Torrijos 4, T 471500, F 483803, 83 rm, garage, wheelchair access, a/c, right next to the W side of the Mezquita.

B *Albucassis*, C/Buen Pastor 11, T 478625, garage, wheelchair access, a/c, clean establishment just N of the Mezquita; **B** *Marisa*, C/Cardinal Herrero 6, T 473142, F 474144, 28 rm, garage, wheelchair access, in the shadow of the Mezquita.

C *Maestre*, C/Romero Barros 4/6, T 472410, F 475395, 26 rm, small clean hotel with garage close to the Plaza del Potro, approach from N because of the one way system; **C** *El Oasis*, Avda de Cádiz 78, T 291350, F 291311, 50 rm, a/c, pool, on the other side of the river, but within walking distance of the historic quarter.

Pensiones: with nearly 30 pensiones in Córdoba, there is plenty of choice. Expect to pay more nr the historic core of the city. **D** *Baghdad*, C/Fernández Ruano 11, T 202854, 15 rm, new, N edge of Judería; **D** *El Triunfo*, C/Luis de la Cerda 79, T 475500, 44 rm, garage, a/c, good facilities, close to the Mezquita; **D** *Séneca*, C/Conde y Luque 7, T 473234, on the N side of the Mezquita, simple hostel with attractive courtyard.

E *Los Arcos*, C/Romero Barros 14, T 485643, 16 rm, wheelchair access, a/c, in quiet cul-de-sac close to the Plaza del Potro with attractive patio; **E** *El Portillo*, C/Cabezas 2, T 472091, bargain accommodation in traditional house just to the E of the Mezquita; **E** *Las Tendillas*, C/Jesús María 1, T 473029, 15 rm, in the commercial centre of town – not quiet.

Youth hostel: *Plaza Judás Leví*, T 290166, impressive new building, 88 beds (2 beds to a room), meals, max stay 3 days.

Camping: *Campamento Municipal*, Avda del Brillante 50, T 472000, 1st category site, pool 10 km N of town but frequent buses run to city; *Carlos III*, Ctra N 1V, Km 429.5, La Carlota, T 300697, pool, tennis, 30 km S of Córdoba.

● **Places to eat**
♦♦♦*Almudaina*, Campo Santo de los Mártires 1, T 474342, stylish local food; *El Blasón*, C/José Zorilla 11, T 480625, expensive, set in historic house; *El Caballo Rojo*, C/ Cardenal Herrero 28, T 475375, Andalucían and old Arab recipes.

♦♦*Los 5 Arcos*, C/Martínez Rúcker 6, T 491505, Arab specialities, just E of the Mezquita; *Boston*, Plaza de las Tendillas, T 485989, Andalucían cuisine, *platos combinados*, reasonable *menu* incl wine; *El Candil*, C/San Felipe 15, T 475305, well prepared local dishes; *El Triunfo*, C/Corregidor Luis de la Cerda 79, T 475500, clean, speedy service, *menu del dia* at 1,100 ptas; *La Montería*, C/Corregidor Luis de la Cerda 77; *Siena*, Plaza de las Tendillas 5, T 473005, good *menu* and *platos combinados*.

♦*Cafetería Monaco*, Ronda de los Tejeres 3, reasonable *platos combinados*; *El Extremeño*, Plaza Benavente 1, T 478314, local and Extremaduran cuisine; *El Tablón*, C/Luis

de la Cerda 75, T 476061, patio, friendly service, close to the Mezquita (and one of the few worth trying in this area); *Mesón de Luna* and *Mesoñ la Muralla* are adjacent restaurants in the ramparts of the Judería – their proximity ensures value for money. For real budget eating, try the *buffet libre Los Patios*, C/Cardenal Herrero 26.

● **Bars**
Tapas bars: there are many excellent *tapas* bars in the old part of Córdoba. In the Judería area try *Bodega Guzmán*; nr the Mezquita is *Taberna de Pepe*, while *Taberna San Miguel* in the Plaza Tendillas should be everyone's first choice. Note that Córdoba's *tapas* bars usually serve Montilla (the sherry look-a-like produced in the S of the province). Many of the *tapas* bars are run by the Sociedad Plateros, a silversmiths' benefit society which has branched out into the running of *bodegas*.

● **Banks & money changers**
Branches of the main Spanish banks are found in the Avda del Gran Capitán and the Ronda de los Tejeres area.

● **Embassies & consulates**
France, C/Manuel de Sandóval 4, T 472314; Monaco, C/Gran Capitán 32, T 474391.

● **Entertainment**
Bullfights: take place throughout the season at the Plaza de Toros de los Califas, which is in the modern part of the city to the NW of the historic quarter.

Concerts: take place on Sun in the Alcázar and there are open air shows in the *Teatro Municipal*, incl the International Guitar Festival. Check with the Tourist Office for details.

Flamenco: Córdoba is famed for its *flamenco*. A national *flamenco* competition takes place every 3 years and there are numerous festivals during the summer months. For some reasonably genuine performances try *Meson Flamenco La Bulería*, C/Pedro Lopez 3, T 483839. Starts 2230; 1,000 ptas for the first drink.

Discos and other nightlife are rather sparse in Córdoba, particularly when compared with other Andalucían cities, but try *Disco 3*, Ctra Trassierra s/n, T 278607; *Saint Cyr Club*, C/Eduardo Lucena 4, T 410055.

Theatre: *Gran Teatro*, Avda de Gran Capitán s/n, T 480237; *Teatro Góngora*, C/Jesús y María 12, T 472165. The tourist office will have details of performances.

● **Hospitals & medical services**
Ambulances: T 295570.

Emergencies: T 291133.

Hospitals: *Casa de Socorro*, Avda República Argentina 4, T 234646; *Cruz Roja*, Paseo de la Victoria, T 293411; *General Hospital*, T 297122.

● **Post & telecommunications**
Area code: 957.

Post Office: *Correos*, C/Cruz Conde 15, open Mon-Fri 0800-2100, Sat 0900-1400. Telegrams, T 472009 or T 470345. Open Mon-Fri 0800-2100, Sat 0900-1900.

Telephones: *locutorio* at Plaza Tendillas 7. Open Mon-Fri 0930-1400 and 1700-2300, Sat 0930-1400.

● **Shopping**
The main shopping streets are to the N of the historic quarter, concentrating along Avda Ronda de las Tejares, Plaza Tendillas and C/Cruz Conde. There are numerous shops around the Mezquita aimed at the tourist trade, but selling some of the traditional craftwork of the Córdoba area such as silverwork, jewellery, leather (known simply as 'cordobanes'), pottery and guitars. There is a flea market every morning in the Plaza de la Corredera, with a larger affair on Sat.

● **Sports**
Golf: *Club Golf Villares*, Ronda Tejares 1, T 474102.

Riding: *Club Hipico*, Ctra Trassierra, Km 3, T 271628; *Cortijo la Ventilla*, Hacienda El Cordobés, Gran Capitan 14001, Córdoba, T 474794.

Swimming: *Piscina Municipal*, Avda del Brillante.

Squash: *Squash Córdoba*, C/Alonso el Sabio 22, T 480981.

● **Tour companies & travel agents**
Viajes Intercontinental, Avda del Gran Capitán 16, T 470694; *Viajes Vincit*, Avda Burgos 1, T 472316.

● **Tourist offices**
C/Torrijos 10, in the Palacio de Congressos, T 471235. Open summer Mon-Fri 0930-1400 and 1700-1900, Sat 1000-1300. Also Plaza Judas Levi, T 470000. Open Mon-Fri 0900-1400 all year.

● **Useful addresses**
Garages/car workshops: *Citroën*, Ctra Madrid, T 260216; *Ford*, Polígono las Quemadas, T 255800; *Peugeot*, Avda de Cádiz, T 292122; *Seat/VAG*, Polígono la Torrecilla, T 295111.

Parking: parking place opp the Mezquita.

● **Transport**
Local Bus: *Bonobús* tickets for 10 journeys available from kiosks for 475 ptas. Most local buses pass through Plaza de las Tendillas. Long distance coaches connect with Badajoz, Cádiz and Madrid (all one daily); Ejica and Málaga (4 daily); Granada, Jaén and Sevilla (5 daily). Most coaches are run by Alsina Graells (office on Avda Medina Azahara 29, T 236474). **Car hire**: Avis, Plaza Colón 35, T 476862; Europcar, Avda Medina Azahara 7, T 233460; Hertz, Ctra de Guadalhorce, T 477243; Ital, Viajes Melia, T 470862. **Coches de Caballos**: (horse drawn carriage) – a sedate way of seeing the city.

Air There is a minor national airport at Córdoba, but any international flights must be made via Sevilla or Málaga. The Iberia office is in Ronda de los Tejeres 3, sales T 471227, reservations T 472695.

Train The station is on Avda de América; an additional RENFE office is on Avda Ronda de los Tejeres 10, T 475884. Information T 479302. The Madrid-Cádiz and the Madrid-Málaga lines meet at Córdoba resulting in frequent trains to many destinations, with 12 running daily to Sevilla, 3 to Algeciras, 2 to Jaén and 3 to Ronda.

EXCURSIONS FROM CORDOBA

Medina Azahara (also known as Madinat al-Zahra) These Moorish ruins may be found some 7 km NW of Córdoba. The complex was begun in 936 by the Caliph Abd Al-Rahman III in honour of his favourite wife, Azahara. No expense was spared in its construction and historians have provided some amazing statistics. 10,000 men and 1,500 camels and mules were used to construct the palace and the associated buildings, which included houses, barracks, baths, markets, mosques, ponds and even an aviary and a zoo. The affluence of the place amazed visitors, some rooms having visual effects (extraordinary for the time) involving crystals providing rainbows and moving bowls of mercury sending sunbeams around the walls. The building materials

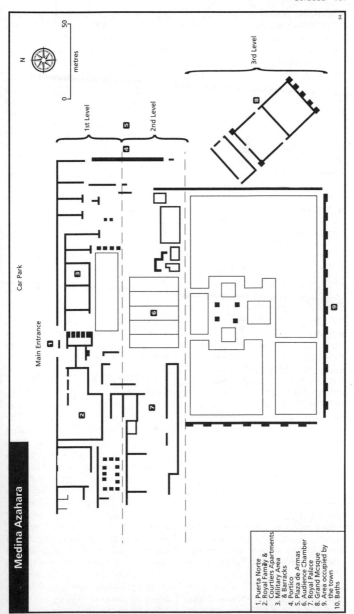

Medina Azahara

Car Park

Main Entrance

1st Level

2nd Level

3rd Level

N

0   50
metres

1. Puerta Norte
2. Royal Family &
   Courtiers Apartments
3. Military Area
   & Barracks
4. Portico
5. Plaza de Armas
6. Audience Chamber
7. Royal Palace
8. Grand Mosque
9. Area occupied by
   the town
10. Baths

were varied in origin, with tiles and bricks taken from Roman sites in Andalucía and marble brought in from North Africa and other places. When complete, Medina Azahara measured 2,000m long by 900m wide, spreading over three terraces leading down to the Guadalquivir valley, while it is estimated that 20,000 people lived within its double walls.

After the death of Abd Al-Rahman III, his successors Al-Hakim II and Al Mansur continued to live at Medina Azahara, but when the latter died decline set in. There was a popular revolt in 1010 and the Medina was looted and then finally destroyed by retreating Berber mercenaries. So the 'wonder of the western world' lasted a mere 75 years. Over the succeeding centuries the site was frequently looted for its building materials, which turn up for instance in the Alcázar at Sevilla.

Today, most of the site consists of ruins and foundations, but excavations continue and there has been some controversial reconstructions, mainly to the palace. This does, however, give some scale and atmosphere to the place. Entry through the Puerta Norte gives a view down over the location. The first level consists of the royal apartments with the rooms built around patios; there were believed to be some 400 houses for courtiers here. To the E is the main military area, the *Dar al-Djund*, including the barracks. This leads to the portico, which was obviously the grand entrance to the Medina, while beyond this was the *Plaza de Armas*, probably a military parade ground.

Dominating the second level is the Royal Palace, with its restored audience chamber where guests were received. Painstakingly pieced together, the chamber shows some delightful marble carving, which unusually for Islamic art work, shows figures of men and animals. Finally, on the lower level, are the foundations of the Great Mosque, revealing five naves. Open 1000-1400 and 1600-1800, Sun 1000-1400, closed Mon. Entrance 250 ptas; free to EU citizens with proof of identity. To reach Medina Azahara, take the Avda de Medina Azahara out of Córdoba. After leaving the industrial suburbs behind, turn right after 4 km. It is another 3 km to the site. For those without transport, buses Nos 1 and 2 will drop you at the main road intersection. Do not confuse Medina Azahara with the privately owned 15th century Monastery of Sam Jeromino which is clearly seen in the woods on the hillside above the medina.

On a day's excursion it is possible to drive on from Medina Azahara a further 15 km along the C431 to **Almodóvar del Río**, following the Guadalquivir with the Sierra Morena to the right. Dominating the town is the 8th century Moorish castle fortified by Abd Al-Rahman III, but heavily restored by the Christians in the 14th century. Today it is privately owned, but visits are possible if the guardian can be located. The sleepy town below livens up only during the second Sun in May when the Romeria de la Virgen de Fátima takes place.

NORTH FROM CORDOBA

Leaving behind the fertile *vega* of the Guadalquivir, the land rises gradually into the **Sierra Morena**, a landscape similar to that in neighbouring Jaén and Huelva provinces. Initially rolling farmland with cereals, the succeeding higher land is well wooded with four species of oak, two of pine, plus areas of garrigue scrub, with deep ravines in places. Although this is popular hunting country (particularly for wild boar and deer), it has a good range of wildlife and has the advantage of rarely being visited by tourists. Amongst the mammals are small numbers of mongoose, lynx and wolves, while otters occur in the rivers and reservoirs. Birds of prey are outstanding, with all three varieties of vultures and five species of eagles. Black Storks also breed. Spring flowers and butterflies are also prolific. There are two Natural Parks in this section of the Sierra Morena, the **Parque Natural de Sierra Cardeña y Montoro** in the NE, and the **Parque Natural de Sierra de Hornachuelos** in the NW. As both have a similar range of species, visitors short of time will probably choose only one to explore, in which case Hornchuelos should be selected as this has the additional scenic attraction of some large reservoirs. There are no towns of any size in the area and the villages tend to be uninspiring and lacking in historical and monumental interest. Accommodation, too, can be a problem, the only hotels being in the villages of Peñarroya-Pueblonuevo and Villanueva, while *pensiones* are sparse on the ground and there are no official camp sites.

SOUTH FROM CORDOBA

Most travellers rush through this area en route to either Málaga or Córdoba, but there are many places worthy of a stop. Known as the **Campiña Cordobesa**, it is a landscape of rolling olive groves and vineyards. On the Granada road, the first settlement of importance is **Espejo**, a small town which has been inhabited since Iberian times. Both the Romans and Moors had important sites here and after the Re-Conquest it had an important role in defending the frontier against the Kingdom of Granada. It was Ferdinand IV who gave the town its name from the word *specula*, meaning 'watchtower'. There is the inevitable hilltop castle, in this case a 15th century Gothic-Mudéjar building, with an impressive keep. If spending some time in the town, try to visit the Gothic parish Church of San Bartolomé and the palacio of the Dukes of Osuna. From Espejo, the route follows the valley of the Guadjoz River to **Castro del Río**, another town with Roman origins. Its castle, of which a fair amount still remains, would have seen much fighting between the Christians and the Moors, the latter having laid siege to it unsuccessfully for several months in 1331. Today there are a number of churches of interest and the town's main industry is the making of olive wood furniture. In **Montilla**, just off the N331, you might wish to visit one of the many *bodegas*, as this town is an important wine-producing centre, giving its name to the drink. Otherwise, there is little else of interest. A little to the W is **la Rambla**, a pottery centre specializing in the spouted drinking vessels known as *botijos*.

East of Montilla is the town of **Baena**, a centre for the production of olive oil and having its own *denominacion de origen*. The huge oil storage tanks can be clearly seen as one approaches the town. The name of the town comes from a Roman called Baius who had a villa in the vicinity. Baena has Moorish origins and there are a number of interesting buildings, including the Church of Santa María, which has a Moorish tower, believed to be the minaret of a former mosque, while there are three Plateresque doors. Unfortunately the building was partially destroyed during the Civil War, when many of its treasures were lost. The castle was built in the 9th century and had many later extensions. There are still some stretches of its walls which form the boundaries of the old quarter and which feature two Almohad horseshoe gates. The centre of the old part of the town is the Plaza de la Constitución, around which are a number of buildings of historical importance, including an 18th century colonaded warehouse, which now operates as the *casa de cultura*. Holy Week is spectacular in Baena, with two notable fraternities, the 'White tailed Jews' and the 'Black Tailed Jews', who parade, rolling their drums, on alternate days. Should they meet (and this is usually arranged) they try to 'out-drum' each other. The din is predictable.

The S of the province becomes hillier as the *Sistema Subbético* is reached. The largest town of this region is **Lucena**, a centre of light industry specializing in furniture, with some 40 retail outlets. The only reason for stopping here would be to look at the church of San Mateo,

Not just a sherry look alike

The wines of the Montilla region in Córdoba province have suffered for years by being considered a cheap version of sherry. Indeed until 1944 the Montilla region sent much of its production to Jerez, (the description 'amontillado' is derived from Montilla), but after that date the law decided that sherry had to be produced within a certain area of Cádiz province. Montilla now has its own *denominación*, and certainly within Córdoba province it is the norm to drink Montilla rather than sherry. Although it does not have the worldwide distribution of sherry, Montilla has become popular in Britain, which imports around 100,000 cases a year, and to a lesser extent in Holland.

Aficionados of Montilla are quick to point out the differences with sherry. Firstly, there is the grape. Whereas sherry is made largely with the Palomino grape, Montilla uses the Pedro Ximenez grape, which is thought to have been brought to the area by a soldier serving in Flanders in the 16th century. Secondly, the climate around Montilla is hotter than in the Jerez area which receives more sea breezes. Consequently, the Montilla develops more sugar and therefore more alcohol content, removing the necessity to fortify the wine with more spirits. Thirdly, the wine is fermented in a slightly different way. There are three pressings, after which the juice is clarified and pumped into *tinajas* – huge pottery Ali Baba type jars, where it remains for 9 months.

After this, the differences in production cease. The wine may develop a *flor* (a yeast cap several inches thick), in which case the wine becomes a *fino*. If not, it becomes the darker *oloroso* and is sweetened. Like sherry, Montilla is blended using the *solera* system, mixing wines of different ages to produce uniform quality and is then aged in oak barrels. The end product is claimed to be a more natural product than sherry and what is more it is retailed at a cheaper price.

Like the *bodegas* in Jerez, the equivalents in Montilla offer tours and tastings. Try the following: *Bodegas Cruz Conde*, C/Marquez 3; *Bodegas Garcia Hermanos*, Avda Marqués de la Vega de Armijo 4; *Bodegas Tomas García*, Llano de Palacio 7; and *Bodegas Perez Barquero*, Avda Andalucía 31.

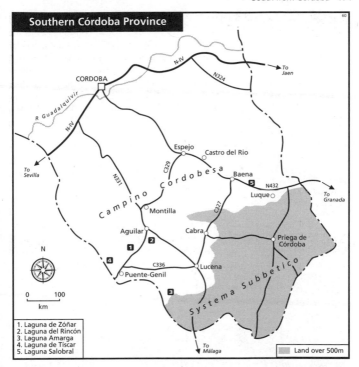

Southern Córdoba Province

To Jaen

CORDOBA

R Guadalquivir

N-IV

N324

N-IV

To Sevilla

Espejo

Castro del Rio

Campiño Cordobesa

Baena

N432

To Granada

Luque

C329

Montilla

C327

Aguilar

2

Cabra

Priega de Córdoba

1

N331

N

4

C336

Lucena

Systema Subbetico

Puente-Genil

3

0   100
km

To Málaga

1. Laguna de Zóñar
2. Laguna del Rincón
3. Laguna Amarga
4. Laguna de Tiscar
5. Laguna Salobral

Land over 500m

which is one of the finest Baroque churches in the province. East of Lucena, on the N331, is the remarkable, but little visited town of **Priego de Córdoba**. An early Moorish settlement, Priego had its heyday in the 18th century, when it produced great quantities of silk and other textiles, creating a wealth which led to the construction of superb Baroque churches. Before touring the churches, obtain a town plan from the tourist office just off the Plaza de la Constitución. The building in which the tourist office is located was the birthplace of Niceto Alcalá Zamora, who was the first president of the Spanish Republic between 1931 and 1936. Note, too, in the square the 16th century fountain with its 180 jets. For sheer atmosphere, head next for the Barrio Villa, which is

the oldest part of Priego and retains much of its original Moorish street plan. There are a number of delightful *plazuelas* linked by winding alleyways festooned with hanging pots of flowers and a promenade, the Paseo de Adarve, which gives wonderful views over the surrounding countryside. The Moorish castillo, with its dominating keep, has been heavily altered and is now privately owned. There is a whole host of Baroque churches and in a short visit it will be impossible to cover all of them. Pick out three or four to study in detail. The following are recommended: the Iglesia de San Francisco, in C/Buen Suceso, with many examples of the work of Juan de Dios Santaella, born in Priego in the early 18th century; the Iglesia de la Asunción in the Plaza de Abad Palo-

Olive oil (*Olea europaea*)

Looking out of an aircraft window at 10,000m over Andalucía, the traveller will notice the chequerboard pattern created by the ubiquitous olive tree. At ground level the impression is confirmed, particularly in Jaén and Córdoba provinces, where the rolling olive groves stretch for endless hectares.

Olive trees were first introduced to Andalucía by the Romans, who trans shipped the product back to Rome. (The best Spanish oil is still exported to Italy and often re-exported as an Italian product.) The Moors extended the cultivation and called the oil *az-zait*, meaning 'juice of the olive'. Spaniards use the term *olivo* for the tree and *oliva* for the fruit, and frequently use the saying *olivo y aceituno, todo es uno*, meaning 'six of one and half a dozen of the other'. Today, Spain is the world's largest producer of olive oil and Andalucía accounts for 20% of this amount, producing some 550,000 tonnes of oil annually.

Many pueblos in Andalucía are proud of their 1,000-year-old trees, which are very fire- and drought-resistant. Methods of harvesting and processing have barely changes since Roman times. The tree blossoms in Spring and the green unripe olives are harvested around Sept. Ripe olives turn black and are harvested later. Some 10% of the harvest is picked for consumption as a fruit and widely used, often stuffed with pimiento or almonds, as a *tapa* or in salads. The remaining 90% is used for the production of oil. These olives will be taken to local factories where they are washed and then ground under cone shaped stones. The resulting pulp is spread on esparto mats and pressed, so that the oil flows out and the 'cheese', which is the residue of the pips and pulp, is left behind. The oil is then filtered through a series of settling tanks, giving pure virgin olive oil.

Selecting a bottle of olive oil from the *supermercado* shelf, however, is not so simple. The label needs to be studied carefully and the percentage of *acidez* noted. The best oil, *Virgin extra*, comes from olives which are picked ripe and milled immediately and which can contain a maximum 1% acidity. *Fino* is allowed 1.5% and *corriente* 3.3%. The higher the acidity, the stronger will be the flavour and therefore the lower the price. *Aciete de Orujo* is made by re-pressing the cheese left over from the first pressing. This is mainly used for industrial purposes, for instance in the production of Castile soap and in carding wool. Some *aciete de orujo* is also refined for cooking oil. To encourage production of high quality oil, a control board, as with wine, issues some *denominación de origen* labels. Of the four already issued, two are in Andalucía, at Sierra de Segura (Jaén) and Baena (Córdoba). In some parts of the S of Spain, oil tasting takes place in the same way that wine is sampled.

It is a sad fact, however, that olive oil consumption in Spain has dropped considerably in recent years. The reasons for this are easy to appreciate. Producing olive oil is expensive as it is a labour intensive industry, whereas alternatives such as corn and sunflower oil lend themselves to the use of machinery in the farming methods and are therefore much cheaper on the supermarket shelf. Secondly, the large numbers of tourists who visit Andalucía are used to a bland cooking oil and restaurateurs have quickly adapted to their cheaper tastes.

Olive oil does, however, have one saving grace – it is HEALTHY. Folklore has always claimed that olive oil contributed to good complexions, efficient digestion and strong hearts. The people of Spain, Italy and Greece have a markedly lower incidence of coronary disease. Modern nutrition, with its emphasis on the 'Mediterranean diet' seems to be confirming this belief. Olive oil contains no cholesterol!

mino, with its amazing *retablo* and *sagrario* (now national monuments); and Iglesia la Aurora in C/Argentina, with a pillared façade and more gems from Santaella inside. This only scratches the surface – there are another half dozen churches to satisfy Baroque buffs. The latter might want accommodation in Priego, where there are four *pensiones* (one extremely cheap), but no hotels. There is a municipal campsite near the bullring.

Environmentalists are also catered for in the Campiña Cordobesa, with a collection of permanent and seasonal semi saline lakes, which are noted for their winter wildfowl. Just SW of the town of **Aguilar**, on the C329, is the largest of the lakes, the **Laguna de Zonar**. Covering some 66 ha, this Reserva Natural comes complete with a hide and an information centre (which regrettably is often closed) and is outstanding for its winter wildfowl. It was formerly one of the of the best spots in Andalucía for seeing the rare White Headed Duck, until the recent introduction of carp which have decimated the subaquatic vegetation. Just off the Moriles-Jauja road is the **Laguna Amarga**, comprising some 16 ha of permanent water surrounded by abundant vegetation, including tamarisk and reeds. Wildfowl are again the main attraction, while Purple Gallinules occasionally breed in the reeds. Both Marsh and Montagu's Harriers hunt over the lake. Just off the Aguilar-Moriles road is the small, but permanent **Laguna del Rincon**. Fringed by often dense vegetation, this lake is reliable for White Headed Ducks, plus a whole range of other winter wildfowl, while Water Rails and Purple Gallinules breed in the reeds. There is an information centre and public hide, but both may be closed during the week. The remaining lagoons (the **Laguna de Tíscar** near Puerto Alegre, and **Laguna Salobral** close to Baena) are semi permanent and can be dry by May, but often attract Flamingoes and passage waders. Because of the salinity of the water, the surrounding vegetation is of the halophytic type. The permanent lagoons have an interesting range of amphibians, including Striped Necked Terrapins and Painted Frogs, while Viperine water snakes are common.

In the extreme SE of Córdoba province, to the E of Lucena and Cabra and to the W of Priego, is the **Sierra Subbéticas Parque Natural**. It consists of limestone sierras, four of which are over 1,000m in height, reaching a maximum of 1,570 in the Sierra Tiñoso, and separated by narrow valleys. The area is lightly wooded, mainly by Cork Oaks, with poplars along the rivers. At the higher levels, raptors are the main attraction with perhaps some 20 pairs of Griffon Vultures. Short Toed Eagles are common in summer, while with luck Bonellis and Golden Eagles may also be seen. The lower levels have a range of typical Mediterranean birds, such as Hoopoe, Bee Eater, Red Rumped Swallows, Black Wheatears and Blue Rock Thrushes. For more risky leisure pursuits, there is the possibility of pot holing and paragliding. Check with the Reception and Nature Interpretation centre at Km 23 on the road between Cabra and Carcabuey. There is also an information centre on the road to Zuheros. One of the main gateways to the park is the small town of **Luque** to the N which was at the centre of Moorish/Christian skirmishes in the 12th and 13th centuries. Its castle dates from the 9th century and a good section of the town walls are still standing. Worth looking at is the Parish Church of La Asunción in Gothic and Renaissance styles.

Granada Province

G RANADA IS Andalucía's most mountainous province, with around half the area over 1,000m in height. With a snow cover for much of the year, the Sierra Nevada forms Spain's premier skiing location and in 1996 it hosted the World Championships.

The city of Granada itself is located at the east end of a fertile plain, while to the south and east the snow capped Sierra Nevada form a perfect backdrop. Granada should be on the itinerary of every visitor to Andalucía, with the Moorish Alhambra being one of the great tourist destinations in the world and the rest of the city offering much more besides.

Northeast of the city, the province has a long 'panhandle' stretching to the border with Murcia. It includes towns such as Guadix, famous for its modern day cave dwellers who have carved their homes out of the soft rock, and Baza, to the east of which the land becomes more arid as the semi desert region of Almería is approached. This area has two Natural Parks, the Parque Natural de la Sierra de Castril along the watershed with Jaén Province, and the Parque Natural de la Sierra de Baza, rising to 2,271m at Santa Bárbara.

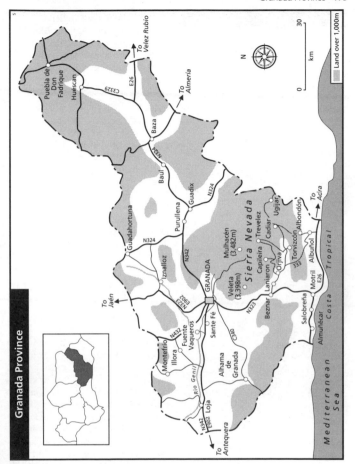

HORIZONS

The **Sistema Penibetico** runs through the south and in the **Sierra Nevada** there are the highest peaks in mainland Spain, rising to 3,398m at Valeta and 3,482m at Mulhacén. The lower slopes of the Sierra Nevada are still clad with forests of oak and pines, but the upper slopes are typically barren scree and Alpine pasture. To the south of the Sierra Nevada, the land slopes down to the **Alpujarras**. A series of wooded valleys drain the mountains reaching the main east/west valley of the Río Guadalfeo ('Ugly River'), with a number of attractive whitewashed villages in good walking country. Further south is the lower range of the **Sierra de Contraviesa**, before the Mediterranean is reached. Granada's portion of the coast is known as the **Costa Tropical**, a generally mountainous shoreline with small, largely unspoilt resorts such as Almuñecar and Salobreña.

GRANADA – THE CITY

(Pop 265,000; *Alt* 689m)

ACCESS The national airport is 17 km to the W of the city, but shuttle buses connect it to the town centre at Plaza Isabel la Católica, cost 300 ptas. Bus No 11 runs a circular route connecting the reasonably central train station on Avda Andaluces and the bus station on Camino de Ronda to the town centre. Once in Granada it is easiest to travel on foot around the lower part of the city, since many of the major places of interest are close together and parking can be a problem.

The capital of the province, Granada stands at the confluence of the Río Genil (which flows W eventually joining the Guadalquivir in Sevilla province) and the Río Darro. The old part of the city is built on the slopes of three hills, contrasting with the more modern development of low rise blocks which sprawl out over the plain to the W. Granada is situated 67 km N of Motril on the Mediterranean coast and 93 km S of Jaén at the eastern end of a fertile upland plain, the **Vega de Granada**. The lofty peaks of the **Sierra Nevada**, the highest mountains in Europe S of the Alps, snow covered for much of the year, lie 30 km to the SE and act as an imposing backdrop to the

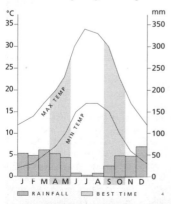

Climate: Granada

town. In addition to travellers coming to absorb the atmosphere of the **Alhambra**, the **Generalife** and the **Albaicín**, visitors also find Granada to be a useful base for both skiers and sunseekers. This accounts for its huge popularity.

HISTORICAL BACKGROUND

Historical records go back to the **Iberian** tribe known as the Turdulos, who made coins on which Granada is named *Iliverir*. Then came the **Phoenicians**, the **Greeks** and the **Carthaginians**. The famous sculpture, the Dama de Baza, dates from the latter period. The **Romans** established a town, known as *Illiberis*, roughly in the location of the Alhambra. The settlement grew in importance under the **Visigoths**, at which time a **Jewish** suburb, named *Garnatha Alyehud*, became established on the southern slopes of the Alhambra. This was significant, because it is believed that the Jewish population assisted the **Moors** in their invasion of the city.

The Moors gave Granada the name *Karnattah* (both names mean pomegranate, the fruit which has now been adopted as the city's symbol). For 3 centuries it was under the control of the Caliphate of Córdoba, but when this declined the capital was moved (in 1013) to Granada where it was to remain for 4½ centuries until it was ended by the Catholic Monarchs in 1492. Granada thrived under both the Almoravids and the Almohads, so that by the end of the 13th century its territory stretched from the coast at Tarifa in the W to Almería in the E. It could survive, however, by paying allegiance to the various Christian kings established to the N and occasionally using Arab power from North Africa. Its most affluent period came during the reigns of **Yusef I** (1334-1354) and **Muhmmed V** (1354-1391), the rulers who were largely responsible for the construction of the Alhambra.

Towards the end of the 15th century, however, things were to change for the worse. Firstly, in 1479, the Christian forces became united with the marriage of Ferdinand and Isabel and their combined armies had, within 10 years, taken Almería, Ronda and Málaga. At the same time the Moors were weakened by internal strife which led to civil war between rival supporters of the Sultan Muley Hassan's, two most influential wives, Ayesha and Zoraya. The feud caused Ayesha to flee to Guadix with the heir Abu Abdullah (better known as Boabdil). He was proclaimed king there in 1482. Known as *El Rey Chico*, Boabdil eventually overthrew both his father and his uncle to become the last king of Granada. *Los Reyes Católicos* began to make impossible demands on **Boabdil**, who tried in vain to rustle up support from the Islamic world. War was declared in

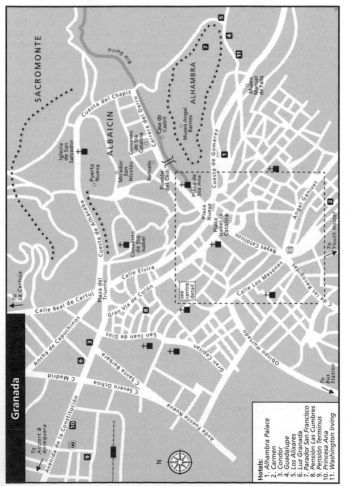

Granada

Hotels:
1. Alhambra Palace
2. Carmen
3. Condor
4. Guadalupe
5. Los Alixares
6. Luz Granada
7. Parador San Francisco
8. Pensión Las Cumbres
9. Pensión Terminus
10. Princesa Ana
11. Washington Irving

Granada

1490 and Granada quickly laid to siege. After 7 months Boabdil gave in and formally ceded the city to the Catholic Monarchs, thus completing the Christian Reconquest.

Harsh times followed for the city, with the Jewish and Moorish inhabitants eventually being expelled. Deprived of many of its craftsmen, traders and merchants, decline set in. There was a brief revival during the Baroque period, when several important monuments were built, such as the monastery of La Cartuja. As with many parts of Andalucía, the Peninsular War was a disaster for the city, with Napoleon's barbaric troops actually using the Alhambra as a barracks, causing untold damage to this monument and many others. *Granadinos* have always had a reputation for being staid, middle class and right wing (a distinct contrast with neighbouring Córdoba) and during the Civil War the local fascists slaughtered literally thousands of left wingers and liberals, including the writer Federico García Lorca – a blemish which the city still struggles to live down.

PLACES OF INTEREST

The **Alhambra** comprises four separate groups of buildings. The **Alcazaba** is a ruined 11th century fortress, which was the only building on the hill when the Nazrids made Granada their capital.

They extended the walls and towers, which are largely intact today. The **Casa Real** (or Royal Palace) was built much later during the 14th century, largely during the reign of Muhammad V. The **Generalife** on the NE side of the hill consists of a series of pavilions and gardens forming the summer palace of the sultans. Finally, there is the **Palace of Carlos V**, a Renaissance building of some worth, sitting uncomfortably amongst the Moorish surroundings. The name Alhambra comes from the Moorish *Qalat Alhamra*, meaning the 'red palace or fort', which could refer to the red building stone or soil, although some Arab chroniclers claim that it derives from the fact that it was rebuilt at night by the reddish light of flaming torches. The Alhambra is best avoided during the heat of summer when the crowds are at their densest, but it is better to see it in the summer than not at all since as the saying goes *"quien no ha visto Granada, no ha visto nada"* (the person who has not seen Granada has seen nothing).

To reach the Alhambra from the city, leave Plaza Nueva by the steep C/Cuesta de Gomérez, reaching after a few hundred metres the **Puerta de las Granadas**, a stone gateway capped with three large pomegranates, the symbol of the city. Here the road forks. Those approaching by car should take the right hand fork which leads eventually to a series of convenient hotels and to the upper entrance and the ample car park. Visitors on foot should labour up the left hand fork to the lower entrance at the **Puerta de la Justicia**, a sturdy stone tower with a horseshoe arch built in the time of Yusef I. In the keystone of the arch is a carved hand, which according to the legend, would prevent Christian entry to the Alhambra unless it reached down with the key. In an effort at crowd control, the tickets

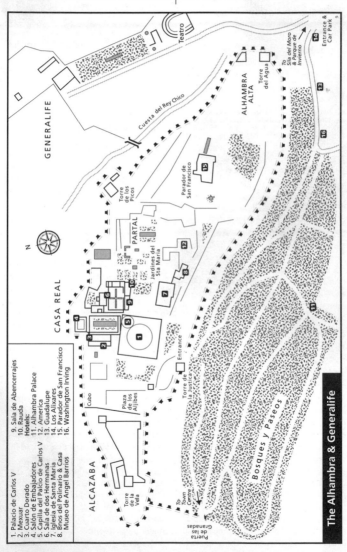

1. Palacio de Carlos V
2. Mexuar
3. Cuarto Dorado
4. Salón de Embajadores
5. Capilla del Palcio de Carlos V
6. Sala de dos Hermanas
7. Iglesia de Santa Maria
8. Museo de Angel Barrios

9. Sala de Abencerrajes
10. Rauda

Hotels:
11. Alhambra Palace
12. America
13. Guadalupe
14. Los Alixares
15. Parador de San Francisco
16. Washington Irving

The Alhambra & Generalife

have a half hour time slot for entry to the Casa Real (once in you can stay as long as you like) and as this is likely to be some time after your initial entry to the Alhambra, there will be time to see first the Alcazaba (if you have used the lower entrance) or the Generalife (if you have come through the upper entrance).

Alcazaba

From the lower ticket office, go through the **Puerto del Vino** and cross the **Plaza de los Alijibes**. This was once a gully separating the palace from the fortress, but was filled in after the Reconquest to contain *alijibes* or large water cisterns. Later the whole area was flattened out to form a parade ground. The cisterns can actually be inspected on Mon, Wed and Fri mornings. Cross the plaza and enter the Alcazaba. This is the oldest part of the whole complex, but most of it was destroyed by Napoleon's departing troops. Much of the central area is taken up with the **Jardín de los Ardaves**, a garden dating from the 17th century. Cross this to reach the **Torre de la Vela**, the top of which gives magnificent views over the city, the river Darro and over to the Albaicín and the caves of Sacromonte, with the snow capped hills of the Sierra Nevada in the opposite direction.

Casa Real

Recross the Plaza de los Alijibes to reach the **Casa Real**, which for all visitors will be the highlight of the day. This Royal Palace dates largely from the 14th century, particularly during the rule of Muhammad V and can be divided into three distinct sections. Firstly there is the Mexuar, a series of chambers used for business; secondly there is the Serallo where important guests were received; and finally there is the Harem, consisting of the private living quarters. Having fallen into decline over the centuries, serious restoration work began in 1860 and is still underway, so that some areas may be closed to the public. Although its exterior is simple, the interior is highly intricate with a variety of orna-

mented ceilings and walls made of tiles and carved plaster work and Arabic inscriptions. There is clever use of light and space, with courtyards and delicate archways set off with fountains and water channels drawn off the nearby Genil and Darro rivers. Water is skilfully used as the central theme throughout the palace, with many pools mirroring the surrounding carvings.

The entrance to the Casa Real leads into the **Mexuar** (1), the place where the Moorish kings held audiences with their subjects and dispensed justice and which held a similar function immediately after the Reconquest. At the far end is a small **Oratory** (2), set at an angle to Mecca. This leads to the **Cuarto Dorado** (3) or Golden Room, which was revamped by Carlos V, although originally Mudéjar. We move next into the **Patio de Cuarto Dorado** (4), a simple courtyard with an ornate façade leading into the Serallo section of the Casa, which was built in the time of Yusef I – and mainly to his design.

The first section of the Serallo is the **Patio de los Arrayanes** (5), named after the neat myrtle hedges alongside the sizeable pool with its simple fountain. Notice here the beautifully carved filigree plaster work. The route now moves into the **Sala de la Barca** (6), which has an exceptional, restored *artesonado* wooden ceiling, thought by some to be in the form of a boat, although the name probably derives from a corruption of the Arabic word *baraka* (blessing or luck). We now arrive at the **Torre de Comares** (7), the most impressive of the towers of the Alhambra, with a height of 45 m and walls 2½ m thick. Inside is the **Salón de Embajadores** (8), by far the largest room in the palace with a ceiling soaring to a height of 20 m. The carved walls here are quite stunning, set off by a large number of windows, doorways and arches, complementing the cedarwood ceiling. The original floor was probably marble, but this has been replaced at some time with earthenware

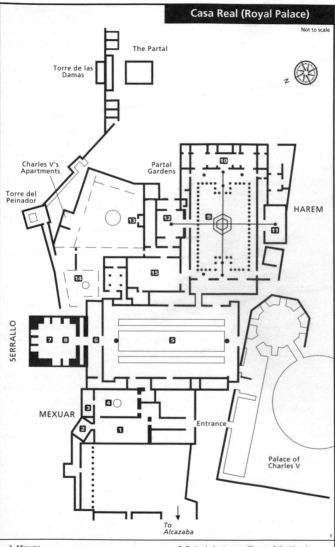

Casa Real (Royal Palace)

Not to scale

The Partal

Torre de las Damas

Charles V's Apartments

Torre del Peinador

Partal Gardens

HAREM

SERRALLO

MEXUAR

Entrance

Palace of Charles V

To Alcazaba

1. Mexuar
2. Oratorio
3. Cuarto Dorado (Golden Room)
4. Patio de Cuarto Dorado
5. Patio de los Arrayanes (Myrtles)
6. Sala de la Barca
7. Torre de Comares
8. Salón de Embajadures (Hall of the Ambassadors)
9. Patio de los Leones (Court of the Lions)
10. Sala de los Reyes (Hall of the Kings)
11. Sala de los Abencerrajes
12. Sala de las dos Hermanos (Hall of the 2 sisters)
13. Peindor de la Reina (Queens Pavilion)
14. Patio de la Reja (Patio of the Grille)
15. Baños Reales (Royal Baths)

tiles with 16th century paving stones around a centre of glazed tiles with a coat of arms. The room has a strong sense of history, for it was here that Boabdil signed the document handing the city over to the Christians. It is also probable that this was the place where Columbus was received by Fernando to discuss his proposed travels to the New World.

We now move into the Harem section of the Casa Real, passing into the **Patio de los Leones** (9), the Court of the Lions, which is undoubtedly the most photographed part of the palace – although you would need to be there out of season to obtain a photograph which excludes the crowds. This beautiful, cunningly constructed courtyard contains a central fountain and pool of water, fed by four channels from the surrounding area and supported by 12 small grey lions. The fountain is a recent addition and it has been argued that the triangles on the heads of two of the lions would make the Star of David, suggesting Jewish origin. The same argument claims that it could not have been Moorish because they represent living animals, although as the nearby ceiling has both men and animals represented, perhaps this argument should not be taken too seriously. The patio is surrounded by arches resting on 124 marble pillars, each with a different capital.

There are a number of rooms leading off the Patio de los Leones. At the far eastern end is the **Sala de los Reyes** (10), the Hall of the Kings, entered by three porches with triple arches. Of particular interest here are the drawings in leather of men and lions, the 10 Moors possibly representing kings, hence the name. These drawings, which have been attached to the beams, are in direct contradiction to Islamic law and it is believed that they may have been the work of a Christian during the latter years of the Moorish rule. To the S is the **Sala de los Abencerrajes** (11). In the fountain at its centre it is said that Abu al-Hassan, the

father of Boabdil, beheaded some 16 members of the Abencerraj family whose leader had fallen in love with his favourite wife Zoraya, although there may be no more to this story than the red streaks in the marble of the fountain. Don't miss the ceiling in this room; with 16 sides each lit by a window and stalactite vaulting to the sides, it is the finest in the Alhambra. On the N side is the **Sala de las dos Hermanas** (12), the Room of the Two Sisters, named after two slabs of white marble in the floor, but possibly the room of the sultan's favourite wife. It opens out onto a *mirador*, known as the 'eyes of the sultana'.

Now following a rather tortuous route the visitor eventually arrives at the **Peinador de la Reina** (13), the Queen's Pavilion, which was originally an oratory for the sultanas, but later the dressing room for Carlos V's wife. Moving through the **Patio de la Reja** (14), which is a 17th century addition, the route moves to the **Baños Reales** (15), the Royal Baths, which are in the Roman style rather than Arabic. The entry room contains four arches forming a square area in the centre surrounded by galleries, the walls of which are richly decorated in a wealth of colours. The baths themselves have white marble walls and floor, with an upper gallery possibly for musicians.

The exit from the Casa Real takes one into the **Partal Gardens** (named after a pavilion or portico) with its central pool guarded by two large stone lions. Rising over the gardens is the **Torre de las Damas**, via which Boabdil is said to have escaped from his father Muley Abul Hassan. The gallery of the tower has an ornamental wood ceiling with a cupola decorated with stars, domes and shells. The highest part of the tower forms a belvedere giving fine views over the Darro valley below.

Palacio de Carlos V

The building was begun in 1526 after Carlos V had pulled down a significant part of the Casa Real to make way for it. The palace was designed by Pedro Manchuca, who was once a pupil of Michelangelo, and is in strong Renaissance style. The work was stopped in 1568 due to a Moorish rebellion and did not resume until 1579, but has never been completely finished. Although claimed to be the best Renaissance palace outside Italy, it sits uncomfortably amongst the delicate Moorish buildings around it (in much the same way the Christian cathedral seems out of place in the Moorish Mosque at Córdoba, which was also the work of Carlos V). The interior is dominated by the central courtyard in the form of a circle surrounded by a portico of 32 Doric columns, with a similar number of Ionic columns in the upper gallery, which is a pattern repeated on the exterior of the building. The courtyard was often used as an arena and even staged bullfights. The ground floor of the palace now houses the **Museum of Hispano-Muslim Art**, while the upper floor is the site of the Granada's **Museo de Belles Artes**. The Alhambra entrance fee does not cover these museums and tickets must be bought at the door.

Generalife

Above the Alhambra on the slopes of the Cerro del Sol is the Generalife, the summer palace of the monarchs of Granada. The name is derived from the Arabic *Gennat-al-Arif* (Garden of the Architect). It was probably built in the 13th century, although it has since been altered several times, particularly after the fall of Granada, although this work was almost certainly carried out by Arab workers. It can be reached from the upper car park entrance and also from the Alhambra via a bridge which crosses the Cuesta del Rey Chico.

The grounds of the Generalife consist of a series of pathways, gardens and fountains, with clever use of shade and running water – ideal for a relaxing hour or two in the heat of summer. The best known area is the **Patio de la Acequia**, with its arched walkway and stretch of gently playing fountains, with at its end the delightful little palace with latticed plasterwork and an upper galleried belvedere. The other main courtyard is the **Patio de los Cipreses**, where the ancient trees are said to have been the setting for romantic intrigues over the centuries, most notably the affair between Boabdil's favourite wife Zoraya and the head of the Abencerrajes clan who was executed for his troubles along with much of the rest of his family. A ticket can be bought to visit the Generalife only, currently 225 ptas.

It should be remembered that a sizeable city was contained within the walls of the Alhambra and whilst most of this has since been reduced to ruins, there are a few other buildings remaining. Of these, by far the most interesting is the **Convento de San Francisco**. Built by Fernando and Isabel in the late 15th century on the site of a Moorish palace, it is now a *parador*. The chances of getting a room here are slight unless a booking is made several weeks ahead, but it is worth strolling around and taking a drink on the delightful patio. Nearby are the remains of a chapel where Fernando and Isabel were originally buried, before being removed (against their instructions) to the cathedral in the city.

Admission to the Alhambra The Alhambra area is open 0900-1645 in winter and 0900-1845 in summer. There are ticket offices at the lower Alhambra entrance and the upper Generalife entrance. There is a combined ticket with tear off slips for all four parts of the site, costing 625 ptas, for the Generalife only 250 ptas. The disabled, *Grenadinos*, Spanish senior citizens and children under 8 may enter free. Remember that there is a time slot for visiting the Casa Real. There is also a 2-day ticket, which is good value and allows for a leisurely visit. During the height of the season there are night time floodlit visits at 600 ptas, on Tues, Thur and Sat 2200-2345. Because of the crowds, it is good advice to try to arrive before the coaches or, alternatively, after they have gone (around 1630).

OTHER PLACES OF INTEREST

The Albaicín Immediately SW of the Alhambra on the far side of the Río Darro is the old Moorish ghetto of Albaicín, its name meaning 'district on the slope of a hill'. It is believed to have been originally occupied in 1227 by Moors driven out of Baza by Ferdinand III and became one of the busiest areas of Moorish Andalucía, shown by the remains of 30 or more mosques and numerous water tanks and fountains. Today, the area is best approached by taking the Carrera del Darro from the Plaza Nueva, alongside the river (with good views of the Alhambra to the right, particularly when floodlit at night) and then striking off left up the Cuesta del Chapiz or the C/de Zafra to ramble along the narrow cobbled streets and alleys, through tiny plazas, past Moorish ramparts and cisterns and the traditional *cármenes* (a combination of houses and gardens). There are, however, a number of interesting sites in the valley, including the **Church of Santa Ana**, dating from the 16th century and located just above the point where the Darro disappears under the city. Nearby, on the left, are the **Baños Arabes**, an 11th century set of public baths, now privately owned but allowing visitors. Some of the columns in the brick built rooms are Roman and there are typical star-shaped skylights. Open Mon-Sat 1000-1400. Also on the Carrera del Darro at No 43 is the **Casa de Castril** in Renaissance style and now the city's Archaeological museum. Behind this building is the **Convento de Santa Catalina**, housed in an old Moorish palace – the nuns' *dulces* have a mean reputation. The main mosque of the Albaicín now has the **Iglesia de San Salvador** built on its site, but the original *patio arabe* was fortunately preserved. The best views

of the Alhambra and the distant Sierra Nevada are obtained from the *mirador* at the top of the hill beside the **Iglesia de San Nicolás**, which can be reached on Bus No 12. The church has little of interest, but note the genuine Moorish fountain outside.

Once up here the **Puerta Nueva** gateway is nearby to the N. From here W, parallel with the Cuesta de la Alhacaba, are some 13th century Moorish walls, marking the oldest area of Moorish Granada. Near the W end is the **Convento of Santa Isabel** on C/San Juan de los Reyes, named after the Queen who received the city at Boabdil's capitulation in 1492. Partially built within an old Nasrid palace of which some arches still remain, the convent's church has a Mudéjar ceiling and a fine Plateresque doorway. Beyond it on Callejón de las Monjas, formerly part of the convent, are the remains of the 15th century Moorish palace of Dar al-Horra built for Boabdil's mother Ayesha la Horra, whose feud with her husband was largely responsible for the Moors loss of Granada. The style of the surviving tower and patio overlooking the Albaicín is reminiscent of the Alhambra itself. It is currently closed for restoration.

Two churches worth a visit are the **Iglesia de San Miguel** on the E side of the attractive Plaza de San Miguel Bajo, built over a mosque and preserving the original ablutions fountain, and the **Iglesia de San José**, in C/Cauchiles, also built over a mosque and maintaining the minaret as a belfry.

Sacromonte This area of gypsy caves has been inhabited for hundreds of years and although some still do live here the majority of the *gitanos* have been rehoused in the city after the floods in 1962. The gypsies return in the evening to perform contrived *flamenco* shows to coachloads of tourists, who are outrageously fleeced with over-the-top prices for drinks and tatty souvenirs, often with a spot of professional pick-pocketing and amateurish fortune telling. Never-

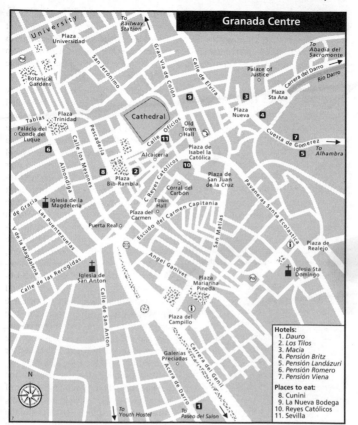

Granada Centre

To Railway Station

University

Plaza Universidad

San Jerónimo

Pol

Botanical Gardens

Plaza Trinidad

Tablas

Palácio del Conde del Luque

6

Alhondiga

de Gracia

Las Puentezuelas

Calle de las Recogidas

Gran Vía de Colón

Pescadería

Calle los Mesones

Cathedral

Calle Oficios

Alcaicería

11

C. Reyes Católicos

8   **2**

Plaza Bib-Rambla

Corral del Carbón

Town Hall

Plaza del Carmen

Puerta Real

V de la Magdalena

✝ Iglesia de la Magdalena

Iglesia de San Anton

Calle de San Anton

Galerías Preciadas

Acera de Darro

To Youth Hostel

Calle de Elvira

Palace of Justice

9

Old Town Hall

Plaza de Isabel la Católica

10

Plaza de San Juan de la Cruz

Escudo del Carmen

Capitania

San Matias

Angel Ganivet

Plaza Marianna Pineda

i

Plaza del Campillo

Carrera del Genil

To Paseo del Salon

1

Plaza Sta Ana

3

Plaza Nueva

4

Carrera del Darro

Rio Darro

To Abadia del Sacromonte

Cuesta de Gomerez

7

5

To Alhambra

Pavaneras Santa Ecolástica

✝ Iglesia Sta Domingo

Plaza de Realejo

i

Pol

N

Hotels:
1. *Dauro*
2. *Los Tilos*
3. *Macia*
4. *Pensión Britz*
5. *Pensión Landázuri*
6. *Pensión Romero*
7. *Pensión Viena*

Places to eat:
8. Cunini
9. La Nueva Bodega
10. Reyes Católicos
11. Sevilla

theless, Sacromonte has plenty of atmosphere and most visitors return feeling that they have had a good, if pricy, evening out.

The **Cathedral** Claimed to be one of the finest Renaissance churches in Spain, most visitors might find this description extravagant. Begun in 1518 on the foundations of a mosque, it was largely the work of Diego Siloé. Squat, towerless and hemmed in by other buildings, the exterior is dull with only the main W façade by Alonso Cano of some merit. The interior, however, has some redeem-ing features, being light and airy and, unusually for Andalucía, possessing some fine stained glass windows by Teodoro of Holland. The nave is flanked by four aisles lined with chapels containing some altarpieces and works by Bocanegra, Cano and Ribera. The stonework of the cathedral is painted white and this makes a sharp contrast with the gold of the Capilla Mayor, where on the columns of the main arch are statues of the Catholic Monarchs at prayer carved by Pedro de Mena. Hours and entrance fee as for the Capilla Real.

The **Capilla Real** (Royal Chapel) Begun in 1506 and completed in 1521, the chapel was designed as a sepulchre for the Catholic Monarchs. Isabel died in 1505 and Fernando 11 years later, both being buried at the Alhambra, but in 1521 their remains were taken to the Capilla Real. The Gothic style building actually has only one façade (it adjoins three other buildings), which has a Plateresque portico embellished with shield and emblems of *los Reyes Católicos*. Inside, the tombs are found in the transept enclosed by a fine Plateresque *reja* by Maestro Bartolemé of Jaén. The tombs are carved from Carrera marble and the Catholic Monarchs are flanked by their daughter Joanna la Loca (the Mad) and her unfortunate husband Felipe el Hermoso (the Fair). The actual coffins are in the crypt underneath, but whether they still contain the monarchs' bodies is debatable as they were desecrated by Napoleon's troops during the Peninsular War. Other features of note are the *retablo* by Felipe de Vigarny containing a wealth of gilded figures and scenes including the handing over of the keys of the city by Boabdil, and the Sacristy which contains Fernando's sword, Isabel's crown and her personal art collection including several Medieval Flemish paintings and her impressive royal jewels. All in all the Capilla Real is of more interest than the cathedral itself. Open Mar-Sep 1030-1300 and 1600-1900; Oct-Feb 1100-1300 and 1530-1800. Entrance 200 ptas.

Alcaicería This is a set of little streets which used to be the Moorish silk market, located around C/Zacatín which was next to the mosque (now under the cathedral). Unfortunately, little of the original market remains following a fire in 1843. Restoration work has been carried out reviving some of the atmosphere, but substituting expensive gift shops for the Moorish bazaars.

Palacio de Madraza Also in C/Zacatín at the N end is this rarely visited palace which was built in the early 1300's for Yusef I and was the prayer college attached to the mosque. Although much restored, it is still possible to see the old prayer hall with its elaborately decorated *mihrab*. Gaining entry, however, may be a problem.

Corral de Carbón (Charcoal House) This is the oldest surviving Moorish building in Granada. It was originally an inn of the type widespread in the early 14th century, before being successively adapted as a granary, a theatre, a centre for charcoal sellers and now a craft centre with artisan workshops. Entry is through a magnificent Moorish horseshoe arch backed by a double gallery arch into a courtyard with a marble horse trough, surrounded by two upper galleries made of brick. Open Mon-Fri 1000-2000, Sat 1000-1400. Entrance free. The Municipal Tourist office is now located here in the office to the left of the entrance.

Hospital de San Juan de Dios Situated in the W of the central area of Granada and about 10 mins walk from the cathedral is the Hospital of San Juan de Dios. It was founded by the Catholic Monarchs in 1492 and has been on its present site since 1504. Entry is through a fine portico with Doric columns, but the most impressive features are the two patios. The outer, larger one has a lower arched gallery decorated with coloured tiles and a typical Andalucían pebble patterned floor with central fountain. The smaller inner patio is full of orange trees and crumbling frescoes. The building is still a working hospital and entry should be discreet. Next door is the **Church of San Juan de Dios**. Begun in 1737, it has an imposing façade capped with two spires. The entrance door has two sets of Corinthian columns, the upper set framing a statue of St John by Ponce de León. The interior is dominated by the High chapel with frescoes and a spectacular *retablo* by JF Guerrero dripping with gold, marble and glass.

One block away from San Juan de Dios in C/Gran Capitán is the **Monastery of San Jeronimo**. It was founded by the Catholic Monarchs in 1492 and the building was completed in 1547, much of the work directed by Siloé. Of exceptional importance are the cloisters, with a double layer of 36 arches, and the church, which has some 18th century frescoes and a magnificent gold *retablo*. On either side of the *retablo* are statues of 'El Gran Capitán' Gonzalo de Córdoba and his wife Maria Manrique at prayer. Open 1030-1330 and 1600-1930; entrance 200 ptas.

Not far from the university on the NW side of the city on C/Real de Cartuja is the impressive Carthusian **Monastery of La Cartuja**. It is located in the Ainada Mar (Fountain of Tears) area of Granada where the Arabs once built their summer residences on land given by 'El Gran Capitán'. It took over 300 years to complete and is a mixture of the styles spanning this period resulting in an overall impression of jumbled opulence, with Baroque dominant. Entry is through a Plateresque porch, with an arch bearing the coat of arms of Spain, over which is a vaulted niche with a 16th century wooden statue of the Virgen. Within, there is a large courtyard with orange trees and box hedges, with the monastery on one side and the Church on the other. The overwhelming wealth of the church is almost too much to take, but note in particular the 18th century Sacristy in brown and white marble and rich decorations. The Sagrario is almost as impressive, while next to the choirstalls are a pair of paintings by Cotán surrounded by gilded carving. It is open daily Mar-Sep 1030-1300 and 1600-1900; Oct-Feb 1030-1300 and 1530-1800. Entrance 150 ptas, free Sun mornings. For visitors without their own transport, the monastery is a good 30 mins walk from the city centre, but the No 8 bus passes nearby.

MUSEUMS

NB Many museums are now free for EU citizens, but you will need your passport as proof.

Casa Museo Federico García Lorca Located 17 km W of the city in the village of Fuente Vaqueros is the birthplace and former home of the dramatist and poet Federico García Lorca, who was shot by right wing Nationalists in 1936. The building is located in C/Poeta García Lorca, just off the main square and is full of Lorca memorabilia. Ureña buses go here approx hourly from Avda Andaluces by the train station. Open 1000-1300 and 1800-2000 during summer and 1000-1300 and 1600-1800 during winter. Closed Mon. Entrance 200 ptas, T 516453.

Casa Museo Manuel de Falla, C/Antequeruela Alta 11. The *Gaditano* composer's home for a number of years. Open 1000-1500. Closed Mon. Entrance 150 ptas.

Museo Angel Barrios The home of this 20th century guitarist is inside the Alhambra grounds and contains information about his life. Open 1500-1800. Closed Sun and fiestas. Entrance 150 ptas.

Museo Arqueológico de la Casa de Castril is housed in a 16th century mansion in the Albaicín with a splendid Plateresque façade. There are some important and well-displayed Neolithic remains from the caves at Los Murceliegos and an excellent Roman section which includes some 4th century Christian lamps. Make sure to see the Moorish room featuring a 4th century bronze astrolobe, which was used to position stars in order to orientate *mihrabs* towards Mecca, as well as converting Muslim dates into Christian ones. Open Tues-Sat 1000-1400. Entrance 200 ptas, T 225640.

Museo Bellas Artes Located on the upper floor of the Palacio de Carlos V in the Alhambra grounds, the sculptures are generally better than the paintings, with works by Diego de Siloé, Alonso

Cano, Pedro de Mena and the de Mora brothers. One of the most important items is a triptych of El Gran Capitán, a 15th century raised enamel from Limo-

ges attributed to Nardon Penicaud. After the beauty of the Alhambra, this museum does not get the attention it deserves. Open Tues-Fri 1000-1400; Sat

Federico García Lorca

🐾 Lorca, undoubtedly the most popular poet of the Spanish speaking world, was born in 1898 in the village of Fuente Vaqueros, a village on the *vega* to the W of Granada. His childhood was spent in Granada and on the family farm, Huerta de San Vincente, where he absorbed the flavour of the Andalucían countryside and the way of life of its people, especially the gypsies. He attended the university in Granada, where he published his first book of poems, and later went on to Madrid university where he studied philosophy. When he was 30, he achieved national fame for the first time with his book of gypsy ballads, *El Romancero Gitano*. On the strength of this success, he went to New York for a year learning English, intermittently attending Columbia university and working on a book of poems, *Poeta en Nueva York*, which was published after his death.

Lorca returned to Spain in 1931 and ran a popular travelling theatre for the Spanish Government. During the next 5 years he produced his best known stage works, including *Bodas de Sangre* (Blood Wedding, 1933), *Yerma* (1935) and *La Casa de Bernarda Alba* (1936), which dealt with the passions and emotions of country people. His most famous set of poems was *Lament for the Death of a Bullfighter and other poems* (1935), beginning with the line *'A las cinco de la tarde'* and stressing throughout the nobility of the gypsies.

Lorca was proud of his Moorish ancestry and despised the post-Reconquest activities of the Christians, suggesting that *Los Reyes Católicos* had destroyed a culture superior to their own. He was also strongly critical of Granada's middle class, believing them to be northerners rather than true Andalucíans. Lorca was an accomplished musician and recognized the historical importance of *flamenco* to the Andalucían culture, organizing Granada's first festival of *cante jondo*, the deep gypsy song.

Lorca was an open *maricón*, or homosexual, with Republican sympathies. Neither trait appealed to the middle classes of Granada, where Lorca had expected to be safe during the Civil War. He was mistaken. In Aug 1936 he was assassinated by a group of Franco's thugs in a gully in the village of Viznar, some 10 km NE of Granada. His body was never found.

The Granada authorities have been slow to appreciate the worth of their most famous son, but visitors on a Lorca 'pilgrimage' have three places which they can visit. Firstly, the house where Lorca was born in Fuente Vaqueros is now a museum to his memory. Secondly, the Huerta de San Vicente where the Lorca family spent the summer, is now a rose garden. The house on the plot is not at the present open to the public, but there are plans for it to be a museum. Finally, at the village of Viznar, where Lorca was shot, there is a monumental garden with a small granite memorial. In Granada there is nothing.

Recommended reading Go no further than Ian Gibson, a British writer based in Spain, who has written three books on Lorca: *Lorca's Granada* (Faber and Faber); *Federico García Lorca* (Penguin) and *The Assassination of Federico García Lorca* (Pantheon).

1000-1300. Entrance 150 ptas, free with EU passport.

Museo Hispano Musulmán (Museum of Hispano-Muslim Art) On the ground floor of the Palacio de Carlos V. Contains many items from the Alhambra, most notably a spectacular 15th century vase, the Jarrón de la Alhambra, a metre and a half in height, together with Moorish ceramics, stucco, carvings, jewellery, etc. There is also an 11th century stone trough with strong relief work on its sides showing antelopes and lions fighting at the foot of a tree. Open Mon-Fri 1000-1400, Sat 1000-1300. Entrance 150 ptas, free with EU passport, T 226279.

Casa de los Tiros Located in the Plaza del Padre Suarez, this building was formerly the Palace of the Princes of Granada and now houses the Museum of the History and Handicrafts of Granada. A fortress like building, it gets its name from the 'tiros' or muskets projecting from the upper windows. Also adorning the exterior are a number of statues of Greek deities such as Hercules, Theseus, Jason, Hector and Mercury. Inside, the Golden Hall has a beautifully painted coffered ceiling. Alongside the small courtyard with its Moorish columns and capitals there is an Alpujarras style kitchen of the type typical of inns in this region. There are other rooms devoted to the gypsy culture, local bullfighting memorabilia and Washington Irving. Local ceramics and wrought iron are well represented, but the painting is generally disappointing. Currently, this museum is closed, but should have re-opened by the time this handbook is published – check with the local tourist office.

Parque de las Ciencias (Granada Science Park) An interactive 'hands on' museum, particularly attractive for children, with plenty of opportunity to take part in experiments. Displays and themes change regularly. Also has a planetarium. Open Tues-Sat 1000-1900, Sun 1000-1500, closed Mon. Entrance 350 ptas, children 250 ptas. Planetarium is 150 and 100 ptas extra.

LOCAL FESTIVALS

A fiesta on the first 2 days of Jan celebrates the end of the Reconquista and the arrival of the victorious King Fernando and Queen Isabel in Granada. In early Feb the *Romería Popular de San Cecilio*, the city's patron saint, takes place with a pilgrimage to Sacromonte Abbey in his honour. During *Semana Santa* at Easter, the traditional processions take place and special viewing stands are erected in Plaza del Carmen. May begins with *Las Cruces de Mayo* when the squares and patios are decorated with floral crosses. In Jun, to mark Granada's major festival of *Corpus Cristi*, there are bullfights and other celebrations. At the end of Jun or beginning of Jul the *International Music and Dance Festival* takes place in the Palacio de Carlos V information from C/Ancha de Santo Domingo, T 225201. 29 Sep is the occasion for another *romería popular*, this time to the Hermitage of San Miguel Alto, and the last Sun in Sep is the *Fiesta de Nuestra Señora de las Angustias* (Our Lady of Sorrows). In Nov the *International Jazz Festival* takes place.

LOCAL INFORMATION

Price guide

Hotels:

AL	over US$90	**D**	US$20-40
A	US$75-90	**E**	US$10-20
B	US$60-75	**F**	under US$10
C	US$40-60		

Places to eat:

♦♦♦	expensive	♦♦	average
♦	cheap		

● **Accommodation**

Most visitors will be coming to Granada on a short stay to see the Alhambra area and must choose between the convenience of more expensive accommodation nr to the main site or cheaper, or noisier options in the city. Those arriving by car should certainly look for garage/parking space. With over 50 hotels (incl

12 in the luxury **AL** range) and around 100 *pensiones*, there is certainly an abundance of choice, reflecting the drawing power of Granada's tourist sites.

There are 2 possibilities within the walls of the Alhambra itself: **AL** *Parador San Francisco*, La Alhambra, T 221440, F 222264, 38 rm, parking, TV, gardens, restaurant, a/c, magnificent and luxurious accommodation inside the Alhambra complex, book well in advance, especially in summer; **B** *America*, Real de la Alhambra 53, T 227471, F 227470, 13 rm, delightful small hotel, formerly a hostel, close to the parador, no restaurant, booking essential, expensive for the facilities but well worth it.

Other hotels in a quiet location close to the Alhambra incl: **AL** *Alhambra Palace*, C/Peña Partida 2, T 221468, F 226404, 144 rm, a/c, wheelchair access, restaurant, parking, garden, luxury in pseudo Moorish style; **A** *Los Alixares*, Avda Alixares del Generalife s/n, T 225506, F 224102, 162 rm, modern, a/c, pool, parking, good views, restaurant; **A** *Washington Irving*, Paseo de Generalife 2, T 227550, F 228840, 68 rm, restaurant, gloomy old fashioned grandeur but conveniently placed nr the Generalife car park, named after the American writer who penned *Tales of the Alhambra*; **B** *Guadalupe*, Avda de los Alijares s/n, T 223423, F 223798, 58 rm, a/c, parking, comfortable, close to the Generalife car park.

The nearest decent *pensión* is: **D** *Suecia*, C/Moninos 2, Huerta Los Angeles, T 225044, 13 rm, in quiet cul-de-sac 15 mins walk from the Alhambra, used by tour parties.

Rec hotels in the central area of town incl: **AL** *Carmen*, C/Acero del Darro 62, T 258300, F 256462, 283 rm, wheelchair access, a/c, restaurant, pool, luxury hotel with all facilities; **AL** *Luz Granada*, Avda de la Constitución 18, T 204061, F 293150, 174 rm, wheelchair access, a/c, garage, disco; **AL** *Princesa Ana*, Avda de la Constitución 37, T 287447, F 273954, 61 rm, garage, a/c, restaurant, central position; **A** *Condor*, Avda de la Constitución 6, T 283711, F 283850, 101 rm, a/c, garage, restaurant, central position; **A** *Gran Via de Granada*, C/Postigo de Velluti 2, T 285464, F 285591, a/c, garage, restaurant, just to the W of the cathedral; **B** *Dauro*, C/Acero del Dauro 19, T 222156, F 228519, 36 rm, a/c, garage, modern and central; **B** *Victoria*, Puerta Real 3, T 257700, F 263108, 69 rm, a/c, restaurant, located in a busy square; **C** *Los Tilos*, Plaza de Bib-Rambla 4, T 266712, F 266801, 30 rm, plain, central, traffic noise; **C** *Macía*, Plaza Nueva 4, T 227536, F 285591, 40 rm, a/c, in busy square beneath the Alhambra.

Pensiones: note that there are, surprisingly, no pensiones in the Albaicín area. Most are located in the district to the SE of the cathedral.

D *Residencia Britz*, Cuesta de Gomérez 1, T 223652, 22 rm, noisy location on the hill leading up to the Alhambra; **D** *Las Cumbres*, C/Cardenal Mendoza 4, T 291222, garage, close to San Juan de Dios; **D** *Lisboa*, Plaza del Carmen 27, T 221413, 28 rm, clean and modern, on busy square nr to the cathedral; **D** *Veronica*, C/Angel 17, T 258145, 14 rm, small friendly hostel S of the cathedral.

E *Landázuri*, C/Cuesta de Gomérez 24, T 221406, 15 rm, on the hill leading up to the Alhambra, restaurant and roof terrace with views of the Alhambra; **E** *Romero*, C/Sillería de Mesones 1, T 266079, convenient position on the corner of Plaza Trinidad, clean rooms, some with balconies over the square; **E** *Viena*, C/Hospital de Santa Ana 2, T 221859, 3 rm, small Austrian owned hostel off the Cuesta de Gomérez.

F *San Jerómino*, C/San Jerónimo 12, T 275040, 5 rm, cheapest in town; **F** *Terminus*, Avda Andaluces 10, T 201423, 28 rm, plain and cheap, in a noisy locality nr the train station.

Something different: **D** *Cortijo La Solana*, La Solana Alta, 18650 Dúrcal, Granada, T/F 780575, 4 rm with balconies and great views in this comfortable country guest house overlooking the Lecrín valley, S of Granada close to the Puerta del Suspiro del Moro, price incl breakfast, American run.

Youth hostels: *Camino de Fuente*, 18779 Viznar, T 543307, F 543448, 108 beds, 12 km from Granada in woodland setting, facilities for the disabled; *Camino de Ronda 171*, T 222638, 78 beds, meals provided, swimming pool, in a sports complex on the edge of town, suitable for wheelchair users, bus No 11 300m, reservations essential.

Camping: *El Ultimo*, Ctra Huétor-Vega, Km 22, T 123069, open all year; *Los Alamos*, Ctras Nacional 342, Km 290, T 275743, pool, open Apr-Oct; *María Eugenia*, Ctra Nacional 342, Km 286, T 200606, pool, 4 km further out, open all year; *Sierra Nevada*, Ctra de Madrid, Km 107, T 270956, large top grade site nr town with modern facilities and pool, open Mar-Oct. All sites on bus routes.

● **Places to eat**

Eating out is no problem in Granada, where there are restaurants and bars to suit all tastes and pockets. Hotel restaurants tend to be pricy, while the Alhambra and Plaza Nueva areas have the inevitable establishments well versed in tourist rip offs. There are a number of regional specialities – try Trevélez ham, cured in the mountain air of the highest village in Spain; omelette *al Sacromonte* and almond soup. Regional desserts contain more than a hint of the Moorish past, with *huesos de santo* ('saints bones') and *barettas*.

♦♦♦*Cunini*, C/Pescaderia 14, T 250777, expensive sea food restaurant; ♦♦♦*Mirador de Morayma*, Callejon de las Vacas 2, T 228290, marvellous location overlooking the Albaicín and the Alhambra – a must for all romantics, local specialities incl *tortilla de Sacromonte*; ♦♦♦*Sevilla*, C/Officios 12, T 221223, traditional restaurant close to the cathedral, Andalucían speciality, said to have been one of Lorca's favourites.

♦♦*Alcaicería*, C/Officios 8, T 224341, atmospheric location in the old Arab market close to the cathedral, good regional specialities; ♦♦*Chikito*, Plaza Campillo 9, T 223364, international cooking in a central location E of the cathedral; ♦♦*Jardines Alberto*, Avda del Generalife, T 224818, small restaurant with good ambience nr the Generalife entrance; ♦♦*Las Perdices*, Avda Andalucía 24, game specialities; ♦♦*Seis Peniques*, Plaza de los Tiros, T 226256, regional and international food.

♦*Casa Cepilla*, Plaza Pescadería 18, good value *menú del día*; ♦*La Nueva Bodega*, C/Cetti Merién 3, T 222401, cheap and cheerful at the bar; ♦*MacDonalds*, C/Recogidas 25, T 264140, for American fast food at a Spanish pace; ♦*Pizzería Burguer Goffi*, C/Pedro Antonio de Alarcón, fast food and takeaways; ♦*Reyes Católicos*, Placeta Sillería 3, T 223928, friendly service and a range of fixed price *menús*.

Tea shops: on Plaza Nueva, try *As-sirat*, Caldereria Nueva 5, wide selection, pleasant atmosphere.

Ice Cream parlours: for a good *heladerías*, try *La Perla* in Plaza Nueva.

● **Bars**

Tapas bars offer some local atmosphere in Campe Príncipe and along C/Acera del Darro, C/Martínez de la Rosa and C/Gran Capitán. Typical *tapas* incl *tortilla al Sacromonte* (omelette with potatoes, peas and peppers), brains in batter and testicles (all finely chopped!), *habas con jamón* (beans with ham) and fried fish and other seafood.

● **Banks & money changers**

All banks are closed on Sat from 15 Jun-15 Sep. Numerous banks and *telebancos* (cash points) in Plaza Isabel la Católica, along Gran Vía de Colón and C/Reyes Católicos, incl some foreign banks.

● **Embassies & consulates**

Belgium, C/Recogidas 66, 1°A, T 251631; France, C/Carlos Pareja 5, T 261447; Germany, Avda de la Constitución 20, T 293352; Italy, C/Dr Martín Lagos 3 – 1°, T 261361. **NB** The nearest British Consulate is in Málaga.

● **Entertainment**

Bullfights: there are regular bullfights, but especially important during Corpus Cristi. The box office is on C/Escudo del Carmen, open evenings only.

Cinemas: there are also 4 cinemas, the best of which is *Multicines Centro*, Plaza de Gracia s/n, T 252996.

Discotheques: only really flourish in the university term time, when some of the lower Sacromonte caves are turned into lively discos. In town there are several *discobares*, such as *La Estrella*, C/Cucherillos, off Plaza Nueva, and *Patapalo*, C/Naranjas 2, nr Plaza del Carmen.

Flamenco: popular and reliable flamenco at *Jardines Neptuno* on C/Arabia from 2200 daily, book in advance, entrance incl drink, 2,500 ptas, T 251112. The shows in the caves of Sacromonte are heavily tourist orientated.

Nightclubs: try *New York*, C/Porton de Tejiero, or *El Cid*, C/Luis Braille 3.

Theatres: there are 2 theatres in Granada: *Teatro Isabel la Católica*, C/Acera del Casino 2, T 223269. Information T 274000; and *Teatro Estable de Granada (Universitario)*, C/Gran Capitán 16, T 202725.

● **Hospitals & medical services**

Hospitals: *Cruz Roja* (emergencies), C/Escoriaza 8, T 222024; *General Hospital*, Avda Coronel Muñez, T 276400; *Hospital Clinico San Cecilio*, Avda Dr Olóriz 16, T 270200; *Hospital San Juan de Dios*, C/San Juan de Dios 15, T 204200; *Hospital Virgen de las Nieves*, Avda de la Constitución 100, T 241000.

● **Post & telecommunications**

Area code: 958.

Post Office: *Correos* in Puerta Real. Open Mon-Fri 0800-2100, Sat 0800-1400. Telegrams Mon-Fri 0800-2100, Sat 0900-1700, Sun 0900-1400.

Telephones: there is a public call centre at C/Reyes Católicos 55. Open Mon-Sat 0900-1400 and 1700-2200.

● **Shopping**
The main shopping streets are to the E of the cathedral, particularly along C/Reyes Católicos and around the square of Puerta Real. The main department store is *Galerías Preciados* on Acera del Darro. There are a variety of craft items which are typical of the area, incl carpets, marquetry work, brass lanterns and *jarapas*, the traditional rugs from the Alpujarras. There are artisan workshops in the Corral de Carbon adjacent to the tourist office.

● **Sports**
There are no fewer than 8 **swimming** pools in the city. There is an **aquapark**, Parque Acuatico 'Aquola', Ctra de la Sierra, Km 4, T 486186. For **roller skating**, Don Patín, C/General Narvaez 14. For sport in general, incl **tennis**, contact Club Omnisport Grenade 74, C/Cañaveral s/n, T 202505.

● **Tour companies & travel agents**
Bonanza, C/Reyes Católicos 30, T 229777; *Ecuador*, C/Angel Ganivet 8, T 223566; *Marsans*, Gran Via de Colón 20, T 222088; *Sacromonte*, C/Angel Ganivet 6, T 225598.

● **Tourist offices**
The main tourist office in splendid new accommodation in the Corral de Carbón, C/Libreras 2, opens weekdays 1000-1400, T 225990. There is also a provincial tourist office at Plaza de Mariana Pineda 10, T 226688, open all the year round, Mon-Fri 1000-1300 and 1630-1900, Sat 1000-1300. Tourist guides are available using a variety of languages – contact Puerta del Vino in the Alhambra, T 229936.

● **Useful addresses**
Garages/workshops: *Citroën*, C/Ribera del Genil s/n, T 814056; *Ford*, Ctra Amarila s/n, T 810111; *Peugeot*, Camino de Ronda 129, T 201761; *Renault*, T 272850; *Seat*, C/Arabial 80-90, T 275254; *VAG*, Ctra Sierra Nevada 30, T 227505; *Volvo*, Camino de Ronda 83, T 254804.

● **Transport**
Local Bus: locally, No 2 from Plaza Bibataubín or Carrera del Genil beside *Galerias Preciados*

for the Alhambra; No 8 for La Cartuja and No 12 for the Albaicín, both leave from beside the Cathedral; No 11 (circular) for the stations and the town centre. Free bus maps are available from the tourist offices and *bonobús* tickets for 10 journeys can be bought in advance from tobacconists and kiosks for 500 ptas. The main inter city bus company serving all major towns in Andalucía and the coast is *Alsina Graells* at Camino de Ronda 97, T 251358. Long distance coaches to other parts of Spain are run by *Bacoma* at Avda de Andaluces 10, T 284251. There are daily buses to Almería (4), Almuñecar (6), Basa (8), Córdoba (7), Guadix (11), Jaén (8), Madrid (1), Málaga (15), Motril (7), Nerja (2), Salobreña (7) and Sevilla (8). **Car hire**: *Alquiauto*, C/Cristo de Medinaceli 1, T 255747; **Atesa**, Plaza de Cuchilleros 1, T 224004; **Avis**, C/Recogidas 31, T 252358; *Europcar*, Avda del Sur 12, T 295065; **Autos Fortuna**, C/Camino de Purchil 2, T 260254; **Autos Gudelva**, C/Pedro Antonio de Alarcón 18, T 251435; **Hertz**, C/Luis Braille 7, T 251682. **Coche de Caballo** (horse drawn carriage): available nr *Correos* on C/de los Mesones. Fix the price before setting off. **Cycle hire**: from *Ski 3* shop at Ctra de Sierra Nevada 46, T 210211. **Taxi**: there are taxi ranks in Plaza Nueva, Puerta Real and outside the Alhambra. *Radio Taxi*, T 151461; *Tele Taxi*, T 280654.

Air National flight tickets and information from Iberia, Plaza Isabel la Católica 2, T 227592 and T 203322. Two flights a day to **Madrid** and **Barcelona** for transit to international destinations and flights each week to **Valencia** (3), **Palma de Mallorca** (3), **Las Palmas** (2) and **Tenerife** (1). The airport is situated 17 km out of town on Ctra Málaga, T 447081. Buses for the airport leave from outside Bar Ventorillo, nr the cathedral.

Train The train station is on Avda de Andaluces, T 271272, reached by the No.11 bus, which follows a circular route. Additional RENFE office at C/Reyes Católicos 63, T 223119. Daily trains run to **Algeciras** (2), **Almería** (3), **Córdoba** (3), **Guadix** (3), **Madrid** (2), **Málaga** (3), **Ronda** (1) and **Sevilla** (3).

EAST OF GRANADA

East from Granada the N342/E26 runs through the panhandle of the province towards the border with Murcia, initially through outstanding scenery with superb views of the Sierra Nevada to the S. Then follows alternating areas of arid steppe and wooded mountains. There are two Natural Parks, the **Parque Natural de la Sierra de Baza** in the S of the panhandle and the **Parque Natural de la Sierra de Castril** in the more remote N, forming part of the Sistema Subbético. There are two major towns in this eastern part of the province, **Guadix** and **Baza**.

GUADIX

Located some 58 km E of Granada and 6 km along the N324 to Almería is the town of Guadix. It is accessible by train, but the station is 20 mins from the town centre. The bus station is only 5 mins from the main sites (Autodia buses in C/Rector Marín Ocete 10). It is on the Río Guadix and the area immediately around the town is a fertile farming region. Julius Caesar is said to have founded the town in 45 BC, setting up silver, iron and copper mines. Later, the Moors, who called it *Wadi-Ash* (the river of life), established a silk industry here and remained until 1489. Guadix achieved notoriety during the Civil war, when some horrendous atrocities were committed. Today it is an agricultural centre, with industries based on esparto grass and the production of cutlery. Some 10,000 people in Guadix still live in well furnished caves dug out of the soft tufa rock of the hillside. It is thought that this troglodyte community, in the Barrio Santiago, was established following the Christian Reconquista of Spain, when fear of Philip II caused local Moors to seek safety underground. There is a **Cave Museum** in the barrio showing traditional implements and furniture. Open 1000-1400 and 1600-1800; Sat 1000-1400 only.

The town's old quarter is almost entirely walled, with an impressive Moorish gateway, the Puerta San Turcuato. The ruined Moorish **alcazaba** dates from the 10th and 11th centuries. It's red sandstone walls are capped with battlements and a central tower, the *torre gorda* gives magnificent views towards the Sierra Nevada. Open 0900-1300 and 1600-1800. Entrance 100 ptas. Also built of red sandstone is the **cathedral**, which although started in 1492 on the site of a mosque, was not completed until the 18th century. Not surprisingly, it shows a variety of styles, with Baroque dominant. The main façade is dominated by Corinthian columns and designed by Vincente Acero. The late-Gothic interior, which is largely the work of Diego de Siloé, is somewhat gloomy, the best features being the Churrigueresque choir stalls. Open Mon-Sat 1030-1300 and 1630-1800; Sun 1030-1400. Outside is the **Plaza Mayor**, arcaded in Renaissance style and much restored after damage during the Civil War. There are a number of interesting churches in the town, including El Sagrario, with a Plateresque façade and Santiago, which has Mudéjar ceilings.

Visitors looking for accommodation in Guadix will find that there are three small hotels and a *pensión*. The best of these is **D** *Mulhacen*, Avda Buenos Aires 41, T 660750, F 660661, 39 rm, garage; but also recommended is **E** *Carmen*, Ctra Granada, Km 226, T 661500, F 661401, garage, a/c; there is little in the budget range, the cheapest being the pensión **E** *Río Verde*, Ctra Murcia 1, T 664581.

There are some villages of interest around Guadix, including **Graena**, where there are thermal baths used since Roman times, **La Pexa**, where there are the ruins of a 9th century Moorish castle, and the pottery village of **Purullena**. Southwest of Guadix is a large flat semi arid depression known as the **Hoya de Guadix**. This steppe area has chalky ground, dissected with gullies and ravines, with esparto grass and a little cereal farming. Although the site has no special protection or status, this is one of the better areas of Andalucía for steppe birds including Little Bustard (probably 100 pairs), Stone Curlew, Black Bellied Sand Grouse, Tawny Pipits and Dupont's Lark.

BAZA

A further 50 km NE is the town of **Baza**, which has a long history. Iberian tribes occupied the area and their most important relic is the *Dama de Baza*, a sculpture which is now in Madrid, although a copy is in the local archaeological museum. The Romans were certainly here, naming

---

Caves – the troglodyte tendency

There is a long history of cave dwelling in Andalucía. Caves at **Boquete de Zafarraya** (Málaga), **Pinar** (Granada) and **Vera** (Almería) show evidence of Neanderthal man, possibly dating back 85,000 years. Relics include bones, tools, ceramics and cooking implements. The cave wall paintings at Pileta near Ronda showing fish, goats and horses are dated as Bronze Age, while the caves at Nerja (Málaga) show that after the Ice Age, Cro-Magnon man inhabited the caves of Andalucía. It comes as something of a surprise, nevertheless to learn that there are still some 35,000 cave dwellers in Andalucía, the largest proportion of them in the **Guadix** area of Granada province. In most cases, however, these are not natural caves, but dwellings which have been excavated by man in the brown Pliocene clay of the area. The custom is believed to date originally from the 16th century, when the *Moriscos* were fleeing from the persecution of Philip II. Today, the Andalucían government has recognized the situation and embarked on a cave improvement programme.

Do not think, however, that such a life is onerous. Many of the better caves in the Guadix area have seven or eight rooms, electricity, sewage disposal, television and even a cave garage. Many of these troglodytes have resisted the pressure to be rehoused in high rise flats (where would they keep their donkey?) after all, caves do not leak or collapse; they are quieter than apartment living; the temperature is a constant 17°C throughout the year; extra room is easily available.

The caves have title deeds like normal houses and are bought and sold in the same way. Community life is often good, with caves converted into discos, bars and churches. It is often thought most cave dwellers are gypsies, but this is not the case. The most famous gypsy troglodytes are those of the **Sacromonte** district of Granada, but, in fact, most of these have been rehoused in apartments in town and only return to their caves at night to fleece the *flamenco* seeking tourists.

The caves have become tourist attractions in recent years and it is not unusual to find a tour bus including a visit to a cave on its itinerary. People fascinated with caves now have the opportunity to 'Rent-a-Cave'. *Promociones Touristicas de Galera* have 14 caves available for daily or weekly rent (4,000 ptas a night or 22,000 ptas a week. The caves take up to seven people in two double or three single rooms. Contact Tourismo Rural Casas Cuevas, Promociones Turísticas de Galera, Avda Nicasio Tomas 12, 18840 Galera, Granada, T 739068.

For cave luxury try the *Cuevas Pedro Antonio de Alarcon*, a newly built cave hotel in a complex of 19 caves. The hotel has richly furnished rooms and all modern amenities, including an excellent restaurant. The price of a two-room cave sleeping four is 7,800 ptas. Contact Cuevas Pedro Antonio de Alarcon, Barriada San Torcuato, 18500 Guadix, Granada, T 958-664986, F 958-661721.

the town *Basti*, while during Moorish times Baza was a silk producing centre and from 1234 onwards it was part of the Nasrid Kingdom of Granada. It was taken by the Christians in 1489 after a long siege. Today it is mainly an agricultural centre, but has a number of interesting remains. The 10th century Moorish **alcazaba** is well and truly ruined, but the **Banos Arabes** are better preserved. Dating from the 10th century, these Moorish baths are some of the oldest in Spain, but they are now privately owned. For admission seek the advice of the tourist office. Elsewhere, the Church of **Santa Maria de la Encarnacion**, with its façade attributed to Diego de Siloé, is worth a visit, while the **Palacio de los Enriquez**, which is a 16th century Mudéjar mansion, still retains some ceilings in the Moorish style. Again, admission may be a problem, so consult the *turismo*. There are several accommodation possibilities in Baza, but nothing in the luxury class. The best hotel is **D** *Robemar*, Ctra de Murcia, Km 175, T 860704, F 700798, 46 rm, wheelchair access, pool; one of the best bargains in the *pensión* range is **E** *Mariquita*, C/Caños Dorados 10, T 701012, garage. The bus station is on Avda de los Reyes Católicos and there are eight buses a day to Guadix and Granada.

South of Baza is the **Parque Natural de la Sierra de Baza**, consisting of a series of elongated anticlines with the upper areas well wooded with oak, pine, rowan, maple and ilex, covering some 52,000 ha. There is a good variety of Mediterranean birds, with important colonies of Egyptian Vultures and Golden Eagles. Mammals include Genets, Beech Martens and Badgers. North of Baza is the large semi arid depression of the **Hoya de Baza**, covering some 80,000 hectares. Much of the area is covered with tamarisk and scrub, with poplars along the watercourses. The area has no special protected status and contains similar species to the Hoya de Guadix, which birders are advised to choose in preference.

20 km NE of Baza, the C3329 leads to the remote town of **Huéscar**, a settlement of some 10,000 people in a mainly agricultural area. It was an important Roman and Carthaginian town. The Moors also occupied it, until it fell to the Christians in 1488. There are the remains of a Moorish castle and some watchtowers, while there are a number of 16th and 17th century mansions of distinction. The collegiate church of Santa María de la Encarnación, with its impressive façade, dominates the town. Huéscar makes a good base to explore the sierras to the N, including the **Parque Natural de la Sierra de Castril**, a deeply incised limestone block with a number of peaks over 2,000m, containing raptors such as Griffon Vultures and Golden Eagles.

WEST FROM GRANADA

The area immediately W of Granada is a fertile plain or *vega* growing a variety of cereals and vegetables. The landscape is also dotted with groves of Black Poplar, a swift growing hybrid tree. The Poplar is felled every 15 years or so, the wood being in high demand for the packaging and paper industries. The N342 *autovia* cuts across the plain ensuring a speedy journey to Antequera and Málaga, but for the visitor who is not in a hurry, there are some diversions worth making. 15 km from Granada and close to the airport, a minor road leads N to the village of **Fuente Vaqueros**, the birthplace of Federico García Lorca. He was born in Jun 1898 in the house of the village school mistress, his mother. The house is now a museum and the neighbouring granary turned into an exhibition and cultural centre. The house is close to the main square of the village and is open Tues-Sun 1000-1300 and 1700-1900; guided tours on the hour. Entrance 200 ptas.

Some 30 km further W is the small town of **Loja**. A flourishing trading centre in Phoenician times, Loja was a strategic military base under the Moors, guarding the western end of the *vega*. It was eventually captured by Ferdinand in 1486 following a long siege after which it is said that over 5,000 Muslims left the town for Granada. The Moorish *alcazaba* has been in ruins since the time of Philip II, but still retains the walls, the Ochavada tower and a well preserved well. There are a number of churches of interest in Loja, all built in the local brown sandstone. Santa María de la Encarnación was built over a mosque to the design of Ventura Rodríguez and has an impressive tower, but it is the Church of San Gabriel which is most impressive. The work of Diego de Siloé, it is one of the best examples of Renaissance in Granada province. Other buildings of note include the 'New' Granary dating from the 16th century and the Palacio de Narváez, a 19th century building in French style with superb gardens.

Just outside Loja, off the minor road to Ventorros are **Los Infiernos de Loja**, a series of waterfalls and rapids flowing through a ravine cut by the Río Genil in the last part of the Sub-baetic range before going on the Iznájar reservoir. They are particularly impressive in the Spring, when the water levels are high.

A few kilometres W of Loja is the small hamlet of **Río Frio**, where the river of the same name flows N to join the Genil. A number of *piscifactorías*, or trout hatcheries, have sprung up here and they in turn have spawned several *ventas* and restaurants, featuring trout as their speciality dishes. This is a favourite stop for Granada bound coaches, while on Sun Río Frio is a popular lunchtime venue for *granadinos* and *malaguenos*.

An alternative, slower and more picturesque route from Granada to Málaga is via the spa town of **Alhama de Granada**, over the **Zafarraya Pass** and down through the **Axarquia** to **Velez-Málaga** and the coast. There are two possible routes from Granada to Alhama. One is from the S outskirts of Granada at Armilla and proceeding along the C340 through Malá and Ventas de Huelma. The other quicker route involves leaving the *autovia* at Moraleda de Zafayona and heading S on the GR131.

ALHAMA DE GRANADA

Perched on a clifftop overlooking a deep gorge created by the Río Alhama, the town gets its name from the Moorish *Al Hamman* meaning 'thermal waters or baths'. Its history, in fact, goes much further back than the Moors as it was occupied in turn by the Iberians, Phoenicians, Carthaginians and Romans (who called it *Artigi*). Both the Romans and the Moors valued Alhama highly as a spa and the baths are still in operation today. To find them take the 340 N out of town (noting the old Roman bridge) and fork right to find a complex of gardens, fountains, a hotel and the baths themselves. Some of the old Moorish 11th century constructions remain, but the present day buildings date from the Middle Ages. The staff at the hotel can show you some of the original Moorish sections of the baths.

The town itself is a delight and one can appreciate Muley Hacen's cry of sorrow "Ay di me Alhama", when he lost the battle here against Christian forces in 1482. Most of the places to see are near to the Plaza de la Constitución, close to which is the **barrio árabe**, with a maze of alleyways following the original street plan. The Moorish **castle** is largely ruined and privately owned. Close by is the 16th century **Iglesia del Carmen**, which looks out over the gorge. The church which dominates the town, however, is the **Iglesia La Encarnación**, a 15th century Gothic building with a Mudéjar pulpit and an *artesonado* ceiling, which the ubiquitous Siloé had a hand in designing. Other buildings worth seeing include the **Posito** (granary) in the Plaza de los Presos, which was built in the 13th century and used for a time as a synagogue, and the **Casa de la Inquisición**, a delightful stone building with a Platteresque façade.

There are a limited number of accommodation possibilities in Alhama, with just two hotels and a *pensión*. The best, but still reasonably priced is **B** *Balneario Alhama de Granada*, Balnearios s/n, T 350011, F 350297, 116 rm, spa hotel at the baths with pool and tennis. There is also **D** *Baño Nuevo*, Balnearios s/n, T 350011, 66 rm, on the same site as the main hotel; and the *pensión* **E** *San José*, Plaza de la Constitución 17, T 350156, 14 rm. Both of the hotels are closed in the winter months.

South of Alhama, the road runs through the **Zafarraya Pass** at the summit of which there is a clutch of *ventas*. Nearby is an enormous Karstic depression (or *polje*), which is excellent for wild flowers, particularly orchids, in the Spring. Also nearby in the Boquete de Zafarraya cave, a Neanderthal skull was discovered in 1883. The route continues S into the Axarquia region of Málaga province, reaching the coast just S of Velez-Málaga.

SOUTH FROM GRANADA

The Sierra Nevada These mountains are snow capped for most of the year and provide a magnificent backdrop for the city of Granada. There is sufficient snow for skiing from Dec to Apr, but surprisingly there are no glacial features such as pyramidal peaks or even glaciers. Three peaks rise above the general level, **Alcazaba** (3,366m), **Veleta** (3,470m) and **Mulhacén** (3,481m). The latter is the highest mountain on the Iberian peninsula, but most of the skiing takes place on the slopes of Veleta, above the purpose built resort of Solynieve. Summer activities include mountain walking, hang gliding and horse riding. The whole area is a Natural Park, covering nearly 170,000 ha, and containing a number of vegetational zones. The lower slopes were once well wooded with oak and pine, but some deforestation has taken place. There is some agriculture in the valleys. The higher areas are rather barren with alpine moorland, scree and bare rock. Despite being a Natural Park and being declared a Biosphere Reserve by UNESCO in 1983, these titles have failed to prevent the degradation of much of the alpine terrain as developers in the ski industry have run roughshod over the conservation interests.

The wildlife, however, remains outstanding. Particularly in summer a trip to the Sierra Nevada makes a refreshing change from the heat of Granada. There are some 2,000 species of plants, of which around 70 are unique to the area; the 200 species of the alpine zone include 40 endemics, such as the White flowered Buttercup, Nevada Daffodil, Glacier Toadflax and the Nevada Violet. There is also a fine range of **butterflies**, including the Nevada Blue which is only seen above 2000m, while there are three or four other blues which are only found in this area. Amongst the 35 species of **mammals** in the Park, the Spanish Ibex, once almost extinct in the area, has now

recovered to over 3000 individuals. The woodlands of the lower slopes provide a habitat for Wildcats, Beech Martens and Badgers. With regard to **birds**, the high peaks and cliffs contain several hundred pairs of Alpine Choughs and other mountain species such as Rock Bunting, Alpine Accentors, Ravens and Black Wheatears. The elusive Wallcreeper is also occasionally reported. The lower slopes have a good range of Mediterranean woodland birds, including Nightingale, Subalpine Warblers, Roller and Golden Orioles. Birds of prey are not particularly common and are confined to Golden Eagles, Peregrines and Bonellis Eagles, with Goshawks in the more wooded areas.

The upper reaches of the Sierra Nevada give some scope for mountain walking and scrambling during Jul and Aug, when most of the snow has gone. A dirt road runs from near the parador down to Capiliera in the Alpujarras, but it is prudent to have a 4WD vehicle for this journey. The ascent of Veleta begins from this road and should take about 3 hrs to the summit. The ascent of Mulhacén normally starts from Trevélez in the Alpujarras and 6 hrs should be allowed for this climb. The *Ruta Integral de los Tres Mil* is an attempt on all the peaks over 3,000m and starts at Jeres del Marquesado to the N of the Sierra Nevada and finishes 3 or 4 days later in Lanjarón in the SW. Although expert rock climbing skills are not required for these routes, walkers should obviously be well kitted out; get an up to date weather forecast (T 249119) and have a detailed map – there is a 1:50,000 map produced by the *Federación Española de Montañismo* which can be bought in bookshops in Granada and in Solynieve.

Access is by the much improved road from Granada, car journey time 35 mins. Check if the road is open on T 480153, information in Spanish and English. There are several viewpoints en route, including one giving views over the

Skiing in the Sierra Nevada

👣 Prior to the second half of the 20th century, few *Granadinos* would have had any reason to go to the Sierra Nevada, particularly in winter. An exception were the 'icemen' who would toil up to the snowline and bring down blocks of ice on mules to sell in the streets of Granada. A few local enthusiasts, however, started to ski on the mountains in the early part of the century, again accessing the Sierra Nevada by mule. They eventually formed the Sierra Nevada Society in 1912 (Spain's third oldest skiing club), but it was not until the 1960's that any serious development started. A 10-year plan begun in 1985 further expanded facilities to a standard which enabled Sierra Nevada to successfully apply to host the 1995 World Skiing Championships. Unfortunately fate intervened in the form of the climate – untypically mild weather not only led to a lack of snow, but temperatures were not cold enough to operate the hydrants for 'artificial snow'. This led to the cancellation of the championships, but they were held successfully the following year.

The Sierra Nevada has several unique features. It is the most southerly ski centre in mainland Europe, but also one of the highest. This means that it has a long season, often lasting until late May, but also good sunshine records. Access is easy. The Sierra Nevada is 161 km from Málaga and the Costa del Sol by good motorway. Alsina Graells run an hourly bus service between Málaga and Granada. Infrastructure improvements for the world championship mean that the 35 km from Granada have been much improved and can be travelled in 45 mins, the road leading directly to the new covered parking with a capacity for 2,800 cars – claimed to be the largest covered parking space in Spain. The resort area, formerly known as Pradollano but now expanded and renamed Solynieve (sun and snow), is not an attractive place by Alpine standards – the treeless slopes around give it little ambience – but this is more than made up for by the excellent skiing facilities.

There are some 2,500 ha of skiable area with 19 lifts (cabins, chairlifts and t-bars) capable of carrying 30,000 people an hour reaching 54 km of marked slopes. There are additionally six off-piste itineraries and a skiable vertical drop of 1,300m. 3.5 km are floodlit for night time skiing at weekends. Snow boarding (practised on a broad single ski, a direct descendant of the skate board) is the latest craze and has its own circuit. Cross country skiing is also catered for, but is less popular than in other areas. Associated facilities include ski schools, banks, supermarkets, boutiques, ski rental and taxis. The hotels are generally modern and many are equipped with jacuzzi, squash, fitness centres, saunas and indoor swimming pools. Après ski is typically Spanish, with heavy emphasis on fiestas.

Equipment hire is no problem and costs around 2,300 ptas a day, 7,500 ptas for 6 days. A lift ticket costs between 2,300 ptas and 3,150 ptas per day according to the season and up to 13,400 ptas a week. Lifts begin to operate at 0900, while closing times vary between 1615 and 1700 according to conditions. Most lifts run up to the Borreguiles area where there are plenty of bunny slopes. Further lifts then run up to more challenging pistes. Lift tickets can be obtained from kiosks in the Plaza de Pradollano and in the lower Al-Andaluz gondola terminal. Ticket windows are open from 0900 to 1720 on Mon to Sat and Sun until 2000. Skiers should bear in mind the quirky hours which Spaniards keep, allowing for late breakfasts and extended lunches. This means that the best times for skiing are between 0900 and 1100 and 1300 to 1500, when the slopes are almost deserted. Try to avoid weekends and fiestas, when the resort can be intolerably crowded.

Some useful telephone numbers Ski conditions: T 249119, a recorded daily update in both Spanish and English. **Road conditions**: T 282400, wheel chains can be rented at garages on the Granada-Sierra Nevada road. **Granada-Sierra Nevada buses**: T 273100, Bonal buses depart daily from the Palacio de Congresos in Granada at 0900 returning from Sierra Nevada at 1700. **Taxis**: T 151461 or 280654. A taxi from Granada to the Sierra Nevada costs around 6,500 ptas.

Accommodation in the Sierra Nevada There are some 15 hotels and just one *pension* in Solynieve. Almost all open only from 1 Dec until 30 Apr. Those that remain open in the summer may reduce their prices from half to two thirds of the winter price. For the central reservation agency T 249111. There is also a national parador at Solynieve T 480200. The cheapest accommodation is at the *Albergue Universitario*, T 480122, which is at Peñones de San Francisco, near the parador.

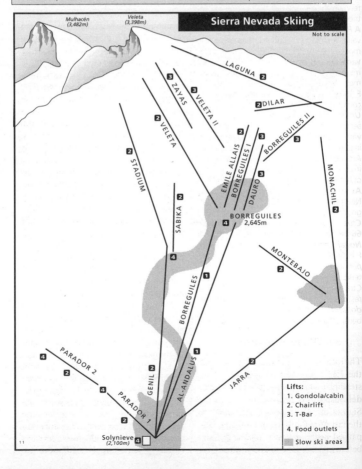

Sierra Nevada Skiing

Genil reservoir. Autocares Bonal run a daily bus service to the Sierra Nevada, leaving at 0900 and returning at 1700, with tickets available at the Bar el Ventorillo beside the Palacio de Congressos on Paseo del Violón on the E bank of the Río Genil. The departure point changes periodically, so check with the tourist office or on T 273100.

● **Accommodation** During the skiing season accommodation is quite expensive, whilst many of the hotels close from Jun to Nov. The few which stay open all the year may halve their prices during the summer and incl: **A** *Parador Sierra Nevada*, Ctra de Sierra Nevada, Km 34, T 480400, F 480458, small, modern; **AL** (winter)/**B** (summer) *Kenia Nevada*, Pradollano s/n, T 480911, F 480807, 67 rm, garage, pool, sports; **AL** (winter)/**C** (summer) *Nevasur*, Pradollano s/n, T 480350, F 480365, 62 rm, few facilities. Cheaper accommodation is provided by the *Albergue Universitario*, where the bus drops off passengers. Solynieve is not a pretty place even with a covering of snow and summer visitors in particular might wish to stay at lower levels. Around Km 22-25 on the road from Granada in an area known as Guejar Sierra, are a cluster of hotels and pensiones, of which the best are: **AL** (winter)/**C** (summer) *Don José*, Ctra Sierra Nevada, Km 22, T 340400, F 159458, 26 rm, good restaurant; **A** (winter)/**B** (summer) *Santa Cruz*, Ctra Sierra Nevada, Km 23, T 470800, 66 rm, pool, sports; **A** (winter)/**C** (summer) *El Nogal*, Ctra Sierra Nevada, Km 21, T 484836, F 470836, 37 rm, restaurant, pool. Of the 3 *pensiones* the most promising is **C** (winter)/**E** (summer) *Puentes de Sierra Nevada*, Ctra Sierra Nevada, Km 17, T 753219, pool, restaurant. **Youth hostels**: *Estación de Pradollano*, 18196 Sierra Nevada, T 480305, 104 beds, cafeteria and sauna, Granada 35 km.

THE ALPUJARRAS

The road S from Granada towards Motril, the E323, leaves the *vega* and climbs steadily to a height of 860m at the **Puerto del Suspiro del Moro** – the Pass of the Sigh of the Moor, named after Boabdil the last Moorish King of Granada, who paused here for a last look at the city before his exile. The road continues S for another 20 km before a side road leads E to **Lanjarón**, the gateway to the Alpujarras. Said to have an Iberian origin, the name comes from *alp* – high place, and *Ujar* – goddess of clear light. This may be fanciful, but it summarizes the beauty of the area, which Richard Ford described as the "Switzerland of Spain".

This remote area is bordered to the N by the Sierra Nevada and to the S by a series of lower ranges, including the Sierras de Lújar, Contraviesa and Gádor. A broad valley runs E-W drained by the rivers Guadalfeo and Andarex. A series of smaller rivers run N-S fed by melting snow from the Sierra Nevada, creating deep valleys and gorges and ensuring that the area stays green for most of the year. The silt laden valleys are extremely fertile, so that agriculture thrives, helped by a equable climate due to the mountains keeping out extreme cold from the N and extreme heat from the S. The original forest of the Alpujarras, consisting of Ilex and Pyrenean Oak, is less common now owing to clearance for agriculture, but there is a wealth of introduced species such as Poplar, Chestnut, Cork Oak and Olive. The White and Black Mulberry trees introduced by the Moors for feeding the silk worms are still found extensively.

When Granada fell to the Christians, many of the Moors fled to the Alpujarras, which under the Nasrids had been divided into administrative areas known as *taas*. Boabdil lived in the *taa* of Laujar. The Moors terraced the valley sides and built irrigation channels and generally left their stamp on the landscape, with street patterns in the villages unchanged over the centuries. The domestic architecture, too, is distinctive. The roofs are invariably flat and constructed of large flat blocks of the local schist laid horizontally. This is covered with a depth of several inches of slate shards. The flat roofs or *terraos* are often used for terraces and cross alleyways making small tunnels. Chimneys are

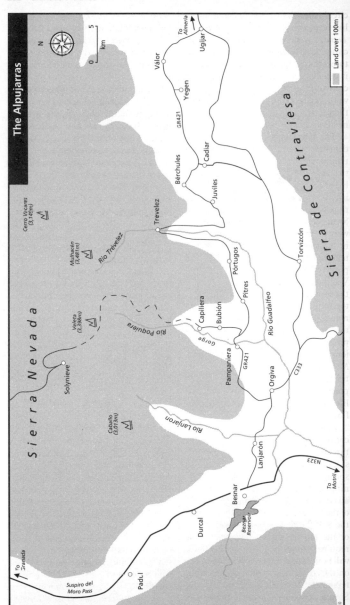

The Alpujarras

Land over 100m

circular in shape with a small mushroom like capping. The walls are made of *launa*, a paste of magnesium and clay, covered with whitewash. Another feature is the exterior gallery or *tinao*, which is usually festooned with flowers. Their craftwork, such as ceramics, esparto work and textiles, still survive, as does their food, particularly delicious sweetmeats such as *pestiños* and *roscos*.

The Christians continued to make demands to force them to adopt Christianity, which eventually led to the abortive revolt in 1570 and this eventually led to the final banishment of all Spanish Moors in 1610. The Alpujarras were re-populated with Christians from N Spain, but a certain number of Moors were obliged to remain to instruct them in the intricacies of the irrigation systems. The area gradually fell into rural poverty, which centuries later the Civil War did little to change. It was not until the second half of the 20th century that the fortunes of the Alpujarras began to revive. This recovery is based largely on tourism and on the purchase of rural properties by Northern Europeans anxious to escape the culture of the *costa*. More discriminating tourists are attracted by the scenery, which gives opportunities for walking tours, the bird life and the immense variety of wild flowers.

Many environmentalists, however, consider that the Alpujarras are under threat, with quarries scarring the hillsides and inappropriate urbanizations springing up, reflecting the lack of planning restrictions. The biggest threat of all is the proposal to dam the headwaters of the Río Trevelez and pipe the water to the S of the region, but as the capacity of the pipe is seven times the needs required, the suspicion is that the water will be used for the *plasticultura* industry on the coast, which will leave the aquifers in the Alpujarras permanently low. So enjoy the area while you can!

There are few monuments to see in the Alpujarras, but the small towns and villages are full of interest and the clear air complements the varied and attractive scenery. The main towns include:

Lanjarón – a spa town going back to Roman times. There are eight springs in all, each containing a different chemical make up which can help a variety of ailments. The bottled water from these springs is marketed all over Spain, while there is a plethora of shops selling herbal remedies to the aged, who throng the streets in summer. Don't let this put you off, as there is plenty to appreciate in Lanjarón. The main street, the Avda de Andalucía, is elegant and shady, while close by is the Moorish castle on top of a rocky hill flanked by a long rocky escarpment. Largely ruined today, it was the scene of a major battle in the Moorish uprising of the late 16th century. The hermitage of Tajo de la Cruz is worth an inspection, as is the 16th century Church of La Encarnación. There is a tourist office at the W end of the village, with helpful multi-lingual staff. It also acts as a travel agency and will book accommodation.

Orgiva, 10 km E of Lanjarón. Orgiva is the administrative centre of the region, being made capital of the Alpujarra by Isabel II in 1839. It is also an important market town. Although frequently mentioned by the Arab chroniclers and although the sons of Muley Hassan and Zoraya lived here, there are few remains of its Moorish heritage around today. The town is dominated by the twin towers of the Church of the Expectación, dating from the 16th century, while the somewhat dilapidated Palacio of the Counts of Sástago looks Moorish, but is in fact 17th century. Anyone in Orgiva on a Thur should certainly visit the weekly outdoor market, which attracts people from miles around and is a sociological experience in anyone's book.

North from Orgiva, are three villages of the High Alpujarras, Pampaniera, Bu-

Gerald Brenen

On the wall of a house, just off a small square in the Alpujarran village of Yegen, is a small plaque which proclaims in blue letters that the English writer Gerald Brenen lived here in the 1920's and 1930's. A modest tribute to one whom many consider to be the greatest English Hispanist.

Brenen was born in 1894 and after a public school education (where according to his biographer he developed most of his hang ups), he fought in the First World War, gaining a Military Medal and the French Croix de Guerre. After the War he settled in Spain, mainly it seems because of the cheap wine and cigarettes, which were lifelong addictions. He ended up in the then remote village of Yegen, with his collection of over 2,000 books, having married the American poetess Gamel Woolsey. It was here that he had a steamy relationship with a 15-year-old peasant girl, resulting in his only daughter Miranda – who the long suffering Gamel agreed to bring up. Don Gerardo, as he was known to the locals, was quite wealthy owing to a number of legacies which came his way, so he did not need to publish work to survive. Study and scholarship were more important and it was not until he was 40 that his first book was published. This was *South From Granada*, a perceptive insight into everyday life in an Andalucían pueblo and since regarded as a sociological masterpiece. Then followed the scholarly *The Spanish Labyrinth* and *The Literature of the Spanish People*. Meanwhile, Brenen had developed a strong Andalucían dialect and a love for the Spanish, admiring their pride in their poverty and their emotions which they carried on their sleeves. It was a two way rapport and his passionate writing found an appreciative readership in Spain. Brenen was also an assiduous correspondent and wrote at length to contemporaries in Britain, especially the Bloomsbury circle. Indeed, his recent biographer, Jonathon Gathorne-Hardy, believes that his brilliant letters will 'eventually prove Gerald's most lasting memorial'.

Gerald Brenen moved to England at the outbreak of the Civil War, and he did

bión and Capiliera, which cling to terraces on the side of the Poqueira valley. The first of these, **Pampaniera**, is approached through the **Poqueira Gorge**, cut by the river of the same name which rises on the slopes of Mulhacén. Pampaniera is an attractive little village and it is no surprise to learn that it has won the Best Kept Spanish Village Award on a number of occasions. There is a pleasant square next to the 16th century, largely brick built, Baroque church, which dates from the 16th century. Look for the *retablo* and the Mudéjar coffered ceiling. The square, known as the Plaza de Libertad, has bars, craft shops (many claiming that they sell no factory made products) and the Sierra Nevada Natural Park Visitors Centre. Here there is a small display showing the natural history, geology and wildlife of the Alpujarras, while there is also a comprehensive collection of books and pamphlets. Particularly recommended for serious trekkers are the handbooks *Andar por Sierra Nevada* and *Andar por La Alpujarra*. Also available are 1:25,000 maps covering 'Pico de Veleta', 'Trevélez' and 'Bérchules'. The multilingual staff also have details of accommodation to rent and arrange treks into the Sierra Nevada on foot or by 4WD vehicle for 1 to 7 days. Just outside the village, perched on the side of the gorge, is the incongruous **Tibetan Buddhist Monastery of Clear Light**, also known as O Sel Ling, the birthplace of the young Osel, who is supposed to be the successor to the Dalai Lama.

Bubión is the next village along the valley. In a stunning position backed by

not return to Spain until 1949, settling in Churriana near Málaga. He continued his writing, preferring this to the academic world and turning down offers of chairs in Spanish Studies at both Oxford and Boston. In his later years Brenen's behaviour became increasingly bizarre. Gathering material for his novel *The Lighthouse Always Says Yes*, he enthusiastically embraced the hippie culture of Torremolinos, despite being in his late 60's. After the death of his wife, he moved in with an Englishwoman 49 years his junior in the village of Alhaurín el Grande. Finally at the age of 90 he returned to England, staying in old people's home in Pinner.

Brenen was always more highly regarded in Spain than in England and the Spanish press spread the idea that he had returned to England against his will. Eventually a delegation from Alhaurín came to Pinner and virtually kidnapped Brenen and returned him to Andalucía. He was installed in a home in Alhaurín and the Regional Government provided a nurse and covered his living expenses, no doubt expecting to receive his vast library. There he lingered on like an ailing Russian president, kept alive as a literary trophy. Brenen eventually died in Alhaurín in Jan 1987.

Today, there is little for *aficionados* of Don Gerardo to see. The home in Yegen has a small plaque. The houses in Churriana and Alhaurín el Grande have both changed hands several times. His manuscripts and books are kept in a locked room in Alhaurín's public library, the key controlled by the moribund Brenen Foundation. There is not even a grave or monument at which to pay homage. Brenen had paid for a plot next to his wife in Málaga's English Cemetery, but awkward to the end, he made a late change in his will and donated his body to medical science. His corpse remains pickled in formaldehyde in the Anatomy department at Málaga University.

Recommended reading: *The Interior Castle: A Life of Gerald Brenen* by Jonothon Gathorne-Hardy, Pub Sinclair Stevenson.

---

the snows of the Sierra Nevada, it is rapidly acquiring the trappings of tourism, but it has a long way to go to catch up with **Capiliera**, 1,300m high at the head of the valley. This village marks the start of the summer dirt road which climbs up to the upper slopes of Mulhacén and Veleta and down to Solynieve. It is also an excellent centre for walking and horse trekking holidays. In Moorish times it had a mosque and two baths and was well known for its silk production. The Church of Nuestra Señora de la Cabeza was in Mudéjar style but rebuilt in the 17th century. It has a carving of the Virgen, which was a gift from Ferdinand and Isabel. There is also a museum devoted to the writer Pedro Antonio de Alarcón, who travelled widely in the 19th century and wrote a book about the Alpujarras.

Returning S to the main E/W high road, a cluster of villages are reached, including Pitres, Pórtugos, Mecina Fondales, Ferreirola and Busquistar, which collectively make up what in Moorish times was known as the *Taa* or *taha* group (a word derived from the Arabic word for obedience). All five villages show the typical domestic architecture of the area, with the gallery-like *tinaos* and walls and roof made of *launa*. **Pitres** is the largest of the group and although less attractive than the villages in the Poqueira valley, has much to make the visitor linger. Its name is thought to come from the Latin *petra*, meaning 'stone', so it was probably occupied by the Romans before the Moors, but remains of the latter can be seen around the village, with the ruins of an old hill-top mosque, a derelict mill and a well.

Just to the E of Pitres is the well-kept village of **Pórtugos**, which itself is unremarkable, but 400 m to the E is a hermitage containing the image of *Nosotra Señora de las Angustias* (Our lady of Sorrows). A steady stream of villagers walk down the hill to look through the grill and pray. A plaque on the wall has a verse attributed to Pedro Antonio de Alarcón (1872-1972), the local writer, which makes clear his opinion on the best parts of Granada province:

> *Viva Graná que es mi tierra*
> *Viva la Puente del Genil*
> *la Virgen de las Angustias*
> *la Alhambra y el Albaicin*

Alongside the hermitage is a wooded valley where a spring emerges, the Fuente Agria, which is rich in iron minerals giving the stream bed a reddish brown tinge. 50m away, next to a picnic site, the stream drops over a cliff known as El Chorreón and through a remarkable vegetated gorge like something out of a rain forest.

The next valley has been cut by the Río Trevélez and with terraces lining the valley sides, this is not so dramatic as the Poqueira. A road leads up one side of the valley to the village of **Trevélez**, returning down the other side. The name Trevélez means 'three districts' and the village is divided into the *alto, medio* and *bajo barrios*. While it has little of real interest, its main claim to fame is that it is the highest village in Spain (and indeed the whole of the Iberian peninsular) at 1,500m above sea level. Trevélez is also the main starting point for treks to the top of Mulhacén and the other peaks of the Sierra Nevada. Next to the bridge over the River Trévelez is a rather charmless square, surrounded by bars, tacky craft shops and *jamonerias*. The mountain ham of Trevélez is famous throughout Spain and is produced from white pigs rather than the usual Iberian black strain. The climate is said to be

ideal for the microbial flora required for the curing. Legend has it that Rossini was once prepared to swap his Stradivarius for a Trevélez ham! Certainly the small square reeks with the aroma of hams and sausages which hang in profusion from the ceilings of every house and shop. A Feast of the Hams is held every year in Aug. The other big event is the *romeria* to Mulhacén which is held on the 5th of every Aug, in honour of the Virgen of the Snows.

The high road continues through the unremarkable, but pleasantly attractive villages of **Juviles**, a silk producing centre in Moorish times, **Bérchules**, overlooking a gorge, and, just off the main route, **Cadiar** with an attractive central square. Cadiar marks the end of the Western Alpujarras and heralds a change in the scenery to a more arid, undulating landscape, particularly as the border with Almería is approached. In the N, the town of **Válor** is worth a visit. Surrounded by well-wooded farmland, the village is characterized by its steep winding streets with the houses covered by the dark grey *launa*. The village is well known for the exploits of one of its 16th century residents, Fernando de Córdoba y Válor who led the Moorish revolt against the Christians in the Alpujarras in 1569. The family's house still stands in the village, which is the venue for the best Moors and Christians festival in the region. Most visitors to Válor will probably make the pilgrimage to the nearby village of **Yegen**, the home for many years of the British writer Gerald Brenen, who wrote the observational study *South of Granada*. His house, 'El Casa del Inglés' can be found in the upper part of the village.

The lower sierras in the S of the Alpujarras are less visited. With a drier climate, agriculture is more difficult and there are consequently fewer villages. Those that do exist, such as **Haza del Lino**, **Albuñol** and **Albondón** (all of which have great views of the Mediterranean) tend to concentrate on wine growing, producing a deceptively strong *rosé*, which is usually available from barrels on the counters of most bars in the Alpujarras.

When to visit the Alpujarras

The scenery and clear air of the Alpujarras ensures that the region receives a steady stream of visitors throughout the year. The summer, however, can be crowded with tourists and finding accommodation can be difficult. Autumn sees fewer visitors, but there is little in the way of bird life and flowers, although the colours of the trees in the valleys can be attractive. The weather in the winter is unreliable and snowfall can be heavy in the higher areas with poor visibility. Spring and early summer are undoubtedly the best times, with flowers at their best, birds in full song and plenty of snow on the peaks. Even in spring, however, the area can be crowded at weekends.

Local information
● Accommodation

Whilst most of the villages will boast a pensión or two, decent hotel accommodation is hard to find and worth booking in advance during the summer and fiesta weekends. The best bets are in Lanjarón and Orgiva, but don't expect anything in the luxury range.

C *Alpujarras Grill*, C/Empalme Orgiva s/n, T 785549, 22 rm, garage, a/c; C *Andalucía*, Avda Andalucía 15-17, Lanjarón, T 770136, 58 rm, pool, restaurant, gardens; C *Miramar*, Avda Andalucía 10, Lanjarón, T 770161, 59 rm, garage, a/c, pool, gardens.

There are 2 good possibilities in the village of Pórtugos, which makes a convenient centre for touring the area: B *Nuevo Malagueno*, Ctra Orgiva-Trevélez s/n, T 766098 F 857337, 30 rm, garage, bar, restaurant, stunning views from rooms. C *Mirador de Pórtugos*, Plaza Nueva 5, T 766014, 23 rm, good restaurant, a *pension* sited on a terrace at the entrance to the Trevélez valley, with, as its name suggests, some marvellous views.

Something different: A *Villa Turistica del Poqueira*, Barrio Alta s/n, Bubion, T 763111, F 763136, 43 rm, self catering units with hotel facilities, the first of Andalucía's 8 Villa Turisti-

cas to be built, for booking contact Turismo Andaluz, CINTA, Ctra N340, Km 189, 29600 Marbella, T 95 2838785, F 95 2836369; C *Alquería de Morayma*, 18440 Cadiar, Granada, T 343221, named after the child bride of the luckless Moorish king Boabdil, this hotel is based on a typical Andalucian *cortijo* near the village of Cadiar, features include a restored mill and an old style bread oven, pool, restaurant serving regional dishes (same ownership as the Mirador de Morayma restaurant in the Albaicin district of Granada).

THE COSTA TROPICAL

The coastal stretch of the province of Granada is known as the **Costa de Granada**, or, more commonly these days, the **Costa Tropical**. It consists of a short stretch of some 60 km from the borders with Málaga province to the boundary with Almería province, but comprises the most attractive coastal scenery within Andalucía. Apart from the area around Motril, where the Río Guadalfeo has built up a flat plain, the shoreline consists largely of tall cliffs with the occasional small cove or fishing village. **Motril**, set slightly inland, is the main town of the area, while the only resorts of any note are **Almuñecar** and **Salobreña**. Because of the physical nature of the coast line and the distance from major airports, the Costa Tropical has resisted the developments which have afflicted the areas to the W, but it is extremely popular with weekenders from Granada.

MOTRIL

ACCESS Road The nearest railway stations are at Málaga and Almería. The N340 coast road bypasses Motril, but buses stop in the town.

Motril is located at the intersection of the E/W coastal route and the N/S Granada road. It is 115 km W of Almería and 3 km inland separated from its port by sugar cane fields. Motril, with a population of 50,000, is the second largest town in Granada province. It's main industries are based on agricultural produce, especially sugar cane, and were developed initially by the Larios gin family. Because of the reliance on this crop the area has often been dubbed 'Little Cuba'. Sugar cane has been grown in this area since the Cathaginians brought it here in the 3rd century, but it was the Moors who developed the refining process in the 10th century. The product has usually been exported via Málaga. More recently, a chemical industry has developed in the port area.

Places of interest

Motril has little to interest the tourist, as its inhabitants will readily agree. Evidence of its Moorish past has totally vanished. Visitors will hardly fail to notice, however, the **Iglesia Mayor de la Encarnación**, which is located in the tree lined avenue at the entrance to the town. Construction began in 1510 and shows a variety of architectural styles including Mudéjar, Baroque and Gothic. The church also doubled as a fortress against Berber pirates, so the overall effect is rather windowless and austere. In the Plaza de España, next to the church, is the dominating statue of Cardinal Belluga, a native of Motril. The *ayuntamiento* or town hall is quite imposing, built in Baroque style by Isidro de la Chica in 1631. A fascinating example of the 'sugar culture' is the **Casa de la Palma**, a colonial style house, which includes one of the few remaining pre-industrial sugar mills in Spain. Add to this list the **Calderón de la Barca Theatre** dating from the end of the 19th century in Neoclassic style and you have the complete inventory of tourist interest in Motril. Not inspiring for a town of its size and it is hardly surprising that few visitors linger for long.

Summer activity at Motril is concentrated at the Poniente beach, where there is a yachting harbour and club, with the possibility of watersports. Nearby is the fishing port and it is worth watching the fish auctions at the Ex-change warehouse. Behind the beach is the only golf course to be found along the Costa Tropical.

Local festivals

The main local festival of Motril's patron saint, the *Virgen de la Cabeza*, takes place on 15 Aug. The **Santuario de la Virgen de la Cabeza**, around which this fiesta is based, is built on the site of the Arab castle which was occupied by Boabdil's mother Aixa, after they were evicted from Granada.

Local information

● **Accommodation**

There is a poor selection in Motril itself, with the best hotel currently closed, but the choice is widened by considering the nearby coastal resorts of **Calahonda** and **Torrenueva**.

B *Costa Nevada*, Avda Martín Cuevas s/n, T 600500, F 821608, 67 rm, garage, a/c, pool, restaurant.

D *Alborán*, C/Varadero Carrera de Mar 1, T 601370; **D** *Los Balandros*, Ctra Nacional 340, Km 336, T 835740, 14 rm, 7 km out of town in the small resort of Torrenueva, pleasant gardens.

E *La Campaña*, C/Princesa 22, T 600007, 34 rm, centrally located budget option.

Camping: *Don Cactus*, Ctra Motril-Almería, Km 11, T 623109, top category, open throughout the year. There are 2 second category sites at Playa Poniente: *Playa de Poniente*, T 820303, and *Playa de Granada*, T 822716.

● **Places to eat**

None of the following is specially rec, but if you need a meal while in Motril, these are possibilities:

◆◆◆*La Caramba*, Avda de Salobreña 19, T 602578, closed Wed.

◆◆*Mesón el Rincón de David*, Avda Rodríguez Acosta 22, T 605686, specializes in ham and cheese dishes, regional wines; ◆◆*Tropical*, T 600450, in the hotel, closed Jul, traditional sea food.

◆ Out of Motril, most of the bargain restaurants are on the seafront at nearby Torrenueva beach, all specializing in seafood and shellfish, incl *el Cordobés*, *Nueva Torre* and *Torre Mar*.

● **Banks & money changers**

There are branches of all the major Spanish

banks and local savings banks in Motril, mainly in the area of Avda Acosta and C/Hernández Velesco.

● **Post & telecommunications**
Area code: 95(2):

Post Office: *Correos* is in C/San Rafael.

Telephones: no *locutorios*, but many cabins around the town.

● **Tour companies & travel agents**
Jumantur, C/Cuevas 1, T 630416.

● **Tourist offices**
There is no office in Motril, but the *ayuntmiento* produces a brochure in Spanish entitled *Motril, Costa Tropical*, which incl a useful town plan. It is stocked by some travel agents.

● **Useful addresses**
Garages/workshops: *Citroën*, Avda Salobreña; *Ford*, Ctra Almería; *Peugeot*, Ctra Almería; *Renault*, Avda Rodríguez Acosta.

● **Transport**
Local Car hire: Autos Joya, C/Cuevas 7, T 823007. **Taxis**: ranks can be found in Avda Andalucía and Plaza Aurora.

Road Bus: to reach the bus station, take C/Nueva out of the town centre, fork right into C/Cruces and the bus station is on the left opp C/Ancha. This is a 10 mins uphill walk out of town, but necessary if you need to book a ticket. The main bus company in this area is Alsina Graells, with the following daily services: 8 buses each way along the coast, 10 to **Granada**; 3 long distance coaches to **Sevilla** via **Córdoba** and 1 to **Jaén** and **Cádiz** and 2 to **Madrid**.

EAST OF MOTRIL

The N340 hugs the coastline for the 50 km to the border with Almería, passing through or bypassing a number of small villages and minor resorts, all backed by the foothills of the Sierra de la Contraviesa. The first three resorts, which have sandy beaches, are **Torrenueva**, **Carchuna** and **Calahonda**. Behind the beach at Carchuna is a conical hill with a small ruined Moorish castle on the top. Another 8 km E is **Castell de Ferro**, with, as its name suggests, yet another castle. Called *Marsa-l-Firruy* by the Moors, it makes a precarious living today on summer tourism and fishing off the rather gritty beach. A diversion inland from Castell de Ferro to its sister village of **Gualchos** is well worth taking if time is at a premium, for this gives the essential flavour of the Alpujarras without going too far inland. The coast road continues through the unremarkable villages of **La Mamola**, **Los Yesos** and **Melicena** before arriving at **La Rábita** close to the border with Almería province. From La Rábita there are two possible excursions inland. One is to the **Cave of Murciélagos** (bats) and the other to **Albuñol**, a village with considerable Moorish flavour. Both sites are on the Murtas road.

WEST OF MOTRIL

Between Motril and the border with Málaga province are the two main resorts of the Costa Tropical, **Salobreña** and **Almuñécar**, the latter with its fishing resort suburb of **La Herradura**. A recent development nearby is **Marina del Este**.

SALOBRENA

Some 4 km W of Motril is the small resort of Salobreña. It is in two parts, an old hill village and a modern beach development, both surrounded by sugar cane fields. The older part has the most spectacular location on the Granada coast and it has a long and interesting history. Founded by the Phoenicians in the 8th century as a trading post, it was known as *Salambina*. It was later occupied in turn by the Carthaginians and the Romans, when it was integrated into the province of Bética. In 713 the Moors arrived and were to stay for 7 centuries, calling it *Salubania*. It was one of Granada's 30 districts and an area of some agricultural and industrial importance. During the Nasrid period (1166-1247), Salobreña was used by Granada's royal families for summer holidays. In 1489 it was conquered by Francisco Ramírez of Madrid, who was made governor by the Catholic Monarchs when he later successfully defended the town against the siege of Boabdil.

After languishing for years in poverty, Salobreña has gained a modicum of prosperity through tourism. The newer coastal area of Salobreña is a purpose built tourist development, but is inoffensive, well planned and consists mainly of low rise apartment blocks and villas, aimed at self catering visitors. The sandy beach is divided into two by a large rock – Peñon Beach has all the facilities, while Guardia Beach stretches away towards the sugar cane fields. The main hotel accommodation is found close to the main coast road.

Places of interest

The **Castillo** was built by the Moors and later remodelled by the Christians. Despite some damage by earthquakes, it was the most important fortress in the coastal part of the province. With steep cliffs on three sides, the only approach was through the houses, making it very siege resistant, especially as a fountain within the castle gave a reliable water supply. It is kidney shaped and consists of two enclosures, one of which contained the prison, which at one time or another held a number of disgraced Moorish kings such as Muley Hacen and Yusef III. A large flattened tower contained the armoury, while another tower protected the entrance. The Tower of Homage is of square construction and contains two large rooms on two storeys. The windows have decorated arches, and Moorish ceramics and glass have been found on the site. To reach it, follow the signs marked 'Castillo' through the narrow roads and alleyways. Open daily 1000-1300 and 1600-2100. Entrance 100 ptas.

The **Iglesia de Nuestra Señora del Rosario** is also worth a visit. It is located on the E side of the Castillo at a lower level. It was constructed in the first half of the 16th century in Mudéjar style on the site of a former mosque and was extensively restored in the 17th and 18th centuries. As with many churches in this area, it has three naves separated by square pillars. The sculptures inside date from the 17th century.

Local festivals

Easter week is marked by traditional *Semana Santa* processions through the old part of town; end Jul – *Fiesta de San Juan y San Pedro*. Aug sees exhibitions and talks as part of a Cultural Week; the *Fiesta de Nuestra Señora del Rosario* takes place in the first week in Oct.

Local information

● **Accommodation**

B *Salobreña*, Ctras Nacional 340, Km 326, T 610037, F 610101, 151 rm, marvellous position on a spur overlooking old Salobreña, pool, tennis, parking, garden; **C** *Salimbina*, Ctra Nacional 340, Km 328, T 610037, 13 rm, restaurant, marvellous site overlooking town and sea. **Pensiones**: there are a number of cheaper *pensiones*, both on the sea front and in the old town, incl **D** *Mari Tere*, Ctra de la Playa 7, T 610126, 20 rm, restaurant, handy for the beach; **D** *Palomares*, C/Fábrica Nueva 28, T 610187, 12 rm, acceptably clean and welcoming; and **E** *Pérez*, C/Del Cristo 28, T 610231, the cheapest in town.

Camping: *El Peñon*, Paseo Maritimo, 2nd category beach side site.

● **Places to eat**

There are a variety of eating places in Salobreña. There are restaurants in the *Hotel Salobreña* and *Hotel Salimbina*.

♦♦♦*Mesón Duran*, Ctra Málaga, Km 341, International cuisine, sea views.

♦ *Chiringuitos* on the beach, such as *Flores* and *Tres Hermanos*, provide good, cheap fish dishes; *Mesón la Bodega*, Plaza de Goya, has ambience along with sherry from the barrel and a reasonable *menu del dia*.

● **Tourist office**

The office is located in Plaza de Goya and has a helpful brochure on Salobreña, but in Spanish only.

● **Transport**

Road Bus: buses stop at the town entrance, just off the coast road. There are 8 local buses in each direction, hourly to **Motril**, 7 buses a day to **Almería**, **Málaga** and, **Granada** and less frequent connections to **Sevilla**.

ALMUNECAR

10 km W of Salobreña lies Almuñécar,

the largest resort on the Costa Tropical. Founded by the Phoenicians some 3,000 years ago and later occupied by the Romans, who left behind an aqueduct and the rather improbable name of *Sexi Firmun Julium*. The Moors wisely dropped that name and called it *Al-Munnakkah*. It was the Moors who built the Castillo de San Miguel on the foundations of a Roman ruin, although it was extensively reconstructed during the time of Charles V and today serves as the local cemetery. In 755, Almuñécar was the spot where Abderramán I landed after he fled from Damascus. Heir to the Omeya Dynasty, he soon became Emir of Córdoba and reigned for over 30 years. Recently, a huge bronze statue in his memory has been erected beneath the castle.

Laurie Lee in *As I Walked Out One Midsummer Morning* described Almuñécar in withering terms at the start of the Civil War, when he was rescued from its rather stony beach by a British destroyer. Today, he would be surprised at Almuñécar's development as a holiday resort, although its future expansion will probably be limited by its distance from Málaga Airport, some 75 km to the W. A headland, the **Peñon del Santo**, divides the coastline into two, with the Playa de San Cristobel to the W and the Playa de Puerta del Mar to the E. Both beaches are of stone or shingle, but backed by attractive *paseos* with a number of *tapas* bars. The inevitable apartment blocks and hotels do not seem to have drastically ruined Almuñécar, which still retains a Moorish atmosphere in the old town behind the castle.

It is well worth visiting the small **Archaeological Museum**, located in the Plaza de la Constitución. The premises themselves are interesting. Known as the *Cuevas de las Siete Gatos* (Cave of the Seven Cats), the place is thought to have been a cellar of Roman construction, probably for the storage of water. Local artefacts are displayed from Phoenician, Roman and Moorish periods, but the star exhibit is an inscribed Egyptian vase dating from the reign of the Pharoah Apophis I. Open Tues-Sat 1100-1400 and 1800-2000. Entrance 100 ptas. Horticulturalists will relish the **Botanical Gardens**, which display more than 400 varieties of sub tropical plants, mainly from Latin America. As a last resort there is always the **Parque Ornithológico**. Almuñécar's most popular attraction, with some 15,000 visitors a year. It is widely advertised as the 'Loro Sexi' (the Sexy Parrot, if you like). Open daily 1100-1400 and 1800-2100. Entrance 300 ptas.

● **Accommodation** There is a variety of accommodation available in Almuñécar, although nothing in the luxury category. Plenty of rented apartments are available. The largest hotel is the **A** *Helios*, Plaza de San Cristóbel s/n, T 634459, F 634469, 232 rm, pool, garage, a/c, suitable for wheelchair users; smaller is **C** *La Najarra*, C/Guadix, T 630873, F 630391, 30 rm, pool, tennis; **D** *Carmen*, Avda Europa 19, T 631413, centrally placed. Amongst the **pensiones**, the following are rec: **D** *Tropical*, Avda de Europa s/n, T 633458, 11 rm, small, comfortable and centrally placed; **E** *Victoria I and II*, 2 pensiones in Plaza de la Victoria under the same management, T 631734, *Victoria II* has a garage, 23 and 26 rm.

Just to the W of Almuñécar is **La Herradura**, set on a beach between the headlands of Cerro Gordo and La Mona. Once a fishing village, it is now becoming a distinctly up market residential area. Nearby is the recently built 'sport port' development of **Marina del Este**. Attractively set in a narrow bay, it has been heavily advertised, but its launch coincided with the property recession of the early 90's and it has been slow to take off.

Huelva Province

HUELVA IS the most westerly and one of the least visited of the provinces of Andalucía. The tidal Atlantic coastline consists largely of lagoons and dunes, often pine covered, with a string of minor holiday resorts such as Ayamonte, Punta Umbria, Mazagón and Matascalañas. In the middle of this shoreline is Huelva, the provincial capital, industrial city and port. East of the capital are a number of locations associated with the voyages of Columbus to the New World, including the monastery of La Rabida and the villages of Palos and Moguer. Further east is the nature reserve of Coto Doñana, one of the top three wetlands in Europe. Bird watchers also flock to the Odiel Marshes to the west of Huelva.

HORIZONS

Huelva has some 425,000 inhabitants, of which a quarter live in the capital. To the west, the Río Guadiana forms the boundary with Portugal, while to the east the Río Guadalquivir is the border with the Cádiz and Sevilla provinces. Across the centre of the province runs an undulating area of farmland, specializing in cereals, fruit and sunflowers. The land rises gently to the north in the rolling hills of the **Sierra Morena**, subdivided into a number of ranges of which the Sierra de Aracena is the most attractive. The main centre here is the town of **Aracena**, while neighbouring **Jabugo** is an important centre for the production of Serrano ham. In the southeast of the Sierra Morena are the **Río Tinto Mines**, worked for centuries and worth a visit if only to appreciate the scale of the desecration of the landscape.

Huelva Province

Not to scale

PORTUGAL

Sierra Morena

Rosal de la Frontera
N433
Jabugo
Aracena
Almonaster la Real
Alájar
Zutre
Minas de Riotinto
To Sevilla
Puebla de Guzmán
Calañas
Nerva
Valverde del Camino
Río Odiel
Río Tinto
Gibraleón
La Palma del Condado
Sevilla Province
Río Guadiana
N431
Niebla
To Sevilla
Ayamonte
Huelva
La Rábida
Almonte
Punta Umbría
Mazagón
El Rocío
N
Atlantic
Ocean
Coto Doñana
Río Guadalquivir
Matalascañas
Cádiz Province

Land over 500m

80

HUELVA

(*Pop* 139,000; *Alt* Sea level to 50m)

ACCESS Air The nearest airport is at Sevilla.

Train The train station, T 246666, is in Avda de Italia, to the E of the town. There are daily express trains to Madrid and Sevilla, and numerous slower trains to Sevilla, where connections can be made to other regional centres. There is also a route W to Almonte on the Portuguese border.

Road The main bus company serving Huelva is Damus SA, Avda de Portugal 9, T 256900, with links to Algeciras, Cádiz and Sevilla, plus local villages.

There is a saying in Spain that when you have been to Huelva once you never return. This is an understandable comment, considering the appearance of the city today. Spain's fourth largest port and the busiest in Andalucía, Huelva's eastern approaches are packed with petro chemical installations and cement works, which pollute the atmosphere and scar the landscape. The Río Tinto estuary, which for centuries has drained the mining area to the N, looks totally dead and lifeless. Penetrate this desolation and the city of Huelva itself, located on a bluff of land between the Tinto and Odiel rivers, is surprisingly attractive. It is a port of some antiquity, having been founded by Phoenician traders over 3,000 years ago, when it was known as *Onuba* (its citizens are still known as *(onubenses)*. The Romans used it as a port for minerals which they extracted from the Río Tinto mines to the N, as did the Moors who knew it as *Guelbah*. Alphonso X *el Sabio* (the wise) recaptured it from the Moors in 1257. Huelva's status as a port was enhanced when Columbus, using crews from the local area, set out from here for his voyages to the New World. It also prospered when it was used as a trading base by the Conquistadors, although it later lost ground to Cádiz and Sevilla. Unfortunately, little of this rich historical heritage is evident today, largely due to the 1755 earth-quake (the same one which destroyed Lisbon). There has recently been a resurgence of prosperity stimulated by the petro chemical industry (set up by Franco in the 1950's), the continuing exports of Río Tinto minerals and spinoffs from tourism.

PLACES OF INTEREST

Museo Provincial, Alameda Sundheim 13. Some would say that the museum is the only thing worth looking at in Huelva and it is certainly not to be missed. Housed in a pleasant modern building, the ground floor consists of sections on archaeology and mining while the upper floor has a fine arts collection. Attention is immediately captured by the huge Roman water wheel in the entrance hall. Found at the Río Tinto mines, it was one of a series used by slaves to raise water from flooded parts of the underground works. From here coloured lines on the floor take you on different tours. The archaeological section is excellent, with artefacts from the Bronze Age through to Moorish times. The displays devoted to mining are also outstanding, particularly the items of Roman origin. The fine arts collection on the upper floor is not distinguished. Visitors who have had a surfeit of heavy religious art at other provincial Andalucían galleries, will probably be relieved that there is not a Murillo in sight, but the alternatives are hardly worth displaying. An exception is the work of the local 20th century artist Daniel Vásquez Diaz, responsible for the murals at La Rábida monastery, who has a number of competent paintings, including one stunning nude and portraits of the poets Ruben Dario and Juan Ramon Jimenez. Open daily (Except Mon) 1000-1400 and 1600-1900, T 259300. Entrance free.

An architectural curiosity in Huelva is the **Barrio Reina Victoria**, along the Avda de Guatemala, which is an estate built by the Río Tinto company to house its British workers around the turn of

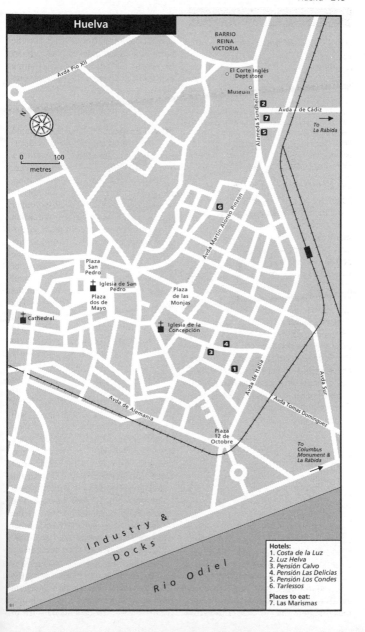

Huelva

BARRIO REINA VICTORIA

Avda Pío XII

El Corte Inglés Dept store

Museum

Avda de Cádiz

To La Rábida

Alameda Sundheim

N

0   100
metres

2

7

5

6

Avda Martín Alonso Pinzón

Plaza San Pedro

† Iglesia de San Pedro

Plaza dos de Mayo

Plaza de las Monjas

† Cathedral

† Iglesia de la Concepción

4

3

1

Avda de Italia

Avda Sur

Avda de Alemania

Avda Tomás Domínguez

Plaza 12 de Octubre

To Columbus Monument & La Rábida

Industry & Docks

Río Odiel

Hotels:
1. *Costa de la Luz*
2. *Luz Helva*
3. *Pensión Calvo*
4. *Pensión Las Delicias*
5. *Pensión Los Condes*
6. *Tarlessos*

Places to eat:
7. Las Marismas

Columbus Monument, Huelva

the century. Much on the lines of those built by the industrial philanthropists in England, it is now decaying badly, despite its designation as being of 'historico-artistic interest'. The wrought iron Río Tinto pier at the mouth of the estuary dates from the same period.

There are one or two churches and convents of interest in Huelva. The **Catedral de la Merced** dates from 1605 and was once a convent. It was designated a cathedral in 1953, largely, it would seem, on the grounds that it was the largest church to survive the 1755 earthquake. Located just N of the Plaza de la Merced, it has a refreshingly white marble interior, but frankly is hardly worth a visit. Two other churches are of more interest. The **Iglesia de la Concepción** in C/Concepción is believed to be the first church in Spain to be consecrated in the name of the Immaculate Conception. First

constructed in the 14th century, it was rebuilt after the 1755 earthquake, retaining the richly decorated choir stalls. It also has paintings by Zurburan. The **Iglesia de San Pedro** in the Plaza of the same name was built in the 15th century over a mosque. The oldest church in the city, it has numerous Baroque modifications including the tower. Of most interest, however, is the **Santuario de Nuestra Señora de la Cinta**. Standing at the end of the tree lined Paseo del Conquero just off the road to Portugal, the sanctuary is a simple white walled affair where Columbus is said to have prayed before setting out on his first voyage. The event is portrayed in traditional 'azulejo' tiles by Daniel Zuloaga. There is also an impressive altar grille. For visitors without private transport, the sanctuary can be reached by local bus – the No 6 from the Plaza de Monjas.

That covers just about everything of interest in Huelva, but for those who just like ambling around a city, head for the attractive Plaza de Monjas, the main square replete with palm trees. Some of the streets leading off the square are pedestrianized and decorated with the occasional modern sculpture.

LOCAL FESTIVALS

On the 5 Jan there is the traditional cavalcade of the Three Wise Kings through the streets of the city. There are the usual Easter processions. On 8 Sep, the feast day of the *Virgen de la Cinta*, the patron saint of Huelva, is celebrated. The Columbus Festival takes place at the end of Jul and the beginning of Aug to commemorate the departure of the caravels and is marked by bullfights, sports events and regattas.

LOCAL INFORMATION

Price guide

Hotels:			
AL	over US$90	**D**	US$20-40
A	US$75-90	**E**	US$10-20
B	US$60-75	**F**	under US$10
C	US$40-60		

Places to eat:			
♦♦♦	expensive	♦♦	average
♦	cheap		

● **Accommodation**

There are half a dozen hotels and 9 *pensiones* in Huelva and booking is not normally a problem. Many visitors, however, incl businessmen, prefer out-of-town hotels in more attractive locations, such as Punta Umbria to the S and Mazagón to the SE. The nearest paradors are at Ayamonte, close to the Portuguese border, and Mazagón.

The best hotel in Huelva is the **AL** *Luz Huelva*, Alameda Sundheim 26, T 250011, F 258110, 106 rm, garage, wheelchair access, a/c, tennis, golf, rooms with views over the river and Columbus statue (but also the petro chemical works).

Also rec are **A** *Tartessos*, Avda Martin Alonzo Pinzón 13, T 282711, F 250617, 112 rm, garage, a/c, centrally placed; **A** *Monte Conquero*, C/Pablo Rada 10, T 285500, F 283912, 168 rm, garage, a/c, wheelchair access, to the W of the town.

C *Los Condes*, Avda Sundheim 14, T 282400, 93 rm, garage, wheelchair access, centrally placed; **C** *Costa de la Luz*, C/José Maria Amo 8, T 256422, centrally placed; **C** *Santa Ursula*, Ctra Huelva-Ayamonte (Peguerillas), T 285211, F 256212, 134 rm, garage, wheelchair access, a/c, pool tennis, golf, northern outskirts of Huelva.

Most of the *pensiones* are located in the area to the SE of the Plaza de Monjas. **D** *San Miguel*, C/Santa María 6, T 245203, 25 rm; **D** *Virgen del Rocio*, C/Tendaleras 14, T 281716, centrally placed, some rooms with a/c.

E *Andalucía*, C/Vazquez López 22, T 245667, 17 rm, some rooms with a/c; **E** *Las Delicias*, C/Rascón 42, T 248392, pleasant patio.

F *Calvo*, C/Rascón 33, T 249016, currently the cheapest place in town.

Youth hostels: *Albergue de Huelva*, C/Marchena Colombo 14, 21004 Huelva, T 253793, 130 beds, meals available, suitable for disabled, city centre location; *Mazagón*, Cuesta de Barca s/n, T 536262, 100 beds, meals available, free kitchen, suitable for wheelchair users, 25 km SE from Huelva on the coast; *Punta Umbria*, Avda Océano 13, Punta Umbria 21100, Huelva, T 311650, 84 beds, meals available, suitable for wheelchair users, directly S of Huelva, but across the river.

Camping: there are 11 camp sites within 30 km of Huelva mainly at coastal locations. The only 1st category site is *Camping Doñana Playa*, Ctra Huelva-Matascalañas, Km 29, T 376281, beach, pool, restaurant.

● **Places to eat**

As Huelva is a fishing port it is no surprise that some good seafood is available.

Seafood: try ♦♦*Doñana*, C/Gran Via 13, T 242773, where local seafood specialities incl sardines with peppers, skate in paprika and clams in saffron sauce; ♦*La Marisma*, C/Padre Laraña 2, T 245272, another good seafood spot with an economical menu.

Those on a budget could try ♦*Pizzeria Napoli*, appropriately located in Avda de Italia 79, T 252396.

● **Banks & money changers**

Most Spanish banks are represented and are mainly located in the streets leading off the Plaza de Monjas.

● **Embassies & consulates**

Denmark, C/Lazo Real 4, 5°, T 240127; Finland, Avda Martin Alonso Pinzón 4, T 249583; **France**, C/Rico 53, 1°, T 257700; **Greece**, C/Marina 19, T 251706; **Netherlands**, C/Marina 19, T 251706; **Portugal**, C/Vázquez López 15, T 245569; **Sweden**, C/Rico 53, 1°, T 257700. Note that the nearest British, Canadian and American consulates are in Sevilla.

● **Entertainment**
Huelva is definitely not the entertainment capital of Andalucía and much of the night life that there is migrates to the nearby coastal resort of Puerto Umberto in the summer.

Bullfights: the Plaza de Toros is located in the W of the city on the Paseo de Independencia. *Aficionados* claim that the best *corridas* take place during the Fiestas Colombinas in Aug.

Cinemas: apart from films at the Gran Teatro, there are 2 multi screen cinemas: *Emperador Multicines*, C/Berdigón 6, T 248100 and *Multicines La Rábida*, C/Rábida 17, T 281403.

Flamenco: supposedly famed for its *flamenco*, the genuine article is hard to find in Huelva. The best bet is *Peña Flamenca de Huelva*, Avda de Andalucía. Otherwise, try *Meson Tablao Solera*, C/Conde 9, or *Pub Bodegones*, Avda Federico Molina 4. Failing these, check with the tourist office.

Discos: again, the liveliest scene is at Puerto Umberto in the summer, but in Huelva itself the best spot is *Alameda*, Alameda Sundheim.

Theatre: *Gran Teatro*, C/Vázquez López 13, T 245703. There is a 'Pueblos de España' theatre display for 1 week during May or Jun, an International Festival of Dance usually in Jul and a 'Classical Theatre Campaign' in the Autumn. There are also occasional theatre performances at the Escuela de Magisterio, C/Cantero Cuadrado.

● **Hospitals & medical services**
First aid: *Casa de Socrro*, Via Paisajística s/n, T 253800.

Hospitals: *Hospital del SAS Huelva*, Avda Federico Mayo s/n, T 242222; *Hospital del SAS Infanta Elena*, Autovía Huelva-Sevilla s/n, T 232100.

Red Cross: *Cruz Roja*, Paseo Buenos Aires s/n, T 261211.

● **Post & telecommunications**
Area Code: 955.

Post Office: *Correos*, Avda Tomás Domínguez 1, T 249184. For telegrams T 248860.

Telephones: no *locutorios*, but plenty of cabins.

● **Shopping**
The main shopping area is around the Plaza de Monjas and incl some pedestrianized streets such as C/Concepción. A branch of the department store *El Corte Ingles* has opened fairly recently at the rear of the museum and provides convenient multi-storey parking as well as a good restaurant. Local craft items incl basketwork, wrought iron goods, ceramics and leather work. There is a street market on Fri in *El Recinto Colombino*.

● **Sports**
Football: the local football stadium is located in the N of the city, Ctra de Sevilla. Football was introduced to the area by English workers of the Río Tinto company – which may explain why the local team habitually languishes at the lower end of the Spanish football league system.

Golf: for golfers, there is the *Bellavista* course at Ctra de Huelva-Aljaraque, T 318083.

Tennis: is available at the club at C/José Avila s/n, Huelva, T 248978.

Watersports: for watersports, contact the *Club Martimo*, Avda Montenegro, T 247627.

● **Tour companies & travel agents**
Bonanza, Avda Martín Alonso Pinzón 8, T 261100; *El Corte Ingles*, Avda Federico Molina, T 280008; *Melia*, Avda Martín Alonso Pinzón 20, T 245811; *Ultratur*, C/Puerto 49, T 252811.

● **Tourist offices**
The **Provincial Tourist Office** is located at Avda de Alemania 14, T 257403. There is also a **Municipal Tourist Office** at C/Cardenal Cisneros 10, T 249586. Both operate normal office hours.

● **Useful addresses**
Garages/repair workshops: *Citroën*, Ctra de Sevilla, Km 637, T 229609; *Ford*, Pol San Diego s/n, T 228512; *Peugeot*, Ctra de Sevilla, Km 638, T 221988; *Renault*, C/Legión España 2, T 254964; *Seat/VAG*, Ctra N431, Km 637.5, T 234051.

● **Transport**
Local Car hire: Avis, *Hotel Luz*, Alameda Sundheim 26, T 258211; **Hertz**, Alameda Sundheim 16, T 258211; **Marina**, C/Río de la Plata 25, T 250199. **Taxis**: *la Merced*, T 244951; *El Rocio*, T 224753; *Teletaxi*, T 250022.

Air The nearest airport is at Sevilla (110 km),

as is the nearest *Iberia* office, T (95) 4228901.

Train The train station is in Avda de Italia s/n. For information T 246666. There are daily trains to Almonaster la Real (2), Sevilla (7) and Zafra (2).

Road Bus: there are a number of bus companies serving Huelva, the main one of which is Damus SA with their station on the Avda de Portugal, T 256900. There are small bus stations in Avda de Italia, Avda Alemania and Avda Federico Molina. There are daily bus services to Aracena (2), Ayamonte (6), Granada (1), Málaga (1), Matascalañas (1) and Sevilla (12).

Boat During Jul, Aug and Sep there is a boat service between Huelva and the resort of Punta Umbria operating between 0930 and 2130.

WEST FROM HUELVA

The W boundary of the city of Huelva is the Río Odiel, which in comparison with the Río Tinto to the E, suffers little from pollution. The estuary to the W and its accompanying marsh land forms the **Natural Park of the Marismas de Odiel**, covering some 7,000 ha of varied habitat. Birders visiting the more famous Coto Doñana should certainly attempt the journey to the Odiel which has a wide range of species, whatever the season. The reserve can be viewed from a number of sites, but undoubtedly the best is the causeway, which runs right down the centre of the area ending in a 10 km man made jetty to the lighthouse. A car is absolutely necessary and makes an excellent mobile hide, being easy to pull off the road in a number of places. The N of the area is not too promising with reclaimed land, presumably for farming, and commercial salt pans. Then follows stretches of freshwater marsh with occasional clumps of trees. Finally there are saltwater marshes and intertidal sands and lagoons. The range of species is enormous, but the stars are undoubtedly the colonies of Spoonbills. There are estimated to be 400 pairs, which if precise, would amount to around a third of the total European population. Grey and Purple Herons also breed along with Little Egrets, Black Winged Stilts and some 300 pairs of Little Terns. In the winter the reserve is attractive to Flamingoes, a variety of gulls and waders, plus small groups of Caspian Terns. Odiel is also as good a place as any to see the rare Spanish Imperial Eagle. Botanists will also be delighted with the salt marsh flowers, which form a carpet of blue and yellow in the spring and early summer.

Most visitors will approach from the SE coast. On arriving at Huelva, cross the Río Tinto bridge, turning left at the Columbus statue and follow the road through the docks to the N of the city. Turn left over the old Odiel road bridge (if you cross by the newer bridge further N you will have to back track on the other side). Take the first left down the road marked rather grandly 'Carretera de las Islas. Dique Juan Carlos I, Rey de España'. The road runs down the centre of the reserve for nearly 20 km.

From the Río Odiel mouth westwards to the Portuguese border is a string of minor holiday resorts, which, due to their remoteness from an international airport, are mainly used by Spaniards. Due S of Huelva is the first of these, **Punta Umbria**. 19 km from the capital and reached via a new road bridge and ferries in the summer, it is not a particularly inspiring resort. It does, however, have a fine sandy beach and with fresh sea breezes it can be a relief from the heat of Huelva. There are half a dozen small hotels (none in the luxury class) and a similar number of *pensiones*, so accommodation is not a problem except in Jul and Aug, when the place can get quite lively. With a small port and a fishing fleet, good seafood restaurants are not hard to find. 4 km W is **El Rompido**, a former fishing village now expanding with tourism. Between the two is the village of El Portil, where there is a small freshwater lagoon, **La Laguna de el Portil**. This 15 ha lake is now a *Reserva*

Natural and amongst its breeding birds are Black Necked Grebes.

West of El Rompido is the mouth of the Río Piedras, which has been ponded back by the growth of a spit known as the Flecha del Rompido, causing extensive salt marshes alongside the river. With the coastal pinewoods, tidal creeks and dunes, there is a variety of habitats and some 2,500 ha of the area, known as the **Marismas del Río Piedras**, now has *Paraje Natural* status. Its unspoilt nature makes it a delightful reserve to visit and a good variety of birds and plants can be expected, particularly in spring. The best viewing is from the fishing village of Puerto de El Terrón on the W bank of the river.

To the W of the Río Piedras is the long sandy beach of Playa de las Antillas, part of which is reserved for naturists. This area comes under the administration of **Lepe**, a few kilometres inland. Lepe, which is in the centre of a fruit growing area, is best known in Spain as the butt of the nation's jokes of the 'How many men from Lepe does it take to change a light bulb?' variety. The inhabitants of Lepe are not that dim, however, as they now host an annual jokes festival, which attracts not only a host of visitors, but most of the better comedians in Spain.

The next resort is **Isla Cristina**, which, as its name implies, was once an island. It is still the second most important fishing port along the Huelva coast, with an important canning factory. Tourism is now becoming increasingly significant, with the population of 18,000 trebling during the summer months. There is an excellent sandy beach, backed by some good fish restaurants. There are a few accommodation possibilities. At the top of the range is **AL** *Riu Canela*, Ctra La Antilla-Isla Cristina, Km 3, T 477124, F 470460, 350 rm, wheelchair access, pool, tennis, a/c, gardens. There is little in the budget range, except **E** *Maty*, C/Catalanes 7, T 331806. Book

well in advance for everything in Isla Cristina during Jul and Aug.

Finally there is the rather scruffy border town of **Ayamonte**, which is the only one with anything in the way of monuments. It is located on the Río Gaudiana opposite the Portuguese village of Villareal de San Antonio, with which it is now linked with a state of the art suspension bridge – formerly one had to rely on 15-min ferry boat voyage. The 15th century Iglesia de San Salvador is worth a visit and if you can find the place open, the tower repays the slog to the top with marvellous views over the river and marshes. Also of interest are the Church of Nuestra Señora de las Agustias dating from the 16th century and the Convents of San Francisco and Santa Clara. The castle has only its foundations remaining, but these appear to have Roman origins.

The area between Ayamonte and Isla Cristina forms yet another nature reserve, the **Marismas de Isla Cristina**. Tidal activity has led to the formation of sand spits protecting areas of salt marsh, tidal creeks and abandoned salt pans. The dunes have extensive vegetation, including Stone Pine and Juniper, while there is a wide variety of salt marsh plants dominated by Glasswort. Breeding birds include White Stork, Black Winged Stilt, Collared Pratincole and Montagu's Harrier. There is a good variety of waders and gulls during the winter months. Access is best from the road/causeway S from Ayamonte towards the beach at Playa de Moral.

NORTH FROM HUELVA

The main route N from Huelva to the Sierra Morena is the N435 which leaves the Sevilla-Huelva route at San Juan del Puerto. Initially it passes through pleasant farmland dominated by cereal growing, bypassing the unremarkable villages of **Trigueros** and **Valverde del Camino**. After the latter the route becomes more hilly, but the road is well engineered and fast. Woodland takes over, much of it Eucalyptus groves. The tree is grown for its wood and regularly coppiced, but drains the soil of its nutrients, so that little else grows in these areas. Environmentalists are quite justified in referring to these areas as 'Eucalyptus deserts'.

Just after passing the village of Zalamea la Real, the C421 leads off E to the village of **Minas de Río Tinto**. Huge open cast mines may not be many tourists' cup of tea, but the sheer scale of the operations and the way the landscape has been desecrated has a certain horrific fascination, and most people find the detour well worthwhile. Minerals have been extracted here from the Devonian and Carboniferous rocks since the time of the Phoenicians. It is the iron content of the rock which has stained the waters and bed of the Río Tinto red and yellow and given it its name. The Romans deepened the mines in an effort to find silver, but this led to flooding problems, which were resolved by the use of a complicated system of slave driven wheels to bring the water to the surface. A number of these wooden wheels have survived and may be seen in the local museum and in the one in Huelva. The mines were less important during the Moorish occupation and when the New World was discovered and cheap minerals were brought back to Spain, the mines all but closed down. In 1873, the mines were sold to an Anglo German consortium and the Río Tinto Mining Company was formed. Large numbers of British workers and managers came to the area and there are a number of quaint reminders of their influence today. The mines reverted to Spanish ownership in 1954.

A quick look around the area will reveal the two huge open cast mines, the *Corte Atalaya* and the *Cerro Colonado*. The former, which has been worked since Phoenician times, is now more or less closed down and the land around it is being landscaped with a mirador (ticket from the museum) and a golf course under construction. The *Cerro Colondao's* viewing platform has now gone, but when driving past, the mining operations can be clearly seen with the enormous earth moving equipment dwarfed by the precipitous side of the quarry. Next to the main mining offices at La Dehesa is a recently unearthed Roman graveyard. Entry is, unfortunately, only by guided tour, but from the roadside a number of stone coffins can be seen lying around under the trees. Driving into the village one can appreciate the paternal nature of the company, which has provided many facilities for the community. Look out for the Barrio de Bella Vista, a Victorian estate provided for the English workers, complete with church and swimming pool. There are remnants of the high perimeter wall which was built to deter fraternization with the 'natives'. Do not leave the area without visiting the Mining Museum, located in the Plaza de Museo near to the Health Centre. This is an absolute gem and has already established itself as one of the major theme museums in Andalucía. Near to the entrance is a large room where audio-visual presentations are made. Then follows a series of rooms devoted to the archaeological aspects of mining from the Chalcolithic period through to Medieval times. The Roman period is particularly well represented with coins, pottery, jewellery and burial items. Naturally enough, there is a superb geological section with fossils, rocks and

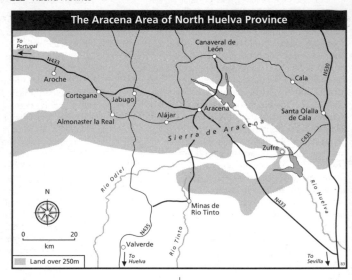

The Aracena Area of North Huelva Province

minerals in abundance. The local flora and fauna are also displayed, although one wonders whether any wildlife at all survives in the lunar landscape outside. There is a fascinating section on the industrial archaeology of the mines, from the setting up of the Río Tinto company to the present day, showing some of the equipment and instruments which were used. For many visitors, however, the most engrossing part of the museum will be the railway section. On taking over the mines the Anglo German company built a railway line to the coast at Huelva to export the minerals, and some of the rolling stock, including two steam locomotives, are displayed in the museum. One is a type 'K' locomotive built in Britain in 1907, while the other is a type 'N' crane locomotive built by Hawthorn Leslie in 1930, which was used in the event of derailments and accidents. The most delightful exhibit, however, is the *Maharajah's Carriage*, which was built in Birmingham in 1892 for Queen Victoria's visit to India. She never went (despite being Empress) and

the carriage was sold to Río Tinto, who used it for the visit to the mines by King Alfonso XIII. It is nowadays considered to be the most luxurious narrow gauge passenger carriage in the world. The Mining Museum is open Mon to Sat 1000-1400 and 1700-2000. Closed Mon and fiestas. Entrance adults 200 ptas, children 125 ptas. Tours around the whole complex, including the museum, the mines and the railway can be booked at the museum. Adults 1,300 ptas, children 1,000 ptas. Tours are on Tues-Sat, leaving at 1400. At weekends and holidays, special trips run on the 30 km of refurbished railway line, pulled by a steam engine. Adults 700 ptas, children 600 ptas.

Visitors going on to Aracena can continue on the C road N passing, just out of Río Tinto, an attractive looking lake with inviting turquoise water. Don't be tempted to swim, however, as a notice states 'Danger, do not bathe. Acid Water'. This says it all! Visitors going on to Jubago or Almonaster la Real should return W to the main N435.

The **Sierra Morena**, which forms the N boundary of Huelva province, consists of well wooded rolling hills, sub divided into a number of lesser sierras. The most scenic is the **Sierra de Aracena**. The area is bisected by the N433, which runs from N of Sevilla to the Portuguese border. Most of the important towns of the region are on, or just off, this routeway. The area has a rainfall over 1,000 mm annually, which ensures that the hills have a good tree cover, with extensive forests of Sweet Chestnut, Cork Oaks and Stone Pines. Both Black and White Poplars line the river valleys. Where trees have been cleared there are often areas of *cistus* scrub, while especially around Aroche there are stands of Eucalyptus. Much of the area S of the town of Aracena consists of the Parque Natural de Sierra de Aracena, covering some 184,000 ha. Both Black and White Storks breed here, while raptors include the rare Black Vulture, plus Red and Black Kites. Amongst the mammals are Stone Marten, Polecat, Genet, Lynx and Mongoose. The plethora of wild boar and deer ensure that this is a popular hunting area. This is also excellent walking country and a guide has been produced – *Andar por la Sierra de Aracena* – unfortunately only in Spanish. Most hotels have the book for reference and with a little persuasion will photo copy relevant sections for you. The Natural Park of the Sierra de Aracena has a network of information centres at Almonaster, Aroche, Cortegana, Cumbres Mayores, Encinasola and Santa Olalla del Cala – all in historic buildings.

ARACENA

The main centre of the Huelva section of the Sierra Morena, Aracena is 104 km from Huelva and 89 km NW of Sevilla. Although having only 6,500 inhabitants, it is the main regional and market centre of the N of the province and makes a good base to explore the area. Dominating the town is the hill to the S capped with a church and a ruined castle. The latter dates from Moorish times and today there is little to see apart from the local courting couples, for whom it is a favourite venue. The walk to the hilltop is a hot drag in summer, but it is possible to drive all the way, passing en route through a striking 16th century brick gateway, which also acts as a belfry. The church, next to the castle, is the Iglesia de Nuestra Señora de los Delores, built by the Knights Templar in the 13th century. Regrettably, it is usually closed. The view from the castle hill over the town is spectacular. Look for the Plaza Alta, a large sloping square beneath the hill, around which most of the older buildings in the town are located. The square is dominated by the Church of Nuestra Señora de la Asunción, complete with stork nests on its towerless roof. The church was begun in 1476 and was still unfinished when the 1755 earthquake severely damaged the structure. A roof was finally fitted in the 18th century, but the building is still not complete and a peep through the cracks in the door will show builders and masons still at work. Nearby is the 16th century *ayuntamiento*, the oldest in the province. In the more modern part of the town life revolves around the attractive Plaza de Aracena, where there are a number of *tapas* possibilities.

Most people come to Aracena, of course, to see the **Gruta de las Maravillas** (the Cave of the Marvels) and in terms of limestone redeposition structures it is probably the best in Spain. It has all the usual formations, such as stalactites, stalagmites, pillars, organ pipes and tufa screens, all discreetly lit. Even the occasional background music (said to be specially written for the cave) does not detract from the formations. Said to be discovered by a boy looking for a lost pig (amazing how many Spanish caves are discovered by small boys), it was opened in 1914, displaying 1,200m of galleries, several large caverns and six incredibly beautiful lakes. The last of the caverns, known as the 'Chamber of the Nudes', has some extraordinary rounded redeposition features resembling various parts of the human anatomy, leaving little to the imagination and ensuring that everyone leaves the caves having had a good laugh. The caves are open 1000-1300 and 1430-1800. Entrance 600 ptas. There are guided tours only and when you buy a ticket you will be told the time of your tour. This may be 2 hrs hence, but this will give you time to visit the numerous bars, restaurants and gift shops around the cave. There is also an excellent geological museum near the booking hall. The collection was donated in 1983 by Francisco Orden Palomino and includes specimens from all over the world (but none of course from the cave).

The local tourist office is also located at the cave, but the staff seem more interested in renting out local apartments. In the streets and squares around the cave is a permanent **Outdoor Museum of Modern Sculpture**. Although none of the sculptors are internationally known and the standard varies from brilliant to ridiculous, the idea is a good one. Pity about the graffiti, presumably added by visiting school parties.

● **Accommodation** There are 2 middle-of-the-range hotels: **B** *Los Castaños*, Avda de Huelva 1, T 126300, F 126287, 33 rm, garage, restaurant, stones throw from the caves, those seeking a quiet night might worry about the disco on the opp corner; **C** *Sierra de Aracena*, Gran Via 21, T 126175, 43 rm, central, wheelchair access, opp childrens' play area in an otherwise quiet part of town. There are 2 budget *pensión* possibilities close to the main square: **E** *Casa Manolo*, C/Barbero 6, T 110014 and **E** *Sierpes*, C/Mesones 19, T 110147, garage, restaurant. **Something different**: **AL** *Finca Buen Vino*, 21293 Los Marines, Aracena, T/F 124034, 4 rm, English run converted farmhouse 6 km W of Aracena. Outstanding food.

● **Places to eat** Choice for eating out in the evening in Aracena is limited. Try the *Meson de Pedro*, next to the *Hotel Sierra de Aracena*.

There are a number of good restaurants around the caves, but many of these close in the evening.

Other towns of the Sierra Morena

There are a large number of towns and villages in the Sierra Morena which will be of only marginal interest to the visitor on a tight schedule. The following are the pick of the bunch. In the E of the region is the wonderfully sited village of **Zufre**, sitting along the top of a ridge. The Paseo de los Alcades (often called the Balcony of the Sierra) gives superb views over the terraced farmland of the surrounding countryside. The village itself has a strong Moorish influence, with its narrow winding streets, whitewashed houses and small squares. The largely brick built parish church, with Renaissance and Gothic elements, was constructed by Hernán Ruiz, who was responsible for the Renaissance part of the Giralda tower in Sevilla. There was some damage from the 1755 earthquake and a new tower was completed in 1758. In the same square as the church is the arcaded *ayuntmiento*, built in the 16th century. Nearby is a large reservoir, the *Embalse de Zufre*, which offers possibilities for fishing. Enquire about permits at the town hall.

West of Aracena are a number of places worth a visit. 18 km W, just S of the N433/N435 crossroads, is the village of **Jabugo**, the centre of the ham industry. The curing factory in the village is the main employer in this area where jobs are at a premium. Reminded by the roadside advertisements showing grinning black pigs, it would be a crime not to sample the finished product and there are plenty of bars and restaurants to choose from. Check the prices carefully, however, as *jamón serrano* can be very expensive. Besides from the *jamón* connection, there is little to see in Jabugo, apart from a rather dilapidated Baroque church, which will almost certainly be closed. A religious curiosity is to be found at the nearby train station of El Repilado. Here a small obelisk marks the spot where, near to a Chinese banana tree, an apparition of the Holy Virgin of Fátima revealed itself to a local girl. The occasional pilgrim can still be seen around.

Just SW of Jabujo is the mountain of San Cristobal, which at 912m is the highest point of the Sierra Morena. To its S is the village of **Almonaster la Real**, which should be on the itinerary of all students of Moorish southern Spain. The name Almonaster comes from the Arabic *Almunia* and the town is dominated by the 10th century mosque on the hill to the S of the town. The important point is that after the Reconquest, unlike most Andalucian mosques, it was not destroyed or altered. This means that today we can see a perfectly preserved minaret, a *mihrab* which may well be the oldest in Spain and an interior with five naves showing some superb brick horseshoe arches, whose columns may have come from the original Roman buildings on the site. To gain entrance you will need a key, obtained from the *ayuntamiento* in the Plaza de la Constitución – and well worth the trouble. While in Almonaster, take a look at the parish church, the Iglesia de San Martin. Dating from the 14th century it has an interesting façade added 2 centuries later in the Portuguese influenced Manuelino style. If possible, time your visit to coincide with the *Cruces de Mayo* festival, held during May and one of the best in Andalucía.

Out on a limb in the W of the area and only 24 km from the Portugese border, is the village of **Aroche**. The town has a long history being first fortified by the Romans, who called it *Arruci Vetus*. Today the village has a hilltop location sitting snugly around its Moorish castle, built by the Almoravids in the 12th century. The most bizarre of the Christian reconstructions was to include within its walls the local bullring. There are two small museums in the village. Near the castle entrance is the Archaeological Museum, displaying artefacts from Aroche and the surrounding area. An oddity is the Museo del Santo Rosario (Museum of Rosaries), which contains a collection of over 1,200 rosaries from all over the world, including donations from Mother Teresa, various Popes, royalty and politicians. Visitors interested in heraldry will find plenty to see in Aroche. A number of aristocratic families built mansions in the village and their coats of arms are displayed in marble on the house fronts. Also of interest is the Hermitage of San Mamés, venue of a *romería* at Whitsun. The building is in Mudéjar style and contains the statue of San Mamés, which, when it was brought here in the 18th century, was the subject of a long and expensive lawsuit, documented in the cashbook of the hermitage.

IN THE FOOTSTEPS OF COLUMBUS

The area immediately E of Huelva has rich connections with **Christopher Columbus** (known in Spain as Cristóbel Colón) and his quest to find the New World. At the narrow tip of land between the mouths of the Río Tinto and the Río Odiel, the **Punta del Sebo**, is the imposing monument to Columbus known as the *Spirit of Exploration*, completed by the American Sculptress, Gertrude Whitney, in 1929. The caped figure stares resolutely out to sea, ignoring the towers of the petro chemical plant which provide a backdrop for the most commonly used photographic view.

Across the river, on a small hill, is the **Monastery of La Rábida**. Built on the site of what was probably an Almohad mosque, this Franciscan monastery was dedicated soon after the Reconquista. The gatehouse dates from this time, while the cloister was rebuilt after the 1755 earthquake. The monastery's church survived the earthquake and is in Gothic-Mudéjar style. Columbus came here in 1491, after failing to gain royal approval of his plans. He met two friars, Antonio de Marchena and Juan Pérez (the latter having formerly been the Queen's confessor) and they took his case to court gaining permission for his venture. The monastery today receives visitors from all over the world who see it as an important symbol of the Hispanic World. Visiting is by guided tour only. Your guide will be one of the Franciscan friars. Commentary is in Spanish only, but at most stops there are small unobtrusive plaques with brief comments in English. The tour begins in a small ante-room where there are frescoes, painted in 1930, by Daniel Vásquez Díaz, a local Huelvan artist. There is also a plaque commemorating the Quincentenery of Columbus's voyages. The next stop is in the cloisters, often known as the Patio de las

Sorting out your hams

🐖 The English words 'ham' and 'gammon' both originate from the Spanish word **jámon**. The thin slices of ham normally eaten in Britain and North America are known as 'jámon york' in Spain, where they are thought of as only being fit for a toasted sandwich or a roll. No, in Andalucía **jámon serrano** is the real thing and it has attracted around it a certain mystique and tradition which foreigners find difficult to understand. Certainly it is popular. Spain consumes 27 millions joints of ham annually and no bar or bodega worth its salt would be seen without festoons of *jamones* hanging from the ceiling. The production of jámon serrano, which is essentially mountain ham from white pigs, has traditionally been a cottage industry, with small farmers keeping a number of free range pigs under oak trees where they eat the fallen acorns. The slaughtered pigs would then be taken to the local curing factory, a small scale affair where the joints would be kept for 2 or 3 months for the curing process. This involves covering the meat with sea salt to sweat, in a carefully controlled micro climate.

Some areas of Andalucía, such as Trévellez in the Alpujarras, are noted for the excellence of their hams. The ham, par excellence, however, is the *pata negra* from the Sierra Morena of Huelva province, which is produced from the brown breed of pigs with black *patas* (feet). They give a fatty meat, but this helps to tenderise during the curing stage, which may last for as long as 18 months. As a result *pata negra* can be extremely expensive.

At the home and the bar, there is a complicated etiquette to produce the wafer thin slices of *jámon*. Ingenious wooden racks with screws and clamps hold the ham steady while it is carved with long, thin, razor sharp knives. Accompanying the *jámon* will be bread or a type of bland biscuit which will not detract from the taste of the ham. Add a glass of cold *fino* and you have a meal fit for a king.

However, you should enjoy the traditional *jámon serrano* while you can, because the old time cottage industry may not last much longer. The lines of *jamones* in bars and bodegas may soon be a thing of the past, owing to EU hygiene laws. Meanwhile the Spanish house wife, who formerly bought ham on the bone and made soup with what was left, is now probably holding down a full time job and will only find time to buy her *jámon* boned and vacuum sealed. Indeed, some 60% of ham is now sold in this way, produced by huge marketing consortiums in the cities of the north. Connoisseurs may sniff, but at least *jámon serrano* will be cheaper – at 3,000 ptas a kilo it needs to be!

Flores. The cloisters contain an Almohad arch, which may have been the original entrance door. Just off the courtyard is the Monks' refectory, where no doubt Columbus would have eaten. The tour now moves into the 14th century church, which is dominated by the 15th century Image of the Crucifixion. There are frescoes from the same period on the walls and in the apse. Also of interest is the 14th century Alabaster image of the Virgen de los Milagros, before which Columbus and his crew prayed before setting sail. Martín Alonzo Pinzón, the right hand man of Columbus, is buried in the church, beneath the Shrine of Santa María as he had requested. On the first floor is the Chapter House, where Columbus, the Pinzón brothers and the friars met to discuss the plans for the voyages. The same room was used on 3 August 1992, by the King of Spain and the whole government to commemorate the 500th anniversary of the event. In the nearby rooms are models of the three caravels, the Niña, the Pinta and the Santa María, plus other artefacts connected with the voyages. The Sala de Banderas or Flag Room contains the standards of the South American countries along with boxes of soil from each – now covered with glass to keep out cigarette ends and other forms of vandalism.

The monastery is surrounded by pleasant tree lined gardens, in which there is a Latin American University and monument celebrating the 400th anniversary of the Discovery of the Americas. This is a stout column with a simple cross on the top. There are guided tours of the Monastery of La Rábida at 1000, 1045, 1130, 1215 and 1300. Tours resume in the afternoon at 1600, 1645, 1730 and 1815. The tour is free, but a donation is appreciated.

Lying between the river and the bluff on which the monastery stands, is the **Muelle de las Carabelas**. At this point, close to where Columbus' flotilla sailed in

1492, are accurate replicas of the Nina, the Pinta and the Santa María, which were built for the 500th anniversary celebrations. Open Tues-Fri 1000-1400 and 1700-2100; Sat, Sun and public holidays 1100-2000. Closed Mon. Entrance 420 ptas, children 210 ptas, T 530597.

Just 5 km N of La Rábida is **Palos de la Frontera**, a town of little attraction where few people would bother to stop if it were not for the Columbus connection. This was the port from where Columbus set sail in 1492 on his first voyage and was the home of many of his sailors, such as the Pinzón brothers. In those days Palos was a prosperous port, its river location sheltering it from the Atlantic winds. Because the people of Palos had offended Portugal, they were forced to serve the Spanish crown with caravels which had been built and fitted out in the town's shipyards. In 1492, the Catholic Monarchs ordered them to supply Columbus and so in this way the cost of the voyage was greatly reduced. Today the river has silted up the bay and a stretch of marshland separates Palos from the water. The inhabitants of Palos tend to revere the Pinzón brothers more than Columbus and there are a number of commemorative monuments and reminders of the past. The 15th century orphanage which took in the Pinzón brothers still stands, while there is a statue of Martín Alonso Pinzón in the main square. His home, at C/Colon 24, is now a museum. La Fontanilla – the fountain with Roman origins where the caravels took on water before setting sail, is now dry, but has had a facelift for the quincentenary. The jetty from where the caravels left was rebuilt for the 400th anniversary, but as this is now a collapsed heap of rotting timber, it is hardly worth the effort of finding it. Better, instead, to take a look at the 15th century Church of San Jorge, with a mixture of styles from Mudéjar to Gothic. The bell tower is pyramid shaped and dates from the 18th century, while the nave has a coffered ceiling and some fine

Columbus – man of mystery

Although Spain has always regarded **Christopher Columbus** as one of its national heroes, it is now generally agreed that he was born in Genoa in Italy (despite the claims of nearly 20 other towns). Columbus, known as Cristóbel Cólon in Spain, was the son of a weaver and began his maritime career at the age of 13, eventually becoming a trading agent. His work must have led him to many parts of the Mediterranean during which time he learnt his skills in navigation, sailing and map reading. In 1476 he travelled to England, being shipwrecked on the way and swimming ashore near Cape St Vincent. He took refuge for a while in Lisbon, before eventually arriving in London in Dec 1476. He spent the winter and spring there before embarking on a ship at Bristol for Iceland.

Columbus then settled in Lisbon, where his brother Bartholomew was working as a cartographer. In 1479 he married Felipa, the daughter of the governor of Porto Santo and their son Diego was born 2 years later. By now he was beginning to formulate his ideas, by reading maps and charts, that the world was 25% smaller than previously thought and that the East Indies could be reached much more quickly by sailing westwards. These erroneous beliefs remained with him until he died. In 1484 he put forward his ideas to King John II of Portugal with the suggestion that he finance a westward crossing. A Royal Maritime Commission rejected his proposals because of his miscalculations and the fact that Portuguese vessels were already rounding the southern point of Africa on their way eastwards.

Disappointed, Columbus moved to Spain with his son, (his wife having died) and stayed at La Rábida Monastery, near Huelva. In 1486 he presented his plans to the Catholic Monarchs, Ferdinand and Isabel. While waiting for their decision he stayed in Córdoba and developed a liaison with a wealthy widow, Beatrice Enríquez de Harana, who eventually produced his illegitimate son Ferdinand. The plans were rejected and Columbus again retreated to La Rábida to lick his wounds. Here he found an ally in the Abbot, Juan Pérez, who had formerly been the confessor to Isabel. The Catholic Monarchs had now completed the Reconquest with the fall of Granada, but as a result were short of funds. The thought of riches from the New World led them the to change their minds and sponsor an expedition. The persistence of Columbus had eventually paid off.

The **First Voyage**, which left Palos on 3 August 1492, was a modest affair with three ships, the 30m decked *Santa María* and two small 15m caravels, the *Pinta* and the *Niña*, captained by the Pinzón brothers, Martín and Vincente. The total of the crews was probably no more than 90. After a brief stop for repairs in the Canary Islands (where Columbus had a continuing love affair with Beatrice Bobadilla) the fleet resumed the voyage westwards. With his crews almost on the point of mutiny, land was sighted on 12 Oct and landfall was made on the island of Guanahani in the Bahamas group. Columbus continued to the island of Cuba, which he named after Juana, one of the Spanish princesses, and Española (later corrupted to Hispaniola and now the Dominican Republic and Haiti). In Dec 1492, the *Santa María* was shipwrecked. A fort, La Navidad, was built with salvaged wood from the wreck and left with a garrison of 35 men, while the *Niña* and the *Pinta* returned home, Columbus arriving back in Palos in Mar 1493 to receive a noble title.

Columbus began planning almost immediately for his **Second Voyage**. This was an altogether grander affair, with 17 vessels and around 1,500 men. The fleet left Cádiz in Sep 1493 and the voyage was to last for almost 3 years. Countless islands were discovered, including Dominica, Guadalupe and Antigua. When he returned to La Navidad, he found that the fort had been destroyed and the men killed by the natives. Columbus abandoned the site and set up the colony of Isabella, which was effectively the first settlement of Europeans in the New World. The natives, however, were becoming increasingly rebellious and Columbus defeated them in a battle in Mar 1495 and sent five shiploads of them back to Spain, which could be claimed to be the start of the slave trade. He then established a new capital, which he called Santa Domingo and set sail for Spain, leaving his brother Bartholomew in command.

Columbus left Cádiz on his **Third Voyage** on 30 May 1498. He made his first landing on a 3-peaked island which he called Trinidad after the Holy Trinity. The following day he sighted the mainland of South America, at what is now Venezuela. He continued along the coast looking for a strait which he was convinced would lead westward. He eventually returned to Española to find the colony in revolt against his brother Bartholomew. Meanwhile, his enemies in Spain had convinced the Catholic Monarchs that the colony should have a new governor, who duly arrived and sent the Columbus brothers back to Spain shackled in irons. Columbus insisted in retaining his irons until personally pardoned by the Queen.

Columbus began campaigning for his **Fourth Voyage**, but by now he had become something of a nuisance to the crown and the only ships he could obtain were four worm eaten caravels. These left Cádiz in May 1502 and after 21 days anchored off Santa Domingo. Here Columbus sensed the onset of a hurricane and made for shelter. A large homeward bound fleet, with many of his enemies on board, ignored his warnings and were annihilated. Columbus then explored the coast of Central America, still searching for a westward passage. The last two caravels of his small fleet finally foundered off Jamaica in Jun 1503. The remains of his party were shipped back to Spain, arriving in Sanlúcar in Nov 1503. He was never to sail again. Christopher Columbus died 3 years later in Valladolid, a wealthy but bitter man.

So how does history rate Christopher Columbus, 500 years after his first voyage? On the debit side he was clearly hopeless at administration, particularly man management. He was also somewhat greedy and self righteous, which in his old age developed into a paranoia about the way it appeared to him that he had been cheated and slighted. On the other hand, he was a brilliant navigator and never lost a boat through his own faulty seamanship and obviously had a natural instinct for the sky, the stars and the wind. He also had an obsessive perseverance to prove that his ideas and concepts about a westward passage were correct. The fact that they were erroneous does not lessen his achievements. The over riding fact remains that it was Columbus who introduced the Old World to the New. The United States have always celebrated the idea of Columbus discovering America and the 400th centenary was held in Chicago. Yet the nearest he got to discovering what is now US territory was the island of Puerto Rico and the US Virgin Islands, which are part of the commonwealth of the USA.

The Columbus story ends, as it begins, with a mystery. Where are his remains? Initially laid to rest in the Franciscan monastery in Valladolid, his body was at some time taken to the Carthusian monastery in Sevilla. About 20 years later, his daughter in law María de Toledo, arranged for the remains of Columbus and her husband Diego (who had died early at the age of 50) to be sent to the cathedral at Santa Domingo where they were buried in the vaults. By 1795, the whole of Hispaniola had been taken over by France and the remains were removed to

Spanish soil – in this case to the cathedral at Havana in Cuba. Just over a century later Cuba gained independence and in 1899 the coffin was disinterred and taken to the cathedral in Sevilla where today it lies in a crypt beneath an impressive monument. However, in 1877, back in Santa Domingo, another coffin was discovered in the cathedral's crypt in which was a silver plate claiming that the remains were those of Christopher Columbus. American examination in the 1960's suggested that the remains were of two bodies, presumably those of Columbus and his son Diego. But the mystery does not end there. Gianni Granzotto, who produced a biography of Columbus in 1986, claims that his remains were never taken from the Franciscan monastery in Valladolid. The monastery no longer exists and above its site is a bar. If the remains are still there then Columbus' body will lie under its billiards room!

Recommended reading In Seach of Columbus, Hunter Davies, Pub Sinclair-Stevenson – Davies recounts the Columbus story, following in his footsteps and tracing the memorabilia; Christopher Columbus - Master of the Atlantic, David A Thomas, Pub Andre Deutsch – a well chronicled and impressively illustrated account of the life of Columbus.

two tone brickwork. Columbus and the Pinzón brothers attended mass here before setting sail. Unfortunately the church is only open at service times. Today Palos no longer has a maritime role, its 6,500 inhabitants largely making a living from agriculture, specializing in strawberry growing.

7 km up river is the altogether more attractive town of **Moguer**, with its delightful square, Baroque mansions and a handful of convents. Moguer provided many of the crew members of the caravels and Columbus frequently visited the town. A tour of Moguer should certainly include the Convent of Santa Clara, which was founded in the 14th century by Alonso Jofre Tenorio, who surrounded it with high walls and battlements. The convent's church is in Gothic-Mudéjar style and has a number of interesting features. The altars, dating from the 17th century, have glazed tiling from Sevilla, while the impressive Mudéjar choir stalls are 15th century. The three sets of cloisters are similar in style to those which were later built in American missions. Columbus often came to the convent and was in correspondence with the abbess, Doña Inés Enriquez. When he returned from his first voyage he spent a night in prayer at the convent, fulfilling a vow he made on surviving a fearsome storm off the Azores. The nuns left the convent around the turn of the century and it is now a museum. Entrance is by guided tour only, at half hourly intervals, Tues-Sat 1100-1400 and 1700-2000; Sun1700-2000. Entrance 250 ptas.

Also of interest in Moguer is the Church of Nuestra Señora de la Granada, surrounded by whitewashed houses and mainly constructed of rather severe brick, but having a tower which is remarkably similar to the Giralda in Sevilla. Moguer was also the birthplace of Juan Ramón Jiménez (1881-1958), the poet and winner of the Nobel Prize for Literature in 1956. During Franco's times, the poet spent 20 years of exile in Puerto Rico, but his body was returned to Moguer in 1958 for burial. The house in which he was born, C/Jiménez 5, is now a museum to his memory. Open daily 1000-1400 and 1630-2000. Entrance 100 ptas. Finally in Moguer, take a look at the 18th century ayuntamiento. Its cream coloured, double arched Neo classical frontage topped by a clock (usually stopped) features on the current Spanish 2,000 ptas banknote.

EAST FROM HUELVA

29 km E of Huelva on the old N431 to Sevilla is the fortified walled town of **Niebla**. It is located where the main road crosses the Río Tinto and its strategic position warranted protection, as the Romans, who called it *Ilipla*, moved their silver by barge down stream. It was the Romans who built the bridge to the SE of the town and which has carried traffic for 2,000 years since. It was blown up during the Civil War, but has since been carefully restored. Niebla is, in fact, the archetypal walled city. The pink sandstone walls stretch for 2 km, completely encircling the town, and are in places 15m wide. They were largely built during Moorish times, when Niebla was *Medina Labla*, capital of a caliphal district and later an independent *taifa*. During the Reconquest, it fell to Alfonso X in 1257 after a 9-month siege in which gunpowder was used for the first time in Spain. Niebla then gradually declined in importance.

Today, the Río Tinto's bed is red and yellow and the water totally lifeless, but the Roman bridge and the Moorish walls of Niebla are intact and invite exploration. There are four horseshoe Arab gates, named Sevilla, Socorro, Buey and Agua. The gate to the E of the town is the most convenient for the visitor as it is closest to the monuments and has ample parking nearby. Close to the main gate is the ruined Church of San Martín, dating from the 15th century and possibly built on the site of a synagogue. The road separates the Bell tower from the apse and the chapel, which is all that survives. The main church is the Iglesia de Santa María de Granada in the Plaza Santa María right in the town centre. The key is available from the *casa de cultura* (an old 15th century hospital) on the next side of the square. The site was occupied by a Visigoth cathedral and a Moorish mosque before the Reconquest. Bits and pieces of masonry from such times seem to be scattered about the entrance area with its 11 lobed doorway. Inside there is a well preserved *mihrab*, some Roman altars and the throne of the Visigoth bishops. The tower is the original Arab minaret. The castle was originally Moorish, but later modified by the Christians (it is usually known as the Castillo de Guzmán today). It was badly knocked about by French troops in the War of Independence and today, with a modicum of restoration, it is mainly used as a cultural centre. Most visitors will be happy to wander around and enjoy the ambience of Niebla. Food outlets, however, are hard to find, but there is a good bar restaurant in Plaza San Martín. Accommodation is also scarce, with only the *pensión* **E** *Los Cazadores*, C/Quepo de Llano 4, T 363071.

THE CONDADO

East of Niebla is an area known as the **Condado**, reflected in the place names of its main town and villages, **La Palma del Condado**, **Rociana del Condado**, **Almonte** and **Bollullos par del Condado**. The name has its origins in the administrative district of Niebla, set up by Henry II of Castile. The area is notable today for its wine production, with over 16,500 ha under cultivation. Palomino and Garrido are the main grapes used, with the white table wine having its own Denominacion de Origin – one of the few decent white wines produced in Andalucía. Some powerful 'sherries' are also produced. The Condado is also famous for the Huelvan regional dish of *migas*, which is essentially breadcrumbs fried in olive oil and garlic, an accompaniment to almost any meat or seafood meal of the province. **Bollullos** is the main centre of the area and makes a welcome stop for visitors who have slogged along the *autovia* from Sevilla. The main street is like an elongated square with numerous bars and outside tables. There are also a number of *bodegas* along the main road running through the town, many of which can be visited. Some, curiously, sell shellfish.

The next village to the S along the

H612 is **Almonte**, which is now bypassed, leading to the extensive pine woods marking the approach to the **Coto Doñana**. The centre of this nature reserve is the remarkable town of **El Rocio**, which, with its sand covered streets and houses with verandas, looks like a set from a Wild West film. The town is, of course, the venue of the Whitsun *romería* to the sanctuary of the image of the Virgen del Rocio held in the Church of Nuestra Señora del Rocio. Dominating the town, the church belies its elderly appearance, having only been built in the 1960's to replace one flattened in the 1755 earthquake. El Rocio is also a mecca for bird watchers, who can be seen in the Spring lining up along the bridge and the paseo with their telescopes trained on the *marismas*. Accommodation in El Rocio is scarce (impossible at the time of the *romería*) and most birders will stay at **Matalascañas** on the coast. This is a purpose built resort located on the coastal dunes, which have been flattened to make way for the featureless hotels, apartment blocks and villas which line the beach. Matalascañas is not a pretty sight, but it makes an excellent base for exploring the area and its beach is wide, sandy and safe. The road back to Huelva runs for nearly 50 km between the massive tree clad dunes and the marshes, until the provincial capital's petro chemical industry hoves into sight.

THE COTO DONANA

The Parque Nacional de la Coto Doñana is one of Europe's best wetland reserves, rivalled only by the Camargue and the Danube Delta. It covers some 50,270 ha and there is a protective zone around it of similar size. The Coto Doñana forms the western edge of the Guadalquivir estuary and consists of a variety of habitats. Firstly, there is the **beach**, with its inter tidal sands, stretching for over 30 km and largely deserted. Inland there is an extensive system of **sand dunes**, initially mobile dunes, but then older dunes fixed with marram grass and the occasional Stone Pines. These pass into **open woodland** with Cork Oaks and Stone Pines, with clearances covered with scrub *(mator-rales)* dominated by Rock Roses, Lavender and Cistus. The woodland clearings are the best places to see the herds of Fallow and Roe Deer along with small parties of Wild Boar. Other mammals include some 25 pairs of the rare Pardel Lynx, which are, however, nocturnal and elusive. The Egyptian Mongoose is more readily seen as are the Polecat and Otter, while there are also three varieties of bat. The camels which used to splash around the wetter areas have now died out due to poaching and old age. The Coto Doñana is above all a wetland and its largest habitats are the **marismas**, marshland which is inundated each winter and spring by the flood waters of the Río Guadalquivir. The fresh water marshes are surrounded by salt pans and rice paddies. These various wetland habitats attract birds in huge numbers and more than 250 species have been recorded. Winter wildfowl from Northern Europe include some 60,000 Grey Lag Geese and over 250,000 ducks and coots. Spring and autumn passage migrants are dominated by waders such as both types of godwit, Ruffs, stints and Purple Sandpiper. It is the breeding birds in the spring and early summer which are the most spectacular. There are a number of large heronries containing Cattle Egrets, Little Egrets, Grey Herons, Night Herons, Purple Herons and Squacco Herons (one, in fact, is right opposite a hide at the park headquarters). Spoonbills and White Storks are always around, while Whiskered Terns and Collared Pratincoles hawk over the water. Glossy Ibis have appeared regularly in recent years. The reed beds and scrub are alive with the calls of Nightingales, Cettis Warblers, Great Reed Warblers and the Purple Gallinule – the emblem of the Coto Doñana. The sky is full of raptors, including Red Kites, Booted Eagles, Short toed Eagles and hundreds of Black Kites. There are an estimated 15 pairs of the rare Spanish Imperial Eagle nesting within the reserve. Azure

Viva La Paloma Blanca!

Follow a car in Andalucía and you may see a sticker in the rear window proclaiming **'SOY ROCIERO'** indicating that the driver is proud of the fact that he has been on the annual Whitsun pilgrimage to El Rocio. This *romería* is unique not only in Andalucía, but is one of the most amazing spectacles anywhere in the world. A mixture of the religious, the profane, the violent and the bucolic, it could perhaps only happen in Andalucía.

It all started in the 13th century when a shepherd found a carved image of the Virgin in a hollow tree. While carrying her home, he stopped for a sleep and when he awoke he found the statue missing. Retracing his steps he found that the Virgin had miraculously returned to her tree. Villagers from Almonte came to his aid and took the statue away, but again she returned, resisting all attempts to move her. Eventually a shrine was built on the spot, where healing and other miracles were often reported.

Today, in Whitsun week, thousands of pilgrims, many in 'brotherhoods' from all over Andalucía, converge on El Rocio to pay their respects to Nuestra Señora del Rocio, La Paloma Blanca, Queen of the Marshes. The object of their devotion is a white, carved, life-sized statue with a gold head dress and six white petticoats, kept in a sanctuary in El Rocio Church. The traditional way for the brotherhoods to travel to El Rocio is by horseback or ornately decorated ox carts, a journey which takes several days, but which is well fortified by alcohol and paella. Each brotherhood carries a *simpecado*, a mini shrine with a portrait of the Virgin. Thousands more arrive by coach, car and 4WD vehicles, many of which have been ferried across the Guadalquivir by the army. During the last few years the number of *Rocieros* has risen to over half a million, posing a serious logistics problem for the local authorities.

On the Saturday evening, each brotherhood files past the shrine to pay their respects to the Virgin. On the Sunday there is an outdoor mass in the square, followed by more drinking and dancing. Monday morning is the highlight of the pilgrimage, when the Virgin is taken from her shrine by the senior brotherhood, the *Hermandad de Almonte* to visit the *simpecados* of the various brotherhoods, greeted by cries of 'Guapa' or 'Viva la Paloma Blanca'. Any pilgrim wishing to help carry the Virgin,or even touch her, must literally fight for the honour and will be thuggishly repelled by the *Almonteños*. Eventually *La Paloma Blanca* – the White Dove – is returned to her sanctuary and the ox carts, coaches and their inhabitants return home to dry out.

Winged Magpies commonly scavenge around the car parks and picnic sites.

Access to large areas of the Coto Doñana is restricted, but the official locations around the fringe of the reserve will satisfy all but the most fanatical of birders.

The bridge and promenade at El Rocío give excellent views of a range of water birds (a telescope is useful here). The SEA (Spanish Ornithological Association) run a delightful little observation centre looking over the water, with telescope, information and English speaking staff. The SEA have their main office in the *Casa de Cultura*, C/Ajolí 44, El Rocio, T 442310. **La Rocina sub centre** is located 500m from El Rocío on the road to Matalascañas, T 406140. There is a 2.5 km trail with a series of hides overlooking a fresh water lake and marsh known as the Charco de la Boca (the second hide is particularly good for Purple Gallinules). There are also areas of pinewood and scrub, plus a large reed bed where Grasshopper Warblers breed.

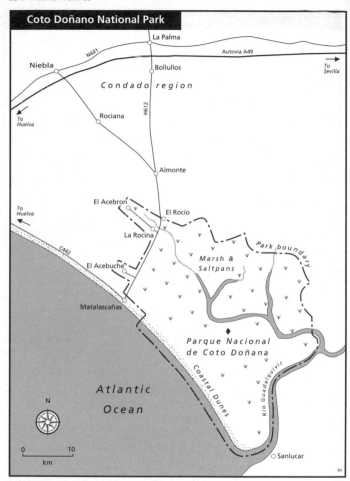

Coto Doñano National Park

La Palma

N431

Autovia A49

Niebla

To
Sevilla

Bollullos

Condado region

H612

Rociana

To
Huelva

Almonte

El Acebron

El Rocío

Park boundary

To
Huelva

La Rocina

C442

El Acebuche

*Marsh &
Saltpans*

Matalascañas

*Parque Nacional
de Coto Doñana*

Rio Guadalquivir

Coastal Dunes

*Atlantic
Ocean*

N

0   10
km

Sanlucar

84

7 km from La Rocina along a minor road through the scrubland is the **Acebron Palace**, an old mansion with a mildly interesting museum. The grounds have mature woodland and a delightful shady walk around a small lake.

The main visitors centre and the Coto Doñana headquarters are at **El Acebuche**, 4 km N of Matalascañas on the C435. The centre includes an educational room with an audio visual presentation, restaurant and shop. On the roof is probably the most photographed storks nest in Andalucía. There are a series of nine hides overlooking a large lake of 33 ha, surrounded by trees and marsh. From late Apr, the trees on the far side support a busy heronry. The last three hides overlook a fenced-in area where there are wildfowl no longer able

235

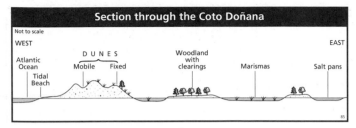

Section through the Coto Doñana

Not to scale

WEST — Atlantic Ocean, Tidal Beach — DUNES: Mobile, Fixed — Woodland with clearings — Marismas — Salt pans — EAST

to fly, but which seem to attract truly wild birds to the location.

It is possible to book Landrover tours of the reserve from El Acebuche. These leave twice a day, last 4 hrs and need booking well in advance. These tours start by driving along the beach and then hurtle up the dunes and in to the woodland. While they give a good indication of the various habitats, they are usually crowded with noisy tourists who have little interest in wildlife and can prove frustrating to the serious naturalist. Visiting groups of birders can hire these for the day and have a little more control over the situation. Contact the centre in advance, T 406722. It is also possible to visit the S edge of the reserve by boat from Sanlúcar (see page 130) and Sevilla (see page 276).

Despite being one of only five National parks on mainland Spain and being designated a UNESCO 'Biosphere Reserve', the Coto Doñana has been under threat in recent years. Firstly, there have been plans put forward for further development at Matalascañas, including a golf course, which will put extra demands on water supply which threatens the water table levels on the reserve. Farmers wish to reclaim more land for agriculture, which will then need more irrigation water, which will also affect water levels. Local people, who see jobs as more important than wildlife, have organized a number of demonstrations and some of the park property and vehicles have been vandalized. Environmentalists throughout Europe have sprung to the rescue of the

Coto Doñana with petitions and pressure through the EU and at the moment an uneasy peace prevails.

When to visit the Coto Doñana

The period between late Feb and mid May is the most rewarding in terms of the maximum number of species, but this will depend entirely on the water level. After a dry winter, breeding conditions can be disappointing. In summer, the *marismas* dry out, the heat is intense and the mosquitoes are irritating. Avoid the Whitsun *romería* at El Rocío.

● **Accommodation** There are 5 small *pensiones* in El Rocío itself: **D** *Doñana Tour*, Plaza Real 29, T 442468, 44 rm; **D** *Isidro*, Avda los Ansares 59, 14 rm, a/c; **D** *Velez*, C/Algaida 2, T 442117; **E** *Cristina*, C/Real 32, T 442413, 24 rm; **E** *La Marisma*, C/Baltasar lll 4, 23 rm. It is probably better to stay in the beach hotels of Matalascañas of which there is a good choice: **A** *La Carabela*, Sector L parc 59, T 448001, F 448125, 275 rm, a/c, wheelchair access, pool, restaurant; **A** *El Cortijo*, Sector E parc 15, T 430259, F 448570, a/c, wheelchair access, restaurant, pool, tennis; **A** *el Flamero*, C/Ronda Maestro Alonso, T 448020, F 448008, 484 rm, a/c, pool, disco, closed Oct to Easter; **A** *Gran Hotel del Coto*, Sector D, T 440017, 467 rm, wheelchair access, pool restaurant, tennis; **A** *Tierra Mar*, Parcela 120, sectro M, T 440375, F 440720, 253 rm, a/c, pool, tennis, disco, restaurant, beachside location. There are also half a dozen *pensiones*, the best of which is **D** *Los Tamarindos*, Avda Adelfas 31, T 430119. The nearest **camp site** is *Rocío Playa*, Ctra Huelva-Matalascañas, Km 45, beachside, 2nd category site.

Jaén Province

THE LANDLOCKED province of Jaén in the northeast of Andalucía is one of the region's least visited areas, yet it has some interesting cities and Natural Parks. In many ways, but particularly in the architecture of its cities, it is more like central Spain than Andalucía, with which it is linked in the north by the strategic Despeñaperros Pass. The capital city, Jaén, has some fine Renaissance buildings, including the cathedral, a pattern repeated in both Baeza and Úbeda. These monuments, funded by textile production, were largely designed by the famed Andrés de Vandelvira.

HORIZONS

The history of the province, however, goes back way beyond Renaissance times. Moorish castles abound in Andalucía, but two of the best examples are found in Jaén province – at **Baños de la Encina** in the north, guarding the Despeñaperros Pass, and at **Alcala la Real** in the south. The mountainous east of the province is dominated by the **Cazorla Natural Park** (strictly speaking the natural Parks of Cazorla, Segura and Las Villas), a series of limestone ridges running northeast-southwest, forming the largest protected area in Andalucía.

Other Natural Parks include the **Sierra Mágina**, immediately southeast of Jaén and part of the Subbética range, while in the north of the province is the **Parque Natural Despeñaperros**, part of the Sierra Morena. Running through the centre of the province is the valley of the **Guadalquivir**. The river rises in the Sierra de Cazorla, running through the Tranco reservoir before swinging W to form a large area of fertile lowland to the N of Jaén and flowing a further 600 km before reaching the Atlantic at Sanlúcar in Cádiz province.

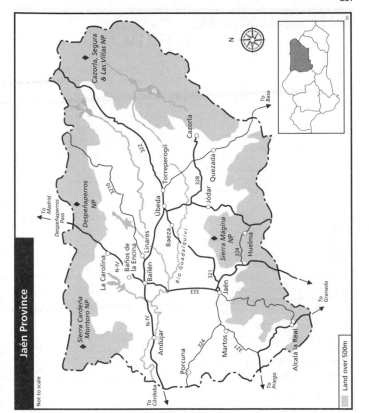

Jaén Province

Not to scale

N

To Basa

Cazorla, Segura & Las Villas NP

Cazorla

Torreperogil

Quezada

Jódar

Úbeda

Baeza

Sierra Mágina NP

Huelma

Río Guadalquivir

Despeñaperros NP

To Madrid

Despeñaperros Pass

La Carolina

Linares

Bailén

Baños de la Encina

N-IV

Sierra Cardeña Montoro NP

Jaén

To Granada

Andújar

N-IV

Porcuna

Martos

Alcalá la Real

To Córdoba

To Priego

Land over 500m

JAEN CITY

(*Pop* 105,000; *Alt* 574m)

ACCESS Air The nearest national airport is at Granada, while the nearest international airport is at Málaga.

Train Jaén is linked by railway with the other Andalucían cities and northwards to central Spain.

Road Jaén is at the centre of a network of roads, but motorways are only just reaching the province. At present an *autovia* is being constructed from Granada to Jaén and this will continue N to connect with the existing *autovia* which runs northwards through the Despeñaperros Pass to central Spain.

HISTORIC BACKGROUND

Jaén was probably an Iberian town, but the first major settlement was built by the Romans who were attracted by local deposits of silver. They named it *Aurigi*, and it was here, legend has it, that Euphrasius introduced Christianity. The Moors took the city in 712 and called it *Yayyan*, turning it into a strategic centre along local caravan routes. The Moorish armies under Muhammad II al-Nasir stopped in Jaén en route to the disastrous **Battle of Navas de Tolosa**, in which they lost much of their territory to Alonso VIII. Jaén itself, which had become part of the Nasrid Kingdom of Granada, was ceded to Fernando III by Muhammad Ibn Nasr in 1246, after which time it played a key role as a Christian frontier town during the final stages of the Reconquista. Jaén was, in fact, used by the Catholic Monarchs as a meeting point by their army prior to the thrust to expel the Moors from Granada. As in many parts of Andalucía, decline then set in, a situation which was not helped by the steady emigration of its citizens to the colonies of the New World. Today, Jaén is the poorest of the provincial capitals of Andalucía, with chronic unemployment both in the city and the surrounding agricultural area. Few tourists visit the city. Those who do are often stared at in some disbelief by the inhabitants, who cannot imagine the purpose of such visits. Jaén is, however, not an unpleasant place and there are a small number of sites worthy of a call – although most visitors would find half a day quite enough to allocate for sight seeing.

PLACES OF INTEREST

The Cathedral Jaén's outsize cathedral was built on the site of the Great Mosque. It was begun in 1492, largely to the design of Andres de Vandelvira, but was not completed until the early years of the 19th century. The exterior is dominated by the W façade in Baroque style with Corinthian columns and twin towers capped with small domes. The architecture elsewhere is undistinguished. The interior is typically gloomy, due to the lack of windows. Worth looking at are the choir stalls, dating from the 16th century and richly carved, and some of the many side chapels, which have the occasional work of art of note. Kept behind the high altar, in a glass case, is a holy relic, a cloth with which St Veronica is reputed to have wiped the face of Christ. Locals are allowed to kiss the glass case on Fri afternoons. The cathedral is open daily 0830-1300 and 1630-1900. There is also a

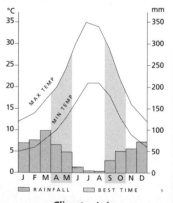

Climate: Jaén

small Sacristy Museum, open on Sat and Sun 1100-1300, which has a few sculptures and other items of interest.

20 mins' walk NW from the cathedral along Cs/Martínez and Molina is the **Palacio de Villadompardo**. This was built in the 16th century over the **Baños Arabes**, which have now been re-

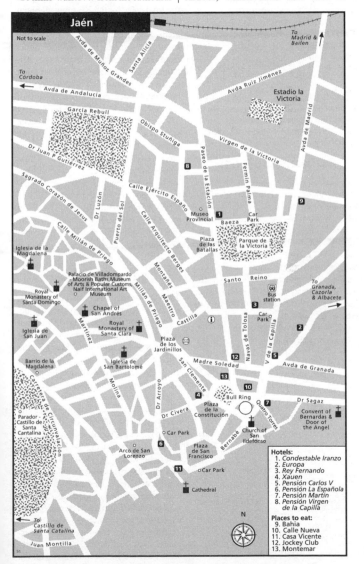

Jaén

Not to scale

To Córdoba

To Madrid & Bailen

Avda de Munoz Grandes

Santa Alicia

Avda de Andalucia

Avda Ruiz Jiménez

Estadio la Victoria

Garcia Rebull

Obispo Stuñiga

Virgen de la Victoria

Avda de Madrid

Dr Juan P Gutiérrez

Sagrado Corazón de Jesus

Calle Ejército Español

Paseo de la Estación

Fermín Palma

Calle Millán de Priego

Dr Luzón

Puerto del sol

Museo Provincial

Baeza

Car Park

Calle Arquitecto Berges

Plaza de las Batallas

Parque de la Victoria

Iglesia de la Magdalena

Palacio de Villadompardo - Moorish Baths, Museum of Arts & Popular Customs, Naif International Art Museum

Montañés

Maestro

Santo

Reino

Bus station

To Granada, Cazorla & Albacete

Royal Monastery of Santa Domingo

Chapel of San Andrés

Royal Monastery of Santa Clara

Millán de Priego

Castilla

Car Park

Navas de Tolosa

V de la Capilla

Iglesia de San Juan

Martínez

Plaza de los Jardinillos

Madre Soledad

Barrio de la Magdalena

Iglesia de San Bartolomé

Molina

San Clemente

Avda de Granada

Parador - Castillo de Santa Cantalina

Cerbera de Circonvalación

Dr Arroyo

Dr Civera

Bull Ring

Plaza de la Constitución

Dr Sagaz

Quatro Torres

Convent of Bernardas & Door of the Angel

Arco de San Lorenzo

Car Park

Bernabé

Church of San Ildefonso

Plaza de San Francisco

Car Park

Cathedral

To Castillo de Santa Catalina

Juan Montilla

N

Hotels:
1. *Condestable Iranzo*
2. *Europa*
3. *Rey Fernando*
4. *Xauen*
5. *Pensión Carlos V*
6. *Pensión La Española*
7. *Pensión Martín*
8. *Pensión Virgen de la Capilla*

Places to eat:
9. *Bahia*
10. *Calle Nueva*
11. *Casa Vicente*
12. *Jockey Club*
13. *Montemar*

Bathing the Moorish way

Andalucía is particularly rich in examples of medicinal baths and spas, which was always a strong Mediterranean tradition, particularly with the Romans. It was the coming of the Moors to Spain, however, which brought this to a fine art, because in the Islamic world bathing was not just for hygiene or pleasure, but part of the religious practice. Known to the Moors as *hamman*, each town would have several public baths, with the main baths close to the central mosque. Wealthy and powerful individuals would have their own private and often luxurious baths. Today, many of these baths have survived, and like those at Alhama de Granada, where the spring water used has medicinal qualities. Others, such as the example in Jaén, were excavated during this century after being built over. There are further baths at Ronda, Alhama de Almería, Córdoba and some of the best preserved of all at Gibraltar.

The organization of the baths followed a fairly standard pattern. Entry was through an open air courtyard and then into an entrance hall, where the visitor was welcomed and moved into the separate areas for men and women. There were then three rooms, the cold, warm and hot. The cold room or *al-maslaj* was for undressing. Clothes were taken off and replaced by towels, slippers and bath robes. The warm room or *bait al-wastani* would have had pools, as would the hot room or *bait al-sajuni*, where the humidity functioned to bring on perspiration in order to clean out the pores – much in the way of present

MOORISH BATHS
JAEN

day saunas. At the side of the pools were areas to rest and have a massage or haircut. The water and air were heated by a wood furnace from which a hypocaust system distributed the warmth under the floor.

The architecture of the baths was also standard. The roofs of the baths were simply vaulted, with star shaped apertures. Other parts of the building would have had traditional tiled roofs. Inside, the floors were of absorbent flagstones, while the walls had decorative glazed tiles. Pillars and rounded arches held up the roof. The pillars were often taken from Roman remains, where these were available.

The baths were usually well staffed with attendants supplying all the bathers requirements. Others would stoke the furnace or have cleaning duties. Barbers and masseurs would ply their trade. For the bathers, however, the baths were a place for lounging, relaxation, gossip and doing business.

opened. The building also contains the **Museum of Arts and Popular Customs** and the **Naif International Art Museum**. All three museums are open at the same time, and, as they are free with an EU passport, they make a profitable visit. The **Baños Arabes**, or Moorish *haman*, are the largest surviving in Andalucía. They were built in the 11th century and the Almohad decoration suggests that they were restored a century later. After the Reconquest in 1246 they fell into disuse and later the buildings became a tannery. At the end of the 16th century the palace of Don Fernando de Torres y Portugal was built on the site, filling the basement of the ruined baths with soil. A local archaeologist rediscovered the baths in 1913 and for the remainder of this century they have been diligently restored. They were finally opened to the public in 1984. The site consists of an entrance hall and rooms for cold, tepid and hot baths. The floors are largely of marble, with brick walls and stone pillars supporting brick horseshoe arches. The ceilings are either cupolas with star shaped windows or half barrel vaults. Their lack of decoration suggests that they were for public rather than private use. The area of the Palacio occupied by the **Museum of Arts and Popular Customs** was a bank in the 17th century. It now includes two of the courtyards of the palace and a columned gallery on two levels. The museum gives a fascinating view of everyday life in the province over the last few centuries. The basement concentrates on agriculture, particularly the production of wine, cereals and olives, with a comprehensive collection of carts and farming implements. The first floor deals with ceramics, textiles and traditional house building techniques. Here you can see the first cast iron bed, which won 1st prize at the London Exhibition in 1851. The second floor looks at various aspects of religion, plus a handful of trades. The **Naif International Art Museum** was opened in 1990 to occupy the remainder of the palace and was the first

of its kind to be set up in Spain. Naive or primitive art has always been under estimated and this museum makes a refreshing change from the heavy religious based art found in most of Andalucía's fine art museums. Naive art is characterized by being created by people who paint with no established methods or ideas learnt at art schools. Their work is generally flat with bright colours, detailed background, foreground and lack of perspective. The simplicity and fantasy make them easy to understand. The collection is based on the legacy of Manuel Mozas, who donated his own collection, which included his own works and those of other artists. Works of numerous Spanish and foreign artists have since been added. The Palace of Villadompardo is open from Tues-Fri 1000-1400 and 1700-2000; Sat and Sun 1030-1400. Closed Mon and fiestas. Entrance 100 ptas, free with EU passport. Visits to the Baños Arabes are by guided tour only. Lady guides round up visitors from other parts of the complex at half hourly intervals.

Many visitors will quite happily call it a day after seeing the cathedral and the palace, but before leaving those with private transport should certainly drive up to the **Castillo de Santa Catalina**, approached via the Ctra al Castillo y Neveral. This castle stands on the hill overlooking the town. It was once an Arab palace built by Ibn Nasr, but, after its capture from the Moorish King Al-Hammar during the Reconquest, it has been much altered and restored. Some secret passages have been discovered leading down to the *barrio* of La Magdalena in the town below, which still has its winding Moorish street plan. The castle is now a *parador* and a path from its car park leads along to a *mirador*, giving magnificent views of the city below.

Back in Jaén, those with more time on their hands could visit the **Museo Provincial** on Paseo de la Estación, which contains a fine collection of archaeological exhibits, the most important of which are the Iberian stone sculptures which were found in the W of the province. The Moorish room has a good collection of coins and ceramics, the latter in the green style which is still prevalent in the pottery of today. The Fine Arts section of the museum is located upstairs, but contains little of quality and is hardly worth the walk.

Church architecture buffs might also find it worth seeking out one or two additional buildings. The **Royal Monastery of Santo Domingo** in C/Santo Domingo in the Magdalena *barrio*, close to the Arab baths, was built in the 14th century and was later the city's university. It then carried out the dealings of the Inquisition, before becoming a school. Although it is not open to the public, the imposing 16th century entrance by Vandelvira can be appreciated. Nearby, in the same *barrio*, is the **Church of La Magdalena**, which was built over a mosque. The original minaret is now the bell tower, which sits remarkably easily with the 15th century Gothic of the remainder of the church. On the opposite side of the town to the NE of the cathedral is the late 14th century **Church of San Ildefonso**, within which is the image of Our Lady of La Capilla, the Patron Saint of Jaén. Finally, there is the **Royal Convent of Santa Clara**, in C/Las Huertas, which dates from the 13th century. Founded by Ferdinand III, it has a figure of Christ with Bamboo, which may be of 16th century Ecuadorean origin.

LOCAL FESTIVALS

Night of 16 Jan – *Fiesta de las Lumbres (fires) de San Antón*; usual Holy Week processions during *Semana Santa*; the *Romería del Cristo del Arroz* pilgrimage on the second Sun in May at the Fuente de la Peña; in Jun *Corpus Cristi* is marked by a procession; 11 Jun – *Fiesta de Nuestra Señora de la Capilla*, Jaén's patron saint, with flowers, processions and dances; 12-20 Oct – *Feria de San Lucas* dates back to the 15th century, hav-

ing been established by the Constable of Castille, Miguel Lucas de Iranzo. This is Jaén's most important fair, with bullfights and sports events; 25 Nov *pilgrimage* to the Castillo de Santa Catalina.

LOCAL INFORMATION

Price guide

Hotels:			
AL	over US$90	**D**	US$20-40
A	US$75-90	**E**	US$10-20
B	US$60-75	**F**	under US$10
C	US$40-60		

Places to eat:			
♦♦♦	expensive	♦♦	average
♦	cheap		

● Accommodation

Considering Jaén's importance as a regional centre, the amount and variety of accommodation is surprisingly small, with only 6 hotels and 4 *pensiones*.

AL *Parador Nacional*, Castillo de Santa Catalina, T 264411, F 223930, 45 rm, a/c, restaurant, pool, in heavily restored section of the castillo, quiet with stunning views.

A *Condestable Iranzo*, Paseo de la Estación 32, T 222800, F 263807, 159 rm, garage, a/c, disco.

B *Europa*, Plaza de Belén1, T 222700, F 222692, 36 rm, garage, a/c, restaurant, central location off the Avda de Madrid; **B** *Rey Fernando*, Plaza de Coca de la Piñera 7, T 251840, garage, a/c, restaurant, central position; **B** *Xauen*, Plaza de Deán Mazas 3, T 264011, 35 rm, a/c, central location.

The *pensiones* are all nr the city centre and on bus routes: **E** *Carlos V*, Avda de Madrid 4, 222091, no rooms with bath, noisy main road; **E** *La Española*, C/Bernado López 9, T 230524, 19 rm, centrally placed a stones throw from the cathedral in quiet pedestrianized area; **E** *Martín*, C/Cuatro Torres 5, T 220633, 14 rm, rough and ready; **E** *Virgen de la Capilla*, C/Cristo Rey 2, T 220024, 29 rm, a/c, cheapest rooms with bath in town, restaurant, nr Museo Provincial.

Camping: no sites nr Jaén, but plenty in the Cazorla Natural Park to the E.

● Places to eat

Local dishes incl *gazpacho* with, unusually, grapes and apples and *enslada de pimientos asados* – salad made with roasted peppers.

♦♦♦*Castillo de Santa Catalina*, T 264411, at the summit for altitude, price and ambience with local specialities; *Casa Vicente*, C/Arco del Consuelo 1, T 262816, priciest restaurant in the city, in old mansion specializing in game and other local dishes; *Jockey Club*, Paseo de la Estación 20, T 251018, expensive, but with a reasonable *menu*; *Montemar*, C/Roldán y Marín 7, T 234262, excellent fish and seafood.

♦♦*Bahía*, Plaza San Roque 1, T 251450; *Batavia*, Paseo Estación 31, T 266032, traditional cuisine; *Zeluan*, Plaza San Francisco 3, T 271860.

♦ Reasonable *platos combinados* and *raciones* in C/Nueva: *La Gamba del Oro*, N°3, T 261613; *Los Moriscos*, N°2, T 253206; *Mesón del Chico*, N°12, T 228502.

● **Bars**

For *tapas* bars, try, again, C/Nueva and the area to the E of the Plaza de la Constitución.

● **Banks & money changers**

The branches of the main Spanish banks are concentrated around the Plaza de la Constitución.

● **Entertainment**

There is nothing in the way of wild nightlife in Jaén. There are a few lacklustre **discos**, mainly along the Avda de la Estación. There are 3 multi screen **cinemas**, the best of which is *Avenida Multicines*, Avda Muñoz Grandes 4, T 264706. The most important bullfights take place during the festivals of *San Lucas* and *Nuestra Señora de la Capilla*. There is an **International Piano Competition** annually during the first week in May and an **International Festival of Song and Dance** later in the year.

● **Hospitals & medical services**

Hospitals: *Centro Hospitalario 'Princesa de España'*, Ctra de Madrid, T 222650; *Hospital del SAS 'Cuidad de Jaén'*, Avda del Ejército Español, T 222408.

Red Cross: *Cruz Roja*, C/Carmelo Torres 1, T 251540.

● **Post and telecommunications**
Area code: 953.

Post Office: *Correos*, Plaza de Jardinillos, open Mon-Sat 0900-1400, T 220112.

Telephones: no *locutorios*, but cabins in most of the squares, incl Plaza de la Constitución and Plaza de San Francisco.

● **Shopping**

Cottage industries thrive throughout the province producing ceramics, rugs, wickerwork, ironwork and guitars. There is a flea market on Thur next

to the train station. The main shopping streets of the city are those branching off the Plaza de la Constitución, such as the Paseo de la Estación, Via de la Capilla and C/San Clemente.

● **Tour companies & travel agents**

Ecomar, C/Navas de Tolosa 14, T 256650; *Halcon*, Plaza Coca de la Piñera s/n, T 259600; *Sacromonte*, Pasaje Mazas s/n, T 222212. For the hire of tourist guides ring Maria de la Cruz Lomez Guidsa, T 257987, or Fernando Gallardo Carpio, T 261468.

● **Tourist offices**

Regional Government Tourist Office, C/Arquitecto Berges 1, T 222737. Open Mon-Fri 0900-1330 and 1700-1900; Sat 1000-1300 except Jul and Aug. There is also a local municipal office at the Diputación Provincial, Plaza San Francisco.

● **Useful addresses**

Garages/car repair workshops: many of the main garages/showrooms are located on the Los Olivares industrial estate. *Citroën*, Ctra Madrid, Km 332.6, T 252542; *Ford*, Pol Los Olivares, C/Mancha Real 2, T 223554; *Peugeot*, Pol Los Olivares, C/Torredonjimeno 7, T 251329; *Renault*, Ctra de Granada, Km 336, T 221550; *Seat*, C/Ortega Nieto 3, T 224000; *Volvo*, Pol Los Olivares, C/Beas de Segura 18, T 263001; *VAG*, C/Ortega Nieto 7, T 261300.

● **Transport**

Local Bus: the bus station is in Plaza Coca de la Pinera. Castillo run regular bus services around the town, stopping in the Plaza de la Constitución. **Car hire**: Autos del Pino, C/La Luna 6, T 250901; Avis, Avda de Granada 7, T 223137; Hertz, Viajes Sacromonte, Pasaje Maza, T 222212. **Taxi**: Avda de Andalucía 47, T 220028; Plaza de la Estación, T 220020; Plaza José Solis, T 220021; Plaza de las Batallas s/n, T 251036; Plaza Coca de la Pinera, T 251026; Plaza de la Constitución, T 265017; Plaza del Valle, T 229055; Plaza de San Francisco, T 265019.

Train The huge RENFE station, T 255607, in Plaza de la Estación, is visited by very few trains since the line S of Jaén was abandoned. There are 2 daily to **Madrid**, 2 to **Cádiz** and a bus at 1730 to nearby **Espeluy** station for connections to other towns in Andalucía, incl **Córdoba** and **Sevilla**.

Road Bus: there are daily buses to **Úbeda** and **Baeza**, with some going on to the **Cazorla**. There are also daily long distance coaches to **Córdoba**, **Madrid**, **Sevilla**, **Granada** and **Málaga**.

SOUTH OF JAEN

The main road from Jaén S to Granada, the N323, initially follows the valley of the Río Guadalbullón through the Sierra Mágina. This mountain region rises to 2,167m at Pico Mágina and forms the **Parque Natural de Sierra Mágina** covering nearly 20,000 ha. There are three distinct vegetation zones in this limestone area. At lower levels is evergreen forest with Holm Oaks, Juniper and Holly. The middle zone comprises Mediterranean forest with largely deciduous trees, while above the tree line is open grassland with brooms. The lower levels support a variety of mammals including wild Boar, Beech Martens, Polecats and Genets and the recently introduced Red Deer. The mammals will be elusive, but the bird life is abundant, including raptors such as Golden Eagle, Bonelli's Eagle, Griffon Vultures and Eagle Owls. Golden Orioles are found along the wooded river valleys and there are Blue Rock Thrushes and Ring Ouzels in the higher spots.

There are a couple of villages in the area worth a diversion. Some 10 km from Jaén, just off the N323 to the W, is the hilltop village of **La Guardia**, dominated by its 8th century Moorish castle, which, unusually, is in the shape of an equilateral triangle. Its ruins have much older elements in its walls, possibly going back to Visigoth times. The other building of note in La Guardia is the ruined church of Santo Domingo, designed by Vandelvira and once part of a Dominican monastery. Further to the SE, and reached by turning off the main road along the N324, is the village of **Huelma**. Located on the S side of the Sierra Mágina in wild scenery, the village has a Moorish castle with several round towers. Below it are narrow whitewashed alleyways with the original Moorish street pattern, leading to the sandstone Renaissance Church of La Immaculada.

Tourists with more time on their hands might wish to take the more leisurely route S from Jaén to Granada, by following the N321 via Martos, Alcaudete and Alcalá la Real. South of the rolling landscape of olive groves is the village of **Martos**, dominated by its ruined Moorish castle of *La Virgen de la Villa*, on the crag which overlooks the town. This particular fortress fell to the Christians in 1225 on St Marta's Day – hence the present place name. The keep and Tower of Almedina are still in good condition. While in the village, take a look at the *ayuntamiento* which was built in 1577 and the 13th century Church of Santa María de la Villa (although later additions in Baroque style dominate). 25 km further S is the small town of **Alcaudete**. Known to the Moors as *Al-Qabdaq*, it changed hands several times during the Reconquest, before finally falling to Alfonso XI in 1340. The ruined fortress of Albendín, which towers over the town, was built in the 10th century with the stones from a former Roman settlement, but only the massive keep remains in good condition. There are various other defensive walls and towers scattered around Alcaudete, particularly along the road to Granada. Nestling beneath the castle is the Church of Santa María, with a mixture of architectural styles, a staggered tiled roof and strongly built tower. A further 26 km S is the town of **Alcalá la Real**, which was first settled by Yemanis in 713. It was later a Moorish stronghold (known as *Al-Kalaat Be Zayde*) with its peak of influence coming in the 12th and 13th centuries when it was an independent *taifa*. It changed hands several times during the Reconquest, finally falling to Alfonso X, who added the suffix *Real* to the place name. All visitors should visit the hilltop castle, the *Forteza de la Mota* and the adjacent church of Santa María la Mayor. The whole site covers some 3 ha, with rocky cliffs forming part of the external walls. There were seven gates to the fortress, one of which, the Puerta de la Imagen, is now the main entrance. The walls were supported by a series of watchtowers, of which 15 still exist – six Christian and the remainder Arab. The Tower of Homage now houses a small archaeological museum, with Roman, Moorish and Christian remains. Coins, skeletons, pottery and weapons, mostly obtained on the site, are all carefully displayed. A few metres away is the Church of Santa María de Mayor, which was built during the time of Alfonso XI, on the site of a mosque. It has been gutted and is in process of being restored by an enthusiastic group of architectural students. There are guided tours of the whole site (tip deserved and appreciated). Access is easy – follow the signs from the town centre to the top of the hill where there is well landscaped parking. The views from the castle over the town and the surrounding olive groves and mountains are stupendous, making this a highly recommended diversion. Overnight accommodation, however, is restricted to the *Pensión Zacatín*, C/Pradillo 1, T 580568.

NORTH FROM JAEN

The area N of Jaén is largely agricultural, with rolling landscape covered with olive groves. On the N side of the Guadalquivir valley are the three, largely nondescript, industrial towns of Linares, Bailén and Andúcar. All are now thankfully bypassed, either by the NIV or the N322. Should a stop be necessary, the visitor will find that the only claim to fame of **Linares** is that the famous bullfighter *Manolete* was gored to death here in 1947. **Bailén** was founded by the Moors, there is scant evidence of it, even in the castle, and today the town is known only for the quality of its ceramics and pottery. **Andúcar**, the most attractive of the three, has some parts of its walls and towers still standing, plus one or two examples of Baroque and Renaissance architecture. The time saved by avoiding the three towns could be used by the discerning traveller to make the 10 km detour northwards from Bailén to the small hill village of **Baños de la Encina**, with its wonderfully preserved Moorish castle. Archaeological remains show that Baños was a Prehistoric settlement. Bronze Age paintings and remains have been found in the nearby caves of la Moneda and Peñalosa. It was occupied by the Arabs in the 8th century and in 967 Al-Hakim II had the fortress built, naming it *Burch al Hamma*, or the tower of the baths. The castle, composed of golden sandy conglomerate and shaped like a ship, is in an excellent state of preservation, despite the fact that it was won and lost six times by the Christians. Entry is through a double horseshoe arch. The walls have restored battlements and no fewer than 14 towers. There is a huge courtyard (used as a parade ground in more military times and now used for village dancing at fiestas). The impressive Tower of Homage gives spectacular views over the village and the nearby reservoir, the Embalse del Rumblar. Viewing hours are informal and depend entirely on the an-

The Battle of Las Navas de Tolosa

It was in the year 711 that the Moors led by Tarik, General of the Caliph's Governor in North Africa, left Tangier with an army of 9,000 men and landed in Gibraltar. Within 5 years they had occupied almost the whole of the Iberian peninsula. By the year 1065, the *taifa* kingdoms still occupied two thirds of Iberia. The Almohad empire at the start of the 13th century covered most of the southern half of Spain and Portugal, with what is now Andalucía firmly in Moorish hands. Whenever the Christians in the N threatened, the Moors were always able to call on reinforcements from North Africa to fight for their cause. But by now the Christian armies were beginning to unite and the allied forces of Castile, Aragon and Navarra faced up to the Almohads in 1212.

The battle was fought some 9 km NE of the village of **Las Navas de Tolosa**, which guarded the Despeñaperros Pass to the N. The Christians had amongst their forces a contingent of mostly French crusaders, along with the men of Peter II of Aragon, Alfonso VIII of Castile and the army of Sancho 'the Strong' of Navarre. The Moorish army of Granada was led by the 4th Almohad caliph, Mohammed al-Nasir. The Moors were soundly defeated and now the fragile balance between the Moors and the Christians was broken, with the Christians having the upper hand. In addition, the people of the Maghreb, seeing the first signs of weakness in the Almohads, decided that they were no longer prepared to come on further military journeys from Al-Andalus.

Although the Moors held on in Granada for a further 250 years, largely through the payment of taxes and tributes, the Battle of Las Navas de Tolosa was the beginning of the end – but a battle which continues today throughout Andalucía in the fiestas of the Moors versus the Christians.

cient guardian and his equally antique key. His surprising agility around the rickety steps usually earns him a tip. If he is not around, enquire at the *ayuntamiento* in the main square. The village of Baños de la Encina itself is worth a stroll around. Take a look at the pretty Plaza de la Constitución and the imposing Iglesia Parroquial de San Mateo, with its Gothic 15th century nave and octagonal Renaissance tower dated 1596. There are also one or two mansions with coats of arms over their doors.

There are two Natural Parks in this area, both part of the Sierra Morena. Immediately N of Andúcar is the **Parque Natural de Andúcar**, covering some 60,000 ha. This is one of the most heavily wooded parts of the Sierra Morena, with Cork Oaks, Encinas and Stone Pines along with large areas of scrub. Woodland birds include Golden Oriole, Azure Winged Magpies, Crested Tits and woodpeckers. There is a good range of raptors including all three vultures, Golden Eagles and Buzzards, while there is a good chance of seeing the rare Spanish Imperial Eagle. This Natural Park also includes the location of Andalucía's second most important *romería* (after El Rocío), to the 13th century shrine of **Nuestra Virgen de la Cabeza**. The original shrine was destroyed during the Civil War by a combination of *Guardia Civil* occupation and Republican bombardment. The hermitage which replaced the shrine has little to commend it, but this does not deter the thousands of pilgrims who converge on the spot at the end of Apr from all over southern Spain to see *La Morenita* (the little dark one).

The other Natural Park is to the E of the Despeñaperros Pass, the **Parque**

Natural de Despeñaperros. This is a small reserve covering 8,000 ha. The natural vegetation and the animal and bird life are similar to the nearby Andúcar Park, and because access is difficult from the *autovía*, birders on a tight schedule might wish to give this one a miss.

EAST OF JAEN

About 50 km E of Jaén are the hilltop towns of **Baeza** and **Úbeda**, justifiably described as architectural gems. It has often been claimed that little of architectural significance in Andalucía came after the Moors, but these remarkable towns are surely the exception, and anyone seeking the Renaissance style should head in this direction. Aided by wealth created by the 16th century wool trade, Úbeda and Baeza were developed by two men – the architect Andres de Vandelvira and the nobleman Francisco de los Cobos, secretary to Charles V. Together they provided a number of civic and public buildings, ranging from churches and universities to granaries and abattoirs, which form classic Andalucían Renaissance masterpieces.

BAEZA

(*Pop* 14,800; *Alt* 790m)

ACCESS Air The nearest national airport is at Granada, while the nearest international airports are at Málaga and Almería.

Train There is a railway station, officially named Linares-Baeza, but this is over 20 km away and bus connections are sparse, particularly at weekends.

Road Baeza is linked by bus with Úbeda, Jaen, Córdoba and Sevilla.

History

Baeza was known as *Viata* to the Romans and was later an important Moorish settlement. Called *Bayyasa* in Arabic, it was the civilian and religious capital of the upper Guadalquivir region, but, in 1227, it was one of the first Andalucían towns to be captured during the Reconquest. For the next 2 centuries it became a warring centre between rival Christian families, earning it the title of the 'Royal Nest of Sparrow Hawks', until Isabel became so exasperated that she tore down much of the Alcazar and the defensive walls. Baeza's main development came in the 16th and 17th centuries, with the

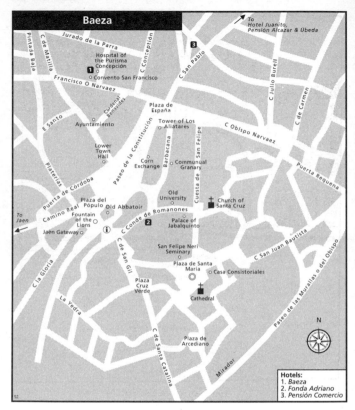

Baeza

Hotels:
1. Baeza
2. Fonda Adriano
3. Pensión Comercio

wealth produced from textiles and agriculture. Today, it gives an overwhelming impression of sleepy Renaissance charm, set off by the honey coloured sandstone of its buildings.

Places of interest

Fortunately, most of the worthwhile buildings in Baeza are concentrated within a small area, so that it is possible to see the best features within half a day if necessary, although a longer stay would certainly be more rewarding. A short walking tour is suggested below.

The centre of the town is the Plaza de España and this merges south-eastwards into the long, tree-lined Plaza de

la Constitución. At its SE corner is the delightful little **Plaza del Pópulo** (also known as the Plaza de los Leones), surrounded by a clutch of interesting buildings. First stop should be at the charmingly old fashioned **Tourist Office** (open Mon-Fri 0930-1330 and 1630-1900; Sat 1000-1230), located in the **Casa del Pópulo** (the House of the People). Formerly the law courts, this attractive Plateresque building was built in the early 16th century. On the W side of the square is the double arched **Jaén Gate**, part of the original walls, and built in honour of Carlos V, who passed this way en route to his marriage with Isabel

Plaza de los Leones, Baeza

of Portugal. Opposite the arch is the old **Abattoir**, dating back to 1540 and displaying the enormous coat of arms of Carlos. Today the town archives are kept here. In the centre of the square is the **Fuente de los Leones** (the fountain of the Lions), which is believed to have been built with stones from the Roman ruins of *Castulo*. Now badly eroded (the lions look more like coypus), the female statue in the centre of the fountain is believed to be that of Hannibal's Iberian wife, Imilce.

Take C/San Gill and C/Obisco Mengibar from the N corner of the square, which will lead to the **Plaza de Santa María**. In the centre of the square is another imposing stone fountain, dated 1569, with a small triumphal arch and the coat of arms of Felipe II. Designed by Ginéz Martínez, who was also responsible for the town's water supply, it is now Baeza's symbol. Dominating the square is the 13th century **Cathedral** (open 1030-1300 and 1600-1900 in winter and 1800-2000 in summer) which was built on the site of a mosque, but comprehensively updated by Vandelvira 300 years later. The nave has three aisles, the sturdy columns supporting low semicircular vaulting. The oldest part of the cathedral is the Puerta de la Luna (Door of the Moon) in 13th century Gothic-Mudéjar, while the other door, in the S wall, is the 15th century Puerta del Perdon, from which an alleyway leads to a *mirador* giving fine views over the rolling landscape of olive groves to the SE. The cathedral is lighter and airier than most and shows to good advantage the 14th century Gothic rose window above the Puerta de la Luna. Don't miss the painted wrought iron grill by Maestro Bartolomé, which encloses the choir. There are also four fine Mudéjar side chapels leading to a small cloister, where part of the old mosque can be seen. If you have 100 ptas to spare, you can persuade a picture to move aside to reveal a silver monstrance. Next to the cathedral is perhaps the most beautiful building in Baeza, the **Casa Consistoriales**, also known as the Palace of Los Cabreras and once the upper Town Hall. Now a national monument, the walls display the coats of arms of Juana the Mad and her husband Philip the Fair.

On the opposite side of the square to the cathedral is the **Seminary of San Felipe Neri**. Dating from the 16th century, the stone walls show the traditional graffiti of successful students. Heading NE the Cuesta de San Felipe leads on the right to the **Iglesia Santa Cruz**. This little church (open 1100-1300) is the oldest in Baeza, being constructed immediately after the Reconquest in 1227 in Romanesque style, although with later additions. The simple white walled interior has some 16th century frescoes, but is mercifully free of monuments and ornamentation – and consequently tourists. On the opposite side of the road and joined to the Seminary is the 15th century **Palacio de Jabalquinto**, undoubtedly the most splendid of the palaces in the town. It was built by Juan Benavides, a relative of Ferdinand; it has a richly ornamental Isabelline Gothic façade topped with an arched gallery, while inside there is an impressive Renaissance courtyard and a majestic Baroque staircase. Turn left into C/Bealto Avila by the **Antigua Universidad**. This old university was opened in 1542 and classes were held for over 3 centuries, but

it was closed down in 1824. Since then it has been a high school and during Jul and Aug it holds classes as part of the Granada International Summer School. The famous Spanish poet Antonio Machado gave French grammar lessons here from 1912 to 1919 and many of his best works come from this period of his life. Visitors are admitted to the 'university' (see the Mudéjar ceiling in the main hall and the superb patio).

Turn right at the end of the Antigua Universidad, passing under an arch into C/Barbacana. Shortly on the right is the **Pósito** (13), the old communal granary. At the end of the street is the **Torre de los Aliatares** (14) or clock tower, once incorporated into the old walls of the town. We are now back in the Plaza de la Constitución, where there are two other buildings of note. On the E side of the square is **La Alhóndiga** (15), the 16th century Corn Exchange, with an impressive façade including a double arcade. A third flat gallery was added later and all three were glassed in. On the opposite side of the plaza is the **Casas Consistoriales Bajas** (16), or the Lower Town Hall, built in the 17th century with impressive arched windows fronted by iron work. The tour ends, where it began, in the Plaza del Pópulo.

There are, however, a number of other buildings which could be visited if time permits. Just to the SW of the Plaza España is the **Convento de San Francisco**. Designed by Vandelvira, it is still impressive, despite the ravages of an earthquake and the attentions of French troops in the 19th century. Along with part of the **Hospital of the Purisma Concepción** next door, it has been converted into a complex of hotel, conference hall and restaurant (Hotel Baeza). Also worth looking at is the **Ayuntamiento**, located to the W of the Plaza de la Constitución. Having also acted as the law courts and a gaol, it dates from 1559 and has an elaborate Plateresque frontage. There are further churches, convents and mansions to attract the dedicated.

Local information
● Accommodation

B *Baeza*, C/Concepción 3, T 748130, F 742519, central position, a/c, restaurant, located in a sympathetically converted convent.

C *Juanito*, Avda Arca del Agua s/n, T 740040, F 742324, 37 rm, garage, wheelchair access, a/c, pricy restaurant, unpromisingly located on main road between sports ground and a derelict factory.

D *El Alcázar*, Ctra de Málaga, T 740028, 34 rm; **D** *La Loma*, Ctra de Úbeda, Km 321, T 743402, 10 rm, restaurant, small modern hotel on the outskirts of town.

E *Comercio*, C/San Pablo 21, T 740100, 31 rm, restaurant, popular and centrally placed, but can be noisy.

Something different: **E** *Fonda Adriano*, C/Conde Romanones 13, T 740200, an old Renaissance mansion in the historic quarter of the town. It is built around a patio (now covered with perspex) and full of azulejos, heads of stags and potted plants and a fountain. All rooms have a bath.

Camping: none in the immediate vicinity, but plenty in the Cazorla Natural Park to the SE.

● Places to eat

♦♦♦*Juanito*, Avda Arca del Agua, T 740040, this hotel restaurant specializes in local dishes and if its photographs in the lobby are to be believed it attracts the great and the good from all over the province and beyond; ♦♦♦*Andres de Vandelvira*, C/San Francisco 17, T 742519, the restaurant attached to the *Hotel Baeza* in the reconstructed ruins of the Convento San Francisco.

♦♦*Sali*, C/Cardenal Benavides 9, T 741365, opp the Ayuntamiento, good *menu del dia*.

● Bars

For *tapas*, try the numerous bars under the arcades around the Plaza de la Constitución.

ÚBEDA

ACCESS Entirely by road; buses run to Baeza, Jaén and Linares. The nearest train station is at Linares-Baeza 15 km to the NW. The nearest national airport is at Granada and the closest international airport is at Málaga.

(*Pop* 28,718; *Alt* 757m) After the charm of Baeza, the traveller might expect its larger neighbour Úbeda to be something of an anticlimax, but this is certainly not the case. It does, however, have a larger area of modern suburbs and if arriving by bus this will give an unfortunate first impression. Úbeda's delight is its large and architecturally outstanding old quarter, full of Renaissance richness.

History

It was known to the Romans as *Betula* because of its location near to the *Bethis*, the Roman name for the Río Guadalquivir. On its foundations Abd al-Rahman II built the Moorish town of *Ub-badat al-Arab*. It was walled in 852 and later occupied by both the Almoravids and the Almohads. It was during Moorish times that the craft industries of pottery and esparto work were developed and which still survive today. It was eventually conquered by Ferdinand III in 1234. The situation in Baeza repeated itself in Úbeda – noble families came to the town, built their mansions and then fought each other for power, causing Ferdinand and Isabel in 1503 to demolish the defensive walls and towers of the town. Its heyday came in the 16th century, during the times of Charles I and Philip II, when the area's textiles were traded throughout Europe, bringing great wealth to the town. The patronage of two noblemen, Francisco de los Cobos (who was Carlos V's secretary) and Juan Vásquez de Molina, plus the genius of the architect Andres de Vandelvira, led to the construction of the wonderful Renaissance quarter of the town. Decline set in, however, in subsequent centuries. Today Úbeda is a mildly prosperous market town producing agricultural machinery along with the more traditional olive oil, esparto and ceramics. Cereals, vines and olives are the main crops grown locally, helped by the Jaén Plan, which has developed irrigation schemes in the area. In 1965, sodium deposits were discovered

8 km from the town, providing further employment. Despite its obvious historical attractions, Úbeda remains something of a tourist backwater, largely due to its geographical remoteness.

Places of interest

Úbeda is neatly divided into old and new quarters, the latter being of little interest. Following the signposts, head straight for the historic section, but remember that there are 46 classified historical buildings and it is impossible to 'do' them all in a day. If time is limited, concentrate on the following, starting at the **Plaza Vásquez de Molina**. Flanked by a collection of honey-coloured Renaissance buildings, it must be one of the most attractive squares in Spain. There are two churches. On the SE side is the **Church of Santa María de los Reales Alcázares**, which was built on the site of a mosque, its cloisters enclosing what was the mosque's patio. The church is, in fact, a hotchpotch of different styles and epochs. The main walls belong to the 17th century, the double belfries to the 19th and the cloisters are Gothic. Inside, there are five naves topped with barrel vaulting, plus a number of interesting chapels. The main chapel stands on the spot where the first mass following the Reconquest was celebrated. Look also for examples of the wrought iron grilles of Maestro Bartolomé. At the back of the church is the **Cárcel del Opisco**, the Bishop's Prison, which was founded as a convent and is now the law courts. The other church is Vandelvira's **Sacra Capilla del Salvador** at the NE end of the Plaza. Ordered by Francisco de la Cobos and originally designed by Diego de Silóe (who was responsible for Granada and Málaga cathedrals) it was built by Vandelvira and the stonemason Alonso Ruiz. The church was originally the chapel of Cobos' mansion, which later burnt down. The main west-facing façade is a mass of ornate Plateresque detail, but it is worth strolling round to the N door to see in the tympanum Vandelvira's trademark, Santiago the Moor slayer. Inside, the single nave has Gothic ribbed vaults and is dominated by the retablo, the work of Michelangelo's pupil Alonso de Berruguette. It is capped with a cupola and fronted by yet another grill by Bartolomé. Entry to the church is via the sacristy on the N side, but you may have to find the caretaker for the key.

Behind the Capilla is the **Hospital de los Honrados Viejos del Salvador**, designed by Vandelvira and constructed in the 16th century for the honoured elderly of the town. Continue past this building to the end of the street to the **Redonda de Miradores**, where a paseo gives superb views of the rolling olive-treed landscape and the Cazorla mountains beyond. Back in the square on the other side of the Capilla is the **Condestable Dávalos Palace**, a large 16th century mansion, originally the residence of Fernando de Ortega, Dean of Málaga. It is now a National Parador and if you cannot afford to stay there, at least look in for a drink and admire the magnificent arcaded patio with a gallery above. At the W end of the Plaza de Vásquez de Molina is the **Palacio de los Cadenas**, named after the chains which were once attached to the columns on the façade. The palace was built for Juan Vásquez de Molina, secretary to Felipe II, and whose family arms are found over the main doorway. Also designed by Vandelvira, the building now houses the *ayuntamiento*, entry to which is via the Plaza de Ayuntamiento to the rear, where you will find the **Tourist Office** (open Mon-Fri 0900-1430; Sat 1000-1230). The buildings in the square are completed by the **Palacio del Marques de Mancera**, now a convent, and the **Antiguo Pósito** or old granary, which in its time has been a prison and is now the police station.

The next area of the old quarter to visit should be the **Plaza del Primero de Mayo**. This is easily reached from the

Plaza de Vásquez de Molina by heading NW along either of the streets on each side of the parador. The Plaza del Primero de Mayo (sometimes known as the Plaza del Mercado) has a totally different atmosphere from the previous square. It is tree-lined and has a delightful bandstand in the centre, along with a palm tree shaded monument to San Juan de la Cruz. Near the Plaza at the end of C/San Juan de la Cruz, is the **Oratory of San Juan de la Cruz**. St John of the Cross was a small friar (reputed to be only a metre and a half tall) who

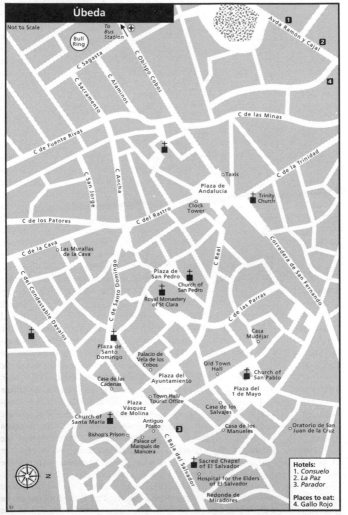

Úbeda

Not to Scale

To Bus Station

Bull Ring

C Sagasta

C Obispo Cobos

C Sacramento

C Alaminos

Avda Ramón y Cajal

1

2

4

C de las Minas

C de Fuente Rivas

C de la Trinidad

C San Jorge

C Ancha

o Taxis

Plaza de Andalucía

† Trinity Church

Clock Tower

C de los Patores

C del Rastro

C Real

Corredera de San Fernando

C de la Cava

Las Murallas de la Cava

C del Condestable Davalos

C de Santo Domingo

Plaza de San Pedro

† Church of San Pedro

Royal Monastery of St Clara

C de las Parras

Casa Mudéjar

Plaza de Santo Domingo

Palacio de Vela de los Cobos

Old Town Hall

† Church of San Pablo

Casa de las Cadenas

Plaza del Ayuntamiento

Plaza del 1 de Mayo

Town Hall/ Tourist Office

Casa de los Salvajes

Plaza Vásquez de Molina

Church of Santa María

Antiguo Pósito

Casa de los Manueles

Oratorio de San Juan de la Cruz

Bishop's Prison

3

Palace of Marqués de Mancera

C Baja del Salvador

† Sacred Chapel of El Salvador

Hospital for the Elders of El Salvador

Redonda de Miradores

N

Hotels:
1. *Consuelo*
2. *La Paz*
3. *Parador*

Places to eat:
4. *Gallo Rojo*

was a writer, poet and mystic. He came to Úbeda in 1591 from the Convent of La Peñuela for treatment to a cut on his foot, but died a painful death from gangrene. The Oratory has a small museum in which the cell where he died can be visited. Various relics and personal objects are on display. The museum is open Tues-Sun 1100-1300 and 1700-1900. Back in the square, the **Iglesia de San Pablo** comprises a variety of styles. The main façade faces S and on either side of its sturdy portal are balconies dating from the 13th century. The W wall is the oldest part of the church and is in the transitional Romanesque style. The N wall is Gothic and is dated 1485, while the tower is Platesresque and therefore later. The main interest in the interior is in the chapels, one of which, the Chapel of Camarero Vago, was possibly the first work carried out in Úbeda by Vandelvira. The Chapel de las Mercedes is earlier and in Isabelline style. On the SW side of the square is the **Ayuntamiento Viejo**, which dates from the 16th century. Italianate in style, it has a number of arches resting on Corinthian columns and from its balconies the local dignitaries presided over the *autos de fé* on the orders of the Inquisition. Ironically, the site of the fires is now marked by the bandstand.

There are a number of buildings of note in the streets leading off the Plaza del Primero de Mayo. The **Casa de los Salvajes** (the House of the Savages) in C/Horno Contado, was built in the 15th century for the Chamberlain of the Bishop of Jaén, Francisco de Vago. The house has acquired its name from the figures on the coat of arms, which possibly depict natives brought back from the Indies by the successors of Columbus. In the same street is the **Casa de los Manueles**, with an impressive Renaissance façade and Baroque coat of arms. SW from the Plaza del Primero de Mayo and close to the Plaza de Ayuntamiento is the **Palacio de Vela de los Cobos**, built

in the mid 16th century by Vandelvira for Francisco Vela de los Cobos and with a superb arcaded gallery. N of the Plaza del Primero de Mayo, in C/Cervantes, is the **Casa Mudéjar**, a 14th century building with pointed horseshoe arches, which now houses an Archaeological Museum (open Mon-Fri 1000-1400 and 1600-1900; Sat 1000-1230).

For most visitors, this will have been quite enough Renaissance architecture for one day, but before leaving Úbeda everyone should make an effort to see the **Hospital de Santiago**. It is located in the W of the town, some 10 mins walk from the Plaza de Andalucía along C/s Mesones and Cobos (those returning to the bus station will pass it anyway). Probably Vandelvira's finest work, it was commissioned by Diego de los Cobos y Molina, the Bishop of Jaén in the mid 16th century. Described as the 'Andalucían Escorial', it is a disciplined and subdued work for Vandelvira. The entrance steps are flanked by lions and above the arch Santiago again slays some Moors. The interior features a graceful arcaded patio with 20 marble columns brought from Genoa in Italy, a superb vaulted staircase and another Vandelvira chapel. The hospital is now a cultural centre and the reception desk can provide a certain amount of tourist literature and information.

Visitors with more time at their disposal could visit a clutch of other churches and convents in the old quarter, including the **Iglesia de San Pedro**, which has a Romanesque apse, the **Real Monasterio de Santa Clara**, dating from 1290, and the **Iglesia de la Trinidad**, with an exuberant Baroque frontage. Also of interest are the **Potters Quarter** in C/Valencia, and some remnants of the old walls in the S of the town, including the gateway, the **Puerta de Granada**. Finally, on the border of the old and new areas in the Plaza de Andalucía is a modern feature which brings a wry smile. It is a statue of a fascist civil war general, which after the war was riddled with bullets. The bullet holes remain today with their self evident message.

Local festivals

Semana Santa – there are the usual processions during Easter Week. 1 May is celebrated with the *romeria*, when pilgrims go the Virgen of Guadalupe. On 1 May, the day of the patron saint, San Miguel, is celebrated with a large fair, fireworks and a flamenco festival.

Local information

● Accommodation

The *parador*, located in the centre of the old quarter, is undoubtedly the place to stay in Úbeda. Decent hotel accommodation is otherwise hard to find, although there is a good range of *pensiones*.

AL *Parador Nacional Condestable Dávalos*, Plaza Vásquez de Molina 1, T 750345, F 751259, 31 rm, a/c, restaurant, luxury and atmosphere. All other accommodation is in the newer part of the town, mainly on and around Avda de Ramón y Cajal.

C *Consuelo*, Avda Ramón y Cajal 12, T 750840, F 756834, 39 rm, a/c, wheelchair access, restaurant, garage; **C** *La Paz*, C/Andalucía 1, T 752140, F 750848, 51 rm, a/c, wheelchair access, restaurant, garage.

D *Dos Hermanas*, C/Risquillo Bajo 1, T 752124, F 791315, 30 rm, garage, a/c, restaurant, upgraded *pensión* on the N outskirts of the town.

Most of the *pensiones* are located on the W side of the town centre. **E** *Casa Castillo*, Avda Ramón y Cajal 20, T 750430, a/c, garage, restaurant, clean establishment close to the bus station; **E** *Los Cerros*, C/Peñarroya 1, T 751621, 18 rm; **E** *Martos*, C/Vandelvira 3, T 756178, close to the bus station; **E** *Sevilla*, Avda Ramón y Cajal 7, T 750612, 23 rm, garage, restaurant; **E** *San Miguel*, Avda Libertad 69, T 752049, in the N of the town, cheapest accommodation available; **E** *Victoria*, C/Alaminos 5, T 752952, 15 rm, a/c, just renovated.

Something different: **AL** *Palacio de la Rambla*, Plaza del Marqués 1, T 750196. The present Marquesa de la Rambla, Elena Meneses de Orozco Gallego de Chave, who is presumably a little strapped for cash, lets out some of the rooms in her sumptuous mansion in the historic quarter. All rooms have TV, CH, minibar, some with their own fireplace, family antiques and old fashioned bath with legs.

Camping: none in the vicinity, but plenty of sites in the Cazorla Natural Park to the E.

● Places to eat

The best restaurant in Úbeda is undoubtedly at the ◆◆◆*Parador*, which serves excellent regional dishes.

Visitors staying in the Avda Ramón y Cajal area could try ◆◆*Restaurant Gallo Rojo*, C/Ramón y Cajal 3, T 752038, which serves good regional dishes. A cheaper option in the same area is ◆*El Olivo*, Avda Ramón y Cajal 6, T 752092, serving reasonably priced *menus* and *platos combinados*.

● Bars

The bars of the hotels mentioned have rather uninspiring restaurants, but good bars. At the *Consuelo*, drinks are still accompanied by a free *tapa*.

● Banks & money changers

Some branches of Spanish banks are located in the newer part of the town, mainly in the roads leading off the Plaza de Andalucía.

● Hospitals & medical services

Hospitals: *General Hospital*, Carretara de Linares, T 797100.

Red Cross: *Cruz Roja*, C/Santiago s/n, T 755640.

● Post & telecommunications

Area code: 953.

Post Office: *Correos*, C/Trinidad 4, T 750031.

● Shopping

The main shopping area of the town is in the newer section in the roads leading off the Plaza de Andalucía. There is a street market on Fri. Local craft specialities incl ceramics, esparto mats and baskets (established in Moorish times), ironwork, carving and gilding.

● Tourist offices

Town Hall, Plaza del Ayuntamiento, open 0900-1430, Sat 1030-1330, T 750897. The reception in the Hospital de Santiago arranges guided tours of the town.

● Useful addresses

Garages/car repairs: *Mercedes*, *Peugeot*, *Renault* and *Seat/VAG* all have garages on the Ctra de Circunvalación. Also *Citroën*, Avda de la Libertad 47, T 754240; *Ford*, Avda Cristo Rey, T 750315.

● **Transport**
Local Bus: local buses serve surrounding villages. **Taxis**: are available in the Plaza de Andalucia T 751213.

Road Bus: the Alsina Graells company operate 9 buses a day to Jaén and Granada and 5 buses a day to Linares. There are daily direct coaches to Granada, Almería, Málaga and Madrid. The bus station is in C/San José, close to the Hospital de Santiago.

EAST OF ÚBEDA

Parque Natural de Cazorla

The Natural Park of the Sierras of Cazorla, Segura and Las Villas forms the largest of the Spanish nature parks, covering a surface area of 214,336 sq km. This mountainous area connects the Sierra Morena with the Subbética chain, closing off the Guadalquivir valley and stretching all the way to the border with Murcia. The park consists of a series of parallel limestone ridges running from NE to SW and there are a number of peaks over 2,000m (6,500 ft). It is one of the wettest areas in Spain with an annual rainfall of over 2,000 mm, plus equal snowfall which ensures that the headwaters of the Guadalquivir are well supplied. The park is heavily wooded, with Aleppo pines at lower levels and Maritime and Laricio Pines higher up. Patches of mixed woodland include Encinas (Holm Oak), Olives and Junipers, while Poplars and Willow occur in the wetter valleys. The whole area is a naturalists delight, with some 1,300 flowering species, including some 30 endemics such as the Cazorla Violet and the Hoop Petticoat Daffodil. Wild Peonies and Gladioli plus a host of orchids are among the outstanding flowers. Amongst the mammals, the game species abound, as many were introduced when the park was a shooting reserve. The bellows of the rutting Red Deer are a typical sound during the Autumn months. Also found are Roe and Fallow Deer, while the Ibex can be seen, usually above the tree line. Predators include Beech Martens, Polecats and Genet. The Pardel Lynx is also occasionally reported. Other mammals include Fox, Badger and Wild Boar, while Otters frequent many of the rivers. Birds are also well represented, with over 100 species nesting within the park. Raptors are outstanding and include all three vultures, four varieties of eagle, Honey Buzzards and Peregrine. The Cazorla is the only place in Spain outside the Pyrenees where the Lammergeier can still be seen, although there is probably only one breeding pair left. Some attempts at re-introducing immature birds have been made. There is also a wide range of woodland birds, including Crossbills and the Firecrest. Butterflies are outstanding in the Spring and early Summer, featuring the Mother of Pearl Blue and the Spanish Argus. Reptiles and amphibians include three species of snake and several lizards and skinks, of which Valverde's Lizard is endemic to the area. The rivers and lakes of the park, on which there are no motorized watersports, are rich in fish such as Carp, Trout, Barbel and Black Perch (anglers will need a permit from the Tourist Office).

From the naturalists point of view, the best time to visit the Cazorla is May and Jun, when flowers are at their best and the summer visiting birds have arrived. Avoid summer weekends and Jul and Aug, when the park is saturated with visitors. Autumn can be very pleasant, but lacks flowers and birdsong. Disruption from snow is not unknown during the winter months. There is very little public transport in the park, and no petrol stations within the park boundary. Signposting is also poor. Beware, too, of the maps of the park in the official glossy brochures, as they can be inaccurate in places. The area is magnificent for walking, but unfortunately there are few marked tracks and those which exist are very short. The best is along the lower Barrossa Gorge. Maps are available at various scales from the Turismo Quercus in Cazorla, but note that this is

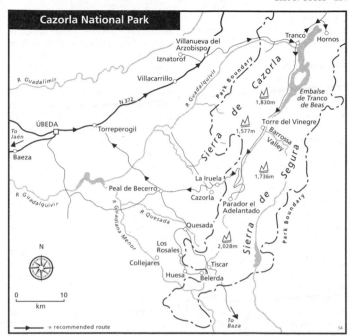

Cazorla National Park

a private cooperative and their main objective is to promote nature tours, 4WD excursions and horse riding. They make no money from independent walkers. There is also an official Natural Park Information Centre in Cazorla, which can help with accommodation. In addition, there is an Interpretation Centre at Torre del Vinegre. Remember to book accommodation well ahead, especially during the summer months.

For visitors who can spend only one day in the Cazorla Natural Park and have their own transport, the route below is recommended and is shown on the accompanying map. It takes a clockwise journey starting and finishing at Úbeda. The trip could just as well be followed in an anti-clockwise direction.

Leave Úbeda eastwards on the N322, bypassing **Villacarillo** after 32 km. After another 6 km, a side road leads N to the

hill village of **Iznatoraf**. For those with a little time, this is well worth a diversion. There is a pleasant square, an imposing Renaissance church, a ruined Moorish castle above some narrow alleyways and some spectacular views from a *mirador* on the N side of the village. Back on the main road turn right just before Villanueva del Arzobispo on a minor road which leads to the park. The scenery improves dramatically and after 10 or so km the road enters a spectacular wooded gorge, eventually arriving at the hamlet of **Tranco**, scattered around the dam of the Tranco reservoir. There are a number of bars and restaurants here, many of which have some accommodation, set amongst the trees overlooking the reservoir. To follow the reservoir SE, you need to cross the dam, but another recommended diversion is to carry straight on NE to the hill top village of

Hornos, perched on a crag dominated by a castle, which, though mostly in ruins, makes an excellent viewpoint over the reservoir. The village has a strong Moorish flavour, with narrow streets and a small stretch of the original walls, complete with a horseshoe arch.

To proceed SE into the park, do not be tempted to take the road shown on the Tourist Office map on the E side of the reservoir – it does not exist! Instead return to Tranco, cross the dam and pass through the park gates (your entry and departure will be noted and you will be asked if you intend to stay the night, and if so, where. The road now continues along the N side of the Tranco reservoir, giving spectacular views of the island in the centre of the lake, the **Isla Cabeza de la Viña**, which in the early 1990's was no longer an island, owing to the low winter rainfall and subsequent drop in water levels. The road continues past the end of the reservoir, now following the Río Guadalquivir towards its headwaters, passing through the hamlet of **Coto Ríos**, before arriving at the **Torre de Vinagre Interpretation Centre**. This is in two sections. The first is the Educational Centre, which has excellent audio visual displays of the history, geology and wildlife of the park. Next door is a 'Hunting Museum', which consists largely of a collection of mounted stags heads, including one bagged by General Franco, and a display of the guns which accounted for them. It is interesting to note the varied reactions of the coachloads of visitors. Young people flock into the educational centre, while the *pensionistas* pour into the hunting museum – it seems that environmental education has not yet reached the older generation.

To follow the **Barrossa Valley** walk, take the road opposite the Centre, cross a stream and after around 2 km you arrive at a trout farm, where there is parking at the start of the walk. The track has recently been widened, so that it is possible for a troop of soldiers to march up it, but it is still a marvellous walk. If few people are around it is as good a place as any in the park to encounter wildlife. The track narrows into a gorge and wooden bridges take the path from one side of the river to the other. At the end of the gorge there is a further track for the adventurous up to what appears to be a simple hydro electric scheme.

The main route through the Park now leaves the Guadalquivir valley and climbs over the **Puerto de las Palomas** (the Doves Pass), where a *mirador* gives superb views back through the valley. The road then drops down past the Park boundary and into the villages of, firstly, **La Iruela** and then to **Cazorla** itself.

Cazorla is the main tourist centre of the park and is located at a height of 900m beneath a steep limestone cliff, the *Peña de los Halcones*. Cazorla has a long history, with both Iberians and Romans living here. It was the Moors who recognized its strategic position and originally built the two castles which dominate the village. Today, there are three busy squares in the town, the Plaza de la Constitución, the Plaza de la Corredera and the Plaza Santa María. In the former is the private Quercus Tourist office, T 720115, and in a street just off the square is the official Natural Park Information Centre, open 1100-1400 and 1600-1900, T 720125. The Plaza de la Corredera is known locally as the *Plaza del Huevo*, because of its supposed egg shape, and here you will find the *ayuntamiento*, located in a Moorish style palace. The third square, the Plaza Santa María, is the most lively and is named after the ruined church, which was designed by Vandelvira, but regrettably destroyed by Napoleon's troops in the Peninsular War. The square is overshadowed by La Yedra, the tower of one of the Moorish castles. Also in this square is the small Museo de Artes y Costumbres, which gives a glimpse of local history crafts and folklore. Open Tues-Sat 1000-1500.

There are a number of other villages just outside the park boundaries, which could be visited by those with a little more time on their hands. In the N of the area is **Segura de la Sierra**, which is easily reached from Hornos and which can be seen from kilometres around, sitting on the top of its conical hill. Its strategic position meant that it was occupied in turn by all the groups who invaded Andalucía from the Phoenicians through to the Moors. The castle, built by the Almoravids and eventually destroyed by French troops during the Peninsular War, has been heavily restored, consisting of two main precincts, several towers, gates, a keep and a well. To look around, you will need a key from the Tourist Office. They will also arrange for entrance to the Moorish Baths in the main square, where you can see cold, tepid and hot rooms, with double horsehoe arches at each end and a barrel vault with star-shaped ventilation holes. To the S of the park, a road runs from **Peal de Becerro**, through **Quesada**, another old Moorish settlement, and over the **Tíscar Pass** through spectacular scenery, before joining the Granada-Basa *autovia* some way to the S.

● **Accommodation The Cazorla area**: **A** *Parador Nacional El Adelantado*, Sierra de Cazorla, T/F 721075, 33 rm, pool, restaurant, functional building in hunting lodge style in a superb setting; **B** *Noguera de la Sierpe*, Coto Rios, T 721601, F 721709, 20 rm, wheelchair access, pool, restaurant, disco. Most other accommodation possibilities are in the villages of Cazorla and La Iruela, outside the park itself. **C** *Los Enebros*, Ctra El Tranco, Km 7, La Iruela, T 721610, pool, tennis; **C** *Río*, Paraje de la Teja, La Iruela, T 720211, 21 rm, delightful views and a bottle of house wine when you settle your bill. For those on a budget, try **E** *Betis*, Plaza de la Corredera 19, T 720540, some rooms looking over the square – but not, of course, quiet. **Something different**: *Villa Touristica de Cazorla*, Ladera de San Isicio, Cazorla, T 710100, one of the first Villa Turisticas to be set up in Andalucía, a pueblo-type development of some 32 cottages in traditional style on the hillside overlooking the village of Cazorla, pool, gardens, restaurant, all rooms have fireplace, terrace, kitchen and TV. **Youth hostels**: C/Mauricio Martínez 6, 23470 Cazorla, T 720329, 76 beds, meals available. **Camping**: there are 3 sites in the Sierra de Segura and 6 in the Sierra de la Cazorla. Most are well equipped and in unspoilt surroundings. The only 1st category site is *Fuente de la Canalica*, Ctra las Acebeas, Siles, T 491004. There are also a number of *camping libre* sites which are free.

Sevilla Province

THE PROVINCE of Sevilla is landlocked, being bordered by Huelva to the west, Cádiz to the south and Málaga and Córdoba provinces to the east. Sevilla, the provincial capital, is on most people's itinerary, due to its wealth of monuments and vibrant atmosphere, and yet the remainder of the province is little visited. This is a pity, because towns such as Carmona, Osuna, Éjica and Estepa have much of interest.

HORIZONS

For centuries its main artery has been Andalucía's largest river, the **Guadalquivir**. Running through the centre of the province, the river's flood plain provides fertile farmland for the production of cereals, vines, sunflowers and olives. But the same silt that fertilizes the soil has also clogged up the river, which is kept navigable to Sevilla only with extensive dredging.

To the N are the wooded hills of the **Sierra Morena** rising to their highest point at a little over 900m. Sevilla province offers little to delay the naturalist, with just three Natural Parks. In the Sierra Morena, is the **Parque Natural de Sierra Norte**, which provides nothing particularly outstanding, but makes a welcome change from the heat of Sevilla. To the S of the capital, there are reserves based on the marshlands on either side of the Guadalquivir. To the E, between the river and the town of Los Palacios y Villafranca, is the **Brazo del Este Parque Natural**, while W of the river a little further downstream is the **Lucio del Cangrejo**, which is part of the 'buffer zone' of the Coto Doñana.

Finally, in the extreme SE of the province, is further high land in the N edge of the **Serranía de Ronda.**

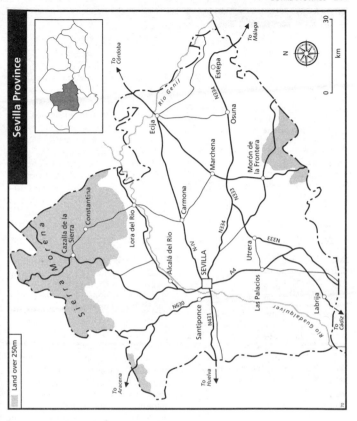

Sevilla Province

Land over 250m

N

To Córdoba

Río Genil

Ecija

To Málaga

Estepa

N334

Osuna

Marchena

Morón de la Frontera

N333

Carmona

Constantina

Cazalla de la Sierra

Sierra Morena

Lora del Río

Alcalá del Río

N-IV

N334

SEVILLA

Utrera

EEEN

A4

Las Palacios

Labrija

Río Guadalquivir

To Cádiz

N630

Santiponce

N431

To Aracena

To Huelva

0   30   km

SEVILLA

(*Pop* 710,000; *Alt* 9m)

ACCESS The city's infrastructure, particularly its communication system, underwent many improvements for EXPO '92.

Air A new airport has been built beside the old one at San Pablo 12 km E of the city for both national and international flights. An hourly bus (route EA) links the airport with the city centre at Puerta de Jerez, via the train station. Price 200 ptas. Taxis are also available, but watch out for fiddled fares. You should be charged approx 2,000 ptas.

Train From the new train station, Santa Justa, catch bus No 70 to the bus station at Prado de San Sebastián near the Plaza de España, or a taxi to Plaza Nueva, the central square, approx 600 ptas.

Road If arriving by car, parking can be difficult, although parking areas, including some underground car parks, have been increased. Theft of, or from, cars is widespread, so no possessions should be left visible inside the car. If staying overnight, try to find a hotel with a garage or secure parking. The **bus** station at Prado de San Sebastián is within walking distance of the centre. Cross C/Menéndez Pelayo and at Plaza Don Juan de Austria turn down C/San Fernando to Puerta de Jerez, where a right turn takes you down Avda de la Constitución past the tourist office and the cathedral.

HISTORY

Both the Iberians and the Phoenicians occupied the site of what is now Sevilla, attracted by the minerals such as silver and copper which were found in the mountains to the N. The Carthaginians arrived around 500 BC and named the place *Hispalis*. Later the Romans came to the area and under Julius Caesar they captured the settlement, renaming it *Julia Romula* or little Rome. This became capital of the Roman province of *Baetica*, while just to the N the city of *Italica* was growing quickly, eventually providing two Roman Emperors in Trajan and Hadrian. After a brief period of occupation by the Visigoths, Sevilla was taken by the Moors under Musa in 712. They changed the name to *Ishbiliyya* and also renamed the river *Wadi El Kabir* (which remains as the present Guadalquivir). The town, despite its own great wealth and status, became subject to the Caliphate of Córdoba, but in 1023 following the disintegration of the Caliphate, Sevilla took the opportunity to declare itself an independent *taifa*. The town was successively ruled by the Abbasids, the Almoravides and the Almohades. It was under the Almohad Emirs that the city achieved its greatest prosperity, especially between 1068 and 1095 under Al-Mutamid, when the silk trade was at its peak.

Sevilla eventually fell in the *Reconquista* in 1248 to Fernando III and thereafter became a favourite residence of the Spanish monarchs. By the 15th century, with the discovery of the New World, Sevilla entered a new age of splendour. The gold from the Indies poured in and by the 1500's it had an estimated population of 150,000, making it one of the most important cities in Europe and the magnet for painters and writers. It is during this period that many of the city's monuments were constructed.

Then followed a period of decline,

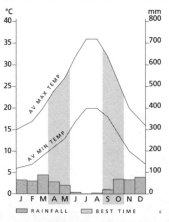

Climate: Sevilla

which began with the silting up of the river, so that the port activities and trade with the Americas moved downstream to Cádiz. Sevilla was later affected by plagues, earthquakes and floods, to say nothing of decadence, while it was unaffected by the Industrial Revolution.

The 20th century has been marked by two exhibitions. In 1929, the Latin America exhibition never achieved the success desired because of the Wall Street crash, but the Plaza de España and the María Luisa Park plus a number of pavilions remain and add to the appearance of Sevilla today. 1992 was marked by the Fifth Centenary of the Discovery of the Americas and by EXPO '92, giving the city a year of wonderful

April contrasts in Sevilla

To be in Sevilla in Apr is a rare experience, with two of the most extraordinary festivals in the whole of Spain, let alone Andalucía. The month begins with *Semana Santa* or Holy Week, when each of the parish churches of the city celebrate Easter. There are over 100 *cofradias* or brotherhoods who organize processions in which there are normally two *pasos* or floats, one of the Virgin Mary and the other of Christ, each carried by scores of *costaleros* or bearers. They are accompanied by bands and march to the beat of drums, followed by members of the brotherhoods in their frightening, slit eyed conical hats and accompanied by penitents, known as *Nazarenes*, who might be walking barefoot. Occasionally an onlooker, often from a balcony, will launch into an impromptu *saeta*, an eerie form of *cante hondo* or deep song in praise of the Virgin. Each procession eventually reaches the official route which leads along the pedestrianized Calle Sierpes and through the cathedral, accompanied throughout by the thunder of drums. The complete journey from and back to their own parishes can take as long as 12 hrs, so it is hardly surprising that there are informal moments when the float is set down and a bearer takes the opportunity to nip into the nearest bar to use the toilet or to have a quick beer. The whole thing makes excellent street theatre. The most popular procession is without doubt that of *La Macarena*, the goddess of the city, who incites an almost pagan adulation and whose *paso* is attributed to Luis Roldán. Indeed, many of the floats are considerable works of art in their own right and the brotherhoods (which include members from across the whole social range) spend much of the year in their preparation.

After the tense human emotion of Holy Week, it is almost inevitable that the *Sevillaños* will let off steam. Two weeks later the *Feria de Abril* takes place. Dating back to 1293, when Alfonso the Wise granted the city a charter to celebrate Pentecost, the Fair is undoubtedly the largest and most vibrant in Andalucía. Since 1973 it has taken place at a permanent fairground in the barrio of Los Remedios. Here, large marquees are set up, many belonging to the more wealthy Seville families, while others are run by organizations such as commercial companies or political parties. The important thing is to have *enchufes* or the right connections – not to have access to the hospitality of a *caseta* means certain loss of face. The majority wear traditional costume, with the women in their colourful flamenco dresses and the whole city resounding to the wail of flamenco, the sound of guitars and the percussion of feet and hands. The climax comes when the great and good of Sevilla parade around in carriages or on horseback, while in late afternoon there are the traditional bullfights at the Maestranza bullring. The continual drinking, dancing, merry making and sheer exuberance of the *feria*, make it unique in Andalucía. Oh to be in Sevilla, now that April's here!

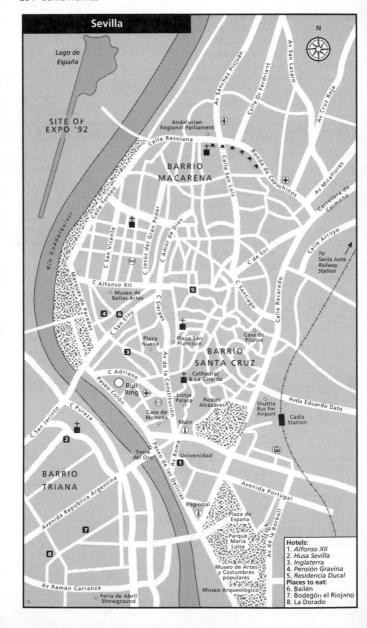

Sevilla

N

Lago de España

SITE OF EXPO '92

Río Guadalquivir

Av Sánchez Pizjuán

Calle Dr Ferdriant

Av Lázaro

Av Cruz Roja

Andalucian Regional Parliament

Calle Resolana

Calle San Luis

BARRIO MACARENA

Ronda de Capuchinos

Av Miraflores

Carretera de Carmona

Calle Torreo

C Jesús del Gran Poder

C Amor de Dios

C de Sol

Calle Arroyo

To Santa Justa Railway Station

C San Vicente

Pol

C Alfonso XII

Museo de Bellas Artes

C Sierpes

C San Eloy

Plaza Nueva

Plaza San Francisco

C Santiago

Calle Recaredo

Casa de Pilatos

BARRIO SANTA CRUZ

Av de la Constitución

C Adriano

Paseo Colón

Bull Ring

Cathedral & La Giralda

Lonja Palace

Reales Alcázares

Shuttle Bus for Airport

Avda Eduardo Dato

Cádiz Station

C San Jacinto

C Pureza

Casa de Moneda

Main i

Paseo de las Delicias

Torre del Oro

Paseo de Roma

Universidad

BARRIO TRIANA

Marqués de Paradas

Avenida República Argentina

Avenida Portugal

Regional i

Plaza de España

Parque María Luisa

Av de la Borboll

Av Ramón Carranza

Feria de Abril Showground

Museo de Artes y Costumbres populares

Museo Arqueológico

Hotels:
1. *Alfonso XII*
2. *Husa Sevilla*
3. *Inglaterra*
4. *Pensión Gravina*
5. *Residencia Ducal*
Places to eat:
6. *Bailén*
7. *Bodegón el Riojano*
8. *La Dorado*

72

publicity along with vast improvements in its infrastructure, including the AVE high speed train link with Madrid.

The post-Franco era saw a number of developments in Sevilla, helped by the fact that both the long standing premier, Felipe González, and his deputy were both *sevillaños*. Whether Andalucía in general, and Sevilla in particular, will receive similar benefits from the new right wing government and its regional allies is doubtful. Despite increasing industrial development in the city (the factories stretching out of Sevilla on the Málaga road are particularly hideous), the unemployment rate remains higher than any other Andalucían city. Probably as a result, petty crime in the city is rife. Much is made of the activity of the *semaforazos*, whose speciality is to break car windows at traffic lights and make off with anything which they can reach. Bag snatching and pick-pocketing are also common. But the situation should not be over exaggerated. The vast majority of visitors to Sevilla will encounter no problems, provided that they take the usual precautions which are detailed elsewhere in this handbook.

PLACES OF INTEREST

The **Cathedral** After Sevilla fell to the Christians in 1248, the existing mosque was retained for a while for Christian worship. In 1401, however, a decision was made to build a new cathedral on the site, designed by Alonso Martínez and on such a scale that people in the future would 'think its architects mad'. It was always thought to be the third largest cathedral in the world after St Pauls in London and St Peters in Rome, but latest calculations based on volume put it in first position – if you don't believe it, look in the Guinness Book of Records. Based on the rectangular plan of the mosque (116m long and 76m wide), extra height has been added, with the central nave rising to 42m and even the side chapels looking like small churches. It is late Gothic in style and took 4 centuries to complete. The mosque's minaret, known today as the Giralda, was retained as the bell tower, while the Patio de la Naranjas, the Moorish ablutions area, has also survived.

The exterior of the cathedral probably has more merit than the rest of the Andalucían cathedrals put together, with some superb stonework and crock-

Processions of a different kind

One is used to processions of all types in Andalucía, but one kind which occurs in Spring is to be avoided like the plague. This is the line of hundreds of furry caterpillars which can be seen in a nose to tail convoy crossing roads and tracks and climbing walls. These are the caterpillars of the **Processionary Caterpillar Moth** *(Thaumatopoea processionea)*, and known in Spain as **Orugas**. The moths lay their eggs in grey, pendulous cotton wool-like 'nests' high in pine trees and on hatching, the gregarious caterpillars make their way to the ground in a nose-to-tail chain in their search to find a place to pupate, which is the next stage in their life cycle.

On no account touch or go near these caterpillars, fascinating though they may be. If their hairs come into contact with the skin they will cause a painful rash and if disturbed their hairs give off a fine dust which can cause respiratory problems. Children can become quite ill and there have been cases of cats and dogs dying after coming into contact with the Orugas.

If you go into a *farmacia* and ask for a remedy, be careful how you pronounce 'Oruga'. The similar sounding 'Arruga' is a wrinkle and *Crema para Arrugas* will not cure a rash caused by a caterpillar!

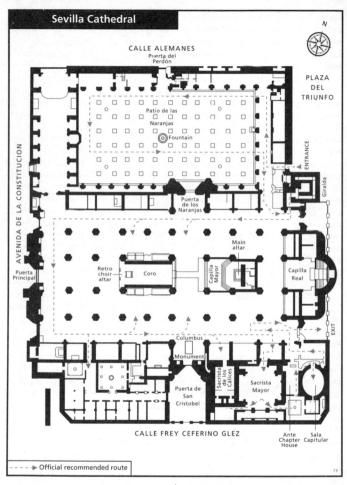

Sevilla Cathedral

CALLE ALEMANES

Puerta del Perdón

PLAZA DEL TRIUNFO

Patio de las Naranjas

Fountain

ENTRANCE

Giralda

AVENIDA DE LA CONSTITUCION

Puerta de los Naranjas

Puerta Principal

Main altar

Retro choir altar

Coro

Capilla Mayor

Capilla Real

EXIT

Columbus Monument

Puerta de San Cristobel

Sacrista de los Calices

Sacrista Mayor

CALLE FREY CEFERINO GLEZ

Ante Chapter House

Sala Capitular

- - - - ▸ Official recommended route

73

eting on its doorways and windows, sturdy flying buttresses and even some stained glass of interest. There are, in fact, seven exterior doors, varying in age, from the Moorish Puerta del Perdón leading into the Patio de las Naranjas to the Puerta Principal, built in the 19th century. The interior is magnificent, combining grandeur, space and solemnity. The five naves based on the Moorish ground plan give a rather box like feeling. In the central area of the main nave, the *coro* or choir leads to the Capilla Mayor, notable for its huge *retablo*, which must be the most impressive altar piece in Europe, if not the world. It is the life work of the Flemish carver Pieter Dancart, although many others contributed before its completion in 1526. Depicting the life of Christ, the screen contains a vast number of figures and scenes, all dripping with gold leaf, but look particularly for the Virgin of the Sea and the scale model of Sevilla as it would have been in the 15th century.

There are no fewer than 20 chapels located around the naves, of which the most important is the Capilla Real or Royal Chapel. Here one finds in an urn the remains of Fernando III, while his sword is kept in the chapel treasury. On either side of the domed chapel are tombs containing the remains of Fernando's wife, Beatrice, his son Alfonso the Wise, Pedro the Cruel and Pedro's mistress María de Padilla. Other chapels worth looking at, mainly because of their artworks, are the Capilla de San Antonio, which contains Murillo's *Vision of St Antony* and the Capilla de San Pedro, with a clutch of paintings by Zurburán showing the life of St Peter, part of a 17th century *retablo* by Diego Lopéz Bueno.

In the SE corner of the cathedral is a fascinating complex of rooms. A delightful ante chamber leads into the oval shaped Sala Capitular or Chapter House, with a superb white and gold domed ceiling. At the far end is the Bishops Throne, inlaid in mahogany, and above this more Murillo's, including probably his best *Inmaculada* and a circle of eight saints, all considered to be from Sevilla. Nearby is the Sacristía Mayor or Main Sacristy (try to locate this building from the top of the Giralda – it is identified by its domed roof with tiled and buttressed cupola). It is also the cathedral's treasury and contains a vast array of art works, books and silver work, including in the centre a huge 4-tier monstrance, said to be nearly 4m high and weighing 475 kgs.

Finally, do not miss the Monument to Christopher Columbus, on the S side of the cathedral, next to the door also named after him. The monument was completed in the late 19th century by the local Sevillan sculptor Arturo Mélida and displays the figures of four kings representing Aragon, Castile, Leon and Navarra carrying the navigators coffin. The remains of Columbus are supposed to be in the crypt below, but the tomb may or may not contain his body – it could be his son Diego or even his grandson Luis. On the other hand the tomb may contain the remains of all three. The truth may never be known.

Proceed now to **La Giralda**, the bell tower of the cathedral and Sevilla's most famous landmark. Elegantly constructed of patterned brick and stone, it dates from the 12th century, a few decades before the Almohads lost control of the city. It was the main minaret on Sevilla's mosque, Islam's second largest mosque at that time. The Emir who ordered its construction in 1184 (12 years after work had begun on the mosque itself) instructed the Maghribian architect, Ahmad Ibn Baso, that it should be more beautiful than any other in existence. It is 100m high and built on a Visigothic base. In Renaissance times balconies were added and a belfry of four diminishing storeys. The tower was originally surmounted by four globes, but these were destroyed by an earthquake in 1568. They were replaced by a *giraldilla* or weather vane, representing Faith, from which the tower's present name has been derived. Unusually, access to the summit is via 35 (seemingly endless) ramps, rather than steps, apparently designed to be sufficiently wide to allow two mounted horsemen to pass. The view from the top is well worth the toil, giving superb views over the pinnacles, buttresses and domes of the cathedral itself, as well as rooftop vistas of the city, which is useful for future orientation for ground level sightseeing. It is also hard to miss the noisy colony of Lesser Kestrels which wheel around the tower in summer.

A combined ticket secures entry to both the Cathedral and the Giralda. Entry 500 ptas. Open Mon- Sat, 1100-1700; Sun and festivals 1000-1400 (Giralda only) and 1000-1600 (Giralda and Cathedral), T 4214971.

The **Alcázar** Work on a Moorish fortress in the Plaza del Triunfo originally began in 712 following the capture of Sevilla. In the 9th century it was transformed into a palace for Abd-Al-Rahman II. The wall which still runs between the Plaza del Triunfo and the Barrio de Santa Cruz dates from this period. During the prosperous rule of the Almohads, the palace was extended further. The Patio del Crucio and Patio del Yeso are remnants of this period, but the fortress was vast, stretching right down to the Guadalquivir. However, much of the existing Alcázar was built in the 14th century for Pedro the Cruel, who employed Moorish architects to undertake the work, many of them from the neighbouring Moorish Kingdom of Granada under Yussef I. Many fragments from earlier Moorish buildings, such as those from Medina Azahara near Córdoba, were incorporated in its construction. Successive centuries saw various additions and restorations, most of which were unsympathetic, but the Alcázar remains one of the best surviving examples of Mudéjar architecture in Spain and has always been a popular place of residence for Spanish royalty when visiting the area.

Entry to the Alcázar is from the Plaza del Triunfo through the splendidly Moorish, red coloured, Puerta del León, the Gate of the Lion – named after a tiled heraldic lion over the main arch. This leads initially into the Patio del León (a caged lion once guarded the entrance) and then into the Patio de la Montería, which has 14th century buildings at each end with galleries and marble and brick columns. This is pure Mudéjar and sets the scene for the interiors to come. At the side of the Patio is the Sala del Justicia, where Pedro dispensed his summary rulings. Firstly, however, the route goes through the Casa de las Americas, built by Isabel to administer

the expeditions to the Americas. These gloomy rooms have little of architectural merit, but it is interesting to muse that the biggest empire in the world at that time was ruled from these quarters. The best part of Isabel's complex is undoubtedly the small chapel, the Capilla de los Navegantes, with a fine *artesonado* ceiling. Above the altar is a large painting, La Virgen de los Mareantes, by the Sevilla artist Alejo Fernández, which is thought to be the oldest representation of the Virgin as protectress of seamen. In the painting, the Virgin spreads her protective mantle over, on her left, Columbus and the Pinzón brothers, while on her right is Carlos I and his retinue. In the foreground is a collection of boats, while in the background a selection of native people lurk, no doubt blessing their good fortune in having new found Christian guardians. All very symbolic.

The tour of the Alcázar now moves into the main palace and from even the small entrance vestibule the combination of carved stucco work, horseshoe arches and *azulejos* so typical of Moorish and Mudéjar architecture is immediately evident. A narrow passage now leads into the Patio de las Doncellas (the Patio of the Maidens) and here one immediately recognizes that the Mudéjar workmen from Granada had certainly seen the Alhambra. This was the main courtyard of the palace and was named after the maidens who would line the upper gallery when visiting ambassadors trooped in. The patio has double columned arches which, with the upper storey, were added by Carlos V and these seem to merge agreeably with the original Mudéjar work. The route passes through the Salon of Carlos V – it appears that when the Kings came to Sevilla in the summer, they preferred to sleep on the ground floor because the rooms were cooler, which in fact was a continuation of a Moorish habit. We now pass into a group of rooms designed for María de Padilla, the mistress of Pedro

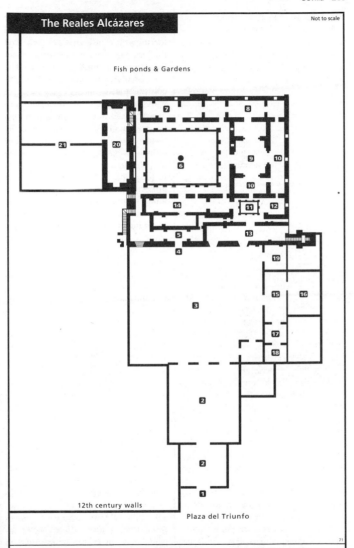

The Reales Alcázares

Not to scale

Fish ponds & Gardens

1. The Lion Gate
2. Courts of the Monteria (Royal Guard)
3. Court of the Lion
4. Main entrance & façade
5. Vestibule
6. Patio de la Doncellas
7. Salon of Charles V
8. Chambers of Maria de Padilla

9. Ambassadors Hall
10. Philip II's rooms
11. Patio de las Muñecas
12. Isabel the Catholic's bedroom
13. Prince's Room
14. Bedchamber of the Moorish Kings

Chamber of American Commerce:
15. Audience Chamber
16. Chapel
17. Fans
18. 19th century bedchamber
19. Stairs to Royal apartments (closed to the public)
20. Chapel
21. Carlos V's Palace

12th century walls

Plaza del Triunfo

the Cruel and who was believed to have some magical hold over him – just as well because he has been described as "tall, handsome with a lisping speech and an insatiable pursuer of beautiful women". Little changes!

The route then leads to the Salon de Embajadores (Salon of the Ambassadors), which has more echoes of the Alhambra. It was named because this was where the Ambassadors were received, but is also sometimes known as 'de la media naranja' after the half orange domed roof. Its arcades of horseshoe arches were inspired by the Palace of Medina Azahara, near Córdoba. Unfortunately Carlos V, in his usual way, made 'improvements' by adding balconies and panels of Royal pictures to mark his marriage on this spot to Isabel of Portugal. Nevertheless, the room is the highlight of the Alcázar and stands comparison with anything in the Alhambra.

Leading off is a small dining room which then brings us to a modest apartment built for Felipe II. We then arrive at the last of the classic rooms of the Alcázar, the Patio de la Muñecars (Patio of the dolls), named after two tiny faces carved in one of the spandrels and reputed to have been built as a playroom for King Pedro's daughter and her maids. But it was also the scene of some dirty deeds. It is probable that it was here that Pedro murdered his brother Fadrique in 1358. It was also the place where the visiting Abu Said of Granada was murdered for his jewels. One, an enormous ruby, was given by Pedro to the Black Prince and it is now in the collection of British Crown Jewels.

The tour now returns to the Vestibule and all that remains is to take a stroll around the Gardens of the Alcázar. This is a somewhat rambling area, the result of several centuries of alterations and additions, but providing welcome coolness and shade. The gardens were often used for balls. One, in 1350, was in honour of the Black Prince, who was greatly impressed by the Moorish dances performed by the Sevillan ladies. When he returned home, the dance became fashionable in England, giving rise, it is claimed, to the 'Morris Dance'. Probably myth, but a nice story! Features of the garden include an unusual myrtle maze, a small pavilion built by Carlos V and some vaulted baths where Maria de Padilla was said to have bathed (and courtiers subsequently drank the water).

Entry to the Real Alcázar costs 600 ptas; Children under 12, OAP's and students free. Open Tues-Sat 10.30-1700; Jun-Sep 1000-1330 and 1700-1900. Sun and festivals 1000-1300. Closed Mon. Owing to the pressure of visitors during the summer months, when satisfactory photography is impossible, a flow control system operates allowing in a certain number of people every half an hour. You are advised to visit early in the morning or late afternoon or preferably out of season.

The **Lonja** Numerous palaces grace Sevilla. The Lonja, on Avda de la Constitución next to the cathedral, was designed for Felipe II by Juan de Herrera and completed in 1598 in pure Renaissance style. Today it houses the **Archives of the Indies**, comprising some 38,000 files, documents, letters amd manuscripts concerning the discovery and colonization of the Americas. Here you can see Columbus's diary and the Mapa Mundi by Juan de la Cosa. Open to visitors 1000-1300, closed Sat and Sun. Free entry.

The **Torre del Oro** This 12-sided tower was built in the early 13th century by the Almohades under Yussef II to protect the city from the Christians when the latter had become a threat following their victory at the Battle of Las Navas de Tolosa. It is located on the E bank of the Guadalquivir and was originally linked by chain to a similar tower on the

Torre del Oro, Sevilla

W bank, being part of the city's fortifications, which once included 166 towers and 12 gates. It gained its name from the gilded tiles which originally decorated it. Today the main part of the tower is made of stone, while the upper section, which is made of brick, was added in the 18th century. It houses a small Maritime museum.

Hospital de la Caridad (Charity Hospital) Located in a back street, close to the Torre del Oro and parallel with the river, the hospital was built in Baroque style in 1676 by Miguel de Manera, a reformed local 'Jack the Lad', to help the destitute – a function which it still fulfils today. The main reason for paying a visit, apart from admiring the colonnaded, plant-filled patio with its two fountains, is to view the paintings in the chapel. These include a number of Murillo's, including one where Manera himself (who commissioned the works) posed as

San Juan de Dios. There are also two paintings by Valdés Leal, one of which, the superb *Finis Gloriae Mundi*, shows a dead bishop being eaten by worms. This apparently obliged Murillo to suggest that it was necessary to hold your nose when viewing the picture. The Hospital is open Mon-Sat 1000-1330 and 1530-1800; closed Sun and festivals; entrance 200 ptas.

The **Plaza de España and María Luisa Park** Sevilla has a number of parks and open spaces, but the best, without doubt, is the Parque de María Luisa, which was founded in 1893 by the widowed Duchess of Monpensier, who donated to the city half of the gardens of the Palace of San Telmo. (The Palace itself, once a Nautical College, is now a Seminary.) The gardens were turned into a park as part of the 1929 Exhibition. Many of the exhibition buildings have survived, in contrast to the EXPO '92 pavilions, and some now function as museums. The Spanish exhibitions were housed in the specially built Plaza de España, a semicircular complex located on the spot where the Inquisition burned the last witch in 1781. In front of the building is a vast square, with a canal and computer-controlled fountains. Unusual blue and white balustraded bridges cross the canal at intervals and lead to tiled seats with *azulejos* depicting the main features of each of the Spanish regions. This is a delightful place to spend the 'dead' hours of the afternoon when everywhere else is closed.

Between the Plaza de España and the cathedral are two other buildings of interest. Alongside the Puerta de Jerez is the **Hotel Alfonso XIII**, built in Baroque style in 1929 for some of the more prestigious guests at the exhibition. Prices are still outrageous, but the interior patio, which is something special, is open to non residents and worth a view. Next door to the hotel is one of the main **University** buildings based in the old

Tobacco Factory, which was made famous by Bizet's opera *Carmen*. Cigarette production continued here until 1965, when the building was taken over by the university. It remains the second largest building in Spain (after El Escorial) and budget travellers might be interested in trying the student's cafeteria.

The **Casa de Pilatos** There are a vast number of mansions and palaces in central Sevilla, but the most impressive, without doubt, is the Casa de Pilatos. Located on the far NW side of the barrio Santa Cruz, it is sufficiently far from the main sites to deter coach parties and therefore visitors are not crowded out by tourists. Those who eventually make it, will therefore probably enjoy it more than the Alcázar. Those who have a map and like a challenge could approach the Casa de Pilatos by wandering through the maze of Santa Cruz, but otherwise go to the end of the pedestrianized C/Sierpes, turn right and head E via the Plaza de la Encarnación and Plaza San Pedro. It was built by the Marquis of Tarifa on his return from the Holy Land and was wrongly thought to be modelled on the house of Pontius Pilate. It is in fact a combination of Mudéjar and Renaissance styles, Moorish and Italianate in flavour, with wonderful patios and probably the best display of *azulejos* anywhere in Andalucía. The house is owned by the Medinaceli family and the various Dukes have meticulously restored the building over the last 50 years. An entry gate leads into a courtyard where the *apeadero* marks where carriages were boarded. The Main Court or Patio Principal is then reached. This one of the great patios of Andalucía. There is a combination of Mudéjar arches and stucco work, traditional tiles, Gothic balconies, Italianate fountains and Roman statuary which merge in harmony. The route leads into a Praetorian Chamber, with a coffered ceiling incorporating the family coat of arms. The tour

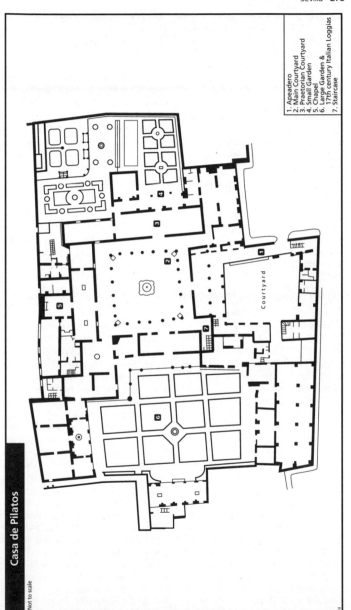

Casa de Pilatos

Not to scale

1. Apeadero
2. Main Courtyard
3. Praetorian Courtyard
4. Small Garden
5. Chapel
6. Large Garden &
   17th century Italian Loggias
7. Staircase

Courtyard

continues into the Small Garden, past a Chapel of Flagellation and into the shade of the formal Large Garden. From here, a four flighted, domed stairway, covered with the most superb *azulejos*, leads to the family quarters. Following the Moorish tradition, they slept on the upper floor in the winter and the ground floor in the summer. This part of the building requires a further entrance fee and many visitors will happily settle for the ground floor, the gardens and the staircase. The Casa de Pilatos is open daily 0900-1900. Entrance 500 ptas, with a further 500 ptas for a guided tour of the upper floor.

La Isla de la Cartuja This 215 ha site on the W bank of the Río Guadalquivir was once notable only for its old monastery, the **Santa María de las Cuevas**, where Columbus frequently visited and where he lay buried for 37 years. After the monastery was closed, it became a barracks for the French forces under Marshal Soult for 2 years during the Peninsular War, before being used as a pottery. The five huge kilns can still be seen towering over the old monastery. The site was then chosen as the location for EXPO '92 and the monastery restored at great cost, becoming the Royal Pavilion. Following the closure of EXPO '92, the Isla de la Cartuja has been developed as a theme park, **El Parque de los Descubrimientos** (The Park of Discoveries), T 4461616, closed Mon. It includes four theme pavilions (Navigation, Discovery, Nature and Future), a digital planetarium and Omnimax space theatre. The Spanish and regional pavilions have been retained. The Park also features a cable car, Banesto panoramic tower, fairground, restaurants, picnic areas and entertainments. Entry 500 ptas just to walk around, 2,000 ptas to visit the pavilions. If you thought that the entry charges to visit EXPO were a rip off, then clearly things haven't changed. The restored monastery may also be visited, Tues-Sun 1100-1830.

MUSEUMS

NB Entrance to all public museums in Sevilla is free for EU citizens with proof of identity.

Museo Arqueológico, Plaza de América, Parque de María Luisa. Located in one of the pavilions which have survived from the 1929 Exhibition, it is the most important of its type in Andalucía. The collection runs from Prehistoric times to the end of the Moorish occupation. Outstanding are the Carambalo Treasures, a hoard of gold coins and jewelry discovered in a Sevilla suburb in 1958. The Roman section is very thorough, with a comprehensive collection of mosaics, kitchen utensils, statuary and tombs, much from the nearby site of Italica. Open Tues-Sun 0900-1430; closed Mon and festivals, T 4232401. Entrance free.

Museo de Arte y Costumbres Populares, Plaza de América, Parque de María Luisa (opposite the Archaeological Museum). Provides a fascinating insight into the traditional crafts, customs and domestic life over the last 300 years in Andalucía. The sections devoted to Sevilla's *Semana Santa* and the Apr *Feria* are particularly good. Open Tues-Sun 0900-1430; closed Mon and festivals. Entry 250 ptas.

Museo Maritimo Located in the Torre de Oro, this small exhibition presents the naval history of Sevilla. Open Tues-Fri 1000-1400. Closed Sat-Mon and festivals. Also closed during Aug. Entrance 25 ptas.

Museo de Belle Artes, Plaza de Museo 9. Claimed to be second only in importance to the Prado in Madrid. The museum is located in a renovated former convent in an attractive square, where the scene is set with a statue of Murillo. The museum certainly concentrates on the rather heavy religious art of its local Sevillan stalwarts, Zurburán, Murillo and Valdés Leal and many visitors feel the lack of balance. Certainly, the small 19th and 20th century collection is uninspiring. The highlight, however, is Room 5, which is the convent's former church, where the light is exceptionally good. Here the vaulting and dome have been restored showing the 18th century work of local artist Domingo Martínez. In the apse of the church are some of Murillo's best paintings, superbly set off by the surroundings. The museum also has some outstanding sculptures, including works by Montañes and Pedro Millan. Open Tues-Sun 0900-1500; Closed Mon and festivals. Entrance 250 ptas.

Museo de Arte Contemporaneo Located in an old building between the cathedral and the tourist office, this Modern Art Museum is something of a disappointment, with many of the works little better than scribbles in felt and ball point pen. The upper floors, however, will reward the climb. Open Tues-Fri 1000-2000; Sat-Sun 1000-1400; Closed Mon. Entrance free.

The Barrios of Central Sevilla Around the central monumental area of Sevilla are a number of districts or *barrios*, each with their own distinct character. Close to the cathedral and much visited is the **Barrio Santa Cruz**, a maze of narrow streets, whitewashed houses, small squares and flower strewn patios. A stroll around this atmospheric *barrio* with frequent stops at its plethora of bars is one of the delights of a visit to Sevilla. Amongst the locations of interest are the Palacio Arzobispal, the Convento de San José with some marvellous Mudéjar plasterwork, the Museo de Murillo, Plaza Santa Cruz and a gateway marking the former entrance to a synagogue – the only surviving evidence of what was once a busy Jewish Quarter. To the N of the Central Busines District of Sevilla is the **Barrio Macarena**. Always solidly working class and rarely visited by tourists, the district is now undergoing a certain amount of gentrification.

Running parallel with the inner ring road is the finest remaining section of the old city walls, including the Puerta de Córdoba with its horseshoe arch. Just across the road is the Hospital de las Cinco Llagas (Hospital of the Five Wounds), the restored building of which now operates as the Andalucían Parliament. At some time in the future the public will be allowed into the debating chamber, which is sited in the Hospital's old church. There are some fine churches in the *barrio*, but the most famous is in fact quite modern. This is the Basilica of Macarena, home of *La Macarena*, the star of the Easter processions. This 17th century image of the *Virgen* is normally located on the *retablo* behind the main altar. Other churches of interest are San Marcos, with some interior horseshoe arches still intact despite Civil War damage, San Julian dating back to the 14th century and San Gil, boasting a Mudéjar tower and ceiling.

The third *barrio* is **Triana**, located across the river to the SW. This was the centre of the city's gypsy community until they were relocated throughout the city. It was the same *gitanos* who made Sevilla the home of *flamenco*. Triana is still the traditional starting point for the annual *romería* to the marshlands of the Coto Doñana. The district has a long standing ceramics industry based on local supplies of clay, which back in Roman times made the amphorae used for the transportation of wheat, olive oil and other agricultural products. Bricks were also produced, but today decorative tiles or *azulejos* are the chief product. If you wish to buy staight from the producer, go to Ceramica Santa Ana on Plaza Callao – you can't miss the amazing tiled façade. Triana was, naturally enough, thought to be the home of Roger de Triana, the sailor on Columbus's *Santa María* who first sighted land on the other side of the Atlantic. Reseach has shown, however, that he came from Lepe, near Huelva.

Flamenco

Holidaymakers visiting Andalucía will find it hard to miss the sound of Flamenco music, mainly emanating from the radios of bars, while the Costa travel agents and tour reps usually have a 'flamenco show' with which to tempt visitors. What they offer, however, is unlikely to be the 'real thing'. Pure flamenco is an essentially private phenenomen and often extremely difficult to find.

The roots of flamenco have attracted much discussion and research. What seems certain is that it has its origins in the minority groups at the time of the Christian Reconquest, such as the Moors, Jews and particularly the Gypsies. The word itself possibly comes from the Jews who lived in Flanders where they were able to live and sing freely. When they came to Spain they were known as 'Fleming-goes'. Other researchers suggest that the name has Arab origins. But the Gypsy connection has continued and it is the gitanos who have preserved the authentic, traditional forms of flamenco and who established the 'laws' of the art in the 19th century, leading to the so called 'Golden Age' in the early 20th century. The stronghold of flamenco has always been in the W of Andalucía in the triangle formed by the cities of Sevilla, Jerez and Cádiz, particularly in their gypsy quarters. Only a small percentage of flamenco performers are non gypsies or payos.

There are four elements to flamenco. Firstly, there is cante or singing, performed in an agonised, melancholy way full of despair and lamentations on the lot of the discriminated minorities. Secondly, there is the toque or guitar playing, on a much lighter instrument than the classical guitar and serving the purpose of not just accompanying the singer, but establishing a rapport and developing a situation where each feeds off the other. During this century, guitar playing has developed as a solo form of flamenco. Thirdly, there is the jaleo,

---

But this has not stopped the residents of Triana erecting a modern statue to his memory – presumably their contribution to the Fifth Centenary celebrations. Triana today sees few tourists, but it is within easy walking distance of the central monuments and has a number of cheap accommodation and eating possibilities.

EXCURSIONS

Local travel agents have information on fairly expensive organized tours of the city, such as those of *Pullmantur* and *Trapastur* including a 3 hrs trip around Sevilla, night cruises, *flamenco* evenings and excursions to nearby towns. Information and departures from C/Almirante Lobo 13. *Sevi-rama*, C/General Sanjurjo 2, T 4560693, run a multi-lingual city tour in open-topped buses, lasting 1 hr. Departures from the Torre del Oro. Tours start 0900 in summer, 1100 in winter and claim to cover over 50 historic monuments. Adults 1,300 ptas, children 800 ptas.

River cruises In summer 9 Cruceros Panorámicos depart from the Torre del Oro daily, 1130-2215. Price 500 ptas, children free. There is a new boat service which takes visitors to the Coto Doñana National Park, leaving the Torre del Oro at 0900 and reaching Sanlúcar at 1300. Then follows an itinerary which is basically the same as that from Sanlúcar described on page 130. Return is by coach, getting back to Sevilla at 2100. The trip can also be done in reverse. Tickets, costing 2,900 ptas, can be obtained from the office next to the Torre del Oro.

Alcalá de Guadaira Located 10 km SE of Sevilla on the N334, this small town is well worth a visit. The spectacular fortress after which the town was named was built by the Almohads on the river Guadaira as part of their defence system

involving percussion sounds produced by shouts, finger snapping, clapping and footwork. Castinets, incidentally, are not part of the traditional jaleo. Lastly, there is the dancing or baile, performed by an individual or a pair. In the second half of the 20th century, group flamenco folk dances have developed such as the Sevillanas and the Malagueñas and flamenco dancing has moved into the theatre with the advent of flamenco ballet.

In the second half of the 20th century, after the repression by Franco, flamenco moved into new areas, stimulated by performers such as Paco de Lucía and the late Isla de la Cameron, linking it with rock, salsa and Latin American and even introducing instruments such as the flute and saxophone. Flamenco rock groups such as Ketama and Pata Negra, developed in the 1990's what has become known as 'flamenco nueva'. The flamenco theatre has also become highly popular, with the performers often trained in ballet and music schools. The latest sensation is Joaquín Cortés, who although a gypsy, has graduated from ballet school and scandalized the flamenco purists by dancing bare chested. Nevertheless, his flamenco stage show, Pasión Gitana, which has as its theme the gypsy culture, plays to full houses wherever it goes.

So what can the flamenco seeking tourist expect? Well it is almost impossible to find genuine flamenco on the costa. Many bars advertise flamenco, but this is basically amateur dancing by schoolgirls to an often scratchy record and largely a complete waste of time. Some shows or tablaos with live musicians can be very entertaining, but they will not be the real thing. This is not to denigrate them, however, and they can provide an enjoyable evening. The best bet is to head for the flamenco clubs or peñas in the larger towns away from the coast, where something spontaneous can always happen or ask the tourist office for details for any *flamenco* festivals being held.

for Sevilla itself. It is one of the best remaining examples of Almohad military architecture and the largest of their fortresses to have survived. Following its capture in 1246 by Fernando III, it was modified for use as a prison by Pedro the Cruel. Also of interest is the Iglesia de San Miguel, which was originally built as a mosque. Alcalá has now increasingly become a dormitory town for Sevilla, and as in Sevilla, cars and their contents are vulnerable.

Italica The Roman ruins of Italica can be found some 9 km N of Sevilla next to the village of Santiponce. For those without transport, the site can easily be reached by bus, which takes 20 mins from the C/Reyes Católicos. The original city was founded in 206 BC by General Publius Cornelius Scipius as a convalescent area for his soldiers wounded in the Battle of Ilipa. The men

called the place *Italica* presumably to remind them of home. Trajan, the first Emperor to hail from a Roman province, was born in Italica. His successor, Hadrian, whilst born in Rome, received much of his education here and whilst he was Emperor he richly endowed the city, building a large new section.

Italica is actually divided into two parts. Firstly there is the *vitus urbs* or old city, much of which lies today under the town of Santiponce. Hadrian built the *nova urbs* or new city, which is the part forming the archaeological site which can be visited today. At its peak, Italica had a population of over half a million, but declined under the Visigoths and the Moors, who finally deserted the site after the Guadalquivir changed its course after some flooding. In the succeeding centuries the site was looted initially for its building stone and later for its artefacts.

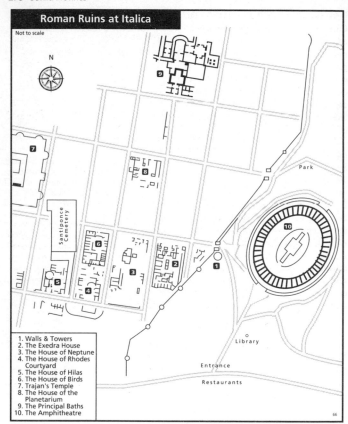

Roman Ruins at Italica

Not to scale

N

Santiponce Cemetery

Park

1. Walls & Towers
2. The Exedra House
3. The House of Neptune
4. The House of Rhodes Courtyard
5. The House of Hilas
6. The House of Birds
7. Trajan's Temple
8. The House of the Planetarium
9. The Principal Baths
10. The Amphitheatre

Library

Entrance

Restaurants

Serious excavation began as early as the late 18th century and has gathered apace during recent years.

What has been uncovered from the farmland is quite remarkable. Most astonishing of all is the huge amphitheatre. Composed of a crumbling conglomerate, it consists of three rows of seats, of which only the lower two rows remain intact. It is estimated that it could hold some 25,000 people – believed to be the third largest in the Roman Empire. Beneath the arena with its central pit, one can wander along the corridors where the gladiators would have strode and look into the pits where the wild animals were kept. An eerie experience. To the W of the amphitheatre is the city, which is laid out on a rough grid plan. Between the well marked roads, which were wide and colonnaded, public buildings would have occupied a whole block. It is believed that the site contained six public buildings and around 50 houses, with probably two in each block. Most of the houses are yet to be excavated, but those which have been uncovered have revealed an amazing collection of mosaics. The houses have been named according to the subjects of the mosaics, so for instance we have the bird mosaic in the Casa de los Pájaros, the Neptune mosaic and the Casa del Planetario, where the mosaic shows planetary divinities, which gave their name to the seven days of the week in the Roman calendar. Also of interest is the Exedra House, with baths for men and women and a number of cement blocks which are thought to be the remains of a dome which covered the exedra.

Italica is open Tues-Sat, 0930-1830 in the summer and 0900-1700 in the winter; Sun 0900-1500 in the summer and 1000-1600 in the winter. Closed Mon and festivals. Entrance 250 ptas, EU citizens free. If visiting in the summer, beware of the heat, as there is little shade. Easter is the most popular time for coachloads of Spanish schoolchildren, who make more noise in the echoing amphitheatre than the original wild animals. There is a string of restaurants along the road opposite the entrance to the site, ranging from the sordid to the reasonably presentable.

LOCAL FESTIVALS

The *Labalyata de los Reyes* (Cavalade of the Magi) takes place early in Jan with the 'Kings' throwing sweets from their floats; the *Semana Santa* celebrations in the week leading up to Easter are arguably the best in Spain, with effigies of Christ and the Virgin Mary being paraded through the streets by the brotherhoods; solemnity is replaced 2 weeks later by the riotous *Feria de Abril*, marked by bullfights, fireworks, dancing and general merrymaking lasting for a week; *Corpus Cristi* is celebrated by a procession through the streets which are decorated by flowers and herbs, while choirboys dance according to a 14th century tradition. Triana holds its own smaller version of the event, the *Corpus Chico*, the following day; *Virgen de los Reyes* on 15 Aug celebrates the patron saint of Sevilla; the *Bienal de Flamenco* takes place in Sep in even years; the *International Jazz Festival* is held in Nov.

LOCAL INFORMATION

Price guide

Hotels:

AL	over US$90	D	US$20-40
A	US$75-90	E	US$10-20
B	US$60-75	F	under US$10
C	US$40-60		

Places to eat:

♦♦♦	expensive	♦♦	average
♦	cheap		

● **Accommodation**

The price of accommodation in Sevilla and the surrounding area still remains ridiculously high in the aftermath of EXPO '92, particularly when one considers the glut of available rooms. Recently the regional tourist authority requested that hotels in Sevilla reduce their prices by 20%, but this sort of action is not in the Andalucián mentality, and few changes have occurred. Hopefully, prices will eventually fall to more reasonable levels. Visitors wishing to stay in Sevilla during *Semana Santa* or the *Feria de Abril* will need to book accommodation well in advance, when prices can often double. Those arriving by car should certainly look for accommodation with a garage. With some 50 hotels and over 100 *pensiones*, there is certainly no lack of choice.

AL *Alfonso XIII*, C/San Fernando 2, T 4222850, F 4216033, 149 rm, luxurious 1920's building, one of the priciest in Spain, garage, pool, a/c, wheelchair access, restaurant, close to the monumental quarter; **AL** *Doña María*, C/Don Remondo 19, T 4224990, F 4219546, 61 rm, garage, a/c, restaurant, pool, nr Giralda; **AL** *Husa Sevilla*, C/Pagés de Corro 90, T 4342412, F 4342707, 128 rm, garage, a/c, located in a quiet part of Triana barrio within walking distance of the monumental area; **AL** *Inglaterra*, Plaza Nueva 7, T 4224970, F 4342707, garage, a/c, wheelchair access, restaurant, central position; **AL** *Macarena*, C/San Juan Ribera 2, T 4375700, F 4381803, 305 rm, garage, a/c, wheelchair access, pool, restaurant, located on the inner ring road close to the regional parliament.

A *Fernando III*, C/San José 21, T 4217301, F 4220246, 157 rm, some with balconies, a/c, pool, relatively quiet, are convenient for monuments, garage, garden; **A** *Monte Carmelo*, C/Turia 9, T 4279000, F 4271004, 68 rm, garage, a/c, quiet, nr the grounds used for the *Feria de Abril* just S of the river.

B *Residencia Murillo*, C/Lope de Rueda 7,

T 4216095, F 4219616, 57 rm, a/c, by the Real Alcázar in the old part of the town, but can be noisy.

C *Ducal*, Plaza de la Encarnación 19, T 4215107, F 4228999, 51 rm, a/c, fairly central, bus routes nearby; **C** *Italica*, C/Antonio de la Peña Lopez 5-9, T 45615922, F 5411518, a/c, nr the station; **C** *Simon*, C/García de Vinuesa 19, T 4226660, F 4562241, 31 rm, a/c.

Pensiones: accommodation queries by telephone on T 4237474, Mon-Sat 1000-2200. The **Barrio Santa Cruz** area, known for basic (but no longer very cheap) rooms, is central, try **C** *San Pancracio*, Plaza de los Cruces 9, T 4413104, 8 rm, clean, popular, shared shower; **C** *Fabiola*, C/Fabiola 16, T 4218346, 13 rm, by the Iglesia de Santa Cruz, simple but clean.

D *Archeros*, C/Archeros 23, T 4418465, 6 rm, small but comfortable; **D** *Florida*, C/Menendez Pelayo 27, T 4422557, 5 rm, clean; **D** *Goya*, C/Mateos Gago 31, 20 rm, right by the cathedral, comfortable; **D** *Gravina*, C/Gravina 46, T 4216414, off C/Alfonso XII, 10 rm, basic; **D** *Nevada*, C/Gamazo 28, T 4225340, 14 rm, nr Plaza Nueva.

There are 3 other *pensiones* on Calle Gravina, any of which is worth a try: **C** *Gala*, N°52, T 4214503, **C** *Granadina*, N°82, T 4213122 and **C** *Romero*, N°21, T 4211353.

Visitors preferring to stay outside Sevilla in a quieter location and travel in daily, might consider accommodation in Alcalá de Guadaira, some 20 mins SE of the city. Rec is: **B** *Silos*, C/Silos s/n, T 5680059, F 5684457, modern hotel built round a Moorish style patio, 54 rm, restaurant, parking.

Something different: **AL** *Hacienda San Rafael*, Cruce de las Cabezas, Ctra NIV, Km 594, T 5898014, F 750349, 10 self catering apartments in a 150-year-old converted olive mill surrounded by fields of sunflowers, wheat and cotton; trad Andalucían courtyard, pool, meals by arrangement. 30 mins from Sevilla, but also handy for Cádiz, Jerez, Ronda and Arcos. Book through Tri Hotel Marketing, 2 Gerrard Rd, Barnes, London, T 0181 563 2100.

Youth hostels: *Fernando el Santo*, C/Issac Peral 2, T 4613150, off Avda de la Palmera, away from the centre but accessible from Plaza Nueva on Bus No 34. Usually crowded, 198 beds with shared bathrooms, TV lounge, meals available, suitable for wheelchair users, airport 14 km, train 7 km.

Camping: **Warning** Because of the heat, camping in high summer can be uncomfortable in the Sevilla area. *Sevilla*, Ctra Madrid-Cádiz, Km 534, T 4514379, 12 km from city, nr airport, hot showers, pool, restaurant, bar; *Villsom*, Ctra Sevilla-Cádiz, Km 554.8, Dos Hermanas, T 4720828, 14 km from the city, pool, showers, open Feb-Nov only; *Club de Campo*, Avda de la Libertad 13, Dos Hermanas, T 4720250, 12 km from the city, pool, restaurant. A Los Amarillos bus runs to Dos Hermanas every 45 mins.

● **Places to eat**
As the home of the *tapas* bar, Sevilla has never been noted for its restaurants. Take care when selecting restaurants nr to the main monuments, which are expensive and serve some appalling *platos combinados*.

♦♦♦*Bailén*, C/Bailén 34, T 4225281, Andalucían home cooking; ♦♦♦*Bodegón el Riojano*, C/Virgen de las Montañas 12, T 4450682, good regional cuisine; ♦♦♦*El Burladero*, C/Canalejas 1, T 4222900, Sevilla's only 4 fork restaurant, international and local cuisine, expensive; ♦♦♦*La Dorada*, C/Virgen de Aguasanta 6, T 4450220, luxury fish and sea food.

♦♦*Las Meninas*, C/Santo Tomás 3, T 4223355, Andalucían cuisine and fish specialities; ♦♦*Victoria Eugenia*, Plaza Villasis, T 4227459, off C/Martín Villa, local dishes; ♦♦*VIPS*, C/República Argentina 25, young people's cafetería with late night music and grocery shop, overpriced.

♦*Casa Cabo*, C/Menendez Pelayo 5, nr Barrio Santa Cruz, good *menú del día* (lunch and dinner); ♦*Casa Diego*, Plaza Curtidores 7, T 4415883, off C/Menendez Pelayo, cheap regional dishes; ♦*El 3 Del Oro*, C/Santa María la Blanca 34, T 4422759, self service Andalucían cuisine in Puerta de la Carne; ♦*El Baratillo*, C/Pavia 12, off C/De Dos de Mayo, T 4229651, good value nr the cathedral.

● **Bars**
As Sevilla is the place which claims to have originated the *tapa*, it is no surprise to find *tapas* bars in profusion throughout the city. Many are bedecked with sherry barrels and hanging hams and are full of atmosphere. Locals generally drink *fino* with their *tapas*. A few outstanding bars can be mentioned. In the Santa Cruz area, *Bar Modesto* should be on everyone's itinerary. In the Triana locality, try *Bar Bistec*, which specializes in spicy snails. In

the central area of the city, *Bar Alicantina* in Plaza Salvador serves great seafood. This selection, however, barely scratches the surface and *aficionados* will soon find their own favourites.

● **Banks & money changers**
Banks are open Mon-Fri 0830-1400, Sat 0830-1300. Closed Sat May-Oct. Banks cluster around Avda de la Constitución, Plaza Nueva and C/Tetuán. There are change facilities out-

side banking hours at the Santa Justa station and in many of the more central hotels. The department store, *El Corte Inglés*, in Plaza Duque de la Victoria, also provides change facilities at convenient hours.

● **Embassies & consulates**
Austria, C/Marqués de Paradas 26, T 4222162; **Belgium**, Avda San Francisco Javier 20, 3A, T 4647061; **Canada**, Avda de

Nibbles – Spanish style

The custom of taking *tapas* is not, historically speaking, a long standing habit. *Tapas* are thought to have appeared in Sevilla in the last century, when legend has it that drinkers protected their glass of *fino* from flies, dust and dripping hams by putting over them a cover or *tapa*. The cover was often a slice of bread and before long enterprising bartenders were putting some food on the bread. The rest, as they say, is history.

'Grazing' – nibbling at small amounts of food – is nowadays a popular way of eating throughout Europe, but nowhere is it more common than in Spain. This may be due to the quirky mealtimes in Spain, with lunch rarely starting before 1400 and dinner beginning at 2200 in the evening, with long gaps to fill the rumbling tummy. Of equal importance, however, is the fact that the *tapas* bar or *tasca* is an essential part of Spanish life, a place where people meet to eat and drink, to gossip, to carry out business and generally pass the time. A *tapas* crawl, hopping from bar to bar and sampling a nibble of food at each one, is one of the delights of Andalucía.

So what should the uninitiated visitor expect and what etiquette is involved? Firstly, *tapas* are usually taken standing at the bar. Expect to pay more if you sit at a table or on a terrace. The various dishes are laid out on the bar, so you can point to the ones you want. The food is served in a small dish called a *concha* or in tiny erathenware casseroles, accompanied by bread (good for mopping up sauces) or a dry breadstick and possibly a small fork. *Tapas* have always traditionally been served cold, but many are now popped into a microwave before serving. In some of the more remote parts of Andalucía you may still be lucky enough to be given a free *tapa* with your drink, but normally expect to pay between 200 and 300 pesetas.

The food provided varies enormously from simple olives and chunks of cheese or tortilla to quite elaborate dishes, particularly in those bars frequented by affluent businessmen. Some bars have their own specialities, which are well known in the area, such as a mountain ham or a seafood dish. But in the majority of bars, as in the Spanish home, the type of *tapas* may depend on what was left over yesterday or what is in season or whether there has been a glut of *sardinas* at the local fish market. If a *tapas* looks particularly good, ask for a *ración*, which can be shared with more than one person.

When choosing a drink to accompany *tapas*, bear in mind that the traditional slurp is a cold *fino* sherry, often drawn from a barrel, but in reality anything goes. A beer, red wine or even carbonated water is quite acceptable. Most Spaniards would draw the line at a gin and tonic, however, while a coffee with a *tapa* is definitely NOT on.

la Constitución 30, T 4229413; **Denmark**, Avda Reina Mercedes 25, 1B, T 4611489; **Finland**, C/Adriano 45, 2B, T 4225079; **France**, Plaza Santa Cruz 1, T 4222896, **Germany**, Avda Ramón de Carranza 22, T 4457811; **Greece**, Ctra de Carmona 30, T 4419000; **Italy**, C/Luis Montoto 107, T 4577102; **Netherlands**, C/Gravina 55, T 4228750; **Portugal**, Pabellón de Portugal, Avda del Cid, T 4231150; **Sweden**, Avda Reina Mercedes 25, T 4611489; **Switzerland**, C/Luis Montoto 112A, T 4575355; **UK**, Plaza Nueva 8, T 4228874/5; **USA**, Pabellón de los EEUU, Paseo de las Delicias 7, T 4231883.

● **Entertainment**

Bullfights: held in the Plaza de Toros de la Real Maestranza, Paseo de Cristóbel Colón, one of the largest bullrings in Spain, from Mar-Apr. Tickets are bought directly from the bullring and also from a kiosk in C/Sierpes.

Cinemas: there are 11 cinemas in Sevilla, some outdoor, some multiscreen.

Concerts: various concerts take place throughout the year, ranging from pop concerts to recitals in the cathedral. There are 5 theatres and 4 outdoor auditoriums in the city. For details, check in *El Giraldillo*, the free monthly magazine which can be obtained from the tourist office.

Discos: plenty of choice here, with the more adult venues carrying through to daylight. Try *Groucho*, C/Federico Sanchez Bedoya 20; *B 60*, C/Betis 60, in Triana; and *Holiday*, C/Jesús del Grand Poder 71. For live jazz you can do no better than *Bluemoon*, C/Cavestany s/n, nr Santa Justa station.

Flamenco: will vary from the 'real thing', which because of the spontaneous nature of this art form, can be remarkably difficult to find, to overpriced shows put on for tourists. Try *Los Gallos*, Plaza de Santa Cruz 11, T 4216981, 2130-0130, probably the best of the 'shows'; *El Arenal*, C/Rocío 7, T 4216492, 2200-0130; for a more spontaneous performance, *Bar Quita Pesares*, Plaza Jerónimo de Córdoba.

● **Hospitals & medical services**

Hospitals: *Cruz Roja*, Avda de la Cruz Roja, emergencies T 4350135; *Hospital Universitario*, Avda Doctor Fedrano s/n, T 4378400; *Hospital General*, Avda Manuel Siurot, T 4558100, emergencies T 4558195; *Real Hospital San Lazaro*, Avda Fedriani s/n, T 4378444.

First aid: *Casa de Socorro*, T 4411712.

● **Post & telecommunications**

Area code: 95.

Post Office: *Correos*, Avda de la Constitución 32, Mon-Fri 0900-2000, Sat 0900-1400. Telegrams by telephone 24-hr service within Spain, T 4222000, outside Spain, T 4226860.

Telephones: *locutorio* in Plaza de Gavidia, open 1000-1400 and 1730-2200.

● **Shopping**

The main shopping street is the pedestrianized C/Sierpes. A large branch of the department store, *El Corte Inglés*, is to be found in Plaza Duque de la Victoria. Local handicrafts include leatherware, *flamenco* costumes, ceramics, fans, gold and silver jewellery. Local markets are held on Thur in C/Feria, on Sun in Alameda de Hercules. There are other Sun markets in Plaza Alfalfa (pets) and Plaza Cabildo (stamps).

● **Sports**

Football: soccer enthusiasts are well catered for in Sevilla, as the city has 2 teams in the First Division of one of the most competitive leagues in Europe. *Real Betis* play at the Benito Villamarín Stadium in the S of the town, while *Sevilla FC* perform at the Sánchez Pizjuan stadium in the eastern suburbs.

Golf: there are 2 local courses: *Club Pineda*, Avda de Jerez s/n, T 4613399 and *Sevilla Golf*, Ctra Isla Mayor, T 5750414.

Horse riding: at *Hipica Puerta Principe*, Ctra de Sevilla-Utrera, Km 11.5, T 4860815.

Parachuting: at the *Parachuting Sports Club*, C/Rodrigo de Triana 62, T 4451267.

Shooting: at *Club el Carambolo*, T 4390401.

Swimming: there are 2 swimming pools, *Piscinas Sevilla*, Avda Cuidad Jardin, and *Piscina Municipal Virgen de los Reyes*, Avda Doctor Fedriani s/n.

Both pools also offer **Tennis**, while there is **Canoeing** and **Rowing** on the Río Guadalquivir. A variety of sports are offered at the *Municipal Sports Centre* at the Poligono de San Pablo.

● **Tour companies & travel agents**

With over 80 travel agents in Sevilla, this is a very small selection: *Viajes Barceló*, C/Reyes Católicos 4, T 4226131; *Viajes Iberia*, C/Tetuán 24, T 4224160; *Julia Tours*, C/Bilbao 22, T 4224910; *Viajes Meliá*, Avda de la Constitución 30, T 4218700; *Torre de Oro*, Avda de la Miraflores, T 4358984; *Universal*, Avda de la Constitución 26, T 4227819.

● **Tourist offices**

Regional Tourist Office at Avda de la Constitución 21 B, T 4221404, open Mon-Fri 0930-1930, Sat 0930-2000, Sun 1000-2000. Very helpful despite being overstretched during the height of the summer. Collect their brochure giving up-to-date times of opening for the main monuments. **Municipal Office** at: Paseo de las Delicias 9, T 4234465, open Mon-Fri 0900-1315 and 1630-1845; **Aeropuerto de San Pablo** terminal building, T 4255046; **Santa Justa** train station, daily 0830-2330.

● **Useful addresses**

Car repairs: *Citroën*, Poligono Industrial Ctra Amarilla, T 4554500; *Ford*, Avda de Andalucía 1, T 4576880; *Renault*, Autopista San Pablo s/n, T 4360100; *Peugeot*, Autopista de San Pablo, Km 537, T 4350450; *Seat/VAG*, Ctra de su Eminencia 2, T 4644766.

● **Transport**

Local Bike hire: from *Biki Rent Sevilla* at Paseo de Colón, Plaza de España and C/del Torneo Bajo, T 4219474, T 4616311. Bikes must be returned to the pick up point. 1 hr costs 400 ptas, half day 1,700 ptas, full day 2,500 ptas, not incl deposit. **Boat hire**: rowing boats for rental by the hour for the canal in the centre of Parque María Luisa. **Bus**: a map of TUSSAM's bus routes is usually available from tourist offices or the special kiosk on Plaza Nueva nr Avda de la Constitución, 50 ptas. Also available are special tourist tickets, *tarjeta turística*, 800 ptas for 3 days, 1,200 ptas for 7 days gives cheap access to frequent users of Sevilla's good public transport system. A *bonobús* for 10 bus trips from kiosks and tobacconists costs 525 ptas with transfers, 500 ptas with no transfers. Useful buses are C1, C2, C3 and C4 which go round the inner ring road. **Car hire**: **Atesa**, Plaza Carmen Benitez, T 4419712; **Avis**, Avda de la Constitución 15, T 4216549; **Europcar**, Aeropuerta, T 4673839; **Hertz**, Avda de la Republica Argentina 3, T 4278887; **Rentalauto**, C/Fernando IV 3, T 4278184; **Sevilla Car**, C/Almirante Lobo, T 4282979. (According to El Pias there are about 2,000 unofficial 'car minders' in Sevilla – all to be avoided.) **Coche Caballo** (horse drawn carriages): carrying up to 4 passengers can be found at the cathedral, Torre del Oro, Plaza de España and Jardines de Murillo. Agree price before setting out, usually approx 3,000 ptas. **Moped hire**: *Alkimoto*, C/Recaredo 28, T 4411115, 3,000-5,000 ptas/day, excluding insurance and 5,000-10,000 ptas deposit. **Taxi**: *Radio Taxi*, T 4580000; *Tele Taxi*, T 4622222; *Radio Teléfono Taxi*, T 4359835.

Air National and international flight tickets and information Iberia, C/Almirante Lobo 3, T 4229801 and T 4218800.

Train The new Santa Justa train station (with exchange facilities) is on Avda de Kansas City, T 4414111 (information), T 4421562 (reservations). The RENFE office is at C/Zaragosa 29. **Cádiz** and **Jerez** departures daily, **Córdoba** and **Huelva** 6 daily, **Málaga** and **Granada** 3 daily. The new AVE high speed trains now make the 340 mile trip to Madrid in just under 2½ hrs (a journey which could previously take 10 hrs), often hitting 180 mph. Moreover RENFE offers a money back guarantee if the train is more than 5 mins late. The trains run to maximum capacity, as airlines cannot compete on price and journey time.

Road Bus: the main bus station is by Prado de San Sebastián in C/Manuel Vásquez Sagastizabál, T 4417111. Several companies operate from here incl Alsina Graells, T 4418811, with frequent services to **Granada**, **Córdoba** and **Málaga**; Comes SA, T 4416858, to **Jerez**, **Cádiz** and **Algeciras**; Los Amarillos, T 4415201, to **Ronda** and **Arcos de la Frontera**. Nearby, on the corner of C/Carlos de Borbón and C/Diego de Raño, the Casal service to **Carmona** leaves approx every hour on the hour.

NORTH AND SOUTH FROM SEVILLA

The road leading **North From Sevilla** quickly leaves the Guadalquivir valley behind and climbs gently into the foothills of the **Sierra Morena**, where in Sevilla province they are at their lowest, being little more than rounded hills. There are in fact three distinct ranges of hills, the Sierra Padrona, the Sierra del Viento and the Sierra Bajosa, none of which rises much above 750m. This area is rarely on the tourist trail, but is popular with *Sevillaños* at the weekends.

There are in fact two or three small towns well worth a visit for tourists with time on their hands, particularly if they have their own transport (local bus connections are poor at best and mostly non existent). The small town of **Constantina** goes back to Roman times and is said to have been named after the Emperor Constantine. There is a fascinating old quarter, the barrio de la Moreria, with a number of distinguished mansions. The parish church of Santa María de la Encarnación has a Mudéjar tower and a Plateresque doorway, while high above the town is a Medieval castle, the Castillo de la Armada. **Guadalcanal**, a further 35 km N, is another historic town situated in the irrigated valley of the Río Sotillo. There is the inevitable ruined castle and a fair stretch of the Medieval walls which still remain. The nearby Hermitage of Guaditoca is the venue of a popular local *romería*.

The main centre of the area is the small town of **Cazalla de la Sierra**, which is linked by daily bus to Sevilla. Occupied in turn by Iberians, Romans and the Moors (who called it *Kazalla*, meaning 'fortified town'), it has a number of historic buildings, including the massive parish church of Nuestra Señora de la Consolación. Today, Cazalla makes its living as a minor centre for agriculture and tourism and as one of the principal

locations for the production of *aguardiente*, a type of brandy made in the area since Roman times.

Much of the hilly area of the northern part of Sevilla province lies within the boundary of the **Parque Natural Sierra Norte**, which covers some 165,000 ha of the Sierra Morena. It's rounded hills are well wooded with Stone Pines, Holm Oaks and Cork Oaks, while the river valleys have stands of Sweet Chestnuts and Poplars. Although not ornithologically outstanding, a good range of raptors can be expected in the summer, including Black and Griffon Vultures, Golden and Booted Eagles and Red Kite. Both Black and White Storks breed. The Wild Boar, Fallow Deer, Rabbits, etc, are widely hunted, while other mammals include the Otter and Wild Cat. There is a Natural Park Reception Centre at Constantina, where details are available regarding walking trails, trout fishing, hire of bikes and horses, and non motorized watersports on the El Pintado reservoir.

● **Accommodation The Sierra Norte**: accommodation is sparse in the N of the province. There is nothing for example at Guadacanal and just one *pensión* in Constantina. Cazalla de la Sierra is the best bet: **A** *Villas Turística de Cazalla*, Ctra de Constantina, Km 3, T 4883308, F 4883312, 39 self catering apartments built in a complex in traditional style, hotel services incl restaurant, indoor and outdoor pool, tennis, bikes and horses for hire; **B** *Posada El Moro*, Paseo El Moro s/n, T 4884326, 15 rm, pool; **E** *La Milagrosa*, C/Llana 29, T 4884260, 6 rm. **Something different**: **B** *Monasterio Cartuja*, Ctra de Constantina, Cazalla de la Sierra, T 4884516, 8 rm, restored Carthusian monastery where pilgrims to Santiago de Compostela once stayed. The monastery's hostel is now the restaurant; family atmosphere, monthly concerts.

There is a choice of parallel roads heading **South from Sevilla** towards Cádiz – the A4 *autovia*, which is a toll road and therefore scarcely used by Andalucíans, and the NIV which is a dual carriageway

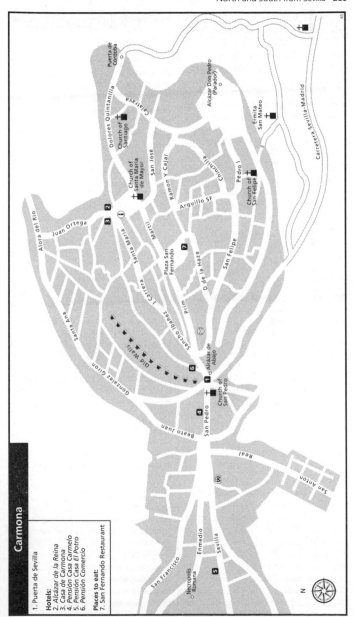

Carmona

1. Puerta de Sevilla

Hotels:
2. Alcázar de la Reina
3. Casa de Carmona
4. Pensión Casa Carmelo
5. Pensión Casa El Potro
6. Pensión Comercio

Places to eat:
7. San Fernando Restaurant

for the whole distance. As the rolling agricultural landscape is generally as dull as the towns of **Dos Hermanas, Los Palacios y Villafranca** and **Las Cabezas de San Juan** (which are thankfully by-passed), there is little reason to stop.

Bird watchers, however, could be tempted by the **Brazo del Este Natural Park**, located between the town of Los Palacios y Villafranca and the Río Guadalquivir. This small site of little over a thousand hectares is located along a former course of the Guadalquivir, which is now a winding reed fringed lagoon, surrounded by rice fields and drainage ditches. Although little visited, this is a superb spot for water birds and probably the best reserve in Andalucía for observing Purple Gallinules. There is a wide range of breeding herons and bitterns, along with rarities such as Little and Spotted Crakes and Collared Pratincole. The reed beds hold Savi's Warblers and Great Reed Warblers. Access is from Exit 3 on the Sevilla-Cádiz *autovia*.

EAST FROM SEVILLA

Two main routeways lead E from Sevilla across the rich undulating farming landscape known as **La Campiña**. The NIV, now an *autovia* for the full distance to Córdoba, by-passes, after 35 km, the ancient town of **Carmona** and then later, on the borders of the province, the town of **Éjica**. The more south-easterly route, the N334 leads to Antequera and Málaga, by passing **Osuna** and **Estepa**, while diversions from this road lead to **Utrera** to the S and **Marchena** to the N. It is tempting to speed along the *autovias* between the major cities, but all of these ancient towns are worth a visit, if time permits.

CARMONA

(*Pop* 23,613; *Alt* 248m)

ACCESS Train There is no railway to Carmona, the nearest station being in Sevilla, as is the nearest airport.
Road   Communications, however, are good, especially via the N IV *autovia*. The Casal company runs a frequent bus service from Sevilla along this route, stopping outside the rather dingy *La Parada* bar on Carmona's main street.

Situated 33 km E of Sevilla on a promontory of the Alcores Hills, Carmona is a picturesque town overlooking the Guadalquivir basin and surrounded by fertile farmland devoted to olives and cereals. It has remained largely unaffected by its proximity to, and easy communications with, Andalucía's capital city.

History
Archaeological remains show that settlement in Carmona goes back to Palaeolithic times, but the most important of the early settlers were the Carthaginians during the 3rd century. The Romans then conquered the town in 206 BC, naming it *Carmo*. It became one of the major fortified towns of the *Baetica* province of the Roman Empire, when most of Carmona's ancient walls were built. The

town achieved its greatest splendour under the Moors, who led by Muza Ben Nosair laid siege to Carmona for some time, taking over after negotiations allowing the Jewish community to remain. (The Jewish presence continued until the 16th century and greatly aided the town's prosperity.) The Moors rebuilt the Roman walls and gateways and constructed two *alcázares* and several mosques. After the collapse of the Córdoba Caliphate, Carmona became capital of its own *taifa* (or small kingdom), until its capture by Fernando III during the Reconquest in 1247.

It was later a favourite residence of Pedro the Cruel, who built a country palace within the castle. In 1630, it was given the status of a city by Philip IV, on the payment of 40,000 ducats. 2 centuries later, horsemen from Carmona played a prominent part in defeating Napoleon's elite Dragoons in the crucial Battle of Bailén.

Places of interest

The two Moorish *alcázares* still stand. The **Alcázar de Arriba** (Upper Palace-Fortress) was extended by both the Almoravids and the Almohads before the building of Pedro's palace. A large part of the structure was destroyed in the earthquakes of 1504 and 1755, leaving only the entrance gate and three towers. In 1976 it was tastefully rebuilt as a *parador* in the style of a Moorish palace. Entry is through an impressive Moorish horseshoe arch and there are some stunning views from the rooms over the surrounding countryside. If you are not keen to pay luxury prices for 4 star accommodation, this monument is best appreciated from the bar, although prices here are not in the budget range either. Just to the N of the *parador* is the **Puerta de Córdoba**, with two octagonal towers of largely Roman origin and marking a sudden end to the town, the old road to Córdoba now being little more than a rough track. The **Alcázar de Abajo** (Lower Palace-Fortress) includes the **Puerta de Sevilla**, a double archway with both Roman and Moorish elements. There is a small museum in the Alcázar, which is currently open on Fri and Sat mornings, entrance 175 ptas. Running N from here is a sizeable stretch of the old **walls** of Carmona.

On the corner of C/Santa María and C/San José is the Gothic 15th century **Church of Santa María de Mayor**. Built over the Moor's Great or Friday Mosque, which itself is believed to have been built over a Roman Temple of Hercules, it retains the Patio de Naranjas, with some fine horseshoe arches. The Mudéjar tower, with its pyramidal capping of tiles, may well contain some elements of the original minaret. The church has a rectangular floor plan with three naves and some intricate stellar vaulting. Note also the superb 16th century high altar and the Visigoth calendar marked on a pillar. Other churches of note are the **Iglesia de San Pedro**, with a 16th century Giralda look-alike tower dominating the main square, and the **Iglesia de San Felipe** which retains some of its original 14th century lancet arches and has a fine coffered ceiling.

Roman Necropolis Located to the W of the town outside the walls (as was the custom in Roman times) is a Roman burial ground which is unique in Spain and comparable only with some examples in Italy. To find the site, take C/San Pedro from the Puerta de Sevilla and proceed along C/Enmedio for some 500m. Excavation of the site, which began in 1881, has revealed over 1,000 tombs dating from the 2nd to the 4th centuries. Some 250 remain in their subterranean chambers and are often decorated with such motifs as birds and flowers. The larger tombs are massive. The most impressive is the *Tumba de Servilia*, named after the separate spaces for servants of the family. The *Tumba del Elefante* is named after a stone carved elephant and has a number of ante rooms which may well have been kitchens, etc, for use at funeral banquets.

There is also a small museum with statues, urns and mosaics. On the opposite side of the road is a modest amphitheatre which is still being excavated and not yet part of the guided tour. Open Jun-Sep, Tues-Sat 0900-1400, Sun 1000-1400; Oct-May, Tues-Fri 1000-1400 and 1600-1800, Sat and Sun 1000-1400. Entrance 250 ptas, free with EU passport.

Local festivals

Late Feb to early Mar, the *Carneval*, which dates back to the 18th century, is celebrated with children parading in fancy dress, dances and competitions. *Semana Santa* is along the lines of that in Sevilla with eight *confradias* (brotherhoods) involved in the processions; the *Feria de Mayo* takes place in mid-May and lasts 4 days. The *Romería de la Virgen de Gracia*, a pilgrimage to the shrine, takes place on the first Sun in Sep. Another pilgrimage, that of *San Mateo*, takes place around the *Ermita San Mateo* to mark the reconquest of Carmona by Fernando III in Sep 1247.

Local information
● **Accommodation**

There are only 5 *pensiones* and 4 hotels in Carmona. Most of the hotels are in the luxury range, while the *pensiones* are expensive for what they offer. Budget accommodation is almost non-existent.

AL *Alcázar de la Reina*, Plaza de Lasso 2, T 4190064, F 4142889, garage, a/c, pool; **AL** *Casa Palacio-Casa de Carmona*, Plaza de Lasso 1, T 4143300, F 4143752, 30 rm, garage, wheelchair access, a/c, pool, good facilities at this luxury hotel; **AL** *Parador Nacional del Rey Don Pedro*, C/Los Alcázares, T 4143300, F 4143752, 30 rm, garage, wheelchair access, a/c, pool, good views from most rooms at this historic site.

D *Casa Carmelo*, C/San Pedro 15, T 4140572, 6 rm, located nr the Puerta de Sevilla in newer part of town, formerly a casino; **D** *Comercio*, C/Torre del Oro 30, T 4140018, 14 rm, restaurant, clean, noisy cockerel next door.

There are a number of possibilities out of town along the *autovia*, but this will cause problems for those without transport: **B** *Palmero*, Ctra N IV, Km 523.7, T 4254945, F 4524946, 27

rm, a/c, pool; **D** *El Aguila*, Ctra Madrid-Cádiz, Km 520, T 4140014, 17 rm.

● **Places to eat**

♦♦♦ All the hotels listed above have good international restaurants. The *parador* serves, in addition, some local specialities such as marinaded partridge and Spinach *a la Carmona*. Another top of the range possibility is *El Ancla*, C/Bonifacio IV s/n, which serves excellent seafood.

♦ At the cheaper end of the spectrum, some of the *pensión* restaurants could be tried, along with some of the *tapas* bars, particularly those around Plaza San Pedro. There are 2 *ventas* on roads out of town which also offer cheap regional food: *Venta el Recreo*, Ctra Viso, Km 13, and *Venta el Tentaero*, Ctra Madrid-Cádiz, Km 506.

● **Banks & money changers**
On C/San Pedro in the newer part of town.

● **Hospital & medical services**
Emergencies: *Paseo de la Feria*, T 4140997, T 4140761.

Hospitals: *Cruz Roja*, Ctra de Madrid, T 4140751.

● **Post & telecommunications**
Post Office: *Correos*, C/ Prim 29, open 0900-1400. Telegraphs 0900-1500.

Telephones: no *locutorios*, but cabins may be found on Plaza San Fernando in the old town and C/San Fernando in the new town.

● **Tour companies & travel agents**
Triana Viajes, Paseo de Estatuto 6, T 4190745.

● **Tourist offices**
The *Oficina de Turismo* is inside the Casa de Cultura, open Mon-Fri 0800-1500 and Sat 0800-1500. The Casa de Cultura itself is open in the afternoon, so it may be possible to get information when the tourist office is closed.

● **Transport**
Local Taxis: Paseo del Estatuto, T 4141359.

Road Bus: casal buses run virtually every hour, on the hour, to **Sevilla** and back for only 240 ptas until 2200. The direct buses are more rapid. Check times at Bar La Parada or, during the summer, the attendant at the nearby ice cream kiosk will have a timetable too. Connections to other towns will have to be made via Sevilla.

ÉCIJA

Located some 52 km W of Córdoba and 54 km E of Carmona, Écija is a tempting half way stop. Sandwiched between the Río Genil and a range of hills, it is known as the 'City of Sun and Towers'. Records show that it is the hottest spot in the region, earning the description *la Sentenilla de Andalucía* – the frying pan of Andalucía. Sightseeing on a summer afternoon is definitely not recommended. There are some 11 towers, 15 bell towers, plus churches, palaces and belvederes which thrust up above the general level of white houses.

There has been a settlement here since Iberian times and it was later an important Roman town known as *Astigi*, which was basically an agricultural centre dealing with olive oil. In Moorish times it was part of the Caliphate of Córdoba, until overrun by Fernando III in 1240. Its main period of prosperity came in the 17th and 18th centuries, based on the *latifundia* or agricultural estates. The wealth produced did not come the way of the landless labourers, but poured into the hands of the landed nobility, who built magnificent mansions and *palacios* in Écija. The Lisbon earthquake destroyed most of the churches in the town, which were then assiduously rebuilt, which explains the large number of Baroque towers in Éjica.

Tourists on a short visit should make for the central Plaza de España, which has the benefit of shady trees, and from where all the major churches and palaces can be reached within minutes. The *ayuntamiento* is also located here and contains the tourist office, as well as a fine Roman mosaic. Most visitors will be content to just wander around and soak up the atmosphere, but make certain to see the church of San Juan Bautista, which has an ornate belfry in white stone – one of the few towers not capped with coloured tiles. Amongst the palaces, the most impressive is the huge Palacio de Peñaflor, with a pink marble portal and a curving balcony running the full length of the façade.

● **Accommodation** For those visitors wishing to stay over, there is a small but varied choice. More comfortable options incl: **B** *Platería*, C/Garcilópez 1A, T/F 4835010, 18 rm, a/c, wheelchair access, restaurant, best hotel in town tucked away in a small quiet side road; **B** *Astigi*, Ctra Madrid-Cádiz, Km 450, T 4830162, F 4835701, 18 rm, a/c, restaurant, disco, out of town. At the cheaper end of the range, there are a couple of *pensiones* close to the *autovia*, but the only budget option in the town centre which can be rec is the attractive, but spartan, **E** *Santa Cruz*, C/Practicante Romero Gordillo 8, T 4830222, 12 rm, nr the Plaza de España.

SEVILLA TO MALAGA PROVINCE

The N334 *autovia* from Sevilla to Málaga via Antequera provides several opportunities for brief stop offs and diversions. After some 30 km, the N333 leads SW to **Utrera**, a small town surrounded by olive groves and ranches rearing fighting bulls. Archaeological finds suggest that there was a settlement here in Chalcolithic times, while there are also Roman remains and a ruined Moorish fort. The parish Church of Santiago El Mayor was built towards the end of the 13th century and its impressive W doorway, the Puerta del Perdón, has some imposing 'barley-sugar' columns. Another church of significance is Santa María de la Mesa, dating from the 15th century and in largely Gothic style, with a Plateresque entrance which served as a model for many of the first churches built in the New World.

South of Utera at **El Palmar de Troya** is the Mount of Christ the King, the headquarters of Clemente, the bizarre, self-styled alternative Pope, Gregorio XVII. For those who are intrigued, there are tours of the building, which is reputed to have over 50 altars.

East of Utrera and some 20 km S of the

N334 is **Morón de la Frontera**, an ancient town which has had continuous settlement from Palaeolithic times to the present. Its Roman name was *Arunci*, but it has been known as Morón since the 3rd century. The ruined Moorish castle is, in fact, largely Medieval. Although destroyed by French troops in 1812, the surviving sections include a rampart walk linking 12 towers and two of the original five gates, plus a Moorish cistern. Near the castle is the Paseo del Gallo, from where there are superb views over the town. Before leaving, take a look at the Church of San Miguel, dating from 1503 in Gothic and Renaissance style, with a Giralda-type tower.

North of Morón and some 7 km N of the N334 is another ancient town, **Marchena**. Although going back to prehistoric times, it was the Moors who built its great walls and four gates, including the Puerta de Sevilla, the Arch of the Rose. After the Reconquest, the town was distinguished by the family of the Dukes of Arcos (which included the *conquistador* Ponce de León) who made Marchena a centre for artistic patronage. Don't miss the Church of San Juan Bautista, which dates from 1490. The remarkable *retablo* contains 14 panels by Alejo Fernández and an alabaster head of St John the Baptist dating from 1593. The church's museum has no fewer than nine paintings by Zurburán, plus the usual books, gold and silver.

The charming town of **Osuna** is located a further 35 km along the *autovia*. As with the neighbouring towns, it has an Iberian past, when it was known as *Urso*. An artefact, the 'Bull of Urso', dates from this time. It was also important in Roman times, when Caesar gave it the status of a colony. Although occupied by the Moors, it was of little importance, falling to the Christians in 1239. 300 years later it came into the hands of the Dukes of Osuna, particularly the Téllez Girón family, who founded many of the buildings still to be seen in the town today, including churches, mansions, the university and the Ducal Palace.

The hilltop above the town is dominated by two buildings, the old university and the collegiate church. The university, which was founded in 1548 by Juan Téllez Girón, is a rather austere, rectangular building in Italian Renaissance style with towers at its four corners and a central atrium. Its chapel displays a good collection of paintings and the main hall has a Mudéjar coffered ceiling. The Collegiate Church of Santa María de la Asunción was founded by the same man, who used some of the finest craftsmen in Sevilla for its construction. The cream stone building has five naves with round Renaissance arches. The main Plateresque door of the church, the Puerta del Sol, was damaged by French troops during the Peninsular War, but remains impressive. The church also has some fine sculptures and paintings, including a Crucifixion by Ribera. Next to the church is the gloomy Plateresque style pantheon which contains the tombs of the various Dukes of Osuna and their families. Visits are by guided tour only, Mon-Fri 1030-1330 and 1530-1900, Sat and Sun 1030-1330; 200 ptas.

Down in the town are a clutch of other churches and convents worth a visit, including the Church of La Merced, with a barrel vaulted ceiling, the Church of Santa Domingo and the Convent of Santa Catalina. There is also a small Archaeological Museum, based in the Torre del Agua, part of the original Almohad fortress, and containing largely local finds. Open 1000-1300 and 1600-1930, entrance 200 ptas.

● **Accommodation** There is a shortage of decent accommodation in Osuna, particularly in the old part of the town, although there are some possibilities close to the *autovia*. The best hotel is **B** *Villa Ducal*, Ctra 334 Sevilla-Málaga, Km 88, T 5820256, 23 rm, a/c, restaurant. Within the old town there is **C** *Caballo Blanco*, C/Granada 1, T 4810184, 14 rm, a/c, wheelchair access, recently renovated, good restaurant and **E** *Las Cinco Puertas*, C/Carrear 79, T 4811243, 15 rm, restaurant, best budget option.

The last historic town in the E part of Sevilla province is **Estepa**. Once a Carthaginain settlement known as *Astapa*, it was involved in the Punic Wars with the Romans, who captured the city in 208 BC. It was later occupied by the Moors, but there is little which remains from this early history, the town being essentially Baroque in character, with a number of churches and convents in this style, including the Iglesia del Carmen, the Iglesia de Santa María and the Iglesia de San Sebastián. Also of interest is the slim 18th century Torre de la Victoria, with some elegant and ornate stonework, which is all that remains of a convent of the same name.

Gibraltar

GIBRALTAR, 127 km southwest of Málaga, is a peninsula some 6.5 km in length and 2 km wide at its broadest point, with an altitude rising to 430m. It is joined to Spain by a low isthmus and separated from North Africa by the Straits of Gibraltar, some 13 km wide at their narrowest point and for this reason has been strategically important for centuries.

The atmosphere in Gibraltar was once like a British naval town set in the Mediterranean, but since the British forces left Gibraltar in 1991, leaving the Rock in the hands of the locally recruited Gibraltar Regiment, the ambience has changed somewhat. Cruise line passengers and tourists from the Costa del Sol have now replaced the British matelot in the pubs and shops of Main St and Gibraltar is struggling to develop its own identity through financial services and tourism.

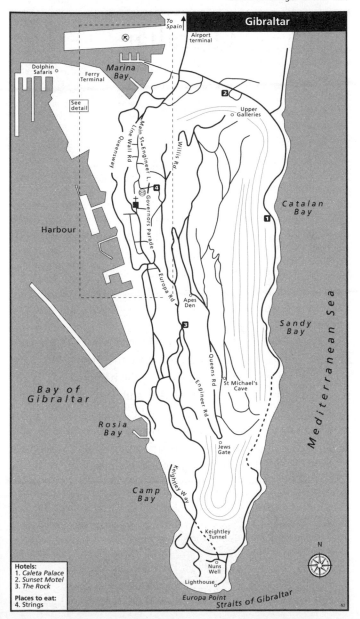

Gibraltar

To Spain

Airport
terminal

Marina
Bay

Dolphin
Safaris

Ferry
Terminal

See detail

Upper
Galleries

Willis Rd.

Line Wall Rd.

Main St

Engineer L.

Governors Parade

Queensway

Harbour

Europa Rd

Apes
Den

Catalan
Bay

Mediterranean Sea

Sandy
Bay

Bay of
Gibraltar

Rosia
Bay

Queens Rd

Engineer Rd

St Michael's
Cave

Jews
Gate

Camp
Bay

Keightley Way

Keightley
Tunnel

N

Nuns
Well

Lighthouse

Europa Point   Straits of Gibraltar

Hotels:
1. *Caleta Palace*
2. *Sunset Motel*
3. *The Rock*

Places to eat:
4. Strings

HORIZONS

The town clusters around the lower slopes on the west side, spreading further west in recent years on reclaimed land. It has a population of around 30,000, of which 20,000 are native Gibraltarians, 6,000 are expatriate Britons and the remainder guestworkers from Morocco or EU countries. However, since the border was reopened in 1985 many Gibraltarians now live in Spain and commute back over the border daily to their work. The Moroccans, who were brought over to work in the dockyards when the border with Spain was closed, now find that they have little work or employment protection. They have mounted a permanent protest outside Government House. The Gibraltarians themselves come from a variety of backgrounds – Spanish, British, Maltese, Jewish, Moroccan and Genoese – and while English is the official language, they will often mix English and Spanish (even within the same sentence) in a curious dialect known as *llanito*. In fact, the mainland Spanish often refer to Gibraltarians as *llanitos*.

ACCESS Air Gibraltar airport was built in WW2 on reclaimed land and a feature of the road into town is that it passes over the runway, which is shared with the RAF, and traffic is stopped as each plane lands and takes off. Only British airlines use the airport and there are no flights to Spain.
Train The nearest train stations are at San Roque and Algeciras, with connections to Málaga, Cádiz and other Andalucían cities.
Road The town itself is accessible by taxi or a 70p/35 ptas bus ride from outside the airport terminal, which is also just beyond the border control. On the Spanish side, the La Linea bus station is a short walk from the border crossing and connections can be made to the towns of the Costa del Sol and other Andalucían cities. **NB** Visitors arriving by car should seriously consider parking at La Linea and walking over the border as there can be very long delays in each direction because of customs action. Ignore rough looking characters on the La Linea side of the border who wish to park and guard your car, as they have no authority whatsoever. A pay and display car park on the E side of the entrance gates, opposite the air terminal, costs 100 ptas an hour. In Gibraltar town, the best bets for parking are at the car park at the cable car terminal at the N end of Main St and next to the war memorial sports ground on the W side of the town where there is a small multi storey car park. Approach both of these car parks via Queensway, NOT through Main St, which is largely pedestrianized. To circumnavigate the Rock via the E side, turn left at the first roundabout after crossing the runway.

The **climate** of Gibraltar is milder and windier than the Costa del Sol. Midday temperatures average 14°C in Jan and 22°C in Jul. The *levante*, an E wind, forces cloud onto the summit of the Rock, increasing humidity and ensuring higher rainfall figures than in neighbouring Spain. There are no rivers or streams in Gibraltar and as the rock is entirely a grey, permeable, Jurassic limestone, it is necessary to collect water via enormous concrete catchments on the E side of the peninsula.

HISTORY

Discoveries during the last century of prehistoric remains in a cave on the North Face of the Rock, have now been shown to be of Neanderthal Age. More recently, another cave has been excavated on the S of the Rock, near Europa Point. Known as Gorham's Cave, it has provided archaeologists with remains dating from up to 100,000 years ago, including bones of hyena, deer, tortoises and tuna. In later times the Phoenicians knew Gibraltar as *Calpe* (note the similarity with the *Penon* at Calpe on the Costa Blanca) and in Greek mythology it formed, along with Mount Ablya on the other side of the Straits, the twin pillars of Hercules. It is doubtful if either the Carthaginians or the Romans had a settlement on the Rock, but the Phoenicians had a town called *Carteia* some 3 km away at the head of Gibraltar Bay. It was from *Carteia*, in 45 AD, that Julius Caesar left to defeat the Carthaginian forces at the Battle of Munda.

Moorish influence in the area began in 711 AD, when Tarik Ibn Zeyed invaded the mainland to start his campaign against the Visigoths. He named the Rock *Gibel Tarik* (or Tarik's Mountain), which has corrupted over time into Gibraltar. Later, under the Almohads, around 1160, Caliph Abdul Mamen constructed some defensive works, reservoirs and a mosque. Gibraltar stayed in Moorish hands until a surprise attack by the Spanish, led by Guzmán el Bueno in 1309, but within 25 years it was regained by the Moors led by the Sultan of Fez after a siege of 4½ months.

The Moors were finally evicted from the Rock in 1462 by the Spanish led by the Duke of Medina Sedonia. They were to stay for a further 240 years until the War of the Spanish Succession. Although Britain supported the Spanish against the French, Gibraltar was taken by a combined Anglo Dutch fleet in 1704 led by Admiral Rooke. The inhabitants were told that they had to support the claimant to the Spanish throne, Archduke Charles of Austria, or leave the Rock. Many did leave and founded a settlement at nearby San Roque, fully expecting to return shortly. Britain, however, gained formal sovereignty over the Rock in the Treaty of Utrecht in 1713 and has remained there ever since, despite Spain's diplomatic and military attempts to regain it.

The most serious attempts came in 1779 when the Great Siege was to last for over 3½ years. During this period the garrison used red hot shot for the first time in warfare. At the start of the next century, Gibraltar's strategic position was fully utilized during the Napoleonic Wars. After Nelson's victory at nearby Cape Trafalgar, his flagship HMS Victory limped into Rosia Bay, with the Admiral's body pickled in a barrel of rum. A number of the crew were buried in the Trafalgar cemetery at the N end of Main St.

Gibraltar played an important strategic role in both World Wars, but particularly the Second, when Hitler formalized Operation Felix, which was a plan to invade the Rock, a scheme which never materialized. During these times the Rock became honeycombed with passages and caverns (augmenting the existing caves) for the storage of ammunition and other arms, making a formidable fortress guarding the Western entrance to the Mediterranean. It was during the Second World War that Winston Churchill, on hearing the legend that if the Barbary Apes left the Rock, then the British would too, insisted for propaganda reasons that their number should never fall below 35.

In the post war period, Franco continued to try to persuade the British to give up the Rock, but in a number of referendums the Gibraltarians have always staunchly wished to remain British. Franco eventually closed the border in 1965, however this only served to make the *llanitos* even more anti-Spanish. After the death of Franco and the entry of Spain into the Common Market, the borders were re-opened in 1985. Controversy, however, continues. In 1988, the SAS killed three suspected IRA terrorists at the Shell petrol station a stones throw from the border, and although there had been some collaboration with the Spanish police, the incident did little to enhance cooperation between the two countries. In recent years, since the departure of the British forces, Gibraltar has made attempts to create some economic independence by forming a sort of financial Isle of Man in the Mediterranean, with mixed results. Accusations of taking a casual attitude towards 'money laundering', plus the crash of BCCI, did not help and many expats on the Costa del Sol lost their life savings as a result. In the early

1990's, relations with Spain took another turn for the worse with the activities of the young Gibraltarian cigarette and drug smugglers, whose fast speedboats proved a difficult target for the Spanish Civil Guard. The election of a new Chief Minister, Peter Caruana, in 1996, may help matters. Although committed to maintaining ties with Britain, he wishes to improve relations with Spain and has promised to clamp down on the activities of the smugglers.

'Smugglers paradise'

Stop at traffic lights in any Andalucían city and the chances are that you will be approached by young men selling cartons of cigarettes. As the Andalucíans are mostly enthusiastic and life long smokers, the cartons do not remain unsold for long. The vendors, known as *Winstonistas*, will almost certainly be selling contraband cigarettes which have entered Spain through Gibraltar. The Spanish tobacco industry is state controlled and the government claims that it is losing hundreds of millions of pesetas annually to the illegal trade from Gibraltar.

The method is no secret. Gibraltar imports vast quantities of cigarettes from USA, 90% of which are exported illegally to Spain, where a packet of Winstons costs around £1.40 as compared with 54p in Gibraltar. The smuggling is carried out by young men known as the 'Winston Boys' using fast speed boats, painted matt black so that they are almost invisible at night. They land the goods on the beach at La Atunara, a seedy fishing village on the far side of La Linea, where they are speedily secreted away. A cargo of 1,000 cartons can earn a profit of £5,000 – not bad for a night's work. The reason for the growth of smuggling is clearly linked with the closure of Gibraltar's Naval dockyard, which once employed 70% of the colony's 13,000 workforce. Now there is an unemployment rate of 11% and a recent estimate claimed that with 250 speedboats operating, over 1,000 Gibraltarians would be involved directly or indirectly in smuggling. Spain's Guardia Civil, of course, try to stop the smuggling, but have achieved only limited success. In a recent attempt to stop a cargo at La Atunara they were pelted with stones and iron bars and had to make an ignominious retreat. The Guardia Civil's helicopters have frequent running battles with the speedboats and there have been fatalities on both sides.

Even more serious has been the move towards the smuggling of drugs from Morocco. The drug runners favourite vessel for this work is the RIB – the inflatables of the type used by the SAS which are capable of speeds up to 70 mph and which can out run any of the boats used by the Gibraltar or Spanish authorities. Little wonder that articles have appeared in the British press suggesting that Gibraltar is a 'smugglers paradise'.

In addition to the smuggling problem there are also accusations of money laundering. Gibraltar has still to comply with over 50 EU directives on a variety of matters. This has created a situation whereby Gibraltar earns little sympathy from either Britain or Spain. The new Chief Minister, Peter Caruana, has promised a clampdown on smuggling, saying that "it is time that Gibraltar stopped being a byword for corruption and contraband". Meanwhile Spain continues its tactic of trying to smother Gibraltar into submission, complaining loudly about the smuggling (though far more drugs and tobacco enter Spain via other routes) and using this to justify its long border delays – an action which simply makes Gibraltarians dig in their heels even more.

PLACES OF INTEREST

The oldest buildings and monuments in Gibraltar are **Moorish**. The most obvious, but not the best Moorish location, is the **Castle**. It was built in 1333, probably on the site of an earlier fortress which may have dated from soon after Tarik's initial occupation of the area in 711 AD. Originally, the castle's defences stretched down the edge of the town where Casemates Gate now stands, but they were destroyed in the various sieges. The main part of the castle remaining is the **Tower of Homage**, the walls of which are pitted with some of the scars inflicted during the various local conflicts. The castle can be viewed from the road above it, while below it is hemmed in by recently built blocks of flats. Entry, however, is not permitted as the castle functions today as Gibraltar's prison and the roof overlooks the exercise yard. At the lower end of the old walls is an ancient gatehouse and nearby is **Stanley's Tower**, originally built in 1160 AD, but renovated several times since. Its clock dates from 1845.

The main location in Gibraltar for any student of Moorish history, however, is to be found in the Museum, where there are some superbly preserved **Moorish Baths**. They are approached from Room 1 of the museum (containing archaeological remains) which leads into the Main Hall of the baths. It is best to start a tour by moving to the Entrance Hall, a room which is thought to have originally been twice its present size, the southern half having been destroyed during the Great Siege. Part of the main flue or hypocaust has been uncovered, which links with the furnace at the E end of the baths. Note, too, the star-shaped apertures in the roof and a vent in the wall which would have let out the steam. Here bathers were given buckets of water to throw over themselves before proceeding into the Main Hall. Here there is a central dome over a series of horseshoe arches, the columns of which are of particular interest, four being Moor-

ish, one Roman and the other three Visigothic. This mixed bag was probably brought here from other sites in the vicinity. The Main Hall originally contained private cubicles for changing and relaxing. Next is a Cold Room, with higher ceilings to retain the cooler temperatures, and containing shallow cold and tepid baths. The next room to the E is the Hot Room, which is entered through a large round arch. It is believed that the steam bath was located at the N end and the hot plunge bath on the southern side. Some of the original lead piping may still be seen and the whole area is in a good state of preservation. Opening times are the same as for the Museum and the tour is included in the entrance fee.

The only other Moorish remnant is the **Nuns Well**, opposite the entrance to Keighley's Tunnel, near Europa Point. The Well is, in fact, an underground Moorish cistern, but acquired its name from the nuns who tended the nearby **Shrine of Our Lady of Europa**. This Shrine is built on the site of a mosque and was made into a Catholic chapel in the mid 15th century. The Image of Our Lady was guarded by a permanent light. Despite being desecrated by both the Turks and the British, the Shrine remains and there is a pilgrimage to the spot each 5 May (Europe Day). Close to the Shrine is a small patch of Moorish pavement. The nearby **Europa Point** has a lighthouse and an observation platform which makes an excellent place for viewing dolphins and migrating seabirds – all with a backdrop of the North African coast when the visibility is clear. The lighthouse, which is 150-years-old and rises to a height of 50m, is the only lighthouse outside of Britain which is regulated by Trinity House.

To view the features of the Upper Rock, it is best to take the **Cable Car**. The lower station is located in Rosia Rd close to the Alemeda Botanical Gardens and the Bristol Hotel. Choose a day when there is no cloud cover on the top of the Rock. The service is open 0930-1715, weather conditions permitting, closed Sun. Fares: adults £4.90, children under 10, £2.45. A £9.20 ticket includes a luncheon voucher for the restaurant at the top, but this is not a good bargain if the visibility is poor. When the conditions are right, the view from the top of the rock can be superb with vistas of the Costa del Sol, Algeciras Bay and the mountains of Morocco. There is a midway stop on the cable car at the **Apes Den**. The so called Barbary Apes (*Macaca sylvanus*) are in fact a species of tail less monkey, the only ones on the mainland of Europe (which is something to be grateful for!). Legend has it that they arrived in Gibraltar via an underground tunnel from Morocco, but the truth is that they were imported for pets by British soldiers and some inevitably escaped. They live in two packs, one at the Apes Den and the other living on the steep slopes of Middle Hill. Visitors are warned not to feed the apes or make sudden movements, as they are not as loveable as they look. Take care also of valuables such as cameras, which the apes take great delight in stealing.

A short walk from the Apes Den leads one to **St Michael's Cave**, which is basically a huge cavern containing all the usual features one expects in a limestone area, such as stalagmites, stalactites, pillars and flow structures, all sympathetically lit. This cave is just one of a whole maze of natural and man-made caves which honeycomb the Rock. During WW2, the cave was prepared for use as a field hospital, but was fortunately never required for this purpose. Today, the main cavern is frequently used as an auditorium for concerts. There are also small dioramas with full sized models of both Neanderthal and Neolithic Man. Experienced pot holers and cavers can, with written permission, explore the Lower St Michaels Caves, where there are over 2 km of passages and a large subterranean lake.

On the North Face of the Rock, overlooking Spain, are some man made passages, known as the **Upper Galleries**. They were constructed during the time of the Great Siege (1779-1783) by British engineers as gun emplacements, ensuring the rock's impregnability. Open 1000-1900 in summer and 1000-1730 in winter.

MORE PLACES OF INTEREST IN GIBRALTAR TOWN

Gibraltar is well supplied with defensive **walls**, **gates** and **fortifications**. Running along the W side of the rock, following the old Moorish sea wall, is **Line Wall**. It stretches from Casemates to Rosia Bay and has been refaced in Portland Limestone, the local limestone being too brittle for this use. It is interesting to note that all the land between the wall and the sea is reclaimed land. The other important wall is **Charles V Wall**, stretching from the S end of Line Wall up to the old Moorish wall. There are two gates in Charles V's Wall, both overlooking the Trafalgar Cemetery. The **Southport Gate** was originally built in 1552, probably on the site of Tarik's original fortifications. It is now a series of gates, one for pedestrians bearing the Spanish royal arms and the other, used by traffic, has arms of Britain, Gibraltar and the then Governor. The most recent series of gates commemorates the referendum of 1967, when the Gibraltarians opted to retain their links with Britain. Higher up, **Prince Edward's Gate**, dating from 1790, is named after Queen Victoria's father. The **Ragged Staff Gates**, near the main entrance to the dockyard, are thought to have gained their name from the crest of Charles V. Finally, at the N end of main street, are the **Casemates**, which have always been the main land defence for over 6 centuries. They were rebuilt extensively after the Great Siege.

The Governor's Residence is still commonly known as 'The Convent' as it

Quickie marriages

👣 Marriage may be out of fashion these days, but if your holiday romance on the Costa is going well and you decide on the spur of the moment to cement the relationship, then Gibraltar might be the place for you. The colony has special regulations which allow 'quickie marriages' by Governor's Special Licence for non-residents.

All you have to do is to prove that you are not married to someone else (which might be difficult if all your documentation is at home 1,000 miles away) and to swear an affidavit at the Gibraltar Registry Office. The paperwork can be completed in 2 days. The cost is £57, which includes the marriage certificate and the ceremony. Well, if Sean Connery took advantage of the regulations, why shouldn't you?

For further details, contact the Marriage Registrar, Marriage Registry, 277 Main St, Gibraltar, T 72289.

was once a monastery of the Franciscan friars. It is an imposing brick and stone Gothic style building with two 'Dutch Ends' and a square Portland stone doorway with roof. It became the official residence of the chief British officer in 1704, before the friars were evicted 8 years later. The 16th century cloisters remain intact, but unfortunately the building is not open to visitors. A colourful Changing of the Guard ceremony takes place monthly outside the residence. (Another tradition, the Ceremony of the Keys, takes place three times a year in Casemates Square.) The convent's Chapel of St Francis was renamed **Kings Chapel** and became the garrison's main C of E place of worship. Worth visiting, the Chapel has the colours of various British regiments plus the tombs of a number of Governors, both Spanish and English.

The Gibraltar Parliament now sits in the **House of Assembly**, which was the old Exchange and Commercial Library. Unfortunately its dignity is somewhat lowered by the plethora of tatty cafes surrounding the building.

PLACES OF WORSHIP

The numerous places of worship reflect the varied background of the Gibraltarians. The oldest building is the Catholic **Cathedral of St Mary the Crowned**. Built on the site of a mosque, some of the early Moorish structures can still be seen, particular on the S side of the building. It was badly damaged during the Great Siege and has been extensively rebuilt, with an imposing yellow and white classical façade and sturdy bell tower. The Anglican **Cathedral of the Holy Trinity** was not built until 1825 and consecrated as a cathedral in 1838. Located in Cathedral Square, it has an extraordinary design, dominated strangely by Moorish style horseshoe arches. The **Great Synagogue**, *Shahar Hashhamayim* in Engineer Lane was founded in 1724, but was destroyed by floods in 1744 and then later during the Great Siege. The present building, for the 750 Jews in Gibraltar today, dates from 1768 and has a Flemish style bell gable.

MUSEUMS

The **Gibraltar Museum** is located in Bomb House Lane, off Cathedral Square, in a reconstructed 14th century building which was formerly officers' quarters. It was chosen as the place for a museum because it was known that Moorish baths lay underneath the site. Rooms 1 and 2 consist of archaeological material covering the Paleolithic to the Moorish periods. The museum's most important archaeological exhibit is now in London's natural History Museum. This is a female skull discovered in Forbes Quarry on the North Front of the Rock in 1848. Its significance was not realized at the time, but modern dating techniques have revealed that it is of Neanderthal age. As the tour guides like to point out, Neanderthal Man should really have been Gibraltar Woman. Other rooms deal with Geology, Zoology and Botany, concentrating on local specimens. In Room 7 is one of the Museum's proudest possessions – an enormous model of Gibraltar as it was in 1850 at a scale of 1:600. It is particularly interesting to see the old Moorish walls before they were swallowed up by the high rise flats. Note, too, how the sea came right up to the town wall before the harbour was constructed in 1894. The displays are completed with sections showing local paintings, a room devoted to the Great Siege and a collection of arms, shot and shell occupying the staircase.

The Museum, which is larger than it appears from the outside, presents a video show every hour, entitled 'The Gibraltar Story'. The Museum is open Mon-Sat 1000-1800, Sat 1000-1400. Entrance £2.00, children £1.00. The Museum is also the main Tourist Information Office. Most items have to be bought.

OFFICIAL TOURS The Gibraltar National Tourist Board has sanctioned an **'Official Rock Tour'** which can be taken by taxi or mini bus with the drivers acting as informative guides. The tours start at a number of points in the town and the route initially goes down the E side of the Rock, stopping at **Catalan Bay** to view the **Water Catchments** before proceeding to the **lighthouse** at Europa point at the southern tip of the peninsula. The route then climbs up to the **Jews Gate** viewpoint. There is then a 30-min stop at **St Michael's Cave** and a further 10 mins at the **Apes Den**. There is an optional stop at the **Upper Galleries**, but many drivers miss this out, before returning to the place of departure. The tour, which takes approximately 90 mins, makes an excellent introduction to Gibraltar, although serious visitors with their own transport might wish to take longer, but would have to cope with the stressful driving conditions on the Upper Rock. Current prices are £16 for a taxi with four people, minibuses £5 pp. Information from Bland Travel, T 79200.

Note that much of the Upper Rock area is unsuitable for wheelchair users, despite the fact that such people are given free entrance to all places on the Official Tour.

WILDLIFE ON THE ROCK

Independent travellers may be tempted to drive up to the well advertised **Upper Rock Nature Reserve**. If you expect to see way marked nature trails, hides, etc you will be disappointed. Narrow roads lead to a kiosk from which there is no escape from a charge of £3. High stone walls and speeding taxis and minibuses shut out any wildlife. Your ticket entitles you to free entry to the Cave and the Apes Den, but if you have already visited them on the 'Official Tour', the term 'rip-off' readily springs to mind. All is not lost for naturalists, however, for the top of the Rock is an excellent place for observing the migration of eagles, vultures and storks during spring and autumn, particularly when the wind is from the W. There is also an **Information Centre** at Jews Gate, jointly administered by a clutch of local environmental organizations. Birders are usually welcome here, as news of sightings can be passed on. There is a limited amount of walking which can be done from the top of the cable car, before precipitous slopes and old gun emplacements put an end to this activity. One of the best ways of seeing some of the wildlife of the upper Rock is to take the cable car to the top and then walk down via some of the quieter lanes and steps.

Much of the upper Rock is comprised of either bare rock or scrub consisting of

Lottery money 19th century style

👣 The **Botanical Gardens** in Gibraltar are only a few years old. Correction. They are nearly 180-years-old, because for most of this time they have been known as the **Alameda Gardens**. What is more, as well the collection of plants, the gardens also have a fascinating history.

They were laid out in 1815 and were the brainchild of the Governor at that time, Lieutenant General Sir George Don (whose tomb may be seen at the Cathedral of the Holy Trinity). To pay for the gardens, Don had the bright idea of legalising lotteries in the colony. Some eight lotteries were held, which soon raised the required money, whereupon Don promptly made lotteries illegal again.

There are features in the Botanical Gardens, however, which go back much later in history. In the lower part, for instance, one can see a small stone ventilation tower which was part of an old Moorish aqueduct. Elsewhere in the gardens are two 18 ton guns which go back to Victorian times. In the upper area there is a memorial to the Duke of Wellington, erected in 1819 and paid for by deducting one day's pay from every soldier currently serving on the Rock – another of Don's money raising ploys. It was little wonder that soldiers often mutinied in those days and ironically the gardens were laid out on the spot where mutineers were often hung. Amongst other features of the gardens are a fountain which is over 150-years-old and a whalebone arch which no doubt originated from the whaling station which used to operate in nearby Algeciras.

Most visitors of course will have come to see the plants – and they will not be disappointed. As well as native Gibraltar specimens, there are flowers, shrubs and trees from other parts of the world which have a similar 'Mediterranean' climate, such the Cape region of South Africa, Perth in Australia, Madeira and the Canary Islands. Particularly impressive when in flower are the numerous Dragon Trees from Tenerife.

The Botanical Gardens are situated on the W side of Europa Rd, next to the Cable Car Station. Entrance is free and in the cool shade of a hot summers day, visitors will be grateful to Governor Don and his lottery money.

dwarf olives, fan palms and broom, with Aleppo Pines at lower levels. Breeding **birds** include Peregrines (which nest on the North Face), Blue Rock Thrush, Scops Owl and Alpine Swift. A target for twitchers will be the Barbary Partridge (Gibraltar is the only place in mainland Europe where it is found). The place to head for is the Mediterranean Steps, a precipitous circular walk from Jews Gate. Migration time can be very exciting, contributing to the 270 odd species of birds recorded at Gibraltar. There is a good range of wild **flowers** from Christmas onwards, including paper white narcissus, Giant Squill and wild Gladioli and wild Iris. Amongst the more exotic butterflies are the Painted lady, Spanish Festoon, Cleopatra, Swallowtail and the enormous Two-tailed Pasha. There are plenty of lizards and geckoes, but **mammals**, apart from the Rabbit and the two groups of Barbary apes, are elusive.

Wildlife enthusiasts may also be interested in Mike Lawrence's **Dolphin Safari**, which has figured on a number of TV programmes. Trips are on a 30 ft catamaran and leave Sheppard's Marina daily, except Mon, at 1000, 1230 and 1500 between May and Oct and last around 2½ hrs. Price £17 for adults and £8 for children, with money returned if no dolphins are seen. Booking is essen-

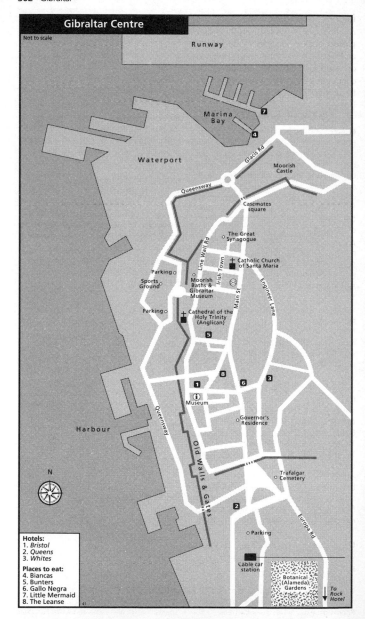

Gibraltar Centre

Not to scale

Runway

Marina Bay

7

4

Waterport

Glacis Rd

Moorish Castle

Queensway

Casemates square

The Great Synagogue

Line Wall Rd

Catholic Church of Santa Maria

Parking

Irish Town

Engineer Lane

Sports Ground

Moorish Baths & Gibraltar Museum

Main St

Parking

Cathedral of the Holy Trinity (Anglican)

5

8

1

6

3

Museum

Governor's Residence

Harbour

Queensway

N

Old Walls & Gates

Trafalgar Cemetery

2

Parking

Europa Rd

Cable car station

Botanical (Alameda) Gardens

To Rock Hotel

Hotels:
1. *Bristol*
2. *Queens*
3. *Whites*

Places to eat:
4. Biancas
5. Bunters
6. Gallo Negra
7. Little Mermaid
8. The Leanse

tial as seats are limited to 12, T 71914. Apart from the resident Common Dolphins, there is a chance to see Striped and Bottlenosed Dolphins and even an occasional Whale. There is an excellent commentary and great views of the Rock from the sea.

LOCAL INFORMATION

● Accommodation

Hotels in Gibraltar are generally more expensive than comparable hotels in Spain. A number of hotels claim to be in the 'luxury' grade, but travellers used to this category may be disappointed. There is little available at the cheaper end of the range and those looking for budget accommodation should consider the *pensiones* in La Linea on the Spanish side of the border.

A *Caleta Palace*, Catalan Bay Rd, T 76501, F 71050, modern hotel on the E side of the Rock, 167 rm, some package tours, sandy beach, pool, restaurant, garage; **A** *The Rock Hotel*, Europa Rd, T 73000, F 73515, 146 rm, TV, garage, pool, restaurant, located on the W side of the rock in a landscaped garden in the best colonial tradition; **A** *Whites* (formerly the Holiday Inn), Governors Parade, T 70500, F 70243, 123 rm, recently refurbished but still with the usual international sterility, pool, jacuzzi, sauna, TV, restaurant.

There are more modest hotels in the town centre incl: **C** *Queens*, 1 Boyd St, T 74000, F 40030, conveniently placed for the cable car, shopping and the Botanical Gardens; **C** *Bristol*, 10 Cathedral Square, T 76800, F 77613, 60 rm, centrally situated, pool, gardens, sauna, TV, restaurant; **C** *Sunset Motel*, 60 Devils Tower Rd, T 41265, F 41245, located beneath the N cliff of the Rock and convenient for the airport, built in 1991 with 36 well fitted rm, but few other facilities; **C** *Montarik*, 1 Bedlam Court, T 77065, central location overlooking Main St, can be noisy, good value; **C** *Continental*, 1 Engineer Lane, T 76900, F 41702, TV, a/c, central location.

D *Gibraltar Beach*, Sandy Bay, T 76191, self catering aparthotel right on the sea.

F *Toc H Hostel*, at the very end of Line Wall Rd, T 73431; try here if you really must stay in Gibraltar on a budget, but at around £11 a night they are almost certainly fully booked. Rooms generally let on a weekly basis.

This list covers just about all the accommodation in Gibraltar – except the prison. Sleeping rough on the beaches is frowned upon by the local police who carry out regular checks in the summer.

Camping: there is literally no room for a camp site in Gibraltar. The nearest sites in Spain are at Algeciras to the W and Manilva in the NE.

● Places to eat

Unlike the accommodation situation, budget travellers will have no problem in Gibraltar when it comes to cheap food. There are numerous pubs, most of which serve some sort of food, usually with an English flavour. The pubs in Main St, such as *The Angry Friar*, *The Royal Calpe* and *The Gibraltar Arms* are inevitably a magnet for both shoppers and tourists, but *The Clipper* in Irishtown and *Sir Winston's Tavern* in Cornwalls Parade are equally good. Passable restaurants, however, have to be searched out.

♦♦♦*Bunters*, 1 College Lane, T 70482, sophisticated international *menú* plus traditional English desserts, fairly expensive, evenings only; ♦♦♦*Strings*, 44 Cornwalls Lane, T 78800, international *menú*, incl Moroccan dishes, closed Mon, fairly expensive, booking advisable; ♦♦♦*The Peacock*, Bell Lane, T 40064, aimed at the lunch time business community, good fresh fish and Gibraltarian dishes.

♦♦*Biancas*, Marina Bay, T 73379, specializes in pizzas, appeals to a youthful clientele, excellent harbour views; ♦♦*Country Cottage*, 13-15 Giros Passage, T 70084, old English cuisine incl roast lamb and Angus steak; ♦♦*Gallo Negro*, Convent Place, T 75654, friendly Italian bistro; ♦♦*Little Mermaid*, Marina Bay, recently opened Danish restaurant with typical Scandinavian specialities and average prices; ♦♦*Maharaja*, 21 Turnbulls Lane, T 75233, the best Indian food on the Rock.

♦ For cheap fish and chips try *Casements Fishery* on the 2nd flr of the International Commercial Centre, open 0930-2130, take away or eat in; ♦*Macs Kitchen*, 245 Main St, T 71155, cheap, acceptable fast food.

Jewish visitors will be interested in ♦♦♦*The Leanse*, a kosher restaurant, 7 Bomb House Lane, conveniently nr to the synagogue, serving international and oriental food, closed Sat.

● Banks & money changers

There are branches of all the main British and Spanish banks, plus some from other European countries, mainly based around the Main St/Line/Wall Rd area. There are also a number of Bureaus de Change, incl one at the airport and 3 in Main St.

Currency: the official currency is the Gibraltar pound and the colony issues its own notes and coins, but in reality British, Spanish currency and even US dollars are widely accepted in all commercial establishments. Gibraltar notes are not exchangeable outside the Rock.

● **Embassies & consulates**
Belgium, 47 Irishtown, T 78553; **Denmark**, Cloister Building, Market Lane, T 72735; **Israel**, 3 City Mill Lane, T 75955; **Italy**, 12 College Lane, T 78123; **Netherlands**, 2/6 Main St, T 79220; **Norway**, 315 Main St, T 78305; **Sweden**, Cloister Building, Market Lane, T 78456.

● **Entertainment**
Casinos: *International Casino Club*, 7 Europa Rd, T 76666. Apart from the gaming tables, there is a restaurant and fine views. Open 2000-0400, entry free.

Cinemas: *Queens*, next to the hotel of the same name in Boyd St. Recently refurbished. Open daily, except Wed; admission £3.00 and £4.00.

Nightclubs: try *Sax*, 1st flr of the ICC, open until 0200; *Penelope*, 3 West Place of Arms, T 70462, set in one of the old town walls.

● **Hospitals & medical services**
UK residents are entitled to free medical treatment provided that they have a temporary address in Gibraltar. Day visitors from UK and other EU nationals must provide Form E 111. *St Bernards Hospital*, T 73941. There is also a *Health Centre* in Casemates Square, T 78337.

● **Post & telecommunications**
Post Office: the main branch is located at 104 Main St, open 0900-1300 and 1400-1700, Sat 1000-1300. Gibraltar issues its own postage stamps. Up to 1886, British stamps were used, then Bermuda stamps were used overprinted with the name 'Gibraltar'. Stamp collectors requiring more information should contact the **Gibraltar Philatelic Bureau**, PO Box 5662, Gibraltar.

Telephones: when telephoning out of Gibraltar, the international prefix is 00 (except for Spain). To call Gibraltar from Spain dial first 9567 (except in Cádiz province where the code is 7). Telegrams, telexes and faxes can be sent from the offices of Cable and Wireless, 25 South Barracks Rd. Telephone cabins in Gibraltar are the traditional British red version.

● **Shopping**
Gibraltar is sales-tax free and therefore has considerable attractions, not only to expatriates on the Costa del Sol, but also to Spaniards living over the border who flock in for their petrol and cigarettes. Be warned that there are limits on the goods you are permitted to import back into Spain and there are often long customs delays. For those who can brave the narrow crowded pavements and busy traffic of the main street, there are branches of well-known firms such as *Safeway* (3 branches), *Marks and Spencer* and *Mothercare*. The larger branch of Safeway opp the airport terminal is well patronized by the Spanish. In the smaller shops in the town centre, the best bargains are in electrical goods, jewellery, watches and perfume, but don't assume you are getting a bargain just because you are buying in Gibraltar. Shopping hours tend to resemble those of the UK rather than Spain.

● **Tour companies & travel agents**
Alpha Travel, 123 Main St, T 79281; *Bland Ltd*, Cloister Building, T 77012; *Calypso Tours*, 21 Horse Barrack Lane, T 76520; *Exchange Travel*, 241 Main St, T 76151; *Herald Travel*, Montagu Pavilion, Queensway, T 71171.

● **Tourist offices**
The main tourist office is now located at the museum. There are sub offices at the airport, in the market place and in the Waterport coach park. In contrast to the Spanish offices, most of the useful material has to be paid for. Some of the offices are staffed by students in the summer – they do their best. The offices are open Mon-Fri 1000-1800, Sat 1000-1400.

● **Transport**
Local Bus: frequent departures from the border to the town centre (70p/35 ptas). There are no formal bus services, but as there are 3 minibus firms and nearly 150 taxis, this is not a problem. **Car hire**: a car is a dubious advantage in Gibraltar and many locals keep their vehicles on the Spanish side of the border. Congestion and parking problems are normal and illegally parked vehicles are enthusiastically wheel clamped. Many international car hire firms have their offices at the airport, incl **Avis**, T 75552; **Budget**, T 79666; **Hertz**, T 42737; and **Europcar**, T 77171 (highly rec), plus a number of local firms who might be cheaper

but not have full back up in Spain. A small car costs around £18-20 a day. If border delays are bad, drivers may have to pick up their car on the Spanish side of the border. When returning the car and catching a plane, remember to leave plenty of time for these customs delays. Do not worry about leaving the car on the Spanish side of the border – this is normal procedure and the hire firm will collect it if you give precise instructions on its whereabouts. **Taxis**: are readily available throughout Gibraltar, with reasonable rates.

Air British Airways operated by the independent carrier GB Airways offer regular scheduled services from London Heathrow, Gatwick and Manchester to Gibraltar. They also fly from Gibraltar to two centres in Morocco. For further information and reservations T (UK) 0345 222111 or Gibraltar T 79300. Monarch Airlines are planning to extend their Crown Service to Gibraltar in 1997. It is worth considering routes via Málaga, which give greater choice and cheaper fares.

Road Bus: Portillo buses run from the Spanish side of the border to resorts on the Costa del Sol and **Málaga**.

Sea Tourafrica International provide a ferry link with **Tangier** sailing on Sun, Mon, Wed and Fri. Return fare for adults is £28. Day excursion with sightseeing tour and lunch for £35, T 77666.

NB A passport is required for entry into Gibraltar. The Spanish customs are usually awkward in view of the widespread smuggling of cigarettes and drugs, so delays for re-entering Spain are common and can last from 20 mins to 7 hrs, depending on the political situation.

Information for travellers

BEFORE TRAVELLING

ENTRY REQUIREMENTS

British citizens need a valid passport. (Note that the temporary British Visitors Passport is no longer acceptable.) Other EU citizens need only their national identity cards, providing their stay is no longer than 90 days. US citizens need a passport and can stay for up to 6 months, but the 90-day rule applies for citizens of Canada and New Zealand. Australians need a visa. This can be obtained on arrival, but only lasts for 30 days. Visitors wishing to stay for longer periods should officially apply for a residence permit *(permiso de residencia)*, although this is widely ignored. Nationalities not mentioned above should consult their nearest Spanish embassy or consulate, as should any visitor wishing to stay for any length of time. Addresses of Spanish embassies and consulates can be found on page 323.

Tourist information

Visitors will probably wish to obtain tourist material, such as brochures and maps, prior to departure. The addresses of Spanish tourist offices can be found on page 323.

● Specialist tour companies

All the major travel and tour companies arrange package tours to Andalucía, generally located at resorts on the Costa del Sol. The more discriminating visitor should not dismiss these tours out-of-hand, however, as they are often exceptional bargains and although the hotels are often noisy and crowded with package tourists, they can make a good base for exploring the interior of Andalucía. The following are a sample only. Full names and addresses can be found under "Useful addresses" on page 323. Two Spanish companies which provide more interesting programmes are: *Magic of Spain*, T 0181 748 7575 and *Mundi Color*, T 0171 828 6021.

More specialist interests are catered for by the following: *Abercrombie and Kent (UK)*, Andalucían safari around Ronda with mules, T 0171 7309600; *Ace Study Tours (UK)*, historical/cultural tours, T 01223 835055; *Andalucía Tours*, horse trekking, English, based in Granada, T 958 610261; *Adventura*, mule trekking and horse riding in the Sierra Nevada, T 01784 459018 ; *Benamorda*, rambling, horse riding, mountain biking, nature tours, based in Málaga, F 95 2152336; *Blackheath Wine Trails*, Bodega tours based at Jerez de la Frontera, T 0181 4630012; *Burro-Adventure*, donkey treks in the Alpujarras, Spanish, Camping de Pitres, Granada, T 958 766112; *Explore Worldwide (UK)*, walking in the Sierra Nevada and the Ronda area, T 01252 344161; *Peng*, offer naturist holidays based at Coast Natura, near Estepona, T 01402471832; *Rancho los Lobos*, horse trekking, English/German, Cádiz, T 956 640429; *Taste of Spain*, specialized tours of Andalucía by jeep, horse or on foot, English, Málaga, T 95 2886590.

The following firms organize bird watching

holidays in SW Andalucía: *Bird Watching Breaks*, T 01305 267994; *Gullivers*, RSPB leaders used, T 01525 270100; *Ornitholidays*, 1/3 Victoria Drive, Bognor Regis, Sussex.

Visitors interested in city breaks, which mainly concern Granada, Córdoba and Sevilla, could contact: *Time Off*, T 0171 235 8070; *Travellers Way*, T 01753 516477.

Students and young people will find the following helpful: *Campus Travel*, T 0171 7303402 and found on most university campuses in Britain.

WHEN TO GO

Andalucía has one of the most agreeable climates on mainland Europe. Winters are mild with some rain, but plenty of sunshine with the clarity of light which delights photographers. Coastal temperatures in Jan average 15-17°C, but it is colder inland, particularly in the mountains, where snow lies on the Sierra Nevada for much of the year. Summers are hot, especially inland, but the coasts have the benefit of sea breezes, particularly in the area from Gibraltar to Cádiz, where the strong *levante* can last for days on end, to the joy of wind surfers. Midday temperatures in Jul are usually 25-30°C and many areas receive no rain at all from May to Oct, although thunderstorms are always a possibility in late summer. Since 1990, the winter rains have consistently failed, so that drought conditions currently prevail with disastrous effects on farming and difficulties with water supply. Fortunately, the wet winter of 1995/6 has restored reservoirs to their normal levels. The port of Almería rarely gets more than 1 or 2 days rain a year and the countryside around is classed as semi-desert.

Tourism is a year-round activity on the Costa del Sol, with many elderly northern Europeans spending the winter here. Spring and Autumn are the peak periods for golf. Naturalists prefer Spring, when the countryside is green, wild flowers are to be seen in profusion and migrant birds have arrived and are in full song. Jul and Aug, as well as being the hottest months, are also the most crowded, with the main resorts humming with activity. For those seeking the sun, watersports and a throbbing night life, this will be the time to come. The height of summer, however, is not the best time to explore the interior of Andalucía, as the heat will be searing. There are attractions for visitors in all seasons, therefore, depending on the interests of the individual.

WARNING Spring, the period between Mar and May, is the peak period for visiting by Spanish school parties. While it is encouraging to find children learning about their historical and environmental heritage, many of the trips seem to have little educational content. Not a clipboard or questionnaire in sight! Visitors from North America and Britain will also be unaccustomed to the decibel level which emanates from large numbers of Andalucían schoolchildren and may find their visits severely inconvenienced.

HEALTH AND INSURANCE

Spain has reciprocal health arrangements with other EU member countries, so British visitors are entitled to care from the Spanish health service, providing that they can show Form E111, which can be obtained from travel agents and main post offices. Travellers are advised, however, that this can be ineffective in practice on short stays and they should obtain a comprehensive travel insurance, which, as well as covering every medical eventuality, will also cover luggage, cancellation, theft and personal accident. No inoculations are required for Spain, but visitors should ensure that their tetanus injections are up-to-date. The usual precautions should be taken against AIDS.

MONEY

● Cost of living

Spain is no longer the cheap destination that it was 20 years ago and visitors will find that the prices on balance are much the same as they are at home. A holiday need not be expensive, however, and budget travellers are well-catered for, providing they shop around for meals, buy fruit and vegetables in season and search out cheap accommodation. Whilst petrol prices are similar to northern Europe, buses are cheap to use and car hire is reasonable, so that travelling within Andalucía should not be a major expense. Drinks of all kinds are ridiculously low-priced, as are cigarettes – particularly in Gibraltar, where there is no purchase tax. Vegetarian, alcoholic smokers will be in their element!

● Credit cards

Major credit cards, such as *Mastercard*, *Visa* and *American Express* are widely accepted, although smaller establishments may only deal with cash. Check restaurants before you eat. They can also be used at cashpoint machines, although you should find out how much commission your bank/card company charges for this service. Eurocheques can also be used if supported by a card. Where shops show the *cirrus* sign, the card only is needed. Visitors should be aware of their credit card numbers and make a note of emergency telephone numbers which will need to be contacted should a card be lost or stolen.

● **Currency**

The local currency is the *peseta*. In recent years the exchange rate has varied from 180 to 200 pesetas to the £ and from 135 to 140 pesetas to the US dollar. Notes in circulation are; 1,000, 2,000, 5,000 and 10,000, while coins are found in denominations of 1, 5, 10, 25, 50, 100, 200 and 500 pesetas. Most coins are duplicated in design. Where this is the case the older, larger coins are due to be phased out. Most visitors will probably wish to carry TCs and they should have no difficulty in cashing them, or foreign notes, in any bank. Hotels and change shops will also cash TCs, but may charge a hefty commission. Cashpoint machines are now found in all towns and cities and will conduct business in a choice of European languages (look for the *telebanco* sign). They will accept most common cards in circulation. In addition to banks, there are *Cajas de ahorros* (savings banks), but some of the smaller branches may be unwilling to cash TCs. Banking hours are Mon to Fri 0830 to 1400, Sat 0830 to 1300, except Jun to Sep when they are closed (perversely, when this is the main holiday season).

● **Taxes**

Variable rates of IVA (the Spanish equivalent of VAT – sales tax) are applied from a basic 6% to 12% or 33% for luxury goods. Major department stores, such as *El Corte Inglís* (Málaga) or *Galerias Preciados* (Granada) operate IVA exemption schemes for non-residents, and this is well worth the trouble for large purchases. Consult their multi-lingual staff for details. IVA is normally included in the stated prices.

GETTING THERE

Visitors to Andalucía have a choice of methods of travelling. Undoubtedly the quickest and most convenient way is by **air**. Those who wish to take their **car** can either drive from the channel ports or take the direct ferries to Bilbao or Santander in Northern Spain. Another pos-

sibility would be to put the car on a train to the S of France and drive on from there. Drivers should be aware that even after they have arrived on Spanish soil, they still have a 650 km journey to reach the border of Andalucía. Further alternatives include **train** and **long-distance coach**.

FROM BRITAIN

By air

The choice here is either by **Charter Flight** or by **Scheduled Flight**. Charter flights are cheaper. They are run by package holiday firms, who sell off un-used seats to 'flights only' passengers. Some very good bargains may be had by taking last minute bookings through the so-called 'bucket shops', who advertise in daily newspapers and magazines such as *Time Out*. The disadvantages of charter flights are that they usually have a fixed return flight, which will be no more than 4 weeks, and they often leave at unsocial hours. It may, nevertheless, be cheaper to take two separate charter journeys than one return scheduled flight. Málaga and Sevilla are the main destinations of the scheduled flights, which are run by Iberia (and its subsidiary Viva) and British Airways. In addition, smaller airlines such as Monarch and Britannia, also run scheduled flights to Málaga, and provide an excellent service with competitive fares. A further alternative is the service to Gibraltar run by GB Air, a subsidiary of British Airways, but as this company has the monopoly of Gibraltar flights, don't expect a cheap fare. Monarch, however, are due to extend their Crown Service to Gibraltar in 1997. Other international airports are Jerez (Iberia) and Almería (various charters).

By train

From London to Málaga by train used to be a 35-hr journey and involved changing trains (and stations) at Paris, and later at Barcelona. The opening of the Channel Tunnel has speeded up this journey considerably, but it is still arduous and will probably only appeal to railway buffs. The cost is more expensive than an average charter flight, although cheaper than most scheduled flights. For students, the *InterRail* pass is an attractive and cheap possibility, which can be obtained from travel agents or British Rail.

For information on travelling by train, contact the British Rail Information Line, T 0171 8342345.

By long distance coach

Buses run from London to Málaga three times a week, a journey which takes in the Dover-Calais ferry and lasts 38 hrs. Another route runs via Paris and Madrid to Algeciras, taking 43 hrs. On these marathon journeys, there are toilet/refreshment stops every 4-5 hrs, but they remain tests of stamina. The fares are on a par with charter flights.

For information on travelling to Andalucía by coach, contact *Eurolines*, National Express, 164 Buckingham Palace Rd, London SW1, T 0171 7300202.

By car and ferry

The most popular route to Andalucía by car is via the ferry services from England to Northern Spain. Scenic routes can be chosen through Spain with hotel stops so that this can be an enjoyable part of a holiday. A long-standing ferry route is that from Plymouth to Santander run by *Brittany Ferries*. This runs twice weekly and takes 24 hrs. Some form of accommodation must be booked and this varies from 4-berth cabins to pullman reclining seats. A recently introduced rival is the *P&O* service from Portsmouth to Bilbao, which takes 30 hrs and runs twice weekly. A cabin is included in the price.

For details of pricing and timetables, contact: *Brittany Ferries*, Millbay Docks, Plymouth, T 01752 221321; *P&O European Ferries*, Channel House, Channel View Rd, Dover, T 01304 203388 or Continental Ferry Port, Mile End, Portsmouth, T 01705 772244.

For readers wishing to drive through France, there are cross-channel routes from Dover, Folkestone, Portsmouth, Weymouth and Plymouth. In addition to the conventional ferries, there is the Hovercraft service from Dover and *le Shuttle* through the Channel Tunnel.

For details of pricing and timetables on cross-channel routes, contact: *Hoverspeed*, International Hoverport, Dover, Kent, T 01304 240101; *Sally Line*, Argyle Centre, York St, Ramsgate, Kent, T 01843 595522; *Stena Sealink Line*, Charter House, Park St, Ashford, Kent, T 01233 647047.

FROM NORTH AMERICA

American and Canadian visitors to Andalucía will need to arrange flights to major European cities and then take connecting flights to Málaga or Sevilla. *Iberia* has flights to Madrid from New York, Miami, Los Angeles and Toronto. It may pay, however, to fly to London or Amsterdam to catch a connecting flight to Andalucía. On the other hand some APEX flights to Madrid throw in a free connecting flight to Málaga, Sevilla or Almería, so it is worth doing some research. There are a number of 'Travel Clubs' in North America which specialize in finding discount flights, such as: *Moments Notice*, 425 Madison Ave, New York, NY 10017, T 212 4860503.

Canadian students should contact: *Travel Cuts*, 187 College St, Toronto, Ontario, M5T 1P7.

FROM AUSTRALASIA

There are no direct flights from Australia and New Zealand to Spain. Most European destinations are 'common rated', so it is possible to have stopovers in a variety of European cities before going on to Andalucía. There are more than 10 airlines working this route, so it is worth shopping around for bargains, such as free car rental, on-going flights or accommodation. Fares will vary according to the season – what is high season in the Antipodes may be low season in Spain.

CUSTOMS

Duty free goods

You may import up to 200 cigarettes or 50 cigars from European countries (double from outside Europe), a camera and a video camera with film, 2 litres of wine, and one litre of spirits (2 litres if under 22%). In practice, customs controls are very slack in tourist areas, but you should abide by these restrictions. You are most likely to encounter difficulties when crossing from Gibraltar back into Spain, when clearance can be very slow on the days when they decide to be difficult. It is also important to bring with you receipts for any valuables you are bringing into the country to avoid any problems when you leave or return to your own country.

When leaving Spain, remember that there are no restrictions for EU citizens on the amount of wine, spirits and tobacco which can be taken home, providing that duty has been paid. The duty free limits are the same as at entry. It is often cheaper to buy duty-paid goods from local supermarkets, than to buy duty-free goods at airports.

ON ARRIVAL

● Opening hours

In Andalucía, more than in any other part of Spain, the afternoon *siesta* is rigidly adhered to, and is an essential part of the rather quirky business hours. The tourist should try to come to terms with this fact and acknowledge that in the heat of the afternoon sitting under a sunshade is preferable to slogging round a historic site. The usual summer working hours are 0930-1330 and 1700-1930, which has repercussions for meal times. Few Andalucíans take lunch before 1400 or eat dinner before 2100. Some tourist shops on the coastal strip may open all day, as will large department stores such as *El Corte Inglés* in Málaga, but this is most unusual in the interior of Andalucía.

The visitor, then, is faced with the problem of how to occupy his time during the afternoon. On the coast, the beach is an obvious solution, but for the visitor exploring inland cities, such as Sevilla, Córdoba or Granada, the best answer may be to check into a hotel just after lunch so that there is an air conditioned room in which to spend the *siesta* hours.

Remember, too, that just about all museums, galleries and monuments close on Mon. Tourist Offices close on Sat afternoons and Sun. Cathedrals and larger churches follow the same hours as museums (and often charge an entrance fee), while small churches are usually locked up and the search for a key can often be a challenge.

● **Tipping**

A service charge is included in restaurant and hotel bills, but an additional 5-10% will be appreciated by the ill-paid waiters. Small tips in this range will be expected at bars and by taxi drivers, guides, porters, cinema ushers and car-park attendants.

● **Toilets**

Public lavatories are hard to find, but this is not usually a problem as there are plenty in bars, hotels and restaurants and other tourist places, which tend to be used by customers and non-customers alike. Ask for the *servicios* or *aseos*. The womens' toilets are labelled *damas* or *señoras*, the gentlemen's toilets labelled *cabelleros* or *señores*. If this is confusing, be reassured by the fact that most toilet doors have the easily recognizable international logos. In some of the more remote parts of Andalucía, 'squat-type' lavatories are still found and it is as well to bring your own supply of paper.

Crime, police & emergencies
● **Crime**

In Andalucía, crime is largely an urban phenomena fuelled by unemployment, drug dependence and easy pickings from tourists. Both Málaga and Sevilla have bad reputations for street crime. The most common forms are bag snatching, pickpocketing, mugging and theft from cars. Sevilla is well-known for its *semaforazos* who smash car windows at traffic lights, steal whatever is available and make off down side streets on mopeds. Visitors staying in villas or apartments should also beware of gypsy women selling tablecloths. While one is distracting attention at the front door, others will be attempting to gain entry at the rear. Pickpockets also often work in pairs, so beware of anyone standing close to you in a crowded place and demanding your attention, as his accomplice will be nearby.

Some simple precautions will reduce the risk of becoming a victim and having a holiday ruined:

● If staying in a city, try to choose a hotel with a lock-up garage for cars.

● Remove all luggage and valuables from cars at night. If it is a private car remove the radio also.

● Do not have cameras and other valuables on display in a car when travelling through a city and make sure that the doors are locked while driving.

● Leave valuables in hotel safety deposit boxes.

● Don't carry handbags unless absolutely necessary or keep wallets in rear pockets.

● Avoid poorly lit and less salubrious areas of cities, especially, late at night.

● Take a taxi, rather than public transport late at night.

To experienced travellers, the above points will be second nature, and most visitors to Andalucía will have no experience of crime of any sort. Northern Europeans and North Americans will feel safer on the streets at night than in their own countries, while women are unlikely to experience any harassment. Indeed, the only molesting will probably come from the ubiquitous timeshare touts.

If, however, a visitor is unfortunate enough to be robbed, they should go immediately to the nearest police station to report the theft, as insurance companies will require a police statement. Be prepared to spend at least half a day there while you queue with other victims and the interminable paper work is completed.

The Spanish authorities are very conscious of the 'Costa del Crime' description and have made considerable efforts in recent years to clean up the image, with extra officers drafted in from other parts of the country for the summer season.

● **Police**

There are three separate police organizations in Andalucía, so the situation may initially be confusing. The **Guardia Civil** wear green uniforms and are less important today than they were in the time of Franco, when they were a reactionary organization. Even today they seem specially selected for their lack of humour. They mainly operate in rural areas or on motor bike traffic control. The **Policía Municipal** are local police who wear blue and white uniforms and spend much of their time directing urban traffic. The **Policía Nacional** wear a brown military-style uniform and can be heavily armed as their duties include guarding public buildings. They deal with most crime investigation and therefore it is to the Policía Nacional that you should go to report a crime or theft. They will issue the documents which insurance companies will require. All three branches of the police are armed and should not be treated frivolously. Be prepared to have some form of identification available and always carry your driving licence when in a car.

Medical services

● **Casas de Socorro (first aid centres)**

Casas de Socorro (first aid centres) are run by the Andalucian Health Service and the *Cruz Rioja* (Red Cross) and are found on beaches, along main roads and in towns.

● **Doctors**

If you need the services of a doctor (*medico*) – there are often multi-lingual ones in the tourist areas – expect to pay a consultation fee of between 3,000 and 5,000 ptas – keep the receipt for insurance purposes.

● **Farmacias (chemists)**

Farmacias (chemists) are identifiable by a green cross and will provide most medicines, often without a prescription. They will give advice about ailments and suggest remedies, as they are used to dealing with people who do not wish to pay a doctor's fee. Local duty chemists will be listed in the window and also in local papers.

● **Hospitals**

The are a number of excellent hospitals throughout Andalucía with emergency departments, plus some private clinics. Any visitor staying on the Costa del Sol for any length of time and regularly using the dangerous N340 coast road, might consider joining *Helicópteros Sanitarios*,

who fly injured motorists speedily to the nearest hospital, probably safer than some of the erratically driven private ambulances, T 2826119. For emergency treatment dial 091 for the *Servicios de Urgencia*.

● **Staying healthy**

As mentioned above, all visitors to the region should have a comprehensive travel insurance, while travellers from EU countries should bring Form E111. The most usual form of illness is a stomach upset caused by an excess of strange food, alcohol or sun. Tap water in Andalucía is normally potable, but in the drought conditions of recent years standards of water purity have fallen. It is perhaps advisable to use bottled water, particularly in rural areas.

WHERE TO STAY

● **Hotels & pensiones**

All accommodation in Andalucía is state-registered and there is sufficient variety to satisfy all requirements. All establishments are shown by blue plaques with white letters – Hotels (H), Residential Hotels (HR), Hostales (Hs), Pensiones (P) and Casa de Huéspedes (CH). Hotels are graded by 1-5 stars and hostels by 1-3 stars, but the distinctions are blurred and a good hostel may be better than a low grade hotel. The term *hostal* is officially being phased out and establishments have to decide whether they are a hotel or a pension. In addition there are *fondas*, which may be inns or simply rooms above a bar. Travellers on a budget should look out for signs saying *camas* (beds) or *habitaciones* (rooms). Be prepared to bargain for this type of accommodation, as owners may be prepared to provide meals as part of the deal.

Many of the hotels in the inland cities are often old, traditional and with a certain gloomy grandeur, which is in direct contrast with the coastal hotels, which tend to be new and in well-landscaped grounds and have facilities such as pools, laundries and nightclubs. The coastal hotels have disadvantages, however, such as noise from discos and package tour parties. The wide range of choice means that there is something for everyone. Should you be dissatisfied with the services provided, ask for the *libra de reclamaciones* (complaints book), which by law all establishments should display. Such a request should ensure that your complaint is dealt heeded.

● **Paradores**

At the opposite end of the scale are the Paradores, which are state-run luxury hotels, often located in historic buildings. They tend to be furnished with appropriate antiques, while their restaurants concentrate on local specialities. Bedrooms are spacious and well-fitted, as are public rooms and bars. Even if you cannot afford to stay in a parador, they are worth wandering around and perhaps having a drink in their well-appointed bars. They are not cheap and booking is essential (there is a strongly-held rumour that rooms are kept open to 1800 for cabinet ministers, after which time visitors may be able to take them without booking!). They can be booked in advance from the Madrid head office at Requena 3, 28013 Madrid, T 559069, F 5593233 and in UK through *Keytel International*, 402 Edgware Rd, London W2N 1ED, T 0171 4028182. Do not be deterred if you arrive at your pre-booked *parador* and they try to persuade you they have no record of your reservation. Polite, firm insistence should secure your room. Particularly recommended *paradores* in Andalucía are those at Arcos de la Frontera, Carmona, Granada, Jaen, Málaga and Úbeda, which are in superb, historic buildings in spectacular locations. There are other *paradores* at Antequera, Ayamonte, Bailén, Cadiz, Cazorla, and Códoba. Those at Mazagón, Mojácar, Nerja and Torremolinos are in modern buildings and less attractive, although the standard of service, of course, remains high.

● **Youth hostels**

Younger visitors might be tempted by Youth Hostels of which there are 147 in Andalucía. A list can be obtained from the English YHA or from local tourist offices in Spain. There are disadvantages, however. Block booking by Spanish school groups is common (which will ensure a sleepless night), while the cost often compares unfavourably with *casas de huéspedes*. They are mainly located in larger towns and cities and may only open for the summer season.

● **Apartments & villas**

On the Costa del Sol, 'residential tourism' is far more important than 'hotel tourism' and consequently there are literally thousands of apartments and villas available for hire, often on a long term basis. Out of season, reduced rates can be negotiated, but check carefully what is included in the rental agreement. Some expatriates are happy for 'caretakers' to stay in their properties while they are away. Be prepared to provide references. Look for advertisements in

the free newspapers, in the windows of *inmobilarios* (estate agents) or simply look for signs saying *Se alquila* (to rent).

● **Camping**

There are 130 official camp sites in Andalucía plus a number of unofficial ones. Many have excellent facilities, particularly those on the coast. They are rated in categories 1-3, depending on their facilities, and many sites have swimming pools, restaurants, sports and supermarkets. They are relatively cheap by European standards – 300 to 500 pesetas a night, with additional charges for cars and caravans. The more popular sites may need to be booked during the summer months and on fiesta weekends, while in the winter months the coastal sites attract large numbers of caravans

Hotel classifications

AL: US$90+. International class luxury hotel. All facilities for business and leisure travellers are of the highest international standard.

A: US$75-90. International hotel with air conditioned rooms with WC, bath/shower, TV, phone, mini-bar, daily clean linen. Choice of restaurants, coffee shop, shops, bank, travel agent, swimming pool, some sport and business facilities.

B: US$60-75. As **A** but without the luxury, reduced number of restaurants, smaller rooms, limited range of shops and sport.

C: US$40-60. Best rooms have air conditioning, own bath/shower and WC. Usually comfortable, bank, shop, pool.

D: US$20-40. Best rooms may have own WC and bath/shower. Depending on management will have room service and choice of cuisine in restaurant.

E: US$10-20. Simple provision. Perhaps fan cooler. May not have restaurant. Shared WC and showers with hot water (when available).

F: under US$10. Very basic, shared toilet facilities, variable in cleanliness, noise, often in dubious locations.

and recreational vehicles. Official camp sites are listed in the regional government's accommodation booklet *Guia de Camping*, available from tourist offices and from Spanish National Tourist Offices overseas. This also includes a decent regional map. For those staying on the coastal strip, *Campings en la Costa del Sol* is a brochure produced in four languages. Reservations may be made through the *Federación Española de Empresarios de Camping*,

Green/rural tourism

Spain in general and Andalucía in particular have been anxious to dispel the image that the area is attractive only to the beach-goer and the lager lout and this has helped to develop the concept of **green/rural tourism**. The idea is to encourage tourists away from the coasts to inland areas, without ruining the rural environment. Fortunately the interior of Andalucía is rich in history, scenery, archaeology and wildlife, so there is much to interest the discriminating tourist. If successful, rural tourism provides jobs for local people and helps to prevent depopulation, particularly of younger people. The *pueblo blanco* of Grazalema, for example, has less than 2,000 inhabitants, which is half the number it had at the turn of the century, while in the village of Cartajima there were only two weddings between 1990 and 1995, which does not make the future birth rate look encouraging.

The government of Andalucía has provided money for rural hotels, *villas touristicas* (self-catering apartment complexes in traditional style) and campsites and given grants for private enterprise schemes. Local handicrafts have been encouraged, such as the woollen goods at Grazalema and the leather making at Ubrique. Local festivals, such as the bull running *Lunes de Toro* at Grazalema have been publicised.

A recent development has been the negotiations between RENFE, the Spanish railway company and the regional government and private companies, to purchase a number of rural railway stations to increase the tourist potential of the area. These stations, which see little use in the age of the car, have facilities such as bars, toilets, outbuildings and parking space which could be put to good use, especially as many are in or near Natural Parks. The station at Benaoján, for example, is now the headquarters of a small company specializing in pot holing and other high risk sports.

Another initiative is in connection with spas and health baths. There are estimated to be over 300 spas in Spain. Many go back to Roman times, but the majority have fallen into disuse. In Andalucía, there are well-known privately run spas such as those at Carratraca and Alhama de Almería, but there are many others which could be rehabilitated and the regional government are actively collaborating with private investors.

All these developments could not take place, however, without an increase in the amount of rural accommodation available, so the Andalucían government has set up the **Red Andaluza de Alojamientos Rurales** (RAAR) – the Andalucían Network of Rural Accommodation. It offers a range of possibilities including rustic cottages, rooms in large haciendas, private rooms in modern homes, hostels, basic camp sites and even old converted cork workers huts. The majority are privately owned and the landlord provides a package of information concerning such things as local swimming pools, hiking trails and riding opportunities. Transport and car rental can also be arranged. This scheme has proved extremely popular and all accommodation can be fully booked at peak holiday periods. To obtain the detailed RAAR brochure and make a booking through the Central Reservation Service, telephone in Spain 34-50-265018 or fax 34-50-270431. In UK, contact *Atlantida Travel*, T 071-2402888.

General Oraa 52-2°D, 28006, Madrid,
T 5629994, F 5637094. Note that inland camp
sites can be few and far between. The province
of Córdoba, for example, has only three listed
sites, Jaén only six, all of which are in or near
the Cazorla Natural Park. An International
Camping Carnet, available from the motoring
organizations, is strongly advised if a lengthy
camping holiday is planned. Camping away
from official sites, whilst not illegal, should be
approached with care. Avoid beaches, urban
areas and private land unless you have permission from the owner. Do not expect sites to be
quiet – blaring televisions, radios and Spanish
children will ensure otherwise.

FOOD AND DRINK

FOOD

Whilst not having the finesse or reputation of
French or Italian cooking, Spanish cuisine has
the benefit of simplicity and healthy ingredients. In Andalucía, there is the added advantage of having a wide variety of fruit,
vegetables and fresh fish, plus the distinctive
Moorish inheritance.

● **When to eat**

Spanish mealtimes reflect the unusual working
day. Breakfast (*desayuno*) is often taken out in
a cafe or bar and rarely before 0930 or 1000.
Lunch (*almuerzo*) is usually the main meal of
the day and will rarely, for the Spaniard, start
before 1400, allowing a siesta before returning
to work. The evening meal (*cena*) is lighter and
not taken before 2100 or 2200. Many Andalucíans will prefer some *tapas* instead of a
full meal in the evening. Away from the tourist
areas, restaurants will stick rigidly to these
timings, but on the coast they will adapt to the
requirements of Northern Europeans.

● **Where to eat**

Traditional Spanish bars and restaurants are
found throughout the region, and the latter
are graded in a fashion. The classification,
however, tends to depend on the facilities and
prices, rather than the excellence of the cooking, so it is probably best ignored. The more
pretentious establishments call themselves
mesones, while the larger hotels will have
expensive dining rooms or *comedores*. In the
coastal resorts, beach bars (*merenderos* or
chirinquitos) can often provide fresh fish food
in an attractive ambience. Also in the resorts
are *buffet libres*, where you can eat as much

as you like for a set price. In the fishing ports
in the W of the province are *freidurías* and
marisquerías, specializing in fish and shellfish.
Sandwich bars, cafeterias and milk bars often
aim at an up-market clientele. Inland, the roadside *ventas*, while varying in quality, often offer
excellent regional game dishes. Over the last
decade the coastal resorts have seen the introduction of numerous international restaurants,
such as Chinese, Indian and Italian, plus a
whole range of American fast food outlets and
'take aways', so that the choice is now wide.
Restaurants are obliged to offer a *menu del dia*
(menu of the day), which provides a 3-course
meal with bread and a drink, generally costing
between 800 and 1,500 ptas. There are confusing terms for the amount of food on offer.
Free *tapa* food provided with a drink is known
as a *pincho*. The average sized tapa dish which
is paid for is known as a *racion*. In some parts
of the region, particularly in the E and inland,
the menu may include several *platos combi-
nadas*, which is effectively a combined plate,
involving meat or fish, plus potatoes and a
vegetable or salad, bread and a drink.

● **What to eat**

Although cooked breakfasts may be available
in the coastal resort areas, Spaniards have a
light continental-type breakfast (*desayuno*)
with rolls or toast (*tostada*) and coffee (*cafe*).
Many Andalucíans prefer a hot chocolate drink
into which they dip thin tube-like doughnuts
(*churros*). Workmen often spread *zurrapa* or
manteca on their rolls, which might best be
described as an orange-coloured dripping containing leftover pieces of meat and sausage –
definitely an acquired taste! Main meals in
restaurants usually consist of 3 courses. Start-
ers are many and varied. In the winter, thick
country soups (*cocidos*) are popular, while in
the summer mixed salads (*ensalada mixta*) are
widely eaten. *Gazpacho*, an Andalucian speciality, is a cold soup containing finely chopped
garlic, onions and peppers. *Tortilla española*, a
Spanish potato omelette, also makes a filling
starter. Main courses will feature fish, meat or

game, but don't expect sophisticated sauces or exotic vegetables. The main item will usually be fried or grilled, smothered in garlic and accompanied by a few fried potatoes. Fresh fish and shellfish are the main joys of Andalucían cooking. With both the Atlantic and Mediterranean to call upon, the variety is enormous. All menus will include *meluza* (hake), *sardinas* (sardines), *calamares* (squid) and *pez espada* (swordfish). Amongst the shellfish, *gambas* (prawns) and *mejillones* (mussels) are the most popular and both figure prominently in *paella*, a rice dish which originated in Valencia. The Andalucían version contains less meat, but is equally good. Fish can be expensive inland and here it is worth trying the game dishes, which include rabbit, partridge, venison, wild boar and hare. *Jamon Serrano* (dried ham) is also superb, particularly in the N of the region, and will be found hanging from the ceilings in many bars and restaurants. But, beware, some varieties are extremely expensive. *Carne* (meat) is generally good and usually served grilled. *Cerdo* (pork) and *cordero* (lamb) are normally reliable, but beef is often disappointing and steak should only be tried at the specialist steak houses which are beginning to appear on the coast. *Estafada*, a meat stew flavoured with cloves, is a typical country dish. Desserts in the cheaper restaurants tend to be limited to *flan* (cream caramel), ice cream and *fruta del tiempo* (fruit in season). It is worth searching for some of the regional specialities, which are usually very sweet and a throwback to the Moorish occupation. You are more likely to find these in the N of the area (see regional descriptions). Cheese is not offered at the end of a meal and is more likely to be found as a *tapa*. Cheese is not, in fact, produced to any great extent in Andalucía. Supermarket shelves, however, are full of interesting Spanish regional cheeses, many of which are worth trying. Vegetarians and vegans will find life difficult in Andalucía, as despite the abundance of vegetables produced in the area, particularly under plastic in Almería, little finds its way onto the menu. Self catering may be the only answer.

DRINK

Alcoholic drinks are plentiful and the supermarket shelves are lined with a huge variety of wines, beers and spirits, all at prices which seem remarkably cheap to visitors from the UK and North America. *Víno* (wine) is widely drunk with meals, but it is usually *tinto* (red). *Rosada* (rosé) and *blanco* (white) are less popular, probably because

their quality in Spain is generally poor. Indeed, in the summer, red wine is frequently produced from the fridge as an alternative to white. At this time of the year, *tinto de verano* (summer wine) is a combination of red wine, ice and lemonade. A stronger version is *sangría*, with the addition of fruit and a liqueur, such as cointreau. Few wines are produced in Andalucía, the main offerings coming from the *rioja*, *valdepeñas* and *navarra* areas. A drinkable wine can be bought from supermarkets for as little as 200 ptas, but the same bottle can cost two or three times as much in a restaurant. Foreign wines are a rarity. Most restaurants will have a *vino de la casa* (house wine), but the quality varies. Try it first, before ordering a bottle.

It is with the fortified wines, such as *sherry*, that Andalucía excels. It is produced in the 'sherry triangle' between Jerez, Sanlucar and El Puerto de Santa María and comes in a bewildering variety of forms. The most popular is *fino* (dry), which is served cold and is the usual accompaniment to *tapas*. Then there is *amontilado* (medium) and *oloroso* (sweet). Similar to sherry is the *montilla*, produced to the S of Córdoba.

Cerveza (beer) is of the lager type and is usually served chilled. It is available in bottles, but the cheapest way to drink beer is in draught form. Ask for *una caña*, which will cost you the equivalent of half a pint for around 100 ptas. The two local brands are *San Miguel*, which is brewed next to the airport at Málaga, and *Cruz Campo*, which is made in Sevilla. Other commonly found varieties are *Victoria* and *Majon*. All are good. A bottle with *sin* on the label will be low, or totally lacking, in alcohol.

A wide variety of spirits are also available and undoubtedly the most popular with Spaniards is *coñac* (brandy). Made in the sherry producing area, its slightly spicy taste makes it instantly distinguishable from the French variety. Some of the more expensive brands are *Carlos 1* and *Gran Duque de Alba*; at the other end of the scale are *Soberano* and *Fundador*. Many Andalucíans start the day with a large *coñac* with their breakfast coffee. The other locally produced spirit is gin, made by the *Larios* family in the eastern part of Málaga province. Optics are unknown in Spanish bars and measures of spirits are often alarmingly large. Of the soft drinks and mixers, *limon* (lemon), *naranja* (orange) and *tónica* (tonic water) are the most common. A delightful thirst-quencher on a hot day is *horchata*, a non-alcoholic drink made from ground almonds and barley.

GETTING AROUND

AIR

Iberia and its subsidiaries operate services between the national airports, but this is an expensive way of travelling around Andalucía and there are more attractive alternatives. Note that there are no services from any of the regional Andalucían capitals to Gibraltar. *Iberia* have special rates available for unlimited travel within Spain, although this is probably not worthwhile if you are only visiting Andalucía.

RAIL

Train buffs recognize that RENFE is Europe's most eccentric railway. It has improved its timetabling and rolling stock considerably over the past decade, but suffers from having an incomplete rail network and a huge length of single-track line, leading to much frustrating time spent in stations and sidings waiting for another train to pass. There are, in fact, over a dozen types of train service, varying from the *AVE* high speed train connecting Madrid to Sevilla (expect to pay twice the cost of the basic fare), down to regional trains which stop at every hamlet. In between there is the *TALGO* which is fast but costly and the *TER* which is much the same. Then there are the *expreso* and the *rápido*, which are neither quick nor fast. If you are travelling to Andalucía from Madrid, you might be advised to book an inexpensive *litera* (bed) on an overnight train, rather than losing a whole day travelling. RENFE has cut a number of smaller lines in recent years and made arrangements with local bus companies to complete these routes. Buying a ticket can be extremely complicated as there is a wide range of discounts and concessions, such as the reductions of between 12 and 50% on 'blue days'. RENFE offers a tourist card which allows travellers to use all lines and all scheduled trains in Spain for periods of 8, 15 or 22 days. The card is also valid on international trains, except the Madrid-Paris *TALGO*. The card is only available to travellers who normally live outside Spain. Details from RENFE's General Agency for Europe in Paris, T 47 235201. A *Spain Flexipass* is available for visitors from North America, allowing 3, 5 or 10 days cheap travel, but the pass must be bought from travel agents in North America before departure. As lengthy negotiations about discounts and fares can go

on at a ticket office, early booking is strongly advisable. Look for the window marked *Venta anticipada*, where tickets can be bought up to 60 days ahead. For last minute bookings, go to the *Venta immediata*. Remember that if you get on to the train without a ticket and hope to buy one from the conductor, he may charge you twice the normal fare.

ROAD

● **Buses**

The main cities of Andalucía are all linked by long distance coach services and this is a cheap and comfortable form of travel. However, the services are run by a number of private bus companies, whose offices may not be at the main bus station, while the *estacion de autobuses* itself may be remote from the town centre. *Horarios* (timetables) are rarely printed, but each separate company will usually display theirs on the wall of the bus station. It is worth getting an overall picture of the bus services from the local tourist office, who will advise you of any cheap period tickets. Buses generally run on time and are clean, cheap and popular. Long distance coaches have air conditioning in summer and often show videos. Book your ticket well before departure, as ticket offices have erratic hours and those who turn up at departure time are likely to encounter a full bus, especially in summer or at weekends. Note also that only minuscule services run on Sun and fiesta days, particularly in rural areas.

● **Car**

If you bring your own right-hand-drive vehicle from the UK, remember that driving is on the right in Andalucía and that overtaking will be hazardous. Canadian and US visitors will have no problem. All foreign drivers are advised to take an International Driving Permit (or EU driving licence), plus insurance and vehicle documentation. Non-EU citizens will also require a Green Card and it is advisable to obtain a Bail Bond in order to avoid imprisonment in the event of a serious accident. You should carry the required documentation whenever you are in the car.

Andalucían roads have improved out of all recognition in the last decade, with the help of EU grants and money to improve the infrastructure for EXPO'92 at Sevilla. Most cities are now linked by *autovia* (motorway) or dual carriageway roads. Some motorways, such as the A4 from Sevilla, have tolls, although there is a free, slower, alternative running parallel. Safety on the notorious N340 between Málaga and Marbella is much improved, although being both a motorway and a local road, it is still highly dangerous. Speed limits are clearly shown, with a maximum of 60 kph in urban areas, motorways 120 kph and other roads 90 kph. Radar speed traps are becoming increasingly common and fines upwards of 15,000 ptas can be expected. Being a tourist is no excuse, but there may be a discount if the fine is paid on-the-spot! Failure to pay will lead to the car being impounded by the Civil Guard.

The standard of Spanish driving still leaves much to be desired; tailgating and dangerous overtaking are national sports and there are none of the road courtesies taken for granted in northern Europe. Particular care should be taken in the summer months when convoys of tired, Moroccan workers in over-laden cars and vans, head through Andalucía to the ferry ports. The first and last weekends in Aug, when large numbers of Spaniards are on the move, are also times when many accidents occur. Road signs are similar to those in the rest of Europe, but note that a car on a roundabout has priority over one seeking to join it. When turning left on a main road, look out for a loop to the right marked *cambio de sentido* as turning directly left is often illegal.

Petrol in Spain is slightly more expensive than in the UK, and considerably more so than in North America. Since the de-regulation of filling stations and the appearance of foreign firms, self-service stations and the use of credit cards are becoming more common, but in the more rural areas, attendant service is the norm. The different fuel types are *normal* (92 octane), *super* (96 octane), *gasolina* (diesel) and *sin plomo* (lead free).

Parking is a horrendous problem in all Spanish cities. The newly affluent Andalucíans all wish to have cars, but unfortunately, as they are largely apartment-dwellers, few have garages. The result is on-street parking. Few Andalucían cities (with the notable exception of Cádiz) have invested to any great extent in underground or multi-storey car parks. This situation has spawned a thriving *grua* (tow-crane) business. Blue curb markings indicate a pay-and-display area. Do not park where there are yellow markings on the curb. If you park illegally (or at fiesta times in the path of a procession), your car will be towed away. Getting it back from the local pound will be both expensive and stressful.

● **Car hire**

Small cars are inexpensive to hire in Andalucía. The large international companies, such as Hertz and Avis, are represented at the main airports and cities, as are smaller local companies who may be able to offer a cheaper deal (although their back-up services may not be so comprehensive). ATESA, a government-owned Spanish firm, is reliable, has air-conditioned cars and offices in all the regional capitals. Many visitors may wish to book in advance in their own countries. Holiday Autos (UK T 0171 4911111/US T 800 4427737) is a worldwide organization and because of its volume of bookings can undercut its rivals and still use reliable local firms. Prices for a Fiesta-sized car at Málaga airport are from 16,500 ptas in the winter to 22,000 ptas in the summer (weekly, unlimited mileage, all taxes). There are also some excellent Fly-Drive deals available provided by the airlines and tour operators.

● **Cycling & motor cycling**

Mopeds and cycles can be hired, particularly on the coast. Cycling is a major sport in Spain (Spaniards have won the Tour de France many times in recent years) and racing cyclists are common on the roads of Andalucía, mainly at weekends. Leisure cyclists are less obvious and mountain bikes have not penetrated the Spanish market to any great extent, despite the suitable terrain. Motorists are obliged by law to give cyclists 2m clearance when overtaking, a manoeuvre which many Spaniards take seriously, often to the detriment of other road users. Cycle helmets are rarely seen, but helmets for moped and motor cyclists are now compulsory but this is a law which is widely disregarded. Mopeds and low-powered motor cycles are an irritating source of noise pollution which the visitor will have to learn to live with. Taking your own bike to Andalucía is well worth the effort as most airlines are happy to accept them, providing they come within your baggage allowance. Bikes can be taken on RENFE, but have to travel in the guards van and must be registered. Remember to take a strong lock, chain or other method of immobilization.

● **Hitchhiking**

Away from the tourist areas, hitching will involve some long, hot waits. Spanish drivers are reluctant to pick up strangers, especially backpackers, and are likely to regard women hitchhikers without rucksacks as prostitutes. Foreign cars are the best bet, but considering the cheapness of buses, this is not a recommended way of travelling and is frowned on by the police.

● **Taxis**
Taxis are reasonably cheap, but not always metered. Since there are supplements (eg at night, from airports, for baggage) it is best to clarify the price in advance. Official rates should be displayed at airports and inside any licensed taxi. There are usually taxi ranks in city centres and it is possible to hail a taxi in the street; look for the *libre* notice on the windscreen or the green light on the roof at night. If you have an address to go to, it is a good idea to write it down on paper to show the driver. Tourist information material will usually quote a local radio taxi number. Tipping should be approximately 10%. Taxis are excellent value within cities and, particularly at night, they are a safe way of travelling. Spanish taxi drivers, however, are notorious for their flamboyant driving and passengers will often need to keep their eyes shut – images of St Christopher on the dashboard are not just for decoration!

COMMUNICATIONS

● **Postal services**
The *Correos* is famous (or infamous) for its unreliability and slow service. Many letters still fail to reach their destinations at busy times, while a letter can take months to travel between neighbouring towns. The service within large cities is usually least satisfactory. Post offices are usually open from 0900 to 1400, but times vary from one city to another and the *correos* may also be open again in the afternoon, but not on Sat. *Poste restante* letters can be collected at the post office. They should be addressed Lista de Correos, followed by the post code, town and province (emphasizing the surname, as letters are often filed under the first name). Be prepared to show some form of identification when collecting mail. When posting a letter look for a yellow box or *buzon*. Post boxes at main post offices may have different destinations – note the local, national and international sections. Be prepared for long queues at the *correos*. For this reason, stamps *(sellos)* are also available at tobacconists (estancos). Allow at least 5 days for a postcard to arrive in UK, longer to North America.

● **Telecommunications**
In contrast to the postal services, *Telefónica* is efficient. The booths are clean and rarely van-

dalized. Instructions are in both Spanish and English, while in addition to coins (100, 25 and 5 ptas), some booths accept phone cards, which can be bought at tobacconists. If you need to reverse charges, make a lengthy call or phone abroad, try to find a *locutorio* – a large cabin with several booths and an exit desk where you settle your bill. Credit cards are usually accepted. Special low level booths are available for disabled travellers in some towns. Many bars and restaurants also have public telephones. When phoning abroad from Spain, dial 07 and wait for the constant high pitched tone, then continue with the country code and the rest of the number. Some country codes include US 1; Australia 61; Canada 1; NZ 64; UK 44. The cheapest times to call are Mon-Fri 2400-0800 and 2200-2400, Sat 0000-0800 and 1400-2400 and all day Sun. Normal rate applies Mon-Fri 1700-2200 and other times are peak rate. When calling Spain from elsewhere, use the appropriate international number, then 34 for Spain, then the provincial code. These are as follows: Almería 50; Cádiz 56; Códoba 57; Granada 58; Huelva 59; Jaén 53. The code for both Sevilla and Málaga is 5, but all 7 digit numbers in Málaga start with 2 and all 7 digit numbers in Sevilla start with 4. Do not use the code if dialling within a province. If phoning another province from within Andalucía, add 9 at the beginning of the code. Some GMS digital mobile phones can now be used in Andalucía, although the service is patchy. Check with your service provider before departure and have the international bar removed.

ENTERTAINMENT

● **Hiking & hill walking**
With its mountains and hills, Andalucía has some marvellous terrain for this activity. It is not a popular Spanish leisure activity, however, so that, regrettably, there are few marked paths except in the Natural Parks, and even there they are sparse. Walkers in agricultural areas run the risk of being attacked by farm dogs, so that a heavy walking stick is a useful accessory. Refer to the regional descriptions for suitable maps. The regional tourist department produce a booklet entitled *Hiking – Andalucía Walking Tours*. It lists 25 walks in each province, produced in quaint English with picturesque maps. Unfortunately, many of the routes simply follow roads.

● **Newspapers**

Of the Spanish national newspapers, *El Pais* is generally regarded as the best and produces an Andalucían edition. Others worth reading are *ABC* and *Diario 16*. The main Andalucían newspaper, produced in Málaga, is *Sur*, which publishes a weekly edition in English. In addition, there are a number of free expat news sheets, of generally abysmal standard and aimed largely at elderly retirees. They can be picked up in bars and on supermarket counters and can be useful for finding accommodation for rent. British daily newspapers are on sale by the early evening of the day of publication in the main tourist areas. Inland, if they can be found, they will be a day or two old. Other European newspapers, plus the *New York Herald Tribune*, are also widely available. English newspapers and magazines are easily obtainable in Gibraltar. Spanish magazines, of which there are a vast number, are typified by their glossiness and their obsession with royalty and gossip. The best English language magazine is the well-produced *Lookout*. Once a modest publication based on the Costa del Sol, it is now available widely throughout Spain.

● **Sports**

Few parts of Europe offer such a variety of sporting activity for the visitor. Local tourist offices can supply full details. There are nearly 100 **Golf** courses in Andalucía, with more in the planning stage. The majority are in Málaga and Cádiz provinces and close to the coast. The better courses are of championship standard and have been designed by the well-known names of the golfing world. Peak times are in spring, when booking is essential. **Watersports** such as sailing, sail boarding, parasailing, water skiing, snorkelling and, of course, swimming, are well catered for along the whole coast. Tarifa is the European 'mecca' for sail boarders. There is a string of marinas and sport ports along both the Atlantic and Mediterranean coastlines, where boats of all types can be hired or instruction arranged. **Tennis** is widely played in Spain and many hotels have their own courts. **Winter sports** take place in the Sierra Nevada at the purpose built resort of Solynieve. **Horse riding** is popular in Andalucía and horses can be hired at numerous stables and equestrian centres, which are usually well-advertised.

● **Television & radio**

You cannot escape Spanish TV, as it is invariably switched on in bars and restaurants (usually at the same time as the radio) whether anyone is watching or not. There are two state-run channels – TVE-1 and 2 – plus *Canal Sur*, which is sponsored by the Andalucían government. In addition, there are three private subscription channels. Whatever the channel, the offerings are uninspiring, being dominated by game shows and sport, particularly basketball, football and bull fighting. Gibraltar TV can often be received in the SW part of Andalucía, showing a good variety of BBC and ITV programmes. Sky TV can also be obtained with a satellite dish and subscription. Short wave radio will pick up the *BBC World Service*. Gibraltar Radio uses the World Service news, while there are numerous foreign language stations in the resort areas.

HOLIDAYS AND FESTIVALS

It is believed that Spaniards take more holidays than any other Europeans. There are 14 national holidays, when everything closes down, plus Andalucían holidays and local *fiestas*. It is worth checking these out to avoid ruining a days sightseeing. Many Spaniards make a *puente* or bridge by adding a day on to a holiday, thereby creating a very long weekend.

National holidays

1 Jan: New Years Day
6 Jan: Epiphany
Mar/Apr: Semana Santa, Holy Week, climaxing on Good Friday
1 May: Labour Day
Jun: Corpus Cristi (movable date)
24 Jun: San Juan – the King's Saint Day
25 Jul: Santiago Day
15 Aug: Assumption of the Virgin
12 Oct: Columbus/National Day
1 Nov: All Saints Day
6 Dec: Constitution Day
8 Dec: Immaculate Conception
25 Dec: Christmas Day

Most Spaniards take their main holiday in Aug. It is this period, plus *Semana Santa* (Holy Week, ending on Good Friday) when hotels are usually full and will require advance booking.

Will you help us?

Our authors explore and research tirelessly to bring you the most complete and up-to-date package of information possible. Yet the contributions we receive from our readers are also **vital** to the success of our Handbooks. There are many thousands of you out there making delightful (and sometimes alarming!) discoveries every day.

So important is this resource that we make a special offer to every reader who contacts us with information on places, experiences, people, hotels, restaurants, well-informed warnings or any other features which could enhance the enjoyment of our travellers everywhere. When writing to us, please give the edition and page number of the Handbook you are using.

So please take a few minutes to get in touch with us - we can benefit, you can benefit and all our other readers can benefit too!

Please write to us at:

Footprint Handbooks,
6 Riverside Court, Lower Bristol Road, Bath BA2 3DZ England
Fax: +44 (0)1225 469461 E Mail travellers@footprint.cix.co.uk

Rounding up

Useful addresses

Spanish embassies & consulates

Australia
15 Arcana St, Yarralumla, ACT 2600, T 062 273 35 55.

Britain
20 Draycott Place, London, SW3 2RZ, T 0171 581 5921.

Canada
350 Sparks St, Suite 802, Ottawa, Ontario, K1R 7S8, T 613 237 2193.

USA
2700 15th St NW, Washington DC 20009, T 202 265 0190; 150 E 58th St, New York, NY 10155, T 212 355 4090.

Spanish tourist offices

Australia
203 Castlereagh St, Suite 21, Sydney, NSW 2000, T 02 264 7966.

Britain
15/17 St James St, London SW1A 1LD, T 0171 4990901.

Canada
102 Bloor ST W, Toronto, Ontario, M5S 1MB, T 4169614079.

USA
665 Fifth Ave, New York, NY 10022, T 212 7598822.

Specialist tour companies

Abercrombie and Kent (UK)
T 0171 7309600

Ace Study Tours (UK)
T 01223 835055

Adventura
42 Greenlands Rd, Staines, Middlesex, TW18 4LR, T 01784 459018

Andalucía Tours
Hotel Salobreña, 18680, Salobreña, Granada, T 958 610261

Benamorda
Sociedad Cooperativa Andaluza de Actividades Turístico-Culturales, Postigo 66, 29492, Jubrique, Málaga, F 95 2152336

Bird Watching Breaks
9 Little Britain, Dorchester, Dorset DT1 1NN, T 01305 267994

Blackheath Wine Trails
13 Blackheath Village, London SE3 9LA, T 0181 4630012

Burro-Adventure
Camping de Pitres, Granada, T 958 766112

Campus Travel
52 Grosvenor Gardens, London SW1, T 0171 7303402 and found on most university campuses in Britain.

Explore Worldwide (UK)
1 Frederick St, Aldershot, Hants, T 01252 344161

Gullivers
Oak Farm, Stoke Hammond, Milton Keynes MK17 9DB, T 01525 270100, RSPB leaders used

Magic of Spain
227 Shepherds Bush Rd, London W6 7AS, T 0181 748 7575

Mundi Color
276 Vauxhall Bridge Rd, London, SW1, T 0171 828 6021

Ornitholidays
1/3 Victoria Drive, Bognor Regis, Sussex

Peng
Costa Natura, near Estepona, T 01402471832

Rancho los Lobos
Estación de Jimena de la Frontera, Cádiz, T 956 640429

Taste of Spain
Apartado 349, 29680 Estepona, Málaga, T 95 2886590

Time Off
2a Chester Close, Chester St, London SW1, T 0171 235 8070

Travellers Way
Hewell Lane, Tardebigge, Bromsgrove, Worcs B60 1LP, T 01753 516477

Writing to us

Many people write to us - with corrections, new information, or simply comments. If you want to let us know something, we would be delighted to hear from you. Please give us as precise information as possible, quoting the edition and page number of the Handbook you are using and send as early in the year as you can. Your help will be greatly appreciated, especially by other travellers. In return we will send you details about our special guidebook offer.

For hotels and restaurants, please let us know:

- each establishment's name, address, phone and fax number
- number of rooms, whether a/c or air-cooled, attached (clean?) bathroom
- location - how far from the station or bus stand, or distance (walking time) from a prominent landmark
- if it's not already on one of our maps, can you place it?
- your comments - either good or bad - as to why it is distinctive
- tariff cards
- local transport used

For places of interest:

- location
- entry, camera charge
- access - by whatever means of transport is most approriate, eg time of main buses or trains to and from the site, journey time, fare
- facilities - nearby drinks stalls, restaurants, for the disabled
- any problems, eg steep climb, wildlife, unofficial guides
- opening hours
- site guides

Glossary

A

Alameda
A promenade, usually tree lined

Alcazaba
A Moorish castle or fortress

Alcázar
Moorish fortified palace

Alijama
Jewish or Moorish meeting place in the city centre, often near the synagogue or mosque

Aljibe
Moorish water cistern

Almohads
Berbers from North Africa who ruled Spain from around 1147 to 1213, succeeding the Almoravids

Almoravids
Fanatical Berbers from the Sahara who controlled much of Spain in the 11th century

AMA
Agencia de Medio Ambiente. The environmental agency of the Regional Government of Andalucía

Artesonado
Mudéjar style wooden ceilings, often beautifully carved and inlaid

Atalaya
Watch towers found mostly along the coast. Those of Moorish origin were usually square, Christian towers mostly round

Ayuntamiento
Town or city hall. Curiously, it also translates as 'sexual intercourse'

Azulejo
Coloured glazed tiles, popular in Mudéjar and later styles

B

Barrio
Quarter or district of a city

Bodega
Wine warehouse or bar

C

Calle
Street – shown by the letter C/ plus the name

Capilla Mayor
The main chapel of a church or cathedral containing the High Altar

Capilla Real
Royal Chapel, as in the cathedrals in Granada and Sevilla

Carretera
Main road or highway

Cartuja
Carthusian monastery

Castillo
Castle

Chiringuito
Beach bar, also sometimes known as a 'Merendero'

Churrigueresque
An exuberant form of Baroque architecture, named after José Churriguea (1650-1723), although his followers were more extreme

Cuidad
City or town

Convento
Monastery or convent

Converso
A Jew who converted to Christianity after the Reconquest

Coro
The choir of a Spanish cathedral. Usually centrally placed and walled in

Correos
Post Office

Corregidor
Royal magistrate

Corrida
Bullfight

Cortijo
Farmhouse, often in the Roman style, with accommodation for both farmer and workers

Coto
Reserved hunting land

Cueva
Cave

D

Dulces
Sweetmeats and cakes made by nuns and sold at convents

E

Embalse
Reservoir

Ermita
Hermitage

F

Feria
Major fair held annually by all Andalucían towns

Finca
Small country farmhouse

Fonda
Small inn traditionally used by traders and other travellers

G

Gitano
Gypsy

Grandee
Member of the higher Spanish nobility

H

Hacienda
Large rural farming estate, often in olive and wine producing areas

Hamman
Moorish baths, also shown in the placename 'Alhama'

Hidalgo
Lowest level of Spanish nobility

I

ICONA
Instituto Nacional para la Conservación de la Naturaleza. The government's Department of the Environment

Iglesia
Church

Isabelline
A form of late Gothic architecture which developed during the reign of Ferdinand and Isabel in the late 15th century, corresponding to the English Perpendicular

J

Jornalero
Landless farm labourer hired by the day

Judería
Jewish quarter of a town

Junta
Government. The Junta de Andalucía is the Government of the Autonomous Region of Andalucía

K

Karst
A dry limestone scenery with much bare rock and caves. Named after the Karst region of Yugoslavia

L

Latifundio
Large rural estate of the type hiring day workers

Lonja
Exchange building used by merchants eg for corn. Can also be a Stock Exchange

M

Marismas
Marshes

Medina
Moorish word for town, but can also refer to the walled centre of a Moorish city

Mercado
Market

Mezquita
Mosque

Mihrab
Prayer niche in the wall of a mosque which faces Mecca

Mirador
A scenic viewpoint

Monasterio
Monastery or convent

Morisco
A Muslim who submitted to Christian rule after the Reconquest

Mozaráb
A Christian living under Moorish rule who was allowed to practice Christianity

Mudéjar
A Moor living under Christian rule. Also applied to a style of architecture built by Moorish craftsmen for their Christian rulers and typified by the use of decorative brickwork, plaster and tiles

P

Palacio
Affluent city mansion

Parador
Luxury state run hotel often housed in ancient premises and specializing in regional dishes

Paseo
An evening stroll or a promenade

Patio
A central courtyard of a public building or house

Plateresque
16th century Gothic style of architecture with elaborate stonework named after its resemblance to the work of silversmiths

Plaza
Square. The Plaza Mayor is the main square of a town and may often be closed in and arcaded

Plaza de Toros
Bullring

Posada
Old type of inn, formerly with stables

PP
Partido Popular. A right wing alliance which came to power under José María Aznar in mid 1996

PSOE
Spanish Socialist Workers' party. Led by Felipe González, it was in power for a number of years in post Franco times

Pueblo
Small town or village

Puerta
Gateway or door. Also a mountain pass

Puerto
Port. 'Puertos Deportivos' are pleasure craft harbours

R

Raptor
Bird of prey, including eagles, buzzards vultures

Reconquista
The Christian reconquest of Moorish Spain, lasting for 700 years but most active under Ferdinand and Isabel, *Los Reyes Católicos*

Reja
Decorative iron grill in a church or on the window of a house

Retablo
Altarpiece, usually ornately carved in wood and gilded

Río
River

Romería
A pilgrimage or procession to a shrine, usually on a saint's feast day

S

Sagrario
Sacristy or chapel in a church often containing relics

Saeta
Song delivered from a balcony as an Easter procession passes

Sala Capitular
Chapter house

Salinas
Commercial salt marshes

SEO
Spanish Ornithologists Association

Sevillana
Popular flamenco dance

Sierra
Mountain range

Sin Numero
Literally 'without number' usually shown as s/n, denoting that a building does not have a street number

Solera
Blending system in the production of sherry

T

Tablao
Flamenco show put on for tourists

Taifa
Independent Moorish Kingdom. The majority were set when the Caliphate of Córdoba collapsed in 1031

Torre
Tower

Torre del Homeje
Tower of Homage. The tallest tower on a fortress, often detached from the main walls

U

Urbanisación
Small housing development with its own facilities, often in a tourist area

V

Vega
Fertile plain

Venta
Rural roadside restaurant

Basic Spanish for travellers

Spanish has been described as an easy language to learn. Certainly it is spoken more or less as it appears and travellers who have fluency in other Latin-based languages such as French or Italian should not find it difficult. Bear in mind that in *castellano* or standard Spanish, *z*, and *c* before *e* and *i* are a soft *th*. Other points to remember are that *ll* approximates to the English *y*, the *h* is invariably silent, while *j* and *g* are pronounced like an *h* when they are at the start of a word. *R*'s, and especially double *r*'s are rolled, often to excess. When *ñ* has an accent or *tilde* above it, the pronounciation is similar to the English *ny*. When consulting a dictionary, remember that *LL, CH* and *Ñ* are considered as separate letters in Spanish.

Emphasis is routine, with stress on the penultimate syllable unless there is an accent. Exceptions are when a word ends in *d, l, r* or *z*, when emphasis is on the final syllable.

The main problem for visitors to south of Spain is the Andalucían dialect (or *Andalu'* as it is popularly known). Spoken at bullet-like speed, consonants, and indeed whole syllables, are frequently omitted, particularly at the end of a word. In addition (as in South American) *ci* and *ce* are pronounced with an *s* rather than the castellano lisp, so that *cerveca* (beer) becomes 'sairvaisa' rather than the Madrid 'thairvaitha'. Andalucians treat all attempts to speak their language with patience and good humour, so that the effort is well worth while.

Numbers

0	cero
1	uno (m) una (f)
2	dos
3	tres
4	cuatro
5	cinco
6	seis
7	siete
8	ocho
9	nueve
10	diez
11	once
12	doce
13	trece
14	catorce
15	quince
16	dieciséis
17	diecisiete
18	dieceocho
19	diecenueve
20	viente
30	treinta
40	cuarenta
50	cincuenta
60	sesenta
70	setenta
80	ochenta
90	noventa
100	cien
200	doscientos
300	trescientos
1000	mil

Days and months

Sunday	domingo
Monday	lunes
Tuesday	martes
Wednesday	miércoles
Thursday	jueves
Friday	viernes
Saturday	sábado
January	enero
February	febrero
March	marzo
April	abril
May	mayo
June	junio
July	julio
August	agosto
September	septiembre
October	octubre
November	noviembre
December	diciembre

Seasons

Spring	la primavera
Summer	el verano
Autumn	el otoño
Winter	el invierno

Greetings

Merry Christmas	¡Feliz Navidad!
Happy New Year!	¡Feliz Año Nuevo!
Happy Birthday	¡Feliz cumpleaños!
Congratulations	¡Enhorabuena!
Good Luck	¡Buena suerte!

Have a nice trip	¡Buen viaje!
Hello/Goodbye	Hola/Adiós
Good morning	Buenos dias
Good afternoon	Buenos tardes
Good evening	Nuenos noches
See you later	Hasta luego
How are you?	¿como está?
Sorry	Perdón/lo siento
Yes/no	Si/no
Thank you	Muchas gracias
OK	Vale
Excuse me	Con permiso
Its nothing/you're welcome	De nada
Do you speak English?	¿Habla Inglés?
Go away!	¡Márchese!
I don't understand	No entiendo

Geography

beach	playa (f)
castle	castillo (m)
cathedral	catedral (f)
countryside	campo (m)
England	Inglaterra (f)
Europe	Europa (f)
fertile plain	vega (f)
France	Francia (f)
forest	bosque (m)
Germany	Alemania (f)
lake	lago (m)
Morocco	Marruecos (m)
port	puerto (m)
Portugal	Portugal (m)
reservoir	Embalso (f)
river	río (m)
road	carretera (f)
sea	mar (f)
Spain	España (f)
street	calle (f)
town/city	cuidad (m)
United States	Estados Unidos (m)
village	pueblo (m)

Hotel and accommodation

air conditioning	aire acondicionado
apartment	apartamento (m)
bath	baño (m)
bed/double bed	cama (f)/cama matrimonial
bill	cuenta (f)
credit cards	tarjetas de crédito
change	cambio (m)
Country Inn	albergue (m)
heating	calefacción (f)
hotel	hotel (m)
hostel	hostal (m)
how much?	cuanto es?
laundry	lavandería (f)
money	dinero (m)
receptionist	recepcionista (f)
room	habitacion (m)
shower	ducha (f)
State run hotel	parador (m)
telephone	teléfono (m)
toilet	servicio (m)
view	vista (f)
waiter	camarero (m)
water (hot)	agua (caliente)

Travel

airport	aeropuerto (m)
arrival	llegada (f)
bus	autobús (m)
bus station	estación de autobuses (f)
car	coche (m)
car hire	aquilar de coches
customs	aduana (f)
departure	salida (f)
duty free	libre de impustos
fare	precio del billete (m)
ferry (boat)	barca (f)
garage	taller (m)
left luggage	consigna (f)
map	mapa (m)
oil (engine)	aceite (m)
papers (documents)	documentación (f)
parking	aparcamiento (m)
passport	pasaporte (m)
petrol	gasolina (f)
puncture	pinchazo (m)
railway	ferrocarril (m)
taxi	taxi (m)
taxi rank	parada de taxis (f)
ticket	billete (m)
ticket (return)	billete de ida y vuelta (m)
What time is it?	¿Qué hora es?
train station	estacíon de trenes (f)
train	tren (m)
tyre	neumático (m)

Food and drink

beer	cerveza (f)
bread	pan (m)
breakfast	desayuno (m)
butter	mantequilla (f)
cheese	queso (m)
coffee	café (m)
dessert	postre (m)
dinner	cena (f)
drink	bebida (f)
egg	huevo (m)
fish	pescado (m)
food	comida (f)
fruit	frutas (f)
lemonade	lemonada (f)
lunch	comida (f)
meat	carne (f)
menu (fixed price)	menu (del día) (m)
milk	leche (f)
olive	olivo (m)
restaurant	restaurante (m)
salt	sal (f)
soup	sopa (f)
sugar	azújar (m)
tea (tea bag)	té (m)
tip	propina (f)
water (bottled)	agua (f) (embotellada)
wine (red/white)	vino (tinto/blanco)

Other common words

after	después
afternoon	tarde (f)
and	y
before	antes de
big	grande
cheap	barato
chemist shop	farmacia (f)
church	iglesia (f)
closed	cerrado
cold/hot	frío/caliente
day/night	día (m)/noche (f)
doctor	médico (m)
enough	bastante

evening	tarde (f)	now	ahora
expensive (too)	caro (demasiado)	open	abierto
film	pélicula (f)	police	policia (f)
forbidden	prohibido	post office	correos (m)
full	lleno	price	precio (m)
good (very good)	bien (muy bien)	shop	tienda (f)
house	casa (f)	shower	ducha (f)
How much?	¿Cuánto es?	small	pequeño
Is there/are there?	¿Hay un ...?	square	plaza (f)
key	llave (f)	stamp	sello (m)
later	más tarde	today	hoy
little	pequeño	toilet	servicio (m)
market	mercado (m)	tomorrow	mañana
more/less	más/menos	What?	¿Qué?
morning	mañana (f)	When?	¿Cuándo?
near	cerca	Where (is)?	¿Dónde (está)?
newspaper	periódico (m)	Why?	¿Por qué?
new	nuevo	yesterday	ayer

Tinted boxes and illustrations

Index

Maps

Map Symbols

Administration

International Border

State / Province Border

Cease Fire Line

Neighbouring country

Neighbouring state

State Capitals □

Other Towns ○

Roads and travel

Main Roads
(National Highways)

Other Roads

Jeepable Roads, Tracks

Railways with station

Water features

River — Rio Guadalquivir

Lakes, Reservoirs, Tanks

Seasonal Marshlands

Sand Banks, Beaches

Ocean

Waterfall

Canals

Ferry

Topographical features

Contours (approx),
Rock Outcrops

Mountains

Mountain Pass

Glaciers

Gorge

Escarpment

Palm trees

Cities and towns

Built Up Areas

Main through routes
Main streets
Minor Streets
Pedestrianized Streets
One Way Street
National Parks, Gardens, Stadiums

Fortified Walls

Airport Ⓚ

Banks Ⓢ

Bus Stations (named in key)

Hospitals ⊕

Market Ⓜ

Police station

Post Office

Telegraphic Office

Tourist Office ⓘ

Key Numbers 1 2 3 4 5

Bridges

Mosque

Cathedral, church †

Guided routes ....

National parks, trekking areas

National Parks and
Bird Sanctuaries ♦

Hide

Camp site Λ

Refuge

Motorable track - - - - -

Walking track ....

Other symbols

Archaeological Sites

Places of Interest ○

Viewing point

Golf course

Footprint Handbooks

All of us at Footprint Handbooks hope you have enjoyed reading and travelling with this Handbook, one of the first published in the new Footprint series. Many of you will be familiar with us as Trade & Travel, a name that has served us well for years. For you and for those who have only just discovered the Handbooks, we thought it would be interesting to chronicle the story of our development from the early 1920's.

It all started 75 years ago in 1921, with the publication of the Anglo-South American Handbook. In 1924 the South American Handbook was created. This has been published each year for the last 73 years and is the longest running guidebook in the English language, immortalised by Graham Greene as "the best travel guide in existence".

One of the key strengths of the South American Handbook over the years, has been the extraordinary contact we have had with our readers through their hundreds of letters to us in Bath. From these letters we learnt that you wanted more Handbooks of the same quality to other parts of the world.

In 1989 my brother Patrick and I set about developing a series modelled on the South American Handbook. Our aim was to create the ultimate practical guidebook series for all travellers, providing expert knowledge of far flung places, explaining culture, places and people in a balanced, lively and clear way. The whole idea hinged, of course, on finding writers who were in tune with our thinking. Serendipity stepped in at exactly the right moment: we were able to bring together a talented group of people who know the countries we cover inside out and whose enthusiasm for travelling in them needed to be communicated.

The series started to grow. We felt that the time was right to look again at the identity that had brought us all this way. After much searching we commissioned London designers Newell & Sorrell to look at all the issues. Their solution was a new identity for the Handbooks representing the books in all their aspects, looking after all the good things already achieved and taking us into the new millennium.

The result is Footprint Handbooks: a new name and mark, simple yet assertive, bold, stylish and instantly recognisable. The images we use conjure up the essence of real travel and communicate the qualities of the Handbooks in a straightforward and evocative way.

For us here in Bath, it has been an exciting exercise working through this dramatic change. Already the 'new us' fits like our favourite travelling clothes and we cannot wait to get more and more Footprint Handbooks onto the book shelves and out onto the road.

The Footprint list

Andalucía Handbook
Cambodia Handbook
Caribbean Islands Handbook
Chile Handbook
East Africa Handbook
Ecuador Handbook
 with the Galápagos
Egypt Handbook
India Handbook
Indonesia Handbook
Laos Handbook
Malaysia & Singapore Handbook
**Mexico & Central America
 Handbook**
Morocco Handbook
 with Mauritania
Myanmar (Burma) Handbook
Namibia Handbook
Pakistan Handbook
Peru Handbook
South Africa Handbook
South American Handbook
Sri Lanka Handbook
Thailand Handbook
Tibet Handbook
Tunisia Handbook with Libya
Vietnam Handbook
Zimbabwe & Malawi Handbook
 with Botswana, Moçambique &
 Zambia

New in Autumn 1997
Israel Handbook
Nepal Handbook

In the pipeline
Argentina Handbook
Brazil Handbook
Colombia Handbook
Cuba Handbook
Jordan, Syria & Lebanon Handbook
Venezuela Handbook

Footprint T-shirt

The Footprint T-shirt is available in 100% cotton in various colours.

Mail Order

Footprint Handbooks are available worldwide in good bookstores. They can also be ordered directly from us in Bath (see below for address). Please contact us if you have difficulty finding a title.

The Footprint Handbook website will be coming to keep you up to date with all the latest news from us (http://www.footprint-handbooks.co.uk). For the most up-to-date information and to join our mailing list please contact us at:

Footprint Handbooks
6 Riverside Court
Lower Bristol Road
Bath BA2 3DZ, England
T +44(0)1225 469141
F +44(0)1225 469461
E Mail handbooks@footprint.cix.co.uk